Introduction to Criminal Justice

Introduction to Criminal Justice

Exploring the Network

Fifth Edition

Steven M. Cox

Western Illinois University

William P. McCamey

Western Illinois University

Carolina Academic Press

Durham, North Carolina

LCCN: 2008011853
ISBN: 978-1-59460-402-7

Carolina Academic Press
700 Kent Street
Durham, NC 27701
Telephone (919) 489-7486
Fax (919) 493-5668

www.cap-press.com

Printed in the United States of America

For Hannah, Monica, Ryan and Lydia
SMC

For Trace and Macy
WPM

Contents

About the Authors

Dr. Steven Cox is Professor Emeritus in the Department of Law Enforcement and Justice Administration at Western Illinois University. He has been teaching, conducting research, and providing training for criminal justice practitioners for the past 35 years both in the United States and abroad. He is author/coauthor of numerous books and articles and serves as a consultant to a variety of criminal justice agencies. Dr. Cox received his Ph.D. at the University of Illinois, Champaign/Urbana.

Dr. William P. McCamey is a professor in the Department of Law Enforcement and Justice Administration at Western Illinois University. He has more than 27 years of teaching, research, and training experience in criminal justice, has served as a consultant to many police and fire agencies, and is author/coauthor of a book and numerous articles in fire science and criminal justice. Dr. McCamey received his Ph.D. from the University of Iowa.

Preface

The field of criminal justice is constantly changing as new laws are passed, new technology is deployed, old social problems continue to fester and surface, and new social problems emerge. The police are accused of racial profiling, of charging innocent people with crimes they did not commit or that did not occur, and of allowing corruption to run rampant in big-city police departments. At the same time, community policing brings relief to neighborhoods plagued by crime and disorder for decades and the police have become guardians of public safety in the battle against terrorists. Overcrowding in the courts leads to a denial of justice for many defendants, but restorative justice offers alternatives to traditional court proceedings and holds out hope for both victim and offender. New supermax prisons are built to house society's most dangerous offenders while new and exciting alternatives to incarceration are explored. Helping students understand the nature and extent of such changes and the interrelationships among them is the goal of this text.

Approach

In this new edition, we again provide a comprehensive, practical view of criminal justice in the United States. We continue to believe that criminal justice can best be understood by viewing practitioners as being interrelated in a variety of both official and unofficial ways. These practitioners conduct business in various components of what is best viewed as a network of interacting individuals whose everyday decisions have consequences not only for others in their agencies, but for criminal justice practitioners in all components of the network, and for the public. Thus we discuss both day-to-day practical aspects of the network and the theoretical model on which the network is based. This approach involves an examination of the role of the public, the uses and abuses of discretion throughout the network, and the effects of political considerations on the day-to-day operations of the criminal justice network.

- Using the network approach instead of the more common systems (police, courts, corrections all pursuing identical goals) approach, we can examine the impact of politics, discretion, and differing goals on the actions of criminal justice practitioners.
- We recognize the public as a crucial player (though often neglected) in the criminal justice network. Without public cooperation, the police would be severely hampered, the courts would not be properly utilized, probation and parole would be totally unworkable, and the entire network would not be financed.
- Similarly, the importance of discretion cannot be underestimated. Discretion plays an important role at all levels of the network—from the use of discretion by citizens in deciding whether to call the police, to the use of discretion by police personnel in determining how to handle calls from the public, to the use of discretion by the prosecutor in deciding whether to prosecute a particular case, to the sentencing discretion of judges.
- Superimposed on the criminal justice network is the political structure of the society in which the network exists, and the influence of political decisions and considerations cannot be overlooked.

In the following pages, we discuss the various components, procedures, and bases of criminal justice in the United States. We define technical terms clearly when they are presented, and we have included numerous practical examples and highlights in an attempt to present the introductory student with a basic understanding of both the theoretical and practical aspects of the criminal justice network.

The Fifth Edition

In this edition not only is there a new co-author, but we have made numerous other changes which include:

- updated references
- discussion of recent cases which have attracted national attention
- coverage of recent trends and concerns in criminal justice

The Fifth edition also features:

- expanded discussion of ethics (Chapter 2)
- expanded discussion of some types of crimes (Chapters 3 and 4)
- discussion of federalism (Chapter 3)
- coverage of the rise in use of methamphetamines
- coverage of Internet crimes in our discussion of white collar offenses (Chapter 5)
- discussion of problem-oriented and community-oriented policing (Chapter 6)
- Coverage of new issues in corrections (Chapter 12) and victim/witness rights (Chapter 11), including the rebirth of restorative justice

Pedagogical Aids

To enhance learning, we have included the following devices in every chapter:

- chapter outlines to provide a road map to reading each chapter
- in-chapter "In the News" boxes to help students see the practical application of what they are reading
- end-of-chapter "Internet Activities" to encourage students to use the net as a research and learning tool
- end-of-chapter summaries and key terms lists to help students prepare for exams
- end-of-chapter "Critical Thinking Exercises" to encourage students to go beyond memorization of terms and concepts in their learning
- An instructor's manual, including testbank, is available
- Instructor Supplements

In Appreciation

A number of people have helped in the preparation of this book. For their encouragement and assistance, we would like to thank Professors Gene Scaramella, Michael H. Hazlett, Giri Raj Gupta, Dennis C. Bliss; Chiefs O. J. Clark, Jerry Bratcher, Brian Howerton, Ralph Caldwell, Mark Fleischhauer; and Chief Probation Officer Courtney Cox.

For substantive contributions we wish to thank Professor Terry Campbell for his insightful contributions to the chapter on corrections and Professor Jennifer Allen for her contributions in the area of restorative justice.

We also want to thank the reviewers of the fifth edition manuscript for their many helpful suggestions:

We welcome your comments concerning the text.

SM-Cox1@wiu.edu
W-McCamey@wiu.edu

Introduction to Criminal Justice

Chapter One

Criminal Justice in the United States: A Network of Interaction

In the News 1.1

EAST SIDE CRIME DRAWS 400

Fear of reprisals from criminals for calling the police was the most often cited concern at an east side listening session on **crime** and safety at La Follette High School Wednesday night.

Yet 32 people stood up in front of nearly 400 people, as well as the city channel TV cameras, and gave their names and addresses and recounted their concerns. The stories ranged from traffic problems to crack houses next door.

Katie Sackett, for example, told about two broad daylight break-ins to her home on Monona Drive in the past year. The first occurred in August 2006 when her garage was broken into between nine and 10 in the morning and a riding mower and a chain saw, among other things, were taken. The second was between 3:15 and 4:20 in the afternoon on Jan. 5 when the house was broken into and "totally ransacked." Sackett said the family had more than $20,000 in insurance claims for destroyed and stolen items.

She said her children were afraid to go downstairs for fear the burglars were back.

Sackett, who has lived in her house for five years, said, "I've never been afraid there before." After Wednesday's meeting, Capt. Jilene Klubertanz of the Madison East Police District said her staff has seen some retaliation, but it has mainly been "nuisance stuff," such as the spray painting on the house that Worthington Park

Neighborhood Association President Tiffany Roberts described during the meeting, "not stuff that endangers people."

But Klubertanz added that the police department has ways to work around fears of retaliation.

She said people can tell the police, "Call me if you need more information instead of coming to my house." The police often need more information or someone to look out a window and say, "Yes, that is the person I called about" for the police to do their job effectively.

Klubertanz said the police also need the kind of citizen feedback they received at the meeting.

She and all the police representatives there were clearly basking in the approval the entire department, individual officers and especially Chief Noble Wray got from a number of speakers.

Former City Council member and County Board Supervisor Carole McGuire got one of the loudest crowd responses of the night when she praised Wray and said he was "ontrack saying we need 30 more officers, if not more." She elicited another cheer when she ordered Mayor Dave Cieslewicz to listen to Wray and said she was mad at the mayor for letting what she called the outer ring of the city deteriorate.

The mayor apparently heard her because he commented in his brief speech at the end of the meeting on McGuire "chewing him a new one."

However, on a more serious note, he also vowed that his budget would include a request for 30 additional officers and that "it will be up to the chief to assign where they go it should not be up to politicians and based on which politician is most popular."

Only a few speakers, most notably including current County Board Supervisor Tom Stoebig and local political party Progressive Dane leader Michael Jacob, questioned the advisability of adding the officers.

Stoebig comment that he was "not sure we're getting results from the 257 cops we've already got" was met with silence. But he got a strongly positive crowd response when he added that increasing the police force was simply dealing with the back end of the problem and that he hoped people would give as much support to county funding of human services programs, which he called preventative measures.

Cieslewicz acknowledged this comment as well, saying in his closing remarks that "the city can't do it alone. We need to partner with the federal government, the state government and the county, which is the chief social service provider in the region."

Jacob urged the city to "give kids a place to be and something to do." He got his biggest audience response from his accolades for neighborhood police officers and Wray's and Cieslewicz's recent statements about turning away from a policy of using fewer neighborhood officers. Jacob said, "Neighborhood officers are critical. They put out fires before they are big."

Rathbu, M.Y. (2007, September 13). East side crime draws 400. *The Capital Times* (Madison, WI), Front, A1. "Copyright *The Capital Times*. Reprinted with permission."

Key Terms

criminal justice network
loose coupling
territorial jealousy
crime control model
due process model
public
racial profiling
presumption of innocence
unofficial probation
justice

Chapter Outline

The Criminal Justice as a Network of Overlapping Components
The Public's Role in the Criminal Justice Network
Some Key Assumptions in the Criminal Justice Network

The Criminal Justice System as a Network of Overlapping Components

The gap between the "ideal" criminal justice system as discussed in academic classes and the daily practice of criminal justice in the United States seems to be growing wider on a daily basis, as the article "East side crime draws 400" illustrates.

Among the questions being asked are: What kind of justice system do we have, or do we in fact have a system? Does the jury system work, or is it time to find an alternative? Are the police held to higher standards than the rest of us? Are any of us really protected by the Constitution? Are all decisions in the justice system ultimately political in nature? Is there no end to the discretion of criminal justice practitioners? In this chapter we begin to address some of these issues by exploring the assumptions on which the criminal justice system is based and the day-to-day realities by which the system operates.

Typical models of the criminal justice system show each component of the system receiving cases from, and passing cases on to, other components. Thus, the police process some alleged offenders and send them on to the prosecutor, who passes some on to court officials, who pass some on to correctional officials, who eventually return some to the society from which they originally came. All this is to be accomplished within a framework designed to protect the innocent and guarantee the rights of the accused. Although these models are not totally inaccurate, they are somewhat misleading in that they fail to indicate:

- The routine pursuit of different, sometimes incompatible, goals by various network components.
- The effects of feedback based on personal relationships inside and outside the criminal justice network.
- The importance of political considerations.
- The widespread, routine use of discretion at all levels of the network.

Many of these models lead us to focus on what the criminal justice system does or does not do, and leads us to overlook the fact that it is not the system itself that acts or fails to act to achieve differentially perceived goals, but individuals (subject, to be sure, to some structural constraints of human origin) to achieve differentially perceived goals. It is more realistic to think of a **criminal justice network**, that consists of a web of constantly changing relationships among individuals, some of whom are directly involved in criminal justice pursuits, others of whom are indirectly involved.

Perhaps the most familiar example of a network is the television or radio network in which stations share many programs, but each station also presents programs that are not aired by other stations in the network. Viewed from this perspective, the criminal justice network appears as a three-dimensional model in which the public, legislators, police, prosecutors, judges, and correctional officials are involved in interactions with one another and with others who are outside the traditionally conceived criminal justice system. The everyday business of criminal justice is accomplished, according to this model, through negotiations among any or all involved parties. In any given negotiation, the various parties may pursue the same or different goals. Interaction among concerned parties may be influenced by both overt (visible) and covert (hidden) pressures and considerations.

The criminal justice network can also be described as a group of loosely coupled organizations. This concept was first developed by social psychologist Karl Weick in 1976. Coupling is the degree to which organizations are linked, connected, related or interdependent (Maguire & Katz, 2001). **Loose coupling**, then, involves various members of the criminal justice network that are loosely connected. In other words, applying this concept, the public, legislators, police, prosecutors, judges and correctional officials are loosely coupled; they are attached but retain a level of individual identity. This is especially true in the exercise of discretion by the police, correctional officials, prosecutors, public and judges. As we will discuss, discretion is a necessary part of the criminal justice network. The loose coupling between the members of the criminal justice network encourages discretion, or a level of freedom, in the decisions and choices they make. Perhaps an example will help clarify this approach.

Suppose a drive-by shooting has occurred in a particular neighborhood. Certain segments of the public (those who live in the locality, for example) are likely to become alarmed and to demand that the police "do something." The mass media may publicize the case widely, bringing additional pressure on the police to find the offender, on the prosecutor to successfully prosecute the guilty party, on the judge to hand down a severe sentence, and, eventually, on parole board members not to grant parole. The police may want very badly to catch the offender to protect those who live in the community and to maintain or develop a positive public image. The prosecutor, in addition to being concerned about protecting members of the community, may be thinking about the effects of favorable or unfavorable publicity on an upcoming election, may strongly desire a conviction. Thus, both the police and the prosecutor are pursuing a common goal — crime control — but both are also pursuing additional, different goals as well. In addition, the police chief may use this case as a basis for requesting more resources, the public may demand more patrols, and political officials may call for the chief's dismissal for failing to prevent such incidents.

Let us suppose that the police arrest a person they think may have committed the crime discussed above, but they do not have what they consider a strong case. They believe they need a confession before they can present a reasonable case to the prosecutor. To obtain such a confession, they may pressure the alleged offender to talk to them so that they can clear the crime by arrest and relieve public pressure. At this point, the prosecutor may step in and tell the police not to use undue pressure, to see that the alleged offender clearly understands his or her rights, and to make certain that the arrestee has access to a lawyer if he or she wants one. These statements by the prosecutor may make it more difficult for the police to obtain their confession and may cause conflict between the police and the prosecutor. Still, both are pursuing the same goal — crime control. In our hypothetical case, the police are concerned primarily with obtaining the facts to control crime, while the prosecutor is also concerned with due process, which may at times make crime control more difficult.

Taking our example one step further, we might ask why the prosecutor would caution the police as indicated above. In the network approach to criminal justice, it becomes clear that the prosecutor is bringing the courts, political considerations, and public opinion into the interactive network. The United States Supreme Court justices have ruled that due process must be followed by all criminal justice network personnel; the Court's decisions have limited police practices concerning search, seizure, and interrogation. Further, these rulings are supposed to represent the will of the people as expressed in the First, Fourth, Fifth, and Fourteenth Amendments to the Constitution (see the Appendix). Of course, the manner in which the Constitution is interpreted at any given time depends, to some extent, on the composition of the Supreme Court, which depends on political appointments made by the President, who depends on votes from the public for obtaining office. Thus, we see that decisions in cases in other locales made by criminal justice personnel who have no knowledge of or concern with this particular case can, nonetheless, affect this case. Any case dealt with by the criminal justice network can be analyzed in this fashion, and a great many activities and decisions that otherwise appear to make little or no sense can be understood.

It is most appropriate, as indicated by the examples above and below, to view the criminal justice system as a network of interrelated, but independent, individuals who are subject to many internal and external pressures, and who work under (and are at the same time developing) a set of operating procedures in pursuit of similar, but not always identical, goals. While public and political influence, legal requirements, and discretionary justice pervade the entire network, each party in the network has goals and problems not shared by other parties. For example, the police are concerned with making arrests, the prosecutor with obtaining convictions, the judge with providing impartial trials, and correctional officials with custody and/or rehabilitation. Although the judge may also be concerned with rehabilitation and custody (in terms of sentencing), she or he is not directly concerned with the physical act of making an arrest; similarly, prosecutors are not directly concerned with keeping people in custody, and correctional officials are not directly concerned with obtaining convictions (except in incidents occurring within the prison walls). Each party, however, is indirectly concerned with what all the other parties do.

The following example may help make the network approach employed in this book easier to understand. Over the past several decades the relationships between drugs and crime have been emphasized by law enforcement and the media. Drugs have been portrayed as direct causes of crime (individuals behaving violently as a result of the influence of drugs) and indirect causes (individuals stealing to get money to buy drugs). As a result, powerful segments of the American public determined that something should be done about the "drug problem." These powerful (in terms of monetary and political resources) groups elected representatives who voted to pass new legislation which made drug-related crimes subject to mandatory imprisonment. Prosecutors, judges, and corrections personnel, guided by these new laws, imprisoned numerous offenders who, while not involved in violent crimes, were in some way tied to drug possession, distribution, or manufacture. The police began seeking forfeiture of cars, boats, airplanes, and houses of those who were found to be in possession of illegal substances, and the courts became involved in deciding the legitimacy of these forfeiture procedures.

The number of drug-related convictions increased significantly, as did the size of the prison population. The vast majority of those imprisoned were not major buyers, importers, or sellers of drugs but the small-time criminals working for them, a point not lost on the media or the public. As the number of inmates receiving mandatory sentences for drug-related crimes grew, prisons became increasingly overcrowded.

In response, some inmates whose crimes were far more serious than those of the drug offenders were given early release to make room for those serving mandatory sentences. The media began to focus on offenses committed by those receiving early release, and the public became concerned about dangerous offenders being set free. To avoid further overcrowding, prosecutors and judges began to use alternative charges to deal with drug-related offenders to avoid mandatory sentencing. Law enforcement officials, taking a hint from prosecutors and the courts, began to modify their behavior with respect to drug-related behavior, and politicians began to reconsider legislation requiring mandatory sentences for drug offenders. The public began to breathe easier because fewer serious offenders were receiving early release, and the media found new issues to present to the public.

Criminal justice, as the example above clearly indicates, is not a one-way street with cases and information flowing only in one direction. It consists of a network of relationships in which any party can both influence and be influenced by any or all other parties, and all may be influenced by public opinion and other factors that are not directly involved in criminal justice, as indicated in "Courts Battling 'CSI' Effect."

Police and public must work together to maintain order.

In the News 1.2

COURTS BATTLING 'CSI' EFFECT

While selecting a jury for a recent rape trial, Vanderburgh County Prosecutor Stan Levco asked potential jurors a question that raised eyebrows.

"Who watches shows like 'CSI' and 'Law & Order?' "

More than half the hands in the jury pool went up.

The question is one prosecutors say they almost always ask potential jurors now.

"Particularly if we don't have spectacular scientific evidence," Levco said.

The question is only the first step prosecutors take to explain to jurors that criminal cases in the real world aren't like those on popular television dramas.

In shows such as "CSI" and "Law and Order," investigators work fast and effortlessly to find stacks of scientific evidence such as fingerprints and DNA, which almost always leads to a conviction in a courtroom. The cases are open and closed in less than an hour.

Almost every night of the week, some form of a legal drama can be found on at least one channel. The surge of legal shows and their popularity in the past decade have caused members of the legal community to coin the phrase "the 'CSI' effect."

"I don't know if it was literally when 'CSI' came on the air, but I think it's raised jurors' expectations unrealistically to what happens routinely," Levco said.

Deputy Prosecutor Donita Farr said speakers at legal seminars she goes to, constantly emphasize the need to explain to juries the difference between television and real cases.

"They even recommend you have an expert come to the trial and explain why there is not physical evidence in a case if there isn't," Farr said.

Christina Wicks, a victim support specialist for the Albion Fellows Bacon Center, said legal dramas increase myths about sexual assault, too.

Wicks said that on television, sexual assault victims typically are shown being interviewed by detectives in hospitals.

"They always have cuts and bruises," she said. "That's why people think someone has to be beaten up and have signs of physical injury, when in most instances there is hardly any physical abuse or injury to a rape victim."

As part of her job as a victim support specialist, Wicks sometimes attends rape trials. She said in a recent case there was no physical evidence connecting the victim to the suspect, but "everything else pointed to him."

"He was still found not guilty," she said. "I was surprised. I think that was extremely due to the CSI effect, because there was no DNA."

Farr deals mainly with sex crimes, but said the "CSI" effect can be seen in all types of criminal cases.

"When you talk to the juries after trials, you find that they all wanted fingerprints to be found on the bullets," Farr said. "In real life, that just doesn't happen. They aren't preserved that way."Farr said she often watches the legal dramas, but she is frustrated to see the fictional detectives swab an entire crime scene with cotton swabs and collect "gobs" of physical evidence.

"I love shows like 'CSI,' too, but they get their DNA results in a day," Farr said. "It's nothing like that in real life. It takes us months to get DNA back, at least."

On television, viewers watch cases solved within an hour, Wicks said.

"But in a courtroom, both sides have to put the puzzle together for the jury, so it is never as clear-cut," Wicks said. "I think that makes the jurors think more often they have reasonable doubt."

Farr said jurors' expectations make trials especially difficult in child-molesting cases."In child-molesting cases, 99 percent of the time there is no biological material," Farr said. Most victims of child molestation do not come forward until long after the crime takes place, she said.

Today, Levco said, his approach to a jury is two-fold.

"First is to educate the jury, if you can, about evidence collection," he said. "And if that is not the case, you eliminate those jurors who expect David Caruso to walk in and give them an open and shut case."

Braser, K. (2006, December 4). Courts battling "CSI" effect. *Evansville Courier & Press*, p. B1.

Criminal justice, in this respect, is like an intricate spiderweb. Pulls or pressures on one part of the web may cause changes in all other parts. Special interest groups define socially harmful activity and persuade voters to elect political officials who represent their interests; the performance of these officials is evaluated in the area of criminal justice. In a variety of ways, both direct and indirect, the goals of one component (the police) are transmitted to the other two (courts and corrections). Indirect communication is often the means employed, even though more direct communication might improve cooperation among components and the overall effectiveness of the network. Suppose, for example, a particular judge feels that personal use of marijuana should not result in criminal penalties for the user. For a variety of reasons, she does not directly communicate her feelings to the prosecutor; instead, she imposes no penalties on marijuana users brought before her. After unsuccessfully prosecuting several such cases, the prosecutor "gets the message" and refuses to prosecute such cases before this judge. For a variety of reasons, the prosecutor may not communicate his or her disinterest in such cases to the police chief, whose officers continue to arrest marijuana users. Eventually, after police officers see that the prosecutor will no longer prosecute such cases, they stop making such arrests. The message has been transmitted, but a considerable amount of time and resources may have been wasted by using this indirect method of communication. Similarly, cooperation among the components might have been improved considerably by a straightforward discussion of the parties involved, but political considerations, personality differences, or **territorial jealousy** (the desire to protect one's turf from others) often hamper such discussion.

One of the major difficulties with viewing criminal justice in the United States as a cooperating, goal-sharing, communicating network is that such a network operates best when consensus about the goals of the network exists. In our society, such consensus exists with respect to certain offenses, but is lacking with respect to many others and with respect to the procedures to be employed in the pursuit of alleged offenders. On the one hand, many citizens and practitioners favor the **crime control**

model, which allows for the arrest and prosecution of individuals who are known to be factually guilty of committing a crime. This model is employed to protect people and their property from harm and for the conservative purpose of promoting order and social stability (Roach, 1999). On the other hand, many prefer the **due process model**, which requires that evidence of guilt presented in court be obtained according to legal guidelines. The due process model relies on equal treatment of all accused persons and guarantees the right to a lawyer. It also imposes certain restraints on actions of the police. For instance, the police might receive a tip from an anonymous caller who states that a specific individual living in a specific hotel room is manufacturing methamphetamine (meth) in the room. Using the crime control model, the police break down the door to the room, find meth and the products used to manufacture it, arrest and charge the offender, and use the meth as evidence in the ensuing trial. Under the due process model, the police must demonstrate that the tip came from a reliable informant, obtain a proper search warrant, and maintain a proper chain of evidence, or the meth will be inadmissible as evidence in court and the defendant will be acquitted. That is, even though the defendant was factually guilty of possessing and manufacturing the meth, he is not legally guilty because the procedures established to safeguard the rights of citizens were violated in this case. The emphasis on crime control versus due process shifts with changes in political administrations, public opinion, and the judiciary; this demonstrates the importance of understanding criminal justice as a network and the lack of consensus regarding the best procedure for dealing with crime and criminals.

Similarly, when the public is uncertain about the desirability of rehabilitation, the enforcement of morality, or the best way to punish offenders, it is difficult for practitioners to cooperate and share goals. Viewing criminal justice as a web of interacting parties, each with a set of goals that may or may not all be compatible with those of others, makes it easier to understand how such events can occur. This view is especially important when we realize that we are dealing not with a small number of criminal justice agencies but with thousands of agencies—each with its own regional variations and each with its own personnel. In addition, we must consider perhaps the most important party to any criminal justice network, the public.

The Public's Role in the Criminal Justice Network

The **public** is the most important part of the criminal justice network for a variety of reasons. Before discussing these reasons, we should point out that the term "public" is somewhat misleading. Actually, we are dealing not with one large homogeneous group called a public, but with thousands of different publics. These publics are divided by factors such as geographical area, race, gender, age, social class, and degree of adherence to law. Many of these publics have unique interests and concerns that separate them on most issues from other publics. Citizens comprise a variety of different publics. As we shall see, this heterogeneity is extremely important for criminal justice. At least as important, however, is the fact that, with respect to any given issue, many of these publics are apathetic about the criminal justice network. A great deal of what happens in the name of criminal justice goes largely unnoticed by most citizens, and pressures to modify the network or the activities that occur within it are often brought to bear by small, vocal groups who have an interest in a particular issue, but who become apathetic again once that issue is resolved.

No matter which of the many publics we are talking about, it is important to recognize the role that each may play in the criminal justice network. First, the vast majority of social control in any society is performed not by the police and courts, but by various segments of the public (families and peer groups, for example). Second, these publics provide resources for and evaluations of the entire network. Without public support, police, court, and correctional officials would be helpless to achieve their goals. Consider, for example, the helplessness of the Los Angeles police in the aftermath of the announcement of the Rodney King verdict. Black citizens took to the streets in protest, looting, burning, and occasionally attacking nonblacks while the police were largely invisible. When public support is absent, the police cannot enforce the laws or maintain order. Further, if citizens refuse to provide information to the police, the police (a largely reactive body) cannot perform their duties. Successful prosecution (or defense) is impossible if members of the public refuse to testify. Ex-convicts cannot be reintegrated into society without the cooperation of the citizenry. Without financial resources provided by the public, none of the criminal justice agencies could hire new personnel, develop new programs, or improve efficiency. From beginning to end, then, there is no doubt that all the many publics or segments play a major role in criminal justice and should not be overlooked when we discuss the criminal justice network. Each segment wants and expects something from representatives of that network:

- Specific types of laws enforced (e.g., liquor violations).
- Specific types of offenders taken into custody (troublesome youth).
- Their property returned.
- A police report so that insurance claims for lost or stolen property can be settled.
- The elimination of the death penalty.

In general, the various publics want their real or imagined problems to be dealt with and resolved officially. In short, publics are involved in the criminal justice network in a variety of ways, and this involvement (or lack of involvement) is crucial to the functioning of the network.

Some Key Assumptions in the Criminal Justice Network

To understand how that network actually functions (as compared with how it functions in theory), we need to look at some of the assumptions on which the network is said to be based. These assumptions include the following:

- The components of the network cooperate and share similar goals.

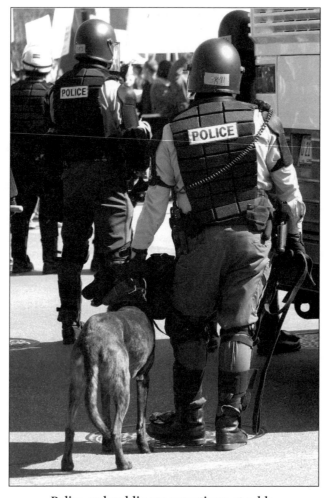

Police and public are sometimes at odds.
Reprinted with permission of iStockphoto.com / Mugur Geana.

- The network operates according to a set of formal procedural rules to ensure uniform treatment of individuals.
- Each person accused of a crime receives due process and is presumed innocent until proven guilty.
- Each accused person receives a speedy, public trial before an impartial jury of his or her peers.
- Each accused person is represented by competent legal counsel, as is the state.
- Innocence or guilt is determined on the basis of the facts.
- The outcome of criminal justice procedures is justice.

We have already dealt with the first assumption—the cooperative, goal-sharing network—and found that cooperation is sometimes lacking and that the various components often have individual, in addition to collective, goals. We will simply add that each component in the network is continually competing with all other components for budgetary dollars.

The second assumption is that the criminal justice network operates according to a set of formal procedural rules to ensure uniform treatment of individuals. To the extent that this assumption is true, race, social class, and gender should have no bearing on the manner in which cases are handled. Similarly, each individual being processed should go through the same clearly delineated steps. There is, however, considerable evidence to indicate that blacks and whites, males and females, and middle-class citizens and lower-class citizens receive differential treatment in the criminal justice network. Blacks in particular face discrimination in the system of criminal justice, beginning with arrest and continuing through incarceration (Mann, 1993; Tonry, 1994). While not all authorities agree that there is a consistent and widespread pattern of discrimination, (Spohn, 2000) argues that certain types of minority offenders are perceived as being more dangerous and are singled out for harsher treatment. Blacks and Hispanics who are young, male, and unemployed are particularly more likely to be sentenced to prison, and receive longer sentences or differential benefits from guideline departures. For example, the Human Rights Watch (2000) concluded that "the war on drugs has been waged disproportionately against Black Americans." They found that Blacks comprise 62.7 percent and Caucasians 36.7 percent of all drug offenders admitted to state prison even though there are reported to be five times more Caucasian drug users than Black drug users. Similarly, Hispanic defendants are imprisoned three times as often and detained before trial for first-time offenses almost twice as often as Caucasians, despite the fact that they are the least likely of all ethnic groups to have a criminal history (Navarrete et. al., 2004) Thus, in many cases minorities convicted of drug offenses, those with longer prior records, those who victimize Caucasians, and those who refuse to plead guilty or are unable to secure pretrial release are punished more severely than similarly situated Caucasians (Spohn, 2000). In addition, since September 11, 2001 racial discrimination problems have intensified and anti-Arab and anti-Muslim sentiments have increased among justice system actors and the population at large (Soros Foundation, 2004). The Foundation concluded that these acts of discrimination often included **racial profiling,** or the use of racial or ethnic stereotypes, as a factor in determining who has been, is, or will be involved in criminal activity.

It is clear that not all defendants go through the same procedural steps when they enter the system. Some are handled by administrative review boards rather than criminal courts (white-collar offenders). Some are prosecuted, others are not. Some are involved in plea bargaining, others are not. Some are convicted and sentenced to prison, while others who are convicted of the same type of offense are not. As we shall see, public opinion, political power, and the exercise of discretion may affect what happens at all levels of the criminal justice network. Assumption number two, then, is at least questionable.

Assumption number three concerns due process and the **presumption of innocence.** No doubt, due process applies in theory to all accused individuals, but what is to guarantee that due process is observed in a practice, for example, like plea bargaining? While several formal procedures have been developed to help ensure that due process is observed in plea negotiations, a great deal of the negotiating remains largely invisible. The more invisible the negotiations, the greater the chance for manipulation by those involved. The fact that guilt is often presumed is apparent in the practice of **unofficial**

probation for alleged juvenile offenders. The juvenile is told by the police, juvenile probation officer, or prosecutor that she or he must meet certain requirements for a specified period of time "or else," which means that the juvenile will be processed through the juvenile court if she or he does not agree to the unofficial probation. Note that the juveniles involved have not been adjudicated delinquent, the facts of the case have not been heard by the court, and the evidence possessed by the authorities is sometimes contested. Where, we might ask, does due process fit into such an arrangement? Nonetheless, such programs exist and are encouraged in many jurisdictions.

With respect to the presumption of innocence, we might simply note that, in general, the police do not believe they arrest innocent people and prosecutors do not believe they prosecute innocent people. There is also evidence to indicate that public defenders do not assume or care whether their clients are innocent (Livingston, 1996, p.460). It may be that judges and juries presume the defendant to be innocent, but it certainly appears that others in the network assume the defendant is guilty. As Grisham (2006) states in introducing his book *The Innocent Man*, "If you believe that in America you are innocent until proven guilty, this book will shock you" (jacket).

Assumption number four, dealing with speedy, public trial before a jury of peers, is clearly questionable. A tremendous backlog of cases ensures that a speedy trial is more an ideal than the reality in many jurisdictions. Since the vast majority of trials involve a guilty plea before a judge, the notions of a "public" trial and a "jury of peers" are called into question. Even when jury trials do occur, the issue of whether the jury consists of peers remains unresolved because of the routine exclusion or excusal of certain types of jurors.

With respect to the assumption that the accused and the state are competently represented, many observers have noted that a significant proportion of lawyers practicing in criminal courts are not competent to do so. Strier (2000) states, "It is no small curiosity that our legal system espouses equality of treatment (equal justice); yet our trial mechanism, more than any other, skews trial outcomes in favor of the side with the better attorney and more money" (p.122). Mann (1993) argues that even if public defenders are effective, their clients typically believe they would be better served by private counsel. As Estrich (1998) indicates, "The right to counsel guaranteed by the Constitution only guarantees the defendant a warm body. The issue for a poor defendant ... is whether he'll even get to meet his lawyer for an interview" (p.97) before going to court. Many defense attorneys have an excess volume of criminal cases in a culture of compromise that tends to assume rather than question a defendant's guilt. According to Joy and McMunigal (2003), the need to obtain concessions from prosecutors in such an environment pressures defense attorneys not to vigorously challenge guilt, police or prosecutor conduct, or the reliability of confessions or eyewitness identifications. They note that the dynamics of negotiating guilty pleas sometimes involves turning defense lawyers into 'double agents' who pressure defendants to plead guilty instead of vigorously representing their clients.

Assumption number six is that the facts of each case will be used to determine innocence or guilt, yet many believe that actual guilt or innocence is the least important factor in determining legal innocence or guilt. Instead, they claim, the resources of the state and defense counsel; the style, presentation, and knowledge of the attorneys involved; and various public and political pressures often determine guilt or innocence.

Finally, assumption number seven concerns the notion of **justice**. If the network or the product of the network is perceived as just by most citizens, we can expect considerable public support for the network. If, however, some groups believe that justice is not uniformly, fairly, or equally applied, we can expect opposition to the network.

In a society such as ours, where citizens are free to voice their dissent and dissatisfaction (within broad limits), it is easy to see that justice is differentially perceived. Those who have little (power, money, status, etc.) often perceive less justice than those who have a great deal. Members of minorities who have been treated as second-class citizens (officially or unofficially) tend to view the network as less just than do members of the dominant group. Both of these points are illustrated by the O. J. Simpson murder case. Because of his considerable wealth, Simpson was able to hire a "dream team" of attorneys who used every conceivable strategy to convince the jury to acquit. When the verdict was announced, it was hailed as a victory by many minority group members and received with a sense of disbelief by many whites.

Victims of crimes and their relatives and loved ones often see little justice in plea bargaining or probation. Offenders seldom see justice in the balance of power between themselves and the state. Justice is often exemplified by the courtroom scene in which the champion of the state (the prosecutor) and the champion of the defense do battle before a jury of 12 (perhaps fewer) "tried and true" persons who decide innocence or guilt on the basis of a presentation of facts with the aid of an impartial mediator (the judge). Today, such scenes are rare, probably occurring in less than 10 percent of all criminal trials. The reality of the criminal trial today involves no jury but a plea negotiated between the prosecutor and defense counsel with the consent of the accused and, sometimes, the judge. In those cases involving jury trials, counsel for the prosecution and defense would each like the jury to believe that he or she is just presenting the facts. In reality, both the prosecution and the defense present the "facts" in such a way as to make their own case look better and to sway the jury. We are all aware that jurors are not chosen simply on the basis of their good intentions. The media, at least in cases receiving national attention, may also have a major impact on both the trial and the perception of justice in general. Whether or not one believes justice is done also depends on the role one plays in the system (e.g., victim, witness, or offender). Again, the O. J. Simpson, Martha Stewart, Michael Jackson, and Enron and Tyco Corporation executives cases are instructive as examples of the points outlined above.

Justice, then, appears to be largely in the eyes of the beholder. Whether or not a particular network for dealing with criminals is seen as just depends, in part at least, on the extent to which the network operates according to the assumptions on which it is based. If these assumptions are not followed in practice, a discrepancy is soon observed between the real and the ideal. As a result, citizens may not know what to expect from the network, may view it as operating on other than an equitable basis, and may believe that justice depends more on access to knowledge and resources required to beat the system than on actual guilt or innocence. Another possible conclusion is that the network simply does not work at all and is not worth supporting. For example, DNA testing has demonstrated that a number of innocent people have been incorrectly convicted. Furthermore, the number of convictions reversed by DNA fail to capture the full scope of the problem since DNA testing is capable of revealing inaccuracy only in cases where evidence such as blood, semen, and hair root were analyzed. There is reason to believe an even greater number of wrongful convictions occur in many cases in which DNA testing cannot be used. Research reveals that most wrongful convictions are based on mistaken eyewitness identification, police and prosecutorial misconduct, false confessions, unreliable informants, faulty scientific evidence and racial bias (Joy & McMunigal, 2003). Consider the following examples that call into question many of the assumptions on which our justice network is based.

The videotaped beating of Rodney King by Los Angeles police officers in the early 1990s led to an acquittal of the officers involved in criminal court, but to a later conviction on civil rights violations in federal court. (Police officers involved were acquitted of criminal charges by a jury in a venue different from the one in which the event occurred, but were later convicted by a federal jury of violating King's civil rights.) This was followed by the criminal court acquittal of O. J. Simpson on murder charges, based, it appears, in part on alleged police misconduct. (If the police can't be trusted to obey the law, should violators be acquitted whatever the evidence?) Simpson was subsequently convicted on wrongful death charges in civil court. (Does wealth provide protection for some in criminal court? Wouldn't someone with fewer resources have been convicted of these crimes? Is race really the overriding issue here, as the response to the acquittal seems to suggest?) The actions of federal authorities at Waco and Ruby Ridge led to considerable criticism of federal law enforcement officials. (Are government officials honest? Were these politically motivated and condoned attacks?) The state of Illinois suspended capital punishment in 1999 as the result of the disclosure of errors and possible police and prosecutorial misconduct. (In convicting offenders and sentencing them to death, have we been sending innocent people to their deaths? Are prosecutors and the police involved in conspiracies?) In Philadelphia, the convictions of dozens of people were overturned as the result of police misconduct and, as we go to press with this book, similar allegations have been made concerning the police in Los Angeles. Abner Louima was sodomized by New York City police officers, one of whom was convicted. New York City police officers also fired 41 rounds at Amadou Diallo, who was holding a wallet, not a weapon, in his hands. Nineteen of the rounds hit Diallo, causing his death. The officers involved were acquitted in a jury trial after the trial had been moved out of New York City to Albany. (Can we trust police officers anywhere? Can we trust the courts to oversee police conduct? Are those segments of the public lacking in political clout routinely treated differently by the police, prosecutors, and judges?) Simultaneously, methamphetamine production appeared to be growing out of control and school shootings were a regular part of the news. (Can't we even protect our children in school? Is the violence that attracts headlines today so different from the violence that occurs in inner-city schools on a continuing basis? Do we care less about one than the other?) The government handling of the Elian Gonzalez case was roundly criticized by the media and the political opposition, as well as by some members of the Cuban community. (How did we single out this boy to be returned to Cuba when so many Cuban refugees are allowed to stay? Do parental rights prevail, or was appeasing Castro the intent of those actions?) Efforts to achieve gun control led to concessions from Smith and Wesson, but concealed-carry laws advanced in several states. (Do we want gun control, or do we want everyone to carry a weapon?) Last, but surely not least, the President of the United States, in politically charged proceedings, was impeached by the House of Representatives on charges stemming from alleged sexual activities in the White House and the subsequent attempt to conceal the activity, but the Senate failed to indict him. (It may be all right to have extramarital sex in the White House, but is it all right to go on national television and lie to the American public about what happened? Did justice or politics prevail, or are the two inseparable?)

In our overview of some of the key assumptions concerning criminal justice in the United States, our intent has not been to convince you that the network does not work. Rather, it has been to point out that the network often does not work in the fashion we say it does or should. As Grisham (2006) notes: "The journey [into the facts cited in *The Innocent Man*] also exposed me to the world of wrongful convictions, something that I, even as a former lawyer, had never spent much time thinking about ... Wrongful convictions occur every month in every state in this country, and the reasons are all varied and all the same,—bad police work, junk science, faulty eyewitness identifications, bad defense lawyers, lazy prosecutors, arrogant prosecutors ... In the cities, the workloads of criminologists are staggering and often give rise to less than professional procedures and conduct. And in the small towns the police are often untrained and unchecked" (p. 356).(The article which opens this chapter confirms Grisham's concerns.) As we proceed through this book, we hope you will continue to question the workings of the criminal justice network, and we hope you will continually compare what you know about the network with the material presented.

In the chapters that follow, keeping in mind certain guidelines will help you comprehend both the ideal and the reality of the criminal justice network. Unquestionably, one of the most important factors to keep in mind is the set of legal statutes and court and administrative decisions that spell out the formal procedures that guide the system. At the same time, to analyze activities within the criminal justice network, it is important to examine the influence of the media, public opinion, political factors, and discretionary justice. Unless we focus on these areas, much of what happens in the criminal justice network will be difficult to comprehend. Why, for example, do we characterize the Supreme Court (generally thought to be the most impartial, scholarly court in the United States) as liberal or conservative? Are political considerations important in this highest of courts? If so, in what ways? And what are some of the effects of such considerations?

Similarly, we might ask why white-collar offenders (who, by many estimates, cost the U.S. public more in terms of dollars annually than robbers, burglars, and other thieves combined) are infrequently handled by criminal courts? Do the various publics view white-collar offenders as criminals? If not, why not? And what are the implications for offenders and society?

In addition to what extent are the police accountable for "adjusting" cases on the street or in the station? To whom are prosecutors accountable for their decisions concerning prosecution? Why do great inequities in sentencing occur among judges? Is discretion a normal and/or necessary part of criminal justice?

Satisfying answers to these and other questions can seldom be found simply by referring to formal procedures, laws, or regulations. References to these formalized procedures need to be supplemented by looking behind the scenes to determine how specific decisions are made within the broad framework of criminal justice. This can best be accomplished by using the network approach.

Summary

1. In this chapter, we have contrasted the real and the ideal of some aspects of criminal justice in the United States. We may have assumed the existence of a system that is more orderly and coordinated than the reality, which may better be viewed as a network of individuals with a diversity of goals.

2. There is little doubt that the police, the courts, and corrections form an interacting network in which changes in one component have clear implications for the other components.

3. The public is an important, perhaps the most important, component of the criminal justice network. What we generally think of as the public actually consists of many different publics with varied interests and concerns, or with no interests or concerns at all, with respect to criminal justice. It is the combination of these publics that supports and evaluates (or fails to support or evaluate) criminal justice agencies and programs.

4. Many of the assumptions on which the criminal justice network is thought to be based are questionable at best in practice.

5. Justice means different things to different people. Whether justice is done in a particular case depends on whether we take the perspective of the defendant, the victim, the police officer, or the jury. Justice, in the ideal sense as the outcome of a battle between two champions before a mediator and a jury, is the exception rather than the rule in criminal cases in the United States.

6. Several important factors are involved in understanding the criminal justice network and its operations. Public opinion, political considerations, media feedback, and the exercise of discretion are important factors in the day-to-day operations of the criminal justice network and should be recognized as such.

Key Terms Defined

criminal justice network A web of constantly changing relationships among individuals directly involved more or less in the pursuit of criminal justice.

loose coupling Describes the extent to which various members and components of the criminal justice network are loosely connected.

territorial jealousy A concern with protecting the turf of one's own agency; sometimes makes cooperation among agencies difficult or impossible.

crime control model A model for procedures to be employed in the pursuit of justice; based on factual guilt.

due process model A model for procedures to be employed in the pursuit of justice; based on establishing factual guilt while adhering to legal guidelines.

public Thousands of different groups divided by characteristics such as age, race, gender, adherence to law, social class, and geographic area; often mistakenly regarded as a cohesive whole, or "the public."

presumption of innocence The belief that an accused is innocent until proven guilty; often lacking among police, prosecutors, and defense counselors.

racial profiling The use of racial or ethnic stereotypes as a factor in the determination of criminal activity.

unofficial probation Probation imposed prior to a determination of guilt or innocence.

justice The belief that various parties involved in a dispute get what they deserve. To some extent, this belief depends on the role of the person doing the perceiving (e.g., is he or she the victim, the offender, or a witness?).

Critical Thinking Exercises

1. What are some of the advantages of viewing criminal justice as a network instead of using a more traditional model?

2. Do all the various components of the criminal justice network have identical goals? Similar goals? Overlapping goals?

3. Why are politics, discretion, and the public important components of the criminal justice network?

Internet Exercise

In this chapter we discussed a network approach to criminal justice. To better understand the network approach you are encouraged to visit the website of the National Criminal Justice Commission (NCJC), at http://www.ncianet.org/cjsce.cfm

1. At the opening menu, read the history and purpose of the Commission. Discuss whether or not the NCJC represents a network approach to criminal justice.

2. Read all nine case examples. Reread the Bank Fraud, Drug Offense, Embezzlement, and Sex Offenses Cases. Discuss the impact on the public and other criminal justice components if the recommendations in these cases are followed.

3. Compare the recommendations with the actual sentences in the Bank Fraud, Drug Offense, Embezzelment and Sex Offense cases. Which is more reflective of public opinion, the recommendations or sentences? Explain.

References

Estrich, S. (1998). *Getting away with murder.* Cambridge, MA: Harvard University Press.

Grisham, J. (2006). *The innocent man.* New York: Doubleday.

Human Rights Watch. (2000). Punishment prejudice: Racial disparities in the war on drugs. Available online at http://www.hrw.org/reports/2000/usa/.

Joy, P.A. & McMunigal, K.C. (2003). Inadequate representation and wrongful conviction. *Criminal Justice Magazine,* 18 (1), 57.

Livingston, J. (1996). *Crime and criminology* (2nd ed.). Upper Saddle River, NJ: Prentice Hall.

Mann, C. R. (1993). *Unequal justice: A question of color.* Indianapolis: University of Indiana Press.

Maguire, E.R. & Katz, C. (2001). Community policing, loose coupling, and sensemaking in American police agencies. *Justice Quarterly,* 19 (3), 503–537.

Navarrete, L., Arboleda, A. & Gendreau, G.D. (2004). Report: U.S. criminal justice system unfair, unjust for Hispanics. Michigan State University. Available online at http://newsroom.msu.edu.

Roach, K. (1999). Four models of the criminal justice process. *Journal of Criminal Law and Criminology,* 89 (2), 671–717.

Soros Foundation Network (2004). Racial discrimination in the administration of justice. Available online at: http://www.soros.org/resources/articles_publications/publications/racialjustice_20040802.

Spohn, C. (2000). Thirty years of sentencing reform: The quest for a racially neutral sentencing process. *Criminal Justice 2000,* 3, National Institute of Justice.

Strier, F. (2000). Adversarial justice. In J. L. Victor, (Ed.), *Annual editions: Criminal justice 00/01* (24th ed.), pp.116–23. Sluice Dock, Guilford, CN: Dushkin/McGraw-Hill.

Tonry, M. (1994). Racial politics, racial disparities, and the war on crime. *Crime & Delinquency, 40* (4), 475–494.

Suggested Readings

Cole, G. F., Gertz, M. G., Bunger,A. (2006). *The criminal justice system: Politics and policies* (8th ed.). Belmont, CA: West/Wadsworth.

Gabbidon, S., & H. Taylor-Greene (2005). *Race, crime and justice.* Oxford, UK: Routledge.

Muraskin, R., & Roberts, A. R. (2004) *Visions for change: Crime and justice in the twenty-first century* (4th ed.). Upper Saddle River, NJ: Prentice Hall.

Roberts, A. (2003). *Critical issues in criminal justice* (2nd ed.). Thousand Oaks, CA: Sage Publication, Inc.

Territo, L., Halsted, J. & Bromley, M. (2004). *Crime and justice in America: A human perspective* (6th ed.). Upper Saddle River, NJ: Prentice Hall.

Chapter Two

Politics, Discretion, Ethics, and the Criminal Justice Network

"In a democratic society, the primary mechanism for holding the police accountable is the political system. Elected officials are responsible for directing the police, along with other government agencies, and for seeing that they reflect the will of the people. In this country, primary responsibility for directing the police falls on mayors and city council members, and to a lesser extent on county commissioners responsible for sheriffs' departments. They do so primarily by appointing police chiefs and controlling police department budgets.

The sad fact of our history, however, is that the political process has often failed in this area. Mayors and city council members have displayed either staggering indifference to police problems or have themselves been the ultimate source of police problems. Most of those elected officials have not cared about police misconduct. Additionally, even today those who are well intentioned lack expert knowledge about the very complex aspects of policing and police administration. Few are able to move beyond clichés about 'professionalism' or 'tough policing' and most fall back on purely symbolic gestures, such as putting more officers on the street. Through all of the nineteenth century and much of the twentieth, these elected officials thought about the police primarily in terms of the potential opportunities for graft or patronage.

Insofar as elected officials have taken an active interest in law enforcement policies, it has been to corrupt [them] or to dictate policies that have undesirable consequences."

Source: Walker, S. (2001). *Police accountability: The role of citizen oversight.* Belmont, CA: Wadsworth/Thomson Learning, p. 9.

Key Terms

> politics
> independent counsel
> power
> authority
> discretion
> full enforcement
> selective enforcement
> testilying
> plea bargaining
> ethics

Chapter Outline

> Politics in Criminal Justice
> The Pervasive Influence of Politics: From the Law to the Police and Courts to Corrections
> Power, Authority, and Politics
> Recognizing the Consequences of Politics in the Criminal Justice Network
> Discretion in Criminal Justice
> Public Discretion
> Police Discretion
> Prosecutorial Discretion
> Defense Counsel Discretion
> Judicial Discretion
> Plea Bargaining as a Form of Discretion
> Correctional Discretion
> Ethics in Criminal Justice

Politics in Criminal Justice

Criminal justice is always practiced within a political context. The introductory quote from Walker (2001) illustrates the relationship between one component of the criminal justice network—the police—and politics. According to Estrich (1998), "The best that can be said of the political debate about crime in America is that it has nothing to do with crime. Politically speaking, crime is a values issue; the value is toughness.... No one tells the truth, and the political dishonesty is distorting and destroying the system" (p.65). A good deal of research suggests that local politics can influence criminal justice outcomes: Wilson's (1968) study of police organizations includes a discussion of the ways that local political culture influences styles of policing; Jacobs and Carmichael (2002), Jacobs and O'Brien (1998), Jacobs and Wood (1999), Walker

Politics and criminal justice are interrelated.
Reprinted with permission of iStockphoto.com / Oleg Prikhodko

(2001), Stucky (2003), and Stucky (2005) suggest that local politics affects criminal justice outcomes in a variety of ways.

The relationship between law and politics has been recognized since ancient times. Yet, it took the social conflicts of the 1960s and 1970s and the intense reaction to violent crime in the early 1990s for us to recognize the fact that criminal justice reflects the values of those individuals and groups with political power. In fact, among the agencies that lend themselves most readily to political manipulation are those of the criminal justice network (Chambliss, 1994; Cole & Gertz, 1998, Feld, 2003). Crime and justice are clearly public policy issues (recall the example from Chapter 1 on mandatory sentencing laws). As the headlines reflect, with an increase in crime the public calls upon political leaders to "do something." In many cases, politicians respond by saying what they believe the public wants to hear, whether or not what they promise is likely to have any dramatic impact on crime (Feld, 2003; Walker, 1998, p. 14). Conservative politicians have been most successful in this respect over the last three decades as they advocated a law-and-order approach and get-tough policies. Nonetheless, Bill Clinton used support of a national police corps and of various gun control measures as a way to neutralize the conservative approaches of both George Bush and Bob Dole in 1992 and 1996. As Walker (1998) points out, "Nonsense about crime is politically nonpartisan"(p. 17).

There is a tendency when discussing the relationships between politics and criminal justice to focus on the negative aspects of those relationships. This is true, perhaps because cases involving political corruption or manipulation of the criminal justice network for personal gain receive a great deal more attention in our society than the day-to-day influence of politics on the network. A moment's reflection, however, is all that is required to note that political input into the criminal justice network is both necessary and desirable in a democratic society. The intermingling of politics and criminal justice is characteristic of all known societies and so may be considered perfectly normal. In fact, a crucial distinction between totalitarian and free nations is that although both develop criminal justice networks controlled by government, governments in totalitarian societies often acknowledge no accountability, while in free societies, criminal justice practitioners are answerable to democratically elected political bodies. The recent focus by the federal legislature and the Justice Department on the actions of federal law enforcement officers in the name of the Patriot Act illustrates this point. In this case, Federal Bureau of Investigation personnel are alleged to have demanded personal data and telephone records of individuals without official authorization through the illegal use of national security letters. Such actions, it is alleged, violate the right to privacy of American citizens and are unacceptable according to Attorney General Alberto Gonzales and Federal Bureau of Investigation Director Robert Mueller (Jordan, 2007, p. A3). Further, the influence of politics on federal prosecutors (including the attorney general) is apparent in headlines such as "Senator: Gonzales should resign" (*Peoria Journal Star,* 2007, March 12, p. A5) and "Dems seek no-confidence vote on Gonzales" (*USA Today,* May 17, 2007) relating to this issue.

The Pervasive Influence of Politics: From the Law to the Police and Courts to Corrections

Law is not written in a vacuum; rather, it is the result of political action. **Politics** may be defined as the process by which tangible (material) and symbolic rewards or resources are differentially distributed or allocated. According to Lasswell (1958) politics is concerned with who gets what, when, and how.

As we indicate throughout this book, criminal justice practitioners work in a network of reciprocal relationships, many of which are shaped by political considerations or are directly political. As Cole (1993) indicates, "the confluence of law, administration, and politics results in a system in which officials who are sensitive to the political process make decisions at various points concerning the arrest, charges, conviction, and sentences of defendants" (p.4). On one level, we are all aware of the importance of political parties in determining who will serve as the prosecutors, judges, police chiefs, and wardens in the criminal justice network. But just how important are political considerations in the day-to-day functioning of the network, and in what ways are they important? In its application, isn't the law supposed to be nonpolitical? Isn't everyone supposed to be treated the same under the law?

In his study of the relationship between politics and the police, Wilson (1968) found that there was little direct, day-to-day political influence on the police in the communities he examined. However, he found that the political culture of the communities was very important in determining the style of law enforcement employed, the type of chief selected, and the nature of departmental activities and policy. Politics are integral to any police operation (Walker, 2001). Personal politics involves using influence for personal gain, while community politics involves democratic control over the police. Although the former may cause a variety of problems, the latter is essential in our society.

Observations indicate that the political form of city government (commissioner, mayor/council, city manager) makes a great deal of difference in the extent to which politics permeates police departments. The role that a mayor may play in the criminal justice network, as well as the potential for conflict among different levels of government and among different components of the criminal justice network, is illustrated by the comments of Mayor Adrian Fenty of the Disrict of Columbia concerning a federal appeals court decision overturning the District's long-standing handgun ban. The decision held that the District cannot prevent people from keeping handguns in their homes. In response to the decision, Mayor Fenty stated, "Today's decision flies in the face of gun laws that have helped decrease gun violence in the District of Columbia" (*Peoria Journal Star*, 2007, March 10, p. A3). Much like the mayoral form of city government, the commissioner form of government places a political figure, who may or may not be acquainted with the complexities of police operations, at the top of the police administrative hierarchy. It may be that a professional city manager is better prepared to deal with such complexities and less likely to permit direct political intervention into police operations.

Regardless of the form of government involved, police, probation, correctional, and court administrators are dependent on the political figures mentioned above for resources. Personnel, equipment, salaries, and benefits are all negotiated through the political representatives of citizens. At the same time, of course, these criminal justice practitioners themselves, as voters and citizens, can influence the outcome of elections and thereby have a voice in selecting the political figures with whom they will negotiate.

We are all familiar with the misuses of political power in relation to police departments. Politicians who use, or attempt to use, the prestige of office to place themselves above the law have become infamous, particularly in recent decades. There are also able politicians who seek office to attempt to correct some of the wrongs that have been uncovered in police departments, courts, or correctional facilities. The police are influenced by political considerations in yet another way. The cases that they prepare must eventually be transferred to the prosecutor for further processing; thus, the policies and desires of the prosecutor influence the kinds of cases sent forward by the police, as well as the manner in which such cases are prepared.

The prosecutor is first and foremost a political figure. Prosecutors are political actors of consequence because they are generally elected or appointed with party support, they have patronage jobs at their disposal, and they exercise considerable discretion. Prosecutors are tied both to the internal politics of the criminal justice network and to local, state, or national political organizations. Since the discretionary powers of the prosecutor are considerable, he or she may be persuaded to take political advantage of the criminal justice position. Thus, charges may be dropped to avoid the possibility of losing difficult cases (and thereby political support), disclosures of wrongdoing by political opponents may be made at opportune moments, and decisions about the types of crimes to be prosecuted may be made for strictly political reasons. A good example of the relationship between the office of prosecutor and politics is the appointment of an **independent counsel** at the federal level. When a sitting president is to be investigated for possible wrongdoing, the attorney general of the United States would normally be in charge of the investigation. However, because the president appoints the attorney general, it is feared that the political connections between the president (the attorney general's immediate boss and political benefactor) and the attorney general may interfere with a complete investigation. The law allows the appointment of a private attorney to conduct the investigation in such cases. Even under these circumstances, however, there is concern as to whether a complete, honest investigation is possible because of the various political pressures brought to bear on the independent counsel. In the investigation of President Bill Clinton's conduct in office, Kenneth Starr was appointed independent counsel. Some were concerned that he might not conduct a thorough investigation because he was appointed by Attorney General Reno and supervised by Reno and a panel of judges. Others were concerned that he used his powers as independent counsel too broadly, costing American taxpayers over $40 million and looking into conduct that was not the immediate subject of his assigned investigation. In this case, many Republicans supported Starr's tactics, while many Democrats were critical, indicating the intermingling of politics and prosecutorial investigation at the highest levels. The shoe was on the other foot when Patrick Fitzgerald was appointed special prosecutor investigating the "leak" of the identity of CIA agent Valerie Plame. In this case, Lewis "Scooter"Libby was found guilty not of the crime of "outing" the agent, but of being less than honest with a grand jury and the Federal Bureau of Investigation. Republicans saw Libby's prosecution as a witch hunt, Democrats as an indication of corruption in the Bush administration. The political context in which the Libby trial occurred is clearly indicated in the headlines of *USA Today* which proclaim "GOP: Verdict about Libby; Democrats say it's bigger" (March 6, 2007), and "Conservatives press Bush for Libby pardon" (March 8, 2007).

The prosecutor, of course, does not have total freedom to exercise his or her discretion, since the police, the publics, and the judges all have vested interests of their own to protect, and they exert varying degrees of pressure on the prosecutor. Some prosecutors are more concerned about advancing their own political careers than providing the legal expertise required by some other components of the criminal justice network. Others, elected to office soon after graduation from law school, may have promising political skills but little or no competence or experience in the courtroom. Many others are basically concerned about providing the services required by the public in a competent, professional manner. In any case, the public has the opportunity to indicate satisfaction or dissatisfaction with the prosecutor at election time. The prosecutor who wishes to continue in office or to advance in the political arena is constrained, to some extent, by the conflicting interests of those who surround him or her, as well as by financial obstacles (Barlow, 2000, p. 366). One example of the interaction between politics and prosecutors involved the firing of eight U.S. attorneys by Attorney General Alberto Gonzales (a political appointee of President Bush). Among the attorneys terminated was one who said he received phone calls from Republican members of

Congress inquiring into the status of ongoing probes of local Democrats. These calls were perceived as applying political pressure to bring indictments. Some of the other attorneys terminated were removed to make room for political allies of the administration. While all these attorneys are political appointees and serve at the will of the President, congressional interference with the role of supposedly independent counsel tends to be seen as inappropriate (Editorial, *USA Today*, 2007, March 7, p. 10A; Johnson, 2007, p. 5A)

The next step in the career ladder of many prosecutors is that of judge, and deeds performed for a political party are often invaluable in obtaining a judgeship. In a number of states, county and circuit court judges are elected directly by the voters. In other states, judges are appointed by the governor from a list prepared by a more or less nonpartisan committee. In either case, the appointments are clearly political, and most judges have records as active political campaigners.

Federal judges are appointed to the bench by the president, with confirmation by the Senate, in a highly politicized process whereby the senior senator of the president's party from the state in which a vacancy exists typically controls the appointment. When federal judges are appointed, partisan politics are clearly not set aside, since the vast majority of all federal judges ever appointed have been members of the same political party as the president who appointed them. That the United States Supreme Court is not exempt from party politics was demonstrated clearly by Woodward and Armstrong (1979) in *The Brethren: Inside the Supreme Court*. From consideration of nominees by the president, through Senate approval or disapproval of such nominees, the appointment process is clearly political. The Court's decision to hear or not hear a case and the decision concerning who will write which opinion are also made in a clearly political context. Finally, we should be aware of the ramifications of a change in the political ideology of the Supreme Court that results from retirements and new appointments. For example, over the past two decades such changes have occurred with respect to defendants' rights as the Court has changed from the liberal Warren Court to a more conservative Court. Consequently, there are fears that erosion of defendants' rights might well continue. Currently, it is believed that there is a division among the justices on many issues with Justices Scalia, Thomas, Alito, and Roberts, seen as generally conservative, and justices Stevens, Breyer, Souter, and Ginsburg, seen as generally liberal. Justice Kennedy is viewed as the swing vote in many cases.

It should be noted that while the president recommends candidates for the federal judiciary, he does not act alone. Candidates are recommended to him by political associates. The senate reviews, and sometimes refuses, his recommendations, again demonstrating the interaction of politics and the justice network at the highest levels. The contentious nature of recent confirmation hearings involving justices Roberts and Alito clearly indicates the importance attached by both liberals and conservatives to the appointment of supreme court justices.

Before leaving our discussion of politics and lawyers, we would like to note the importance of the many local and state bar associations, as well as the American Bar Association, to the criminal justice network. These associations commonly screen and recommend candidates for positions in the judiciary and thereby play a key role in determining the level of competence and the extent of partisan politics in the network.

In addition, they demonstrate the manner in which organizations not included in the traditional systems model influence the criminal justice network.

In the field of corrections, once again the impact of political decisions on the criminal justice network can be clearly seen. The political appointment of wardens has been a significant handicap in developing good correctional programs. In addition to playing a key role in determining the type of custody or treatment an individual receives while in prison, political considerations are generally involved in determining the makeup of the parole board, which decides if and when an individual will be released from prison. In the majority of jurisdictions, parole board members are appointed by the governor with legislative confirmation.

Probation officers are generally appointed by the chief judge of a circuit or by a panel of judges. In locally administered probation offices, political considerations play an important role in determining who will be appointed to the probation officer's job. In state-administered probation departments, the influence of political considerations may be less apparent. Today, the majority of states have eliminated local administration in favor of statewide administration of probation. However, there is little doubt that local interests still play a part in the selection and retention of probation personnel in indirect ways.

We would be remiss if we did not also mention the increasing impact of global politics on the practice of criminal justice in the U.S. As concern over terrorism and terrorists has increased, major changes have occurred or have been proposed in policing, prosecution, the courts, and corrections. Law enforcement personnel at all levels are increasingly responsible for protecting airports and other transportation networks, water supplies and public utilities, and public places from the threat of terrorist activities. Prosecutors have new tools to work with, some of which have raised serious questions about civil liberties in America. New forms of court tribunals have been proposed and implemented, also raising serious issues concerning the rights of citizens. And prisoners have been kept in covert locations around the world as well as in overt facilities in which questionable practices have been alleged. There is no indication that the need for criminal justice practitioners to keep abreast of international events and their impact of the U.S. will diminish in coming years.

Power, Authority, and Politics

We can define **power** as the net ability of persons or groups to recurrently impose their will on others despite resistance (Blau, 1964; Robbins, 2005, pp. 391–394; Weber, 1947). The exercise of power depends on the ability to supply and to withhold rewards and/or punishment. As mentioned earlier in this chapter, politics may be defined as the process by which rewards are differentially allocated. Power and politics, then, are inextricably interwoven. The legitimate use of power by persons in specially designated positions may be termed **authority** (Robbins, 2005, p. 456). In other words, we agree to grant people in certain positions the right to use certain types of power. The granting of this right is a political process that involves elections or appointments by others in positions of authority. Thus, we elect an individual to the office of president, and this individual consequently has the right to exercise certain types of power based on the authority of the office. Similarly, the president may appoint federal judges who then have certain powers as a result of their offices. The municipal fire and police commissions around the country are appointed by mayors and/or councils and then appoint individuals to the position of police officer. The police officer may then use certain types of power that go with the position.

Appointment or election to office does not give the appointee the right to use all forms of power or to exercise power indiscriminately. We consider an officer holder's behavior legitimate to the extent that an officeholder uses power in accordance with the rules of appointment or election. The use of powers other than those prescribed or in situations other than those specified as appropriate for the office involved is considered illegitimate. For example, the police officer who uses deadly force in self-defense while on duty is exercising legitimate power. The same officer who uses deadly force against a fleeing adolescent who has committed a minor misdemeanor is overstepping the boundaries of his or her authority and using power illegitimately.

The exercise of power from positions of authority requires that the person occupying the position of authority be granted the right to hold the position by those over whom authority is to be exercised. In a democratic society, this granting normally involves an election process or an appointment process. In a totalitarian society, the granting may be passive, as when citizens fail to resist by revolution or coup. Power and authority are not unilateral. They involve the consent (either passive or active) of those governed. A major difference between democratic and totalitarian societies is the procedure by which those exercising illegitimate power from positions of authority may be removed from office. In our society, for example, illegitimate use of the powers of office led a president to resign from office. Had he not done so, impeachment proceedings might have removed him. Citizen dissatisfaction with the performance of a public official may lead to a turnover in the presidency every four years, the recall of a judge, or the suspension of a police officer. In totalitarian societies, these peaceful means of addressing wrongs that involve politics, power, and authority may be of little value, and revolution may be the only alternative available.

Recognizing the Consequences of Politics in the Criminal Justice Network

It should now be clear that political considerations are a necessary, normal, and desirable part of the criminal justice network. The political process is the most certain way for us to maintain control of the network and direct its practitioners to serve societal goals. When we elect and remove from office the individuals who control key resources in the criminal justice network, we determine the direction and practices adhered to by those who exercise varying degrees of authority over us. We control the criminal justice network to the extent that we select officials who operate openly and we take the time to exert our political influence by monitoring the conduct of these officials and removing from office those who fail to meet our expectations.

There are, however, some very real dangers in the politics of criminal justice. There are those who argue that criminal justice is a game played by those who have wealth and political power against those who have neither. To the extent that these charges are true, we might expect to find resentment and hostility toward the criminal justice network among those who have little or no political power. It is clear that such resentment and hostility exists. Some, though not all, studies have shown that upper-income groups hold more favorable attitudes toward the police than lower-income groups, that blacks at all levels of income have negative attitudes toward the police, and that more blacks than whites feel the police are disrespectful to them (Hurst, McDermott & Thomas, 2005; Johnson, 1997; Schuck & Rosenbaum, 2005; Smith, 2005; Weitzer & Tuch, 2004) Studies also indicate that minorities may be treated by criminal justice practitioners in ways that stigmatize, brutalize, and reinforce minority stereotypes and oppression in our society (Feiler & Shely, 1999; Leiber & Stairs, 1999; Schaefer, 2000; Weitzer & Tuch, 2004). Public defender and assigned counsel programs experience virtually every imaginable kind of financial deficiency. There are neither enough lawyers to represent the poor, nor are all the available attorneys trained, assisted by ample support staffs, or sufficiently compensated (Estrich, 1998, pp.96–'99; Lee, 2004). Finally, we have to carefully assess the demands from criminal justice practitioners that certain portions of their operations remain covert.

Discretion in Criminal Justice

The exercise of discretion is another necessary, normal, and desirable part of criminal justice. But the invisibility of practitioners involved in plea bargaining and the political considerations involved in decisions to prosecute a case, hear a case, or grant parole often lead to suspicion and distrust. The exercise of discretion by practitioners in the criminal justice network has been a controversial issue for a number of years (Gelsthorpe & Padfield, 2003). Many students of criminal justice have been concerned about the largely invisible, and therefore uncontrollable, nature of discretionary justice.

There is little doubt that if we define **discretion** as the exercise of individual choice or judgment concerning possible courses of action, discretion is a normal, necessary, and even desirable part of the criminal justice network. The exercise of discretion in the criminal justice network is extensive (Gelsthorpe & Padfield, 2003). In what ways do individuals in various components of the network exercise such discretion? What are the consequences of the exercise of discretion for the network, for practitioners, and for those being processed? Is it possible to control discretion?

Public Discretion

One of the reasons we feel so strongly that the public must not be overlooked or underestimated as a component of the criminal justice network is that members of the public have discretionary powers of considerable magnitude. With respect to observed

Police exercise discretion in making traffic stops and in searching vehicles.
Reprinted with permission of Holger Mette / Fotolia.

criminal or suspicious acts, each citizen may exercise discretion in terms of reporting or not reporting, testifying or not testifying, telling the truth or not telling the truth, and so forth. Evidence indicates that over half of the crimes occurring in the United States go unreported as the result of this exercise of discretion (Perkins & Klaus, 1996, p.3; Rand & Rennison, 2002). As a consequence, the police do not investigate a large proportion of all crimes committed since they do not know (except in the relatively rare case of on-view or proactive police work) that they exist. Similarly, the prosecutor is helpless to prosecute offenders in cases where testimony on the part of witnesses is required to substantiate charges if citizens refuse to come forth to testify or testify falsely.

Among the reasons for failure of citizens to cooperate are the beliefs that the police are ineffective in arresting offenders, that prosecutors give away too much in plea bargaining, that judges hand out sentences that are too lenient, and that the entire criminal justice network is too time-consuming and uncertain (Conklin, 1998, pp. 54–56).

The exercise of discretion with respect to specific criminal activities, however, constitutes a relatively small part of the wide range of discretionary activities available to the public. Voting for politicians who campaign for or against stricter law enforcement, supporting or failing to support bond issues intended to improve police services, aiding or failing to aid in the social integration of ex-convicts, and obeying or failing to obey laws are all within the scope of public discretionary activities. At the most basic level, then, members of the public, as they exercise discretion, serve as gatekeepers for the criminal justice network.

Police Discretion

The police serve as the second level of gatekeepers for the criminal justice network. Among their discretionary powers are arrest or nonarrest, life or death, citation or verbal reprimand, investigation or lack of investigation, and many more. Just as the police may be unable to arrest an offender without citizen cooperation, the prosecutor may be unable to prosecute if the police fail to make a legal arrest. For a variety of reasons, a police officer may decide not to enforce the law. He or she may consider enforcement of certain laws a waste of police resources. The personal characteristics of the offender, departmental regulations, the time of day, the place in which an encounter occurs, public expectations, and previous court decisions may all influence the officer's decision (Alpert, MacDonald & Dunham, 2005). The realization that **full enforcement** is seldom possible or desirable, that **selective enforcement** can be an effective technique, or a personal belief that the law is inappropriate may also affect an officer's action.

In addition, the police sometimes take less than proper action to avoid due process of law. Observers of police departments have found that police may fabricate charges or details of incidents to benefit themselves in court proceedings. The process has been referred to as **testilying**, rather than testifying (Cunningham, 1999). This option is open to police as a discretionary aspect of their work. Harassment, either mental or physical, can be viewed as a discretionary measure.

If laws were written in perfectly clear language, if they contained no contradictions or ambiguities, if there was no difficulty in applying the principles stated in laws to particular situations, and if all officers were thoroughly familiar with all laws, deciding whether or not a particular law has been violated would be a simple and straightforward task for the officer. Unfortunately, these conditions, taken either singly or in combination, are seldom met. The law in the United States is a huge, complex, sometimes contradictory, and constantly changing collection of prescriptive and proscriptive rules. The large number of professionally trained legal experts, lawyers, and judiciary officials who make their living arguing over different interpretations of the law gives some indication of the ambiguities and complexities involved in applying the law. A police officer is not, and for that matter does not need to be, a lawyer, but familiarity with the basics of law is required if the officer is to discharge his or her responsibilities appropriately. However, even the best police training programs provide limited information on the law. Consequently, most of the police officer's understanding of the law is achieved indirectly. Through the informal instruction and advice offered by colleagues and supervisors, in-service training programs, cramming for promotional exams, self-initiated reading, day-to-day work experiences, and experiences in the courtroom, however, police officers quickly acquire what might be called a working knowledge of the law. For all practical purposes, this working knowledge is the law as it functions in the day-to-day activities of police officers. It is this work-generated interpretation of the law, which may or may not correspond with the interpretations of lawyers and judicial officials, that guides the officers as they carry out their law enforcement duties.

The law explicitly grants some discretionary powers to police officers and creates a framework within which other discretionary judgments may legitimately be made. It is one measure of the importance of discretion in police work that these are among the first items that become incorporated into the officer's working knowledge of the law. The officer understands, for example, that certain leeway is permitted in determining whether or not probable cause for a search is present (though legislation and court rulings have increased the confusion surrounding the legal latitude granted the officer in these matters). It is also common knowledge among officers that the overlap that frequently exists among laws gives police officers the opportunity to pick and choose which laws, if any, will be cited once a suspect is apprehended. Thus, the officer can choose to "throw the book" at a suspect by citing violations of several laws or can charge the suspect with a more or a less serious offense than circumstances might warrant. In a variety of ways, then, the law, as interpreted and understood by the police officer, creates the framework within which, and sometimes around which, police discretion is exercised (Conser & Russell, 2000; Cox, 1996).

Deciding whether or not a violation of law has taken place is perhaps the most basic, though perhaps not the most consequential, discretionary judgment a police officer makes. If the officer decides that no violation has taken place, there are usually no further formal consequences for anyone involved. If the decision is that an offense has occurred, the officer has the power to set in motion a highly complex, very expensive, and extremely inconvenient set of procedures that may end with the deprivation of a suspect's liberty. To be sure, the officer's judgment that a violation of the law has occurred is by no means the last word on the subject. Prosecutors and judges may eventually reverse the officer's decision, but it is typically the first judgment made by an official of the criminal justice network and, as such, must be considered a basic discretionary power.

Although determining whether or not an offense has been committed is a basic discretionary decision, it is probably not the most consequential so far as the exercise of police discretion is concerned. In essence, it is a technical judgment, dependent on the officer's knowledge of the law and capacity to apply the general principles embodied in the law to the particular events that have occurred. However difficult this judgment may be (and it is difficult in many instances), it is a decision that merely sets the stage for a far more consequential one—deciding whether or not to take official action. If the police officer decides not to arrest, the remainder of the legal machinery in the criminal justice network does not normally come into play. Once an officer decides to take official action in a criminal matter, he or she again exercises discretion with respect to the number and type of charges to be brought against the defendant. The case is then turned over to the prosecutor, who makes a number of discretionary decisions.

Prosecutorial Discretion

"Viewed in broad perspective, the American legal system seems to be shot through with many excessive and uncontrolled discretionary powers, but the one that stands out above all others is the power to prosecute or not to prosecute" (Davis, 1971, p.181). Discretionary activities on behalf of the prosecutor include deciding whether or not to prosecute a given individual, what charges to file, whether or not to plea-bargain, how much time and money to devote to a particular case, what type and how much evidence to share (under discovery motions) with the defense, and, in some cases, what type of sentence or punishment to recommend if the defendant is found guilty. Like the police officer, the prosecutor operates within a network that places limits on the amount of discretion he or she may exercise (Miller & Eisenstein, 2005). Economic considerations, political considerations, public opinion, the law, and expectations of other network practitioners all influence the decisions made (Barlow, 2000, pp. 365–66; Johnson, 2005). (See "In the News" 2.1) ("Prosecutors as truth seekers, ministers of justice").

In the News 2.1

PROSECUTORS AS TRUTH SEEKERS, MINISTERS OF JUSTICE

Most states have ethics rules designed to make prosecutors in the American criminal-justice system act as "ministers of justice," seeking the truth and just punishment for offenders.

Prosecutors wield immense power to authorize arrests, bring charges, dismiss charges, recommend punishment, help prisoners win early release or work to keep them behind bars.

When prosecutors cheat, the consequences can be devastating. Earlier this year when Durham County, N.C., prosecutor Ray Nifong withheld DNA evidence, three Duke University lacrosse players faced possible long prison terms on false charges of raping an exotic dancer. After the cheating was revealed, Nifong resigned, was disbarred and briefly jailed.

"Prosecutors in our system have enormous power — a frightening amount of power," said Hal Harlowe, a Madison criminal-defense attorney who was Dane County's elected district attorney from 1983 to 1989. "They have the power to cost people thousands of dollars and … they can destroy people with just an accusation."

Prosecutors are called on to assess what the law requires and what's reasonable and fair while weighing the rights of the accused, of victims and of society to be protected from its worst elements.

Despite their lofty calling, prosecutors in the United States have suppressed evidence that points to a suspect's innocence, knowingly used false testimony, fabricated evidence, coerced witnesses and made false statements to juries, said Peter Joy, a Washington University law professor who studies prosecutor misconduct.

1 LICENSE REVOKED

In Wisconsin, prosecutors have been disciplined for behavior ranging from bribery, forging documents and providing false information to police to making misrepresentations to the court, drug use and meeting with defendants without their attorneys' permission. The punishments ranged from private reprimands to temporary loss of their law licenses. Only one prosecutor's law license has been revoked.

Experts disagree about whether it's a widespread problem, or relatively unusual. Even when prosecutors are caught cheating, they rarely face sanctions, Joy said in an article published last year in the Wisconsin Law Review. "With impunity, prosecutors across the country have violated their oaths and the law, committing the worst kinds of deception in the most serious cases," Joy wrote. "They do it to win. They do it because they won't get punished."

In a 2003 study, the Washington, D.C.-based Center for Public Integrity found that local prosecutors nationwide have "stretched, bent or broken rules to win convictions."

Keith Sellen, executive director of the state Office of Lawyer Regulation, which handles misconduct complaints against lawyers, declined to say how many complaints against prosecutors his agency has received, citing the confidentiality of the lawyer-discipline system.

Sellen said his office investigates all allegations, and rarely finds merit in the complaints, which often are filed by convicts and their lawyers. He added that regulators recognize that to do their jobs, prosecutors must have great **discretion**.

NOTORIOUS CASE

In one notorious Wisconsin case, former Winnebago County District Attorney Joseph Paulus was convicted in 2004 of taking bribes to fix 22 cases and sentenced to nearly five years in federal prison. Paulus also will serve a two-year state term for the offenses.

Despite several complaints filed against Paulus, state regulators never disciplined the errant prosecutor until after he was federally convicted in the scheme. Sellen said that's because it took the FBI to root out evidence.

"In general, prosecutor discipline is quite rare," said Ellen Yaroshefsky, a clinical professor and director of the Cardozo Law School's Jacob Burns Ethics Center in New York City.

However, she believes there's increasing awareness among attorneys and the public that prosecutor misconduct is a problem.

RELUCTANT TO COMPLAIN

One check on misconduct is defense attorneys who spar with prosecutors. Under Wisconsin Supreme Court rules, lawyers are required to report ethical violations by other lawyers.

Practically speaking, however, defense attorneys rarely complain about prosecutors, Yaroshefsky said, because they must deal with prosecutors on every case, bargaining with them to get the best deal for their clients.

"No defense lawyer wants to alienate the decision-maker over what (punishment) their client will get," Yaroshefsky said.

Dane County Prosecutor Brian Blanchard said he's aware of only a few complaints filed against his staff since he took office in January 2001. None has made it as far as the Supreme Court — except a complaint against Paul Humphrey.

Joy believes top prosecutors can play a key role by "setting clearer guidelines within their offices, and disciplining those prosecutors who do not live up to their obligations."

Yaroshefsky said cheating by prosecutors will remain unless unethical behavior is met with more serious and frequent consequences.

Blanchard said he believes prosecutor misconduct is rare in Wisconsin, in part because prosecutors want to maintain good reputations with defense lawyers.

Still, mistakes can happen.

"In a higher volume system, there's more potential for mistakes in the sense that things are coming fast," Blanchard said. "Everybody's overburdened — defense lawyers, judges, prosecutors."

By the numbers

25

Elected district attorneys, assistant district attorneys and municipal attorneys disciplined for unethical and illegal conduct among the 1,420 attorneys who've been disciplined by the Wisconsin Supreme Court since 1985.

2,000

Cases where prosecutor misconduct was a factor in dismissals, reversed convictions or reduced sentences in the U.S. since from 1970 to 2002.

9,000

Cases nationally in that time in which judges cited misconduct but called it harmless.

107

Wisconsin cases appealed on allegation of prosecutorial cheating or error from 1970 to 2003.

29

Wisconsin cases where a judge reversed or remanded convictions, sentences or charges because of prosecutor misconduct during that time. Sources: Wisconsin Office of Lawyer Regulation records, Center for Public Integrity, "Harmful Error: Investigating America's Local Prosecutors," 2003.

GO ONLINE: For a list of disciplinary actions taken against Wisconsin prosecutors, see www.madison.com/wsj

FOR HELP

To report unethical behavior by an attorney or prosecutor, contact the Wisconsin Office of Lawyer Regulation at (608) 267-7274 or (877) 315-6941. More information also is available at www.wicourts.gov under Office of Lawyer Regulation.

To report unethical behavior by a judge, contact the Wisconsin Judicial Commission at (608) 266-7637 or www.wicourts.gov under Committees and Reports and click on Judicial Commission.

State Journal archives

Dane County District Attorney Brian Blanchard, known for prosecuting a scandal in the Wisconsin Legislature, says members of the legal profession may make mistakes because of heavy workloads, but corrupt prosecutors are rare in the state.

Hall, D.J. (2007 September, 30). Prosecutors as truth seekers, ministers of justice. *Wisconsin State Journal* (Madison, WI). Front, p. A6. "Copyright *Wisconsin State Journal*. Reprinted with permission."

Defense Counsel Discretion

Defense counsel, in conjunction with the defendant, has discretionary powers as well. He or she must decide whether to plea-bargain, what plea to enter, what motions to file, how much time and effort to devote to a given case, whether or not to accept any given case (at least when private counsel is involved), and so forth. In addition, the attitude of defense counsel toward plea bargaining (demanding or reasonable, for example) may be related to the likelihood of success in reaching a compromise. Again, there are constraints that to some extent shape the decisions made, but the exercise of discretion by counsel obviously occurs frequently and has important consequences (Zelnick, 2003).

Judicial Discretion

Judges decide whether objections that attorneys make to the questions asked of witnesses by other attorneys should be sustained or overruled. They decide whether evidence may be admitted or must be excluded, whether there is sufficient evidence to let the case go to the jury for a decision on the factual question of guilt, or whether a mistrial must be declared as a result of some serious error that would prejudice the case. They may have great influence over the jury through their attitudes, their rulings, and their charges. They will also have an impact on those who testify and those who are parties in the trial. Judges, too, are in positions that permit considerable discretionary activity. Some are more lenient than others in admitting certain types of evidence. Some have reputations for being "maximum sentence" judges, while others may be regarded as "bleeding heart liberals." Some are more trusting of police testimony and less inclined to pay strict attention to technicalities than others. Disparities in sentencing individuals who have committed similar crimes are yet another example of judicial discretion (Dripp, 1996; Johnson, 2005). At the level of the United States Supreme Court, judicial discretion is even involved in deciding whether or not to hear a particular case. The discretion exercised by judges may not have the immediate life-or-death impact that sometimes characterizes police discretion, but the long-term effects of sentencing decisions may have the same impact.

Plea Bargaining as a Form of Discretion

Plea bargaining is a form of discretion that involves at least the defendant, the defense counsel, and the prosecutor. In some cases it may also involve the police and the judge. Since bargained or negotiated pleas account for the vast majority of guilty pleas in the United States, plea bargaining is a key part of the criminal justice process (Palermo, White, & Wasserman, 1998). All parties involved exercise discretion in bargaining over the charges to be filed and the sentence to be imposed (see "In the News" 2.2 below). The defendant may exercise her or his discretion in deciding whether or not to enter into plea negotiations. The same is true of defense counsel and the prosecutor. Once they agree to negotiate, the opposing parties attempt to gain concessions from each other. The extent to which the parties are willing to grant such concessions depends on their individual judgments (discretion) as to what may be gained in return. The judge, in some jurisdictions, exercises his or her discretion in determining whether or not to accept a negotiated guilty plea along with the attendant conditions. In some cases, the prosecutor may talk to the police officers involved in the arrest or investigation before deciding what concessions, if any, to grant in the negotiations.

In the News 2.2

BARGAINING FOR JUSTICE

The plea deal allowing a man accused of sexual assault on a 4-year-old boy to avoid serving time in prison raises questions about justice, punishment and the welfare of victims. The case involved a Manchester man, Andrew James, accused of felony sexual assault on a child younger than 10 years old, which carries a penalty of up to life in prison and a $50,000 fine or both. But the prosecution in the case believed that the only way it could obtain a conviction in a jury trial was by forcing the 4-year-old victim to testify. Instead, it agreed to a plea deal that would secure a guilty plea in exchange for a sentence of 30 months to five years of jail time, all of it suspended.

The offender will be required to complete sex offender treatment and to register as a sex offender. If he fails to complete treatment to the satisfaction of his probation officer, he would have to serve his jail term. The case calls to mind that of Mark Hulett, which gained national attention last year when Judge Edward Cashman sentenced Hulett to only two months in jail for sexual assault. Cashman did so because corrections policy would not have provided sex offender treatment for Hulett until the end of his jail term, and Cashman believed Hulett needed treatment sooner rather than later. Getting him out of jail sooner was the only way to achieve that end.

The brouhaha that followed the sentencing of Hulett forced the Corrections Department to change its policy so that prisoners are able to get treatment when they need it. Hulett later received a longer sentence.

The case of Andrew James hinges on a different problem. On the one hand, there is the public's expectation that punishment in criminal cases is measured in time served in jail. On the other hand, there was the judgment of the prosecution that taking the case to trial was the only way to obtain a lengthy jail sentence for James and that doing so would harm the young victim.

It is a sad truth that the victims of sexual abuse are sometimes victimized twice: once by the offender and a second time by the judicial system. Even adult victims of sexual abuse are often unwilling to go through the process of a criminal trial. The trauma for a 4-year-old boy might be even more severe. That was the judgment of the prosecutors in the James case.

Plea bargains are often characterized as a form of compromised justice, but they are often the only way to obtain a conviction in a case. If every case had to go to trial, the justice system would be hopelessly bogged down.

But the outrage provoked by the crime to which Andrew James has pleaded guilty is hardly quelled by the sentence he received. It is clear that James has gotten away with something. And yet if the prosecutor's judgment is accurate about the potential for damage to the victim, it may be that the sentence obtained by the prosecution is the best that could be gained in this case.

James' criminal record does not indicate he is a good citizen. He is on notice. He must either cooperate with treatment or he will be headed for jail. It may be that in the end, he will not have gotten away with it after all.

Moats, D. (2007, January 11). Bargaining for justice. *Rutland Herald* Record Number 701110307

As has been pointed out, none of the discretionary powers exercised is without limits. Each participant in plea bargaining is constrained by the facts of the case, resources available, and the goals of other participants. Again, the network model allows us to analyze the workings of criminal justice practitioners as they go about their day-to-day duties.

Correctional Discretion

The exercise of discretion also occurs frequently and regularly among correctional officials. Probation and parole officers decide what conditions to impose on their charges and how strictly to enforce such conditions. In juvenile cases, for example, the judgment of a probation officer can determine whether a probationer may marry, move out of state, or join the armed forces.

Although parole boards operate according to specific regulations, discretion plays an important part in determining when and if parole or early release will occur. The discretionary powers of prison wardens to make inmate assignments and to allow minor infractions of prison rules to go unpunished by instructing guards as to the type of conduct they consider worthy of note are considerable. Similarly, prison staff members exercise their discretion in determining what to overlook and what to report to the warden.

Although we have not attempted to discuss all the types of discretion in the day-to-day operations of the criminal justice network (for example, the discretion exercised by political figures in determining whether to try to influence the decisions of the police or prosecutor, or the discretion exercised by offenders in deciding when and how to commit a crime), it should be clear that discretion plays an important role at all levels of the network. Network participants, of course, are limited as to the amount and type of discretion they may employ by the factors we have discussed above. Still, the range of alternatives available at any given place in the network is sufficient to make it difficult to predict with certainty exactly what actions, if any, will be taken, except perhaps in cases involving serious predatory crimes (and even these are sometimes not predictable). Selective reporting of crimes, selective enforcement of laws, and selective processing of those against whom the law is enforced are necessary and normal activities in the criminal justice network. Criminal justice, as we know it, could not exist without discretion. We should not lose sight, however, of the fact that the exercise of discretion sometimes confuses those who participate in or observe the network. When the exercise of discretion becomes whimsical or haphazard, predictability is lost, and for those in a democratic society, the network may cease to be perceived as one dispensing justice.

Ethics in Criminal Justice

Closely related, perhaps inseparable, from notions of discretion and politics in criminal justice is the issue of ethics. The word **ethics** has a number of meanings. In its most general sense, it refers to the sum total of human duty, the moral obligation of human beings to act in ways that are good, just and proper. Applied ethics may be viewed as dealing with standards created by and/or for professionals, and specialized ethics may be seen as those that apply to a particular profession. For a specialized area of ethics to emerge, certain conditions must be met. The area must have some special features that make it difficult to bring under the domain of general, conventional ethics; that is, the ethics of the area must be in some way different from conventional ethics (Close & Meier 1995; Delattre, 2002; Pollock, 2007; Souryal, 2003).

Criminal justice practitioners possess at least two capacities whose use raises special ethical problems: They are sometimes entitled to use coercive force, and they are sometimes entitled to lie and deceive people in the course of their work. Because of these two special capacities, it is imperative that criminal justice practitioners exercise discretion within an ethical framework. The ethics of criminal justice practitioners have consequences that are of concern not just to practitioners but also to those outside the area, because practitioners who engage in unethical practices may offend the moral sensibilities of sizable numbers of people.

Ethical considerations are paramount where certain types of misconduct cannot be or are thought better not controlled by other means (law, supervisory review, or public opinion). Usually, these areas involve considerable discretion on the part of practitioners who consumers must trust to be ethical. Unethical behavior destroys the confidence of those who trust criminal justice practitioners not only in the individual practitioners involved, but also in the network itself. Governors convicted of racketeering, police officers sodomizing prisoners, juries acquitting defendants who appear clearly guilty, and presidents who are impeached do little to inspire confidence in the criminal justice network or in the ethics of governmental officials.

Of course, the actual decision to violate ethical standards comes down to the individual (Cox, Campbell & McCamey, 2002). Thus, the practice of criminal justice can safely be entrusted only to those who understand what is morally important and who respect integrity. Without such understanding and respect, no codes or rules or laws can safeguard other citizens from the danger of misconduct by police, prosecutors, judges, wardens, and other criminal justice practitioners.

It may be argued that so many gray areas exist in the practice of criminal justice that black-and-white decisions become impossible. While reasonable people may debate the existence of probable cause for a vehicle stop, reasonable doubt in a criminal case, or judicial dispositions of probation versus incarceration, there are some acts that are clearly unethical: stealing; brutally violating human and civil rights; planting evidence, obtaining retroactive search warrants, or forcing people to sign disclaimers; lying under oath; and disclosing confidential information. Although most of us would agree that such behaviors are inappropriate among criminal justice practitioners, there is ample evidence that they occur with some degree of regularity (Cunningham, 1999; Dripp, 1996; Smith, 1997; Smith & Holmes, 2003). Although the proportion of criminal justice practitioners involved in unethical conduct is probably relatively small, their conduct tarnishes the image of all practitioners.

Summary

1. The relationship between law and politics has long been recognized, but events in the first decade of the twenty-first century indicate just how important this relationship can be.

2. Although cases that involve the negative impact of politics on criminal justice receive a great deal of attention, we need to be aware of the many positive aspects of politics in the criminal justice network as well.

3. Societal values (both positive and negative) are transmitted to the network through the political process. The creation of law is a political act.

4. From police to prosecutors, judges, and correctional officials, the political culture shapes policies and practices. Prosecutors and judges are politicians, and police chiefs, wardens, and probation and parole officers are political appointees. It makes little sense, therefore, to think of the criminal justice network as outside the realm of politics.

5. Power (the ability to influence others) and authority (the right to use certain forms of power in certain circumstances) are critical components of the criminal justice-political network. Authority does not allow individuals to use power indiscriminately, and the exercise of authority requires either the active or passive consent of the governed.

6. Political considerations are a necessary, normal, and desirable part of the criminal justice network. They provide a way for concerned citizens to influence the scope and direction of the network. However, if political access is not uniformly available to all citizens, resentment and hostility among those denied such access may be expected.

7. Discretion, or the exercise of individual choice or judgment, is an important part of the criminal justice process. Although choices and judgments made by participants in the criminal justice network are limited by the resources available, the expectations of other participants, the law, and other factors, there is still considerable latitude in the decision-making process. Discretion is a normal, necessary part of criminal justice, but it can be misused and abused. When the exercise of discretion leads to unpredictability or to predictable favoritism in the criminal justice network, it is likely that the network will be characterized as unjust.

8. Ethical values are derived from many sources and range from general beliefs about life to specialized ethics applied to specific criminal justice practitioners. Specialized ethics are essential for criminal justice practitioners because they sometimes have the rights to deceive others in the course of their duties and to use deadly force, and because much of what they do is invisible to outsiders. Although there are some gray areas in the practice of criminal justice, there are also many areas where proper conduct is obvious to all of us. When criminal justice practitioners fail to engage in ethical conduct, they tarnish the image of all those involved in the network.

Key Terms Defined

politics The process by which rewards or resources are differentially distributed or allocated.

independent counsel A private counsel retained by the U.S. Attorney General to investigate high-ranking government officials.

power The ability of persons or groups to impose their will on others despite resistance.

authority The right of specially designated persons to use power in a legitimate fashion.

discretion The exercise of individual choice or judgment concerning possible courses of action; a normal and necessary part of the criminal justice network.

full enforcement Enforcing all the laws all the time.

selective enforcement Enforcing some laws at one time and place and others at other times and places.

testilying Police making intentionally false statements under oath in court.

plea bargaining A form of discretionary activity in which the charges to be filed and/or the sentence to be recommended are negotiated by at least the defendant and his or her counsel and the prosecutor.

ethics Standards of right and wrong behavior.

Critical Thinking Exercises

1. Discuss the complex relationships among law, politics, and the criminal justice network. Are these relationships always negative in nature? Why or why not?

2. What are the relationships among power, authority, and politics? How do these relationships affect the criminal justice network? Give a specific, recent example.

Internet Exercises

The issue of ethics in criminal justice has stimulated many criminal justice organizations to develop formal codes of ethics, and some of those organizations publicize their codes on the Internet. You can access the Benton, Missouri, police code of ethics at http://www.aocds.org/code_of_ethics.htm

Read the Orange County code of ethics then answer the following questions:

1. What are the highest priorities in this code of ethics? Are they appropriate? Are there any additions you would make if you were developing your own code?

2. What are the expectations for police officers who are off duty? Are these reasonable? Are these expectations communicated during educational and skills training?

3. What role does discretion play in the code of ethics? If you were designing a training workshop, how would you communicate the importance of these concepts to the participants?

4. The code provides no provisions for violations. What types of sanctions do you think should be imposed for violations of fundamental duty, confidentiality, and acting officiously?

References

Alpert, G. P., & Dunham, R. G. (1997). *Policing urban America* (3rd ed.). Prospect Heights, IL: Waveland Press.

Alpert, G. P., MacDonald, J. M. & Dunham, R. G. (2005). Policing suspicion and discretionary decision making during citizen stops. *Criminology, 43* (2), 407–435.

Barlow, H. D. (2000). *Criminal justice in America*. Upper Saddle River, NJ: Prentice Hall.

Blau, P. M. (1964). *Exchange and power in social life*. New York: Wiley.

Chambliss, W. J. (1994). Policing the ghetto underclass: The politics of law and law enforcement. *Social Problems, 41* (2), 177–94.

Close, D., & Meier, N. (1995). *Morality in criminal justice: An introduction to ethics.* Belmont, CA: Wadsworth.

Cole, G. F. (1993). *Criminal justice: Law and politics* (6th ed.). Belmont, CA: Wadsworth.

Cole, G. F., & Gertz, M. G. (1998). *The criminal justice system: Politics and policies* (7th ed.). Belmont, CA: West/Wadsworth.

Conklin, J. E. (1998). *Criminology* (6th ed.). Boston: Allyn and Bacon.

Conser, J. A., & Russell, G. D. (2000). *Law enforcement in the United States.* Gaithersburg, MD: Aspen Press.

Cox, S. M. (1996). *Police: Practices, perspectives, problems.* Boston: Allyn and Bacon.

Cox, S. M., Campbell, T. & McCamey, W. P. (2002). Ensuring police ethics: Doing the right thing: Why a few police officers find it so difficult. *Illinois Law Enforcement Executive Institute Forum, 2* (2), 1–8.

Cunningham, L. (1999). Taking on testilying: The prosecutor's response to in-court police deception. *Criminal Justice Ethics, 18* (1), 26–40.

Davis, K. C. (1971). *Discretionary justice: A preliminary report.* Chicago: University of Illinois Press.

Delattre, E. J. (2002). *Character and cops: Ethics in policing* (4th ed.). Washington, DC: AEI Press.

Dripp, D. A. (1996). *Trial, 32,* 60–62.

Estrich, S. (1998). *Getting away with murder: How politics is destroying the criminal justice system.* Cambridge, MA: Harvard University Press.

Feiler, S. M., & Sheley, J. F. (1999). Legal and racial elements of public willingness to transfer juvenile offenders to adult court. *Journal of Criminal Justice, 27* (1), 55–64.

Feld, B. (2003). The Politics of race and juvenile justice: The "due process revolution" and the conservative reaction. *Justice Quarterly, 20* (4): 765.

Gelsthorpe, L. & Padfield, N. (2003). *Exercising discretion : Decision making in the the criminal justice system and beyond.* United Kingdom: Willan Publishing.

Hurst Y. G., McDermott. M. J., & Thomas, D. L. (2005).The attitudes of girls toward the police: differences by race. *Policing, 29* (4), 578–594.

Johnson, J. (1997, September). Americans' views on crime and law enforcement. *NIJ Journal,* 233,9–14.

Jacobs, D. and Carmichael, J. T. (2002). Subordination and violence against state control agents: Testing political explanations for lethal assaults against the police. *Social Forces, 80,* 1223–1251.

Jacobs, D. and O'Brien, R. M. (1998). The determinants of deadly force: A structural analysis of police violence. *American Journal of Sociology, 103,* 837–862.

Jacobs, D. and Wood, K. (1999). Interracial conflict and interracial homicide: Do political and economic rivalries explain white killings of blacks or black killings of whites? *American Journal of Sociology, 105,* 157–190.

Johnson, B. (2005). Contextual disparities in guidelines departures: Courtroom social contexts, guidance compliance, and extralegal disparities in criminal sentencing. *Criminology*, 43 (3), 761–797.

Johnson, K. (March 7, 2007). Ousted U.S. attorney says he felt 'leaned on' by senator's call. *USA Today*, p. 5A.

Jordan, L. R. (2007, March 10). FBI under fire for security letters. *Peoria Journal Star*, p. A3.

Kerr, B., & Mladenka, K. R. (1994). Does politics matter? A time-series analysis of minority employment patterns. *American Journal of Political Science*, 38, 918–943.

Lasswell, H. (1958). *Who gets what, when, and how?* New York: Macmillan.

Lee, K. M. (2004). Reinventing Gideon v. Wainwright: Holistic defenders, indigent defendants, and the right to counsel. *American Journal of Criminal Law*, 31 (3), 367–443.

Leiber, M. J., & Stairs, J. M. (1999). Race, contexts, and the use of intake diversion. *Journal of Research in Crime and Delinquency*, 36 (1), 56–86.

Miller, L. L. & Eisenstein, J. (2005). The federal/state criminal prosecution nexus: A case study in cooperation and discretion. *Law & Social Inquiry*, 30 (2), 239–269.

Palermo, G. B., White, M. A., & Wasserman, L. A. (1998). Plea bargaining: Injustice for all? *International Journal of Offender Therapy and Comparative Criminology*, 42 (2), 111–23.

Peoria Journal Star. (2007, March 10). Court overturns Washington, D.C. handgun ban, p. A3.

Peoria Journal Star. (2007, March 12). Senator should resign. *Peoria Journal Star*, p. A5.

Perkins, C., & Klaus, P. (1996, April). *Criminal Victimization, 1994*. Washington, DC: U.S. Department of Justice.

Pollock, J. M. (2007). *Ethical dilemmas and decisions in criminal justice* (5th ed.). Belmont, CA: Thomson Higher Education.

Rand, M. & Rennison, C. (2002). True crime stories? Accounting for difference in our national crime indicators. *Chance Magazine*, 5 (1), 47–51.

Robbins, S. (2005). *Organizational behavior*. 11th ed. Upper Saddle River, NJ: Pearson Prentice Hall.

Roth, B., & Knapp, S. (2000). Taking a chisel to our rights. *AFT on Campus*, 19 (8), 12–16.

Schaefer, R. T. (2000). Racial and ethnic groups. (8th ed.). Upper Saddle River, NJ: Prentice Hall.

Schuck, A. M. & Rosenbaum, D. (2005). Global and neighborhood attitudes toward the police: Differentiation by race, ethnicity and type of contact; [1]. Journal of Quantitative *Criminology*, 21 (4), 391.

Smith, B. (2005). Ethno-racial political transition and citizen satisfaction with policing. *Policing*, 28 (2), 242–255.

Smith B. W. & Holmes, M. D. (2003). Community accountability, minority threat, and police brutality: An examination of civil rights criminal complaints. *Criminology, 41* (4), 1035–1064.

Smith, M. B. E. (1997). Do appellate courts regularly cheat? *Criminal Justice Ethics, 16* (2), 11–19.

Souryal, S. S. (2003). *Ethics in criminal justice: In search of the truth.* (3rd ed.) Cincinnati, OH: Anderson.

Stucky, T. D. (2005). Local politics and police strength. *Justice Quarterly, 22* (2), 139–170.

USA Today. (2007, March 6). GOP: Verdict about Libby; Democrats say it's bigger p. 1A.

USA Today. (2007, May 17). Dems seek no-confidence vote on Gonzales Available online at: http://www.usatoday.com/news/washington/2007-05-17-gonzales.

USA Today. (2007, March 7). Editorial: Political pressure taints firing of top prosecutor, p. 10A.

Walker, S. (1998). *Sense and nonsense about crime and drugs: A policy guide.* (4th ed.). Belmont, CA: Wadsworth.

Walker, S. (2001). *Police accountability: The role of citizen oversight.* Belmont, CA: Wadsworth/Thomson.

Weber, M. (1947). *The theory of social and economic organization.* London: William Hodge.

Weitzer, R. & Tuch, S. A. (2004). Race and perceptions of police misconduct. *Social Problems,* 51 (3), 305.

Wilson, J. Q. (1968). *Varieties of police behavior.* Cambridge, MA: Harvard University Press.

Woodward, B., & Armstrong, S. (1979). *The brethren: Inside the Supreme Court.* New York: Simon and Schuster.

Zelnick, K. H. (2003). In Gideon's shadow: The loss of defendant autonomy anad the growing scope of attorney discretion. *American Journal of Criminal Law,* 30 (3), 363–400.

Suggested Readings

Anonymous. (2006). Politics and progress in federal judicial accountability. *Judicature,* 90 (2), 52–55.

Braswell. M. C., McCarthy, B. R., & McCarthy, B. J. (2005). *Justice, crime and ethics.* Cincinnati: Anderson Publishing.

Cheek, K. & Champagne, A. (2005). Judicial politics in Texas: Partisanship, money and politics in state courts. New York: Peter Lang.

Cox, S. M., Campbell, T. & McCamey, W. P. (2002). Ensuring police ethics: Doing the right thing: Why a few police officers find it so difficult. *Illinois Law Enforcement Executive Institute Forum*, 2 (2), 1–8.

Estrich, S. (1998). *Getting away with murder: How politics is destroying the criminal justice system.* Cambridge, MA: Harvard University Press.

Gelsthorpe, L. & Padfield, N. (2003). *Exercising Discretion: Decision-Making in the criminal justice decision and beyond.* Devon: Willan Publishing.

Lee, K. M. (2004). Reinventing Gideon v. Wainwright: Holistic defenders, indigent defendants, and the right to counsel. *American Journal of Criminal Law*, 31 (3), 367–443.

Leighton, P. & Reiman, J. (2001). *Criminal justice ethics.* Upper Saddle River, NJ: Prentice Hall.

Lyles, K. L. (1996, Spring). Presidential expectations and judicial performance revisited: Law and politics in the federal district courts. *Presidential Studies Quarterly*, 26, 447–72.

McGrath, B. (2000, April 26). In circuit court races, it's old-fashioned politics. *Chicago Daily Law Bulletin*, 5.

Wahlbeck, P. J. (1997, August). The life of the law: Judicial politics and legal change. *Journal of Politics*, 59, 778–802.

Weber, M. (1947). *The theory of social and economic organization.* London: William Hodge.

Wilson, J. Q. (1968). *Varieties of police behavior.* Cambridge, MA: Harvard University Press.

Woodward, B., & Armstrong, S. (1979). *The brethren: Inside the Supreme Court.* New York: Simon and Schuster.

Chapter Three

Law and Criminal Law—Essential Ingredients of Criminal Justice Systems

Two problems need resolving before any society can implement an institutionalized pattern of criminal justice. First, the laws must be delineated. Next, the manner of enforcement must be specified. The way a society resolves these problems involves the essential guarantees of any legal system. These activities are of equal importance and provide a sound basis for diagramming the basic foundation of legal systems ... an institutionalized pattern of justice rests on the definition of rules (substantive law) and the determination of their enforcement (procedural law). In turn, delineation of rules specifies the requirements to be met for something to qualify as a law and the criteria used in deciding whether a particular behavior is criminal.

Source: Reichel, P. L. (2005). *Comparative criminal justice systems.* 4th ed. Upper Saddle River, NJ: Pearson/Prentice Hall, p. 73.

Key Terms

law
folkways
mores
sanctions
functions of law
conflict model
substantive law
procedural law
statutory law
case law
precedent (stare decisis)

Law covers almost every facet of life.
Reprinted with permission of iStockphoto.com / William Mahar.

civil law
criminal law
plaintiff
preponderance of evidence
beyond a reasonable doubt
crime
actus reus
mens rea
strict liability offenses
felony murder rule
canon law
common law
courts of equity
federalization

Chapter Outline

Law
The Origins, Nature, and Functions of Law
Criminal Law
Law in the United States
Federal and State Law

Law

We all are born and we all live, work, play, and die within the parameters of complex cultural systems. From the moment of birth (and even before birth) until death, we are affected directly and indirectly by a seemingly infinite number of rules and regulations. For example, there are rules and regulations governing the hospitals in which we are born, and the physicians and nurses who assist at birth. Other rules and regulations govern the schools we attend, the leisure-time activities in which we engage, our rights as employers and employees, and even our funeral procedures.

Among these rules and regulations are some that we come to regard as laws. These laws touch everyone—they regulate virtually every aspect of human behavior in modern societies. Try to imagine American life without laws. Something as simple as driving to the corner convenience store would be extremely risky without laws. One could drive at any speed on either side of the street (or down the middle), pass through intersections without regard for others, and park anywhere and in any fashion. Further, without laws, a company manufacturing cars could build unsafe vehicles, that could result in the deaths of innocent people, and have no fear of being held liable. As these examples illustrate, laws help create stability, protect private and public interests, provide for the orderly resolution of conflict, and uphold certain traditions and institutions or bring about change in these traditions and institutions.

What, exactly, is law? Putting the question to a number of citizens might lead to such responses as "the cops are the law," "the judge is the law," and "law consists of the rules we play by." Although each of these responses is partially accurate, none will suffice to explain in meaningful form what the law is.

Law is a complex, dynamic, social phenomenon. It is more than the sum total of persons who actively participate in the administration of rules. It consists of rules administered, decisions rendered, legislation passed, and interpretations handed down by specially designated individuals who have been given the authority to impose sanctions of specified types on those who violate these rules, decisions, and interpretations. Law is a formal means of social control involving the use of rules that are created, interpreted, and enforceable by specially designated persons in a particular political community (Davis, Davis, & Foster, 1962; Hoebel, 1954). According to Schmalleger (2002) the law functions to provide the following to all members of society.

- protect members of the public from harm
- preserve, maintain social order and support fundamental social values
- distinguish criminal violations from civil wrongs
- deter people from criminal activity
- express communal condemnation of criminal behavior
- punish those who commit crimes
- rehabilitate offenders and
- assuage victims of crimes

The Origins, Nature, and Functions of Law

Sources of law are the materials of which legal rules are fashioned once distinctively legal obligations have emerged in society. Customs based here on religions, there on secular traditions, decisions by judicial bodies or other notables, written rules, standards of justice, and, possibly, authoritative writings about law constitute these materials. Singly, or more frequently in combination, these are the sources common to all legal orders (Ehrmann, 1976, p. 21; Lippman, 2007, p. 7).

How do these "distinctively legal obligations" emerge in a society? How do certain rules and regulations become recognized as less formal customs or mores, and how are they enforced in different ways?

We might speculate that the following developments occurred in the evolution of law (Blumer, 1969; Cox & Fitzgerald, 1996, chap. 2; Durkheim, 1938). Humans interacting with each other over time developed expectations concerning proper and improper (normal and abnormal) behavior of individuals in certain positions. Chiefs, priests, hunters, wives, warriors, and cooks were all expected to perform in certain ways. This role-associated behavior might have varied to some extent as different individuals filled the role of chief or priest, for example, but certain expectations of the position and not the individual who occupied the position remained. Behavior that met these expectations was considered normal; that which failed to meet the expectations was considered abnormal, or deviant (Edwards, 2006). That is, it became customary for individuals occupying certain roles (positions) to behave in certain ways. It is not a big step from saying that chiefs behave in a particular way to saying that chiefs should behave in a particular way, ought to behave in a particular way, or must behave in a particular way (Becker, 1963; Durkheim, 1947; Malinowski, 1926; Wolff, 1950). Initially, those who violated the expectations of others could be sanctioned through the application of group pressure. Violations of these expectations may be considered violations of **folkways** (customs) or **mores** (religious or ethical standards), and **sanctions** (punishments) for violating folkways and mores include gossip, ostracism, and, in some cases, excommunication (Sumner, 1906).

As communities grew in numbers, specialization became necessary. The once homogeneous community became diversified. Conceptions of normal and abnormal behavior were no longer consensual. Behavior accepted as normal among warriors might be defined as deviant by farmers, yet each specialized group needed the others to survive. That is, each group had to be able to depend on the performance of certain tasks by other groups. Failure to perform needed tasks could have dire consequences. Ensuring performance (contracts) became too important to leave solely to informal or group pressure. Some tasks had to be performed. To ensure that tasks were performed, certain individuals were appointed to look for behavior that violated expectations. These specially designated individuals were given the power to use certain types of sanctions (arrest, fines, and even death) to ensure compliance with expectations or to punish those who failed to comply. The legal rights and obligations of all parties in the community had been specified, and formal institutions for ensuring that rights were protected and obligations were fulfilled emerged. Law became important as one form of social control.

Although the concept of law has probably existed in all societies, law in the sense of formal or written rules enforceable by specially designated persons has evolved over time and is particularly characteristic of complex societies. Whereas custom, tradition, and religion could once be used to handle most disputes, modern industrial societies rely more heavily on legislative and administrative law to deal with rapidly changing social conditions (Ehrmann, 1976). These laws are based, of course, to a great extent on custom, tradition, and precedent.

In the attempt to understand the origins, nature, and **functions of law**, it is important to recognize that law is the result of political action. One school of thought says that in a democracy, law represents the views or values of the majority of citizens and results from consensus (Dahrendorf, 1959). Another widely accepted model is the **conflict model**, which indicates that conflict between interest groups with varying degrees of power leads to the formation of law (Becker, 1963; Quinney, 1975). According to proponents of this model, coalitions form among the many groups existing in society with respect to specific issues. The more powerful the coalition (in terms of money, prestige, and political skills), the more likely it is to create or pass the laws it desires. Since the interests of these groups vary over time, the coalitions formed are temporary and constant change characterizes the society. There is no single stable, identifiable majority on all issues. The two approaches may both be correct: in the initial stages of the development of law, the conflict model clearly applies, but with time and practice, consensus develops (Glaser, 1978).

The discussion above indicates another important characteristic of law—its dynamic nature. The law constantly changes as the interests of groups and individuals change, which leads to the election of new political figures, the appointment of new judicial officials, the passing of new legislation, and the handing down of new court decisions. Although it is easy to talk about the law as if it were something real and concrete, numerous scholars have pointed out the difficulties in saying exactly what the law is at any given time. Thus, Ehrlich (1936) spoke of the living law, Holmes (1986) discussed law as what the courts are likely to do in a given place at a given time, and Weber (in Rheinstein, 1956, pp.486-93) emphasized the difference between the normative aspects of a legal proposition and what actually happens in a given time as a result of these normative aspects.

Regardless of time and place, law helps perform certain functions. Law defines relationships among individuals and groups by specifying rights and obligations, and may be used to help tame the use of naked force to assist in the orderly resolution of conflict, to dispose of problem or "trouble" cases (those that arise repeatedly), and to help society adapt to changing conditions (Hoebel, 1954, pp.275-76). Perhaps the way the law may be used to perform these functions will become clearer if we take a look at several different ways of classifying law.

Substantive law is the body of law that creates, discovers, and defines the rights and obligations of each person in society (Hoebel, 1954, p.275; Lippman, 2007, p. 5). The two key elements of substantive law are specificity and penalty. That is, substantive law specifically defines proscribed (prohibited) behaviors and specifies the penalties that may be administered to those who commit such acts. Laws concerning sexual assault, medical malpractice, income tax evasion, and so forth, are substantive in that they specifically define the acts constituting sexual assault, malpractice, and tax evasion, and specify the consequences for engaging in these acts.

Procedural law is the body of law that specifies the manner in which substantive laws will be applied. If the law is to be used in the orderly resolution of conflict, specific, predictable procedural steps must be followed. Thus, we have developed rules concerning the seizure and admissibility of evidence, the circumstances under which a confession may be legally obtained and admitted in court, the use of informants, and so on.

The law may also be viewed in terms of statutory law versus case law. **Statutory law** consists of those laws passed by a legislative body and is typically codified and published as revised at the federal, state, and local levels. **Case law** is derived from court decisions that are sometimes based on statutory law and sometimes arrived at in the absence of statutes. In handing down case law, the deciding judge usually takes into account past case decisions involving similar conditions, or **precedent** (*stare decisis* is an equivalent term). The United States Supreme Court is the ultimate authority for creating and deciding precedent. The ultimate sources of formal or written law are the federal and state constitutions. Constitutions of states and the United States Constitution provide fundamental laws, power for government, and individual protections from the government (Ross, 2005, p. 26). The United States Constitution is the highest source of law in the country. For example, Article VI, Section 2 of the U.S. Constitution provides that

> This Constitution, and the Laws of the United States, which shall be madein Pursuance thereof; and all Treaties made, or which shall be made, underthe Authority of the United States, shall be the supreme Law of the Land; and the Judges in every State shall be bound thereby, any Thing in the Constitution or Laws of any State to the Contrary notwithstanding.

Finally, for our purposes, law may be divided into civil and criminal categories.

The "**civil law**" is the portion of the law that defines and determines the rights of the individual in protecting his person and his property. The "**criminal law**" is that body specifically established to maintain peace and order. Its purpose is to protect society and the community from the injurious acts of individuals. The same act causing injury to person or property, a civil wrong called a "tort," may also be a breach of the peace, also known as a "crime." The wrongdoer may then be subject to both civil and criminal proceedings. (Lippman, 2007, p. 4; Ross, 1967, p.14) This situation occurred, for example, in the O. J. Simpson case, with Simpson being convicted in civil court and acquitted in criminal court. Additional examples include battery, rape, theft, criminal libel, and criminal damage to property, which are all torts and also crimes (Gardner & Anderson, 2000).

Differences between criminal and civil law are apparent in the manner in which cases are filed in court and cited in the legal literature. In such citations, the **plaintiff**, or person initiating the action, is always listed first. The plaintiff in all criminal cases will be a governmental entity—federal, state, or local—since the state is considered an "injured party" in such cases. In civil cases, the plaintiff will normally be a private party. It is possible for a governmental entity to be a plaintiff in a civil matter, but as a rule of thumb, the distinction outlined above holds. Moreover, in a civil action the plaintiff must prove that (1) the defendant owed some legal or contractual duty, and (2) that a breach of duty by the defendant resulted in harm to the plaintiff (Ross, 2005, p. 22).

Another difference between civil and criminal law concerns the nature of the sanctions involved. Sanctions in criminal cases are said to be punitive, while those in civil matters are generally compensatory (although they may also be punitive or exemplary). In criminal cases, the intent is to punish for wrongs done to society (the state); in civil cases, the intent is to award compensation for harm, damages, or suffering to the individual.

In addition to the differences listed above, there are important procedural distinctions between civil and criminal law. The most basic of these is in the standard of proof required to establish guilt. In civil proceedings, a "**preponderance of evidence**" must exist to support a guilty verdict. A preponderance of evidence can mean that the probability of the defendant having done what is claimed is just over 50 percent. In other words, following a preponderance of evidence criterion a judge or a jury can rule in favor of the plaintiff if they conclude that it is more likely than not that the allegations against the defendant are true (Schmalleger, 2002, p. 46). In criminal proceedings, guilt must be established "**beyond reasonable doubt**." A higher standard of proof is required in criminal cases compared to the preponderance of evidence standard used in civil cases. The United States Supreme Court has not precisely defined "reasonable doubt" and has left this task to states to communicate the essence of the concept to a jury (Schmalleger, 2002, p. 46). Many states define the concept differently. For example, a Nebraska jury instruction which was held to be constitutional by the United States Supreme Court in 1994 defined reasonable doubt as " … an actual and substantial doubt arising from the evidence, from the facts or circumstances shown by the evidence, or from the lack of evidence" (*Victor v. Nebraska*, 511 U.S. 1 (1994). For an additional discussion of "reasonable doubt" see "In the News 3.1" ("Jury seeks clarity on reasonable doubt").

In the News 3.1

JURY SEEKS CLARITY ON REASONABLE DOUBT

BARNSTABLE - Under the stony gaze of the man credited with defining the concept of reasonable doubt, jurors yesterday finally asked their first question in the Christa Worthington murder trial.

After 3½ days of deliberation, the jury asked Judge Gary Nickerson to clarify that concept. Judge Lemuel Shaw of West Barnstable, whose bust sits in a nook in the main session of Barnstable Superior Court where the Worthington case is being heard, pioneered the standard in an 1850 ruling.

Shaw's language has been modernized slightly, but it's the script followed by Massachusetts judges, including Nickerson.

Guilt for a crime — in this case murder, aggravated rape and aggravated burglary — is proved beyond a reasonable doubt "if, after you have compared and considered all of the evidence, you have in your minds an abiding conviction, to a moral certainty, that the charge is true," Nickerson told jurors. Even if prosecutors establish a strong probability, "that is not enough," the judge said.

Jurors also asked Nickerson to explain which parts of the case were subject to a reasonable doubt determination. Nickerson said the reasonable doubt standard must be applied to the elements of a crime — in other words, the legal pieces that make up each charge — but not to each and every detail of fact. The standard must also be applied to the question of whether the statement of defendant Christopher McCowen to police was voluntary, Nickerson said.

Over the course of the trial, defense attorney Robert George tried to inject reasonable doubt into the case several times. George argued that vital evidence, such as an exterior genital swab from Worthington's corpse, was not tested for DNA. He also wants jurors to believe the incriminating statement McCowen gave to police the night of his arrest was not valid because he was high on Percocet and marijuana, has a very low verbal IQ and was intimidated during the interview.

In addition, George repeatedly indicated there were other suspects, including ex-boyfriend Tim Arnold, over the course of the three-year murder probe before his client was arrested. And then there's Jeremy Frazier, the man who McCowen said during his interrogation was Worthington's real killer."When they're focusing on reasonable doubt, they're really focusing on the heart of the case. It also shows me they're taking this very seriously," Marc Perlin, associate dean and professor of law at Suffolk University Law School in Boston, said of the jurors. "The longer they're out the better it is for the defendant."

The concept of reasonable doubt in U.S. criminal law was solidified in Commonwealth v. Webster, a gruesome murder case, when Shaw was the state's chief justice. Webster, a Harvard medical school professor, was executed by hanging for murdering another man, whose body parts were found in Webster's library and in the Charles River, according to Judge H. Gregory Williams.

Williams and four other justices lingered yesterday afternoon in judge's chambers in Barnstable District Court, and each said no one has yet come up with a better definition than Shaw did 150 years ago.

"If you try to defer from that, you do so at your own peril," Judge Joseph Reardon said of the state Supreme Judicial Court's preference to stick to Shaw's definition. A 1994 challenge to those well-tested instructions made it all the way to the U.S. Supreme Court, but Shaw's version came through unscathed.

Reasonable doubt is still hard to explain to jurors, the judges said in their chamber. Even in civil cases and for misdemeanor criminal charges, jurors wrestle every day with the concept, Judge Joan Lynch said.

Abstract. Abstruse. Call it what you will, but Williams perhaps termed it best.

"It's a metaphysical concept," he said.

Russ, H. & Williams, E. (2006, November 11). Jury seeks clarity on reasonable doubt. *Cape Cod Times*, available online at: http://www.Capecodonline.com Record number: 11557517DBA54540

Because this book deals with the criminal justice network, most of our attention is devoted to criminal law. It should be noted, however, that there are numerous, complex relationships between civil and criminal law. Thus, a finding of guilt or innocence in criminal court may be used in civil proceedings resulting from the same case.

Criminal Law

In this section we examine the characteristics of criminal law, but first we must define crime. According to Tappan (1960), "**Crime** is an intentional act or omission in violation of criminal law, committed without defense or justification, and sanctioned by the state as a felony or misdemeanor" (p.10). Included in Tappan's definition are five specific elements that, taken together, establish the criteria necessary for the violation of criminal law: (1) an unjustifiable act or omission, (2) mental state or intent, (3) a union of intent and action, (4) the existence of a statute prohibiting the act, and (5) the existence of a prescribed penalty.

The act (*actus reus*), or omission considered criminal, must be defined by law. For example, under common law (still followed in some states), the crime of rape occurs only when there is penetration of the sexual organ of the victim by the alleged offender; in a battery, physical contact must occur; in criminal homicide, one person's life must be taken by another person without justification (Skelton, 1998, pp. 85-88).

Notice that thoughts of committing a crime do not, in and of themselves, violate criminal law (many of us have probably secretly planned the "perfect crime"!). There must be some action in furtherance of these thoughts for a crime to occur. Failure to act constitutes one type of action. Therefore, failing to file an income tax report and failure to register for the draft when required to do so are criminal acts because legal requirements mandate that both be performed by certain categories of individuals. In some cases, an individual may feel a moral obligation to act but not be legally required to do so. Thus, a passerby seeing a drowning person may feel morally obligated to help but will not be guilty of a crime if he or she fails to do so because there is no legal requirement that he or she act.

Criminal law recognizes that some acts, which are generally considered criminal, are justifiable under specific circumstances. In such cases, the actor must prove that she or he committed the act with justification. Thus, a police officer in the line of duty may intentionally take the life of another citizen (homicide) without committing a crime if the officer observes a person unjustifiably kill another during the commission of a serious felony or the officer reasonably believes that his or her own life, or the life of others, is in immediate danger from a felon. Such actions may constitute "justifiable homicide." Criminal acts committed under duress (at gunpoint, for example) may also fall into this category.

The mental state of the actor (*mens rea*) is another important element of criminal law. An act alone is not enough for the commission of a crime. Thus, one who kills another by accident (without an accompanying culpable mental state) does not commit criminal homicide.

Proper investigative techniques help determine whether the elements of a crime are present. Reprinted with permission of iStockphoto.com / Chris Bernard.

There are four commonly recognized culpable mental states: intent, knowledge, recklessness, and negligence. These mental states are typically identified and defined in the criminal codes of various jurisdictions. There are a few circumstances under which the law does not require proof of a particular mental state. One such exception consists of **strict liability offenses** which is a special category of offenses that requires no culpable mental state and presents a significant exception to the principle that all crimes require a conjunction of action and *mens rea* (Schmalleger, 2002, p. 57). Strict liability offenses make it a crime to simply do something, even if there was no intention of violating the law. In enacting statutes to enforce rules concerning traffic, liquor, purity of food, and hunting, modern legislative bodies chose not to create true crimes, but rather strict liability offenses (Gardner & Anderson, 2000). For example, a driver who did not realize he failed to obey a stop sign and clearly possessed no intent to violate the traffic law is still guilty of a traffic offense. The only relevant issue in a strict liability offense is whether or not the violation occurred. Did the driver fail to stop at the stop sign? If so, a violation occurred. Another exception is the **felony murder rule**. Under this rule, offenders may be held responsible for the consequences of acts that occur during the commission of certain felonies even though the offenders do not intend the acts to occur or the consequences to follow. In such cases, the intent to commit the felony is regarded as sufficient to make the felon responsible for the consequences that follow. For most crimes, specific actions are required to prove mental state. For example, laws concerning shoplifting may require that shoplifters leave the store in which they have shoplifted before a charge of shoplifting can be sustained. These laws are based on the premise that as long as the shoplifters stay in the store they can argue that they intended to pay before leaving (even though they have hidden several items on their persons). For other crimes (most felonies, for example) general intent is all that is required. The intent to commit a felonious act may make the perpetrator responsible for all consequences following the commission of the felony, even though such consequences are unforeseen.

In our society, several categories of persons cannot be convicted of crimes because they are said to be incapable of forming a culpable mental state. Among these are juveniles under a certain age (though the age in question has changed dramatically in recent years), those who have been declared insane, and the severely retarded. These persons may be dealt with through legal means (commitment hearings, for example) other than criminal proceedings. Some of these categories of individuals who are exempt from criminal prosecution have caused considerable controversy. This controversy has resulted in a series of attempts to change laws to assess greater responsibility to those who claim insanity as a defense. For example some jurisdictions have created guilty but mentally ill statutes that provide for both punishment as a criminal and mental health treatment for the offender.

As we have noted, neither an act alone nor an intention alone is sufficient for the commission of a crime. Intent and act must typically coexist for a crime to be committed. Further, the act considered criminal must be prohibited by law at the time it is committed; otherwise, no crime has occurred. Finally, criminal codes must specify the punishments that may be administered for particular crimes to avoid capricious punishment.

As we have noted, criminal laws reflect the moral and ethical beliefs communicated by society. Murder, for example is considered morally wrong, and most people would not murder another person even if it were not forbidden by all jurisdictions in the United States (Gardner & Anderson, 2000). In other words, murder is a violation of criminal law and the moral law. This moral or ethical commitment to the law is known as the "law behind the law" (Gardner & Anderson, 2000). Many believe the importance of this concept of a "law behind the law" is that it compels most people to conform to certain standards whether or not they are being watched by police officers. Public order would certainly suffer without informal controls such as these, since there are not enough police to enforce every criminal law.

There are many other aspects of criminal law and numerous exceptions to the general rules stated here. Some of these are discussed in later chapters. The overview presented in this chapter should help you better understand the general nature and functions of law.

Law in the United States

Although there is evidence that laws were codified as early as the twenty-fifth century B.C., the first complete surviving code, the Code of Hammurabi, originated in the eighteenth century B.C. This code deals with subjects ranging from specific punishments for specific crimes to medical malpractice. The Mosaic Code, including the Ten Commandments, was developed 500 to 1,000 years later. The impact of the Ten Commandments, prohibiting behaviors such as murder, adultery, and perjury, is well established. Roman law was codified about 450 B.C. and became the basis for **canon law,** or the law of the Roman Catholic church. These various codes were tied together in the Napoleonic Code in 1804.

In Britain, the kings traditionally dispensed law throughout the country by traveling around and establishing court at various locations. In general, the same laws were applied throughout the country; thus, the law came to be referred to as **common law.** When canon law came to England, **courts of equity** (in which decisions were based more on conscience than on strict interpretation of common law) were also established, and the two systems coexisted for a number of years. In 1215 the Magna Carta, the basis for British civil liberties, became the law, and over the following years British common law continued to develop on the basis of customs, tradition, and precedent. This common law became the most important single aspect of the legal system in the new country, America.

When the colonial period ended in 1776, a new governmental system had to be developed. The federal Constitution, written in 1787, established the executive, legislative, and judicial branches of government; it also included a system of checks and balances among the branches and between state and federal governments. The Constitution became the law of the land in 1789 and, with 27 amendments, remains so today. The 27 amendments ensure freedom of worship and speech, ensure trial by jury, abolish slavery, extend voting rights to all citizens, protect privileges and immunities of citizens, and guarantee a variety of other civil rights.

Of the 27 amendments, five are particularly important for the criminal justice network. These amendments establish, clarify, and regulate many elements of procedural law. The Fourth Amendment regulates arrests and searches by prohibiting unreasonable searches and seizures. The Fifth Amendment affects grand jury proceedings, self-incrimination, and double jeopardy, and provides for due process of law. The Sixth Amendment regulates interrogation and criminal prosecution by establishing the right to counsel, trial by jury, and the speedy trial doctrine. It also establishes the rules of venue, the right to confront witnesses, and the right to call one's own witnesses. The Eighth Amendment prohibits excessive bail as well as cruel and unusual punishment. The Fourteenth Amendment applies all basic constitutional privileges at the state level through due process and equal protection for all. Although many of these amendments have been interpreted and refined through court decisions, they remain the fundamental source of procedural law.

Federal and State Law

Prior to the ratification of the Bill of Rights, the Constitution said little about federal criminal law. State courts had concurrent, and often primary, jurisdiction over designated federal crimes. This made sense because crime and order maintenance on an everyday basis were principally matters of local interest. However, after the Civil War, Congress enacted federal civil rights legislation and gave federal jurisdiction to violations in the event citizens were denied their rights or when state courts refused to enforce federal law. This brought crimes such as murder and assault under federal jurisdiction in certain types of cases (Brickey, 1995). This trend continued into the twentieth century with passage of the Lindbergh Act (dealing with kidnapping across state lines), the Fugitive Felon Act (prohibiting interstate flight to avoid prosecution for certain violent crimes), the Comprehensive Crime Control Act of 1990, and the Violent Crime Control and Law Enforcement Act of 1994 (Brickey, 1995). This process of extending federal jurisdiction to civil causes of action and criminal prosecutions that could be maintained in the state courts is known as **federalization** (Young & Hindera, 1999).

The federal government's involvement in maintaining law and order at the local level is the topic of considerable debate. On the one hand, federal duplication of state criminal law strains the federal system to its limits. At the same time, federal intervention limits the discretion of states to respond to local concerns (Brickey, 1995). Additionally, both federal and state law, as we have noted elsewhere, are heavily politically motivated. As a result, under the current get-tough philosophy, crimes such as those involving drugs often result in mandatory prison time. Because they are so numerous, they clog the federal court system (which is ill equipped to deal with the large volume of these crimes), as well as the federal prison system. In addition, it appears that Congress sometimes passes legislation aimed at destroying the intent of Supreme Court decisions. In June of 2000, for example, the Supreme Court handed down a decision reaffirming the need for the police to issue a Miranda warning. This decision resulted from a case brought under the guise of a law passed by Congress in 1968 that attempted to circumvent the Miranda warning by allowing acceptance of "voluntary" confessions without Miranda. Finally, state and federal laws sometimes conflict (as in the case of the legal use of marijuana in some states although such use is prohibited under federal law). Thus, individuals may be law-abiding from one perspective while criminal from another. On the other hand, citizens who cannot receive equitable treatment in state courts may have a better chance in federal court (as in the case of Rodney King, whose police assailants were acquitted in state court but convicted in federal court). Federal laws that deal with hate crimes are another positive example, since not all states have treated such crimes seriously. Still, according to the American Bar Association's Task Force on the Federalization of Criminal Law, the amount of behavior subject to federal criminal law has dramatically increased in the past few decades. The task force notes that there seems to be no underlying principle that governs the manner in which Congress criminalizes conduct, and also notes that these laws are often passed without the resources required to implement them (Mountjoy, 1999).

The conflict between state and federal law further illustrates the network approach to understanding criminal justice. Clearly, politics, local standards, and state and federal legislatures and courts are all involved in this conflict. Changes in policies or practices at one point in the network create repercussions throughout (Smith, McCall & McCall, 2006). See "In the News 3.2" (" 30 Years later - Madison voters passed a law in April 1977 that permits possession of small amounts of marijuana in private places").

In the News 3.2

30 YEARS LATER – MADISON VOTERS PASSED A LAW IN APRIL 1977 THAT PERMITS POSSESSION OF SMALL AMOUNTS OF MARIJUANA IN PRIVATE PLACES

Thirty years ago, Madison was at the forefront of the effort to bring the nation's marijuana laws in line with growing public opinion that, among adults, smoking a joint is akin to drinking a beer.

But after three decades, Madison's historic ordinance permitting possession of small amounts of marijuana remains at odds with state and federal laws, putting city police in a difficult position.

And Madison advocates are still pushing for Wisconsin to join other states that have relaxed their laws against pot. "Once again, from the bottom up, we're seeing an upswing in activism," said

Gary Storck, co-founder of the Madison chapter of the National Organization for the Reform of Marijuana Laws and a medical marijuana activist and patient.

On April 5, 1977, Madison voters passed what is now the nation's second-oldest municipal ordinance still on the books decriminalizing possession of small amounts of marijuana.

The binding referendum — which made its way onto the ballot after proponents obtained 8,800 signatures — went beyond an ordinance the City Council adopted just two months earlier by eliminating any penalty for private possession of small amounts of pot.

Minutes after the February law was adopted, "several persons lit up marijuana cigarettes in a hallway outside the council chambers," the State Journal wrote at the time.

By the time Madison's referendum passed, five states — Oregon, Colorado, Alaska, Ohio and California — had decriminalized pot. Madison's ordinance also followed a similar measure in Ann Arbor, Mich., the oldest municipal decriminalization law still in existence.

"RELAXED ATMOSPHERE"

Madison's ordinance 23.20 allows possession of up to 112 grams of marijuana -just under four ounces, or about 112 joints — or up to 28 grams of cannabis resin, or hashish, in a private place. It prohibits possession in a public place without a prescription or order from a physician or other practitioner, violations of which are subject to a $109 fine.

Selling the drug is also still prohibited.

But Madison police Lt. Sandy Theune, commander of the Dane County Drug Task Force, questions whether it would be appropriate for city police to say, "Hey, just feel free" — even in a private home.

"It's still not 100 percent legal," because of state and federal law, Theune said, but "I think it's pretty well known that there's something of a relaxed atmosphere about marijuana in Madison."

Still, Theune said, police are likely to confiscate marijuana, and, depending on the circumstances, could seek to press charges under state law. "There's not always a black-and-white answer to what will an officer do."

"It depends on who it is ... on both sides," said Ben Masel, a fixture on the marijuana legalization front for decades.

Discretion ultimately rests with the district attorney's office, which determines whether to file charges under state law. In March, District Attorney Brian Blanchard, citing a lack of resources, said his office will no longer file criminal charges against individuals possessing less than 25 grams of marijuana - just under an ounce, or about 25 joints.

Public use has declined dramatically in Madison in the years since the passage of the city ordinance decriminalizing pot, as federal authorities have continued to crack down on marijuana as part of the "war on drugs," Storck said. "Back then, Madison was a lot more free about cannabis," he said, adding that it was common to walk into the Memorial Union Rathskeller and find people smoking pot in a corner. "Everybody was doing it."

ANNIVERSARY CELEBRATION

But not everybody agreed on its effect.

Despite a national task force report in 1972 that recommended decriminalizing pot for personal use, the federal Drug Enforcement Administration has steadfastly opposed relaxing the law.

Such moves, the DEA said, would hurt children and public safety by creating increased dependency and treatment needs and open the door to the use of other drugs, while increasing health risks, delinquent behavior and impaired driving. It also argues that the potency of marijuana today is much greater than it was in the 1970s.

Advocates such as Storck counter that there was potent pot back then, and he likened responsible marijuana use by adults to using alcohol or tobacco. Storck is hoping the anniversary of Madison's ordinance will renew debate, as well as support for changing state law.

About 50 people attended a 30th anniversary celebration of the ordinance last week at a Williamson Street cafe.

The commemoration was marked not with raucous chants or demonstrations, but with a PowerPoint presentation on events leading up to passage of the law.

A band performed "cannabis tunes," including Bob Dylan's "Rainy Day Women #12 and 35" with the popular refrain "everybody must get stoned" for the laid-back audience, some of whom stepped outside to smoke pot.

Despite federal prohibitions, other states and municipalities have followed Madison. Twelve states have now decriminalized marijuana for personal use, and 12 states — many of the same ones — have legalized marijuana for medical use.

"SKY HAS NOT FALLEN"

Madison's experience has played a role in the passage of marijuana reform in other cities and states, he said. "The sky has not fallen," St. Pierre said. "They are still productive people. The children are born with 10 fingers and 10 toes."

A Zogby poll commissioned by NORML in March found that 49 percent of Americans supported removing criminal penalties for the personal use of marijuana by adults, while 48 percent were opposed.

In Wisconsin, Storck said, "There's some very hopeful things happening."

Last year, then-Rep. Gregg Underheim, R-Oshkosh, introduced a medical marijuana bill after he was diagnosed with cancer, but the bill did not make it out of committee in the Republican-controlled chamber. This year, Rep. Mark Pocan, D-Madison, said he plans to join Rep. Frank Boyle, D-Superior, in introducing similar legislation.

Sen. Jon Erpenbach, D-Middleton, chairman of the Senate Health and Human Services Committee, said he plans to hold a hearing on medical marijuana in the Democratic-led Senate this fall.

But Rep. Leah Vukmir, R-Wauwatosa, who chairs the Assembly Committee on Health and Healthcare Reform, said she will continue her opposition to medical marijuana because of concerns about its safety.

Vukmir, a nurse, said she believes it is better for patients to use medications that have been approved or may soon be available than to have people grow their own marijuana.

"I will refuse to put members through the circus of a hearing for a bill that is not going to go anywhere," Vukmir said. "This is nothing more than a backdoor attempt to legalize marijuana, which is not going to happen on my watch."

POT LAWS COMPARED

Madison ordinance 23.30: Possession of up to 112 grams (just under 4 ounces) of marijuana in a private place is not a crime and is not subject to forfeiture.

Possession is prohibited in public without a prescription or order from a physician or other practitioner and is subject to a fine, which is now $109.

Wisconsin: Possession of any amount of marijuana is punishable by up to six months in jail and a fine of $1,000 for the first offense, which is a misdemeanor.

The state allows conditional release or alternative sentencing, such as drug treatment, for people facing their first prosecution. After successfully completing their sentence, defendants' criminal records may be cleared of the charge. Second and subsequent drug offenses are felonies, punishable by up to 3½ years in prison and a $10,000 fine. Upon conviction of a drug offense, the offender's driver's license is suspended for 6 months to 5 years.

Federal: Possession of any amount of marijuana is punishable by up to one year in jail and a minimum fine of $1,000 for a first offense, which is a misdemeanor.

For a second offense, also a misdemeanor, penalties increase to a 15-day mandatory minimum sentence with a maximum of two years in prison and a fine of up to $2,500. Subsequent convictions carry a 90-day mandatory minimum sentence and a maximum of up to three years in prison and a fine of up to $5,000.

Joseph W. Jackson III - State Journal

Over the last three decades, marijuana use has moved indoors in Madison.

JOSEPH W. JACKSON III - State Journal archives

Smoking a joint in public - normally not one as large as the one revelers in this October 1979 photo appear to be firing up - used to be common in Madison.

\State Journal graphic\

Federal and state laws prohibit possession of any amount of marijuana, but the Dane County district attorney's office won't file criminal charges for possession of less than 25 grams of pot — or about 25 joints — while a Madison ordinance allows private possession of up to 112 grams of marijuana.

Source: National Organization for the Reform of Marijuana Laws / Marijuana laws by state

However, Madison and Dane County's ordinances decriminalizing possession of small amounts of marijuana is trumped by state and federal law.

0 - Federal and state

25 - Dane County

112 - Madison ordinance

Correction: The full name and title of Allen St. Pierre was omitted from a story on marijuana laws on Tuesday's front page. St. Pierre is executive director of the National Organization for the Reform of Marijuana Laws.

(correction published 4-11-07)

Cullen, S. (2007, April 10). 30 years later—Madison voters passed a law in April 1977 that permits possession of small amounts of marijuana in private places. *Wisconsin*

State Journal, **Front, p. A1.** "Copyright *Wisconsin State Journal.* **Reprinted with permission.**"

Summary

1. Law is a complex phenomenon. Among the multitude of rules and regulations developed by societies over time, some come to be designated as laws. These laws help us resolve conflict in an orderly way by establishing rights and obligations of individuals and groups.

2. Law is dynamic (constantly changing) and is one form of social control that helps societies adapt to changing conditions.

3. Law is the result of political action and of conflicts of interest among individuals and groups rather than the will of the majority, at least in most cases.

4. Criminal law is only one type of law and is characterized by requiring higher standards of proof than, for example, civil law.

5. A crime is an unjustifiable act that is typically accompanied by intent. The combination of act and intent that violates a specific statute prohibiting the act in the presence of a specified punishment constitutes a violation of criminal law.

6. The body of criminal law may be analyzed in a variety of ways, using categories such as substantive versus procedural law, case versus statutory law, and so on.

7. In the past few decades, Congress has passed a number of laws at the federal level that limit states' discretion in responding to local standards. Some of these, such as the hate crimes law and civil rights legislation, provide equity across state lines. Others have led to an overloading of federal courts and crowding of federal prisons as the result of political concerns rather than a comprehensive, rational plan to address crime.

Key Terms Defined

law A complex, dynamic, social phenomenon consisting of legislative rules and court decisions as they are administered and interpreted by specifically designated individuals in a political community.

folkways Customs or traditions.

mores Ethical or religious standards.

sanctions Punishments.

functions of law Law defines relationships among individuals and groups, helps regulate the use of force, may assist in the orderly resolution of conflicts, helps dispose of "trouble cases," and may help society adapt to changing conditions.

conflict model A model that views law as emerging from conflict between interest groups with varying degrees of power.

substantive law Law that creates, discovers, and defines the rights and obligations of each person in a society; key elements are specificity and penalty.

procedural law Rules that specify the manner in which substantive law is to be applied.

statutory law Law passed by a legislative body.

case law Law derived from court decisions.

precedent (stare decisis) Court decisions that provide guidance as to how future similar cases might be decided.

civil law The portion of law that defines and determines the rights of individuals in protecting person and property.

criminal law Law established to maintain peace and order by protecting society from injurious acts of individuals.

plaintiff Party initiating court action.

preponderance of evidence A probability of just over 50 percent that the defendant did what is claimed.

beyond a reasonable doubt An actual or substantial doubt arising from the evidence, from the facts or circumstances shown by the evidence, or from the lack of evidence.

crime An intentional act or omission in violation of criminal law.

actus reus The act constituting a crime.

mens rea A guilty mind; criminal intent.

strict liability offense A special category of offense that does not require a mental state.

felony murder rule A rule which holds that those who commit certain kinds of felonies are responsible for all consequences of their acts, including unforeseen or unintended consequences.

canon law Church or religious law.

common law Law based on court decisions that become widely accepted.

courts of equity Courts in which decisions are based more on conscience than on strict interpretation of the law.

federalization The process of extending federal jurisdiction to civil causes of action and criminal prosecutions that are typically handled in state courts.

Critical Thinking Exercises

1. Discuss how law develops and how it differs from folkways and mores. What or who determines whether a norm will become law? What are some of the basic functions of law? What legal machinery and societal actions are necessary if these functions are to be performed successfully?

2. What are the basic requirements for a violation of criminal law? What are some of the exceptions to these requirements? Why do these exceptions exist?

Internet Exercises

The common law has played a major role in the development of the current criminal law in the United States. Access the web site http://www.wisegeek.com/what-is-common-law.htm.

Read the information concerning common law then answer the following questions:

1. In what country did the common law originate?
2. List and explain the three courts from which the common law derives its power.
3. What role does *stare decisis* play in the common law?
4. Is common law still followed in practice today?

References

Becker, H. S. (1963). *The outsiders: Studies in the sociology of deviance.* New York: Free Press.

Blumer, H. (1969). *Symbolic interaction: Perspective and method.* Englewood Cliffs, NJ: Prentice Hall.

Brickey, K.F. (1995). Criminal mischief: The federalization of American criminal law. *Hastings Law Review*, 46: 1135-1174.

Cox, S. M., & Fitzgerald, J. D. (1996). *Police in community relations: Critical issues* (3rd ed.). Madison, WI: Brown and Benchmark.

Dahrendorf, R. (1959). *Class and conflict in industrial society.* Stanford, CA: Stanford University Press.

Davis, F. J., Davis, E. E., & Foster, H. H., Jr. (1962). *Society and the law: New meanings for an old profession.* New York: Free Press.

Durkheim, E. (1938). *The rules of sociological method.* Chicago: University of Chicago Press.

Durkheim, E. (1947). *The division of labor in society.* New York: Free Press.

Edwards, M. A. (2006). Law and the parameters of acceptable deviance. *Journal of Law & Criminology, 97* (1), 40-101.

Ehrlich, E. (1936). *Fundamental principles of the sociology of law* (W. L. Moll, Trans.). Cambridge, MA: Harvard University Press.

Ehrmann, H. W. (1976). *Comparative legal cultures.* Englewood Cliffs, NJ: Prentice Hall.

Gardner, T.J. & Anderson, T.M. (2000). *Criminal law.* 7th ed. Belmont, CA: Wadsworth Thomson Learning.

Glaser, D. (1978). *Crime in our changing society.* New York: Holt, Rinehart and Winston.

Hoebel, E. A. (1954). *The law of primitive man.* Cambridge, MA: Harvard University Press.

Holmes, O. W. (1986). The path of law. In W. Murphy & C. H. Pritchett (Eds.), *Courts, judges, & politics: An introduction to the judicial process*, 4th ed. (pp. 20-23). New York: Random House.

Lippman, M. (2007). *Contemporary criminal law: Concepts, cases, and controversies.* Thousand Oaks, CA: Sage.

Malinowski, B. (1926). *Crime and custom in savage society.* London: Routledge and Kegan Paul.

Mountjoy, J. J. (1999). The federalization of criminal laws. *Spectrum, 72* (3), 1-4.

Quinney, R. (1975). *Criminology: Analysis and critique of crime in America.* Boston: Little, Brown.

Reichel, P. L. (2005). *Comparative criminal justice systems.* 4th ed. Upper Saddle River, NJ: Pearson/Prentice Hall.

Rheinstein, M. (1956). *Max Weber: Law and economy in society.* Cambridge, MA: Harvard University Press.

Ross, D. L. (2005). *Civil liability issues in corrections.* Durham, NC: Carolina Academic Press.

Ross, M. J. (1967). *Handbook of everyday law.* Greenwich, CT: Fawcett.

Schmalleger, F. (2002). *Criminal law today.* 2nd. ed. Upper Saddle River, NJ: Prentice-Hall.

Skelton, D. T. (1998). *Contemporary criminal law.* Boston: Butterworth-Heinemann.

Smith, C. E., McCall, M. & McCall, M. (2006). Criminal justice and the 2004-2005 United States Supreme Court term. *The University of Memphis Law Review, 36*, (4), 951-1012.

Sumner, W. G. (1906). *Folkways.* Boston: Ginn.

Tappan, P. (1960). *Crime, justice, and correction.* New York: McGraw-Hill.

Victor v. Nebraska, 511 U.S. 1 (1994). In Schmalleger F. (2002). *Criminal law today.* 2nd ed. Upper Saddle River, NJ: Prentice-Hall.

Wolff, K. H. (Trans.). (1950). *The sociology of George Simmel.* New York: Free Press.

Young, C. D., & Hindera, J. J. (1999). Judicial intergovernmentalism: The impact of federalization on the American court system. *Public Administration Quarterly, 22* (4), 407-25.

Suggested Readings

Edwards, M. A. (2006). Law and the parameters of acceptable deviance. *Journal of Law & Criminology, 97* (1), 40-101.

Lippman, M. (2007). *Contemporary criminal law: Concepts, cases, and controversies.* Thousand Oaks, CA: Sage.

Meares, T. L., & Kahan, D. M. (1998). Laws and (norms of) order in the inner city. *Law and Society Review, 32* (4), 805-38.

Mountjoy, J. J. (1999). The federalization of criminal laws. *Spectrum, 72* (3), 1-4.

Smith, C. E., McCall, M. & McCall, M. (2006). Criminal justice and the 2004-2005 United States Supreme Court term. *The University of Memphis Law Review, 36,* (4), 951-1012.

Umphrey, M. M. (1999). The dialogics of legal meaning: Spectacular trials, the unwritten law, and narratives of criminal responsibility. *Law and Society Review, 33* (2), 393-423.

Chapter Four

Types of Crime: I

In the News 4.1

SEX OFFENDERS IN NORTH PORT GET GREETING

Every time a sex offender moves to town, Sgt. Tony Sirianni is among the first to say welcome.

Welcome, and don't screw up. Sirianni offers a handshake and strict instructions on what the sex offender or predator must do to avoid a felony charge for failing to comply with the state's sex offender registry laws.

And under a program ordered by the City Commission, officers in Sirianni's specialized unit knock on sex offenders' doors once a month and make sure they are living at the same home, driving the same car and working at the same place as they had reported to the state.

"We don't mess around," said Sirianni, who supervises the traffic and neighborhood stabilization unit that is responsible for the face-to-face checks on the convicted rapists and child molesters. "They all know what kind of tightrope they walk on."

Such programs, while not mandated by law, were a reaction to several highly publicized child abductions and killings in Florida, from Carlie Brucia to Jessica Lunsford.

Unrelenting reminders

The house calls are not intended to harass the offenders who have already completed their sentences, police say. But discouraging them from living here, where the number of sex offenders per capita is higher than anywhere else in Sarasota County, is an extra benefit, they say.

For Glen Simms, 36, the status checks are a regular reminder of what he says was a case of bad judgment seven years ago involving his boss' 17-year-old daughter.

Simms moved with his wife to North Port after serving jail time in Manatee County for a charge of unlawful **sexual** activity with a minor.

"I'd like to put it behind me," he said Wednesday while waiting to pick up his 3-year-old daughter from day care. "Thanks to the North Port police, they remind me of it every month."

Achieving results

Just over six months into it, police have discovered several violations of the state's registry laws, but none of the offenders has been charged with a new sex crime.

The status checks are not required by state law, and few neighboring law enforcement agencies do them. A Florida law passed after Jessica Lunsford's 2005 kidnapping, rape and murder requires sex offenders and predators to check in, in person, at their local sheriff's office twice a year.

About 88 percent of offenders are in compliance with that, said Kristen Perezluha, a spokeswoman for the Florida Department of Law Enforcement.

She said the department does not keep data on how many local law enforcement agencies have implemented programs similar to North Port's, but such approaches seem to be on the rise.

"It's definitely great to have agencies closely monitoring the sex offenders and predators who reside in their jurisdiction," Perezluha said. "It definitely helps to be vigilant."

A sex offender, according to Florida law, is anyone convicted of a sex crime, though some convicted before 1993 are not in the registry. Those convicted of multiple sex crimes in a certain time frame are labeled sexual predators.

Punta Gorda and Venice police also conduct monthly checks, and the Manatee County Sheriff's Office is gearing up for a similar program.

Police in Punta Gorda reported a decline in the number of offenders living there after they began their program in 2005. The small Charlotte County city never had a huge number of sex offenders, but the number did drop from five to three, said Deputy Chief Albert "Butch" Arenal.

Since then, others have moved to town, but "Most who have moved in have moved out," he said.

Police there also distribute fliers with the sex offender's picture and contact day-care centers and other facilities when one moves to town.

Sobering numbers

The number of sex offenders and predators in North Port has risen through the years as the population has exploded. At 78 sex offenders, the city has a per capita rate twice as high as in the unincorporated area of Sarasota County and four times the rate as Venice. North Port's sex offender ratio is slightly higher than in the city of Sarasota, though these numbers vary widely throughout the year as offenders are released from jail or change residences.

Police believe the abundance of affordable rental homes compared to the rest of the county probably attracts offenders to the city.

Police Officer Aaron Nick, who is part of Sirianni's unit, says many of the offenders live with relatives or have families of their own.

"The vast majority tend to be around minors," Nick said while making checks earlier this week. "That's one of the things that really struck me."

The responses Nick gets when he makes his house calls vary. Some offenders open the door with a smile; many are hostile.

"A lot of them are starting to get a little resentful of this," he said while driving away from a home. "Especially with the homicide."

After the September rape and killing of 6-year-old Coralrose Fullwood, a case which remains unsolved, Nick and his colleagues fanned out with other investigators and checked in on each of the city's offenders and predators, asking about their whereabouts during the time of the crime.

And in the nearly five months since the girl's body was found in a wooded lot in her neighborhood off Chamberlain Boulevard, investigators have been back to some of their homes seeking information.

Sirianni, whose unit also does DUI checkpoints, monitors gang and street-level activities, and does highway interdiction, says the monthly status checks could probably have the same impact if they were done less frequently. But because the community is still uneasy about the Coralrose case, it's worth it.

"The city is happy we do more than enough," he said.

Key Terms

statutory law
case law
felonies
misdemeanors
malum in se
malum prohibitum
homicide
murder
suicide
malice aforethought

felony murder rule
manslaughter
battery
assault
aggravation
rape
sodomy
deviate sexual conduct
deviate sexual assault
rape shield statutes
statutory rape
robbery
armed robbery
aggravated robbery
theft (larceny)
identity theft
account takeover
application fraud (true name fraud)
phishing
burglary
arson
hate crimes
stalking
Uniform Crime Reports (UCR)
time clock
offenses known to police
offenses cleared by arrest
National Incident Based Reporting System (NIBRS)
victim survey research
National Crime Victimization Survey (NCVS)
National Crime Security Survey (NCSS)
self report studies
The Institute for Social Research

Chapter Outline

Some Important Distinctions
Crimes against the Person
    Homicide
    Assault and Battery
    Forcible Rape
    Sexual Predators or Sexually Dangerous Persons
    Other Sex Offenses
Crimes against Property

In Chapter 3, we noted differences between substantive and procedural law and between civil and criminal law. In this chapter, we discuss several types of crime to familiarize the reader with some important elements of such crimes. A comprehensive examination of criminal law is well beyond the scope of an introductory text, but an overview of some types of crime should enable the reader to examine, analyze, and interpret, in general, any given criminal code. Because each state enacts its own criminal code, there is considerable variation among the states in the definitions of specific crimes. We recommend that each reader familiarize him- or herself with relevant state statutes to gain a more detailed understanding of the various offenses discussed therein. In addition, most criminal justice programs devote an entire course to the study of criminal law and will acquaint the reader with a more thorough understanding of basic concepts, special designations, and the application of the criminal code in that particular jurisdiction.

Criminal law is enacted by legislative (state and federal) bodies (**statutory law**) and interpreted and/or modified by court decisions (**case law**). Criminal law, then, represents some of society's values (that a specific behavior is wrong), and because these values are subject to change, criminal codes undergo periodic revisions. In most cases the state or federal prosecutor initiates action in the court system for a violation of a criminal law. Such a violation is only possible when the behavior in question is defined by statute. It is important, therefore, that both students and practitioners keep abreast of changes in relevant codes. This can be accomplished by periodically reviewing the revised statutes published by the various states.

The laws discussed in this chapter have been developed over time (many originate in British common law) and have undergone numerous revisions. These laws are not necessarily the ones most frequently violated, but they do cover violations that are considered serious by most, if not all, states.

Some Important Distinctions

The offenses discussed in this chapter are generally divided into two categories: crimes against the person and crimes against property. Crimes without complainants, organized crime, and white-collar/corporate offenses are presented in Chapter 5. Before proceeding to a more detailed discussion of these offenses, we should distinguish between certain offenses on the basis of the punishment associated with each. **Felonies** are usually offenses punishable by sentences of more than one year in state or federal prisons. In many cases additional procedures accompany felony charges such as the guaranteed right to an attorney if the person charged cannot afford to hire counsel. **Misdemeanors** are offenses punishable by sentences up to one year, usually in a county or local jail, although some states maintain institutions specifically for misdemeanants. Examples of misdemeanors include simple assault, battery, driving while under the influence of alcohol, and minor thefts. In addition to incarceration, both categories may be accompanied by fines. In some instances a crime could be either a misdemeanor or felony depending on the specific facts. For example, domestic battery is often a misdemeanor, however if the defendant possessed a weapon while performing the domestic battery or the victim was pregnant the charge becomes a felony in many states. However, felony charges may be reduced through plea bargaining or prosecutorial discretion to misdemeanors. And, in some states, the crimes associated with domestic violence are misdemeanors while in another state the same facts would constitute a felony. Many local ordinance violations and petty offenses are punishable by fine only. Petty offenses often involve receiving a ticket or some form of citation and almost never involve a jury trial.

In addition to the distinction between felonies and misdemeanors, we may categorize crimes as *malum in se*, or acts that are wrong in and of themselves, or *malum prohibitum*, or acts that are wrong merely because they are prohibited. Examples of the former include most crimes against the person (murder, rape, and battery) and some property crimes (theft, arson, and burglary). Virtually every society deems these behaviors inappropriate. Examples of the latter include the use of marijuana, underage drinking, and prostitution. Even jurisdictions that prohibit such behaviors may define them in disparate terms.

We would be remiss not to mention attempts to commit offenses. Generally, a person commits an attempt when he or she intentionally commits an act that constitutes a substantial step toward committing that offense. Thus, an individual who intentionally fires a weapon at another person, without legal justification, has attempted murder even if he or she has a bad aim. It is also possible to transfer this intent to an unintended victim. Suppose "A" shoots at "B" with the intent to kill her but misses and seriously injures bystander "C" who "A" had no intention to kill. The intent to kill may be transferred to "C" and "A" may be charged with the attempted murder of "C."

Crimes against the Person

Homicide

Homicide is generally considered the most serious felony. In fact, it is the only crime that carries a penalty of death in the United States. Homicide is of interest not only because of its severity but also because it is a fairly reliable barometer of all violent crimes. In the U.S. no other crime is measured as accurately or precisely (Fox & Zawitz, 2007). The term literally refers to the killing of a human being and is often thought to be synonymous with murder, but murder is only one category of homicide.

Any time one human being kills another, a homicide occurs. However, it does not necessarily follow that a crime has been committed because the law distinguishes among justifiable homicides, such as state-sanctioned execution, the use of deadly force in self-defense that is authorized under common law and police use of deadly force in some circumstances; criminal homicides, murder, and manslaughter (voluntary and involuntary) or killings neither justified nor excused; and excusable homicides involving killings while insane and accidental killings (Samaha, 2005, p. 283). Problems can be encountered when attempting to distinguish between excusable and justifiable homicides. Individuals threatened with imminent great bodily harm or death are permitted in most states to use reasonable means to prevent that harm. If the threatened person has legal cause to kill in self defense and does so intentionally, the result is usually justifiable homicide rather than excusable homicide (Reid, 2004, p. 207).

Historically, for a homicide to have occurred, the death of the victim had to occur within a given time period—usually a year and a day—after the attempted killing. The rule was intended to prevent murder charges from being initiated long after an attack. The assumption was that medical science was not advanced sufficiently to determine the cause of death in these circumstances (Reid, 2004). Advances in forensic science have resulted in the elimination of this rule in many states, however federal circuit courts continue to adhere to this principle (Klotter, 2004). Also, as modern medical science is now able to maintain cardiorespiratory systems even after the brain stops functioning, brain-death statutes have been substituted for the common law in determining when a person is dead (Uniform Determination of Death Act, 1987). For a homicide to occur, it must also be shown that the alleged victim was alive at the time of the offense and that death was not the result of the actions of an intermediate party (e.g., medical personnel who failed to provide an available lifesaving injection) but the consequence of the offense itself.

As we focus our attention on criminal homicides, keep in mind that the types are differentiated primarily on the basis of the intent of the perpetrator. Murder and voluntary manslaughter generally require proof of a specific intent to kill or to cause great bodily harm. Involuntary manslaughter and manslaughter resulting from the driving of a motor vehicle normally require only a general criminal state of mind. In either case, the key elements of criminal homicide include the killing of one human being by another without lawful justification.

Murder occurs when one human being is killed by another without lawful justification and with malice aforethought. A detailed examination of this definition explains exactly what murder is and is not. First, we note that murder involves the "killing of one human being by another." This tells us that killing oneself (commonly defined as **suicide**), killing an animal, and the killing of a human being by an animal, unless directed by a human being, are not murder. Second, we note the words "without lawful justification." These words indicate that the killing of one human being by another is not murder if the affirmative defense of lawful justification can be proved. Finally, we note that **malice aforethought** is required for murder to exist. The phrase simply means that an intention to seriously harm someone or to commit a serious crime must exist for a murder to take place and that the killing of one human by another that results from an accident is not murder because no such intention exists. It is indeed this specific phrase that distinguishes murder from other types of criminal homicide, as we will see below.

It is not our intent to analyze each definition of an offense in a step-by-step way as we have for murder. However, we encourage the reader to adopt this technique to better comprehend the nature of any given statute. Exact comprehension of any statute is difficult, even using this technique, because some of the words used to define a criminal act are unclear, ambiguous, or both. In the case of murder, the terms "killing," "human being," and "lawful justification" have empirical referents and are relatively easy to comprehend. "Malice aforethought," however, refers to a state of mind, and there is some confusion concerning what the term actually means. In common law and in the minds of many today, malice involves ill will or hatred, whereas aforethought indicates premeditation; but, as we have indicated above, ill will or hatred are no longer required.

Actually, malice may be categorized as either expressed or implied. An example of expressed malice might involve a person's lying in wait, holding a pistol in another person's garage, and firing the pistol at the garage owner when he or she enters the premises. Implied malice is involved in cases in which there was no actual intent to kill. In other words, implied malice is an indirect concept that can be proven by an objectively dangerous act and subjective conscious disregard for human life despite awareness of danger (Weinstock, 1999). In such cases, the action (or failure to take action) of the offender is considered so serious that he or she may be held criminally accountable (culpable) for the consequences of his or her actions even though he or she did not specifically intend those consequences (see the discussion of the felony murder rule below).

Some jurisdictions distinguish between first- and second-degree murder. Generally, such a distinction is predicated on the presence of expressed malice aforethought in first-degree murder. Evidence of lying in wait, the deliberate use of poisons or intoxicants, and the brutal nature of the killing may be used to demonstrate the expressed malice aforethought and to obtain a first-degree murder conviction. The final decision usually rests with a jury, which subjectively applies the circumstances to the letter of the law.

Another form of murder, often defined as first-degree murder, involves the **felony murder rule**. This doctrine holds that deaths resulting from the attempt or commission of certain felonies are the responsibility of the perpetrator and, in some jurisdictions, his or her accomplices. Today, the felony murder rule is most frequently applied when a death results from an inherently dangerous felony (such as robbery, rape, kidnapping, or arson), although historically it has been applied in other types of cases (Klotter, 2004). The justification for this rule is that it places upon the perpetrator of certain felonies the possible finding of "guilty of murder" if he or she creates a substantial risk that could result in the loss of life. Generally, homicides that involve malice aforethought but fail to meet the requirements of first-degree murder are defined as murder in the second degree in jurisdictions that make such distinctions. Thus, second-degree murder may result from the commission of less dangerous felonies or misdemeanors, from the commission of an act intended to cause bodily harm, or from other actions that imply a significant disregard for human life (such as firing a weapon at a passing vehicle).

Manslaughter is an unlawful homicide committed without malice aforethought and is a distinct category of crime rather than a degree of murder (Reid, 2004). There are two categories of manslaughter: voluntary and involuntary (or negligent or reckless). Voluntary manslaughter involves an intent to kill but is distinguished from murder by the circumstances that precede the commission of the act. If great provocation existed, if the offender acted in the "heat of passion" from that provocation, or if the accused acted in a "blind rage," these factors may serve to mitigate the malice, and the offender may be charged with voluntary manslaughter rather than murder. In determining whether an act is murder or manslaughter, a jury faces the difficult tasks of determining the degree of provocation, passion, or rage involved and the extent of provocation necessary to transform murder into manslaughter. In attempting to resolve such dilemmas, the courts have developed some general guidelines. For example, it is generally agreed that merely using words is not sufficient provocation to transform a murder to manslaughter (*Mullaney v. Wilbur*, 1974). Some action — such as a battery, mutual combat, the commission of adultery (*Dabney v. State*, 1897), or resistance to an unlawful arrest — is required. The courts have consistently held that the provocation must be immediately related to the killing. That is, the killing must occur while the offender is in a provoked passionate state. As the court stated in *In re Fraley*, "the law will not permit a defendant to deliberate his wrong, and avenging it by killing the wrongdoer, set up the plea that his act was committed in the heat of passion" (*In re Fraley*, 1910). It is important to understand that in these circumstances, the law is not meant to imply that it is permissible to kill (as it is permissible to do with respect to self defense or in many states to protect the life of another person) (Reid, 2001, p. 189).

The distinguishing feature of involuntary manslaughter is its unintentional nature. (This is the reason for the frequent reference to negligent manslaughter and why deaths resulting from automobile accidents are frequently categorized as involuntary manslaughter or a similarly defined offense.) Gross negligence or recklessness is a key element of this offense. Because many of us have committed reckless or negligent acts at one time or another, a standard of gross negligence is required. The established standard requires a definite disregard for the safety of others in the conduct leading to a death. Examples include the unsafe operation of a motor vehicle (*Commonwealth v. Welansky*, 1944), failure to employ reasonable care in hunting game, and failure to provide proper exits in buildings. Some states have developed misdemeanor manslaughter laws that are similar to the felony murder doctrine. The basis for these laws is the belief that the commission of some misdemeanors (generally, *malum in se* offenses) implies negligence and, therefore, that the offender is responsible for any deaths resulting from the commission of these offenses.

Punishment of homicide varies according to the category of homicide involved. The most severe punishments, including death, are generally reserved for first-degree murder. Many states now provide for "natural life" (life without the possibility of parole) sentences for offenders convicted of first-degree murder who do not receive the death penalty. The length of sentence usually decreases, moving downward from second-degree murder to involuntary manslaughter. We advise the reader to examine the homicide statutes of his or her state to obtain a better understanding of the prescribed punishment associated with each offense.

Assault and Battery

Obviously, not all crimes against the person result in the victim's death. The unlawful application of force by one individual against another may constitute a **battery**, and the attempt or threat to commit a battery may constitute an **assault**. Some jurisdictions combine the two offenses, whereas others treat them separately. A popular misconception is that a serious injury must result for a battery to occur. It is the unlawful application of force, not the result of that application, which constitutes battery. Such actions as striking with one's fist, kicking, holding the victim, and any touching if it is unlawful, may constitute the force necessary for a battery (Klotter, 2004; *Scruggs v. State*, 1974). It is unnecessary that the victim's body or even his or her clothing be touched, because touching anything connected with the person may constitute a battery. For example, the intentional snatching of a dinner plate from a restaurant patron by the manager in a loud and offensive manner was sufficient to support the charge of battery (*Fisher v. Carrousel Motor Hotel*, 1967). Further, spitting on another or striking another with a thrown projectile has been deemed battery, even if the recipient was not the intended target. Batteries can also include administering poison, communicating a disease, and deliberately exposing a person to inclement weather (*Pallis v. State*, 1899; *State v. Lankford*, 1917; *Woodward v. State*, 1932). Of course, not all contact, or even all violent contact, constitutes battery. Contact sports, such as boxing, football, and wrestling, are generally exempt from battery rules as long as the contact is within the rules of the game. Similarly, the parent who physically disciplines his or her child does not commit a battery unless such discipline is excessive. The reasonable use of physical force against another in self-defense may also be justified and therefore is not a battery.

Actions that place a person in "reasonable apprehension" of being battered (threat) or an attempt to batter may constitute assault. Thus, the unlawful attempt to strike another or otherwise cause injury constitutes an assault. If the attempt is consummated (successful), a battery has occurred. Some interpretations of assault statutes seem to require awareness on behalf of the victim that he or she is in danger of being battered, whereas others simply require a criminal state of mind on the part of the offender. Interpretations also vary with respect to whether the offender has the ability to commit a battery or only the apparent ability. Threatening another person with a soft rubber knife might be an assault under the latter interpretations but not under the former.

The key issue in determining whether an assault has occurred is whether reasonable apprehension exists on behalf of the victim. Generally, words alone do not appear to be sufficient to generate the necessary apprehension; rather, they must be accompanied by some threatening act or behavior on behalf of the offender.

Some jurisdictions include aggravated assault and aggravated battery in their criminal codes. Factors in **aggravation** include attempts to conceal identity, brandishing or displaying a deadly weapon, and committing assaults or batteries on specially designated professionals (e.g., teachers, police officers, or firefighters) while they are officially performing their duties (*Moreland v. State*, 1916).

In some jurisdictions, no battery can occur without an assault (the consummated battery includes the threat or attempt to batter), and battery and assault are merged into a single statute.

Forcible Rape

Traditional definitions of **rape** generally involve the following elements: (1) sexual intercourse, (2) by a male with a female other than his wife, (3) against her will and without consent, and (4) by force or threat of force, or while she is unconscious. Again, the definition may be broken down into its component parts to help us comprehend the nature of the offense.

Traditionally, sexual intercourse requires penetration of the female sex organ by the male sex organ. Lewd fondling or caressing and oral or anal sexual contact were defined as batteries, indecent liberties, or **sodomy**, but did not constitute rape. Today, many jurisdictions refer to these offenses under the headings of **deviate sexual conduct** (lewd fondling, for example) and **deviate sexual assault** (crimes involving penetration).

Historically, the courts have adhered to a principle of spousal immunity and have excepted forced intercourse by a husband on his wife from the category of forcible rape. The underlying assumption seems to have been that marriage is a permanent consent to sexual intercourse. Today, however, most states have theoretically eliminated this exemption; nonetheless, there are still few husbands convicted for the rape of their wives. Another modification being witnessed involves the gender of the offender and victim. Under the traditional definition of rape, it was virtually an all-male offense, and victims were exclusively female. Today, in some jurisdictions the word "person" has been substituted for "male" and "female," making it legally possible for a male to rape another male or for a female to rape a male (*State v. Flaherty*, 1929). Some states have also specified a minimum age for the offender.

There is considerable controversy over what constitutes consent on behalf of an alleged rape victim. In general, a victim who is incapacitated by the use of alcohol or other drugs, who is unconscious, who is mentally ill or severely retarded, or who is a victim of deception or fraud is incapable of giving a valid consent. However, some courts have held that the victim must resist to the utmost and that any form of sub-

mission, prior to forced penetration, constitutes consent. For example, an alleged offender was acquitted of rape when it was disclosed during cross-examination that the
victim had a knife in her possession at the time of the incident but made no attempt
to retrieve it from her purse and defend herself (*Peoria Journal Star*, 1977, p.C-14).
Opinions such as this are rare today, however, and most cases hinge on factors such as
the number of assailants, the presence of a weapon, and evidence of penetration. Further, most states have passed **rape shield statutes** which ban the introduction of evidence of a victim's past sexual conduct at a rape trial. Many states have also relaxed the
prompt reporting rule that prohibited prosecution unless the person promptly reported
the rape (Samaha, 2005; Spohn & Homey, 2002).

The element of force or threat of force in rape is somewhat ambiguous. Cases in
which a battery occurs are relatively easy to discern. It is equally clear that the presence
or use of a deadly weapon is not required to prove that force was imminent. Torn clothing, cuts, bruises, or teeth marks are frequently used to indicate that force accompanied sexual intercourse. Generally speaking, courts have held that coercion sufficient
to accomplish the intended result (i.e., sexual penetration) fulfills the force or threat
of force requirement for rape.

Sexual Predators or Sexually Dangerous Persons

Recently, several states have passed laws that require community notification when
a convicted sex offender moves into a neighborhood, as well as requiring that sex offenders register with law enforcement officials in the communities in which they live.
For example, in Illinois a sex offender must register in person annually for a period of
10 years with the law enforcement agency having jurisdiction where they reside
(I.S.O.F., 2007). In many states sex offenders are prohibited from being present on
school grounds with out special permission and are prohibited from residing with in
a specified distance of school, playground or facility providing education
programs. These laws, often referred to as sexual predator laws, are variations of a New
Jersey law known as Megan's Law (See the introductory article at the beginning of this
chapter). Such laws pit protection of children and victims against the offender's right
to privacy and have thus been controversial. Even more controversial are laws that allow
the courts to commit offenders legally declared sexual predators or sexually dangerous
persons to mental health facilities subsequent to serving their prison terms (*Chicago
Daily Law Bulletin*, 2000; Kazak, 2000). See "In the News 4.2" ("Jessica's Law: 21 States
and Counting").

In the News 4.2

JESSICA'S LAW: 21 STATES AND COUNTING

Led by state Sen. John McKinney, R-Fairfield, and state Sen. Louis C.
DeLuca, R-Woodbury, the Senate Republican Caucus reintroduced Jessica's

Law for Connecticut at a press conference last week in Hartford. At the same time, a new bill, the Internet Child Protection Act, was announced.

According to Connecticut General Assembly's Web site, Senate Bill 899 (Jessica's Law) An Act Concerning the **Sexual** Assault or Exploitation of Children would increase the penalties and monitoring of persons convicted of **sexual** offenses when the victim is under 13 years of age.

Senate Bill 900 [Internet Child Protection Act] An Act Concerning the Penalty for Enticing a Minor would increase the penalty for and supervision of a person who uses a computer to entice a child under 13 of age to engage in prostitution or **sexual** activity for which such person may be charged with a criminal offense.

McKinney, who represents Weston, Easton and Newtown as well as Fairfield, introduced both bills.

The original Jessica's Law was passed in Florida in 2005 after the abduction, rape and murder of 9-year-old Jessica Marie Lunsford by a repeat sex offender. It's difficult to think of a more reprehensible act, and 21 states seem to agree as they have adopted legislation similar to Florida.

The question we're posing to our colleagues in the majority is simple, Do you believe, yes or no, that a criminal who sexually assaults a child should go to jail for 25 years to life? asked McKinney in a press release distributed by the Senate Republican Office. I believe, and the Senate Republican Caucus believes, that they should.

Jessica's Law for Connecticut would legislate that individuals convicted of sexually assaulting a child 12 years of age or younger be sentenced to 25 years in prison for a first offense and life imprisonment for a second offense. Those convicted of promoting child prostitution, or employing a child under 13 in pornography would also be subject to the provisions of the law.

Additionally, released child **predators** would be on probation for the rest of their life and would be required to wear a GPS [Global Positioning System] tracking device.

Under the terms of the Internet Child Protection Act, the same penalties would apply to pedophiles convicted of using a computer to entice a child under 13 into having sex. The penalty for enticing children aged 13-15 would be a mandatory 10-year sentence for a first offense.]

Two additional provisions of SB900 would establish an Internet **Predator** Task Force Unit within the State Police and create an Internet Safety Course for elementary and middle school students. Both are excellent ideas.

Jessica's Law is not without opponents. Some question its efficacy while others question whether the restrictions placed on released offenders will make it too hard for them to reintegrate into society. Another issue is the cost involved.

McKinney also pointed out that, while there would be no judicial discretion in sentencing, there would still be flexibility in the legal system prior to sentencing.

This is an important point. When the mandatory minimum sentences are so great, the system needs to be able to weed out cases where there may be extenuating circumstances. Although it is hard to imagine what those circumstances might be, we have to allow for the possibility. On the other hand, there is absolutely no reason why recidivistic **predators** shouldn't be dealt with severely.

Though the initiative was introduced with political overtones, surely the concerns reflected in Jessica's Law are universal.

As to the Internet Child Protection Act, it's time all of our laws started catching up with what's happening online.

Author unknown. (2007, February 2). Jessica's Law: 21 States and Counting. *Greenwich Citizen (CT)* Available on line at: http://www.greenwichcitizen.com/ Record number 5142991

A sexually dangerous person is any person suffering from a mental disorder, which has existed for not less than a year, who has demonstrated the criminal propensities to commit sexual offenses and sexual assaults or the sexual molestation of children. Sexually dangerous persons in Illinois are required to register every 90 days (ISOF, 2007).

Other Sex Offenses

Although forcible rape is usually considered the most serious of the sex offenses, a number of other offenses are worthy of mention. Some jurisdictions hold that a female under a given age (usually 15 to 18) cannot legally consent to sexual intercourse. If vaginal intercourse occurs, the male participant may be charged with **statutory rape** or a similarly defined offense. Historically, statutory rape involved underage females, but many states also include male victims. Statutory rape is usually a strict liability offense, meaning that the perpetrator does not have to be aware of the minor's age. However, in some jurisdictions a reasonable mistake of fact concerning the minor's age could constitute a defense to a criminal charge (*People v. Hernandez*, 1964; Reid, 2004). Other states have categorized sexual contact (other than intercourse) as indecent solicitation of a minor, sexual exploitation of a child, or contributing to the sexual delinquency of a minor (*Illinois Compiled Statutes*, 2005, chap. 720 ILCS, sec. 5/11-6, 5/11-9.1).

As indicated above, another trend in criminal law is to reduce the overall number of sex offenses by incorporating all forms of sexual penetration (vaginal, oral, and anal, and the insertion of foreign objects) into the crime of sexual assault. In addition, cases involving weapons, minors, and family members are termed "aggravated sexual assault" and carry stiffer penalties (ILCS, 2005, chap. 720, sec. 5/11). While historically a number of sexual acts, including oral/genital and anal/genital contact, were prohibited under the general heading of sodomy, the current trend is to accept a variety of forms of sexual penetration and/or contact if they occur privately and between consenting adults.

There clearly are numerous other sex offenses, but space does not permit a detailed examination of all such offenses. We encourage the reader to carefully examine his or her own state's criminal code under such headings as adultery, fornication, prostitution, incest, and indecent exposure.

Crimes against Property

Robbery

Robbery is a unique crime in that it can be characterized as both a crime against property and a crime against the person. In addition, unlike homicide and aggravated assault, most robberies involve victims and offenders who have no prior personal relationship. Robbery involves taking property (theft) from another person by force or threat of force (assault, battery, or murder). The theft must occur in the presence of the victim but need not involve taking property from the person of the victim. As long as the property is within the general proximity of the victim and is under the victim's control (e.g., cash stolen from the teller at a bank) and as long as force or threat of force is used (e.g., the presence of a weapon) with the intent to permanently deprive the victim of the use of the property, a robbery has occurred. Threat of deadly force is not required—pushing, jostling, or striking with a fist are sufficient to prove the force element in robbery. Thus, the pickpocket who is caught trying to remove the victim's wallet and who struggles with the victim to pull the wallet away has now used force and has crossed the line from theft to robbery. Similarly, threats to destroy valuable property or to inflict bodily injury have consistently been found sufficient to substantiate a robbery charge.

Graduations of robbery are fairly common. Armed or aggravated robbery (involving the use or presence of deadly weapons) is the most serious form of the offense and is subject to the most severe punishment. Many question whether a robbery or **armed robbery** occurred when a perpetrator verbally claimed to possess a weapon or uses a finger in the pocket of a jacket to appear as though armed with a weapon. In many states this scenario constitutes a form of **aggravated robbery** which involves taking property from a person or presence of a person through the use of force or threatened use of force while indicating verbally or with actions that they are armed with a deadly weapon, even when no weapon is present (ILCS, chap. 720, sec. 5/18-5).

The law protects the property of citizens as well as their persons. The list of crimes against property is quite extensive, and we illustrate the nature of these crimes by focusing on three in addition to robbery: theft, burglary, and arson.

Larceny/Theft

Theft (**larceny**) occurs when one obtains unauthorized control over the property of another with the intent to permanently deprive the rightful possessor of the use of that property. Many statutes include receiving stolen property and obtaining property through deception (e.g., embezzlement) or under false pretenses under the general heading of theft. Like most crimes against property, theft is a crime against the right of possession, not necessarily ownership, and statutes usually protect both actual and constructive possession. Actual possession involves physical control over the property. For example, Jones is walking down the street carrying some packages. Smith takes one of the packages, runs away, and later sells the contents of the package. Smith has committed a theft involving actual possession. Constructive possession occurs when the property involved is outside the owner's control but the right of ownership has not been relinquished. For instance, Jones drives his car to Brown's house and leaves it there. While Brown is distracted by a fire truck, Smith steals the car. Although neither Jones nor Brown had actual possession of the auto, Jones still maintained constructive possession and was thus the victim of auto theft.

Because theft is a crime against the right of possession, it is possible for a person to be charged with stealing his or her own property. An apartment owner who signs a legally binding contract to rent an apartment complete with furnishings (stereo, refrigerator, stove, and furniture) relinquishes possession to the renter for the duration of the lease. If the apartment owner enters the apartment without the renter's knowledge and removes some of the furnishings with the intent to keep them permanently, he or she may be technically guilty of theft even though the items belonged to him or her. Thus, one does not have to own the property stolen to be the victim of a theft; he or she must simply have legal possession of the property. The property involved may be either real property (e.g., land or buildings) or personal property (all other property).

The issue of intent to permanently deprive an individual of his or her property is frequently a key element of theft cases. If you borrow a rake from a neighbor's garage to use for an afternoon, you have not committed theft because you did not intend to deprive the neighbor of the permanent use of the rake. If, however, you pick fruit from your neighbor's tree and eat it, you have unquestionably deprived the owner/possessor of the permanent use of the fruit and are subject to prosecution for theft.

The issue of intent to permanently deprive arises frequently in shoplifting cases. When a person conceals merchandise and passes the checkout lanes without paying for it or leaves the store, the intent to permanently deprive is relatively easy to demonstrate in court. If, however, an overzealous security guard confronts the person concealing the merchandise at the time the merchandise is concealed, the necessary element of intent to permanently deprive is more difficult to prove. The shoplifter can make an argument that he or she intended to pay for the items at the checkout lanes.

Automobile theft presents some of the same problems. Does the teenager who, without permission, takes an auto to go to the mall and then leaves the auto unharmed intend to permanently deprive the owner of the use of the auto? As a solution, most states have enacted "joyriding" or "unauthorized use of a vehicle" statutes. The intent to permanently deprive is not a necessary element of these statutes.

In most instances, theft is divided into two categories, depending on the dollar value of the items involved. The dividing line varies (in some states it's $300), but the lesser dollar amounts are defined as petty (or misdemeanor) theft and the more substantial sums grand (or felony) theft. As you might expect, the penalties tend to increase with the value of the property stolen.

Identity theft is a more recent crime that involves wrongfully obtaining and using another individual's personal data in a way that involves fraud or deception, typically for economic gain (NCJRSa, 2006). There are two major types of identity theft. **Account takeover** occurs when a perpetrator wrongfully acquires an existing credit card account, Social Security number, drivers license information, ATM card, telephone calling card and purchases products and/or services using the card or the number and expiration date. Another form of identity theft known as **application fraud or true name fraud** involves a person using Social Security numbers and other identifying information to create new accounts in another person's name (Privacy Rights Clearinghouse, 2006). See "In the News" 4.3 ("Thousands of records exposed—WIU breach releases data on up to 240,000 people").

In the News 4.3

THOUSANDS OF RECORDS EXPOSED — WIU BREACH RELEASES DATA ON UP TO 240,000 PEOPLE

A recent security breach in a Western Illinois University computer system could compromise the records of as many as 240,000 people, school officials said Friday.

Mitch Davidson, the director of the University Computer Support Services, said that on June 5 someone hacked into one of the school's computer systems that houses personal information on students.

That information includes names, addresses and Social Security numbers as well as credit card information on anyone who purchased something over the Internet from the school's bookstore or who stayed in the hotel in the University Union.

Academic information, such as grades and transcripts, were not accessed.

School officials said they don't know for sure if the records were viewed or copied.

Davidson said the school has not had any reports of any of the records being used improperly, but one of the biggest concerns over their possible use is **identity theft**.

Free credit reports are available online, and further information about how those exposed could protect themselves is available from the Federal Trade Commission at: www.consumer.gov/idtheft/

WIU is working to form a total list of record holders in the system and separate any duplicates. Davidson estimates the system has information on between 200,000 and 240,000 people. WIU's Office of Public Safety is investigating the breach.

School officials dealt with the breach the day it happened but did not release a statement notifying the public until Thursday.

WIU spokesman John Maguire said the school acted quickly to deal with the breach but then took the time to put a plan together to deal with the issue.

He said no cost estimate is yet available of lost employee time and the postage it will cost to mail out information to all of the affected record holders.

Maguire said the school hopes to begin mailing the letters Monday.

The school runs numerous routine checks on its computer system as well as spot checks, Davidson said. The computer hacker was in the system for a "relatively short period of time" that Davidson said may be possible to measure in minutes.

"Some scans are ongoing," Davidson said. "We found (someone) who had been within the system who did not belong there."

This is not the first university in the nation to experience such a problem. Davidson said 29 schools nationwide have had similar situations, including Ohio University, Harvard, Stanford and George Mason.

"About 30 percent of the break-ins in the past 12 months have been at colleges or universities," he said.

Pospeschil, J. (2006, June 17). Thousands of records exposed—WIU breach releases data on up to 240,000 people. *Peoria Journal Star,* **p. A1.**

During 2003 and 2004 a form of identity theft involving "phishing" gained prominence. **Phishing** involves creating and using emails and Web sites designed to appear like those of prominent, well-known legitimate businesses, financial institutions, and government agencies to deceive internet users into disclosing their personal information including financial information, usernames and passwords (National Criminal Justice Reference Service, 2006a). Most states have enacted laws that criminalize identity theft and the federal government created the Identity Theft Assumption and Deterence Act and later the Identity Theft Penalty Enhancement Act of 2004 which identified the offense of aggravated identity theft. While these forms of theft remain a multi-billion dollar problem for individuals and business, incidents of identity theft declined in 2006 with significant drops in fraudulent new-account openings (*Chicago Tribune,* 2007). Researchers attributed the decline to better consumer education and awareness, as well as increased use of online banking and financial sites that allow individuals to monitor their accounts more often.

Burglary

How many times have you heard someone cry, "I've been robbed!" when they returned to find a window or door broken and their television set or stereo removed?

Burglaries are among the most frequent of the property crimes.
Reprinted with permission of iStockphoto.com / Paul Hebditch.

Actually, these individuals have been burglarized (and are also victims of theft), not robbed. Traditionally, **burglary** involves breaking into and entering the dwelling of another, at night, with the intent to commit a felony in the dwelling. The use of force to enter such a dwelling constitutes breaking into. The courts have held that the amount of force required may be exceedingly little, such as turning a doorknob (*State v. Perry*, 1914) or raising an unlocked window (*State v. McAfee*, 1957).

Most jurisdictions now hold that one who enters a building lawfully but remains inside without authorization after the building is closed commits breaking in. This type of entry may be referred to as constructive breaking and applies to acts of deception used to gain entry.

Unlawful entry must also occur for a burglary to transpire. The entry may be very slight: Reaching inside to extract some article is sufficient. Constructive entry, involving the use of a trained animal, rope, or other device, may also establish the necessary element of the offense.

Burglary statutes today cover not only the dwellings of others but also telephone booths, unoccupied buildings, automobiles, aircraft, watercraft, and other forms of transportation or conveyance. If a breaking and entering occurs in a hotel or vacation residence, it is still classified as a burglary of the household whose member or members were staying there at the time the entry occurred (Bureau of Justice Statistics, 2006). Some jurisdictions list special crimes, such as residential or aggravated burglary, which involve the burglary of a dwelling and carry stiffer penalties. Similarly, modern statutes have eliminated the requirement that the breaking and entering occur at night.

With burglary, like theft, the element of intent may be difficult to prove. The prosecution must prove both the intent to enter and the intent to commit a felony or theft once entry is gained. One who falls asleep in a library and awakens after the library is closed has not committed a burglary, nor has the individual who enters the wrong apartment while reasonably believing it to be his or her own. This sometimes happens when an intoxicated person breaks into an apartment or house near and similar to his or her own, believing that a spouse has locked him or her out. In such a case, there is no intent to enter unlawfully, and even though a physical break-in occurs, the individual has not committed a burglary, although he or she may be civilly liable for any damages that occurred.

There is some disagreement regarding the second form of intent to commit a felony or theft. Some courts have held that the intent to commit any felony will suffice, whereas other jurisdictions specify an intent to commit dangerous felonies. Most statutes state an intent to commit a felony or theft, recognizing that some thefts are not felonies. The intent is relatively easy to prove if the offender is caught with stolen property or when the burglar uses a knife or gun to threaten others at the scene. The intent to commit a felony or theft is more difficult to prove when the burglar is caught making his or her entry. The presence of a torch, burglary tools, explosives, or a weapon may be sufficient to indicate such intent. It need not be shown that the accused did, in fact, commit a felony or theft, only that he or she intended to do so.

Arson

Arson poses a serious threat to both human life and property. Arson involves the willful and unlawful burning of a building or structure and is often motivated by crime concealment, revenge or spite, monetary gain, malicious vandalism or mental illness (Office of the State Fire Marshal, 2007). At one time, arson was limited to burning dwellings belonging to another, but contemporary statutes include all buildings and structures and many forms of personal property. Some states have created special crimes with stiffer penalties for the arson of a building or structure that is the dwelling place of another.

A general criminal state of mind, rather than a specific intent to commit arson, is all that is required by most arson statutes. An act intended as vandalism or an act of extortion that leads to an unlawful burning may constitute arson as well. In certain cases, gross negligence may also result in prosecution for arson.

Total destruction of the property is not required to prove arson. Similarly, the arsonist need not be physically present to ignite the fire. A bomb, explosive, or delayed ignition device may also be used to commit arson.

Arson for profit has become a major problem in the United States. Arson fires on average cause proportionately higher losses than fires from other causes (USFA, 2004). Furthermore, 84 out of 100 confirmed cases of arson are unsolved and in the United States approximately 2 percent of all arson cases result in the offender's conviction for

**Arson is among the most difficult crimes to investigate.
Reprinted with permission of iStockphoto.com / Daniel Cardiff.**

the crime of arson (interFIREonline, 2007). Burning one's own property to defraud an insurer has become almost fashionable among some property owners experiencing financial difficulties. Ideally, the culprit hopes that the evidence of arson will be destroyed in the fire or explosion. Many insurance carriers will not issue payment when there is a suspicious origin of the fire.

A more recent development is the creation of aggravated arson statutes. Arson of an occupied building or arson that results in injury to police or fire personnel responding to the fire are deemed aggravated and often carry harsh penalties.

Other More Recent Additions to Criminal Law

Although many of the acts discussed in this chapter have been defined as criminal for centuries, we cannot lose sight of the fact that new laws are continually enacted in response to specific societal problems. In the past decade or so, we have seen several new crimes emerge in response to societal behavior patterns. Among these are hate crimes and stalking.

Hate crimes are defined as "the violence of intolerance and bigotry, intended to hurt and intimidate someone because of their race, ethnicity, national origin, religion, sexual orientation, or disability" (Department of Justice Community Relations Service, 2001, p. 1). See "In News" 4.4 ("Such Actions Tantamount to Terrorism").

In the News 4.4

SUCH ACTIONS TANTAMOUNT TO TERRORISM

In 1998, James Byrd was murdered by three White supremacists in Jasper, Texas. Byrd, a Black man, was beaten severely and dragged for three miles behind a truck. Evidence suggests he was alive while he was being dragged.

Last week in Scottsdale, two gay men were accosted and beaten outside a local restaurant by a group of thugs who called them "fags." One victim was sent to the hospital. Luckily, the physical wounds will heal. The emotional wounds will remain.

What is the connection between these two crimes? There is the obvious bigotry that is the motivation behind them. There is the sense that, whatever problems one person might have with another group of people, those problems can be solved by inflicting pain on members of that group. It's savage.

When a violent crime is motivated by hate, we as a community are rightfully indignant. The violent crime is an affront to our common ethics as people who value peace and individual freedom. But the system that allows the hatred to fester does not garner the same outrage from the community. It should.

Some people doubt if we should have hate-crime laws for cases such as this. I understand their concerns. Such laws appear to create a special punishment for thought and, however distasteful a thought may be, thought is not a crime in a free society. However, when thought translates into action, then motive does matter and should not be ignored.

Hate crimes attack more than the victim. They are an attack on civil society itself. To exact physical pain and suffering on people for their identity is to engage in terrorism and, therefore, warrants more severe punishment. Thank goodness Arizona does have specific punishments for hate crimes, including those perpetrated because of sexual orientation.

It may be difficult to prove these two were the victim of a hate crime, however. This is because nobody claims to have seen the incident, despite it having occurred in the doorway of the restaurant.

There is the crime that garners no outrage but should force us all to look inward. Why do we have a society that tolerates this type of hatred? For while the violence may outrage us, intolerance of homosexuals is still the most acceptable form of bigotry in today's society.

Huffman, L. (2006, December 27). Such actions tantamount to terrorism. *The Arizona Republic, (Phoenix, AZ)*, p. 11.

Hate crimes can target either groups or individuals and usually involve another offense, such as assault, battery, criminal trespass, criminal damage to property, mob action, or, in rare instances, homicide. Both the additional offense and the designation of the target are necessary elements to obtain a conviction under a hate crimes statute. On June 11, 1993, the U.S. Supreme Court issued a unanimous decision upholding the constitutionality of Wisconsin's hate crimes enhancement statute, removing any doubt that legislatures could increase the penalties for crimes in which the victim is targeted because of his or her race, religion, ethnicity, or sexual orientation. Since that decision, virtually all states have adopted some type of hate crimes statute. Such statutes typically specify stiffer penalties than the predicate offense (Illinois General Assembly, 2007, chap. 720, sec. 5/12-7.1). Over the past twelve years Congress has passed several pieces of hate crime legislation including the Hate Crime and Prevention Act of 1999; Church Arson Prevention Act of 1996; Hate Crimes Sentencing Enhancement Act; and Hate Crimes Statistics Act of 1980 (National Criminal Justice Reference Service, 2006b). In spite of these statutes, research indicates there has been an increase in the number of hate crimes in recent years, indicating that hate is alive and well in the United States (Haider-Markel, 1998). Data compiled by the Federal Bureau of Investigation indicate that in hate crime incidents the most common types of offenses were intimidation; destruction, damage or vandalism; and assault or aggravated assault (National Criminal Justice Reference Service, 2006c). Racial and ethnically motivated incidents were the most likely to be violent. However, two-thirds of those incidents motivated by religion involved a property offense, most commonly vandalism (Strom, 2001). Young offenders were responsible for most hate crimes.

Society's increased focus on domestic violence has resulted in the addition of stalking statutes to many state criminal codes. **Stalking** involves the intentional or deliberate following of another person or placing that person under surveillance and either threatening that individual or placing the victim in reasonable apprehension of bodily harm. Typically, estranged spouses or lovers are perpetrators of stalking. Some jurisdictions have also created the offense of aggravated stalking when injury occurs, the victim is unlawfully restrained, or the offender violates an order of protection or a restraining order (ILCS, 2005, chap 720, sec. 5/12-7.3, 7.4). In addition, the federal government enacted the Federal Interstate Stalking Law, U.S.C. Title 18, sec. 2261A (amended 2000) which makes it a federal crime to travel across state lines to stalk someone. This law requires the stalker to have intent to kill, injure, harass, or intimidate the victim, who must be placed in a situation that causes reasonable fear of death or serious bodily injury. The victim's family members, spouse or intimate partners are also protected by this law (MCAVA, 2000). An additional provision of this federal law makes it an offense to stalk someone across state lines using regular mail, e-mail, or the internet (i.e. cyberstalking).

Measuring and Understanding Crime

Official crime statistics are available at the national level in the **Uniform Crime Reporting Program** (**UCR**), prepared annually by the Federal Bureau of Investigation

(FBI). The FBI claims that the UCR covers about 291 millions inhabitants, or 93 percent, of the total national population, with the most complete reporting coming from urban and suburban areas and the least reporting from more rural areas. Today, most jurisdictions participate in the UCR regardless of their size. For comparative purposes, a crime rate is calculated and standardized by multiplying the rate by 100,000. In addition to crime counts and trends, the UCR findings presented in the report, *Crime in the United States*, includes data on crimes cleared, persons arrested, and law enforcement personnel (Federal Bureau of Investigation, 2007b). In 2005 the Federal Bureau of Investigation discontinued the printed version of this publication. Although the FBI statistics are the most comprehensive ones available at the national level, they are subject to a number of sources of error. First, reporting is voluntary and not all agencies report. Second, the Uniform Crime Reporting Program (UCR) is based on reports prepared and submitted by individual police agencies, and reporting errors made by each agency are added to those made by other agencies in the final report. (Such errors include mistakes in calculations and mistakes in placing offenses in the appropriate categories.) Third, statistics in the UCR fail to indicate whether the alleged offender was actually apprehended and subsequently convicted for the reported offense. If we are interested in the number of offenders for certain types of crime in a certain time period, UCR data are useful, but if we want to know something about the actual extent and nature of criminal behavior, these data are considerably less valuable. Last, the UCR also includes **time clocks** that indicate how frequently specific offenses occur across the United States. The fact that a certain offense occurs every three seconds is unrelated to most citizens' potential to be the victim of that particular offense. It should be noted that many of the weaknesses associated with the UCRs are also noted by the FBI in *Crime in the United States* on its Web site: http://www.fbi.gov/ucr/ucr.htm.

There are a variety of official statistics available at the local and state levels. Most police departments tabulate statistics on **offenses known to the police** (those offenses observed by or reported to the police) and **offenses cleared by arrest.** Of all official statistics, offenses known to the police probably provide the most complete picture of the nature and extent of certain types of illegal activities (not including white-collar, organized, corporate, or political crime). Even when we consider the Index Offenses— criminal homicide, aggravated assault, forcible rape, robbery, burglary, felony theft, arson, and auto theft—there is considerable evidence to indicate that less than 50 percent of these crimes are reported to the police (Livingston, 1996, p.63). If estimates are reasonably accurate, the police are able to arrest a suspect in only about one out of five Index Offenses reported, which means that about 80 percent of those offenses reported to the police are not included in statistics based on crimes cleared by arrest.

Official statistics may be collected at a number of levels in the criminal justice network. However, each level includes some possible sources of error. Figure 4.1 indicates some sources of error that may affect official statistics collected at each level in the criminal justice network. Each official source of statistics has appropriate uses, but generally speaking, the sources of error increase as one moves through each level of the network. Another source of error may involve the use of slightly different definitions of certain crimes in certain jurisdictions.

Figure 4.1 *Some Possible Sources of Error at Specified Levels of the Criminal Justice Network*

	Levels at Which Data May be Collected	Sources of Error in Official Statistics
Police	1. Offenses known to police	All offenses not detected
		All offenses not reported to or recorded by the police
Police	2. Offenses cleared by arrest	Errors from Level 1
		All offenses that do not lead to arrest
Prosecutor	3. Offenses leading to prosecution	Errors from levels 1 and 2
		All offenses that result in arrest but that do not lead to prosecution
Criminal Court	4. Offenses leading to a conviction	Errors from levels 1, 2, and 3
		All offenses prosecuted that do not lead to conviction
Correctional Facilities	5. Offenses leading to incarceration	Errors from levels 1, 2, 3, and 4
		All offenses leading to conviction but not to incarceration

Source: Adapted from Cox, Allen, Hanser, and Conrad, *Juvenile Justice, 6th ed.*, Sage Publications, 2008.

Finally, there are two additional sources of error that may affect official statistics. First, in our current criminal justice network, there is a strong tendency for those who are least able to afford the luxury of private counsel and middle-class standards of living to be overrepresented at all levels in the criminal justice network. Whether official statistics report actual differences in the nature and extent of crime by social class or whether they reflect the inability of members of the lower social classes to avoid official labeling as readily as their middle-class counterparts is not entirely clear, although there is considerable support for the latter explanation. Second, it is important to remember that agencies collect and publish official statistics for a variety of purposes (such as justifying next year's budget request). This does not mean that all or even most agency personnel deliberately manipulate crime statistics for their own purposes, but all statistics are open to interpretation and may be presented in a variety of ways to suit the needs and purposes of the presenters.

It is apparent that using official statistics to assess the nature and extent of crime is like looking at the tip of the iceberg; that is, a substantial proportion of crime remains hidden beneath the surface. Although much crime that is not reported to or recorded by officials occurs, there is no precise method to determine just how much crime remains hidden. Attempts to assess the nature of criminal activity have involved victim survey research and self-report studies.

The National Incident-Based Reporting System (NIBRS)

The limitations associated with the UCR resulted in the development of a new collection method for crime data. The NIBRS is an incident-based reporting system that allows police agencies to collect data on individual crime occurrences. Administered by the Federal Bureau of Investigation, the NIBRS includes information on the place where a crime occurred, weapon used, type and value of property damaged or stolen, personal characteristics of the offender and the victim and the nature of the relationship between the two, the disposition of the complaint and additional data (Fagan, 2007). The NIBRS can furnish more detailed, accurate, meaningful crime data compared to the traditional summary reporting.

Victim Survey Research

Our knowledge of hidden crime has improved considerably over the past several years through the use of **victim survey research**. The best example of victim survey research is the **National Crime Victimization Survey (NCVS)** conducted by the Department of Justice. Samples of about 150,000 citizens over age 12 are analyzed every six months on a nationwide basis, and these citizens are asked to indicate whether (and, if so, how often) they have been the victims of crime in a specified time period. Households selected for the interview remain in the sample for three years. Respondents who indicate they have been victimized, unlike respondents in self-report studies, are not admitting to participation in illegal behavior and may therefore be more honest than self-report respondents. Victim survey research indicates that somewhere between 50 and 66 percent of all serious crime in the United States goes unreported to the police (Livingston, 1996, p.63). Rates for reporting vary by crime, and respondents indicate a variety of reasons for failing to report their misfortunes to criminal justice officials. The data indicate that most homicides and auto thefts are reported to the police, whereas rapes, aggravated assaults, burglaries, robberies, and thefts are not. The NCVS provides information concerning the circumstances of the crime, the characteristics of the offender (for some offenses), and the personal characteristics and actions of the victim regardless of whether or not the crime was reported to the police. Supplements are added periodically to the NCVS to obtain information on current topics such as school crime. Since 1995 the NCVS has experienced sample reductions due to the escalating costs associated with the collection of data. At the same time, the rate of crime has remained at a low level. According to the Bureau of Justice Statistics (2006), the combination of fewer respondents and less crime has resulted in diminished ability to detect statistically significant year-to-year changes in crime rates.

Although victim survey research has expanded our knowledge of the crime picture considerably, it too has limitations. Obviously, we cannot collect data on homicidal victimizations from victims; we generally do not ask questions about white-collar, corporate, political, or drug-related crime; and victims of some types of crime (e.g., rape) may be hesitant to report. Undoubtedly, some under- and overreporting occurs as the result of misinterpretations of the questions asked. Memory also affects the validity of victim reports.

Comparison between the UCR and NCVS

Many similarities exist between the Uniform Crime Reporting Program (UCR) and the National Crime Victimization Survey. They both measure an overlapping, but not identical, set of crimes. However, significant differences exist between the two programs. For example, the UCR provides timely data on crimes reported to law enforcement agencies. The NCVS is the primary source for the characteristics of criminal victimization and the number and type of crimes not reported to law enforcement. The NCVS collects data on nonfatal crimes against persons age 12 and older, reported and not reported to the police, from a national representative sample of U.S. households. Many members of the criminal justice network use these reports to explore trends between reported crimes and crimes reported by law enforcement agencies. Discrepancies between these reports can indicate changes in police procedures, shifting attitudes towards crime and police, and other societal changes (Bureau of Justice Statistics, 2007).

National Computer Security Survey

The National Computer Security Survey (NCSS) was designed to estimate the prevalence of computer security incidents (such as fraud and theft of information) against businesses and the resulting losses incurred by businesses (Bureau of Justice Statistics, 2006b). The Survey was conducted in 2006 by the Rand Corporation, and collected data concerning the nature and extent of computer security incidents; monetary costs and consequences of these incidents; types of offenders, and types of computer security measures used by companies in the U.S.

Self-Report Studies

Recognizing that official statistics provide a false dichotomy between criminals (those officially labeled) and noncriminals (those who may engage in illegal behavior but avoid the official label), Short and Nye (1958) and others decided to use self-report studies from juveniles to compare the nature and extent of delinquent activity on the part of institutionalized (labeled) and noninstitutionalized (nonlabeled) juveniles. **Self-report studies** of delinquent behavior were obtained by distributing questionnaires to both labeled and nonlabeled juveniles. These questionnaires allowed respondents to indicate what types of crimes they had committed and the frequency with which the acts had been committed. Short and Nye concluded that delinquency among noninstitutionalized juveniles is extensive and that there is little difference in the extent and nature of delinquent acts committed by noninstitutionalized and institutionalized juveniles. In addition, Short and Nye indicated that official statistics lead us to the misbelief that delinquency is largely a lower-class phenomenon, because few differences in the self-reported incidence of delinquency exist among juveniles in lower, middle, and upper social classes. The conclusions reached in similar studies (Akers, 1964; Porterfield, 1946; Voss, 1966) generally support those of Short and Nye.

Self-report studies are subject to criticism on the grounds that those who serve as respondents may under- or overreport their illegal activities. Some researchers have included questions designed to detect deception. Clark and Tifft (1966) used follow-up interviews and polygraph examinations to assess the extent to which deception occurred in their self-report study and found that all respondents made corrections on their original questionnaires when given the opportunity. Three-fourths of all the changes increased the frequency of admitted deviancy, all respondents underreported their misconduct on at least one item, and over half overreported on at least one item. Clark and Tifft concluded that "those items most frequently used on delinquency scales were found to be rather inaccurate" (p.523).

The Institute for Social Research, based at the University of Michigan, annually surveys approximately 2,500 high school seniors concerning their involvement in criminal activity. The Institute's findings relating to drug use, violent crime, and property offenses are frequently used to measure the success of various school-based and government-sponsored prevention programs. For example, the Institute reported at the end of 2006 that illicit drug use by U.S. teens (8th, 10th, 12th grades) had declined but prescription drug use (such as Oxycontin and Vicondin) remained high (ISR, 2006).

In conclusion, the use of self-report scales as the only means of determining the extent of crime or delinquency is risky. However, these scales provide information that can be cross-checked in a variety of ways (e.g., through police records) and allow comparisons between official and unofficial estimates of crime.

An Overview of Crime in the U.S.

We have described the methods for measuring crime in the U.S. and now turn to a discussion of the crime problem and the characteristics of those who are the victims of crime. Each of these measurements assists in the development of an understanding of the problems of crime in the U.S. We will examine condensed aggregate data from each source, but in order to achieve a true picture of crime it is important that you review all sources of crime data.

National Crime Victimization Survey Data

The NCVS data released in 2006 reported that the violent crime rate remained unchanged between 2004 and 2005, while the property crime rate declined because of a decrease in household theft. However, the violent crime rate for 1993 to 2005 declined 58 percent, from 50 to 21 victimizations per 1,000 persons age 12 and older (Bureau of Justice Statistics, 2006c). Together, violent crime and property crime rates in 2005, as estimated by the National Crime Victimization Survey, were at the lowest levels reported since 1973—the first year that such data was available. In 2006 there were an estimated 18 million property crimes (burglaries, motor vehicle thefts, and household thefts); 5.2 million violent crimes (rapes or sexual assaults, robberies, aggravated assaults, and simple assaults); and 227,000 personal thefts (picked pockets and snatched purses). In 2005, according to victims included in the NCVS, 47 percent of violent crimes were reported to the police, an increase from 43 percent in 1993. Specifically, 38 percent of rapes and sexual assaults were reported to law enforcement as were 42 percent of simple assaults, 52 percent of robberies, and 62 percent of aggravated assaults. The proportion of property crimes reported to the police also increased from 33 percent in 1993 to 40 percent in 2005. For example, approximately 83 percent of motor vehicle thefts were reported to police.

Uniform Crime Report Data

More than 17,000 municipal, county, state, tribal, and federal law enforcement agencies reported arrest and offense data in 2005. The offense of forcible rape was the only reported violent offense to experience a decrease when compared to 2004 data (Federal Bureau of Investigation, 2006). The estimated volume of robbery increased 3.9 percent, murder and nonnegligent manslaughter increased 3.4 percent, and aggravated assault increased 1.8 percent. Burglary was the only property crime to reveal an increase in 2005. According to *Crime in the United States*, law enforcement agencies cleared 45.5 percent of violent crimes and 16.3 percent of property crimes in 2005. The FBI estimated that law enforcement agencies in the U.S. made 14.1 million arrests in 2005. Law enforcement agencies reported that their staffing rate was 3.5 officers per 1000 residents. See Figure 4.2, Percentage Change by Population Group from Crime in The United States (2008) on the next page.

Preliminary data for the first six months of 2007 indicated that law enforcement agencies reported a 1.8 percent decrease in the number of violent crimes when compared with the same time period in 2006 (Federal Bureau of Investigation, 2008). The number of property crimes decreased by 2.6 percent when compared with the reported data for the first six months of 2006. Figures for 2007 indicated that reported arson decreased 9.7 percent in the first half of the year when compared to 2006 data (Federal Bureau of Investigation, 2008).

Figure 4.2   Percentage Change by Population Group

Population group	Number of agencies	Population	Violent crime	Murder	Forcible rape	Robbery	Aggravated assault	Property crime	Burglary	Larceny-theft	Motor vehicle theft	Arson
Total	11,673	245,160,625	-1.8	-1.1	-6.1	-1.2	-1.7	-2.6	-1.3	-2.1	-7.4	-9.7
Cities:												
1,000,000 and over	10	25,080,811	-4.1	-6.5	-14.2	-4.3	-3.3	-0.9	+3.5	-0.3	-7.5	-3.3
500,000 to 999,999	22	14,663,740	-2.3	-5.0	-8.0	-2.2	-1.9	-2.8	-3.7	-0.9	-7.8	-15.9
250,000 to 499,999	35	12,312,747	-5.1	0.0	-6.8	-3.4	-6.2	-4.8	-3.1	-4.1	-9.4	-6.9
100,000 to 249,999	185	27,606,579	+0.1	+0.9	-7.1	+2.4	-0.4	-2.2	-0.1	-1.9	-7.0	-6.2
50,000 to 99,999	381	26,155,379	-0.7	+3.2	-3.5	+0.7	-1.1	-4.0	-1.2	-3.9	-9.5	-15.8
25,000 to 49,999	661	22,769,358	-0.2	0.0	-3.4	+3.9	-1.6	-2.8	-1.5	-2.5	-7.5	-5.6
10,000 to 24,999	1,464	23,211,182	+1.1	-0.7	-4.2	+0.4	+2.1	-1.9	-0.5	-1.7	-7.3	-11.0
Under 10,000	5,753	18,851,973	+0.3	-3.5	-2.8	-2.7	+1.4	-2.6	-1.3	-2.7	-5.3	-12.8
Counties:												
Metropolitan[1]	1,304	52,214,353	-1.9	+4.9	-6.0	-0.6	-2.0	-2.6	-3.6	-1.7	-5.1	-8.6
Nonmetropolitan[2]	1,858	22,294,503	+1.1	+1.3	-3.5	+3.4	+1.7	-1.4	-0.8	-1.4	-3.9	-13.8

1 Includes crimes reported to sheriffs' departments, county police departments, and state police within Metropolitan Statistical Areas.
2 Includes crimes reported to sheriffs' departments, county police departments, and state police outside Metropolitan Statistical Areas.

Characteristics of Crime Victims

In this section we will discuss several social and demographic characteristics which distinguish victims and nonvictims of crime in the United States. Reid (2006) concluded that young people, men (except for rape and sexual assault), African Americans, Hispanics, divorced or separated people, the unemployed, the poor, and residents of central cities were the most frequent victims of crime. These patterns of victimization were consistent with the victimization data reported for 2005 by the National Crime Victimization Survey. Males, African Americans, and persons age 24 or younger continued to be victimized at higher rates than females, Caucasians, and persons age 25 or older. With respect to gender, males were victims of overall violent crime, robbery, total assault, aggravated assaults and simple assaults at higher rates than females (Bureau of Justice Statistics, 2006c). Females in 2005, as in the past, were more likely to be victims of rape or sexual assaults. Even though males are much more likely than females to be violent crime victims, many studies have concluded that fear of violent crime is greater among females, mainly because of the crime of forcible rape (Reid, 2006). When men are the victims of violent crimes, the perpetrator often is described as a stranger; women are much more likely to be attacked by someone they know than are men (Siegel, 2001). Furthermore, violent crimes against females are more likely to be reported to the police than crimes against males.

In 2003 the NCVS altered the definition of race and ethnicity, and respondents were allowed to self-identify with more than one race. This prevented long term comparisons with past data. However, in 2005 African Americans were more likely to be victims of violence than persons of other races. Persons of two or more races were victims of overall violence at significantly higher rates then Caucasians, African Americans and Hispanic victims. Consistency with prior data collection was also observed in the age of the victims. A general pattern of decreasing crime rates for persons of older age groups was observed in 2005. Persons age 16–19 experienced robbery at rates higher than persons in other age groups except for ages 20–24. The association between age and victimization is undoubtedly related to the lifestyle shared by young people. Most adolescents ages 12 to 19 are attacked by offenders in the same age category, whereas a majority of adults are victimized by adult criminals (Siegel, 2001). A general pattern of decreasing victimization for persons residing in households with higher incomes was reported by the NCVS in 2005. Specifically, those living in households with an annual income under $7,500 were more likely to be victims of robbery and assault crimes than members of households with incomes that exceeded $35,000 or more. Also, lower annual income households experienced the highest levels of burglary victimizations. Location of the residence also revealed an interesting pattern. As expected, urban residents experienced overall crimes of violence, robbery, and assault at rates higher than those for suburban and rural residents. However, for the crimes of rape or sexual assault, suburban and rural residents had statistically similar rates of victimization (Bureau of Justice Statistics, 2006c). In addition, rural residents reported experiencing more burglaries than suburban residents, but fewer burglaries than urban residents.

Summary

1. By analyzing the definitions of the various crimes step-by-step, we can better understand the exact nature and requirements of these crimes.

2. The general distinction between felonies and misdemeanors has been discussed, as have differences between crimes that are *malum in se* (evils in themselves) and *malum prohibitum* (evil because they are prohibited).

3. Criminal homicides, rape, and robbery are among the most serious of the crimes against the person. The elements of these offenses, as well as those of the property crimes of theft, burglary, and arson, have been briefly analyzed in this chapter.

4. In addition, several new crimes and the laws used to attempt to control them were discussed.

5. There are a variety of ways of collecting information concerning crime. The Uniform Crime Reports and the National Crime Victimization Survey are the most widely used sources of crime statistics.

Key Terms Defined

statutory Law enacted by legislative bodies.

case law Law based on court decisions.

felonies Offenses punishable by a sentence of more than one year in prison.

misdemeanors Offenses punishable by up to one year in jail.

acts malum in se Acts that are wrong in and of themselves.

acts malum prohibitum Acts that are wrong because they are prohibited.

homicide The killing of another person.

murder The premeditated and unlawful killing of another person.

suicide Killing oneself.

malice aforethought The intention to seriously harm someone or commit a serious crime.

felony murder rule A rule stating that an accidental killing that occurs during the commission of a felony may be termed murder.

manslaughter An unlawful homicide committed without malice aforethought.

battery An intentional, unprovoked, harmful physical contact by one person (or an object controlled by that person) with another.

assault An act that creates in one person the reasonable fear of being battered by another by reason of threat or attempt to batter.

aggravation An act that increases the seriousness of the crime in question.

rape Sexual intercourse by force or threat of force without lawful consent.

sodomy Sexual contact between the sex organs of, or an object controlled by, one person with the mouth or anus of another.

deviate sexual conduct Generally, lewd fondling or sexually "knowing" another without consent and without sexual penetration.

deviate sexual assault Generally, sexual contact involving penetration of the mouth, anus, or sex organs of one person by another without consent.

rape shield statute Prevents introduction of the victim's past sexual conduct at a rape trial

statutory rape Intercourse with a person under a specified age.

robbery The illegal taking of property from another by force or threat of force.

armed robbery The commission of a robbery while armed with a deadly weapon.

aggravated robbery The commission of a robbery while indicating verbally or with actions that a person is armed with a deadly weapon when no weapon is present.

theft (larceny) Taking unauthorized control over the property of another with the intent to permanently deprive the rightful possessor of the property.

identity theft Wrongfully obtaining use of another's personal data in a way that involves fraud and deception for the purpose of economic gain.

account takeover Wrongfully acquiring an existing credit card, social security number or drivers license number to purchase products.

application fraud (*true name fraud*) Wrongfully using identifying information to create a new account in another person's name.

phishing Creating e-mails or Web sites to deceive internet users into disclosing their personal information.

burglary Generally, breaking into and entering the dwelling of another with the intent to commit a felony.

arson The willful and unlawful burning of a building or structure.

hate crimes Crimes that target victims on the basis of race, creed, color, national origin, sexual preference, or religion.

stalking The intentional or deliberate following of another person, or placing another person under surveillance and either threatening that person or placing the person in reasonable fear of bodily harm.

Uniform Crime Reporting Program (UCR) Reports prepared by the FBI concerning reported crimes in the United States.

time clocks Clocks showing the number of crimes occurring per minute.

offenses known to the police Offenses reported to or observed by the police.

offenses cleared by arrest Offenses for which one or more individuals has been made available for prosecution.

victim survey research Research that collects reports concerning experiences of crime victims.

National Incident Based Reporting System *(*NIBRS*)* An incident based reporting system that allows police to collect data on individual crime occurrences.

National Crime Victimization Survey (NCVS*)* Report prepared by the Department of Justice concerning crimes occurring in the United States.

National Computer Security Survey (NCSS*)* Estimates the prevalence of computer security incidents against businesses.

self-report studies Studies asking respondents to report their criminal activities.

Institute for Social Research University of Michigan-based survey research center.

Critical Thinking Exercises

1. What sources of information would you use to obtain the most accurate picture of crime in the United States? What are some of the limitations of each source of information?

2. Are there consistent threads through the various types of behavior classified as crimes? If so, what are those threads?

Internet Exercises

The crime of murder is often intriguing and fascinating to the college student. Recently, law enforcement agencies have developed an extensive literature base on serial killers. Access the serial killers Web site at www.crimelibrary.com/serial_killers/index.html

After you read this site, answer the following questions:

1. What distinguishes serial murder from other types/forms of murder?
2. What role does insanity play in the motives for serial killings and as an affirmative defense?
3. Who are the victims of serial killers, and how are they selected?
4. What effect does child abuse and the mother-son relationship have on serial killers?

References

Akers, R. L. (1964). Socioeconomic status and delinquent behavior: A retest. *Journal of Research on Crime and Delinquency*, 1, 38–46.

Bureau of Justice Statistics (2006a). *After many years of declining, burglary rates have stabilized.* U.S. Department of Justice. Available online at: http://www.ojp.usdoj .gov/bjs/glance/burg.htm.

Bureau of Justice Statistics. (2006b). *National computer security survey.* U.S. Department of Justice. Available online at: http://www.ojp.usdoj.gov/bjs/survey/ncss/ncss.htm.

Bureau of Justice Statistics. (2006c). *Violent crime rate unchanged during 2005, theft rate declined.* U.S. Department of Justice. Available online at: http://www. ojp.usdoj.gov/bjs/pub/press/cv05pr.htm.

Bureau of Justice Statistics. (2007) *The nation's two crime measures.* U.S. Department of Justice. Available online at: http://www.ojp.usdoj.gov/bjs/pub/html/ntcm.htm.

Chicago Daily Law Bulletin. (2000, September 29). Justice clarifies sexual predator law, p. 5.

Chicago Tribune. (2007, February 2). ID-theft losses decline by 12 percent, p. 3.

Clark, J. P., & Tifft, L. L. (1966). Polygraph and interview validation of self-reported deviant behavior. *American Sociological Review,* 31 (4), 516–23.

Commonwealth v. Welansky, 316 Mass. 383, 53 NE 2d 902 (1944).

Dabney v. State, 21 So. 211, 113 Ala. 38 (1897).

Department of Justice Community Relations Service (2001). *Hate crime: The violence of intolerance.* U.S. Department of Justice. Available online at: http://www.usdoj.gov/crs/pubs/crs_pub_hate_crime_bulletin_1201.htm.

Fagan, J. A. (2007). *Criminal justice.* Boston, MA: Allyn and Bacon.

Federal Bureau of Investigation. (2008). *Crime in the United States.* Available online at: http://www.fbi.gov/ucr/prelim2007/index.html.

Federal Bureau of Investigation. (2007). *Uniform crime reports.* Available online at: http://www.fbi.gov/ucr/ucr.htm#cius.

Fisher v. Carrousel Motor Hotel, 424 S.W. 2nd 627 (1967).

Fox, J.A. & Zawitz, M.W. (2007). Homicide trends in the U.S. Bureau of Justice Statistics. U.S. Department of Justice. Available online at: http://www.ojp.usdoj.gov/bjs/homicide/homtrnd.htm.

Haider-Markel, D. P. (1998). The politics of social regulatory policy: State and federal hate crime policy and implementation effort. *Political Research Quarterly,* 51 (1), 69–88.

Illinois General Assembly. Illinois Legislative System. Available online at: http://www.ilga.gov/legislation/ilcs/ilcs/asp.

Illinois Sex Offender Information. (2007). Illinois State Police. Available online at: http://www.isp.state.il.us/sor/faq.cfm?CFID=45276CFTOKEN=71936591.

In re Fraley, 109 P. 295, 3 Okla. Crim. 719 (1910).

Institute for Social Research. (2006). *Illicit drug use down among teens, prescription drug use remains high.* University of Michigan. Available online at: http://www.ns.umich.edu/htdocs/releases/study.php?id=3065.

InterFIREonline. (2007). *Underwriting against arson.* Available online at: http://interfire.org/features/underwrite.asp.

Kazak, D. R. (2000, December 20). "Sexually dangerous" man sent to prison. *Chicago Daily Herald*, p.6.

Klotter, J. (2004). *Criminal law*. (7th ed.). Cincinnati, OH: Anderson Publishing Company.

Livingston, J. (1996). *Crime and criminology*. (2nd ed.). Upper Saddle River, NJ: Prentice-Hall.

Minnesota Center Against Violence and Abuse (2000). *Federal interstate stalking law*. Available online at: http://www.mincava.umn.edu/documents/factsh1/factsh1.html.

Moreland v. State, 188 SWI, 125, Ark. 24 (1916).

Mullaney v. Wilbur, 421 U.S. 684 (1974).

National Criminal Justice Reference Service. (2006a). *Identity theft*. Office of Justice Programs. Available online at: http://www.ncjrs.gov/App/Topics/Topic.aspx?Topicid=70.

National Criminal Justice Reference Service. (2006b). *Hate crime*. Office of Justice Programs. Available online at: http://www.ncjrs.gov/spotlight/hate_crimes/summary.html.

National Criminal Justice Reference Service. (2006c). *Hate crimes: Facts and figures*. Office of Justice Programs. Available online at: http://www.ncjrs.gov/spotlight/hate_crimes/summary.html.

Office of the Fire Marshal. (2007). *Arson is a felony crime*. Available online at: http://www.state.il.us/osfm/Arson/ArsonIsAFelonyCrime.htm.

Pallis v. State, 26 So. 339 (1899).

People v. Hernandez, 393 P.2d 673 (Cal. 1964).

Peoria Journal Star. (1977, January 7). Man, 22, acquitted of rape, to face parole, pardon board, p. C14.

Porterfield, A. L. (1946). *Youth in trouble*. Fort Worth, IN: Potisham Foundation.

Privacy Rights Clearinghouse. (2006). *Reducing the risk of identity theft*. Available online at: http://www.privacyrights.org/fs/fs17-it.htm.

Reid, S. T. (2001). *Criminal law*. 5th ed. New York, NY: McGraw-Hill Companies, Inc.

Reid, S. T. (2004). *Criminal law*. 6th ed. New York, NY: McGraw-Hill Companies, Inc.

Reid, S.T. (2006). *Crime and Criminology*. 11th ed. New York, NY: McGraw-Hill Companies, Inc.

Samaha, J. (2005). *Criminal law*. 8th ed. Belmont, CA: Wadsworth Publishing Co.

Scruggs v. State, 161 Ind. App. 666, 317 N.E. 2d 807 (1974).

Short, J. F., & Nye, F. I. (1958). Extent of unrecorded juvenile delinquency: Some tentative conclusions. *Journal of Criminal Law, Criminology, and Police Science*, 49 (4), 296–302.

Siegel, L.J. (2001). *Criminology, theories, patterns, and typologies*. 7th ed. Belmont, CA: Wadsworth/Thomson Learning.

Spohn, C., & Homey, J. (2002). *Rape law reform: A grassroots revolution and its impact.* New York: Plenum.

State v. Flaherty, 146 A. 7 (1929).

State v. Lankford, 12 A. 13 (1917).

State v. McAfee, 100 S.E. 2d 249 (1957).

State v. Perry, 145 N.W. 56 (1914).

Strom, K.J. (2001). *Hate crimes reported in NIBRS.* Bureau of Justice Statistics, U.S. Department of Justice. Rockville, MD: National Institute of Justice.

Uniform Determination of Death Act (1987). 120 U.L.A. Pocket Part 287. In Klotter, J. (2004). *Criminal law* 7th ed. Cincinnati, OH: Anderson Publishing Co.

United States Fire Administration (2004). *Attacking the crime of arson: Report on American fire investigation units.* Available online at: http://www.usfa.dhs.gov/fireservice/subjects/arson/.

Voss, H. L. (1966). Socioeconomic status and reported delinquent behavior. *Social Problems*, 13, 314–24.

Weinstock, R. (1999). Drug and alcohol intoxication: Mens rea defenses. *American Academy of Psychiatry and the Law*, 24 (1), 1–3.

Woodward v. State, 144 So. 895 (1932).

Suggested Readings

Dix, G.E. & Sharlot, M.M. (1999). *Criminal law.* 4th ed. Belmont, CA: Wadsworth Publishing Co.

Dressler, J. (2003). *Cases and materials on criminal law.* 3rd ed. St. Paul, MN: West Publishing Group.

Kaplan, J. (2004). *Criminal law cases and materials.* 5th ed. NY: Aspen Publishing.

Schamalleger, F. (2005). *Criminal law today: An introduction with capstone cases.* 3rd ed. Upper Saddle River, NJ: Prentice Hall.

Simon, R., & Ahn-Redding, H. (2005). *Crimes women commit: The punishment they receive.* Lanham, MD: Lexington Books.

Smith, C.E., McCall, M., & McCluskey, C.P. (2005). *Law and criminal justice: Emerging issues in the twenty-first century.* NY: Peter Lang.

Chapter Five

Types of Crime: II

In the News 5.1

FORMER ANTELOPE MAN SENTENCED TO 20 MONTHS IN PRISON FOR FRAUDULENTLY OBTAINING MICROSOFT SOFTWARE: Defendant Cracked Code Needed to Activate Software Causing More Than $500,000 in Losses

Sacramento—United States Attorney McGregor W. Scott and Sacramento County Sheriff John McGinness announced today that Darren McWaine, aka Darren Macwangwala, David Marsh, Dave Watts, and Darren McWayne, age 35, formerly of Antelope, California was sentenced to 20 months in prison for his role in a scheme in which he stole more than $500,000 worth of Microsoft software.

This case is the product of an extensive/ joint investigation by the Sacramento Valley High Tech Crimes Task Force, which is comprised of more than 30 federal, state and local law enforcement agencies, and the United States Postal Inspection Service. Microsoft also assisted with the investigation.

According to Assistant United States Attorney Robin R. Taylor of the Computer Hacking and Intellectual Property Unit ("CHIPs Unit"), who is prosecuting the case, defendant McWaine previously admitted in court that from approximately November 1999 through January 2004, he fraudulently activated more than 179 subscriptions of Microsoft Developer Network Software, Universal Edition (MSDN), which was use by developers to create computer products compatible with Microsoft software. The initial subscription for the MSDN retailed at approximately $2,799, and could be renewed annually for approximately $2,299.

According to the documents filed in court, a legitimate purchaser of the MSDN software would receive a 15-digit Product Identification Numbers ("PID numbers") or activation number from Microsoft which could be used to activate a software subscription via the Internet, phone, or mail. Defendant McWaine admitted that as part of the fraud, he obtained legitimate PID numbers and then, by manipulating the digits of those numbers, created new and unauthorized PID numbers.

After logging onto Microsoft's computer, defendant McWaine would test a PID number he fraudulently created to determine if it would activate an MSDN subscription. If the PID number he created worked, the computer would generate a certain response. He then used these fraudulently created PID numbers to activate software subscription for himself and others, without the permission of, or payment to, Microsoft. To conceal his identity from Microsoft, McWaine used more than 15 aliases and multiple false addresses.

The defendant, as part of his sentence, was ordered to make restitution to Microsoft for its losses. Additionally, he will serve a three-year term of supervised release following his prison term.

Scott, M. W. (2007, January 25). **Former Antelope man sentenced to 20 months in prison for fraudulently obtaining Microsoft software: Defendant Cracked Code Needed to Activate Software Causing More than $500,000 in Losses. Computer Crime and Intellectual Property Section, Department of Justice. Available online at: http:// www.cybercrime.gov/**

Key Terms

crimes without complainants
prostitution
white-collar crime
business-related crime
fraud
organized crime
Continuing Criminal Enterprise (CCE) statute
terrorism
transnational crimes

Chapter Outline

Crimes without Complainants
Prostitution and Related Offenses
Drug Offenses
Drugs and Crime
Gambling
White-Collar Crime
Fraud
Organized Crime

Computer Crime and Cyber Crime
Terrorism and Transnational Crime

In this chapter, we discuss two categories of crime that have been surrounded for some time by controversy: **crimes without complainants** and white-collar crimes. The former, often called crimes without victims (Schur, 1965), involve the provision of goods and services that are in demand but illegal. The latter are crimes committed by persons who occupy positions of trust in business, medicine, law, and other areas (Sutherland, 1939). As we analyze these crimes, we indicate why they remain controversial, the procedures involved in dealing with individuals involved in such crimes, and the consequences of these crimes for society.

Crimes without Complainants

Schur's discussion of crimes without victims, published in 1965, led to considerable controversy. His initial analysis focused on abortion, homosexuality, and drug addiction as crimes without victims in the sense that they all involve "the willing exchange, among adults, of strongly demanded, but legally proscribed, goods or services" (Schur, 1965, p.169). In the years following the publication of Schur's book, both abortion and homosexuality were largely decriminalized. Others, following Schur's lead, began to include in the general category of crimes without victims prostitution, gambling, and pornography/obscenity (Smith & Pollock, 1975; Walker, 2005). In addition, some people view prostitution, drugs, homosexuality, and abortion as crimes without victims; others view the participants involved as victims without crimes (Meier & Geis, 1997). The debate concerning whether or not these activities involve victims has raged for some time. Most recently, for example, the spread of AIDS has raised questions as to the victimless nature of prostitution and drug abuse, and some contend that engaging in unlawful conduct of any kind is likely to produce victims (Bastian, 1995). We prefer to use the term "crimes without complainants" because it accurately describes the majority of such activities in the sense that the supposed victims of these acts seldom file complaints. Whether they see themselves as victims and whether society should consider them victims are issues that are indeed difficult to resolve. It is clear, however, that attempts to legislate morality and to enforce such legislation produce serious consequences for those involved in the criminal justice network (Duster, 1970; Walker, 1998, 2005; Weisheit, 1990). Among those consequences are the necessity for the police themselves to serve as complainants with respect to such activities and the tremendous costs in police resources (time and money to pay informants and to make drug buys, place bets, and so on), prosecutorial resources, court time, and rehabilitation programs. Most importantly, consensus exists among those who study crimes without complainants that there is seldom any payoff, or return for the investment made, in attempting to enforce laws regulating these activities (Nadelmann, 1998). It is common knowledge that the street-level drug pusher is replaced within hours (perhaps minutes) of his arrest, that the prostitute is often back working the streets before the arresting officer has finished the arrest reports, and that gamblers and addicts return to their habits more often than not, regardless of the punishment or rehabilitation programs prescribed.

Prostitution and Related Offenses

Prostitution involves agreeing to, or engaging in, sexual acts for compensation. James (1977) defined prostitution as any sexual exchange in which the reward for the prostitute is neither sexual nor affectional. Although it has traditionally been treated as an offense committed by women, today it is widely recognized that the offender may be of either sex (Weinberg, Shaver, & Williams, 1999). The offense is generally a misdemeanor, and the most common punishment on conviction is a fine. Patronizing a prostitute, allowing a house to be used for purposes of prostitution, soliciting (arranging or offering to arrange) for a prostitute, pandering (compelling or arranging for a person to commit prostitution), and pimping (making money from the prostitution of another) are also generally prohibited by law. Despite the numerous laws that prohibit prostitution and related activities, however, these activities continue to flourish more or less openly throughout the world and certainly in every major city in the United States (Vito & Holmes, 1994). Many people believe that prostitution ought to be legal, with no regulation whatsoever regarding how it is carried on, except for already existing laws concerning public decency (Meier and Geis, 1997). Others believe that prostitution should be decriminalized but that practitioners should be licensed and subject to periodic testing for venereal diseases and HIV. Still others maintain that for reasons of morality or for the betterment of the position of women, prostitution should remain outside the sanction of the law (Meier & Geis, 1997). Law enforcement efforts to reduce the incidences of these activities sometimes succeed in forcing participants to move from one location to another, but the elimination of such activities seems highly unlikely in spite of some new attempts (Nelson, 2004). The demand and willingness to pay for sexual services virtually ensures the supply, as is characteristic of all the activities covered by the umbrella term "crimes without complainants." Furthermore, some view the prostitutes as primarily responsible for the problem, while some view the clients as responsible, and the prostitutes as victims (Maloney & Mobley, 2002, Raphael & Shapiro, 2004). Of course, others view prostitution as a private matter and reject government intervention. The morals, values, and beliefs of the public affect how a particular community addresses prostitution. Recognition of this fact has led a number of countries to legalize prostitution and at least some jurisdictions in the United States (e.g., some counties in Nevada) to follow suit (Davis, 1993). In a study by Monto (1999) the average age of first prostitution encounter among arrested men was 24 years of age with a median of 21, though ages of first encounter ranged from 9 to 62 years of age. (See "In the News" 5.2.)

In the News 5.2

Acquitted 'john' wants off the Web —
Police chief says leaving information posted on Internet
informs public of 'successful outcome'

A second man featured on the Peoria police Web site has been found not guilty of soliciting sex, but his mug shot will remain until August.

"Why are they arresting people when they're not committing a crime?" asked Jason, who was found "not guilty" last week by a Peoria County jury.

"I feel like I've been slandered," said the 26-year-old Pekin man, who requested his last name not be published. He is among 29 men featured since July on the Peoria Police Department's Web site, which includes the mug shots and personal information of those arrested on solicitation of sex charges, commonly called "johns." The information is posted for one year, regardless of how the cases are decided in court.

"I am not guilty. I didn't do what they are cracking down on," Jason said. "I would never cheat on my wife."

Police Chief Steven Settingsgaard declined to comment about any specific case but said recently it's only fair to leave the information posted so the public can see when someone is acquitted.

"If your picture appears for several months, and the public knows of your arrest, they will not know you were found not guilty if you are simply removed," Settingsgaard wrote in response to other messages on the subject posted on the Journal Star's Web site.

If a "john" is acquitted, a red-letter caption appears under his mug shot saying he is "not guilty."

"Leaving the photo with the indication that you were found not guilty informs the same public of your successful outcome," Settingsgaard wrote.

Apparently, the public is interested. After the Journal Star began a three-day series last week examining those arrested on solicitation of sex charges, the Police Department's Web site, www.peoriapd.com, was flooded with traffic.

On March 5, the day the series started, 3,756 people viewed the "johns" information on the department's home page, an increase of more than a 1,000 percent over the previous week's daily average of 315 views.

That number jumped even more on March 6, when prostitutes' information also was added. More than 11,600 views were recorded that day, and the week's daily average was 4,176 views.

Jason says he's not happy that many people still see his mug shot each day, adding he's endured unneeded stress since his arrest in August.

At trial last week, the defense said Jason and his friends were riding their motorcycles in the 1600 block of Northeast Madison Avenue when they saw who they thought was a prostitute.

"He was dared to go up to her and say something to her," Jason's defense attorney, Jerry Hall, said Monday. "He was on a dare and was in over his head."

According to the police report, Jason stopped his motorcycle and began talking to the woman, who actually was a police decoy. Police say he asked about prices for sexual favors and agreed to meet the woman at her house which led to his arrest. Hall said although his client was talking to a prostitute, he did not break the law since there was no exchange of money or anything of value offered to the decoy, something required in the solicitation law.

"What (the officer) interpreted to be an offer was not there," Hall said. "She was saying, 'I'll do this for so many dollars.' I told the jury that's no different than me going to a car dealership and asking about the price of cars."

Settingsgaard, however, stands behind his officers and defends his department's Web postings, regardless of a court verdict.

"If you are on our Web site, you approached an undercover officer and either offered money for sex, or sex for money. That is it," he wrote in his message on the Journal Star site.

"Not being charged does not negate that you were arrested. Not being convicted does not negate your arrest," he wrote.

Williams, L. (2006, March 14). Acquitted 'john' wants off the Web—Police chief says leaving information posted on Internet informs public of 'successful outcome.' *The Peoria Journal Star,* p. A1.

Limited research exists concerning the prostitution of juveniles. However, the development of the National Incident-Based Reporting System (NIBRS) permitted the identification of certain patterns. For example, police reported more contacts with male juvenile prostitutes than with female juvenile prostitutes (OJJP, 2004). Furthermore, police were less likely to arrest juvenile prostitutes than adult offenders. Today, juvenile prostitution involves complex problems that include a variety of different contexts. International rings and interstate crime operations traffic young girls to distant locations with promises of employment and money (Flowers, 2001). Parents advertise and prostitute their children over the Internet (Hofstede Committee Report, 1999). In addition, some gangs require juvenile members to engage in sexual acts for money as a part of initiation. Runaway and homeless youth on city streets are recruited by pimps and engage in survival sex (OJJP, 2004).

Drug Offenses

The sale, manufacture, distribution, and possession or use of all narcotic (opium-based) drugs, alcohol, cocaine, certain stimulant (amphetamine) drugs, barbiturates,

A majority of jail inmates are dependent on drugs or alcohol. Reprinted with permission of iStockphoto.com / Robert Back.

marijuana, and most hallucinogenic drugs are regulated by both federal and state laws. This includes "club drugs," which is a vague term that refers to a wide variety of drugs including MDMA (Ecstasy), GHB, Rohypnol, ketamine, methamphetamine, and LSD (NIDA, 2004). These violations of the law are known as drug-defined offenses. According to the Bureau of Justice Statistics (2006), in 2002 more than 66% of jail inmates were found to be dependent on drugs or alcohol, or abusing them.

Another form of drug offenses involves drug-related crimes which are motivated by the user's need for money to support continued use and the offenses connected to drug distribution (ONDCP, 2000). Additional examples of this form of drug offense include violent behaviors that result from drug effects. For example, in a classic study of homicide, Wolfgang (1958) concluded that alcohol was involved in about 66% of the homicides he researched. In approximately 40% of the homicides both the offender and the victim had been consuming alcohol. Our society, however, can be characterized as a drug-using or -abusing society, and attempts to regulate the use and traffic of some drugs while allowing others to be used without such regulations have been highly unsuccessful. For example, we allow adults to use tobacco and alcohol (gateway drugs to controlled substances) quite freely even though tobacco has been determined by the Surgeon General of the United States to be harmful to the health of the user, and alcohol to be among the most frequently abused and dangerous of all drugs (Golub & Johnson, 2001; Kane & Yacoubian, 1999; Kao, Schneider & Hoffman, 2000). At the same time, we prohibit marijuana use among the general population even though test results concerning its effects are contradictory, and we prohibit the use of heroin even though there is no evidence that when taken in regulated doses under sanitary conditions, such use would be harmful (Weisheit, 1990). According to data from the 2006 National Survey on Drug Use and Health, an estimated 20.4 million Americans age 12 or older were currently (past month) illicit drug users, meaning they had used an illicit drug during the month prior to the survey interview. This estimate represents 8.3 percent of the population age 12 years or older. Illicit drugs in this study included marijuana/hashish, cocaine (including crack), heroin, hallucinogens, inhalants or prescription-type psychotherapeutic used nonmedically (U.S. Department of Health and Human Service, 2006). During the past 30 years drug related offenses have probably received more attention than any other category of crime (Klotter, 2004). Despite the efforts of state and federal agencies and the addition of state and federal laws, the use of illicit drugs continues to be one of the most difficult problems facing law enforcement. Additional confusion concerning the regulation of drugs often involves the illegality accompanying the sale, use, possession or manufacture of certain substances, while addiction to a drug itself is not a crime. The addict is not a criminal unless he or she is engaged in one of the prohibited activities.

The same rules of supply and demand, and the same outcomes of enforcement attempts discussed earlier with respect to prostitution, apply to drug-related offenses. The fact that many drugs of choice are illegal results in a black market that is characterized by relatively high prices for such drugs. To obtain money to purchase these drugs, users may turn to burglary, theft, robbery, or prostitution. The incidence of these crimes then increases, placing further demands on the resources of the criminal justice network. This cycle is perpetuated when attempts to rehabilitate users fail and they return unemployed to society to take up their old habits.

The criminal justice network has responded to the "grow your own" and "make your own" trends associated with marijuana, methamphetamine, and gamma hydroxybutyrate (GHB). Although large amounts of marijuana are grown and distributed through established criminal syndicates, the proliferation of decentralized smaller networks with concealed growing fields, which market their product on the local level, places greater demand on limited law enforcement resources. Similarly, crank, a form of methamphetamine, can be manufactured with over-the-counter ingredients in a relatively short time span. Law enforcement officials in the Southwest and Midwest devote valuable hours to locating and dismantling these illegal, clandestine labs. GHB, the main ingredient in ecstasy, can also be manufactured in clandestine laboratories by amateur chemists. Some of these drugs pose considerable health risks involving fire, explosion, and the use of ingredients with unknown properties.

The criminal justice network has been actively involved in the so-called war on drugs for a large part of the twentieth century (Vito & Holmes, 1994; Walker, 1998, 2005; Nademann, 1998). The Office of National Drug Control Policy (ONDCP) establishes policies, priorities and goals for the "war on drugs." The U.S. strategy concerning illegal drugs has three key components: preventing drug use before it starts; intervening and healing those who already use drugs; and disrupting the market for illicit substances (ONDCP 2007). The core elements of the market-disruption strategy involve eradication of illicit crops, interdiction of drugs, and an attack on the drug organizations. A majority of the strategy relies on the involvement of law enforcement and enforcement of the law to reduce the availability of drugs in the U.S. and cause a decline in the purity or increase in price. The role of law enforcement in the war on drugs was evident in the prohibition of alcohol in the early part of the century which placed law enforcement in a difficult dilemma. Although the use of alcohol was prohibited and the police were responsible for enforcing the law, many Americans objected to Prohibition and flaunted their use of alcohol. Thus, the criminal justice network was ineffective in enforcing an unpopular law. Today, society has taken a more reasonable approach to curbing alcohol abuse. Many citizen support groups advocate "sensible drinking" and work with criminal justice practitioners to educate the public rather than simply trying to enforce an unpopular moral code.

Public support for drug interdiction has been consistently strong. Drug Awareness Resistance Education (DARE) is available in many school districts, and the criminal justice network enjoys cooperative relationships with many community groups. Attempts to reduce drug use have focused on alcohol, marijuana, cocaine and its derivative products, and more recently, the resurgence of LSD and other hallucinogens. However, most evidence indicates that our efforts to curb drug abuse have not been highly effective, and some argue that legalization of at least some currently proscribed drugs is an option that ought to be explored (Walker, 1998, 2005).

Drugs and Crime

Drugs are related to crime in a number of ways. As we previously discussed it is a crime to possess, manufacture and distribute illegal drugs. However, drugs are also related to crime through the effects they have on the user's behavior, and by generating violence and other illegal activity in connection with drug trafficking (ONDCP, 2000). In 2004, 17% of State prisoners and 18% of Federal inmates said they had committed their current offense to obtain money for drugs (Bureau of Justice Statistics, 2006). Furthermore in the same study 32% of State prisoners and 26% of Federal inmates said they committed their current offense while under the influence of drugs. Among State prisoners, drug offenders (44%) and property offenders (39%) reported the highest incidence of drug use at the time of the offense. In other words, according to Reid (2006), those who are arrested frequently test positive for recent drug use and in many cases drugs are associated with violent crime. Up to 80% of all people arrested for violent crimes test positive for some type of drug (Feucht, 1996). However, any finding concerning a relationship between drugs and crime should be interpreted with some caution. We know most crimes are the result of a variety of factors (personal, situational, cultural, and economic) and drugs are likely to be only one factor in this relationship (ONDCP, 2000). In addition, another factor that must be considered is the possibility that inmates who complete self report surveys exaggerate or minimize the relevance of drugs before or during the commission of a crime.

Gambling

Another common, though often illegal, practice in our society involves placing a bet or wager on the outcome of some event. As Gardiner (1967) noted, public attitudes toward gambling are often more permissive than the statutes that are common to the United States: "Gambling is either positively desired or else not regarded as particularly reprehensible by a substantial proportion of the population" (p.134). The Commission on the Review of the National Policy toward Gambling (1976) made the following observation: "Gambling is inevitable. No matter what is said or done by advocates or opponents of gambling in all its various forms, it is an activity that is practiced, or tacitly endorsed, by a substantial majority of Americans. That is the simple, overriding premise behind all the work of this Commission" (p.1). That this remains true is illustrated by the fact that gambling is legal in some states and counties (e.g., in Atlantic City, New Jersey, and in some counties in Nevada, Wisconsin, Minnesota, and Illinois) although, presumably, it is subject to licensing and regulation by the state. Also, some types of gambling are legal in many states (e.g., state-operated lotteries, on- and offtrack horse race betting, bingo games, Indian reservation casinos, and riverboat casinos) (Walker, 1998, p.235).

The major objection to gambling appears to be its perceived relationship to organized crime. The Commission on the Review of the National Policy Toward Gambling (1976) determined that "there is no uniformity of organized crime control of gambling throughout the country; in some cities such control exists; in others, not. The Commission regrets the notion that organized crime controls all illegal gambling or that all illegal gambling provides revenues for other illegal activities" (p.4). The Commission's report, however, indicated that some proceeds of some illegal gambling went to organized crime consequently, many law enforcement officials continued to believe that gambling was a major source of income for organized crime and therefore should be eliminated or strictly controlled. The Commission's report was reinforced by Kenney and Finckenauer (1995, pp.272–73), whose discussion of organized crime concluded that many ethnic/international organized crime groups were involved in gambling, demonstrating once again the global nature of crime enterprises. Other research concluded that legalized gambling does not lead to higher crime rates (Walker, 1998, p.236). In any case, the enforcement of gambling laws is extremely difficult because of the many forms that exist and the demand for gambling activities. Although most local law enforcement officials are willing to concede that control of social gambling (e.g., a card game at an individual's home or the weekend office football, basketball, or baseball pools) is impossible, these same officials may, from time to time, make serious attempts to curtail more organized forms of gambling (e.g., bookmaking or punchboards). State and federal officials are also concerned about illegal gambling because winners are not inclined to declare their winnings at income tax time. At the same time, however, revenues from legalized gambling play an important part in the economic picture of municipalities and states where they are licensed.

Despite selective local, state, and federal law enforcement attempts to control organized gambling, it is unlikely that such attempts will be successful as long as there is a public demand for such activities. In fact, the rise in riverboat casino gambling and on-line gambling, the increased number of government-operated lotteries, and the adoption of pari-mutuel betting by some states may indicate the government's concession that gambling is inevitable and can serve as a viable source of revenue. These changes, however, do not relieve the criminal justice network of all gambling-related responsibilities. Many gamblers become addicted to the activity and withdrawal is difficult for most and almost impossible for some (Milton, 2006). It is difficult to estimate the costs of gambling addiction on familes and the workplace, but most authorities would agree that it is considerable.

Legalized gambling requires regulation, and even where state-controlled gambling exists, illegal gambling has not been totally eliminated. As is often the case with the other crimes without complainants, the payoff for criminal justice personnel is often minimal in terms of the resources expended.

White-Collar Crime

The term **white-collar crime** was coined in 1939 by Edwin H. Sutherland, although the concept itself was not new at that time. The term, as used by Sutherland, referred to crimes committed by persons of respectability and high social status in the course of their occupations. There have been many attempts to refine and particularize this definition, and it is probably safe to conclude that today the term "white-collar crime" is used as an umbrella to cover most crimes committed by guile, deceit, and concealment, whether or not they are committed by persons of "respectability and high social status" (Clinard & Quinney, 1973, pp.206–23; Shapiro, 1990). Commonly referred to as **business-related crime** (Reid, 2006), the term now includes such offenses as antitrust violations, computer and internet fraud, credit card fraud, phone and telemarketing fraud, bankruptcy fraud, healthcare fraud, environmental law violations, insurance fraud, mail fraud, government fraud, tax evasion, financial fraud, securities fraud, insider trading, bribery, kickbacks, counterfeiting, public corruption, money laundering, embezzlement, economic espionage, and trade secret theft (Cornell Law School, 2006).

The overall costs of white-collar crime are difficult to measure accurately, but in economic terms, the annual cost to Americans is probably over $300 billion (Cornell Law School, 2006). More difficult to measure are costs that result from loss of public confidence in business and the professions. For example, unnecessary surgery, ghost surgery, reports issued by nonexistent or nonfunctioning medical laboratories, occupational diseases and injuries, fraud committed by computer over the Internet, and the intentional release of hazardous waste materials erode public trust in the professions and industries involved and cause health-related problems and deaths, the costs of which are tremendous (Kappeler, Blumberg, & Potter, 1996, 2004). Penalties assessed often appear trivial in comparison with the profits realized by white-collar offenders.

Although white-collar crime is clearly widespread, the frequency with which it occurs cannot be determined by looking at police records or the Uniform Crime Reports. The extent of white-collar crime remains largely unknown, and, perhaps partly because of the nebulous nature of these offenses, public reaction to the offenders remains largely unorganized. Traditionally, legislators have remained relatively unconcerned about passing statutes designed to reduce the incidence of white-collar crime. Recently, however, Congress has been playing close attention to "cyberspace" crime, passing legislation such as the Computer Fraud and Abuse Act, the Digital Millennium Act, and the No Electronic Theft Act (Andreano, 1999). Still, municipal police continue to have few, if any, personnel who are properly trained to investigate such crimes; prosecutions remain few, and criminal court action is infrequent (Kappeler, Blumberg, & Potter, 1996, 2004). White-collar offenders often include individuals, but corporations are also subject to prosecution for law violations (see "In the News" 5.3).

In the News 5.3

MIAMI COUPLE SENTENCED FOR HEALTH CARE FRAUD AND STRUCTURING VIOLATIONS AND MORTGAGE FRAUD

R. Alexander Acosta, United States Attorney for the Southern District of Florida, Jonathan I. Solomon, Special Agent in Charge, Federal Bureau of Investigation, Miami Field Office, and Charles E. Hunter, Acting Special Agent in Charge, Internal Revenue Service, Criminal Investigation, announced that defendants Luis Delgado and Rita Cardoso, of Miami, husband and wife owners and operators of several health care businesses located in Miami-Dade County, were sentenced on February 12, 2007, by United States District Court Judge Jose E. Martinez in Miami, Florida. Cardoso was sentenced to 65 months' imprisonment, followed by 3 years of supervised release, and was ordered to pay $4,457,032.20 in restitution. Defendant Delgado was sentenced to 51 months' imprisonment and was ordered to pay $3,694,324.02 in restitution.

Cardoso and Delgado had pled guilty in October 2006 in separate cases. According to the charges and the evidence, between May 2000 and May 2003, defendant Delgado owned and operated Advance Equipment Supplies & Pharmacy Inc. ("Advance"), a durable medical equipment company. Similarly, between January 2001 and October 2003, defendant Cardoso owned and operated Millenium Medical Equipment Supplies, Inc. ("Millenium"), and Health Medical Services of South Florida, Inc, both durable medical equipment companies. Durable medical equipment ("DME") is designed for a medical purpose and repeated use, and includes items such as prosthetic limbs, back braces, knee braces, and wheelchairs.

According to the evidence, Cardoso and Delgado fraudulently billed Medicare for more than $17 million for durable medical equipment, structured their bank withdrawals to avoid triggering the banks' requirement of filing currency transaction reports with the Department of Treasury, and conspired to commit wire and mail fraud.

More specifically, Cardoso and Delgado submitted numerous fraudulent claims to Medicare from their respective companies, seeking reimbursement for the cost of durable medical equipment that was either not provided or which was not medically necessary. To effectuate this scheme, Cardoso, Delgado and other members of the conspiracy created prescriptions falsely stating that Medicare beneficiaries needed specific durable medical equipment. They also purchased patient signatures and fraudulent prescriptions from patient brokers, who were paid approximately $100 per patient for this information.

Cardoso and Delgado structured withdrawals from their respective companies' bank accounts in amounts below $10,000 to avoid the banks' filing of currency transaction reports ("CTRs"). A bank or other financial institution is required by federal law to file a CTR with the Department of the Treasury for each financial transaction that involves more than $10,000. Covered financial transactions include deposits, withdrawals, exchanges of currency, or other payments or transfers by, through, or to the bank or other financial institution. To evade this reporting requirement, both Cardoso and Delgado recruited and paid others to cash checks for them, all under $10,000.

In March 2005, Cardoso and Delgado devised a mortgage fraud scheme to get money out of properties that Cardoso owned either individually or jointly with Delgado. In this scheme, the defendants agreed to use the identity of Delgado's aunt to apply for mortgage loans to make it appear as if the aunt was purchasing properties from them. Cardoso and Delgado falsified information regarding the aunt's assets, employment, and income in loan applications and related documents. Cardoso and Delgado also used the aunt's identity to purchase a home for themselves. Through this fraud, the defendants obtained approximately $1.8 million from lenders.

Mr. Acosta commended the investigative efforts of the Federal Bureau of Investigation and the Internal Revenue Service, Criminal Investigation Division. The case was prosecuted by Assistant United States Attorney Lois Foster-Steers.

A copy of this press release may be found on the web site of the United States Attorney's Office for the Southern District of Florida at: http://www.usdoj.gov/usao/fls. *Related court documents and information may be found on the web site of the District Court for the Southern District of Florida at:* http://www.flsd.uscourts.gov/ *or on* http://pacer.flsd.uscourts.gov/

The penalties for white-collar crime offenses include fines, home detention, community confinement, costs of prosecution, forfeitures, restitution, supervised release, and imprisonment (Cornell Law School, 2006). In many cases the prosecution of a white-collar crime offender is substantially different from other criminal prosecutions. For example, a corporate insider who possesses knowledge of a white collar crime may, in one federal district, turn and blow the whistle and be hailed as a hero, becoming in the process a star prosecution witness. A virtually identical insider, in another district, may be required to enter a felony guilty plea and serve time as part of his/her cooperation agreement with the government (Wisenberg, 2005, p.1). Because in most cases those who commit white-collar offenses are not particularly likely to be treated as criminals, they often do not view themselves as criminals, and, except for periods of anger and frustration, the public does not view these offenders with the same distaste as they do other criminals. Coupled with the fact that white-collar crimes are often undetected and difficult to prosecute because of their complexity, these attitudes do little to help reduce the likelihood of such offenses. Perhaps looking at fraud as an example of white-collar crime will illustrate some of the difficulties associated with prosecution.

Fraud

Fraud involves obtaining the property of another by misrepresenting a material fact. The accused must also intend to permanently deprive the owner of the use of that property. In this offense, the property is relinquished willfully by the owner, and the illegal act centers on the misrepresentation that induces the relinquishing. Although fraud is often predicated on deceit, some frauds go unreported, while others are not prosecuted because the victim was a willing participant in the fraud.

The misrepresentation must be of a material fact and not an opinion or a prediction. For example, if a car salesman claims that a car will be the "fastest, hottest car in town," he is not misrepresenting a material fact; he is simply giving an opinion or possibly a prediction. On the other hand, if he alleges that the car has accumulated only 10,000 miles but the odometer was turned back and the car actually has been driven 50,000 miles, he has misrepresented a material fact.

The misrepresentation must be known by the offender and must be one that a "reasonable person" would not be aware of. In the previous example, if a second party purchases the auto, thinking it has been driven only 10,000 miles, and without detecting the misrepresentation sells it to a third party, then no fraud has occurred. A person who purchases the Brooklyn Bridge or the Eiffel Tower has gone beyond the standards of reasonableness to claim fraud.

As with theft and embezzlement, the accused must intend to permanently deprive the owner of the use of the property. Courts generally hold that once ownership has passed, the fraud has transpired.

Some of the more commonly known frauds involve the work of con men that play on people's greed or willingness to get rich quick. Credit card fraud has become a crime of major proportions in the United States, along with securities fraud, savings and loan fraud, mail fraud, consumer fraud, health care fraud, fraudulent transfer of a motor vehicle, forgery, and fraud by government officials (Vito & Holmes, 1994; Reid, 2004, p. 366; Kiessig, Karpf & Linkin, 2006) (see "In the News" 5.1).

Fraud among retailers and wholesalers is common as well. Such practices as false advertising, violations of truth in labeling, and use of false weights and measures are detected frequently enough to suggest that they commonly occur. Like other types of white-collar crime, these offenses are often difficult to detect but are very rewarding to their perpetrators. Consider, for example, a supermarket chain that has 100 stores. If the chain were to misrepresent the weight of every package of steak sold by adding only 1 ounce to the actual weight of a package of steak, if the cost per ounce for steak was 20 cents, and if each store in the chain sold 100 packages of steak in a day, the additional profit to the chain would be 20 cents times 100 times 100, or $2,000 per day, or $14,000 per week, or over $700,000 per year! Still, each customer would be paying only an additional 20 cents per package. In addition, the risk involved is minimal compared with the potential return because few customers take their steak home and weigh it; even those who did so might believe their own scales to be in error; those who were suspicious would be unlikely to take much definite action to recoup only 20 cents; and even if the violation were somehow detected, most customers would not become overly irate at the loss of a few dollars over the period of a year or so.

Not all frauds are targeted toward consumers. Friedrichs (1996, 2006) has noted that several frauds are perpetrated with the government as the intended victim. Tax cheating or evasion, welfare scams, false Medicare claims, and inflated expenses on government-funded projects result in huge losses for the government and its taxpayers.

Insurance companies are also frequent victims of frauds. Clients exaggerate losses and have been known to stage automobile accidents and fake falls or spills. Forty to fifty percent of all auto theft claims may be false, at an annual cost of more than $6 billion (Friedrichs, 1996, 2006). Health care fraud is clearly a major problem in the U. S. (Hubble, Mauro & Moar, 2006).

There are some organized attempts to prevent or reduce the incidence of white-collar crime. The National District Attorneys Association (NDAA) through the American Prosecutors Research Institute developed a White Collar Crime Unit. The Unit provides training and technical assistance to prosecutors for white collar crimes including telemarketing fraud, Internet fraud, identity theft, cyber crime, and other scams. The NDAA recognizes the increasing number of senior citizens and that they are the victim of many of these scams (NDAA, 2007). An additional attempt to combat white-collar crime involves the National White Collar Crime Center (NW3C) which provides a national support network for organizations that prevent, investigate, and prosecute economic crime, cyber crime, and other high-tech crime. Specifically, NW3C provides computer crime specialists, curriculum developers, enforcement analysts, intelligence technicians and training coordinators to state and local law enforcement agencies (Bureau of Justice Assistance, 2002). In addition, there are numerous community-based groups across the country oriented toward publicizing and confronting a variety of white-collar offenses and offenders through the use of civil suits (Chibe, 2006; Coleman, 1994, p.158).

No consideration of white-collar crime would be complete without reference to the work of Ralph Nader and his associates. Nader is convinced that illegitimate practices are widespread in corporate America and that there ought to be more severe, criminal penalties for white-collar criminals. Nader and his associates combat white-collar crime through both publicity and recourse to legal processes, and they have been identified, to some extent at least, with the establishment of the Environmental Protection Agency, and the Occupational Safety and Health Administration (Friedrichs, 1996, 2006). Nader appears to remain convinced that the American public will rise up and take action against white-collar offenders if they are made aware of the extent and seriousness of

Numerous attempts are being made to deal more effectively with white collar offenders. Reprinted with permission of iStockphoto.com / Sean Locke.

the problem and if they can be organized. However, there is a great deal of evidence to indicate that, although some segments of the public do become concerned about some types of white-collar crime, the concern is short-lived. Most citizens, in fact, appear to be apathetic about this type of crime.

Organized Crime

The long-standing prevalence of prostitution, gambling, drug use, and other crimes without complainants has made them attractive "business" ventures for criminal syndicates. **Organized crime** involves a self-perpetuating criminal conspiracy that exists to profit from providing illicit goods and services through the corruption of public officials and the use or threat of force (Kenney & Finckenauer, 1995, pp.25, 28). Today the Federal Bureau of Investigation (2007a) estimates that global organized crime reaps illegal profits of approximately $1 trillion per year. Although there is a wide variation of definitions, law enforcement and criminological researchers are consistent in associating the following attributes with organized crime:

1. Nonideological.
2. Hierarchical.
3. Limited or exclusive membership.
4. Self-perpetuating.

5.   Willingness to use illegal violence and bribery.
6.   Specialized division of labor.
7.   Monopolistic.
8.   Governed by explicit rules and regulations. (Abadinsky, 1997, 2006).

Although they may employ illegal means, organized criminal syndicates often operate under rational business principles. Maximum profit is predicated on public demand for illicit goods and services and efficient delivery of "products" through a formally organized system. In addition, payments for political protection are not uncommon (Kenney & Finckenauer, 1995).

Although the most celebrated organized crime unit has been the Mafia, or La Cosa Nostra, organized crime as defined here includes street gang activities, drug distribution networks, and racially or ethnically based criminal syndicates (Economist, 1998). Organized crime now includes many globally recognizable criminal syndicates that have emerged on the scene, including Chinese triads, the Japanese yakuza, Colombian and Mexican drug cartels, Nigerians, the Russian Mafia, enterprises based in Hungary and Romania, and the Jamaican posses (note the global nature of the organized crime network). One can argue that conventional street gangs (e.g., the Bloods, Crips, Vice Lords, and Gangster Disciples) now constitute organized crime syndicates with their attempts to generate huge profits in the drug and weapons markets. We should note that not all organized crime activities are criminal. In an attempt to fend off the Internal Revenue Service (one common prosecutor of organized criminals), many criminal syndicates engage in legal business activities, often entered through illegal means, in an attempt to launder their illegally obtained profits (i.e., financial markets, labor unions, construction, and waste hauling industries). According to the Federal Bureau of Investigation (2007a) the investigation of national and international organized crime syndicates currently involves using undercover operations, surveillance, confidential sources, intelligence analysis and sharing, forensic accounting, multi-agency investigations, and the power of racketeering statutes.

One attempt to help control the spread of organized crime was the passage of the Racketeer Influenced Corrupt Organizations (RICO) Act of 1970. RICO, actually Title IX of the Organized Crime Control Act of 1970, was intended to combat the infiltration of organized crime into legitimate business. RICO focuses on the conspiratorial nature of most organized criminal syndicates and on a series of illegal activities related to the investment of funds in legitimate enterprises that may constitute racketeering. Additional activities chargeable under RICO include the following: sports bribery, counterfeiting, embezzlement of union funds, alien smuggling, mail and wire fraud, money laundering, theft from interstate shipment, and interstate transportation of stolen property (Title 18, USC, sec 1961 (1)). Convictions for RICO carry lengthy prison sentences and heavy fines and provide for forfeiture of all assets associated with the conspiracy (Kenney & Finckenauer, 1995). Although RICO was constructed to attack fully developed criminal syndicates, it has been extended to a number of organizations and to crimes of violence, corruption, and fraud. Some drug syndicates are prosecuted under the **Continuing Criminal Enterprise (CCE)** statute (21 U.S.C. 848). Similar to RICO, the statute makes it illegal to commit or to conspire to commit a continuing series of violations (three or more) of the 1970 Drug Abuse Prevention and Control Act when the offenses are committed in concert with five or more persons. This statute permits the prosecution and conviction of drug lords, who obtain substantial income from drug transactions without direct participation.

Computer Crime and Cyber Crime

Many include the terms computer crime and cyber crime in the definition of white-collar crime. However, we have included a separate discussion of these terms since the rapid advances in computer and internet technology have permitted criminals to develop a variety of new criminal acts. **Computer crime** encompasses crimes committed against a computer, the materials contained therein such as software and data, and its uses as a processing tool (Chik, 2006). Computer crime includes such activities as hacking, denial of service attacks, unauthorized, use of services and cyber vandalism. **Cyber crime,** according to Chik (2006), describes criminal activities committed through the use of electronic communications media. One of the greatest concerns involves cyber fraud and identity theft through such methods as phishing, pharming, spoofing, and through the use of online surveillance technology. The cyber crime forums gird a criminal economy that robs U.S. businesses of $67.2 billion per year according to a Federal Bureau of Investigation projection (USA Today, 2006, p. 1). An interesting characteristic of these types of crime is that they are usually nonconfrontational and more difficult to detect than traditional crime because the perpetrator can act with ease and speed without fear of being recognized (Klotter, 2004, p. 333). As a result, most states and the federal government realized that the existing common laws did not apply to many computer and cyber crimes, thus requiring states to enact new computer-specific legislation. Another characteristic of this type of crime is the lack of evidence and the low reporting of the violations to law enforcement agencies. In 2002, according to the Computer Security Institute survey, only about one-third of all computer intrusions were reported to law enforcement (Garfinkel, 2002). And the Internet Crime Complaint Center (2006) reported that 45 percent of all complaints that were received involved online auction fraud in which three-quarters of the perpetrators were men. The typical victim in these online frauds was between 30–40 years of age with the highest losses involving Nigerian letter fraud with a median loss of $5,100 per victim (Federal Bureau of Investigation, 2007b). The Federal Bureau of Investigation (2007c) claims the people initiating computer intrusion "runs the gamut.... from the computer geeks looking for bragging rights ... to businesses trying to gain an upper hand in the marketplace by hacking competitor websites, from rings of criminals wanting to steal your personal information and sell it on black markets ... to spies and terrorists looking to rob our nation of vital information or launch cyber strikes."

Terrorism and Transnational Crime

Since the terrorist attacks of September 11, 2001, American criminal justice practitioners at all levels have increasingly focused on preventing future such attacks. The issue confronting practitioners from federal through state to local officials is how best to accomplish this task while protecting the due process rights of the citizens of a democratic society. While there is no single universal definition of terrorism, we will use the definition presented by the Federal Bureau of Investigation which states that **terrorism** includes the unlawful use of force and violence against persons or property to intimidate or coerce a government, the civilian population, or any segment thereof, in furtherance of political or social objectives (Federal Bureau of Investigation, 2000, p. i)

Since terrorists sometimes orginate from countries other than the countries in which they conduct their attacks, their crimes may be viewed as **transnational crimes,** or crimes that extend into and violate the laws of several countries (Adler, Mueller, & Laufer, 2000). Transnational crimes include aircraft hijacking, computer crimes, corruption of public officials, environmental crimes, illicit drug trafficking, piracy, trade in human body parts, and trafficking in persons, among others (Reichel, 2005).

In an attempt to deal with terrorism and transnational crimes, efforts have been undertaken by international and national criminal justice agencies. In the United States, the agencies most involved with such crimes include federal agencies such as the Department of Homeland Security, the Department of Justice, and the Department of State. At the state level, state police agencies and state homeland security departments operate. And, at the local level, county and municipal police and a variety of other first responders are involved in the attempt to thwart the efforts of terrorist, respond to terrorist acts, and apprehend those responsible for such acts. Further, a series of new and often controversial laws [including, for example, the Patriot Act] have been passed in an an attempt to make identification, apprehension, and conviction of terrorists/transnational criminals easier for law enforcement personnel. These laws are controversial because they permit the government to intervene (in some cases covertly) into the daily lives of Americans in ways which would have been unthinkable prior to the attacks of September 11, 2001. They also permit the detention, interrogation, and trial of suspected terrorists in ways that critics argue are unconstitutional (and perhaps immoral as well). They argue that Franklin was right when he noted in 1775 that "They who can give up essential liberty to obtain a little temporary safety deserve neither liberty nor safety." (*The Quotable Franklin, 2007)*. Those who support such laws believe that giving up some civil liberties in the interest of protecting the population is reasonable.

Summary

1. Crimes without complainants involve the provision of goods and services that are in demand but illegal. These offenses include illegal drug manufacture, sales, and distribution; prostitution; gambling; and obscenity/pornography.

2. Because complainants rarely come forth voluntarily with respect to these offenses, the police themselves often serve as complainants.

3. The costs involved in developing these cases are high, and the payoff is minimal. Attempts to legislate morality generally lead to such results.

4. Nonetheless, a considerable proportion of the resources of various components of the criminal justice network is expended on crimes without complainants.

5. White-collar crime involves offenses committed by people in the course of their occupations or professions. Tax evasion, embezzlement, consumer fraud, and medical malpractice are examples of white-collar crime.

6. The costs of white-collar crime are high in terms of both economic considerations and loss of confidence and trust in government, industry, and the professions. Still, despite numerous crusades to arouse the public, white-collar offenders are seldom treated or thought of as criminals.

7. Only organized, sustained action on behalf of a concerned public is likely to reduce the incidence of white-collar crime, and such action appears unlikely at this time.

Key Terms Defined

crimes without complainants Crimes that provide goods and/or services that are in demand but illegal and in which the police themselves typically serve as complainants because citizens are usually not willing to accept this role.

prostitution Engaging in, or agreeing to engage in, sexual acts for compensation.

white-collar crime Crime committed by guile, deceit, or concealment, typically by people in positions of trust.

business-related crime Offenses such as computer crimes, product liability, embezzlement, insider trading, and credit card fraud.

fraud An act that involves obtaining the property of another, with the intent to permanently deprive the owner of the use of that property, by misrepresenting a material fact.

organized crime Criminal conspiracies providing illicit goods or services through the corruption of public officials and the use or threat of force.

Continuing Criminal Enterprise (CCE) statute Statute used to prosecute drug syndicates.

computer crime Crimes committed against a computer and materials contained therein.

cyber crime Crimes committed through the use of electronic communication media.

terrorism Includes the unlawful use of force and violence against persons or property to intimidate or coerce a government, the civilian population, or any segment thereof, in furtherance of political or social objectives.

transnational crimes Crimes that extend into and violate the laws of several countries

Critical Thinking Exercises

1. What is the importance of the distinction between crimes without complainants and crimes without victims? In your opinion, are crimes without complainants also crimes without victims? What similarities and differences do you see between crimes without complainants and white-collar crimes?

2. What would you consider an effective means for attempting to combat white-collar crime and crimes without complainants? What is the likelihood that your suggestions would be effective in our current society?

Internet Exercises

The use of club/rave drugs is becoming an epidemic in many regions of the United States. Access the Lake County, Illinois, Web site on club/rave drugs at www.lakecountymeg.org.

Read the PowerPoint presentation; then answer the following questions:

1. What are the five basic drugs used at rave parties?

2. Compare and contrast the effects of GHB (liquid ecstasy) with ecstasy (MDMA).

3. Develop a list of warning signs (indicators of use) to help parents and teachers identify club drug use.

References

Abadinsky, H. (1997). *Organized crime* (5th ed.). Chicago: Nelson-Hall.

Abadinsky, H. (2006). *Organized crime* (8th ed.). Belmont, CA: Wadsworth.

Adler, F., Mueller, G.O.W., & Laufer, W. S. (2000). *Criminal justice: An introduction.* (2nd ed.). Boston: McGraw-Hill.

Andreano, F. P. (1999). The evolution of federal computer crime policy: The ad hoc approach to an ever-changing problem. *American Journal of Criminal Law,* 27 (1), 81–103.

Bastian, L. (1995). Criminal victimization 1993. Washington, DC: U.S. Department of Justice.

Bureau of Justice Assistance (2002). National white-collar crime center. U.S. Department of Justice. Available online at: http://www.ncjrs.gov/pdffiles1/bja/184958.pdf.

Bureau of Justice Statistics (2006, October). Drug use. U.S. Department of Justice. Available online at: http://www.ojp.usdoj.gov/bjs/abstract/dudsfp04.htm.

Chibe, R. J. (2006). A golden age of white-collar criminal prosecution. *Journal of Criminal Law and Criminology, 96* (2), 389–396.

Chik,W.B. (2006). Challenges to criminal law making in the new global information society: A critical comparative study of the adequacies of computer-related criminal legislation in the United States, the United Kingdom and Singapore. A paper presented at the VI Computer Law World Conference, September 6–8, 2006, University of Edinburgh, Scotland.

Clinard, M. B., & Quinney, R. (Eds.). (1973). *Criminal behavior systems: A typology* (2nd ed.). New York: Holt, Rinehart and Winston.

Coleman, J. W. (1994). *The criminal elite: The sociology of white-collar crime.* New York: St. Martin's Press.

Commission on the Review of the National Policy toward Gambling. (1976). Gambling in America. Washington, DC: U.S. Government Printing Office.

Conklin, J. E. (1998). *Criminology* (6thed.). Boston: Allyn and Bacon.

_____(2006). *Criminology* (9th ed.). Boston: Allyn and Bacon.

Cornell Law School (2006). White-collar crime. Legal Information Institute. Available online at: http://www.law.cornell.edu/wex/index.php.White-collar_crime.

Davis, N. J. (1993). *Prostitution: An international handbook on trends, problems, and policies.* Westport, CT: Greenwood Press.

Donziger, S. R. (1996). *The real war on crime: The report of the National Criminal Justice Commission.* New York: Harper and Row.

Duster, T. (1970). *The legislation of morality: Law, drugs, and moral judgment.* New York: Free Press.

Economist. (1998). Out of jail and on to the street, 349 (8097), 29–30.

Federal Bureau of Investigation. (2000). *Terrorism in the United States, 1999.* Available online at: http://www.fbi.gov/publications/terror/terror99.pdf.

Federal Bureau of Investigation (2007a). Organized crime. U.S. Department of Justice. Available online at: http://www.fbi.gov/hq/cid/orgcrime/ocshome.htm.

Federal Bureau of Investigation (2007b). Internet crime. U.S. Department of Justice. Available online at: http://www.fbi.gov/page2/march07/ic3031607.htm.

Federal Bureau of Investigation (2007c). Computer intrusions. U.S. Department of Justice. Available online at: http://www.fbi.gov/cyberinvest/computer_intrusions.htm.

Feucht, T. (1996). *Drug use forcasting* 1995. Washington, DC: National Institute of Justice. IN.

Flowers, R.B. (2001). *Runaway kids and teenage prostitution.* Westport, CT: Greenwood Press.

Friedrichs, D. O. (1996). *Trusted criminals.* Belmont, CA: Wadsworth.

_____(2006). *Trusted criminals* (3rd ed.). Belmont, CA: Wadsworth.

Gardiner, J. A. (1967). Public attitudes toward gambling and corruption. *Annals of the American Academy of Political and Social Science*, 374, 123–34.

Garfinkel, S. (2002). The FBI's cyber-crime crackdown. *Technology Review.* In Victor, J. & Naughton, J. (2007). *Annual editions of criminal justice.* Dubuque, IA: McGraw Hill Contemporary Learning Series.

Golub, A. & Johnson, B. D. (2001). Variation in youthful risks of progression from alcohol and tobacco to marijuana and to hard drugs across generations. *American Journal of Public* Health, 91 (2), 225–232.

Hofstede Committee Report (1999). *Juvenile prostitution in Minnesota*. St. Paul, MN: Minnesota Attorney General's Office.

Hubble, T. D., Mauro, A. C. & Moar, D. (2006). Health care fraud. *The American Criminal law Review, 43* (2), 603–662.

James, J. (1977). Prostitutes and prostitution. In Sagarin, E. & Montanino, F. eds. *Deviants: Voluntary actors in a hostile world*. Morristown, NJ: General Learning Press.

Kane, R. J., & Yacoubian, G. S., Jr. (1999). Patterns of drug escalation among Philadelphia arrestees: An assessment of the Gateway theory. *Journal of Drug Issues*, 29 (1), 107–120.

Kao, T., Schneider, S. J. & Hoffman, K. J. (2000). Co-occurence of alcohol, smokeless tobacco, cigarette, and illicit drug use by lower ranking military personnel. *Addictive Behaviors*, 25 (2), 253–262.

Kappeler, V. E., Blumberg, M., & Potter G. W. (1996). *The mythology of crime and criminal justice* (2nd ed.). Prospect Heights, IL: Waveland Press.

_____(2004). *The mythology of crime and criminal justice* (4th ed.). Prospect Heights, IL: Waveland Press.

Kenney, D. J., & Finckenauer, J. O. (1995). *Organized crime in America*. Belmont, CA: Wadsworth.

Kiessig, T. M., Karpf, B. W. & Linkins, J. R. (2006). Financial institutions fraud. *The American Criminal Law Review, 43* (2), 527–575.

Klotter, J.C. (2004). *Criminal law* (7th ed.). Cincinnati, OH: Anderson Publishing Co. Maloney, P. & Mobley, G. (2002). *Controlling prostitution: A multimodality approach*. White Paper. Memphis, TN: Memphis Shelby Crime Commission.

Meier, R.F. & Geis, G. (1997). *Victimless crime? Prostitution, drugs, homosexuality, abortion*. Irvine, CA: University of California.

Milton, S. (2006). Addictions without substances series: The conundrums of gambling. *Drugs and Alcohol Today, 6* (3), 37–42.

Monto, M.A. (1999). Focusing *on the clients of street prostitutes: A creative approach to reducing violence against women-summary report*. Rockville, MD: National Institute of Justice.

Nadelmann, E. A. (1998). Commonsense drug policy. *Foreign Affairs*, 77 (5), 111–126.

National District Attorneys Association (2007). *White-collar crime*. Available online at: http://www.ndaa-apri.org/apri/programs/senior_fraud/wcc_home/html.

National Institute of Drug Abuse (2004). *NIDA community drug alert bulletin:Club drugs*. Available online at: http://www.drugabuse.gov/ClubAlert/ClubDrugAlert.html.

Nelson, W. F. (2004). Prostitution: A community solution alternative. *Corrections Today, 66,* (6), 88–92.

Office of Juvenile Justice and Delinquency Prevention (2004). *Prostitution of juveniles: Patterns from NIBRS*. Washington, DC: U.S. Department of Justice. Available on-line at: http://www.ojp.usdoj.gov/ojjdp.

Office of the National Drug Control Policy (2000). *Drug related crime*. Washington, DC: Executive Office of the President. Available online at: http://www.whitehouse drugpolicy.gov/publications/factsht/crime/index.htm.

Office of the National Drug Control Policy (2007). *National drug control strategy*. Washington DC: Executive Office of the President. Available online at: http://www.white housedrugpolicy.gov/publications/policy/ndcs06/.

Quotable Franklin. Available online at: http://www.ushistory.org/franklin/quotable/quote04.htm.

Raphael, J. & Shapiro, D. L. (2004). Violence in indoor and outdoor prostitution venues. *Violence Against Women, 10* (2), 126.

Reichel, P. L. (2005). *Comparative criminal justice systems*. 4th ed. Upper Saddle River, NJ: Pearson/Prentice Hall.

Reid, S.T. (2004). *Criminal law* (6th ed.). New York, NY: McGraw-Hill.

Reid, S.T. (2006). *Crime and Criminology* (11th ed.). New York, NY: McGraw-Hill.

Schur, E. M. (1965). *Crimes without victims: Deviant behavior and public policy*. Englewood Cliffs, NJ: Prentice Hall.

Shapiro, S. P. (1990). Collaring the crime, not the criminal: Reconsidering the concept of white collar crime. *American Sociological Review*, 55 (3), 346–65.

Siegel, L.J. (2001). *Criminology theories, patterns, and typologies*. (7th ed.). Belmont, CA: Wadsworth/Thomson Learning.

Smith, A. B., & Pollock, H. (1975). *Some sins are not crimes: A plea for reform of the criminal law*. New York: New Viewpoints.

Sutherland, E. H. (1939). *White collar crime*. New York: Holt, Rinehart and Winston.

U.S. Department of Health and Human Services (2006). *National Household Survey on Drug Use and Health*. Washington, D.C.: Substance Abuse and Mental Health Services Administration. Available online at: http://www.oas.samha.gov/NSDUH/2k6NSDUH/2k6Resultscfm#High.

USA Today (2006, October 11). p. 1. Available online at: http://usatoday.com/tech/news computersecurity/infotheft/2006-10-11-cybercrime-hacker-forums_x_htm?csp =N009.

Vito, G. F. & Holmes, R. M. (1994). *Criminology: Theory, research, and policy*. Belmont, CA: Wadsworth.

Walker, S. (1998). *Sense and nonsense about crime and drugs: A policy guide* (4th ed.). Belmont, CA: Wadsworth.

_____(2005). *Sense and nonsense about crime and drugs: A policy guide* (6th ed.). Belmont, CA: Wadsworth.

Weinberg, M. S., Shaver, F. M., & Williams, C. J. (1999). Gendered sex work in the San Francisco Tenderloin. *Archives of Sexual Behavior, 28* (6), 503–21.

Weisheit, R. (1990). Challenging the criminalizers. *The Criminologist, 15* (4), 1–5.

Wisenberg, S. L. (2005). White-collar crime: The crash course. Find Law. Available online at: http://profs.lp.findlaw.com/collar.index.html.

Wolfgang, M.E. (1958). *Patterns of criminal homicide.* Philadelphia: University of Pennsylvania Press.

Suggested Readings

Abadinsky, H. (2006). *Organized crime* (8th ed.). Chicago: Nelson-Hall.

Chibe, R. J. (2006). A golden age of white-collar criminal prosecution. *Journal of Criminal Law and Criminology, 96* (2), 389–396.

Duke, S. B., Bandow, D., & Jonas, S. (1995). Drug prohibition: An unnatural disaster. *Connecticut Law Review, 27* (2), 569–697.

Friedrichs, D. O. (2006). *Trusted criminals: White collar crime in contemporary society.* (3rd. ed.). Belmont, CA; Wadsworth.

Hubble, T. D., Mauro, A. C. & Moar, D. (2006). Health care fraud. *The American Criminal law Review, 43* (2), 603–662.

Kerr, O. (2006). *Computer crime law.* St. Paul, MN: West Publishing Group.

Kiessig, T. M., Karpf, B. W. & Linkins, J. R. (2006). Financial institutions fraud. *The American Criminal Law Review, 43* (2), 527–575.

Lombroso, C. & Ferrero, G. translated with new introduction by N. H. Rafter & M. Gibson. (2004). *Criminal woman, the prostitute, and the normal woman.* Durham, N.C.: Duke University Press.

Lyman, M.D. & Potter, G.W. (2006). *Organized crime* (4th ed.) Upper Saddle River, NJ: Prentice Hall.

Milton, S. (2006). Addictions without substances series: The conundrums of gambling. *Drugs and Alcohol Today, 6* (3), 37–42.

Potterat, J. J., Rothenberg, R. B., & Muth, S. Q. (1998). Pathways to prostitution: The chronology of sexual and drug abuse milestones. *Journal of Sex Research, 35* (4), 333–40.

Raphael, J. & Shapiro, D. L. (2004). Violence in indoor and outdoor prostitution venues. *Violence Against Women, 10* (2), 126.

Schur, E. (1965). *Crimes without victims.* Englewood Cliffs, NJ: Prentice Hall.

Stoil, M. J. (1994, July/August). Gambling addiction: The nation's dirty little secret. Behavioral *Health Management, 14,* 35–37.

Sutherland, E. H. (1939). *White collar crime.* New York: Holt, Rinehart and Winston.

Chapter Six

The Police

"Municipal police in the United States operate in a climate of constant change. We expect them to continue to perform traditional tasks related to law enforcement and order maintenance while solving problems, organizing communities, and preventing terrorism. Further, we expect them to perform these diverse tasks by exercising discretion wisely within an ethical framework. Many of us are suspicious of their motives and uneasy in their presence. On one hand, we recognize the police role in an orderly society; on the other, we would prefer that they intervene in our lives only if and when we need them. Much of the current criticism of the police, and dissatisfaction among the police, results from confusion as to their role and the misleading and sometimes unreasonable expectations that arise as a result. Sir Robert Peel developed and promoted a model for municipal police that has often been ignored in our society, but many of the basic tenets of the model have been resurrected in the form of community policing. We have come to realize once again that a basic requirement for an effective, efficient, civil police is a meaningful partnership with other citizens. Only when such a partnership exists can the police perform their tasks as problem solvers, service providers, and occasional law enforcers. Only then will the public provide the support and resources necessary for the successful performance of these tasks."

Cox, S. M. (2003) adapted from *Contemporary Municipal Policing*, Boston, MA: Allyn and Bacon, p. xiii.

Key Terms

> social control
> community policing
> SARA process
> due process
> crime control
> arrest

booking
chain of evidence
mediation and negotiation
directed patrol
split-force policing
accreditation
Peace Officers Standards and Training (POST) Boards
assessment centers
probationary officer
corruption
grass-eaters
meat-eaters
perjury
emotional abuse
physical abuse
noble cause corruption
private or contract police

Chapter Outline

The Role of the Police in Social Control
From Watchmen to Crime Fighters to Community Organizers
Community- and Problem-Oriented Policing
Current Police Functions
Police Law Enforcement Procedures
Police Order Maintenance Activities
Police Organizations
Some Variations on the Traditional Police Organization
Selection, Training, and Education of the Police
Police Misconduct
Police Corruption
Typs of Police Corruption
Physical and Emotional Abuse
Noble Cause Corruption
Private or Contract Police

As the official agency most accessible to and most frequently used by the public, the police play a crucial role in the criminal justice network. As gatekeepers for the other official criminal justice agencies, some 670,000 police officers in more than 17,000 police agencies are a vital link between the public and the remainder of the network.

The Role of the Police in Social Control

There are at least two distinct means of attempting to persuade people to adhere to group expectations or norms. The first involves the use of informal or group pressure.

The second involves the use of formal pressure or legal coercion. Both are clearly important to **social control**, which may be defined as the process of attempting to persuade persons or groups to conform to group expectations. Police activities in the form of legal coercion are likely to be unsuccessful in preventing violations of legal norms (laws) unless they are supplemented by informal, group, or social pressure to conform. This is so because successful legal coercion depends on reasonable rates of detection and apprehension. The ratio of police officers to other citizens in the United States (roughly 670,000 to 300,000,000, or 1 to 450) should be enough to convince us that the likelihood of detection and apprehension of criminals by the police is quite low. The various groups that constitute the public (families, peers and religious groups, for example) must take an active part in social control if those who violate norms are to be detected and apprehended. It is important, therefore, to realize that the police are only one of many groups involved in the social control process and that their efforts will fail unless they receive cooperation from these other groups (Renauer, 2007).

From Watchmen to Crime Fighters to Community Organizers

Nowhere perhaps, is the importance of the public to the criminal justice network clearer than in a historical discussion of the development of the police. In the Western world, citizens have been formally responsible for assisting in the maintenance of public order and the enforcement of law for centuries. In both England and colonial America, male citizens were called on to serve terms as watchmen who were responsible for protecting their cities and towns from invasion from the outside, and fire and criminals from the inside. In addition, these watchmen were given the responsibilities of containing those afflicted with plague, preventing commercial fraud, and enforcing licensing regulations (Rubinstein, 1973). These watchmen were paid little, held in low esteem by the public and subject to considerable manipulation by the wealthy, who wished to use the law for their own benefit (Barlow, 2000, p.163; Conser & Russell, 2000, p.40).

As crime became an increasingly complex problem, watchmen were recognized as inadequate for the protection of other citizens from criminals. The watchmen were unorganized, untrained, and undependable. In addition, they were operating under a system of laws that many people considered barbaric, so citizen support was often lacking. Reformers such as Jeremy Bentham, Edward Chadwick, and Patrick Colquhoun, who recognized the importance of public support for successful law policing and believed prevention to be an important part of policing, called for drastic changes in the law (Uchida, 2001). They called for the development of a centralized, organized, mobile, preventive force to deal with the crime problem. As towns became larger and citizens continued to refuse to perform police duties voluntarily, some cities began to pay their watchmen, but seldom enough to allow them to make a living (Johnson, 1981, p.7). In America, there were strong objections to the creation of an organized police force because many citizens were afraid it might be used as an instrument of government oppression. However, in the late eighteenth and early nineteenth centuries, an increasing demand for public order led to a growing consensus about the need for an organized police force (Richardson, 1974).

Although there were several localized police forces operating in England in the early 1800s, the first municipal force was the London police force, organized in 1829 under the direction of Sir Robert Peel. This force, the Metropolitan Police, was organized to help allay public fears arising from an increasing number of crimes being committed with impunity in and about the city of London. Peel believed that the police could be effective only if they were centrally organized, had the support of the public, exhibited a restrained demeanor, and understood the norms of the community in which they policed.

The London police were organized according to territories, or beats, which they patrolled in such fashion that they could be fairly easily located by those desiring their assistance. The beat patrol concept was soon adopted in cities and towns throughout Europe and the United States. With the emergence of community policing in the United States during the 1980s, policing had come full circle. The concepts on which Peel based the first municipal police force were once again front and center on the police stage.

Between 1830 and 1860, most large municipalities in the United States created police departments based on the British model. In the 1830s and 1840s, Philadelphia, New York, and Boston established full-time, centralized police departments (Conser & Russell, 2000, p. 54). As other cities followed suit, policing began to take on different forms. Vigilance committees were organized in areas unprotected by police departments, and private police forces (Pinkertons in 1855, Wells Fargo in 1852, Brinks in 1859, and Burns in 1909) were established by the railroads and other industries (Fischer & Green, 1998).

In the United States, the police were in frequent conflict with some segments of the public as a result of their attempt to enforce vice laws, which did not have widespread public support (Richardson, 1974, pp. 29–30). In addition, hiring and promotion were based on political patronage systems in many cities, which made the impartial administration of justice by competent police officers highly suspect. Despite attempts beginning in the 1870s to introduce reforms to reduce direct political influence, the political image remained (Walker, 1999, p. 26).

In the first part of the twentieth century, the introduction of the automobile led to further police community relations problems since many middle- and upper-class citizens who had previously supported crime control efforts by the police were now, themselves, subject to the actions of traffic officers. Another early police problem involved communication, and this problem, to a great extent, negated the advantages of an organized, mobile police force, since the police could not be summoned, and could not summon other officers to assist them, without the use of messengers or face-to-face contact. The invention and use of the telegraph, telephone, two-way radio, and patrol car made rapid, relatively certain communication possible by the 1930s in many police departments. Now many police administrators felt that crime (in the urban areas, at least) could be greatly reduced, if not eliminated. Public expectations concerning police performance were raised, and the public responded by dramatically increasing requests for services to the police, who were the only public service agency (other than the fire department) available 24 hours a day, every day. The police soon found themselves unable to respond adequately to all these service requests, found little time available for crime-related activities, and found public dissatisfaction growing. At the same time, police administrators began to realize that they had underestimated the ingenuity of offenders, who rapidly achieved the same level of communication and mobility attained by the police. By the middle of the twentieth century, the police (particularly those in large urban centers) were having difficulty living up to their image as crime fighters, and the public knew it. In attempting to be all things to all people, the police found themselves unable to perform all the services requested, capable of solving only about one in five reported major crimes, and unable to find ways out of these dilemmas. Police misconduct of various types, public distrust, and increasing demands for services based on unrealistic public expectations remained unresolved dilemmas. The police continued to attempt to improve their professional image, along with the quality of life of those they serve, by returning to some of the principles originally espoused by Sir Robert Peel over 150 years ago.

In the early 1900s, August Vollmer, chief of police in Berkeley, California, became a strong advocate for police professionalism. Working with the Wickersham Commission appointed by President Hoover in 1929, Vollmer surveyed police in America. On the basis of his findings, Vollmer believed the police should be removed from the direct influence of politics and should be college-educated and well trained. He became a trainer, an educator, and an author of numerous works on the police. He was also an innovator in police technology and a strong supporter of police ethics. He established foundations for hiring and training police officers that remain the model today. One of Vollmer's followers, O. W. Wilson, authored several popular police administration texts and later became the superintendent of the Chicago Police Department. Wilson, William Parker (chief of the Los Angeles Police Department from 1950 to 1966), V. A. Leonard (author of several police texts in the 1950s), Richard Sylvester (chief of District of Columbia Police from 1898 to 1915), and J. Edgar Hoover (director of the Federal Bureau of Investigation from 1924 to 1972) were among others who called for increasing professionalism and initiated major changes in American policing (Conser & Russell, 2000). These calls for reform and change continued in the 1970s, 1980s, and 1990s, and still echo in the twenty-first century.

The professional image of the American police suffered major setbacks in the 1960s and 1970s. Although the police were better trained, better educated, and better equipped than ever before, police-community relations, particularly with minority communities, became increasingly problematic. Major riots occurred in cities across the United States between 1964 and 1968, almost all of which began with police encounters with minority citizens. In the aftermath of the riots, the Kerner Commission (*Report of the National Advisory Commission on Civil Disorders,* 1968) pointed to several apparent shortcomings of the professional model of policing. Officers had become alienated from the people they were to serve, partly as a result of aggressive police tactics, partly as a result of increasing awareness of civil rights on behalf of minority Americans, and partly because the police did not, in terms of race, gender, and ethnicity, represent the public. These difficulties continued throughout the 1970s, compounded by studies which indicated that routine patrol, long considered the backbone of traditional policing, was probably not the best way to employ police resources (Kelling, et al., 1974). By the end of the decade, the police reform movement was stagnant and the future of the professional policing model was in question. It was apparent that traditional, law enforcement-oriented policing had not achieved the lofty goals established earlier in the twentieth century. As the 1980s began, problem-oriented and community-oriented policing appeared to be ways to revive the reform movement and solve at least some of the problems that historically plagued American police.

Community- and Problem-Oriented Policing

Nowhere is the network concept better illustrated than in the development and implementation of community-oriented policing (now typically referred to as community policing). Defining the exact meaning of community policing is difficult because the term refers to a variety of initiatives tailored to different communities. In general terms, however, **community policing** refers to a philosophy of policing that emphasizes a cooperative approach between the police and other citizens focusing on alleviating community problems with the intent of improving the quality of life in the community (Eck & Rosenbaum, 1994; Cox, 1996; Rosenbaum, 2000; Anonymous, 2005a). It is important to note that community policing is not a program, but a different approach to policing. Whereas traditional policing deals with treating the symptoms of crime by handling calls or incidents, community policing, through the use of problem-oriented policing (POP), attempts to identify and attack the underlying problems that lead to calls (Goldstein, 1990). This is often accomplished by going through four steps — scanning, or detailing the nature of the problem; analysis, or obtaining answers to the questions who, what, why, when, and how; response, or identifying possible solutions and selecting those most likely to work; and assessment, or determining whether the chosen solution worked. These four steps are commonly referred to as the **SARA process** (Goldstein, 1990).

To adequately address underlying problems, community police officers are encouraged to form partnerships with residents of the areas they police, with other public service agencies, and with private service providers. Officers are empowered to attempt nontraditional approaches in dealing with the problems and are rewarded for innovative and creative programs and solutions. This approach represents almost the exact opposite of traditional policing, which has typically rewarded officers for following in the footsteps of generations of officers. In fact, officers who innovate in traditional departments are viewed as troublemakers. Regardless, officer discretion is at a premium in community policing, as are the abilities to develop proactive programs and new solutions to old problems (Smith, Novak & Frank, 2005). Accountability, openness to public observation and input, community organization skills, and customer-oriented or personalized police service are encouraged.

It must be noted that some research shows that despite efforts at implementation in various police agencies, POP, as practiced by most police officers, falls short of the ideal model and it may be unreasonable to expect every police officer to continuously engage in full-fledged POP (Cordner & Biebel, 2005).

Organizational changes are required if the philosophy of community policing is to be implemented. Permanent beat assignments are required. Control must be decentralized so that officers are free to deal innovatively with problems encountered, and to create solutions that may differ from one neighborhood or beat to another (Anonymous, 2005a). And the police must be willing to admit that they are not the only persons who can contribute to order maintenance, law enforcement, and crime prevention.

Community and problem-solving policing strategies are now accepted by many police officers in the United States while others continue to resist the required changes. The lack of long-term commitment by community participants makes community policing difficult to sustain (Glensor, Correia, & Peak, 2000, p. 3). Is community policing a panacea for law enforcement and order maintenance? Probably not (Roh & Oliver, 2005). But it is clear that traditional policing has failed to deal effectively with numerous issues and community policing is an alternative strategy that is worth a try.

Only careful evaluation of ongoing programs will allow us to determine the success of community policing. The few evaluations that have been conducted have shown either positive (Lurigo & Rosenbaum, 1994) or ambiguous (Lurigo & Skogan, 2000) results. In a review of community policing efforts in six American cities ranging in size from 38,000 to 1,500,000, Weisel and Eck (2000) found that "regardless of the type and longevity of community policing effort, and the variety and intensity of implementation activity, a solid core of personnel (about 75 percent) believe community policing is here to stay and their behaviors are likely to reflect that perception" (p. 270). Others (Kerlikowske, 2004) argue that we should bring an end to the era of community policing, take the best of what we learned over the last half century, and move on. What we have learned, among other things, is that in every facet of police work, we need to inform, discuss with, and value members of the community. If the network perspective of criminal justice is accepted, community policing would appear to be a step in the right direction because it recognizes the interrelationships among the police, other service agencies, and the public (see "In the News" 6.1).

In the News 6.1

Chief plans to introduce community-oriented policing

Friendly, service-oriented and approachable.

That's the kind of police department Chief Michael Murphy hopes to create in Warminster.

To do so, he plans to give every officer and civilian employee in the department more power to make decisions so they can help keep small problems from becoming big ones.

That type of law enforcement — known as community-oriented policing — harkens back to the days of officers walking a beat, and it represents an about-face from the type of department Murphy inherited when he took over six months ago.

"It had been a fairly autocratic agency, with decisions made by the chief and passed down as doctrines from on high," Murphy said. "I'm a firm believer in having people who work for you be creative decision makers. They're the ones who are out there."

The autocratic style Murphy refers to was only part of the Warminster Township Police Department's problem. The department's image was tarnished by Murphy's predecessor,

James Gorczynski, who is in jail after pleading guilty to charges that included stealing federal drug forfeiture funds and selling bogus overtime and holiday compensation hours to officers under his command.

Also hurting the department's image was the conviction and jailing of an officer who engaged in online sex chat with what he thought was a 13-year-old girl. The officer also arranged to meet the girl in person, only to discover "she" was really an undercover police officer.

Evidence of the department's image problem — which Murphy hopes to improve with community-oriented policing — comes in the form of a recent survey answered by about 125 people with whom the department recently had contact.

From the survey, the department learned two things, according to Lt. Christopher Springfield:

"We provided very good service. However, (a significant percentage of the public expected poor service. That's an attitude we need to change."

Change for the department is to come in two ways over the next five years — through the training of officers and support staff, and with the help of the community.

Springfield said the department plans to teach officers and staff to provide "customer service."

That includes listening to people, empathizing with them by looking at problems from their perspective and helping solve those problems. The department also plans to provide employees with values training, which they can utilize to make decisions in the absence of authority.

"If we create a good working relationship with them, people will be more than willing to help us create a safer environment for them," Murphy said. "We want them to tell us what their problems are, what they see as the issues in their neighborhoods. Sometimes what we think are the most inconsequential problems are monumental to people."

He cites as an example of community policing a loud neighbor complaint. It might be that the elderly person making the complaint is homebound and has no one to care for him, he said.

An officer could take the initiative to call the Area Agency on Aging for help or reach out to a family member.

Normally, the police department wouldn't get involved beyond dealing with the noise complaint, he said. "We've never encouraged our officers to take that kind of initiative."

The idea of empowering police department employees is part of a philosophy that stresses crime prevention by addressing factors that contribute to crime. It represents a fundamental shift from traditional, reactive policing methods.

"One theory is that this is, in fact, old-school policing," said Gilbert Moore, a spokesman for the Office of Community Oriented Policing Services in Washington.

Moore said community-oriented policing, which started in the late 1970s or early 1980s, has seen a dramatic increase in popularity in law enforcement circles since the mid-to-late 1990s.

He points to a study by the Justice Department's Bureau of Justice Statistics, which found that the percentage of local police officers assigned to community policing grew from 4 percent to 21 percent between 1997 to 1999.

By 1999, 64 percent of the police departments in the country — representing 86 percent of the U.S. population served by local police — had full-time officers engaged in community policing.

In 1997, only 34 percent of local departments, serving 62 percent of the population, had community-oriented policing officers.

Exactly how community-policing works varies from department to department, depending on a community's needs, Moore said. However, its fundamental tenants are the same.

They include working with organizations within the community to come up with practical solutions to solving problems and helping residents feel like they have a direct link to their police department. They also involve an organizational shift, with as much authority as possible given to officers out on patrol, he said.

Murphy first proposed the idea of community-oriented policing to the Warminster supervisors when he interviewed for the chief's position. He'd already experienced its success in Upper Dublin, where he was the deputy chief, and he knew it was working in other area townships, such as Abington and Bensalem.

"We thought it was a good thing," said supervisor chairman Richard Luce Jr. "We're in favor of it."

The township's only concern, Luce said, is that the initiative not affect the budget. He added, however, that, "Solving problems at the lowest level doesn't cost anything. It's just a mindset."

For Abington, which has a community policing unit but also has had a department-wide community policing initiative for the past decade, officers are encouraged to park their cars and walk and to talk to merchants and residents.

They're also encouraged to ask people what their problems are and to look beyond crime and traffic control and at quality of life issues and how they can help citizens, said Deputy Chief John Livingood.

Looking beyond typical law enforcement duties is "that obvious next step in serving your community," he said.

It's also a step his officers like taking.

"We encourage them to take ownership for their beat, to solve problems," Livingood said. "I think they like that."

Murphy is confident his officers will like it too.

"The work force today is much different than 30 years ago," Springfield said. "Employees are much more educated and qualified, and they want to have a say. They don't just want to be told what to do.

"We've been listening to the officers in the department, and a lot of this co-incides with what they're telling us they want to do."

Arthur, J. S. (2005, November 16). Chief plans to introduce community-oriented policing: That's a dramatic change for a Warminster police department that has suffered more than its share of image problems. *The Intelligencer*, p.1A.

As noted in chapter two, increasing concern over terrorism and terrorists has led to changes in law enforcement. As law enforcement personnel have become increasingly responsible for protecting the public from the threat of terrorist activities, the need for public cooperation has grown as has the importance of interagency cooperation and communication. The police, by themselves, are unlikely to be able to foil terrorist plots as indicated in the following quote

> The American law enforcement community has not been very proactive with respect to counterterrorism activities, particularly at the state and local levels. For the most part, the burden of counterterrorism has been placed squarely on the shoulders of federal law enforcement agencies. Now, however, it is clear that policing at all levels must assume some responsibility for and commitment to the containment of domestic terrorism. This new priority has created a number of concerns for criminal justice administrators, ranging from budgetary deficiencies and training issues to investigative techniques and expanded police powers, which may be subject to constitutional abuse in the name of national defense (McCamey, Scaramella, & Cox, 2003, p. 323).

Scrivner (2004) questions whether law enforcement can maintain the advances in community policing in light of the post 9/11 demands to secure the homeland. With public assistance and interagency cooperation, the possibility of intervening before terrorist activities occur and of apprehending those who do commit terrorist acts is heightened.

Terrorism has led to changes in police tactics and access to public and private facilities. Reprinted with permission of iStockphoto.com / Chris DeRidder.

Current Police Functions

Although the police may be technically responsible for the full enforcement of statutes, in reality, they selectively enforce the law (as we indicated in Chapter 1). To be sure, they make every attempt to enforce laws prohibiting predatory crimes, but even these are subject to selective enforcement on the basis of whether violations are observed and reported, whether the victim is willing to serve as a witness/complainant, the seriousness of the offense, and numerous other factors. With respect to less serious but more common offenses, the police often tailor their efforts to specific geographic locations and/or times. For example, the police cannot fully enforce traffic laws prohibiting speeding. While an officer is writing a citation to one offender, several others may escape his or her attention. Further, as members of the criminal justice network, police officers often tailor their activities on the basis of decisions of prosecutors and judges. Police officers who see violations relating to the use of marijuana, for example, may initially arrest violators, but if the prosecutor or judge routinely dismisses such cases, the officers will in all likelihood alter their enforcement patterns so that their behavior conforms to the expectations of others (including the public) in the network.

The police are visible representatives of authority whose decisions, to a great extent, determine whether or not other components of the official criminal justice network will take official action. They are largely a reactive agency, dependent on public cooperation and information. The police are "members of the public who are paid to give full-time attention to duties which are incumbent on every citizen, in the interests of community welfare and existence" (Davis, 1978, p.7). This makes apparent the importance of the point that we have repeatedly emphasized: Public cooperation is necessary if the police are to perform their functions effectively. Yet, there is little doubt that public cooperation with the police leaves a great deal to be desired. Many segments of the public are uncooperative with the police, and some are openly hostile a good deal of the time. Other segments either criticize the police for being unable to do anything about the crime problem, or appear largely apathetic. The police are equally critical of and hostile toward some segments of the public. What are the major functions that the public expects the police to perform? Why are the police often judged ineffective? What do the police expect from the public?

The police in the United States are primarily providers of services. Among the services they provide are law enforcement, order maintenance, and crime prevention. In community policing departments, these services are provided largely through the use of problem-solving techniques and police-community partnerships. In more traditional departments, the police have attempted to provide the services with little input from or attention to the public. Traditional agencies have often been unsuccessful in satisfying public demands for these services because successful performance requires public cooperation. When members of the public take their responsibilities seriously, a high level of police performance is possible. When members of the public fail to accept their responsibilities, or when the police fail to participate in partnerships with the public, the police are not likely to be highly effective. Large segments of the American public appear to be willing to leave law enforcement largely to the police. Failure to report crimes, failure to assist victims of crimes in progress, a desire not to get involved, and failure to assist police officers upon request are commonplace. The prevailing attitude seems to be "it's not my job" or "it's none of my business." Thus, the police have been left to handle the tasks of law enforcement themselves. While the vast majority of police work involves providing services that have little to do with criminal conduct, the ability to detect crime and apprehend criminals remains a critical part of policing. These tasks are particularly difficult, perhaps impossible, to accomplish without public support.

Police officers in metropolitan areas typically spend their working hours responding to one service request after another. Some time may be spent on routine patrol, even though the value of such patrol is seriously in doubt. Other services commonly provided by the police include the following:

- Checking security of buildings.
- Regulating traffic.
- Investigating accidents.
- Transporting prisoners and the emotionally disturbed.
- Providing information.
- Escorting funeral processions and parades.
- Finding lost children.

- Providing first aid.
- Making public speeches.
- Handling calls about animals.
- Handling domestic disputes.
- Enforcing licensing regulations.
- Fingerprinting.
- Administering breathalyzer tests.
- Staffing and managing jails.
- Using the computer to file reports and to collect information.
- Engaging in problem-solving activities.
- Seeking to improve quality of life in the community.

Police Law Enforcement Procedures

There are certain crime-related tasks that the police are expected to perform. Generally speaking, the police are held responsible for the following crime-related tasks:

1. Prevention
2. Recording
3. Investigation
4. Apprehension
5. Arrest
6. Interviewing and interrogation
7. Booking
8. Acceptance of certain types of bail or temporary detention
9. Collection and preservation of evidence
10. Recovery of stolen property
11. Transmission of reports to the prosecutor in usable form
12. Testifying in court

As we discuss each of these areas, recall our previous discussions of the exercise of discretion and the influence of politics at all levels in the criminal justice network.

With respect to crime prevention, the police are generally expected to provide programs to educate the public, to provide deterrent patrol, to make house and building checks, and to use informants and intelligence sources to stop criminal acts from occurring. With respect to the latter, police conduct is limited by considerations of **due process**. To maintain a relatively free society, we have decided that due process is at least as important as **crime control**. This has become clear in recent years with the emphasis on preventing racial profiling by the police.

Although crime prevention programs developed by the police may deter some crimes, it is clear that prevention is one area in which public cooperation is critical. Prevention is made even more difficult by the fact that there is no visible end product to prevention programs, so it is difficult to justify resources to support such programs.

A second crime-related duty of the police is to record crimes reported by the public or observed by police officers. Such recording is important, since both our local and national official statistics on the incidence of different types of crime depend on accurate recording. Further, information recorded and shared with other agencies may be useful in solving crimes, arresting offenders, or preventing additional offenses. Once a citizen exercises his or her discretion to report an offense to the police, the police exercise their discretion as to whether the report should become part of the official record. When the report is accepted as worthy of attention, it becomes a crime known to the police.

Having accepted a crime report, the police are expected to investigate the incident. A great deal of discretion is used by the police in deciding whether or not to expend police resources on an investigation, and if an investigation is to be conducted, how extensive it should be. Investigations range from simply making a preliminary report describing stolen property (used largely for insurance purposes) with little or no follow-up, to investigations of homicide that require the crime scene be sealed off, complete inventories of evidence be made, and many persons be located and interviewed. Investigations such as the former are often conducted in a matter of minutes, while the latter may take months or years.

The use of informants is common in police departments. Informants can often provide information that cannot be obtained in any other way, and where they have been shown to be reliable, informants may be important in helping prevent crime and/or in apprehending offenders. Perhaps nowhere is the use of discretion by the police more clearly illustrated than in dealing with informants. To obtain valuable information, the police frequently overlook minor violations by informants. It is not uncommon, for example, for the police to be aware of the fact that an informant is in possession of illegal drugs and, in fact, to provide the informant with funds that they know will be used to purchase such drugs. The discretion not to arrest is exercised in the hopes of obtaining information about more serious offenses committed by others.

When an investigation turns up a likely suspect, the police are expected to apprehend that suspect and, where appropriate, to make an arrest. At the point of arrest, the police officer possesses considerable discretionary power although she or he is influenced by the law, departmental policy, and other network constraints. Still, there is often no one physically present to supervise the officer's actions, and she or he may respond to a variety of cues other than legal ones. The age, gender, race, dress, prior history, or location of a suspect may all influence the officer's decision, which is crucial because if the police officer decides not to arrest, the matter is, practically speaking, closed. It is the exercise of discretion by individual police officers in thousands of police-citizen encounters every day that helps shape public attitudes toward the police (and, we might add, the exercise of discretion by members of the various publics that help shape police attitudes toward them).

If the officer arrests one person for a particular offense but allows another who has committed the same offense to go free, the arrested party (when he or she knows about the discrepancy) can hardly be expected to feel the criminal justice network is just. When one officer ignores a particular offense, but another arrests everyone who commits that offense, the public is confused. Police officers, exercise of discretion, therefore, plays an important part in shaping relations between the police and the public.

The process of arrest itself is quite complicated. Generally speaking, however, a police officer is empowered to make an **arrest** when he or she has a warrant or signed complaint, sees someone commit a felony or misdemeanor, or has reason to suspect that someone has committed a felony. The actual point at which an arrest occurs depends on the officer's intent to arrest and the citizen's understanding of that intent. When the officer says, "You are under arrest!" the intent is quite clear provided the officer is speaking the same language as the arrestee. It is less clear when the officer says, "You, stay here. I want to talk to you." Further, a police officer exercising discretion may try to use this ambiguity to gain time to decide whether or not to make an arrest. For the most part, arrests based solely on suspicion are illegal. But, at what point does suspicion become probable cause or a reasonable belief? It is at this stage, during or just after the arrest, that the suspect is informed of his or her Miranda rights (to remain silent, that anything said may be used in a court of law, and to contact a lawyer) (*Miranda v. Arizona*, 1966). Depending on the suspect's desires or the suspect's lawyer's advice, interviewing and/or interrogation may occur. Even arrest, a function that all of us would agree is important to the police, is not as simple as it first appears.

When a suspect has been arrested and made available for prosecution, the police say the crime has been cleared by arrest even though the suspect is never prosecuted for the crime or is eventually determined to be not guilty. With respect to the crimes classified by the Federal Bureau of Investigation as Index Offenses (criminal homicide, forcible rape, aggravated assault, robbery, burglary, grand theft, arson, and auto theft), the police are successful in clearing by arrest about 20 to 25 percent. In other words, about four out of five Index Offenses are not cleared by arrest. This inability of the police to clear crimes by arrest is both caused by and causes public belief that the police are ineffective.

Once an arrest is made, the police are responsible for informing the suspect of the charges against him or her, for booking, and for interviewing or interrogating the suspect. The **booking** process involves taking an inventory of the suspect's property, fingerprinting, and photographing. Also at this stage, the police may inform the suspect that he or she is eligible for bail and, under certain circumstances (generally in the case of misdemeanors), may accept bail and release the suspect from custody. If bail is not allowable or if the suspect cannot make bail, the police may detain him or her in a holding cell or, in the case of a county sheriff, in a jail until the suspect makes bail or goes to trial.

From the time of the initial investigation through arrest, interviews, and interrogations, the police are responsible for collecting evidence (physical and testimonial) concerning the crime in question. The collection of evidence depends on the skill of the investigator and available clues. The preservation of evidence to be presented in court requires that a **chain of evidence** begin when the evidence is first collected and continue until the evidence is presented in court or determined to be of no value. The chain of evidence must be fashioned in such a way that location and control of the evidence can be documented at every point from discovery to presentation, and often involves the investigative division of the department. Investigators handle most of the serious criminal cases and are specially trained in crime scene investigation and evidence preservation. In larger departments, there may also be criminalists or crime scene technicians, fingerprinting experts, polygraph operators, and juvenile officers in the investigative division. The chain of evidence typically begins when a patrol officer or investigator finds what he or she considers evidence, and collects and tags or clearly identifies the evidence. He or she then turns it over to an evidence custodian or technician, who gives the officer or investigator receipts for the evidence. The chain of evidence typically concludes with the presentation of the evidence in court by the officer or investigator who originally collected the evidence. This officer signs a receipt for the evidence custodian when he or she removes the evidence from the evidence locker or room.

During the investigation and collection of evidence, the police officers involved are also interested in recovering stolen property that will eventually be returned to its rightful owner. Similarly, the officers involved in the arrest and investigation are aware that they must proceed in such a way that they can establish both a factual and legal (following due process) case against the suspect that the prosecutor can use in court. Police reports form the starting point for the prosecutor's case, and inadequate performance in any of the areas we have just discussed may make prosecution either impossible or unsuccessful. The same is true of the last requirement of the police — testifying in court. Inaccurate or perjured testimony can lead not only to the release of guilty persons or the conviction of innocent persons, but also to serious repercussions for the officer personally and the police image in general (Cunningham, 1999). It is important, therefore, that police officers take and retain complete, accurate notes during the investigation; that they be honest; and that they be unafraid to admit they don't know when, in fact, they don't know. Only when police testimony meets these standards can we expect public cooperation with, and support of, the police.

Police Order Maintenance Activities

As we have repeatedly indicated, law enforcement activities are a small, though critical, part of policing. The police spend far more time attempting to maintain order. To accomplish this goal, they engage in **mediation and negotiation**. That is, they mediate disputes between parties and attempt to negotiate settlements that will restore order. Typically, these techniques involve compromises suggested by the police officer. For example, an officer receives a complaint of loud music. She may talk to the person responsible for the music, indicate that it is bothering others, and ask that the volume be turned down. The officer may then talk to the complaining party, indicating that the responsible party has agreed to turn down the volume, but also noting that there needs to be some give-and-take between neighbors and that the partygoers are just trying to have a good time without injuring others. Or a police officer may try to mediate a dispute between a youth who frequently runs away from home and his parents. The officer may ask the parents to try to be more understanding of the youth's needs and desires, and vice versa. He may point out to both parties that taking official action will only drive the parties further apart and suggest that they try to strike a compromise.

Negotiating and mediating are among the most frequent activities in which the police engage. Officers frequently attempt to negotiate settlements to avoid official action (law enforcement). As is the case with law enforcement, negotiation and mediation require reciprocity on behalf of the other citizens with whom the police are involved. Research by Zhao, He, and Lovrich (2003) indicates that police core-functions of crime control, the maintenance of order, and the provision of services remained largely unchanged in the era of community policing although there have been efforts to address these functions at a higher level of achievement.

Police Organizations

To achieve the goals of providing service by maintaining order and enforcing the law, many police agencies have developed organizational structures similar to the one depicted in Figure 6.1

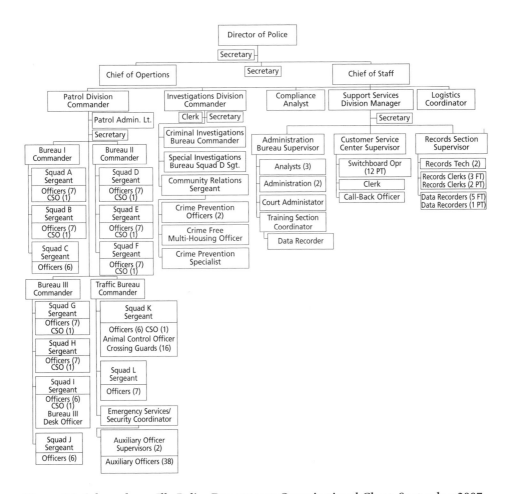

Figure 6.1 Schaumburg, Ill., Police Department Organizational Chart, September 2007

There are many variations on this formal organizational structure. Note that this chart concerns the police department only and does not show that the department is accountable to a mayor, city manager, or commissioner, and the public.

The operations division is normally the largest division in terms of personnel and other resources, and the duties of patrol officers and investigators have been outlined previously. The other division commonly found in police departments may be referred to as the administrative division or staff services division. Primary functions of this division are record keeping, communications, research and planning, training and education, and sometimes logistics. In some departments, most of these functions are performed by sworn officers, but there is a clear-cut trend toward hiring civilian employees to perform the majority of these tasks.

Although some departments have divided the tasks mentioned above differently, most follow this division of activity. Normally, a division commander in charge of each division reports to the chief of police or a deputy chief of police. These division commanders have shift commanders, field supervisors, and staff personnel under their control as well as line officers and/or civilians. In metropolitan departments, several precinct headquarters are established throughout the city, and each precinct may be organized as indicated above, or various types of services may remain centralized, to be called for when the need arises.

In most instances, police departments maintain a paramilitary structure that stresses use of the chain of command in issuing orders and directives and solving problems. Although this structure has some advantages in terms of discipline and control, it is resistant to change. In addition, it fails to promote communication and interaction among members of different divisions and, in fact, often promotes a sense of competition among departmental personnel, which may not always have beneficial consequences. In some departments, patrol officers and investigators seldom interact because of rivalry between division commanders, physical separation of facilities, and aloof attitudes on the part of the investigators. In addition, patrol officers tend to view investigators as glory seekers.

Many students of the police believe that a paramilitary structure is one reason the police have not kept pace with the private industry in adapting to changing conditions. When followed to the letter, such formal organizational structure is often quite cumbersome. Partially as a response to the inflexibility of the formal organizational structure, informal arrangements often arise among various divisions and individuals, which may speed up organizational procedures or impede such procedures. Thus, a police lieutenant who wants to change the activities of his or her shift personnel may not go to the patrol commander, who would then have to go to the assistant chief, who would then have to seek the chief's approval. Instead, the lieutenant may see the chief after hours or may discuss the idea with an alderman or the mayor over drinks to gain support. Similarly, individual patrol officers and investigators may meet informally to discuss a case and share information that their immediate supervisors may not wish to share as a result of divisional rivalries. In organizational structures, then, it is important to consider both the formal and informal arrangements that characterize the agency in question.

Some Variations on the Traditional Police Organization

A number of attempts have been made in recent years to make police departments more flexible and responsive to the needs of both the public and other criminal justice agencies. As noted earlier, one strategy employed by some departments to improve services and efficiency is community policing (variations of which have been referred to as neighborhood policing, team policing, or neighborhood service teams). As originally conceived, police officers, each having some special training, are assigned as a team to serve a particular geographic area. The team is responsible for providing services to area residents 24 hours a day and operates under the direction of a field supervisor who coordinates the team's efforts with those of the larger department. The rationale for this style of policing is that such teams will be more familiar with area problems and more familiar to area residents. Further, decentralized control should result in greater flexibility and responsiveness to the varying needs and desires of different neighborhoods (Eck & Rosenbaum, 1994; Duff, 2006). In contemporary community policing, most city agencies are involved in an attempt to build partnerships between agency personnel and neighborhood residents. The police-community partnership proceeds by trying to restore pride to the neighborhood through organizing general cleanup projects, closing crack houses, improving conditions in neighborhood schools, and helping rediscover a sense of community. Such partnerships have long existed in San Diego, which now has more than 800 volunteers, and are being developed in cities such as Denver where more than 350 volunteer citizens could eventually be trained to handle routine operations such as data entry and gathering DNA and fingerprint evidence at property crime scenes (Anonymous, 2006). These volunteers perform many routine duties that would otherwise have to be performed by sworn officers. The effectiveness of such programs remains to be determined, but some seem to be enjoying at least moderate success.

In an attempt to improve community relations and provide better services (to say nothing of complying with affirmative action guidelines), many police departments now employ women and racial/ethnic minorities. The change from a predominantly white male occupational subculture has come about slowly and with considerable resistance. Nonetheless, the evidence is quite clear: Women and minorities perform police duties as well as white males (Cox, 1996, pp.141–60; Walker 1999, pp.230–32). (See "In the News" 6.2.)

In the News 6.2

Police officers first, women second ...

Though they are a small minority in the Midland Police Department and some people make the mistake of not taking them seriously enough, female police officers continue to effectively protect Tall City residents and risk their lives every day.

Margarita Vengas has been a patrol officer for seven years and said she loves her job. As a single mother who originally studied to become a teacher, Vengas said she made the tough choice to follow her dream of becoming a police officer and has never looked back.

At 5 feet 3 inches tall, Vengas said her job can get difficult, but she said the key to her success is letting people know of her confidence.

"I don't think there has been a call that I didn't think I could handle. I deal with people who are a lot bigger than me, but you have to be confident," Vengas said. "There are those calls where those people don't like women telling them what to do, but you have to set your mind to what your doing."

As one of four siblings who works in law enforcement, Vengas said her family supports her profession.

"My mom worries, everyone worries, and I worry about my brothers and my sister, but we do support each other. We know the dangers out there, but we also know the rewards and challenges," she explained.

"Me being a single mom, it's sometimes hard to leave my children, but I get to go home and take them to school, volunteer at their schools and take them to the mall. Then, I get to go to work."

Officer Molly Porter, who started with the department as a patrol officer about 1½ years ago, said she has never had a dull moment since putting on her uniform and was welcomed onto the force with open arms.

"It's definitely an interesting job. Obviously you stick out more than you want to, but everyone welcomed me," Porter explained.

Porter said though she has to be more aware of her surroundings as a female police officer, she's comfortable and confident in her ability to protect the streets of Midland.

"You just have to be more on guard; you're not as big as any other officer. I'm comfortable with the tactics that I learned in training. Just learn as much as you can and protect yourself as best as possible," she explained.

Police Department officials reported that on April 1, 1969, Melba Elaine James was the first female police officer to join the MPD. Today, of the 153 police officers at the MPD, 16 are females, as are three of the six recruits training for the department.

Vengas said she's not bothered to be one of the very few who actually accomplish becoming a patrol officer.

"My squad is seven guys and I am the only female. I'm the only female officer who works at midnight, but I'm just one of the guys," she said.

"I would have to say there are very few who have made it to become a police officer out of several that have tried. The whole process is hard, and knowing that I am one of the few females who made it makes me proud that I am a police officer."

While many may think being a female police officer has many disadvantages, these female officers agree that being a woman has its advantages.

"You may not come off as aggressive as the men do; sometimes you can just talk someone down," Porter explained.

Though their gender may be obvious when they stand among their male colleagues, both Vengas and Porter said there isn't much of a difference in how the MPD officers do their jobs.

"I like working the streets; I really enjoy working the night shift," Vengas said. "The bonding that you can count on your coworkers makes your job a lot more fun and allows you to have confidence."

Porter and Vengas suggest that any women or young girls aspiring to be police officers must realize protecting the streets at all costs is a job that they will love.

"Sometimes you do have to work twice as hard; a lot of times you will have to deal with people who don't like you," Vengas explained. "But knowing that you're doing your job and you're doing it well, that's all you need to be worried about. And don't ever forget that you are human."

Porter also offered suggestions for women who want to protect the citizenry.

"It's a physical job. Be as strong as you can possibly be. Take good care of yourself," Porter said. "You've got to be up to the physical challenge. And get your education."

Regardless of gender, Vengas said it is important to always follow your dreams, whatever they may be.

"If it is your dream, do whatever you have to do to achieve it," she said.

Bradley, L. (2007, June 3). Police officers first, women second ... *Midland Reporter-Telegram*, Record number 11989BE25AC19048

As time passes, and members of minorities continue to gain supervisory positions, further structural changes in police departments may be expected (Maglione, 2002; Schulz, 2002). For example, at the end of 2000, there were at least 157 female chiefs of police in the United States. About half of these chiefs managed municipal agencies and another 40 percent headed college/university agencies. Roughly 16 percent of these chiefs indicated racial/ethnic minority status (Schulz, 2002, p. 25)

Over the past 40 years, there has been a serious attempt to increase the number of black and other minorities serving as police officers based on the belief that increased diversity will improve police-community relations. This has been done in spite of the fact that there is little empirical evidence that an officer's race is actually related to his/her behavior towards citizens. However, at least some research does suggest that officer race is related to arrest outcomes and that there are differences between white and black officers in the decision to arrest (Brown & Frank, 2006). Major differences in the

In an increasingly diverse society, minority officers are essential to effective police community relations. Reprinted with permission of iStockphoto.com / Jacom Stephens.

way in which black and white officers view their jobs and the opportunities for promotion afforded in policing have also been noted (Bolton, 2003; Sun, 2003).

No discussion of changes in police organization and practices would be complete without a brief mention of technological changes. Personal, notebook, and on-board computers, as well as voice stress analyzers, have made possible virtually instant analysis of crime and accident trends, recall of information on suspects, and analysis of the frequency, duration, and type of activities engaged in by departmental personnel. Computers and cameras mounted in patrol vehicles provide not only instant access to information concerning vehicle registrations, licenses, and wants or warrants, but also instantaneous communications with other police vehicles and headquarters. This rapid communication capability, coupled with greater willingness to experiment on behalf of many police administrators, has enabled the police to become more responsive to changing conditions (Couret, 1999; Green, 2003). For example, "On the Beat" is a television program produced by the North Miami Beach Police Department in Florida in order to increase community awareness of and involvement with the law enforcement community while marketing the department and providing a personal connection to the community (Anonymous, 2005b).

At the same time, the use of citizen or media based surveillance equipment enables the public to assess the performance of the police as never before. Long-range camera and video recorder lenses and audio equipment allow citizens to observe officers while on patrol and in encounters with other citizens. Such devices have been used to incriminate police officers abusing their positions as well as to help identify and locate suspects (Green, 2003).

As a result of research conducted in Kansas City and elsewhere, the effectiveness of patrol officers on routine patrol has been questioned. This cornerstone of police work is defended by many police administrators, but evidence indicates, in some cities at least, that routine patrol does not prevent crime, improve citizen satisfaction, or cut down response time. These findings suggest that valuable police resources have been, and are currently being, wasted. If this is so, a thorough rethinking of police operations is required. Such rethinking has already occurred in many police departments that now employ various types of **directed patrol** strategies to improve efficiency. **Split-force policing** involves designating certain areas high-risk, assigning certain officers to those areas, and saturating the areas with patrols, both overt and covert. In the meantime, other designated officers are responsible for handling service requests and routine patrol in the area. Suspect-oriented policing techniques involve assigning officers to concentrate on known offenders or suspects (Gaines, Kappeler, & Vaughn, 1994, pp.166–71). In addition to identifying and using special types of patrol strategies, many departments have broadened their patrol approach by adding bicycle patrols, aircraft patrols, boat patrols, and foot or mounted patrols (Reaves & Goldberg, 1999).

Another change in policing involves the **accreditation** of police departments. The objectives of accreditation include developing standards against which agency performance may be measured and developing procedures that facilitate objective assessment of police performance. Given the strong American tradition that police power should be decentralized, it has been nearly impossible to establish generally accepted standards of quality in law enforcement. There are almost as many points of view concerning how different police functions ought to be performed as there are police departments. Nonetheless, a number of state and national police organizations are involved in attempting to develop standards for police departments.

The Commission on Accreditation for Law Enforcement Agencies (CALEA) was established in 1979 and administers a voluntary accreditation program aimed at achieving excellence, efficiency, and professionalism among police agencies. The Commission has established a number of standards by which to evaluate police agencies. These standards are tailored to fit agencies of various sizes and to help police agencies evaluate themselves. If an agency desires to be evaluated by a team of assessors working for the Commission, it submits an application. The agency is then sent a questionnaire that is used to determine the standards that apply to that particular agency. A self-assessment is then conducted by agency personnel, and if the agency desires, an on-site assessment by a team of assessors follows. The on-site assessment is then reviewed by the Commission to determine whether the agency will be accredited. Currently, at least 688 agencies have been accredited, a large number have been reaccredited, and altogether over 900 agencies are involved in some stage of the process (Commission on Accreditation for Law Enforcement Agencies, 2005). Some 25 percent of full-time local and state police officers in the United States are officially in the accreditation process (CALEA, 2007)

Peace Officer Standards and Training (POST) boards in 48 states set requirements for becoming certified as a police officer. These boards certify police officers who meet predetermined standards of training and education, and who pass standardized written examinations. The certification process is intended to ensure a minimum level of knowledge among police officers throughout the state and is an important step toward professionalization. Some states, such as Illinois, also have voluntary certification for the chiefs of police with the same goals in mind.

The implications of police certification and accreditation are far-reaching. Transfer between departments and lateral entry would be facilitated among certified officers. The overall level of training among law enforcement personnel should improve. Finally, the overall level of service provided to the public should improve. Yet accreditation, in particular, has not been unopposed. Some states have decided to develop their own standards for accreditation as opposed to accepting the national standards of CALEA. Costs related to accreditation have also been subject to criticism.

These and numerous other adaptations being made in police agencies throughout the United States indicate that the organizational structure of police departments can take a variety of forms and still permit the police to play their roles in the criminal justice network. Let us now turn our attention to a discussion of the procedures used to fill those roles.

Selection, Training, and Education of the Police

It is clear that adequate police performance in all the areas mentioned above requires specially selected, specially trained, and, perhaps, specially educated personnel. How are such personnel selected? What type of education and how much training do these personnel require?

Standards for police officers vary across the United States, but certain considerations appear to be important in most jurisdictions. Generally speaking, potential police officers must meet some or all of the following criteria, which are governed by the Civil Rights Act of 1964, the Equal Employment Opportunity Act of 1972 (EEOA), the Americans with Disabilities Act (ADA) of 1990, and the Civil Rights Act of 1991, as well as by numerous court decisions:

1. Age: minimum age is typically 19 to 21 at time of first employment.
2. Height and weight are in proportion to each other; to test for body fat composition.
3. Education: generally, a high school diploma or GED, but more departments now require some college credits.
4. Agility test: to evaluate physical capabilities required by the job.
5. Written test: to measure aptitude and/or intelligence.
6. Psychological exam: to determine mental fitness for the job; may be required only after an offer of a job has been made.
7. Medical exam: to ensure that no disabilities that might prevent the applicant from performing the essential functions of the job exist at the time of initial employment; may be required only after an offer of a job has been made.
8. Polygraph exam: to determine honesty.

9. Background investigation: to ensure character of applicant.
10. Oral interview: to determine applicant's reactions to job-related issues (Cox, 1996; Walker, 1999).

Many of the traditional requirements for becoming a police officer have come under attack in the past 25 years. Realistically, a number of these requirements have been applied subjectively with the effect (if not the intent) of excluding females and minorities from police work. We have known several police officers who have advanced through the ranks of their respective departments who did not meet existing height requirements at the time of their initial employment. Yet, they were hired, while others who met these requirements were not. One police captain told us that he was measured with his boots on, while others were measured in bare feet. In short, height might exclude certain applicants, but if those responsible for hiring felt a certain individual would make a good police officer, the height requirement could be manipulated. As another example of subjectivity, agility tests at one time were set up in such fashion as to routinely exclude women. But these tests have since been shown to have little or no relationship to activities performed by police officers. Today, tests of physical agility must be based on job task analyses.

Psychological exams are generally considered unreliable (scores for the same individual are subject to considerable variation over time). In addition, analyzing scores of potential police officers often involves comparing the scores they obtain with an "ideal" profile. Because no one knows what the characteristics of an ideal police officer are, such testing seems highly questionable. Still, liability issues related to negligent hiring lead most police agencies to continue to require psychological exams.

Written tests vary tremendously in content and form. Some are job-related or situation-specific; others are general aptitude or intelligence tests. The validity of most of these tests in terms of predicting successful performance as a police officer is yet to be established.

Similarly, the oral board interview is extremely subjective. Although race, gender, dress, and the like are formally excluded from the criteria to be considered by the board in most jurisdictions, the authors, who have repeatedly served on such boards, note that these variables are frequently subjects of discussion among board members and undoubtedly influence the ratings received by applicants. Affirmative action programs have, in many locales, improved the chances that applicants will be selected without regard to race or gender, although informal pressures clearly counteract such programs in some areas.

As Gray (1975) and Falkenberg, Gaines, and Cox (1990) aptly point out, all these selection procedures may be used for covert as well as overt purposes. Overtly, the procedures are designed to fulfill the requirements of the formal police organization. Covertly, they may be used to satisfy the requirements of the police subculture. This subculture, or police fraternity, has developed over the years as the police and other citizens have increasingly come to view each other as "we" and "they." To the police, "we" consists of other police officers (members of the fraternity). These members are expected to be loyal to the police subculture, trustworthy, willing and able to use force, authoritarian, and so forth. "They" consists of everyone who is not a police officer, who cannot be regarded as loyal to the subculture, trustworthy, and so on. As one police officer recently put it, "We work in our little world that those outside don't understand." To some other citizens (members of racial minorities, for example), the police constitute the "they" group. This relationship between the police and other citizens is caused by, and helps maintain, a gap in communication.

At any rate, the requirements of the police subculture are often made known to police selection boards. As a result, most new recruits, though certainly not all, meet both formal and informal requirements for the job. Using the network approach, let us examine how these informal or subcultural requirements can influence hiring procedures even though the law may prohibit their consideration.

The authors are aware of several cases in which police chiefs, mayors, city managers, or council members have contacted selection board members informally to express their feelings concerning who should be hired to fill a police vacancy. In one case, a police chief indicated to the president of a selection board that he wanted no more college graduates hired because they were too intellectual and very likely to move to another department in a short time. In another, a chief of police informed two of the three board members that the department really needed a minority officer.

Informal suggestions or pressures such as these may, of course, be ignored by board members. Theoretically, they must be ignored because the applicant is to be rated on the formal qualifications discussed above, and, short of a consent decree agreement, there is no formal mechanism for adding or detracting rating points for reasons involving race, gender, or creed. Practically speaking, however, members of selection boards are often political appointees, appointed precisely because they are willing to listen to the desires of the police chief or police commissioner. The authors know of a case in which a college professor was appointed to a board of fire and police commissioners. His idea of the selection process was that applicants should be rated strictly on the basis of their qualifications, regardless of race, gender, or creed. He felt informal pressures should be prohibited or ignored, and refused to listen to those not on the board who tried to influence him. He was a rather persuasive fellow and was able to persuade one or both of the two more conservative board members to support him on some occasions. When he resigned from the board, several police officials confided they were not disappointed. Now, they said, someone who "understood the requirements of real police work" would be appointed and things would run more smoothly.

In some instances, particularly in the selection for upper ranks in police agencies, **assessment centers** are employed as a solution to some of the difficulties mentioned above. Assessment center personnel work on the basis of job task analyses to create job-related exercises. A team of independent assessors evaluates candidate performance on those exercises. The team facilitator then typically recommends one or more candidates to the mayor, city manager, and/or chief of police. The value of assessment centers rests on the accuracy of the job task analyses and the training of the assessors. There is some evidence that assessment centers, though costly, are better at predicting future on-the-job success for police officers than are paper-and-pencil tests (Pynes & Bernardin, 1992; Swanson, Territo & Taylor., 1998, 2004).

Applicants who successfully meet the requirements outlined above and are selected for police work generally go to a training institute or academy where they receive training in a subjects ranging from self-defense and weapons through first aid to criminal law and human relations. According to Magers & Klein (2002), "Nationally recognized standards for entry-level police academy training have not been established; therefore, police basic training standards dramatically vary from state to state" (p.103). As of 2000, the lowest number of training academy hours mandated was 320; the highest number of mandated hours was 1,118; and the mean number of training hours required of entry-level recruits was 516 (Magers & Klein, 2002, p. 108).

Successful completion of a training program leads to the status of **probationary officer**, a status that normally lasts from 6 to 24 months. During the probationary period, the new officer receives on-the-job training from senior officers and supervisors. If the recruit successfully completes the probationary period, he or she becomes a full-fledged police officer.

As we indicated earlier in this chapter, many of the criteria involved in the selection of police officers have been questioned. One area of controversy worthy of mention here is that of education. Do college-educated individuals make better police officers than non-college-educated individuals? Are certain types of college programs preferable to other types? Is level of education an important variable to consider when selecting police officers? If so, why do most municipal and county local police agencies still require a high school diploma or GED rather than some college as a condition of employment ?

In the past 100 years, there has been a cry for professional police. While training may help make the police more technically proficient, many believe the real hope for professionalism rests with education, since educational requirements are a basis for most highly regarded professions in our society (e.g., medicine, law, teaching). The issue of education is complicated by financial considerations. In an era of increasing concern over cost effectiveness, are the higher salaries required to hire and retain college-educated police officers justifiable? There is some evidence to indicate that college-educated officers are likely to have fewer citizen and disciplinary complaints filed against them than are non-college-educated officers (Kappeler, Sapp, & Carter, 1992; Roberg & Bonn, 2004; McFall, 2006; Mayo., 2006), and the emphasis on community policing would also seem to dictate the need for better-educated officers (Varricchio, 1998). The advent of community policing has caused many police departments to look for applicants who are more likely to be successful at solving problems and building community relationships and who are more service oriented as opposed to adventure oriented (Miller and Hess, 2008). Whether or not these differences are worth higher salaries and whether or not other differences, which have not yet been detected, exist are still areas of controversy. In addition, the issue of whether criminal justice or law enforcement college programs are more or less desirable than liberal arts programs remains unresolved. According to Roberg and Bonn (2004), only about 1 percent of police agencies currently require a college degree for entry level positions. The debate over the need for higher education in policing continues, with an emphasis on empirical research to help provide answers to questions concerning the necessity or desirability of advanced education for police officers.

Police Misconduct

No discussion of the police would be complete without considering police misconduct. In recent years, newspaper headlines dealing with alleged police misconduct have become all too common. Police performance has been subject to a good deal of moral controversy, partly because the police deal with moral issues on a regular basis, partly because their behavior has sometimes offended the moral sensitivities of observers. The police engage in discretionary behavior regularly, and other citizens must place a good deal of trust in their conduct with little in the way of assurances that their conduct is subject to adequate control (Cox, 1996; Cox, Campbell & McCamey, 2002, p. 4; Cuny, 2002, p. 9).

Police misconduct may be broadly divided into two categories: **corruption,** and physical and emotional abuse; these may be either organizational or individual in nature. Both categories include numerous subcategories, the categories often overlap, and both are violations of the ethical standards of police officers (Hyatt, 2001, p. 75). Applied specifically to police officers, ethical conduct is especially important because of the authority granted officers and because of the difficulty of overseeing the daily behavior of police officers on the street.

Police Corruption

In 1894 the Lexow Commission reported that corruption was systematic and pervasive in the New York City Police Department. The next 15 years found similar investigations and similar findings in almost every major American city (Bracey, 1989, p.175). Bribes from bootleggers made the 1920s a golden era for crooked police, and gambling syndicates in the 1950s were protected by a payoff system more elaborate than the Internal Revenue Service (Lacayo, 1993, p. 43). In 1971, Frank Serpico brought to light police corruption in New York City, and the Knapp Commission investigation which followed uncovered widespread corruption among officers of all ranks. Of particular importance was the identification of grass-eaters and meat-eaters by the Knapp Commission. **Grass-eaters** are police officers who accept graft when it is available but do not actively solicit the opportunity to obtain graft. **Meat-eaters** are police officers who are more widely involved in corruption and actively solicit the opportunity for personal financial gain (Knapp Commission on Police Corruption, 1972). One might believe that meat-eater police officers are a more serious problem than grass-eaters. They do commit more crimes, but the Knapp Commission concluded that the grass-eaters were a more significant problem. They outnumbered the meat-eaters by a significant number. In addition, their illegal activity created a "wall of silence" behind which the meat-eaters could operate with impunity (Roberg, Novak & Cordner, 2005). Barker (1996, 2006) expanded this typology and created three additional types of police officers. The "white knights" are totally honest officers and take an extreme stance on ethical issues. According to Roberg, Novak & Cordner (2005) these officers are in the minority and are not deviant. Next, the "straight-shooters" are honest but willing to overlook some of the indiscretions by fellow officers. Finally, rogues are considered an aberration even by the meat-eater police officers. Rogues engage directly in criminal activities and in high-visibility shakedowns of citizens. For example, in the 1980s, more than 30 officers in Philadelphia were convicted of taking part in a scheme to extort money from drug dealers. In Miami in the mid- 1980s, about 10 percent of the city's police were either jailed, fired, or disciplined in connection with a scheme in which officers robbed and sometimes killed cocaine smugglers on the Miami River, then resold the drugs. In 1993, 22 years after Serpico's disclosures in the same department, Michael Dowd and 15 to 20 other New York City police officers led "a parade of dirty cops who dealt drugs and beat innocent people [which] has shocked the city during seven days of corruption hearings" (Frankel, 1993b, p.3A; CNN Interactive, 1997).

Police corruption occurs when a police officer acts in a manner that places his or her personal gain ahead of duty, resulting in the violation of police procedures, criminal law, or both (Lynch, 1989). According to Barker and Carter (1986), "Corrupt acts contain three elements: (1) they are forbidden by some law, rule, regulation, or ethical standard; (2) they involve the misuse of the officer's position; and (3) they involve some actual or expected material reward or gain" (pp. 3–4).

Types of Police Corruption

It is difficult to estimate the proportion of police officers directly involved in corruption, but it is probably small. Still, the actual number of police officers involved nationwide is quite large, and these officers attract a good deal of negative attention when their corruption is made public. Although most police officers are not directly involved in corrupt activities, large numbers do appear to condone such activities by their failure to speak out or take action against corruption (Cox, 1996).

Barker and Carter (1986) identified a number of types of police corruption. Corruption of authority involves officially unauthorized gains by police officers that do not violate the law. Included here are things such as taking free liquor or meals, free entertainment admissions, police "discounts," free sex, and other free services. The difficulty with accepting such gratuities is that the officer never knows when the corruptor may expect or request special services or favors in return. This, of course, may never happen, but if it does, it places the officer who has accepted the gratuities in a difficult position, though he or she may certainly refuse to grant the requests. In addition, it becomes difficult to draw a line between such gratuities and other types of corrupt activities in terms of monetary value and violation of ethical standards.

Kickbacks constitute a second type of police corruption. Here, tow truck operators, lawyers, bondspeople, and others reward police officers who refer customers to them. The difficulties inherent in such referrals are obvious, but in some departments they, too, are condoned unless a public issue arises as a result.

A third type of corruption involves opportunistic theft from victims, crime scenes, and unprotected property. Shakedowns involve police officers who accept bribes for not making an arrest or writing a citation. While the officer may not actively seek such bribes, he or she may indicate a willingness to consider "other alternatives" offered by guilty parties.

Some police officers engage in protection of illegal activities for profit. They accept payments and/or services from those engaged in gambling, prostitution, drug sales, pornography, code violations, and other activities in return for doing nothing about such activities and sometimes for creating obstacles to investigations of these activities. Protecting the illegal behaviors often requires a good deal of organization. It does little good for one officer to look the other way when gambling occurs if his or her replacement for days off and vacations, or officers on other shifts, fails to protect the parties involved.

The fix involves quashing prosecution following arrest or taking care of tickets for profit. Police actions here may range from failure to show up in court when testimony is required to losing tickets, to perjury. Direct criminal activities include burglary, robbery, battery, intimidation, and other clearly criminal actions committed by officers. Finally, internal payoffs involve one police officer paying another (typically a superior officer) fees for assignments of particular types, promotions, days off, and so on. Although one type of corruption does not necessarily lead to another, where one finds more serious types of corruption, one is also likely to find most of the less serious types.

Police corruption has been recognized as a problem in this country for at least 100 years, and various reform movements and departmental programs to reduce or eliminate corruption have been attempted. Why, then, does police corruption remain problematic? The answer seems to lie, in part at least, in the relationship between the police and the larger society. It has been said that the police are a reflection of the society or community they serve, and this is nowhere more true than with respect to police corruption. If other citizens stopped offering bribes, free services, and other gratuities, and started reporting all police attempts to benefit in unauthorized fashion from their positions, it would be very difficult for corrupt police officers to survive.

Physical and Emotional Abuse

In 1991, the world watched as a home videotape of Los Angeles police officers beating Rodney King was repeated dozens of times on major news networks. In 1993, two Detroit police officers were sentenced to prison for beating to death motorist Malice Green (Ferguson, 1993). Similar incidents occurred during the same time period in New York City, Atlanta, Washington, DC, and Denver. In 1997, Abner Louima was brutally tortured by a New York City police officer who was later sentenced to 30 years in prison for the act (Frey, 2001, p.232; Walker & Katz, 2008).

Police misconduct is not limited to corrupt activities, but includes **perjury** (lying under oath), **emotional abuse** (psychological harassment), **physical abuse** (the use of unnecessary or excessive force), and murder, as well. To some extent, perjury and other forms of unauthorized deception serve as links between corruption and other forms of misconduct. What is the difference, for example, between a police officer who commits perjury to fix a ticket in return for payment from the defendant and one who commits perjury to cover up having used physical force unnecessarily against a defendant? How does one draw the line between lying to informants and drug dealers and deceiving one's superiors? Once perjury and deception gain a foothold, they tend to spread to other officers and to other types of situations until, in some cases, the entire justice system becomes a sham. This is the case, for instance, when police officers perjure themselves in criminal cases in which the defendant is also committing perjury, where the respective attorneys know that perjury is occurring, and where the judge knows that none of the parties is being completely honest. The outcomes of such cases seem to ride on who told the most believable lie, or the last lie. The overall impact is to increase the amount of suspicion and distrust of the justice system among all parties, which is certainly not the desired end product if we wish citizens to participate in and believe in the system. It is difficult for citizens to believe in the system in cases where police misconduct has occurred and the officers involved are trying to cover up the misconduct.

Police officers who stop other citizens without probable cause and/or harass them, and police officers who use force unnecessarily, must attempt to justify their actions or face relatively severe sanctions. As indicated previously, police officers, like those in other occupational groups, sometimes employ stereotypes and divide the world into "we" and "they," or insiders versus outsiders. Those who are perceived as outsiders are often labeled, and occasionally these labels are used openly to refer to the members of groups so designated. The use of racial slurs is but one example of the kind of harassment under consideration. Other special categories and labels are created for particular types of deviants, for example, drug dealers, homosexuals, prostitutes, and protestors. The police, of course, are supposed to represent all other citizens, regardless of race, creed, nationality, gender, sexual orientation, or political beliefs. When they use dehumanizing terms or harass others, the impression may be that since they represent government, they are expressing the attitudes of those who govern, though in fact they may be expressing personal dislikes, contempt, or hostility.

Members of minority groups, particularly in high-crime areas, report that psychological and emotional abuse is a routine part of encounters with the police. Although his study is now dated, Reiss (1968) provides information concerning the incidence of police psychological mistreatment of other citizens:

> What citizens object to and call "police brutality" is really the judgment that they have not been treated with the full rights and dignity owing citizens in a democratic society. Any practice that degrades their status, that restricts their freedom, that annoys or harasses them, or that uses physical force is frequently seen as unnecessary and unwarranted. More often than not, they are probably right. (pp. 59–60).

It is clear, then, that what constitutes police brutality is, at least in part, a matter of definition, and that police definitions and those of other citizens may not always be the same. What some segments of the public see as police harassment or brutality, the police are likely to view as aggressive policing, necessary for their survival on the streets as well as for maintaining some degree of order and crime control. Is a police officer in a high-crime area where many residents are known to carry deadly weapons harassing a citizen when he or she approaches cautiously, pats the citizen down for weapons, appears suspicious, and calls another officer for backup?

What is clear is that the perception that such incidents occur is widespread, especially in minority communities in cities of all sizes across the country (Lersch, 1999). For example one out of every four police officers in an Illinois survey (26.2 percent) and one in six officers in an Ohio survey indicated that they had witnessed racial harassment by their fellow police officers (Crank, 1998). Perception becomes the reality for those involved, whether or not the perception is grounded in reality. The perception creates hostility and resentment on behalf of some citizens, who view themselves as particularly likely to be victims of harassment and brutality, and on behalf of the police, who view themselves as particularly likely to be harassed, challenged, and criticized by certain segments of the population.

In spite of these misgivings on both sides, the vast majority of police encounters with other citizens continue to be carried off without physical brutality on the part of either party. This observation holds true with respect to police misconduct in general. Although there have been improvements, the police are not, and likely never will be, perfect, as the incidents described above clearly indicate. Still, through recruitment and retention of police officers who understand the importance of ethics and personal integrity, and by providing them with appropriate laws, training, resources, public support, and role models, we can minimize the likelihood of their misconduct.

Noble Cause Corruption

One final type of corruption, which overlaps many of the different categories discussed above, must be noted. **Noble cause corruption** involves the argument that illegal actions may be justified by the fact that the public good will ultimately be served by such actions. For example, use of illegal wiretaps may be employed when there is insufficient probable cause to obtain a warrant for the wiretap. The fact that the wiretap ultimately resulted in discovery of a criminal conspiracy is then used to argue that had the police not used the illegal wiretap, the conspirators would never have been caught. Similarly, use of torture by government agents may be justified on the basis of the fact that information obtained through such torture ultimately resulted in saving the life of a victim of a crime. However, as Delattre (2002, pp. 185–186) notes:

> Yet in law enforcement as well as other national affairs, we are driven to the question whether illegal actions that violate the rights of citizens are ever morally right or excusable. I call that the question of 'noble cause' corruption. Are police ever justified, or do they ever deserve to be excused, in breaking fundamental laws, not for personal gain, but for a purpose that appeals to our basic moral sensibilities? ... since ends do not necessarily justify means, a good end cannot justify a means in a context that makes it wrong and evil.... where civilizing law does have a hold, as in America, violations of fundamental civil liberties and laws, violations of oaths of office, abuses of authority and

power—all betrayals of the public trust—area wrong and cannot be justified by any end.

Private or Contract Police

Across the United States the number of people living in townhouses, condominiums, gated communities, as well as those visiting and doing business in shopping malls, concert halls, sports arenas, banks, transportation hubs, and many other places are protected by private and public police officers. According to Cronkhite (2001, p. 10), there are at least as many private as public police officers. This raises concerns about the standards which govern such police personnel and the relationship between private and public police. In general, **private police** operate in relative freedom compared to their public counterparts and governing standards differ dramatically from one state or agency to the next (Joh, 2004). Others, like Sklansky (2006) have questioned the ramifications of privatized policing for American democracy—do those with wealth and power deserve more or better protection than those with less? Whatever the answers to current questions concerning private police, it appears that they will play an increasingly important role in our society. Cooperation between private and public policing appears to be essential for the benefit of all concerned.

Summary

1. The evolution from the watch and ward system to the notion of protect and serve occurred over several centuries in both England and America.

2. Increasing public concern over crime, rapidly growing population, urbanization, and industrialization led to the development of the Metropolitan Police in London in 1829.

3. The territorial strategy of the London police was adopted by most American cities by the end of the nineteenth century.

4. By the mid-twentieth century, technological advances (telephone, radio, automobile) led to the belief that crime would soon be controllable. However, increasing numbers of calls for service and the adaptability of offenders placed serious strains on police resources. Additionally, the tremendous variety of services demanded by the public (and often promised by the police) made it difficult for the police to meet public expectations.

5. The role of the police has become increasingly multifaceted, including provision of a variety of services in order maintenance and law enforcement. The police have attempted to provide these services by offering better training to officers and by encouraging officers to seek advanced education.

6. Still, in the 1960s the professional image of the police suffered serious setbacks as the result of racial disturbances in urban areas, almost all of which were triggered by police encounters with minority citizens.

7. The emphases on fighting crime, handling incidents, and providing a plethora of other services eventually led the police to recognize that they could not meet all expectations by themselves. The result was a movement toward problem-oriented and community-oriented policing (actually representing a return to many of the principles of the original London Metropolitan Police Act).

8. Community policing represents an attempt to formalize relationships among the police, the public, and other social and public service agencies in the pursuit of improved quality of life in the community. These approaches require both philosophical and organizational changes in policing to consistently address the problems underlying the symptoms the police have traditionally attempted to treat. The success of these approaches is yet to be determined, but they clearly illustrate the importance of the network concept in criminal justice.

9. In an attempt to meet public expectations and legal requirements, police selection and training procedures are constantly being modified. Although selection procedures leave much to be desired, innovations such as the use of assessment centers show promise as better predictors of successful job performance than more traditional paper-and-pencil tests. Recruits selected are expected to be mentally and physically fit, of reasonably good character, and able to fit into the police subculture.

10. Formal basic training is required for virtually all full-time law enforcement officers, and the training is becoming increasingly comprehensive in nature. Once training at an academy or institute has been completed, the new officer goes through a probationary period and she or he is regularly evaluated during this period by senior and supervisory officers.

11. The need for education, once assumed to be a prerequisite for professionalization, is currently being reevaluated; further research is needed in this area, especially as community policing becomes more widespread. In the meantime, an increasing number of police departments require at least some college education as a condition of initial employment.

12. In this chapter, we have discussed both traditional, paramilitary police organizations and some of the more recent changes in these organizations. Attempts are being made to solve problems caused by centralization — rigidity, single promotional channels, and the chain of command — by decentralizing, offering dual career programs, and placing less emphasis on authoritarianism. Additionally, strategies such as community policing to improve cooperation and communication between the police and the public are being implemented.

13. The effectiveness of routine patrol has been rethought, and more realistic alternatives (such as split patrol and targeted or directed patrol) are being tried. Many of the traditional requirements for entry-level police officers have been revised to meet legal (EEOA, ADA) guidelines, and increasing numbers of women and minorities are being employed as police officers.

14. Police misconduct, including corruption and emotional and physical abuse, have been and remain problematic for the police. From acceptance of gratuities through participation in criminal activities, an unknown number of police officers attempt to gain unauthorized rewards while compromising the integrity of their positions. Other

officers feel compelled to harass [those with whom they come in contact] either psychologically or physically.

15. Although most officers refrain from engaging in either type of misconduct, many fail to take the necessary steps to bring corruption and brutality to a halt. These activities often involve other components of the criminal justice network when they result in perjury.

16. Both the public and police administrators could greatly reduce the incidence of police misconduct by taking it seriously and removing those involved in misconduct from the ranks of the police.

17. Cooperation between private and public police must improve as the former increase in numbers in coming years.

Key Terms Defined

social control The process of persuading persons or groups to conform to group expectations.

community policing A philosophy of policing in which police officers are assigned to specific geographic areas to form partnerships with neighborhood residents to solve problems and improve the quality of life for all concerned.

SARA process A model in problem-oriented policing that uses scanning, analysis, response, and assessment to address problems.

due process A concept of justice designed to ensure the rights of individuals as guaranteed by the Constitution and that various court decisions are enforced.

crime control A concept of justice emphasizing the importance of factual guilt and minimizing the importance of legal guilt or due process.

arrest The process of taking an individual into official custody.

booking The recording of facts about a person's arrest, including fingerprinting, inventorying personal property, and photographing.

chain of evidence A method of preserving evidence in such a way that it can be accurately accounted for from the time it is seized until the time its usefulness has been determined (generally, in court).

mediation and negotiation Processes used by police officers in the interest of order maintenance in their attempts to settle disputes between parties.

directed patrol Patrol that focuses on specific areas, as opposed to routine, nonspecific patrol.

split-force policing Patrol strategy based on the use of saturation patrols, both overt calls and covert, in high-risk areas as well as designating other officers for routine patrol in those areas.

accreditation Acknowledgement of compliance by a police agency with a set of nationally recognized standards established and evaluated by professional police organizations.

Peace Officer Standards and Training (POST) boards Licensing boards for police officers.

assessment centers Selection process based on job task analyses and conducted by independent assessors who are specially trained to evaluate performance.

probationary officer A person who has successfully completed all the requirements for being a police officer and is obtaining on-the-job training (generally, for 6 to 18 months) while being evaluated in terms of potential for becoming a full-fledged police officer.

corruption Acting in a manner that places unauthorized personal gain ahead of duty, resulting in violation, of police procedures and/or criminal law.

grass-eaters Police officers who accept graft when it is available but do not solicit.

meat-eaters Police officers who actively solicit corruption for personal gain.

perjury Lying under oath.

emotional abuse Psychological harassment.

physical abuse The use of unnecessary or excessive force.

noble cause corruption Involves the argument that illegal actions may be justified by the fact that the public good will ultimately be served by such actions.

private or contract police Police personnel employed by private corporations.

Critical Thinking Exercises

1. It has been said that the police and the public are, or should be, one. What historical basis for this statement can you find? What contemporary basis? Can the police successfully perform their functions without the support of the public?

2. Are the terms "law enforcement" and "policing" synonymous? If not, in what ways are they different?

3. Discuss the concept of community policing. How is it related to problem-oriented policing? How does it illustrate the concept of the network approach to criminal justice?

Internet Exercises

A number of organizations provide support for law enforcement. Among these are the International Association of Chiefs of Police (IACP) and the Commission on Accreditation for Law Enforcement Agencies (CALEA).

1. Locate the website for CALEA at http://www.calea.org. What are some of the recent developments with accreditation discussed on the website?

2. Go to: http://www.theiacp.org/

   a. What are some of the types of training offered through the IACP? (International Association of Chiefs of Police)

b. Would you be able to search for a job in law enforcement using this site?

c. Could you learn about some of the latest law enforcement technology by using a link from this source? How?

References

Anonymous. (2005a). Does Community Policing Work? *Police, 29* (12), 40.

Anonymous. (2005b, Winter). Law enforcement uses cable tv as marketing tool. *Community Links,* 13.

Anonymous. (2006). Denver volunteers aid police investigations. *Crime Control Digest, 40*(8), 3-5.

Barber, R. R. (1996). Neighborhood service team. *FBI Law Enforcement Bulletin, 65* (1), 17–22.

Barker, T. & Carter, D. L. (1986). *Police deviance.* Cincinnati. Pilgrimage.

Barker, T. (1996). *Police ethics: Crisis in law enforcement.* Springfield, IL: Charles Thomas.

Publishers. In Roberg, R, Novak, K. & Cordner G. (2005). *Police and society.* Los Angeles, CA: Roxbury Publishing Company.

_____(2006). Police ethics. *Crisis in law enforcement.* Springfield, IL: Charles Thomas.

Barlow, H. D. (2000). *Criminal justice in America.* Upper Saddle River, NJ: Prentice Hall.

Bolton, K. B. Jr. (2003). Shared perceptions: Black officers discuss continuing barriers in policing. *Policing,* 26 (3), 386–400.

Bracey, D. H. (1989). Proactive measures against police corruption: Yesterday's solutions, today's problems. *Police Studies,* 12 (24), 175–179.

Brown, R. A. & Frank, J. (2006). Race and officer decision making: Examining differences inarrest outcomes between black and white officers. *Justice Quarterly, 23* (1), 96–127.

Campbell, L. P. (1991 March 24). Police brutality triggers many complaints, little data. *Chicago Tribune,* p.10.

CNN Interactive (1997). Serpico resurrects his decades-old criticism of NYPD. Available online at: http://www.cnn.com/US/9709/23/serpico.brutality/.

Commission on Accreditation for Law Enforcement Agencies. (2005, October). *Update.* Available online at: http://www.calea.org/Online/newsletter/No87/87index.htm.

Commission on Accreditation for Law Enforcement Agencies. (2007). *News Release.* Available online at http://www.calea.org/Online/NewsRelease/newsrelease0308 2007.htm.

Conser, J. A., & Russell, G. D. (2000). *Law enforcement in the United States.* Gaithersburg, MD: Aspen.

Cordner, G. & Bieble, E. B. (2005). Problem-oriented policing in practice. *Criminology & Public Policy, 4* (2), 155–181.

Couret, C. (1999). Police and technology: The silent partnership. *American City & County, 114* (9), 31–32.

Cox, S. M. (1996). *Police: Practices, perspectives, problems.* Boston: Allyn & Bacon.

Cox, S. M., Campbell, T. G. & McCamey, W. P. (2002). Doing the right thing: Why a few police officers find it so difficult. *Illinois Law Enforcement Executive Forum, 2* (2), 1–7.

Crank, J. (1998). *Understanding police culture.* Cincinnati: Anderson Publishing Company. In Roberg, R., Novak, K. & Cordner, G. (2005). *Police and society.* Los Angeles, CA: Roxbury Publishing Company.

Cronkhite, C. L. (2001). American criminal justice trends for the 21st century. *Crime and Justice, 16*, 9–35.

Cunningham, L. (1999). Taking on testilying: The prosecutor's response to in-court police deception. *Criminal Justice Ethics, 18* (1), 26–40.

Cuny, D. (2002). Ensuring police ethics: Issues and best practices. *Illinois Law Enforcement Executive Forum, 2* (2), 9–26.

Davis, E. M. (1978). *Staff one: A perspective on effective police management.* Englewood Cliffs, NJ: Prentice Hall.

Delattre, E. J. (2002). *Character and cops* (4th ed.). Washington, D. C.: The AEI Press.

Duff, H. W. Jr. (2006). Concerned Reliable Citizens' Program. *FBI Law Enforcement Bulletin, 75* (8), 8–11.

Eck, J. E., & Rosenbaum, D. P. (1994). The new police order: Effectiveness, equity, and efficiency in community policing. In D. P. Rosenbaum (Ed.). *The challenge of community policing: Testing the promises* (pp. 3–23). Thousand Oaks, CA: Sage.

Falkenberg, S., Gaines, L. K., & Cox, T. C. (1990). The oral interview board: What does it measure? *Journal of Police Science and Administration, 17* (1), 32–39.

FBI National Press Office. (1999, July 15). *NCIC 2000 begins operation.* Washington, DC: Federal Bureau of Investigation: http://www.fbi.gov/pressrm/pressrel/ncic 2000.htm.

Ferguson, C. (1993, October 13). Cops get long terms for beating. *USA Today*, p.1A.

Fischer, R. J, & Green, G. (1998). *Introduction to security* (6th ed.) Boston: Butterworth-Heineman.

Frankel, B. (1993a, September 30). You'll be in the fold by breaking the law. *USA Today*, p.1A.

Frankel, B. (1993b, October 7) For NYC Cops, license for crime. *USA Today*, p.3A.

Frey, R. G. (2001). The Abner Louima case: Idiosyncratic personal crime or symptomatic police brutality? In M. J. Palmiotto (Ed.). *Police misconduct: A reader for the 21st century* (pp. 232–41). Upper Saddle River, NJ: Prentice Hall.

Gaines, L. K., Kappeler, V. E., & Vaughn, J. B. (1994). *Policing in America.* Cincinnati: Anderson.

Glensor, R. W., Correia, M. E., & Peak, K. J. (Eds.). (2000). *Policing communities: Understanding crime and solving problems.* Los Angeles: Roxbury.

Goldstein, H. (1990). *Problem-oriented policing.* New York: McGraw-Hill.

Gray, T. C. (1975). Selecting for a police subculture. In J. H. Skolnick & T. C. Gray (Eds.). *Police in America.* Boston: Little Brown.

Green, D. (2003). *Changes in policing. Law & Order.* Available online at: Proquest (340532111) http://proquest.umi.com/pqdweb?did=340532111&sid=1&Fmt=4 &clientId=3480& RQT=309&VName=PQD.

Hyatt, W. D. (2001). Parameters of police misconduct: In M. J. Palmiotto (Ed.) *Police misconduct: A reader for the 21st century* (pp.75–99). Upper Saddle River, NJ: Prentice Hall.

Joh, E. E. (2004). The paradox of private policing. *Journal of Criminal law & Criminology, 95,* (1), 49–138.

Johnson, D. R. (1981). *American law enforcement: A history.* St. Louis: Forum Press.

Kappeler, V. E., Sapp, A. D., & Carter, D. L. (1992). Police officer higher education, citizen complaints, and departmental rule violations. *American Journal of the Police, 11* (2), 37–54.

Kelling, G. L., Pate, T., Dieckman, D. & Brown, C. (1974). *The Kansas City preventive patrol experiment: A summary report.* Washington, DC: Police Foundation.

Kerlikowske, R. G. (2004). The end of community policing: Remembering the lessons learned. *FBI Law Enforcement Bulletin, 73*(4), 6–11.

Knapp Commission on Police Corruption (1972). *Report on police corruption.* New York: George Braziller. In Roberg, R., Novak, K. & Cordner, G. (2005). *Police and society.* Los Angeles, CA: Roxbury Publishing Company.

Lacayo, R. (1993, October 11). Cops and robbers. *Time,* 43–44.

Lersch, K. M. (1999). Police misconduct and minority citizens: Exploring key issues. *Justice Professional, 12* (1), 65–82.

Lurigo, A. J., & Rosenbaum, D. P. (1994). The impact of community policing on police personnel. In D. P. Rosenbaum (Ed.). *The challenge of community policing: Testing the promises* (pp.147–63). Thousand Oaks, CA: Sage.

Lurigo, A. J., & Skogan, W. G. (2000). Winning the hearts and minds of police officers: An assessment of perceptions of community policing in Chicago. In R. W. Glensor, M. E. Correia, & K. J. Peak (Eds.). *Policing communities: Understanding crime and solving problems* (pp. 246–56). Los Angeles: Roxbury.

Lynch, G. W. (1989). Police corruption from the United States perspective. *Police Studies, 12* (4), 165–170.

Magers, J. & Klein, L. (2002). Police basic training: A comparative study of states' standards in the United States. *Illinois Law Enforcement Executive Forum, 2,* (2), 103–113.

Maglione, R. (2002, March). Recruiting, retaining, and promoting women. *The Police Chief,* 19–24.

Mayo, L. *(2006).* College education and policing. *The Police Chief, 73,* (8), 20.

McCamey, W. P., Scaramella, G. L. & Cox, S. M. (2003). *Contemporary municipal policing.* Boston, MA: Allyn & Bacon.

McFall, E. (2006). Changing profession requires new level of education. *The Police Chief, 73*(10), 45.

Miller, L.S. & Hess, K. M. (2008). *Community policing: Partnership for problem solving* 5th ed. Belmont, CA: Thomson Higher Education. *Miranda v. Arizona,* 384 U.S. 436 (1966).

Palmiotto, M. J. (2001). *Police misconduct: A reader for the 21st century.* Upper Saddle River, NJ: Prentice Hall.

Pynes, J., & Bernardin, H. J. (1992). Entry-level police selection: The assessment center as an alternative. *Journal of Criminal Justice, 20* (1), 41–52.

Reaves, B., & Goldberg, A. L. (1999). *Law enforcement management and administrative statistics, 1997: Data for individual state and local agencies with 100 or more officers.* Washington, DC: U.S. Department of Justice.

Reiss, A. J. (1968). Police brutality ... Answers to key questions. In M. Lipsky (Ed.) *Police encounters.* (pp. 57–83) Chicago: Aldine.

Renauer, B. C. (2007). Is neighborhood policing related to informal social control? *Policing, 30* (1), 61.

Report of the National Advisory Commission on Civil Disorders. (1968). New York: Bantam Books.

Richardson, J. F. (1974). *Urban police in the United States.* Port Washington, NY: Kennikat Press.

Roberg, R. & Bonn, S. (2004). Higher education and policing: where are we now? *Policing, 27*(4), 469.

Roberg, R., Novak, K. & Cordner, G. (2005). *Police and society.*(3rd. ed.) Los Angeles, CA: Roxbury Publishing Company.

Roh, S. & Oliver, W. M. (2005). Effects of community policing upon fear of crime: Understanding the causal linkage. *Policing, 28* (4), 670–684.

Rosenbaum, D. P. (2000). The changing role of the police. In R. W. Glensor, M. E. Correia, & K. J. Peak (Eds.). *Policing communities: Understanding crime and solving problems* (pp. 46–66). Los Angeles: Roxbury.

Rubinstein, J. (1973). *City police.* New York: Farrar, Straus and Giroux.

Schulz, D. M. (2002, March). Law enforcement leaders: A survey of women police chiefs in the United States. *The Police Chief,* 25–28.

Scrivner, E. (2004). The impact of September 11 on community policing. In Fridell, L. & Wycoff, M.A. (Eds.). *Commuity policing: The past, present, and future.* Washington, DC: Police Executive Research Forum.

Sklansky, D. A. (2006). Private police and democracy. *The American Criminal Law Review, 43* (1), 89–106.

Smith, B. W., Novak, K. J., & Frank, J. (2005). Explaining police officer discretionary activity. *Criminal Justice Review, 30* (3), 325.

Sun, I. Y. (2003). Police officers' attitudes toward their role and work: A comparison of black and white officers. *American Journal of Criminal Justice, 28* (1), 89–109.

Swanson, C. R., Territo, L. & Taylor, R. W. (2004,). *Police administration: Structures, processes, and behavior.* (6th ed.) Upper Saddle River: Prentice Hall.

Uchida, C. D. (2001). The development of the American police: An historical overview. In R. G. Dunham & G. P. Alpert (Eds.). *Critical issues in policing: Contemporary readings* (pp.18–35), Prospect Heights, The Waveland Press.

Varricchio, D. (1998). Continuing education: Expanding opportunities for officers. *FBI Law Enforcement Bulletin, 67* (4), 10–14.

Walker, S. & Katz (1999). *The police in America: An introduction* (3rd ed.). Boston: McGraw-Hill.

_____(2008). *The police in America: An introduction.* (6th ed.). Boston: McGraw-Hill.

Weisel, D. L., & Eck, J. E. (2000). Toward a practical approach to organizational change. In R. W. Glensor, M. E. Corriea, & K. J. Peak (Eds.) *Policing communities: Understanding and solving problems* (pp. 257–71). Los Angeles: Roxbury.

Zhao, J., He, N., & Lovrich, N. P. (2003). Community policing: Did it change the basic functions of policing in the 1990s? A national follow-up study. *Justice Quarterly, 20* (4), 697.

Selected Readings

Brown, R. A. & Frank, J. (2006). Race and officer decision making: Examining differences in arrest outcomes between black and white officers. *Justice Quarterly, 23* (1), 96–127.

Cox, S. M., Campbell, T. G. & McCamey, W. P. (2002). Doing the right thing: Why a few police officers find it so difficult. *Illinois Law Enforcement Executive Forum, 2* (2), 1–7.

Delattre, E. J. (2002). *Character and cops.* (4th ed.). Washington, D. C.: The AEI Press.

Glensor, R. W., Correia, M. E., & Peak, K. J. (Eds.). (2000). *Policing communities: Understanding crime and solving problems.* Los Angeles: Roxbury.

Jones, L. D. (2003). Matrons to chiefs in one short century: The transition of women in U. S. law enforcement. *Women Police, 37* (2), 6.

Krimmel, J. T. & Gormley, P. E. (2003). Tokenism and job satisfaction for policewomen. *American Journal of Criminal Justice, 28* (1), 73–89.

Moore, M. M. (2002, March). How effectively does your police agency recruit and retain women? *The Police Chief,* 29.

Sklansky, D. A. (2006). Private police and democracy. *The American Criminal Law Review, 43* (1), 89–106.

Skolnick, J. H. (1994). *Justice without trial: Law enforcement in democratic society* (3rd ed.). New York: Macmillan.

Stevens, D. J. (2001). *Case studies in community policing.* Upper Saddle River, NJ: Prentice Hall.

Sun, I. Y. (2003). Police officers' attitudes toward their role and work: A comparison of black and white officers. *American Journal of Criminal Justice, 28* (1), 89–109.

Walker, S. & Katz, C. (2008). *The police in America: An introduction* (6th. ed.). Boston: McGraw-Hill.

Chapter Seven

The Courts and Court Personnel

It is the spirit and not the form of law that keeps justice alive.

Earl Warren

People who love sausage and people who believe in justice should never watch either of them being made.

Otto Bismark

Justice is incidental to law and order.

John Edgar Hoover

Justice maybe blind, but she has very sophisticated listening devices.

Edgar Argo

Quotations about Justice. (2007). The Quote Garden.
Available online at: http://www.quotegarden.com/justice.html

Key Terms

jurisdiction
venue
stare decisis
precedent
lower courts
magistrates
trial courts
de novo

circuit courts

appellate courts

state supreme court

magistrate judge

district courts

en banc

Uniform Code of Military Justice

U.S. Supreme Court

writ of certiorari

Rule of Four

speedy trial

dispute resolution programs

independent counsels

prosecutor (state's attorney, district attorney, prosecuting attorney)

information

public defenders

defense counsel

adversary system

judge

probation officers

court managers

chief judges

clerk of the court

court administrators

Chapter Outline

Courts
    Basic Concepts
    The Court Systems
    State Court Systems
    The Federal Court System
The Sixth Amendment and Speedy Trials
Court Personnel
    The Prosecutor
    Defense Counsel
    The Relationship between the Prosecutor and Defense Counsel
    The Judge
    The Probation Officer
Managing the Courts
    Chief Judges
    Court Clerks
    Court Administrators

The United States Supreme Court building. Reprinted with permission of iStockphoto.com / Visual Field.

Courts

In the previous chapter, we discussed the front line of the criminal justice network: the police. In this chapter, we focus our attention on another component; namely, the court system. The basic function of the court is to determine the legal outcome of a dispute. In the criminal justice network, this process usually involves the determination of guilt or innocence of one accused of a criminal violation. Disputes in civil matters often concern the determination of monetary damages, custody of children, and injunctions against certain business practices, to name only a few.

Although the determination of guilt or innocence is central to the function of the criminal court, it is by no means the only function. The court is also responsible for determining bail, conducting preliminary hearings, ruling on the admissibility of evidence, and determining the appropriate sentence when a finding of guilty has been reached.

One of the major responsibilities of the court is to provide impartiality to the criminal justice network. This goal is to be achieved by using neutral bodies as decision makers (judges and juries) and by allowing both parties — the prosecution and the defense — to present their arguments in open court. The court operates under formal rules of procedure to guarantee objectivity. For example, there are limitations as to how evidence may be introduced, what types of evidence may be admitted, and what types of questions may be asked. Questions that are clearly leading are generally not allowed, evidence that was obtained illegally is inadmissible, and evidence admitted must be material (i.e., it must relate to a relevant issue in the case in terms of the charges against the accused). The procedures often evolve from interpretations and are subject to be challenged in the future.

The court system is not a new phenomenon, although methods of trial have varied greatly throughout history. Some techniques that have been used are trial by ordeal (in which the accused had to withstand some physical ordeal, such as walking through heated plowshares blindfolded) and trial by battle (in which the defendant challenged his or her accuser to combat, the outcome of which determined the outcome of the case).

Today, we employ a more formalized system of presenting evidence, both physical and testimonial, in a court, following a strict procedural format. Although historically the courts and court personnel have been held in high esteem, criticism and scrutiny of this branch of the criminal justice network have increased considerably in recent years. Many blame the courts for allowing too many defendants to go free or for issuing sentences that appear exceptionally lenient. Others blame the courts for overcrowding the prisons by sentencing too many defendants to incarceration. One of the major complaints is that the court process is very slow, frequently delaying trials for long periods of time for various reasons. More recently, critics have charged that cases have been tried in the media by allowing television crews in the courtroom. In this chapter, we provide a general overview of the court systems, both federal and state, in the United States. We begin by looking at some basic concepts.

Basic Concepts

One of the most fundamental concepts concerning the court system is that of **jurisdiction**, or the authority or power to hear a case. No court in the land has unlimited jurisdiction. Even the U.S. Supreme Court is restricted to hearing specific kinds of cases (discussed later in this chapter).

As a general rule, a distinction is made between courts possessing general jurisdiction and those with specific, or limited, jurisdiction. A court of general jurisdiction has the power to hear a variety of cases. For example, many county or district courts hear both criminal and civil cases involving such issues as murder, probate, divorce, and suits for monetary damages. Courts with specific, or limited, jurisdiction can hear only a narrow range of cases. The juvenile court can hear only cases involving youth in a specific age group; thus, it has a fairly limited jurisdiction. Also, some states maintain magistrate and/or police courts that are restricted to hearing cases carrying a narrowly defined punishment, usually petty offenses and some misdemeanors. Community courts, drug, mental health and family courts have recently been developed to address specific problems in the community. For example, community based courts relate to quality of life issues in the community such as prostitution, shoplifting, turnstile jumping and unlicensed vending (Sviridoff et. al., 2002). Drug courts were formed in recent years to address addiction, rehabilitation and trafficking issues. The highly addictive, easy to manufacture nature of methamphetamine resulted in the development of these limited jurisdiction courts (Huddleston, 2005).

A distinction is also made between courts of original jurisdiction and those with appellate jurisdiction. Original jurisdiction means the court is empowered to hear the case initially. Appellate jurisdiction means that a specific court can hear a defendant's appeal of conviction from the court of original jurisdiction. The power to hear cases is defined through statute, the Constitution, or previous court decisions.

A key related concept is that of **venue**, which is commonly referred to as the place of trial. Under normal conditions the trial will take place within the legally defined geographical area in which the alleged offense was committed. This may be on a municipal, county, or regional basis. Obviously, if you were charged with committing an offense in Los Angeles, California, you would be tried in that vicinity rather than in Dallas, Texas. It should be noted that the possibility to have a change of venue, or location of the trial, does exist. If the defendant can show that he or she cannot obtain a fair trial in the geographical jurisdiction of trial, a petition may be filed with the court to have the venue changed to a neutral jurisdiction. This is a matter not of right but of privilege. Generally, reasonable grounds for the requested change must accompany the petition. One of the more common grounds is that pretrial publicity about the crime or defendant(s) has biased potential jurors.

There are situations in which more than one court has jurisdiction. For example, when a federally insured bank is robbed, both the state in which the bank is located and the federal court system would have jurisdiction. These situations are often referred to as cases involving concurrent jurisdiction. An excellent example of concurrent jurisdiction is the Rodney King case. In that case, officers who used force to arrest Mr. King were first tried in California state court and found not guilty. The same defendants were later tried in federal court under civil rights statutes. As a practical matter, usually one court will waive (give up) jurisdiction, and the defendant will be tried in only one court. Cases in which only one court has jurisdiction are referred to as involving exclusive jurisdiction.

The terms stare decisis and precedent are also important in the understanding of the court system. **Stare decisis** means "let the decision stand." When a court issues a ruling on a matter of law, future cases should abide by or adhere to the **precedent** or legal rule set forth by the earlier case. Consider the following quote: "It is … a fundamental jurisprudential policy that prior applicable precedent usually must be followed even though the case, if considered anew, might be decided differently by the current justices. This policy … is based on the assumption that certainty, predictability and stability in the law are the major objectives of the legal system; i.e., that parties should be able to regulate their conduct and enter into relationships with reasonable assurance of the governing rules of law" (*Moradi-Shalai v. Fireman's Fund Insurance*, 1988). For example, if a court rules at one point in time that a defendant charged with a capital offense must be represented by counsel, then, as a rule of law, all future defendants in capital cases in that court must also be represented by counsel. Such decisions may be applied prospectively (only in subsequent cases) or retrospectively (to past cases as well). Most decisions are applied prospectively. Overturning a precedent is usually not an easy task. Chief Justice Roberts of the United States Supreme Court during confirmation hearings said, to overturn a precedent "… the Court would first have to consider a series of objective criteria, two of which stood out: whether a precedent fostered stability in the nation; and the extent to which society had come to rely on an earlier ruling, even a dubious one" (Walsh, 2005, p. 1).

As you can see, the concepts defined here are important in determining how and where the law will be enforced. A system without such formalized concepts and subsequent rules enforcing them would be chaotic and inconsistent.

The Court Systems

The United States has what is commonly called a dual court system. This system employs thousands of judges, court administrators, clerks, bailiffs, and other court personnel with an estimated budget in the billions of dollars. The federal court system hears cases involving violations of acts of Congress with separate court systems in the District of Columbia, Puerto Rico, the Virgin Islands, Guam, American Samoa, and the Northern Mariana Islands. In addition, state court systems hear cases concerning violations of state statutes. This dual system is a product of the Tenth Amendment to the U.S. Constitution. As we previously stated, there are circumstances in which a single act can violate both an act of Congress and a state statute (concurrent jurisdiction). In general, the role of the federal government in the criminal justice system is limited. It is estimated that 80 to 90 percent of all criminal cases will be heard in the state courts. However, the recent trend to federalize criminal law by expanding federal criminal jurisdiction beyond concerns with federal property and interstate commerce is having an impact on the number of criminal cases now heard in federal court.

State Court Systems

If one were asked to describe the state court system of the United States, the most definitive term used would have to be "variation." The states have considerable latitude in the organization of their court systems. Because no single system adequately depicts the systems of all 50 states, we encourage each student to examine his or her own state's statutes to obtain a better understanding of how the state court system is structured. What follows is a general overview of state court systems.

State court systems are divided into three levels: appellate courts, trial courts of general jurisdiction, and trial courts of lower jurisdiction (lower courts). These levels are arranged hierarchically.

Lower courts are usually courts of limited jurisdiction. They are empowered to hear only cases of a minor nature (e.g., traffic cases and misdemeanors) with lower levels of punishment. The lower court system is probably one of the most neglected areas of study in the criminal justice network even though most of the public's experience with the court system is at this level. There are about 13,500 such courts staffed by approximately 18,000 judicial officers in the United States (Neubauer, 2005, 2007). During 2003, state courts heard over 100 million disputes (Schauffler, Lafountain, Kauder, and Strickland, 2004). Most of these cases were traffic cases, however the authors noted an increase in caseloads related to criminal, civil, domestic relations, juvenile and traffic cases (Schauffler *et al.*, 2004). Attitudes about the courts and the criminal justice network in general are often based on experiences and impressions gained from lower courts.

The lower court system has been severely criticized for the way it processes cases. Most lower courts are characterized by an emphasis on speed and routinization. They are basically courts of assembly-line justice where one can answer a charge with a guilty plea and pay a standardized fine within a matter of minutes or even seconds. Some critics argue that lower courts serve as a system of sentencing rather than seeking truth.

The lower courts have also been criticized for neglecting constitutional procedures. Informality, rather than the rules of courtroom procedure, predominates (Neubauer, 2005, 2007). Sentences are often imposed with lightning speed and practices that would be condemned in higher courts are commonplace in lower courts (Neubauer, 2005, p. 425). In addition, lower courts are not courts of record; that is, they do not keep written records of proceedings unless requested by, and paid for by, defendants. Despite these criticisms, the lower court system fulfills an important function. Most court cases are heard in lower courts (perhaps up to 90 percent). If they were abolished, other courts would have to handle the cases now heard by the lower courts. Presently, many of the other courts have such overloaded dockets that there is a backlog of cases, and a considerable time gap exists between the act in question and the decision of the court. If we did not have a lower court system, the lag would increase, defendants would spend more time in jail, other criminal justice personnel would be overworked, and important cases might be overlooked or slighted in an effort to lessen the backlog. Despite the many criticisms of the lower system, it fulfills a necessary function, and its abolition without provisions for some alternative would result in grave consequences for the entire criminal justice network.

There have been many attempts to upgrade the lower court system. Historically, the lower court system was often staffed by justices of the peace. The justice of the peace system is still in existence today and consists of approximately 15,000 nonlawyers who often conduct court at their place of business (Neubauer, 2005, p. 428). Records are often ill kept, if they are kept at all, and many facilities depend on whatever the justices can afford. Justice of the peace courts have been held in living rooms, on front porches, and in the backs of stores (see "In the News" 7.1).

In the News 7.1

A Day in the Life: Justice of Peace well named

HOLLOWAY — The office of Justice of the Peace is well-named, at least in the way it is handled by Artie Cole.

Cole, justice of the peace for Ward 11, said a part of his responsibility is to "keep the peace" among his neighbors.

"When this job came open, people came to me and asked me to run. They said they wanted someone who would be fair," he said.

Being fair and following the law are probably the greatest attributes a JP can have, he said.

"A justice of the peace has a lot of power. He could hurt some people if he wanted to," Cole said.

But for Cole, "It's a way of giving back to the community."

He got a taste for the job by watching his uncle, Fred Redwine, serve as Ward 11 JP for 25 years.

"I remember watching him perform weddings and I thought to myself 'I can do that,'" said Cole who has held the job for 10 years.

For most of his day, however, Cole is an employee of Ferrellgas, a propane wholesale and retail company.

He is the operations manager for Ferrellgas in this area and has been with the company for 27 years.

Sitting in the Ferrellgas operations center on La. Highway 28, he takes telephone calls from a variety of customers and businesses.

He also receives calls from people needing help.

Cole can hold hearings in civil suits up to $3,500, preside over eviction hearings, write warrants for misdemeanor arrests, issue orders for sequestration and marry people in a hurry.

He holds court at 7 p.m. every Tuesday and Thursday.

"Most of the evictions that I deal with, the people know they're going to be evicted. The reason I have to follow through with the eviction, they are not going to leave until they are evicted," he said.

In many cases, the person being evicted doesn't even bother to show up for the hearing.

Cole recently opened court to hear the petition of eviction sought by Scott Nugent, a landlord whose tenant stopped paying rent after the first month. She did not appear at the hearing.

Cole approved the eviction petition for Nugent and explained that he could take the defendant's property as collateral against the debt. If after 30 days the tenant has not paid the debt, Nugent can sell the property to satisfy his claim or "put it in the road ditch."

"But you can't keep it," Cole said.

"I have a question about leaving it in the road ditch," Nugent said. "Can they get me for littering?"

Cole's answer? Not unless there are items that might blow around if left unsecured — because roadside disposal is provided for in the law.

Cole and Nugent were the only people present for the official proceedings, but there are times small room at the sheriff's substation at Holloway is filled and people are standing outside on the porch.

That's when Cole likes to have Constable Tony Paul present.

Paul, well over six feet tall, is a formidable presence and needs to say little to quiet a crowd, Cole said.

Then, there are the weddings, on riverbanks, boat docks, in houses, wherever they might be held.

"A lot of people don't know when they get a marriage license they have to wait three days (to get married)," Cole said. "That's why they come to me. I can waive the three days."

Morgan, R. (2007, May 20). A Day in the Life: Justice of Peace Well Named. *Alexandria Daily Town Talk*, p. 01E.

Currently, one of the more common lower-level court systems is the magistrate system. **Magistrates** are members of the bar who are either elected or appointed (depending on the jurisdiction). They are limited to hearing specific types of cases but are generally better qualified than their predecessors; they are familiar with constitutional guarantees and court procedures; and they can, and in some states are empowered to, perform other functions, such as issuing warrants and conducting bail hearings.

Some jurisdictions also have police courts and traffic courts, which are also known as municipal courts. These too are considered lower courts and are limited in their jurisdiction. Some of the problems commonly associated with justice of the peace courts also plague these lower courts.

The second level of the state court system consists of the **trial courts**, also known as district, superior, circuit, or county courts. These courts have general jurisdiction and hear both civil and criminal cases as well as appeals from lower courts in some jurisdictions. Trial courts are courts of fact because they are forums where a judge or jury listens to the facts presented in the case and determines whether the defendant is guilty or not guilty (Champion, Hartley, and Rabe, 2008).

The stereotyped image of the court often produced by the media, characterized by proper decorum, flowing orations, and extreme formality, is based primarily on the trial courts. Unlike cases in the limited courts where trials generally last a few minutes, cases heard in trial courts may run for days or, in some instances, weeks and months. Unlike the lower courts, trial courts are characterized by full-time court personnel, sophisticated methods of record keeping, the use of juries, more emphasis on formality, and the protection of constitutional guarantees. There is also a lesser degree of routinization in sentencing in the trial courts than in the lower courts.

Although the trial courts are courts of general jurisdiction, most of their cases are civil rather than criminal. Some jurisdictions maintain separate specialized trial courts to hear each type of case. Trial courts hear some 31 million civil and criminal cases annually (Neubauer, 2005, p.82) and over one million adult felons are convicted annually in these courts (Bureau of Justice Statistics, 2006b). In some jurisdictions trial courts hear appeals from the lower courts, but, as a practical matter, this occurs infrequently (less than 10 percent of the time) and does not generally tax the resources of the trial courts. If an appeal is heard from a lower court, it may be heard **de novo** (over again; anew) because many lower courts do not keep adequate records of their proceedings.

Trial courts are often organized on a county or a regional (multicounty) basis. Historically, trial courts were county courts. The county court system was to some extent impractical because many small counties could not afford to maintain their own courts and, before transportation was modernized, county inhabitants often encountered difficulty in traveling to the county seat. As a result of these and other factors (including greater emphasis on governmental efficiency), **circuit (or regional) courts** appeared. These courts may cover considerable geographical area and are characterized by the use of judges who move from courthouse to courthouse on either a scheduled or an as-needed basis.

The third level of the state court system consists of **appellate courts**, including the **state supreme court** and intermediate courts of appeals. The presence of intermediate courts of appeals is characteristic of the more largely populated states as a method of relieving the caseload of the state supreme court. It should be noted that 39 states maintain intermediate courts of appeals (ICAs) (Neubauer, 2005, p.85). Where such courts exist, they typically consist of three-judge panels and are usually organized on a regional, statewide, or multicounty, basis (one intermediate appellate court for a specific number of county or district courts). For most criminal appeals the intermediate courts of appeals must accept the case because the courts' jurisdiction is mandatory. Because intermediate courts of appeals have some discretion to decide whether to hear civil appeals, not all civil cases are necessarily accepted (Bureau of Justice Statistics, 2004). These courts are normally restricted to appellate jurisdiction; that is, they can only review cases based on trial records. In other words, appellate courts do not determine guilt in criminal cases or liability in civil cases, nor do they ensure that trial proceedings in lower courts are flawless. The primary function of the appellate court is to assess whether or not errors have been committed at trial (Bureau of Justice Statistics, 2004). In some jurisdictions, they are limited by law to hearing cases arising from specific lower courts or cases involving less than a specified dollar value. Again, as with cases in courts of general jurisdiction, most cases heard at this level are civil rather than criminal. In states that employ intermediate appellate courts, decisions are largely finalized at this level because very few cases are heard by the highest court.

At the top of the state court hierarchy we find the state supreme court, or, as it is referred to in some jurisdictions, the state judicial court or the supreme court of appeals. Like the United States Supreme Court, the state supreme court frequently exercises its discretion over the types of cases it chooses to hear. If the request to hear the case is denied by the state supreme court, the litigation is terminated and the ruling of the intermediate court of appeals stands (Bureau of Justice Statistics, 2004). In some states, death penalty cases are automatically reviewed by the state supreme court.

In cases requiring an interpretation of state statutes or the state constitution, the state supreme court has the final decision unless that statute or portion of the state constitution is inconsistent with the U.S. Constitution. State supreme courts are composed of three to nine judges who primarily hear civil cases and review cases on their record (by reviewing the transcripts). Additional powers they may possess include issuing judicial assignments, confirming the nomination of judges, and reviewing cases of alleged judicial misconduct.

There have been some attempts to simplify the administration of state courts by establishing a unified court system, which would shift local control to a centralized management structure. Such a shift would lead to centralized administration, rule making, and judicial budgeting as well as to statewide financing for the courts. This reform would limit the ability of lawyers to choose the court in which their cases are heard and would largely destroy local control of the courts.

The Federal Court System

The other branch of the dual court system is made up of the federal courts. These courts are empowered to hear both civil and criminal cases. The federal system consists of U.S. magistrate courts, U.S. district courts, U.S. courts of appeal, and the U.S. Supreme Court.

Congress created the position of U.S. **magistrate judge** in 1968. These judges are the equivalent of state trial court judges of limited jurisdiction and a subcomponent of the federal **district courts**. They are selected by district court judges and appointed for eight-year terms if full-time. Some part-time magistrate judges are appointed for four years. These judges perform a multitude of tasks, ranging from holding initial appearances in felony cases to setting bail to issuing warrants. They also handle a variety of civil matters and in general reduce the caseload of district court judges (Champion et. al, 2008 pp. 38–46; Neubauer, 2005, pp.52–74). The U.S. district courts were created by Congress in the Judicial Act of 1789. These 94 courts are the trial courts of the federal system. Each state has at least one, and some of the larger states have as many as four federal district courts, with the number of judges ranging from 2 to 28. The District of Columbia and U.S. territories maintain federal district courts as well. Judges in federal district courts are appointed by the president of the United States, with Senate confirmation, for life terms.

The federal district courts were created to lessen the demands on the U.S. Supreme Court. As we will see, the Supreme Court hears only a small portion of the cases it is asked to hear. By establishing the district courts to hear the actual cases, Congress has provided an alternative to the Supreme Court. In fact, the district courts hear about 400,000 civil and criminal cases annually, excluding misdemeanor and bankruptcy cases (Neubauer, 2005, p. 60).

The criminal jurisdiction of the U.S. district courts includes all cases where a federal criminal statute has been violated. Examples include kidnapping, the assassination or attempted assassination of the president, postal violations, violations of federal fish and game laws, and cases involving interstate transportation of stolen goods as well as interstate flight to avoid prosecution. The federal courts also maintain jurisdiction over cases where a constitutional question, such as search and seizure, is involved. Again, we should note that in some instances, concurrent jurisdiction might exist with a state court. The civil jurisdiction of the district courts is limited to suits in which (1) a federal question is raised; (2) the suit involves citizens of two or more separate states and the amount in controversy exceeds $75,000; (3) a citizen of one state sues another state; or (4) a prisoner petitions the court claiming that his or her rights under federal law are being violated.

Within the federal court system are intermediate appellate courts: the United States Court of Appeals for the Federal Circuit. Created in 1891, these courts were established to reduce the number of appeals made to the Supreme Court. Defendants have a right to appeal the decision from the federal district courts. Most, but not all, appeals from the federal trial courts will be heard at this level, and for most, the final decision will be rendered here.

Prior to 1949, these intermediate appellate courts were referred to as circuit courts of appeals. Today, the geographical division of circuits is maintained, but judges are not required to travel to various locations to hear cases as they did in the past. There are 12 regional circuits each of which has a court of appeals: 11 are composed of three or more states and one is for the federal circuit. Each circuit is identified by a number. Circuit courts are generally located in the larger metropolitan areas, and the appellant must travel to the location of the court to have his or her case heard.

Each court of appeals has at least 2 permanent judgeships; larger circuits have as many as 28. Judges are nominated by the President and confirmed by the United States Senate for life or good behavior. The Constitution sets forth no specific requirements for becoming a federal judge. However, members of Congress, who typically recommend potential nominees, and the Department of Justice, which reviews nominees' qualifications, have developed their own informal criteria (U.S. Courts, 2007). The most experienced judge who has not reached his or her sixty-fourth birthday will serve as chief judge of the circuit. In most instances, cases will be heard by three-judge panels, with two considered a quorum. In certain circumstances all judges will hear a case — a process called sitting **en banc**. A case heard en banc usually involves a constitutional issue and is worthy of input from a larger number of judges.

The courts of appeals maintain appellate jurisdiction and only review records of lower courts rather than retrying cases. These appellate courts review the records for interpretation and application of law (both statutory and constitutional) but do not generally decide issues of fact (i.e., whether a defendant was provided with counsel at required times or whether there was an error in admitting evidence or instructing the jury). The courts of appeals also review and enforce the decisions of 19 quasi-judicial tribunals, including the Food and Drug Administration and the National Labor Relations Board. Currently, over 66,000 cases are heard annually in U.S. courts of appeal (U.S. Courts, 2006a).

We should also briefly mention a number of specialized federal courts created by Congress. These courts hear only a limited range of cases and deal primarily with civil cases. Among the types of cases heard by these courts are tax disputes, patent disputes, and cases relating to the **Uniform Code of Military Justice** (laws governing individuals serving in the military).

The court of last resort for both the federal and the state systems is the **U.S. Supreme Court**, which is composed of nine judges, appointed by the President and confirmed by the Senate, who sit for life or good behavior (McGuire, 2005). They may be removed by impeachment or voluntary retirement. The President also appoints one of the judges as chief justice. The chief justice assumes administrative duties (e.g., assigning one of the judges to write the Court's decision) but has no greater authority than the other judges in the determination of each case.

By statutory provision the Court convenes the first Monday each October and sits until mid-June, unless all cases have been decided prior to that time. Many of us have heard someone proclaim, "I will take this case all the way to the Supreme Court." Realistically, this is very unlikely. In most instances, an appellant must petition the Court to hear his or her case. The Court receives 7000 case appeals annually. However, the Court hears oral arguments by attorneys in only approximately 100 cases per year. Of these the Court delivers formal written opinions in 80-90 cases. The publication of the term's written opinions, including concurring opinions, dissenting opinions, and orders, is approximately 5000 pages long (Supreme Court of the United States, 2007). If the Court decides to hear the case, it issues a **writ of certiorari**, or a demand for the transcripts of the proceedings to be sent to the Court for review. In order for all of the justices to hear a particular appeal, the case must pass a screening, known as the **Rule of Four**. In other words, four of the nine justices must agree that the case has constitutional merit or national importance and that it should be heard by the entire court. If a case receives four or more votes from the justices it is placed on the docket and scheduled to be heard by the Court (Champion, et. al., 2008). In special circumstances, arguments may be presented, as in the decision of the constitutionality of the death penalty, but they are limited to a specific time frame. The Court operates on the basis of majority opinion, with six members constituting a quorum. One judge who voted with the majority is assigned by the chief justice to write the Court's opinion, or the chief justice personally writes it. In addition, any other member may write a concurring opinion (if in the majority) or a dissenting opinion (if in the minority). Neither opinion has an impact on the case, but in the future it may be a basis for changing the precedent set in the present case. When the topic of the opinion is controversial, such as abortion or the death penalty, it is not unusual for justices to express individual opinions. For example in *Furman v. Georgia* (1972) all justices wrote separate opinions (Champion, *et. al.*, 2008).

The Court was established by the U.S. Constitution; however, its status as the supreme determinant of legal issues was not conferred at its inception. One of the important factors in the development of the Supreme Court's authority was the case of *Marbury v. Madison* (1803). This decision gave the Court the power of judicial review. In essence, it held that the authority of the U.S. Constitution shall supercede acts of Congress and that the Constitution should be interpreted by the Court.

The Supreme Court is somewhat unique in that it maintains both original and appellate jurisdiction. The Court has limited original jurisdiction in cases involving treaties made by the federal government, controversies in which the U.S. government is a party, and disputes between two states, to name only a few areas.

The Court also has been granted appellate jurisdiction by Congress, and most of its work involves this responsibility (cases of original jurisdiction account for less than 1 percent of the Court's activities). We previously noted that the Court has considerable discretion in determining which cases it hears. Although this is basically true, the Court is required to grant review when (1) a federal court holds an act of Congress to be unconstitutional; (2) a court of appeals finds a state statute unconstitutional; (3) a state's highest court holds a federal law to be invalid; and (4) an individual's challenge to a state statute is upheld by a state supreme court.

We should note the different decisions the Court can reach. If it affirms the decision, the lower court's decision is held to be correct, and the case is finalized. It may also reverse the lower court decision in part or in total. Frequently, a petition will raise several issues and the Court may find that some issues were handled properly while others constitute errors and will remand the case (send it back to be retried with modifications) to the court of original jurisdiction. In some instances, there are such serious constitutional errors that the original decision is completely overturned.

The Sixth Amendment and Speedy Trials

As guaranteed by the Sixth Amendment, "In all criminal prosecutions, the accused shall enjoy the right to a public and **speedy trial**." In this area, courts are the targets of considerable criticism (see "In the News" 7.2).

In the News 7.2

Toothless speedy trial law is abused and ignored

One thing the state Legislature can do in this session is pass a speedy trial law with some teeth in it.

The current law is widely ignored by judges and attorneys alike, allowing trials to drag on and on and on ...

The law reads: "Unless good cause be shown, and a continuance duly granted by the court, all offenses for which indictments are presented to the court shall be tried no later than two hundred seventy (270) days after the accused has been arraigned."

It's the "unless good cause be shown" part that makes this law pretty useless. Judges think nothing of granting continuance upon continuance. Meanwhile, witnesses forget or move away and the whole case gets weakened.

Mississippi courts have interpreted this law as protecting the defendants. The idea is that a defendant has a right to a speedy trial. Many defendants have deliberately abused this by delaying their trials and then trying to get their charges dismissed for taking longer than 270 days.

This is exactly what happened in the case of Guice v. the State of Mississippi. Phelan Terrell Guice delayed and delayed. He fired his attorneys, causing more delays. When he finally was convicted, he appealed on the grounds that he didn't get a speedy trial.

The Mississippi Supreme Court ruled five to four against Guice. The majority opinion pointed out that Guice himself was the cause of the delay, so his guilty verdict should not be thrown out because it took longer than 270 days.

But four judges dissented, raising the whole issue of speedy trials and the responsibility of judges to recognize the public benefit of a speedy trial.

In other words, not only does the defendant have the right to a speedy trial, but so does the public.

Justice Oliver Diaz began his dissent stating, "I am compelled to dissent because the majority ignores the unambiguous pronouncement of our Legislature, entangles state and federal law, and ignores the binding precedent of the United States Supreme Court. This has resulted in a miscarriage of justice for not only Phelan Terrell Guice, but all Mississippians. This case presents a question which we have addressed many times before: at what point is the statute providing that criminal defendants be tried within 270 days after arraignment violated?"

Further down in the dissent, Diaz adds, "In adhering to a faithful interpretation of the statute, we not only fulfill our proper role under the state constitution—we also safeguard our society from the plague of crime and injustice. The right to a speedy trial belongs not only to the accused—it also benefits society."There are several interesting aspects of this decision. First, it is clear that the court needs more direction from the state Legislature. The speedy trial law needs greater specificity. In particular, the Legislature needs to clarify the penalties for failure of judges to follow the speedy trial law.

Freeing killers is no way to punish a judge. By the same token, allowing judges to continually violate the speedy trial law will condemn society to an ever more frozen criminal justice system.

This could be simply rectified without costing any taxpayer money. All we need is for the Legislature to exercise its responsibility and clarify the remedies.

Here's one idea: Create a requirement that all judges try 50 percent of their cases within 180 days, 75 percent within 270 days and 95 percent within 360 days. Judges who fail to meet these ratios will be warned to remedy the situation within six months. If they remain out of compliance after six months, they would be removed from office.

By relying on percentages, judges would retain flexibility since there will always be some cases that have justifiable delays. Removing judges is a much better remedy than releasing killers.

In the Guice decision, the Mississippi Supreme Court is practically begging the state Legislature to do something.Half a century ago, our courts were trying most cases within two months, as Diaz notes in his opinion. With all our advances in technology, how can our courts have gotten 10 times slower?

Emmerich, W. (2007, January 27). **Toothless speedy trial law is abused and ignored.** *The Sun Herald,* p. C2.

Failure to provide speedy trials is one of the leading areas of concern. In reality, most of the people who obtain speedy trials do so only by pleading guilty in a lower court. At the trial level, it is not uncommon for the trial to commence at least a year after arrest in felony cases, although many times the delays are at the request of the defendant. Delays in civil cases are often much greater, exceeding three or more years in some cases. Delays also plague the appellate courts, and appeals are often not finalized until years after a decision was reached at the trial level. In recent years, appellate courts have instituted procedural changes, such as limiting oral arguments and minimizing the number of published opinions, in an effort to reduce their caseloads.

A major question surrounding this problem is the definition of speedy trial. The President's Crime Commission recommended a maximum of 81 days between arrest and trial for those defendants not detained in jail and 71 days for those who are detained (President's Commission on Law Enforcement and Administration of Justice, 1967). This was only a recommendation, and no jurisdiction is bound by it. In fact, few cases at the trial court level are processed within this time frame. At the federal level, Congress has applied the Speedy Trial Act of 1974 (1975) to the federal system (Criminal Resource Manual, 1997). The act holds that only 70 days may elapse between the filing date or the defendant's initial appearance in court and the trial. In 1972, the U.S. Supreme Court established a Constitutional threshold for determining whether a defendant has been denied a speedy trial (*Barker v. Wingo*). All 50 states have crafted speedy trial statutes that apply within their court systems as well. These statutes typically set specific times in which the defendant must be brought to trial depending on whether the accused is in custody or not. Although such efforts are commendable, few defendants, at either the trial or the appellate level, actually receive speedy trials, again, due in part to their own actions. For example, defense attorneys may ask for continuances to avoid appearing before certain judges or to maximize their fees.

Why should we be concerned about court delay or backlog? First, it has tainted the image of the justice network in the eyes of the public, who have little respect for a network that moves so slowly. Second, and closely related, it has necessitated the practice of plea bargaining or pleading guilty for consideration. Roughly 90 percent of all felony convictions are processed by negotiation rather than by trial (Brown & Langan, 1998, p.3, Neubauer, 2005, p. 11). Victims, the public, and the police are frequently unhappy about this practice, but if it were to be discontinued now, the delays would be unconscionable. Third, delay can cause undue financial and/or emotional hardship, both on those defendants who remain in jail and on their families, particularly if the defendants are eventually found innocent. Guilty defendants who are released on bail may commit additional illegal acts while awaiting trial. Repeated delays also cause hardships for victims and witnesses who must appear in court on numerous occasions.

With such negative effects, why does the problem persist? The most common reasons for court delay are a shortage of judges and courtrooms, the use or abuse of continuances by attorneys, the filing of too many petty cases, and inefficient methods of court administration. It has been noted that the increase in the number of criminal prosecutions under federal law has resulted in a greater backlog of civil cases in federal court. This is because the court must give priority to the criminal cases because of the criminal defendant's right to a speedy trial. Prisoner lawsuits have also dramatically added to the federal court dockets. However, efforts such as the Prison Litigation Reform Act have resulted in a reduction in these cases. Neither the number of courtrooms nor the number of judges has kept pace with population increases or with increases in criminal prosecutions on civil cases. Legislatures have been hesitant or unwilling to appropriate adequate funds for judicial budgets. "In times of fiscal crisis, the tensions among the three branches of government become more pronounced. The depth and duration of the recent economic downturn have made courts particularly vulnerable. Court systems all over the country have experienced cuts, stemming from revenue reductions to state governments that have affected the capacity of those systems to deliver justice to the public (Anonymous, 2005, p. 152).

Additionally, a lawyer sometimes waives a defendant's right to a speedy trial by asking for a continuance. Undeniably, the continuance may be necessary to uncover evidence or to aid in the development of the case for the defense. But, as Blumberg (1967) and Neubauer (1999, p.124), among others, have argued, it is also used as a method to collect fees. The continuance may be part of the defense strategy. Banfield and Anderson (1968) found that the longer a case was continued, the more likely it was that the defendant would not be found guilty. As the time between the crime and the trial increases, witnesses are more difficult to locate and cannot always testify accurately to what has transpired months or years ago (Listokin, 2007).

As previously noted, most court cases are civil rather than criminal. Citizens are quite willing to file suit with respect to almost any issue. The result is court congestion. One recommendation to remedy this situation is to use quasi-judicial tribunals to arbitrate claims involving less than a specified dollar amount, thus allowing judges to handle more trials. Some jurisdictions have adopted alternative **dispute resolution programs** in an attempt to resolve matters in the community that would otherwise be heard in court (Brown, 2005). However, the problem of court delay is very complex and will not be resolved simply. An effort involving the court system, the government, and the public is needed if change is to occur.

Inefficient court administration is a contributing factor to court delay. Traditionally, the chief judge is primarily responsible for the administrative duties of the court as well as for hearing cases. These duties include (1) preparing the budget; (2) scheduling cases; (3) assigning and overseeing personnel; and (4) maintaining records. Unfortunately, many justices are not qualified to handle all these responsibilities. Law schools do not traditionally offer courses in court administration, so, unless the judge has prior experience in this area, these tasks are often not effectively or efficiently performed (Jacob, 1997).

There has been a movement over the past two decades to employ professional managers to perform the administrative functions of the courts. The assumption is that a trained and/or experienced administrator can more effectively perform these duties, allowing the judge more time to hear cases. The federal courts, and some larger jurisdictions in the state courts, have employed court administrators with considerable success. Experimentation with court administrators and computerization has led some to believe that these changes will help decrease the court backlog at both the trial and the appellate level because witnesses are better notified and records better kept. Despite the commonsense appeal and the success enjoyed by courts using these techniques, there have been criticisms. Some argue that employing court administrators diminishes the authority of the chief judge in that he or she loses the power to supervise other judges. It is also contended that the practice is too impersonal (too businesslike) and that the court is supposed to process cases individually not like freight (Hoffman, 1991; Reinkensmeyer, 1991).

Finally, there is the problem of expense. Federal funding has supported the hiring of many court administrators and the use of computer systems. Whether or not these positions can be maintained when funding expires remains to be seen, as many states find it difficult to allocate enough funds to increase the size of the judiciary, let alone hire other personnel or enter the computer age (Hartley & Bates, 2006).

Court Personnel

In the typical course of events, an alleged offender first encounters the police and then either a public or private defense counsel, or the prosecutor. Because the prosecutor is the person to whom the police present their case with respect to an alleged offender, let us turn our attention first to that officer of the court.

The Prosecutor

Called by a variety of names—state's attorney, district attorney, prosecuting attorney—prosecutors are found at federal, state, and local levels. There are also prosecutors known as **independent counsels**—private attorneys appointed because public prosecutors are too closely tied to government officials being investigated—who conduct investigations and bring charges when warranted. A good example is the case of President Bill Clinton, who was investigated by Kenneth Starr, an independent counsel. Because President Clinton appointed Attorney General Reno, cries of partisanship would surely have been raised had she taken on the investigation herself. Appointing Starr as an independent counsel basically removed the attorney general from the fray. Similarly, President Bush appointed Patrick Fitzgerald as independent counsel to investigate the Valerie Plame case, in which administration officials were alleged to have disclosed the identify of Plame as a CIA agent, because asking Attorney General Alberto Gonzalez (a Bush appointee) to investigate the case would have been inappropriate. As you can see, the activities of a prosecutor involve him or her in all aspects of the criminal justice network.

Typically, the cases processed by the prosecutor originate with a law enforcement agency, and smooth working relationships between these agencies and the prosecutor's office are essential if the criminal justice network is to be effective and efficient. Grand juries work under the supervision of the prosecutor and rely on the prosecutor for information, evidence, and advice. The role of the prosecutor in plea bargaining is detailed elsewhere in this chapter, as is his or her role in establishing court dockets and recommending sentences to the judge. Parole boards and probation officers also rely on the prosecutor to provide information relevant to their functions. Their willingness to use alternatives to incarceration determines to some extent whether such programs will survive.

There are about 2,400 state prosecutors' offices employing roughly 78,000 support staff (Bureau of Justice Statistics, 2006). The basic function of the **prosecutor** is to represent the people (the state) in criminal proceedings. This function is accomplished through the charging process and the trial process. Charging is a two-step process. In step one, the prosecutor decides whether or not to file criminal charges against an individual. In step two, the prosecutor decides the nature of such charges. Any charges filed must be based on the facts of a particular case and on the law as it relates to that case.

To make a charging decision, the prosecutor reviews case records, presents the case to a grand jury, or files an **information** (a formal accusation). The prosecutor may go through a preliminary hearing and a series of negotiations with defense counsel in determining whether to file charges and, if so, what charges are to be filed.

When a prosecutor decides to proceed to criminal trial, she or he becomes the state's champion, who engages in courtroom combat (generally verbal) with the defense. The final decision about whether an alleged offender will be brought into court rests with the prosecutor. If the prosecutor decides not to take the case into court, no further official action is likely to be taken on the case in question. The prosecutor, then, exercises an enormous amount of discretion in the criminal justice network. Whereas the police officer may open the gate to the official justice system, the prosecutor may close that gate. The prosecutor may do this without accounting for his or her reasons to anyone else in the network (except, of course, to the voters who elect the prosecutor to office, and the elections often take place long after the case has been decided). The decision not to prosecute (nollee prosequi) in addition to the discretion in determining the number and severity of charges renders the prosecutor a very powerful figure in the court process.

Clearly, under some circumstances, the prosecutor would be foolish to proceed with court action. For example, lack of evidence, lack of probable cause, or lack of due process may make it virtually impossible to prosecute a case successfully. However, a number of somewhat less legitimate reasons exist for failure to prosecute. Evidence indicates that the prosecutor may fail to take cases to court for political reasons (e.g., when the person in question is a powerful, local political figure) or because the caseload of the prosecutor includes an "important" or "serious" case (i.e., one in which successful prosecution will result in favorable publicity). As a result, the prosecutor may screen out or dismiss a number of "less serious" cases, such as burglary and assault. In short, the prosecutor is the key figure in the justice system and is recognized as such by both defendants and defense counsel (Misner, 1996).

As Pollock (1994) indicates:

> Whether to charge or not is one of the most important decisions of the criminal justice process. The decision should be fair, neutral, and guided by due process, but this is an ideal; often many other considerations enter into the decision ... despite the ideal of prosecutorial duty, an individual factor in prosecutorial discretion is that the prosecutors want to and must win; therefore their choice of cases is influenced by this value, whether it is ethically acceptable or not.... To give one person who participated in a brutal crime immunity to gain testimony against others is efficient, but is it consistent with justice? To not charge businesspeople with blue law violations because they are

good citizens is questionable if other businesses are prosecuted for other ordinances. (p.153)

Of course, not all prosecutors employ the tactics and techniques discussed above;
abuses do happen. Sometimes prosecutorial abuse occurs as the result of a desire for
revenge, but perhaps more often it results from lack of adequate training on behalf of
the prosecutor or his or her staff. A brief look at the reasons for becoming a prosecutor and the processes through which this occurs will help us understand how and why
such abuses occur.

The position of prosecutor may be attractive for a variety of reasons. For those attorneys who wish to become judges or state or federal legislators, it is an excellent starting point. It is, then, attractive to some individuals interested primarily in political careers rather than in prosecution. For young attorneys just out of law school, the
position of assistant prosecutor ensures a steady income while it provides opportunities to make contacts on which to build a private practice. Some of these assistants
eventually become prosecutors to further their political ambitions or to gain notoriety
as criminal lawyers, or because the tremendous power and discretion accompanying
the position attracts them. Finally, some attorneys become (and some remain) prosecutors because they are committed to the practice of criminal law and to representing
the state in criminal cases.

A variety of other functions are performed by most prosecutors. These include acting as the chief law enforcement official in a specific jurisdiction; reviewing, authorizing and prosecuting felony and misdemeanor criminal law violations and ordinance
violations; juvenile delinquency offenses; allegations of child abuse and child neglect;
participating in mental health commitment hearings; and assisting victims of criminal offenses and initiating civil law actions to obtain financial support for children
(Prosecutor's Duties, 2004). Whereas police, defense attorneys, judges, and probation
officers tend to specialize in specific phases of the criminal justice process, the duties
of the prosecutor involve all of these areas (Neubauer, 2005, p. 126). The chief prosecutor must also administer his or her own office and engage in the political activities
essential to remain in office. Increasingly, prosecutors are also becoming involved in
the development and operation of teen courts and community conflict resolution
groups of one type or another.

We should note that the prosecutor, although he or she is the state's champion, is
obligated to protect the rights of the defendant as well. On taking office, prosecutors
take an oath, which requires them to seek justice, For example, he or she must present
evidence to show that a defendant is not guilty when it comes to his or her attention.

Because we have previously discussed the political process by which the prosecutor
is selected, we will simply point out, once again, the importance of understanding political affiliations and considerations when considering the prosecutor's role.

Defense Counsel

There are two major categories of defense counsel: private and public. According to
the Bureau of Justice Statistics (2001) nearly two thirds of federal felony defendants

and 82 percent felony defendants in the most populous counties in the U. S. were represented by public defenders. Generally financed by some governmental body (state, county, or a combination), **public defenders** represent indigent clients, who cannot afford to retain private counsel. The total cost of this representation in 1999 was over $1.2 billion (Bureau of Justice Statistics, 2001). For many young lawyers interested in criminal law, the position of public defender represents a stepping-stone. In most jurisdictions the public defender is paid a relatively low salary, but the position guarantees a minimal income, which can be supplemented by private practice. As a rule, caseloads are heavy; investigative resources are limited; and many clients are, by their own admission, guilty. The public defender, therefore, spends a great deal of time negotiating pleas and may spend very little time with his or her clients. As Estrich (1998) indicated:

> The right to counsel guaranteed by the Constitution only guarantees the defendant a warm body. The issue for a poor defendant is not whether his attorney will lie for him, create reasonable doubt where there isn't any, or undermine truth-telling witnesses but, quite literally, whether he'll even get to meet his lawyer for an interview to give his side of the story before they face the state in court. (p.97)

As a result, public defenders often enjoy a less than favorable image among their clients.

Some public defenders seem to have little interest in using every possible strategy to defend their clients. On numerous occasions, prosecutors and judges make legal errors to which the public defender raises no objection. In addition, appeals are sometimes not initiated by public defenders even when chances of successful appeal seem good. As Lee (2004, p. 367, footnotes omitted) notes, "Many people may have heard about the drunk lawyer, the drugged lawyer, the mentally ill lawyer, or the sleeping lawyer-all of whom, according to our jurisprudence, provided effective assistance of counsel. Although these stories are the more well-known examples of what is wrong with indigent defense, the problems cover a wider gamut that includes unimplemented (often unenforceable) standards, weak (or non-existent) organizational structures, attorney incompetence, unrealistic workloads, and inadequate funding. The problems infesting indigent defense are many. Sleeping lawyers are simply the more conspicuous symptoms of a deeper dysfunction over the last forty years."

There are also public defenders who pursue their clients' interests with all possible vigor, even to the point of alienating the judges who initially appointed them. On the whole, public defenders have been found to be equally as effective at defending indigent clients compared with private counsel, thus contradicting long-standing criticisms portraying indigent defenders as incompetent, ill-equipped, and poorly trained (Champion, 2008, p. 128). However, Champion (2008) admits there is probably an element of truth in both views of the public defender or assigned-counsel systems. This is particularly true in large urban jurisdictions where defender offices are staffed with new attorneys with little or no criminal trail experience. They often encourage their clients who are often innocent to plead guilty to a lesser criminal charge in exchange for a short jail term or probation (Champion, 2008, p. 126). As Barlow (2000, p.377) notes,

"Public defenders cannot forget that they are paid by the government. This fact puts them in an odd situation, considering that their job is to defend clients whom their employer prosecutes. They are sworn to do their best for their clients, but they are paid by their judicial adversary." Still, a study by Hanson and Ostrom (1998, p.283) found that public defenders fare reasonably well in court in comparison to private attorneys. "How frequently do indigent defenders gain favorable outcomes for their clients? Are they more successful than, less successful than, or equally as successful as privately re-tained counsel in gaining favorable outcomes? The evidence gained from an examina-tion of felony dispositions in the nine courts [studied] is that indigent defenders gen-erally are as successful as privately retained counsel." (See "In the News" 7.3.)

In the News 7.3

Public defender's office struggles

The continuing growth in the number of criminal court cases filed in Blount County hasn't pushed the District Public Defender's Office to the brink of dysfunction yet, but Mack Garnerknows it coming. "We're not there, but two death penalty cases would put us there," said Garner, who has held the office since 1990. "There would go virtually half my staff for what could be six months or a year."

The Public Defender's Office employs four full-time and two part-time at-torneys. During the 2005–2006 fiscal year, his office handled about 4,100 cases. This year, the case load is approaching 4,500. The State Comptroller's Office estimates that Garner's office is about six positions short of recom-mend staffing levels. Garner, though, said he could make do with just two.

"With three (additional) attorneys, we would be set for several years," Gar-ner said. "Two attorneys would probably solve our problem. The comptrol-ler's study is probably excessive. We don't need that many."

During the recent budget deliberations, the Blount County Commission, how-ever, took no action on Garner's request to fund an additional $89,171, which includes the cost of benefits and $52,152 in salary, to add a full-time attorney to his staff.

During a recent day in Alcoa city court, Garner and his assistants plowed through 50 cases, devoting about 12 minutes to each. That kind of pace makes it hard to provide the quality of service that people deserve, he said.

"I try to do all my work by telephone because we simply don't have an hour to spare to talk to a person about a case," he said "I'm not sure all of our clients know what's going on because everything happens so fast."

Since the county added the General Sessions Court Section IV seat that Judge David R. Duggan holds, the demand for public defender services has in-creased, Garner said, but despite the workload, his staff is getting the job done.

"The reason we're not in crisis is my lawyers are great lawyers," he said. "Some of my lawyers, it seems, are never sick or miss work. All of my (assistants) are way, way above average. It would be very difficult to get better representation than what we're providing. That's how we've managed to avoid the crunch."

The Public Defender's Office is not alone in increasing workloads. Blount General Sessions Judge William Brewer said that the overall number of cases in the Blount County system is still on the rise.

"I can't tell you the numbers, but there is a lot more criminal cases now as compared to two years ago," he said. "We have a more active probation office that is, in turn, supervising folks who have been convicted of a criminal offense and are more actively making sure they comply with the rules of probation. If they do not, violation of probation warrants are issued. That has increased the case load. Just in general, the number of cases has gone up as it has over the years. We've got plenty to do."

According to Circuit Court Clerk Tom Hatcher, whose office oversees administration for the County Circuit, General Sessions, Juvenile and Traffic Court divisions, the number of cases filed in Blount County has grown from 20,668 in the 2002–2003 fiscal year to 29,763 in the 2005–2006 fiscal year. That's a 44 percent increase in four years.

District Attorney General Mike Flynn said his office is feeling the strain as well.

"We're managing to keep up with the increased workload, but it's not going to be too much longer until we reach a point where we'll need additional assistance if this continues," Flynn said.

Currently, Flynn's office employs six state-funded assistant district attorneys and one funded through a driving under the influence (DUI) grant. Flynn said one of the these assistants is funded by diverting funds from another authorized position.

"Right now, we're using a criminal investigator slot as an assistant to keep up with the case load," he said.

There is some hope that Garner's office might be able to get funding for one new attorney position from the state. He'll find out in August when the State Public Defenders Conference meets to discuss how to divvy up 19 new positions among the 31 districts in the state.

"Given our percentage of the (staffing) deficit is among the highest in the state, I dearly hope the conference will see fit to allot us one of the positions," Garner said.

County Commissioner David Graham said that the Public Defender's Office serves a population that private lawyers don't." These are the folks that don't have the means for representation," he said. "We should really consider looking at (funding a new position) seriously next budget year."

Garner said his clients are not the only people being hurt by the workload."Victims are having to come back to court six or seven times because the cases are being reset," he said. "It's not fair to the public. I hope the county can see fit to (fund) it. We need to make our criminal justice system as good as the rest of the county. Everybody deserves a lawyer.

Everybody deserves a fair trial. How your case comes out should not depend on whether you're rich or poor."

Davis, J (2007, June 30) Public defender's office struggles. The Daily Times (Maryville, TN). Available at: http://www.dailytimes.com Record number 73286655288831

Research has led to the following conclusions concerning public defenders: They tend to resolve their cases more expeditiously than private attorneys; such resolution doe not compromise the rights of defendants; public defenders and prosecutors tend to be equally experienced; and the outcomes of criminal appeals are not significantly different for the two groups (Hanson, Hewitt, & Ostrom, 1992; Williams, 1995).

It is, perhaps, most interesting that while differences between private and public counsel do exist with respect to dismissals and not-guilty verdicts, these do not indicate an overwhelming superiority of private attorneys over public defenders. There are relatively few private attorneys making good money from the private practice of criminal law. In fact, most good law schools offer few courses in criminal law, and most graduates of these schools have little or no interest in practicing criminal law. This is so, among other reasons, because of the type of clientele involved, difficulties in collecting fees, and the reputation generated by legal practitioners who openly solicit cases in the halls and courtrooms of courthouses and practice law out of their briefcases (Estrich, 1998).

Whether **defense counsel** is private or public, his or her duties remain essentially the same. The duties are to see that the client is properly represented at all stages of the system, that the client's rights are not violated, and that the client's case is presented in the most favorable light possible, regardless of the client's involvement in criminal activity. And these duties are to be fulfilled while adhering to the Code of Professional Conduct, which requires that lawyers neither lie in court nor suborn perjury. To accomplish these goals, the defense counsel is expected to battle, at least in theory, the prosecutor in adversary proceedings. Here, again, the difference between theory and practice is considerable. Sobel (2004, p. 5) indicates that "During the past three years, the American Judicature Society (AJS) has devoted substantial resources in promoting improvements to the administration of the criminal justice system. AJS has observed that inadequate assistance of defense counsel is a prevalent factor in wrongful convictions."

The Relationship between the Prosecutor and Defense Counsel

In theory, adversary proceedings result when the champion of the defendant (defense counsel) and the champion of the state (prosecutor) do battle in open court where the truth is determined and justice is the result. In practice, the situation is quite

Attorneys are obligated to represent their clients in an ethical and competent manner. Reprinted with permission of iStockphoto.com / Kriss Russell.

often different because of considerations of time and money on behalf of both the state and the defendant.

The ideal of adversary proceedings is perhaps most closely realized when a well-known private defense attorney does battle with the prosecutor in court. Prominent defense attorneys often have competent investigative staffs and considerable resources in terms of time and money to devote to a case. Thus, the balance of power between the state and the defendant may be almost even. This balance of power is generally not the case when defense counsel is a public defender who may be less experienced than the prosecutor and generally has more limited access to an investigative staff than the prosecutor. For a variety of reasons, then, both defense counsel and the prosecutor may find it easier to negotiate a particular case rather than to fight it out in court, since court cases are costly in both time and money.

Most adult criminal cases in the United States are settled by plea bargaining. In fact, it has been suggested that justice in the United States is not the result of the **adversary system** (in which prosecution and defense argue their cases in court), but is the result of a cooperative network of routine interactions between defense counsel, the prosecutor, the defendant, and, in many instances, the judge (Neubauer, 2005, p. 285).

In plea bargaining, both prosecutor and defense counsel hope to gain at least partial victories through compromise. The prosecutor wants the defendant to plead guilty, if not to the original charges then to some less serious offense. Defense counsel seeks to get the best deal possible for his or her client, which may range from an outright dismissal to a plea of guilty to some less serious offense than the original charge. The nature of the compromise depends on conditions such as the strength of the prosecutor's case and the seriousness of the offense. Most often the two counselors arrive at what both consider a just compromise, which is then presented to the defendant to accept or reject. As a rule, the punishment to be recommended by the prosecutor is also negotiated; thus, the nature of the charges, the plea, and the punishment are negotiated and agreed on before the defendant actually enters the courtroom. The adversary system, in its ideal form at least, has been circumvented.

To the prosecutor, defense counsel, and the court, the benefits of plea bargaining are clear. The prosecutor is successful in prosecuting a case (she or he obtains a conviction), defense counsel has reduced the charges and/or penalty against his or her client, and all parties have saved time and money by not contesting the case in court. The dangers in plea bargaining, however, should not be overlooked. First, the defendant might have been found not guilty even if he or she had been tried in court (Langer, 2006). Second, because negotiations occur most often in secret, there is a danger that the constitutional rights of the defendant may not be stringently upheld. For example, the defendant does not have the chance to confront and cross-examine his or her accusers. Finally, the judge is often little more than a figurehead in cases settled by plea bargaining. In a court case, the judge has the responsibility to see that the trial is conducted in the best interests of both the offender and society as well as the responsibility to ensure due process. Neither of these can be guaranteed in most cases involving plea bargaining.

Because of some of the difficulties characteristic of plea bargaining, some jurisdictions have taken action to greatly reduce or eliminate the practice. For example, a ban on plea bargaining in Alaska gave prosecutors greater charging powers. With greater power over charging decisions, prosecutors in Alaska were more careful to screen those cases destined for trials (Champion, 2008, p. 341). Subsequent bans on plea bargaining by prosecutors by various jurisdictions, such as New Hampshire, have revealed similar results, with a substantial increase in charge bargaining (Herzog, 2004).

The future of plea bargaining remains uncertain, while some recommend retention with modifications, whereas others recommend abolition. Regardless of the outcome of such recommendations, plea bargaining currently illustrates quite clearly the value of the network approach in understanding criminal justice. Plea bargaining occurs because of a variety of factors relevant to different components of the criminal justice network. Among these are (1) a desire for convictions on behalf of prosecutors; (2) a desire for acquittals or charge reductions on behalf of defendants and defense counsel; (3) a desire on behalf of all practitioners and the public to conserve valuable resources (time and money); and (4) overcrowding of prison facilities. These and other factors impinge on prosecutors, judges, and defense attorneys when they consider plea bargaining as an alternative.

The Judge

At the state trial court level approximately 9,200 judges hear cases. As of 2006, there were 678 federal district court (trial court) judges in the various circuits (U.S. Courts, 2006b).

Theoretically, the judge is the most powerful figure in the justice network, although he or she often allows the prosecutor to usurp most of this power. The **judge** decides matters of law (is certain evidence admissible?), supervises the selection of juries, instructs jurors, presides over the trial, often does the sentencing, ensures that defendants understand the consequences of different pleas and that any plea entered is voluntary, and, in bench cases, also decides matters of fact. He or she is supposed to perform these duties impartially, attending only to facts that are legally relevant to each individual case. However, political and/or financial considerations sometimes outweigh the requirement for neutrality or impartiality.

Most research indicates that the power and discretion of the judge are demonstrated most clearly in the area of sentencing. Sentencing disparity may be due to the judge's perceptions of the dangerousness of certain types of offenders, age, gender, race/ethnicity, social class, or other factors. Some judges may be more lenient than others in imposing sentences. Steffensmeier and Demuth (2006) found that female defendants received greater leniency in sentencing than male defendants and that Black and Hispanic defendants received less favorable treatment than White defendants. The findings of this study suggest that Black and Hispanic female defendants benefit more from their gender than had previously been thought. Attorneys for both the prosecution and defense learn over time which judges are more likely to be lenient in which types of cases and often attempt to schedule cases accordingly.

The judge, prosecutor, and defense counsel are, in the vast majority of cases, members of the legal profession who have graduated from law school and who have become licensed to practice law by passing a bar (law) examination. A great deal of on-the-job training characterizes individuals filling all three positions because unlike some other countries, we do not require extensive training after graduation from law school and prior to employment for lawyers who occupy these positions. Individuals filling these three roles form their own more or less cooperative network as they work with one another on a regular basis. In addition, each has ties with other components in the criminal justice network. Such ties may be beneficial in that cooperation among members of the courthouse workgroup may help the court system run smoothly. However, such ties may also result in wrongful convictions when the various members of the workgroup do not fulfill their obligations in a professional manner (Leipold, 2005; Medwed, 2005).

The Probation Officer

Another officer of the court is the probation officer. As of 2005, almost 4.2 million people were on probation (federal, state or local), so the need for probation officers is clear (Bureau of Justice Statistics, 2007). Unlike the judge, prosecutor, and defense counsel, the probation officer is not likely to be a lawyer. Nonetheless, evidence suggests that probation officers have considerable impact on judges and prosecutors, particularly with respect to sentencing. **Probation officers** are generally civil service employees at the state level and appointees of the courts at the county level. Although training and educational requirements vary considerably among the states, there is a definite trend toward hiring college graduates as probation officers. In some states (Illinois, for example), the tendency is to appoint those with some graduate work or a master's degree. By 1990, the majority of states required college degrees for entry-level probation positions.

The rationale for requiring a college education is clear when the duties of the position are analyzed. In addition to being an officer of the court, and therefore an authority figure to probationers, the probation officer is expected to be a caseworker/therapist and, in many instances, a community liaison officer (working with local industries and businesses as well as with social agencies).The tasks typically performed by probation officers include: (1) conducting a presentence investigation; (2) making recommendations to the trial court judge on sentencing; (3) supervising probationers, including electronic monitoring and intensive supervision; (4) recommending revocation of probation when necessary; and (5) serving as a role model for probationers (Petersilia, 1999). As the probation officer accomplishes these tasks, he or she must attempt to maintain a reasonably close and friendly relationship with probationers to help change the behaviors that resulted in conflict with the criminal justice network, but the probation officer must also maintain sufficient distance to take authoritative action when appropriate. Like other officials in the criminal justice network, the probation officer exercises considerable discretion in the performance of duties. The extent to which conditions of probation are enforced and the extent to which technical violations of probation (as opposed to the commission of a new crime) lead to official action are largely determined by the probation officer, who is often required to fulfill the duties outlined here while managing a relatively heavy caseload.

Given the scope and nature of probation work, it is easy to understand the trend toward hiring better-educated individuals to fill probation positions. Unfortunately, salaries in the probation field have often lagged behind those of other criminal justice employees, making it difficult to recruit and retain probation officers with such educational backgrounds.

Managing the Courts

Traditionally, American courts have been independent and self-governing because of their role as a check and balance on the other two branches of government. At the federal level, many support functions, such as budgeting, docket control, and statistical analysis, are performed by the Administrative Office of the United States Courts. Historically, the concept of a judicial system has not been completely adopted in most states. Although there has been a trend toward unified state court systems, there is so much variation that most state judiciaries should still be classified as nonsystems because of local jurisdictional autonomy, complexity, and lack of centralized control.

In most states, there are three distinct sets of **court managers**: chief judges, court clerks, and court administrators.

Chief Judges

Judges have always been responsible for the administration of their courts. Individual judicial autonomy has resulted in a variety of uncoordinated and inconsistent administrative practices. Judges are often as involved with the many aspects of management as with adjudication. Unfortunately, most judges are not trained in management. The result is that most lawyers who become judges are not adept at analyzing patterns of dispositions or at managing large dockets.

The chief judge faces the same problems. The **chief judge** has general administrative responsibilities in his or her jurisdiction. Since most chief judges assume their position by virtue of seniority, there is no guarantee of effective management. Election of the chief judge (by other judges) may produce a strong and effective manager or a middle-of-the-road candidate.

Court Clerks

Clerks of the court play an important role in the administration of local judiciaries. They are responsible for docketing cases, collecting court fees, arranging for jury selection, and maintaining court records. Historically, they have competed with judges for control over judicial administration. Since they are elected officials in most states, they can function somewhat independently from the judge. As with judges, many clerks are not trained to manage the local courts (Neubauer, 2005, p.108).

Court Administrators

One solution to some of the court problems addressed above has been the creation of a professional group of trained **court administrators** to assist judges in administrative and nonjudicial functions (as discussed earlier). Nonjudicial functions are those associated with the business management of the courts. These may include record keeping, data gathering and analysis, research and planning, budget preparation, management of physical space and supplies, management of support personnel, docketing of court cases, and dispensing of information to the public. Business management plays a support role to the judicial function of the courts and is essential for more effective and efficient court operations.

In 1937, Connecticut established the first centralized office of court administrator, with a number of other states following after World War II. By the 1980s, every state had established a statewide court administrator (Neubauer, 1999, p.112). Because the position is relatively new, several aspects of the court administrator's role are still being debated. Most arguments center on qualifications and administrative relations with other agencies.

Since the creation of the Institute for Court Management in Denver, Colorado, in 1970, an increasing number of colleges and universities have been offering programs in court administration at the undergraduate and graduate levels. However, there is still no agreement regarding the skills and qualifications a court administrator should possess. Many believe managerial expertise is needed and a law degree is unnecessary. Conversely, many judges believe a law degree is essential. Some contend, for example, that court administrators who are hired for their business backgrounds have been ineffective because they know too little about the courts and the law. The need for a well-trained, professional class of court administrators is not a new subject to those who work in and study the profession. In the early 1970s, there were discussions and partnerships among educators, court managers, and legal professionals that focused on the need for quality management in our courts. They concluded that court managers needed skills that were not found in law schools, but were instead found in schools of public administration, public policy, criminal justice, and business.

Over time, the academic programs that sprang from this early cooperation largely disappeared (e.g., the University of Southern California and American University programs), or altered their missions to meet new market needs (e.g., the University of Denver Masters in Judicial Administration). Recently, there was some renewed attention to court management in higher education, but questions have been raised about whether these efforts are enough to reach students. Today, the need for effective court managers is greater than ever.

As we have seen, federal, state, and local courts face numerous challenges to functioning effectively. As Hartley and Bates (2006, p. 81) note, "They must handle rapid case-load growth, accommodate increasingly diverse and foreign language-speaking populations, keep pace with technological advances, coordinate with other governmental and nonprofit agencies, and conduct community outreach and education programs. They must do all this, and more, under ever-tighter budgets and increased spending accountability." Thus, "Today, the need for effective court managers is greater than ever. It is time for the judicial system to renew and institutionalize its partnership with academia in order to create the next generation of court managers."

A second area of concern centers on the relationship between the court administrator and other judicial agencies. Often clerks view this position as a threat and resent the intrusion; yet, to be effective, the court administrator requires the type of data that only the clerk can provide. Court clerks have played an important role in resisting the creation of court administrator positions. If the position is created, court clerks can significantly reduce the administrators' effectiveness by not cooperating.

There can also be friction between judges and administrators. Some judges are reluctant to delegate responsibility over important aspects of the court's work; for example, case scheduling. The distinction between administration and adjudication is not entirely clear. A court administrator's proposal to streamline court procedures may be seen by judges as intruding on how they decide cases (Neubauer, 2005, p.108). Despite their potential for improving the efficiency of the court, court administrators have encountered opposition from both clerks and judges. Most have not been given full responsibility over the court's nonjudicial functions. If the issues concerning qualifications, authority, and accountability can be resolved, court administrators could significantly increase the efficiency of the courts.

Other persons routinely involved in court operations include court reporters and bailiffs. Their roles tend to be more specific and less controversial than those of the court managers.

Summary

1. A number of concepts are common to all types of courts in the United States: jurisdiction (general, limited, exclusive, concurrent, original, and appellate), venue, stare decisis, and precedent (on which courts generally rely).

2. The court system of the United States consists of two more or less distinct systems: state and federal.

3. There is considerable variation among the states systems, but most states employ a three- or four-tiered hierarchy, whereas the federal system is three-tiered.

4. Lower courts typically hear minor cases and are the most numerous of the courts.

5. Trial courts hear both civil and criminal cases and are known as courts of general jurisdiction.

6. Appellate courts normally review cases based on trial records from the lower courts.

7. Most cases heard in trial and appellate courts are civil rather than criminal.

8. The supreme courts at state and federal levels are the courts of last resort and hear a relatively small number of cases.

9. There are serious problems of court delay at all levels. There are many identifiable causes and proposed solutions to court delay, but the problem is complex and difficult to solve satisfactorily.

10. The extent to which criminal justice practitioners are involved in a network in their daily operations is clearly illustrated by court personnel.

11. The prosecutor, perhaps the most powerful individual in the network in terms of discretion, takes into consideration a variety of factors in deciding whether and how to prosecute cases. Among these factors are community norms, political party affiliation, his or her relationships with the police, defense counsel, and judges, prior court decisions, and so on.

12. Defense counselors, judges, and probation officers also take into account these factors as well as the recommendations and desires of the prosecutor and one another in processing cases.

13. The extent to which plea bargaining occurs and the nature of the bargains depend upon these factors and on the extent of overcrowding in jails and prisons.

14. Local public defenders and probation officers are often appointed to their positions by judges who consider the prosecutor's recommendations in making such appointments. Judges and prosecutors are either elected by the public or appointed by other politicians who are elected by the public.

15. Judges, prosecutors, public defenders, and probation officers are assisted in their functions by individuals appointed or elected to help run the courts in an orderly way.

16. A lack of trained court administrators, court managers, and court clerks characterizes the current court scene.

Key Terms Defined

jurisdiction The authority to hear a particular case.

venue The place of trial.

stare decisis Let the decision stand; a policy of following principles laid down in previous decisions.

precedent Decision handed down previously in a similar case.

lower courts Courts of limited jurisdiction, empowered to hear only cases of a minor nature.

magistrates Judges limited to hearing only specific types of cases, usually in lower courts.

trial courts Courts with general jurisdiction (usually over both civil and criminal matters) to hear cases.

de novo Over again; anew.

circuit courts Trial courts serving a particular geographic region or circuit.

appellate courts Courts hearing appeals from lower courts.

state supreme court Court of last resort in a state.

magistrate judge Federal equivalent of state trial court judges of limited jurisdiction.

district courts Trial courts of the federal system.

en banc With all judges sitting together.

Uniform Code of Military Justice Laws governing individuals serving in the military

U.S. Supreme Court Court of last resort (highest appellate court) in the nation.

writ of certiorari An order from a higher court asking a lower court for the record of a case.

Rule of Four Four of the nine justices of the United States Supreme Court are required to vote to hear a case in order for the entire Court to hear the case.

speedy trial Trial for which the time period between arrest and trial is reasonable.

dispute resolution programs Community programs designed to help relieve court congestion by resolving issues through negotiations.

independent counsels Private attorneys appointed because public prosecutors are too closely tied to government officials being investigated.

prosecutor (states attorney, district attorney) An attorney representing the people (the state); also called the state's attorney, district attorney, prosecuting attorney.

information A formal accusation by the prosecutor.

public defenders Defense counsel paid from public funds.

defense counsel An attorney representing the defendant.

adversary system The system of law in the United States involving the opportunity of both prosecution and defense to present their cases at a trial presided over by a neutral judge.

judge An attorney (generally) elected or appointed to preside over court cases.

probation officers Individuals appointed to serve as officers of the court who supervise probationers and provide a variety other services to the court.

court managers Judges, court clerks, court administrators who provide support functions such as budgeting, docket control, and statistical analysis.

chief judge A judge with general administrative responsibilities in his or her jurisdiction.

clerks of the court Responsible for docketing cases, collecting court fees, arranging jury selection and maintaining court records

court administrators Assist judges in administrative and non-judicial functions.

Critical Thinking Exercises

1. Why is our court system called a dual court system? Explain, in general terms, the organization and functions of each component. How do we deal with cases that might be tried in both state and federal courts?

2. Discuss the role of the U.S. Supreme Court. What factors play a role in determining whether a case is heard by the Supreme Court? Is it true that anyone can take a case all the way to the Supreme Court? What obstacles, if any, make this difficult to accomplish?

3. Why is the prosecutor such an influential and important figure in our criminal justice network? To whom is the prosecutor ultimately accountable for his or her actions? What is the role of politics in prosecution? Are you comfortable with the considerable power of the prosecutor?

4. Discuss the courtroom work group in terms of its potential impact on defendants and victims. From your perspective, do we have an adversarial system of justice? Why or why not?

Internet Exercises

Most citizens experience the court system at the lower-court levels of their state. Click on Arizona's Limited Jurisdiction Courts: http://www.supreme.state.az .us/guide/Ltd_jurisdiction.htm.

After reading the materials, answer the following questions:

1. Discuss the municipal court system in Arizona in terms of court personnel, geographic jurisdiction, and subject matter jurisdiction.

2. What are the geographic boundaries of the justice of the peace courts, and how do they differ from the magistrate courts in the types of cases they hear?

3. List and explain the qualifications for becoming a justice of the peace. Is this the type of individual you want hearing your case?

After monumental decisions in *Gideon v. Wainwright* and *Argersinger v. Hamlin*, the role of the public defender has become very important for the court process. You can find Iowa's State Public Defender website at: http:// www.spd.state.ia.us.

After reading the materials presented, answer the following questions:

1. What types of individuals does the public defender represent? Explain the types of cases he or she can become involved with.

2. What advantages does the public defender system offer to criminal defendants?

3. What is the state appellate defender, and what types of clients does he or she represent?

References

Abraham, H. J. (1998). *The judicial process* (7th ed.). New York: Oxford University Press.

Anonymous. (2005). Ensuring adequate funding for the courts. *Judicature, 88* (4), 152–155.

Austin, J. (2004). The proper and improper use of risk assessment in corrections. *Federal Sentencing Reporter, 16* (3), 194.

Banfield, L., & Anderson, C. D. (1968). Continuances in the Cook County criminal courts. *University of Chicago Law Review, 35*, 279–280.

Barker v. Wingo, 407 U.S. 514 (1972).

Barlow, H. D. (2000). *Criminal justice in America.* Upper Saddle River, NJ: Prentice Hall.

Blumberg, A. (1967). *Criminal justice.* Chicago: Quadrangle.

Brown, G. V. (2005). A community of court ADR programs: How court-based ADR programs help each other survive. *Justice System Journal, 26,* (3), 327–343.

Brown, J. M., & Langan, P. A. (1998). *State court sentencing of convicted felons, 1994.* Washington, DC: U.S. Department of Justice.

Bureau of Justice Statistics. (2001). *Indigent defense statistics.* Available online at: http://www.ojp.usdoj.gov/bjs/id.htm.

Bureau of Justice Statistics. (2004). *State court organization 2004.* Available online at: http://www.ojp.gov.bjs/pub/ascii/sco04.txt.

Bureau of Justice Statistics. (2006). *Prosecution statistics.* Available online at: http://www.ojp.usdoj.gov/bjs/pros.htm.

Bureau of Justice Statistics. (2006b). *Courts and sentencing statistics.* Available online at: http://www.ojp.usdoj.gov/bjs/stssent.htm.

Bureau of Justice Statistics. (2007). *Probation and Parole Statistics.* Available online at: http://www.ojp.usdoj.gov/bjs/pandp.htm.

Champion, D. J. (1998). *Criminal justice in the United States* (2nd ed.). Chicago: Nelson-Hall.

Champion, D.J., Hartley, R. D. & Rabe, G.A. (2008). *Criminal courts: Structures, process and issue* (2nd ed.) Upper Saddle River, NJ: Pearson Prentice Hall.

Criminal Resource Manual (1997). *Speedy trial act of 1974.* Available online at: http://www.usdoj.gov/usao/reading_room/usam/title9/crm0028.htm eousa/foia.

Daly, K. & Bordt, R. L. (1995). Sex effects and sentencing: An analysis of the statistical literature, *Justice Quarterly,* 12, 141–151.

Editorial. (1998). Too poor to be defended. *Economist, 347* (8063), 21–22.

Estrich, S. (1998). *Getting away with murder: How politics is destroying the criminal justice system. Cambridge,* MA: Harvard University Press.

Hanson, R. A., Hewitt, W., & Ostrom, B. J. (1992, Summer). Are the critics of indigent defense counsel correct? *State Court Journal,* 20–29.

Hanson, R. A. & Ostrom, B. J. (1998). Indigent defenders get the job done and done well. In G. F. Cole & M. G. Gertz (Eds.). *The criminal justice system: Politics and policies* (pp.264–288). Belmont, CA: Wadsworth.

Hartley, R. E. & Bates, K. (2006). Meeting the challenge of educating court managers. *Judicature, 90* (2), 81–90.

Herzog, S. (2004). Plea bargaining practices: Less covert, more public support? *Crime and Delinquency,* 50, 590–614.

Hoffman, R. (1991). Beyond the team: Renegotiating the judge-administrator partnership. *Justice System Journal, 15,* 211–33.

Holmes, M. D., Daudistel, H. C., & Taggart, W. A. (1992). Plea bargaining policy and state district court caseloads: An interrupted time series analysis. *Law and Society Review, 26,* 139–59.

Holten, G., & Jones, M. E. (1982*). The system of criminal justice* (2nd ed.). Boston: Little, Brown.

Huddleson, W. (2005). *Drug courts: An effective strategy for communities facing methamphetamine.* National Institute of Justice. Rockville, MD: Bureau of Justice Assistance Clearinghouse.

Jacob, H. (1997). Governance by trial court judges. *Law and Science Review, 31,* 3–37.

Langer, M. (2006). Rethinking plea bargaining: The practice and reform of prosecutorial adjudication in American criminal procedure. *American Journal of Criminal Law, 33* (3), 223–300.

Lee, K. M. (2004). Reinventing Gideon v. Wainwright: Holistic defenders, indigent defendants, and the right to counsel. *American Journal of Criminal Law, 31* (3), 367–433.

Leipold, A. D. (2005). How the pretrial process contributes to wrongful convictions. *The American Criminal Law Review, 42* (4), 1123–1166.

Listokin, Y. (2007). Crime and (with a lag) punishment: The implications of discounting for equitable sentencing. *The American Criminal Law Review, 44* (1), 115–141.

Lopez, A. S. (Ed.). (1995). *Latinos in the United States: History, law, and perspective.* New York: Garland Press.

Maguire, K., & Pastore, A. L. (1998). *Bureau of justice statistics sourcebook of criminal justice statistics, 1997.* Albany, NY: Hindelang Criminal Justice Research Center.

Marbury v. Madison, 1 Cir. 137 (1803).

McGuire, K. T. (2005). Are the justices serving too long? An assessment of tenure on the U.S. Supreme Court. *Judicature, 89* (1), 8–16.

Medwed, D. S. (2005). Looking forward: Wrongful convictions and systemic reform. *The American Criminal Law Review, 42* (4), 1117–1122.

Misner, R. (1996). Recasting prosecutorial discretion. *Journal of Criminal Law and Criminology, 86,* 717–58.

Moradi-Shalal v. Fireman's Fund Insurance Companies (1988). 46 Cal. 3d 287,298.

Neubauer, D. W. (1999). *American courts and the criminal justice system* (6th ed.). Belmont, CA: Thomson Wadsworth.

_____(2005). *American courts and the criminal justice system* (8th ed.). Belmont, CA: Thomson Wadsworth.

_____(2007). *American courts and the criminal justice system* (9th ed.). Belmont, CA: Thomson Wadsworth.

Ostrom, B., & Kauder, N. (1996). *Examining the work of state courts, 1995.* Williamsburg, VA: National Center for State Courts.

Petersilia, J. (1999). Probation in the United States: Practices and challenges. In J. L. Victor (Ed.), *Annual editions: Criminal justice 99/00*, pp.160–65. Sluice Dock, Guilford, CT: Dushkin/McGraw-Hill.

Pollock, J. M. (1994, 2003). *Ethics in crime and justice: Dilemmas and decisions* (2nd ed.). Belmont, CA: Wadsworth.

President's Commission on Law Enforcement and Administration of Justice. (1967). *Task force report: The courts.* Washington, DC: U.S. Government Printing Office.

Prosecutor's Duties (2004). Available online at: http://www.otsegocountymi.gov/prosecutor/duties.htm.

Public Citizen. (2003). Federal district judges are vastly outnumbered by state judges. Available online at: http:// www.citizen.org.

Quotations about justice (2007). Available online at: http://www.quotegarden.com/justice.html.

Reinkensmeyer, M. (1991). Compensation of court managers: Current salaries and related factors. *Judicature, 75,* 154–62.

Rubenstein, M. L., & White, T. J. (1979). Plea bargaining: Can Alaska live without it? *Judicature, 62,* 266–79.

Schauffler, R., LaFountain, R., Kauder, N., & Strickland, S. (2004). *Examining the work of state courts, 2004.* Washington D.C.: Bureau of Justice Statistics.

Smith, S., & DeFrances, C. (1996). *Indigent defense.* Washington, DC: Bureau of Justice Statistics.

Sobel, A. D. (2004). Fulfilling the promise of Gideon. *Judicature, 88* (1), 5–7.

Steffensmeier, D. & Demuth, S. (2006). Does gender modify the effects of race-ethnicity on criminal sanctioning?: Sentences for male and female White, Black, and Hispanic defendants. *Journal of Quantitative Criminology, 22* (3), 241–261.

Sviridoff, M., Rottman, D., Weidner, R., Cheesman, F., Curtis, R., Hansen, R., & Ostrom, B. (2002). *Dispensing justice locally: The impact, costs and benefits of the mid-*

town community court. National Institute of Justice/NCJRS. New York, NY: Center for Court Innovation.

Supreme Court of the United States. (2007). *The justices' caseload.* Available online at: http://www.supremecourtus.gov/.

Tonry, M. (1995). *Malign neglect: Race, crime and punishment in America.* New York: Oxford University Press.

United States Courts (2006a). Judicial Business of the United States Courts. Available online at: http://www.uscourts.gov/judbus2006/contents.html.

United States Courts (2006b). *Federal court management statistics.* Available online at: http://www.uscourts.gov/fcmstat/index.htm.

United States Courts. (2007). *Federal judges.* Available online at: http://www.uscourts.gov/faq.html.

Walsh, E. (2005). Minority retort. *The New Yorker.* Available online at: http://www.newyorker.com/archive/2005/08/08/050808fa_fact.

Williams, J. (1995). Type of counsel and the outcome of criminal appeals: A research note. *American Journal of Criminal Justice, 19,* 275–85.

Suggested Readings

Cardoza, B. (2005) *The nature of the judicial process.* Mineola, NY: Dover Publications.

Hartley, R. E. & Bates, K. (2006). Meeting the challenge of educating court managers. *Judicature, 90* (2), 81–90.

Meador, D.S. (2001). *American courts.* St. Paul, MN: West Publishing.

Neubauer, D. W. (2007). *American courts and the criminal justice system* (9th ed.). Belmont, CA: Wadworth/Thomson Learning.

Rosen, J. (2007). *The Supreme Court: The personalities and rivalries, that define America.* Virginia Beach, VA: Time Books.

Scott, K. M. (2006). Shaping the Supreme Court's federal certiorari docket. *Justice System Journal, 27* (2), 191–209.

Segal, J., Spaeth, H. & Benesh, S. (2006). *The supreme court in the American legal system.* New York, NY: Cambridge Press.

Stookey, J. A. (2004). A cooperative model for preventing wrongful convictions. *Judicature, 87* (4), 159–163.

Chapter Eight

Pretrial Procedures

In the News 8.1

Attorney for Fred Russell wants change of venue;
He also wants blood samples excluded from evidence

Francisco Duarte, attorney for Fred Russell, filed documents Friday requesting Russell's blood samples be tossed out as evidence and asking that the trial be moved outside of Whitman County.

Duarte claims the state's "mismanagement" led to the destruction of Russell's blood samples and does not allow Russell and his defense team "an adequate opportunity to challenge the evidence since he would have no ability to have the sample independently tested."

The samples, taken at Gritman Medical Center in Moscow more than two hours after the June 2001 crash, showed Russell's blood alcohol level at 0.12, which is above the 0.08 percent legal limit.

Police allege Russell was speeding and intoxicated on June 4, 2001, when he caused a four-car crash on the Pullman-Moscow Highway in which three Washington State University students were killed and four others were injured.

Russell fled the country in October 2001 shortly before the start of his trial for vehicular homicide and vehicular assault and lived and worked under an assumed name in Dublin, Ireland, until his capture in October 2005. He fought extradition, including applying for political asylum, but was brought back to the United States by U.S. marshals after Irish courts rejected his attempts to remain.

Russell has been held without bail at the Whitman County Jail since his return on Nov. 9.

Duarte also claims media coverage of the case has tainted any chance for an impartial jury, arguing Russell cannot have a fair trial in Whitman County. If the trial continues, Duarte is asking that it be moved out of eastern Washington.

Duarte also filed pretrial motions that argue Washington State Patrol Trooper Michael Murphy did not have lawful authority to detain and arrest Russell at the hospital following the accident. Murphy, according to Duarte's motion, had no reason to assume Russell was intoxicated at the time of the accident.

Assistant State Attorney General Lana Weinmann is prosecuting the case on behalf of Whitman County. County Prosecutor Denis Tracy has stepped aside because he was Russell's defense attorney in a 1997 drunken driving case.

A pretrial hearing will begin July 23. The jury trial is scheduled for Oct. 8.

Anonymous. (2007, July 4). Attorney for Fred Russell wants change of venue. *Lewiston Tribune.* p. 3D.

Key Terms

48-hour rule
probable cause
initial appearance
indigent
bail
nulla poena sine crimine
bail bondsperson
preventive detention
release on recognizance (ROR)
supervised release or conditional release
grand jury
ex parte proceeding
bill of indictment
prima facie case
information
preliminary hearing
arraignment
nolo contendere
motion for discovery
motion for disclosure

Chapter Outline

Initial Appearances
The Administration of Bail
    Consequences of Bail
    Protecting Society

In this chapter, we focus our attention on the various stages of the criminal justice process prior to an actual criminal trial. Although the stages in the pretrial process have not received the same attention as the trial, they are of considerable importance. We must keep in mind that our criminal justice network is supposed to be based on the principles of innocent until proven guilty and due process of law for all those accused of criminal wrongdoing. Inherent within these principles are attempts to ensure that only those rightfully accused will proceed to the trial stage. Many of the pretrial processes, then, act as a sieve to filter out cases that lack necessary levels of proof for a finding of guilt. These stages are beneficial to the citizenry in that they prohibit the state from administering arbitrary punishment.

The pretrial stages are also beneficial to the government and the taxpayer because they help eliminate expensive and time-consuming trials when there is little probability of conviction. Because of the emphasis on due process, these stages also protect the rights of the accused specified in the U.S. Constitution and the Bill of Rights (the first 10 amendments to the Constitution). We must keep in mind that the criminal justice network includes an adversary system consisting of two opponents: the state (prosecution) and the defense (the accused). As we have indicated, the balance of power rests with the state. Due process is an attempt to keep the scales of justice balanced despite this imbalance of power.

In this chapter, we examine the six stages in the pretrial process: the initial appearance, the administration of bail, the formal charging of the accused, the preliminary hearing, the arraignment, and the concepts of discovery and disclosure. Most of our attention focuses on the pretrial stages as they apply to felony cases. We identify differences as they apply to lesser offenses. In addition, we indicate and discuss some of the more controversial stages and practices. There is, for example, considerable debate over bail, the use of grand juries, and the plea of not guilty by reason of insanity. We examine proposed changes in these areas and address their ramifications.

Initial Appearance

After an accused has been taken into custody by the police, he or she is to be taken without unnecessary delay before the nearest and most accessible magistrate (judge), and a charge should be filed (Ferdico, 1999, 2004). The definition as to what constitutes "unnecessary delay" has been constantly reinterpreted in a series of cases: *McNabb v. United States* (1943), *Mallory v. United States* (1957), and *Gerstein v. Pugh* (1975). The current standard, the **48-hour rule**, decided in *County of Riverside v. McLaughlin* (1991), holds that delays of up to 48 hours may be constitutional. The Court concluded that when a probable cause determination is not made within 48 hours, the defendant no longer has the burden to show unreasonable delay. The burden shifts to the State to show the existence of an emergency or other extraordinary circumstance. Delays caused by police procedures such as lineups, fingerprinting, and booking are usually considered reasonable. In addition, delays caused by the unavailability of the magistrate and by weekends and holidays are generally considered justifiable. However, in *People v. Edward Mitchell* (2004) the Court found that the delay is a factor to be considered when determining whether a confession is voluntary.

There are many responsibilities of the presiding magistrate at this stage. First, the judge is responsible for determining if **probable cause** existed for the arrest. If it is determined that probable cause did exist, the accused will be held for further criminal processing. If not, the defendant is released, and no formal charges are filed. This is the first stage of the filtering effect of pretrial procedures. Prior to this, both the public and the police have exercised discretion in reporting offenses or suspicious circumstances and affecting the arrest. Ideally, as the result of the **initial appearance**, only those cases in which there is a reasonable belief that a crime did occur and that the accused is the perpetrator of the act will be processed for further court action.

If probable cause is found, the accused is informed of the charges against him or her and is generally given a written copy of those charges. The magistrate will also inform the defendant of his or her right to counsel as guaranteed by the Sixth Amendment to the Constitution and interpreted by the Supreme Court. Initially, the right to counsel was applied at the federal level, with some controversy as to whether the doctrine applied to state proceedings. In *Gideon v. Wainwright* (1963), the court held that counsel must be provided in state felony proceedings. In *Argersinger v. Hamlin* (1972), the court extended the right to counsel to all cases where the penalty was imprisonment. The magistrate will appoint counsel if the accused is **indigent** (without funds). States and localities use several methods for delivering indigent criminal defense services: public defender programs, assigned counsel programs, and contract attorneys. The federal system also has several programs for the delivery of indigent criminal defense services: public defender organizations, community defender organizations and panel attorneys (Bureau of Justice Statistics, 2007a). In 1999 an estimated $1.2 billions was spent to provide criminal defense in the Nation's 100 most populous counties. Indigent criminal defense programs in these counties received approximately 4.2 million cases during 1999 (Bureau of Justice Statistics, 2007a).

If the charge is a misdemeanor, the case is often heard at this time. In many instances the defendant will plead guilty and the judge will impose a standardized fine as sentence, although there may be circumstances that warrant incarceration. In felony cases the judge may also inform the accused of the next stage in the process, usually setting a date for a preliminary hearing. Another function of the judge at the initial appearance is the administration of bail.

The Administration of Bail

One of the most controversial pretrial procedures involves setting bail. Simply stated, **bail** is the practice of releasing a defendant prior to trial with the promise that he or she will appear before the court as directed. As we will see, the issue of bail is extremely complex.

The practice of bail is traceable to England, as are many other facets of the American criminal justice network. Because judges often rode circuits and court was not held for months at a time, the English would release defendants prior to trial on the oath of responsible individuals who would ensure that the accused would be present when the trial commenced. This practice was maintained by American settlers but was altered by requiring the posting of a bond by the accused or by someone on his or her behalf. The practice was formalized by the Judiciary Act of 1789, through which the practices of admitting defendants to bail (except in capital cases) and permitting considerable discretion in the determination of bail became routine in the American criminal justice network.

Constitutionally, there are few guidelines regarding bail. The Eighth Amendment provides that bail shall not be excessive. There is no federal constitutional right to bail, but if bail is provided by state legislation, it cannot be excessive. This ambiguous mandate has generated conflict in several areas; for example, does "excessive" pertain to the financial capabilities of the accused, the nature of the charge, or some other criterion?

Before addressing these specific questions, let us first examine the practice of bail. Bail involves the posting of cash, property, or securities by the defendant or someone on his or her behalf. Originally, the manifest function of bail was to ensure that the accused would be present for trial or other pretrial procedures. In most jurisdictions, bail is set by the court as a monetary sum. The defendant or another party (legally, the surety) usually posts 10 percent of that sum in cash, property, or securities and pledges to pay the remaining 90 percent if the defendant is not present for trial (called skipping or jumping bail). Of the defendants who had State felony charges filed against them in the 75 most populous counties during 2002, 62 percent were released by the court prior to the disposition of their case. Thirty-eight percent were detained until case disposition, including 6 percent who were denied bail (Bureau of Justice Statistics, 2007b). In this study, about one-third of the released defendants were either rearrested for a new offense, failed to appear in court as scheduled, or committed some other violation that resulted in the revocation of their pretrial release (see "In the News" 8.2).

In the News 8.2

POLICE SAY LOW BAIL A PROBLEM, EVEN REPEAT OFFENDERS CAN GET OUT OF JAIL FOR CHEAP

Modesto police found 78 shaved ignition keys in the front seat of a stolen white Nissan when they pulled it over March 22, court records show.

They arrested the driver, 22-year-old Jonathon Ray Hernandez of Modesto, on suspicion of auto theft and booked him into jail. It wasn't Hernandez's first arrest. Court papers tell the story of a spree that started in January and lasted until mid-April. Hernandez was in and out of jail during that time. He would eventually plead no contest to charges of stealing 12 cars in less than four months — many while he was out on bail.

In Stanislaus County, which has the highest per capita car theft rate in the country, Hernandez is not unique.

One way to bring the car theft rate down, local authorities say, is to make it harder for people accused of car theft to go free on bail while awaiting trial. In some instances, those arrested can arrange credit for a bail bond and get out for nothing down or as little as $300.

This week, Assistant District Attorney Carol Shipley sent a memo asking local judges to quadruple the county's standard bail in auto theft cases — from $10,000 to $40,000.

Shipley also asked the 12 judges who handle criminal cases in Stanislaus County to consider a new rule adding $20,000 to the bail if a person is already out on bail, probation or parole at the time he or she is arrested.

Repeat offenders made up a significant percentage of people arrested on suspicion of car theft, Shipley's memo says. Of 234 people arrested in a 12-month period, 48 were on probation or parole after another offense. That's about 20 percent.

Shipley argued that California counties with higher bail rates than Stanislaus have lower theft rates: Fresno County sets bail at $15,000 and San Joaquin at $20,000.

Don Lundy, administrator for Stanislaus County Superior Court, said the judicial team, headed by Judge Hurl Johnson, will review the request, then make a recommendation to the county court's seven-member executive committee. The higher-level committee is expected to review the request within two weeks.

But Lundy noted that the law already provides a way officers can request higher bail for repeat car thieves, or any other repeat offenders. "That's available for them, if they want to use it." The county's bail schedule also allows $25,000 to be added at booking, without going to a judge, if authorities know that the person was out on bail.

Tim Bazar, the county's public defender, said he doubts the county's high rate of car theft is connected to the relatively affordable $10,000 bail.

He noted some counties with lower theft rates share Stanislaus' $10,000 standard bail amount.

In Riverside County, bail is $5,000, but theft rates are 44 percent lower than in Stanislaus County.

"So it seems to me that the amount of bail does not seem to be related to whether they have a big problem with auto theft in the community," Bazar said.

Bazar said prosecutors and police already can ask for higher bail in the case of repeat offenders.

Sgt. Carlos Castro, of the Stanislaus County Auto Theft Task Force, said it's true that police can request higher bail in specific cases. But "we don't want to inundate the court with bail enhancements," he said.

"We're selective on who we pick those for. We don't want to use it on a guy who's got two arrests," he said. "We use it on the guys that steal 10 or 15 cars, that are a real thorn in our side."

Castro argued raising the bail amounts would keep more defendants in jail, while awaiting trial: "What it does is to make it a little more difficult for the average Joe to be able to bail out."

Bail bonding organization officials say they share his concern for public safety, but say raising bail too high could put it out of reach of the poor. That is important because bail allows a person who has not been tried or found guilty to keep a job and continue supporting his her family. Experts say part of the reason bail increases are even being discussed across California is a trend in the bail industry toward offering credit.

Traditionally, an arrested person pays the bail bond fee — usually 10 percent — up front. But now, some bondsmen offer credit, with a low 3 percent down payment, or none.

"They can get out on $0 to $300 down, if they have good credit," said Sgt. Rick Gilstrap of the Stanislaus County Auto Theft Task Force.

One Modesto bail bondsman, who offers payment plans, said the market is driving the trend." Just like credit card companies these days, it's gotten more and more competitive, with more people coming into the business," said Vernon Sutherland, who has 15 years' experience in Modesto.

Some bail agents' professional groups deplore the trend toward offering credit.

"It reflects badly on the bail industry," said Stephen Krimel, a Santa Rosa attorney who is spokesman for Professional Bail Agents of the United States.

Krimel said he believes that when agents discount bail too much, they can't make enough money to take care of a bondsman's core responsibility — getting the defendant to court.

The California Bail Agents Association has backed legislation that would restrict bail agents' ability to offer credit.

But Krimel said decision makers need to consider issues of equal access to justice.

"If you take the credit element out, you have a gross potential for causing more problems for the lower income and indigent," he said. "There are a lot of families that can't come up with 10 percent of $10,000 or of $20,000."

Maggie Kreins, president-elect of the California Bail Agents Association, said it would be counterproductive to raise bail so high that it becomes inaccessible to those who are not rich.

"If you raise it too high, they'll just sit in the jail," she said. "Then the jails become overcrowded."

That can result in jail authorities releasing people who should be incarcerated, she said.

Craddock, B. (2005, November 2). Police say low bail a problem, even repeat offenders can get out of jail for cheap. *The Modesto Bee* (CA). sec. A, page A1.

The amount posted and the pledge for the remainder is commonly referred to as the bail bond, and the party other than the defendant, who posts the amount and pledges for the bond, is referred to as the bail bondsperson. If the accused is present for trial, the amount posted (or a portion of it) may be returned or, on conviction, may be used to pay a fine or attorneys' fees, or it may serve as an appeal bond. In some jurisdictions, the amount posted is not returned.

Consequences of Bail

In theory, bail is intended to ensure that a defendant appears before the court and answers charges. Suffet (1966) referred to this as the manifest function of bail. Earlier, we raised several questions concerning the administration of bail. We must add to this list the question of how successfully bail realizes its intended purpose.

Under our judicial system, we adhere to a policy of **nulla poena sine crimine** (no punishment without a crime). Although the intention of bail may not have been to alter this legal doctrine, in practice it has, and sometimes dramatically. Some defendants spend months in jail awaiting trial simply because they cannot afford to post 10 percent of the bail bond. Bail is often attacked as discriminating against the poor. Although defendants from the upper classes or those engaged in lucrative criminal ventures can make bail more readily, is their financial status indicative of the likelihood of appearing before the court? As a result of the inability of many accused to obtain bail money, the professional **bail bondsperson** has become a central figure in the bail controversy. It is not uncommon for a bail bondsperson to be as much (or more) of a determining factor than is the offense in deciding who will or will not be held in confinement prior to trial. In theory, the bondsperson posts the required 10 percent and pledges to pay the remainder if the accused fails to appear. In return he or she charges the accused a percentage of the bond. Defendants are usually required to pay the bonding company 10 percent of the bail bond set by the magistrate. For example, if the bond is set at $25,000, the defendant will pay the bonding company a nonrefundable fee of $2500 (Champion, Hartley, and Rabe, 2008). Thus, in theory, the bondsperson is risking considerable financial loss and must exercise caution in selecting clients. In practice, some bail bondspersons simply adjust their fee according to the risk they are taking. It is sometimes argued that a bail bondsperson generates additional crime by charging such high fees that the accused must commit another crime to pay off the bondsperson. They have also been known to engage in illegal relationships with other criminal justice personnel. Investigations have shown that bail bondspersons pay referral fees to police officers, and it has been alleged that in some instances they split fees with judges (Galliher & McCartney, 1977). It is also argued that bail bondspersons occasionally employ unethical practices in retrieving clients who fail to appear. Unlike the police, who are regulated by the Fourth Amendment, they have often literally kidnapped defendants to ensure their appearance. Chamberlin (1999), on the basis of his analysis of bail-enforcement agents, found that despite their rather shady reputation, they are better at what they do than are traditional law enforcement officers (Johnson & Warchol, 2003). It is clear that without much regulation a bail bondsperson often exercise considerable power over other citizens.

Protecting Society

Another alleged consequence of bail has been to protect society from dangerous offenders. Jurisdictions commonly designate specific offenses as nonbailable in an attempt to protect society, or bail may be set in an amount high enough to ordinarily preclude the release of particular defendants. The rise in both crime and the fear of crime in the 1970s and early 1980s led to the Bail Reform Act of 1984. This act, passed by Congress, provided for the **preventive detention** of defendants charged with violent crimes or perceived as a high risk to commit additional crimes prior to trial (Corrado, 1996). Although some scholars criticized Congress, the Supreme Court later upheld the practice *in United States v. Salerno* (1987). In practice, the high bail seldom protects society (Fagan & Guggenheim, 1996). As we have indicated, bail may actually generate more crime under certain circumstances. In addition, criminals involved with syndicates can meet bail even when it is set high. Again, we see that financial advantage can easily overcome the intent of bail.

The Determination of Bail

What factors should the court consider in setting bail? Historically, the nature of the charge and the defendant's criminal record are important criteria in setting bail. Some judges recognize that factors extraneous to the offense are also relevant in determining the defendant's probability of appearance. Such factors as residence in the community, employment, and the presence or absence of relatives and friends in the community are considered in the administration of bail. Additional extralegal factors associated with bail are race and ethnicity. Research indicates that there are four elements of the pretrial process that result in more frequent pretrial detention of minorities:

1. Black and Hispanic defendants are more likely than white defendants to be denied bail.
2. Hispanic defendants are less likely to receive a nonfinancial release option (release on recognizance) than either white or black defendants.
3. The amount of bail required for release is higher for Hispanic defendants than while defendants; there is no black-white difference in bail amounts.
4. Hispanic and black defendants are more likely than white defendants to be held on bail because of an inability to post bail. Indeed, the inability to "make bail" accounts for the majority of black and Hispanic defendants' overall greater likelihood of pretrial detention. (Demuth, 2003; Demuth & Steffensmeier, 2004; Turner & Johnson, 2005).

An experiment sponsored by the Vera Foundation, entitled the Manhattan Bail Project (Vera Institute of Justice, 1972), made substantial contributions concerning the determination of bail. The New York City project began in 1961 and involved the use of law students who interviewed defendants to determine present or recent residence at the same address for six months or more, current or recent employment for six months or more, relatives in New York City with whom the defendant was in contact, prior criminal record, and residence in New York City for 10 years or more. It was assumed that these factors would be relevant to pretrial release.

After this information was obtained, the staff commenced to determine whether to recommend that the defendants be released on recognizance, or released without posting bond. If the staff recommended **release on recognizance (ROR)**, the recommendation was forwarded to the arraignment court, where defendants were randomly assigned to experimental and control groups. Those in the experimental groups had their recommendation given to the judge, prosecutor, and defense attorney; those in the control group did not. The findings were interesting: 60 percent of those in the experimental group were granted ROR, whereas only 14 percent of the control group was released. Thus, the presence or absence of the recommendation is of great importance in releasing defendants. In general, those who were released did in fact appear. Those who failed to appear generally did so because of illness, confusion over the legal process, or family emergencies. This project was the forerunner of numerous other projects designed to circumvent the often discriminatory nature of bail (O'Rourke & Salem, 1968). Today, the use of ROR is common at all levels and in all jurisdictions.

In a later and more sophisticated experiment, Des Moines, Iowa implemented a supervised release program that attempted to expand the ROR concept and to prepare some clients for probation (Boorkman, Fazio, Day, and Weinstein, 1976). Defendants who did not meet ROR criteria were counseled and supervised prior to trial. Attempts to secure employment, reunite or maintain family ties, and otherwise become a viable member of the community served to ensure appearance at trial. More recently, pretrial intensive supervision has been used to conserve jail resources and prevent pretrial offending (Barlow, 2000, pp. 395–97).

The use of recognizance bail recognizes that the nature of the charge is not the only factor relevant to a defendant's pretrial release. Factors that tie the accused to the community should also be considered in determining bail. The practice of releasing defendants on their own recognizance has several advantages:

1. It maintains or upholds the principle of no punishment without crime (many defendants can avoid being detained in jail because of lack of money).

2. It limits the negative impact of pretrial detention in terms of costs to the taxpayer.

3. It makes bail more equitable (those without financial advantage have the same opportunity to be released as the financially advantaged).

A signature bond is similar to a ROR and is used for minor offenses such as traffic law violations and petty offenses. The signature bond is much simpler since there are no prequalifications and no one makes an assessment of the defendant's flight risk or danger to the community (Fagan, 2007). Police officers in most jurisdictions have the discretion to issue a signature bond or individual or personal recognizance bond and release the traffic offender immediately with their signature, which is a promise to appear in court. If the person fails to appear, the court often issues a warrant for their arrest.

A final bail alternative involves **conditional release or supervised released**. These forms of release can involve third party custody (i.e., parents) and involve the defendant agreeing to a number of court-ordered terms and restrictions. Common terms of conditional release include the participation in a drug or alcohol treatment program, attendance at anger-management classes, compliance with court issued restraining orders, and regular employment (Fagan, 2007).

The Effects of Monetary Bail

We previously stated that recognizance bails reduce the negative impacts of bail on defendants. In this section, we identify negative impacts that may result from the practice of setting monetary bail.

First, bail may encourage plea bargaining. Some innocent defendants may agree to plead guilty and receive probation or a fine rather than be detained in jail prior to trial. Thus, the principles of justice are subverted. Second, those who cannot make bail may suffer from being detained in jail. It is estimated that over 50 percent of America's jail population are there awaiting trial. Although there has been considerable jail reform, conditions in many of these jails are bad at best. Inmates are subjected to prolonged boredom, assault, homosexuality, poor physical conditions, substandard medical care, and exposure to convicted criminals. Those who will later be found innocent, as well as those who will be found guilty, are faced with these conditions before a determination of guilt. Third, as a result of being confined, the accused may encounter current or future employment problems. His or her family may be forced to request government assistance, and his or her absence alone may be disruptive. Additionally, the stigma of spending time in jail may follow the individual regardless of the outcome of the case. Finally, pretrial confinement may affect the outcome of the case. An accused that undergoes pretrial confinement may lack the ability to assist in his or her defense. Research by Rankin (1964) found significant differences in receiving or not receiving prison sentences between defendants making bail and those being jailed continuously. This may be due to the fact that those defendants most likely to be denied bail are also those convicted of prior offenses, charged with violent offenses, or on probation or parole at the time of their arrest (Reaves, 1998).

In conclusion, bail is a highly discretionary practice with numerous, complex side effects. In its present form, bail cannot ensure that defendants will appear, that the public will be protected, or that justice will be done. The use of recognizance bonds may help alleviate some of the discrimination in setting bail, but the issue of monetary bail remains controversial.

Formal Charging or Accusation

Before an actual criminal trial commences, there must be a formal accusation of the accused. The process of accusation is basically a review of the evidence to ensure that the evidence is substantial enough to warrant further processing of the defendant. Here, again, we see the criminal justice network employing a filter. Those cases that appear to be lacking in evidence are rejected or filtered out, thereby saving the taxpayers money, limiting the stigma facing the accused, and reducing congestion in the courts. The process of formal accusation is usually reserved for felonies and some serious misdemeanor cases. Traffic cases, petty offenses, and minor misdemeanors are usually handled routinely and do not involve a detailed review of the evidence. In many of these cases, the defendants answer to charges by pleading guilty at the initial appearance. The American network of criminal justice uses two basic means of accusation: grand jury indictment and prosecutorial information. The next two sections examine these two procedures and discuss the strengths and weaknesses of each.

The Grand Jury

The Fifth Amendment holds that "No person shall be held to answer for a capital or otherwise infamous crime, unless on a presentment or indictment of a Grand Jury." The **grand jury** was created in England to ensure that arbitrary charges were not brought against the citizenry by the government. We must remember that, in that era, the judicial and executive branches of government in England were not totally separate.

The Crown could, and did, have charges brought against those who spoke out or otherwise opposed the government. In theory, if not in practice, grand jury members were charged with reviewing the facts of a particular case and determining the validity of the charges. Like many other aspects of the English criminal justice system, the concept of the grand jury was adopted as part of the American legal system during the colonial period.

The grand jury is an accusatory jury only and should not be confused with the petit (or trial) jury, which determines innocence or guilt. The two juries differ in size, purpose, level of proof required and other areas. Still, as one component of the justice network, both give members of the public an opportunity for input into the network. Table 8.1 highlights the major differences between grand and petit juries.

Table 8.1 Distinctions between Grand and Petit Juries

	Grand Jury	Petit Jury
Purpose	Formal accusation	Determination of guilt or innocence
Size	16–23 members	6–12 members
Level of proof required	Probable cause	Beyond a reasonable doubt
Secrecy	Secret proceedings	Public proceedings
Rules of evidence	Can consider inadmissible evidence	Strict rules of evidence
Presiding authority	Prosecutor	Judge

Although the Fifth Amendment provides for the use of grand juries, they are not used in all felony cases. Federal courts employ grand juries as mandated by the Fifth Amendment. State courts, not obligated to follow this mandate, vary in their use of grand juries. Some states require grand jury review in all felony cases, whereas others require it only in cases involving the possibility of a death sentence or life imprisonment; still others permit proceedings to commence on a prosecutorial information without grand jury review. It should also be noted that, in those jurisdictions requiring grand jury review, the defendant can waive the proceedings.

The grand jury normally has two functions. The first, the presentment, permits the grand jury to act as an investigative unit. The grand jury has the power to investigate possible criminal activity of a general nature, meaning such activities as police and political corruption, organized crime activities, and offenses against the public at large. It does not investigate specific crimes. The final report and recommendations of the investigation are called the presentment. If the investigation is productive, charges will be sought.

The second and more common function is the accusatory role. In jurisdictions where the grand jury is employed, grand jury members review evidence and determine if it is substantial enough to warrant prosecution. In this role, they represent the community conscience. It should be remembered that grand juries simply weigh the strength of the evidence. They do not decide guilt or innocence.

In virtually every federal jurisdiction, there is at least one grand jury sitting every day. Generally, most federal grand juries sit for five days a week for a period of one month. However, for cases involving complex and long-term investigations (organized crime, terrorism, drug conspiracies, political corruption) the term can be extended for six month increments up to three years (American Bar Association, 2007).

Grand jury procedures are nonadversarial. Witnesses are called and answer questions from the prosecutor. A grand jury proceeding is an **ex parte proceeding**; that is, it is for only one party: the prosecution. The prosecutor decides which witnesses to call and who will receive immunity. The basic questioning is performed by the prosecutor but grand jury members are permitted to ask questions at the end of a witness's testimony (American Bar Association, 2007). Counsel for the accused is not present in the courtroom, nor is the accused, unless he or she is testifying. There is no right to cross-examination during grand jury hearings. The only parties present at the technically secret proceedings are the judge, prosecutor, grand jury, and witnesses, who are called individually. If the evidence is sufficient for a prima facie case, the grand jury will issue a **bill of indictment** charging the accused with a specific crime or set of crimes. A **prima facie case** is one in which "on the face of it," the evidence without any objections or contradictions is of such a nature that probable cause exists to charge the individual with a crime. A bill of indictment offers certain advantages because it can be sealed. If an indictment is sealed, the decision of the grand jury remains secret and is not disclosed to the public or the defendant (Fagan, 2007). The warrant for arrest of the defendant as a result of the indictment does not have to be immediately served. This scenario is typical in complex or long-term grand jury investigations that involve multiple defendants.

Because the grand jury hearing is nonadversarial, it is subject to rules and regulations that differ from those governing the trial process. The grand jury hearing is similar to the trial in that witnesses must take an oath and are subject to charges of perjury if they give false testimony. Witnesses also have the right against self-incrimination. A grand jury may rely on evidence that would be inadmissible at a trial. The Supreme Court held in *Castella v. United States* (1953) that hearsay evidence and in *United States v. Calandra* (1974) that evidence obtained illegally can be admitted during grand jury proceedings. The basis for these decisions is that the proceedings are nonadversarial. The grand jury is only a fact-finding body, not a determiner of guilt; thus, evidence that cannot be admitted at the trial may still be heard by the grand jury.

Occasionally, prosecutors will use the grand jury as a method of screening politically sensitive cases. For example, a prosecutor wanting to test the community's reaction to a controversial case may proceed before the grand jury. If no bill of indictment is issued, the prosecutor may opt to drop the charges and not proceed with the case. This practice benefits the state financially and protects the prosecutor politically, but it also opens the possibility of abuse on behalf of the prosecutor (Gibeaut, 2001).

Grand juries usually consist of 16 to 23 members, with each jurisdiction deciding on the number of members by statute. Selection is usually from those age 18 and over who are residents of the jurisdiction and who possess U.S. citizenship. Usually, grand juries are selected randomly from voting lists or other such means of registration (motor vehicle license lists, public utility lists). According to Kalmanoff (1976), grand juries are not proportionately representative by race, age, or income. The grand jury has also been criticized as being costly and subject to easy manipulation by the prosecution (Frankel & Naftalis, 1977). Unlike potential jurors in regular criminal or civil trials, grand jurors are not screened for biases or other improper factors (American Bar Association, 2007). Although such criticisms may be sound, the grand jury remains one of the methods of involving the citizenry in the criminal justice process. In fact, in Virginia, a law was passed giving grand juries the authority to conduct investigations and require witnesses to testify rather than depending solely on evidence gathered by the police and prosecutors (Organized Crime Digest, 2001). (See "In the News" 8.3.)

In the News 8.3

Grand jury pace draws criticism

Each time the Greenville County grand jury meets, it considers about 900 indictments in a single day. The group of 18 citizens went through 7,321 charges from Jan. 1 to Aug. 31 and returned indictments on all but one, according to the Greenville County Clerk of Court's Office.

The grand jury system was set up as a check against prosecutorial vendettas and hasty indictments. But with the grand jury blazing through so many cases, some have raised questions about how effective the panel can be.

Furman University political science professor Don Aiesi called the grand jury a "rubber stamp" for the Solicitor's Office. "The system isn't working," he said. "It has not functioned effectively as any kind of buffer."

Thirteenth Circuit Solicitor Bob Ariail said the grand jury hears about two-thirds of the cases that pass through his office. The panel rarely refuses to indict because solicitors weed out the weak cases and dismiss them, he said.

"We don't take junk to the grand jury," Ariail said.

The grand jury's job is to hear the state's evidence and decide if there is probable cause to hold a trial. Unlike most hearings in the criminal justice system, the defendant has no right to be present, have counsel or introduce evidence.

The Solicitor's Office doesn't oversee the grand jury. The panel reports to Chief Administrative Judge Gary Hill, who declined comment, citing judicial ethics.

Defense attorney Stephen Henry said he has been arguing in some cases that indictments should be quashed because of how many cases are run through the system. But the grand jury is a secret process, he said, making his argument tough to prove.

"If I could bring in one grand jury foreman to testify under oath, I think all this would be over," Henry said.

The county's grand jury meets once a month. Panel members start hearing cases at 9 a.m. and usually finish by 6 p.m., although they wrapped up at about 3:45 p.m. last month, Arial said.

The grand jury has given solicitors specific instructions on what it wants to know, Ariail said. Solicitors have communicated those instructions to law enforcement officers who present cases to the grand jury, he said.

In DUI cases, for example, the jury may want to hear only about "where the stop took place, what the bad driving was and what the Breathalyzer is," Arial said.

"Bam, bam, bam — you're talking three seconds to present these cases," he said.

The U.S. Constitution guarantees defendants a grand jury hearing in federal cases, but the U.S. Supreme Court has said that states can use a different system, said Andrew Siegel, assistant law professor at the University of South Carolina.

Even with the option, there often is little support for eliminating grand juries at the state level, he said.

Solicitors like them because they are friendly to the prosecution, Siegel said. Defense attorneys see grand juries as a check on prosecutorial power, at least in some cases, and there is no guarantee they would be replaced with anything better, he said.

"The real question is whether you treat the grand jury as archaic and do away with it," Siegel said, "or take steps to reinvigorate the grand jury."

State Sen. Ralph Anderson, D-Greenville, pledged in an interview with The Greenville News to learn more about the grand jury and consider legislation before the Legislature reconvenes in January.

Until he was contacted by The News, he didn't know about the grand jury's workload or the high percentage of indictments it returns.

"It can't be fair," said Anderson, a member of the Senate Judiciary Committee.

Alongi, P. (2006, October 19). Grand jury pace draws criticism. *The Greenville News*, p. 1A.

Information and Preliminary Hearings

Most felony cases today proceed on the basis of an information rather than an indictment. An **information** is a written charge issued by the prosecutor rather than the grand jury. When an information is issued, a preliminary hearing will be scheduled. Several states only require a preliminary hearing for felony cases. The **preliminary hearing** serves the same purpose as the grand jury: to establish probable cause. If probable cause is established, the accused will stand trial; if not, the charges are dismissed and the accused is given his or her freedom. However, the prosecution is not prohibited from refiling charges later.

Although the functions of the grand jury and the preliminary hearing are similar, the procedures involved differ significantly to ensure that only those rightfully accused stand trial. As we noted previously, grand jury proceedings are not open to the public, are conducted ex parte, and are not subject to some of the rigid rules of evidence. In contrast, the preliminary hearing is usually conducted before the judge or magistrate in open court, the accused is represented by counsel and is permitted to cross-examine prosecutorial witnesses as well as to call his or her own witnesses, and the defense can challenge the legality of the prosecution's evidence. Even in jurisdictions that require grand jury hearings, many defendants waive the hearing and go forward on an information because they gain the opportunity to challenge the evidence at a preliminary hearing, which they could not do if they were accused by the grand jury. It is often argued that the preliminary hearing is closer to the concept of due process.

In addition to waiving the grand jury, the accused can also waive the preliminary hearing. Reasons for such a waiver may include speeding up the process, gaining some compensation in the process of plea bargaining, and avoiding negative publicity that may result from the hearing (e.g., sex crimes and other crimes that invoke strong social response). The advantages of proceeding with the preliminary hearing include the possibility of having the case dismissed and avoiding the stigma of trial and having the opportunity to examine the prosecution's evidence so that the defense can better calculate trial strategy.

As we have seen, there are two distinct methods of formal accusation. Both are designed to determine probable cause; however, they differ as to rules, decision makers (prosecutor or judge), and the openness of the proceedings. Although the information affords the opportunity to confront witnesses and challenge evidence, the grand jury permits the decision to be made by the citizenry. As a practical matter, most cases proceed on the basis of an information, and grand juries are not routinely impaneled in many jurisdictions.

Arraignment

The arraignment in felony cases usually occurs shortly after the return of an indictment or the issuance of an information. In minor cases, the arraignment occurs at the time of the initial appearance. At the **arraignment** the judge reads and explains the charges to the defendant in open court. The defendant, who has a right to be represented by counsel, is then asked to plead, or answer, to the charges. Although jurisdictions vary in the pleas they will accept, the most common are not guilty, guilty, not guilty by reason of insanity, and nolo contendere. A plea of once in jeopardy is also possible, though it is used infrequently.

If the accused pleads not guilty, the plea will be recorded and a date set for trial. If the accused fails to enter a plea, he or she will be considered as standing mute, and the court will enter a plea of not guilty on the defendant's behalf. Usually, any conditions of bail will be continued at this time. It is possible, however, to have the present conditions reconsidered on request.

Most defendants enter a plea of guilty. As previously mentioned, the process of plea bargaining accounts for a substantial majority of guilty pleas. Estimates concerning the frequency of guilty pleas range from 60 to 90 percent of all felony cases. On the surface, it may appear that a plea of guilty negates some of the formalities of the proceedings. Obviously, it saves both the court and the defendant time and money, but because it constitutes a waiver of due process, there is a formal requirement to question the defendant concerning his or her guilty plea. By pleading guilty, the accused is relinquishing the Fifth Amendment right against self-incrimination and the Sixth Amendment rights to trial by jury, to a public trial, and to confront witnesses against him- or herself. The Supreme Court requires judges to question defendants who plead guilty. Through various decisions, the Court has required the right to counsel during plea negotiations (*Brady v. United States*, 1969), the need for a public record showing that the defendant voluntarily pled guilty (*Boykin v. Alabama*, 1968), and the necessity that a prosecutor's promise be kept (*Santabello v. New York*, 1971). The judge must ascertain, by questioning the defendant, that he or she is aware of waiving the constitutional rights and that the plea is being entered voluntarily. In addition, the judge must inform the accused of the statutory provisions for sentencing someone convicted of that particular offense. In many cases, the accused will enter the guilty plea and the prosecutor will recommend a specific sentence in accordance with a bargain they have reached, often with the knowledge of the judge. The judge will then pass sentence. In other cases, a separate sentencing hearing will be set at a later date. This is more likely if the accused pleads guilty without engaging in plea bargaining.

As we have indicated earlier, the plea of not guilty by reason of insanity is one of the most controversial aspects of the criminal justice process. Jurisdictions vary in the labels used and the terms for accepting this plea, which in essence holds that the accused did in fact engage in the criminal conduct but lacked the ability to form the necessary mental element of intent and/or is incapable, because of a mental condition, of aiding counsel in his or her defense.

To the public, the finding of not guilty by reason of insanity is tantamount to an acquittal. In reality, those defendants who are so adjudicated may be subjected to longer confinement than if they had pled guilty. In many cases, a defendant found not guilty by reason of insanity is committed to a state mental hospital until he or she is found mentally healthy. Technically, this could be a few days, but it could also mean until death. In some jurisdictions defendants are placed in mental hospitals and may be tried if they are later declared sane. The frequency of the plea of not guilty by reason of insanity is greatly exaggerated. It usually occurs during the course of murder or serious assault cases, which seems to heighten public attention. Estimates of its successful use range from 2 to 5 percent. The actual decision of sanity is left to the court. In most jurisdictions, once the plea is entered, the accused must undergo psychiatric examination. Evidence resulting from this examination is presented in court, and the jury must then reach a decision.

The insanity plea is fraught with problems. First, the term is strictly a legal one. Psychologists and psychiatrists are concerned with mental disorders that are extremely difficult to define and diagnose, yet we expect them to make pinpoint decisions in court. Second, conflicting psychiatric testimony in court often confuses and baffles jury members who are not familiar with the terminology used or conditions discussed. Finally, it is very time consuming. Usually, both the prosecutor and the defense provide one to three expert witnesses to testify to the mental state of the accused. Such testimony consumes valuable time, is often contradictory, and serves to further confuse the jury.

In the early 1980s, a number of politicians called for the abolition of the insanity defense. While it has not been abolished, several changes in the law have occurred. Some jurisdictions have established an assumption of sanity and placed the burden of proving insanity on the defense. This approach lessens the likelihood of a successful insanity defense. Some jurisdictions have also developed a "middle ground" defense of guilty but mentally ill. Under such laws, a defendant may be found guilty and sentenced like any other defendant but is also ensured of receiving treatment for her or his mental illness. Although the defense is plagued by serious problems and is in need of reform, to abolish it goes against one of the long-held foundations of law: Criminals must have the mental capacity to know that they are acting wrongfully. This is the same principle that protects infants and the severely retarded from criminal charges.

The plea of **nolo contendere** is essentially a plea of guilty. Its literal translation is "no contest." The consequence of a plea of nolo contendere is that it cannot be entered into the record of a subsequent civil proceeding. For example, A is driving a vehicle while under the influence of alcohol and runs into B's house. If A enters a plea of nolo contendere to the criminal charge of driving under the influence, B cannot use the plea as evidence of responsibility in a civil proceeding to hold A responsible for damages to the house. It does not mean that A cannot be held civilly responsible, only that his plea cannot be used in this regard. Other evidence (e.g., a breath or blood test or eyewitness accounts) may be used to find A liable. Courts vary widely on the acceptance of nolo contendere pleas. Only about half the states allow such a plea, and most limit the plea to specific offenses.

The plea of once in jeopardy is fairly infrequent. As the Fifth Amendment states, "nor shall any person be subject for the same offense to be twice put in jeopardy of life or limb." By pleading once in jeopardy, the defendant is contending that the current charge violates the Fifth Amendment. Usually, through counsel, the defendant will supply evidence contending that the accused has already been held accountable for this act. The court may review such a plea at that time or postpone the arraignment until it has had time to review the evidence.

Pretrial Motions and Hearings

In cases where the defendant pleads not guilty at the arraignment, there are usually several motions and hearings on those motions prior to the actual criminal trial. Most of these motions will be filed by the defense attorney. We must remember that these, in effect, are requests to the court, and usually the judge must issue a ruling on such requests. Some of the more common motions follow.

Motion for Change of Venue

Under the principles of due process, the defendant has the right to a trial in the jurisdiction in which the alleged crime occurred. This principle is called venue, meaning

Pretrial motions play an important role in many criminal cases.
Reprinted with permission of Forgiss / Fotolia.

"place of trial." The rationale is that local norms, values, and attitudes should be reflected in jury composition.

The motion for a change of venue is usually reserved for the defense, in which the defense is asking to have the trial moved to another venue—county, district, or circuit. Usually, the motion is based on the contention that the defendant cannot obtain a fair trial in the court of original jurisdiction because of prejudice against him or her. For example, X, who has a prior criminal record, is accused of murdering Y, the only doctor in the county. X was formerly an employee of a local granary that went bankrupt and left many farmers in the community with heavy financial losses. Some factors, such as prior record, occupation, and nature of the crime and victim, may bear heavily on X's right to a fair trial. If X files for a change of venue, he or she must provide evidence or testimony to establish that prejudice and hostility exist. The judge makes the decision, and even if the request is denied initially, it may be honored later, particularly if there is difficulty selecting and impaneling the jury.

Motion for Continuance

Although the defendant's right to a speedy trial is guaranteed by the Sixth Amendment, it is quite common for trials to take place months and even years after the act for which the accused is being tried. Although there are many reasons for this delay, one of the most common is simply that there has been a request for a continuance.

Either party may ask for a continuance. These motions are usually made shortly after arraignment, but they can be made at any time. Motions for continuance must be accompanied by an explanation of the reasons additional time is needed. Some of the more common reasons are illness, unavailability of witnesses, defense counsel's workload being in conflict with the trial date, or defense counsel's inability to be prepared. In addition, the court may arrange for a continuance if it finds it is in the interest of justice, usually meaning that the docket is overcrowded and space and/or court personnel will not be available on the stated date of trial.

Motions for Suppression and Exclusion of Evidence

In 1961 in *Mapp v. Ohio* (see Appendix), the Supreme Court held that evidence obtained or seized illegally was inadmissible in criminal trials at the state level. From that time forward, defense attorneys have made motions to exclude evidence on the grounds that it has been obtained in violation of the Fourth Amendment. These motions are usually filed prior to the trial, and the judge conducts a hearing to determine the legality of the search that produced the evidence in question. These hearings are very important because the evidence in question is often the tie between the defendant and the crime, and without this evidence, the prosecutor may have only a circumstantial case. In addition, confessions made by the defendant may be subject to suppression motions if the confessions were made involuntarily, without counsel, or without the defendant's being informed of his or her rights pursuant to the Miranda decision (*Miranda v. Arizona*, 1965; see Appendix). Again, even if the judge suppresses the confession, this is not tantamount to an acquittal. Only the confession is suppressed. Other evidence, such as fingerprints, eyewitness identification, and possession of stolen property, may still be introduced to increase the likelihood of obtaining a conviction.

Motion for Discovery

In most states, the defense has the right to discovery, that is, to examine the prosecutor's evidence, including a list of proposed witnesses, prior to trial. The rationale for a **motion for discovery** is to ensure fairness in the trial. Motions to exclude and suppress evidence often occur after the granting of a motion for discovery. The United States Supreme Court has held that due process requires disclosure of certain information prior to the trial (*Brady v. Maryland*, 1963). States vary in how broadly they apply discovery. Some allow full or complete discovery, whereas others are not as liberal. There is also the possibility of reciprocal discovery, in which both parties examine their opponent's evidence, but very few jurisdictions have adopted this practice.

Motion for Disclosure

The **motion for disclosure** is usually filed by the defense. If granted, the prosecution must produce a list of witnesses they intend to call with each witness's last known address. This list does not preclude the prosecution from calling additional witnesses if there is good cause for those witnesses' to not have been included on the original list. Like discovery, the purpose of disclosure is to provide the defense with the opportunity to plan a strategy and to investigate the credibility of the witnesses. Like many other pretrial procedures, these motions are designed to balance the scales of justice.

Motion for Dismissal

The defense will also frequently make a motion for judicial dismissal of the charges. If previous motions (e.g., exclusion and suppression) have been granted, the case may be weakened to the point that there is insufficient evidence on which to proceed. Motions to dismiss during pretrial stages do not bar prosecution at a later date if new evidence is uncovered.

Summary

1. The period from arrest to actual trial may be a very active one. Many activities are designed to ensure that the defendant will be afforded due process of law. Some of these procedures are brief and relatively uncomplicated, whereas others are very demanding in both time and energy. Many of the proceedings, such as bail and the use of grand juries, have been subject to controversy.

2. At the initial hearing, usually held within 48 hours of arrest, a probable cause determination is made.

3. Bail is the process of releasing a defendant prior to trial based on the promise that he or she will appear for the trial.

4. There are several proposals in various states to modify pretrial procedures. Most are attempts to shore up the insanity defense and to ensure that dangerous criminals are not released on bail.

5. Although pretrial procedures are beset with problems and may require reexamination, we must not lose sight of the fact that they also aid an already overcrowded court docket, save tax dollars by filtering out cases in which evidence is lacking, and afford constitutional protections to the accused.

Key Terms Defined

48-hour rule A standard for unnecessary delay, in which an accused must be taken before a magistrate within 48 hours of arrest to determine whether probable cause exists to detain him or her further.

probable cause The presence of sufficient facts to convince a reasonable person that some official action (arrest or charging) should be taken.

initial appearance The first appearance of a person taken into custody before a judge (magistrate), at which time a decision is made as to whether probable cause to proceed exists and the person is notified of the charges against him or her and informed of his or her constitutional rights.

indigent A person who is lacking the funds to hire their own attorney.

bail The practice of releasing a defendant prior to trial with the promise that he or she will appear before the court as directed or will forfeit money or property (or some portion of it) accepted by the court as a guarantee of such appearance.

nulla poena sine crimine No punishment without a crime.

bail bondsperson A person who puts up bail money for others for profit.

preventive detention Detention in jail between arrest and trial to prevent further injury or damage.

release on recognizance Release on the promise to appear before the court at the appointed time without posting bail.

supervised release or conditional release Release of a defendant prior to trial without bail under the supervision of an assigned counselor.

grand jury An investigative body whose duty is to determine whether to indict an accused.

ex parte proceeding A proceeding at which only one party is represented (as in the case of the grand jury, where only the prosecution is allowed to present a case).

bill of indictment Formal accusation issued by a grand jury.

prima facie case Case in which "on the face of it" or "at first sight," the evidence is such that probable cause exists to charge the individual with a crime.

information A formal, written accusation made by the prosecutor.

preliminary hearing A probable-cause hearing in a criminal case.

arraignment A court hearing at which the defendant is formally charged and asked to enter a plea.

nolo contendere No contest (essentially, a plea of guilty).

motion for discovery A motion to be allowed to examine the evidence of the other side prior to trial.

motion for disclosure A motion to be provided with a list of the witnesses to be called at a trial.

Critical Thinking Exercises

1. What are some of the problems associated with the use of bail? Can you think of any ways to solve these problems so that bail might be effectively and fairly administered?

2. Compare and contrast the two methods of formal accusation. What are the advantages of an indictment over an information, or are there no advantages? Are there any dangers inherent in the use of an information? If so, what are they?

Internet Exercises

Pretrial procedures may seem rather complicated for those never having been arrested and arraigned. There are some organizations dedicated to helping defendants and the curious to understand these procedures.

1. What is the mission of the National Association of Pretrial Services Agencies? http://www.napsa.org/.

2. What other websites can you find that deal with pretrial issues? What sorts of information do they contain?

References

American Bar Association (2007). Frequently asked questions about the grand jury system. Available online at: http://www.abanet.org/media/faqjury.html.

Argersinger v. Hamlin, 407 U.S. 25, 37 (1972).

Barlow, H. D. (2000). *Criminal justice in America.* Upper Saddle River, NJ: Prentice Hall.

Boorkman, D., Fazio, E. J., Jr., Day, N., & Weinstein, D. (1976). *Community-based corrections in Des Moines.* Washington, DC: U.S. Government Printing Office.

Boykin v. Alabama, 395 U.S. 238 (1968).

Brady v. Maryland, 373 U.S. 83 (1963).

Brady v. United States, 397 U.S. 742 (1969).

Bureau of Justice Statistics (2007a). *Indigent defense statistics.* U. S. Department of Justice. Available online at: http://www.ojp.usdoj.gov/bjs/id.htm.

Bureau of Justice Statistics (2007b). *Pretrial release and detention statistics.* U.S. Department of Justice. Available online at: http://www.ojp.usdoj.gov/bjs/pretrial.htm.

Castella v. United States, 350 U.S. 359 (1953).

Chamberlin, J. (1999). Private-sector enterprise (bounty hunters). *Economist, 351* (8124), 26–27.

Champion, D.J., Hartley, R.D. & Rabe, G.A. (2008). *Criminal courts structure, process and issues.* Upper Saddle River, NJ: Prentice Hall.

Corrado, M. L. (1996). Punishment, quarantine, and preventive detention. *Criminal Justice Ethics, 15,* 3–13.

Demuth, S. (2003). Racial and ethical differences in pretrial release decisions and outcomes: A comparison of Hispanic, black and white felony arrestees."*Criminology, 41,* (3), 873–908.

Demuth, S. & Steffensmeier, D. (2004). The impact of gender and race-ethnicity in the pretrial release process. *Social Problems, 51* (2), 222.

Fagan, J.A. (2007). *Criminal justice a brief introduction.* Boston, MA: Allyn and Bacon.

Fagan, J., & Guggenhiem, M. (1996). Preventive detention and the judicial prediction of dangerousness for juveniles: A natural experiment. *Journal of Criminal Law and Criminology, 86,* 415–48.

Ferdico, J. N. (1999).*Criminal procedure for the criminal justice professional* (7th ed.) Belmont, CA: Wadsworth. (2004). *Criminal procedure for the criminal justice professional* (9th ed.)Belmont, CA: Wadsworth.

Frankel, M., & Naftalis, G. (1977). *The grand jury: An institution on trial.* New York: Hill and Wang.

Galliher, J. F., & McCartney, J. L. (1977*). Criminology: Power, crime and criminal law.* Homewood, IL: Dorsey Press.

Gerstein v. Pugh, 420 U.S. 103 (1975).

Gibeaut, J. (2001, January). Indictment of a system. *American Bar Association Journal, 87,* 34–40.

Gideon v. Wainwright, 372 U.S. 335 (1963).

Johnson, B. R. & Warchol, G. L. (2003). Bail agents and bounty hunters: Adversaries or allies of the criminal justice system? *American Journal of Criminal Justice, 27* (2), 145.

Kalmanoff, A. (1976). *Criminal justice enforcement and administration.* Boston: Little, Brown.

Mallory v. United States, 354 U.S. 449 (1957).

Mapp v. Ohio, 367 U.S. 543 (1961).

McNabb v. United States, 318 U.S. 332 (1943).

Miranda v. Arizona, 384 U.S. 348 (1965).

Organized Crime Digest, 22, Legislature toughens grand jury system. (2001, January 31). 11.

O'Rourke, T. P., & Salem, R. G. (1968). *A comparative analysis of pretrial procedures. Crime and Delinquency, 14* (4), 367–73.

People v. Edward Mitchell, No. 99 CR 19684 (02) (2004).

Rankin, A. (1964*). The effect of pretrial detention.* New York University Law Review, 39, 641.

Reaves, B. A. (1998). *Felony defendants in large urban counties 1994.* Washington, DC: U.S. Department of Justice.

Riverside County, California v. McLaughlin, 500 U.S. 144 (1991).

Santabello v. New York, 404 U.S. 257 (1971).

Suffet, F. (1966). Bail setting: A study of courtroom interaction. *Crime and Delinquency, 12* (4), 318–31.

Turner, K. B. & Johnson, J. B. (2005). A comparison of bail amounts for Hipanics, Whites, and African Americans: A single county analysis. *American Jounral of Criminal Justice, 30,* (1), 35–56.

United States v. Calandra, 414 U.S. 358 (1974).

United States v. Salerno, 481 U.S. 789 (1987).

Vera Institute of Justice. (1972). *1961–1971: Programs in criminal justice.* New York: Author.

Suggested Readings

Burns, R., Kincade, P., & Leone, M. C. (2005). Bounty hunters: A look behind the hype. *Policing, 28* (1), 118–139.

Demuth, S. & Steffensmeier, D. (2004). The impact of gender and race-ethnicity in the pretrial release process. *Social Problems, 51* (2), 222.

Ferdico, J. N. (2004). *Criminal procedure for the criminal justice professional* (9th ed.) Belmont, CA: Wadsworth.

Richman, D. C. (1999). Grand jury secrecy: Plugging the leaks in an empty bucket. American *Criminal Law Review, 36* (3), 339–56.

Schlesinger, T. (2005). Racial and ethnic disparity in pretrial criminal processing. *Justice Quarterly: JQ, 22* (2), 170–193.

Chapter Nine

Criminal Trial

In the News 9.1

BRIGHT DEFENSE COST $221,000 — BUT BILLS FOR THE 15-MONTH CASE STILL ONLY HALF THE STATE AVERAGE.

PEORIA — Those charged with the task of defending admitted serial killer Larry Bright spent more than $221,000 to spare him the death penalty.

According to figures released from the state treasurer's office, Bright's three attorneys, a mental health expert and investigators have submitted bills totaling $221,515, said John Hoffman, a spokesman for the office that administers the Capital Litigation Trust Fund through which the attorneys and others were paid.

That figure doesn't include any submissions from Peoria County State's Attorney Kevin Lyons though he had previously estimated that his submissions to the trust fund would be considerably less than by the defense.

Even so, the cost for Bright's 15-month case is about half that of the state average of $500,000, Hoffman said.

Bright, who will be 40 next week, pleaded guilty May 30 to murdering seven women and causing an eighth to die by a drug overdose. He agreed to give up all his appeal rights and be sentenced to life in prison in exchange for Lyons not seeking the death penalty.

Had his case gone to trial, it would have likely cost tens of thousands more, said Jeffrey Page of Springfield, one of Bright's attorneys. Under state law, the trust fund will reimburse attorneys for their time at a rate of $141.71 an hour. Also reimbursed are work-related expenses such as travel and copying, among other things.

The fund was created in 2000 to help both sides recoup the costs associated with capital cases and to insure that a defendant would have the best possible defense if the case were to go to trial.

"It's just obscene that I would even comment on where I think our case would fit into the state average because I can't get by how outrageous and nutty the state average is.

The figures tell me that whenever the state is paying, the case will be milked like a cow," Lyons said.

But he credited Page and others for pursuing the plea agreement, saying the pot of state money encourages defense attorneys to string cases out rather than resolve them.

So far, $17.2 million has been paid out statewide since the trust fund was created. That excludes Cook County, which handles its own finances because of the sheer number of cases there.

The most expensive trust fund case has been the 2004 trial of Cecil Sutherland, who was convicted and sentenced to death for killing a 10-year-old girl. That case, held in Jefferson County, resulted in $2.3 million in bills to the trust fund.

Page admits there are lawyers who abuse the system, but said there have been safeguards put in place to prevent that. Still, he said, money should not be a factor when a life is at stake.

For those who gawk at the high price, Page has the answer.

"Then you need to put pressure on the Legislature and your governor and try to persuade them to get rid of the death penalty if you think it costs too much," he said. In Peoria County, there have been two death penalty cases besides Bright since the fund was established — Jarvis Neely and Jayson Schertz.

Neely was convicted of killing a Peoria police officer and sentenced to life in prison.

His case took 22 months and cost $123,752.

Schertz pleaded guilty in June 2004 to fatally shooting a rural Chillicothe woman while high on crack cocaine. He was sentenced to 53 years in prison. The total bill for his case was $69,139, none of which went to Lyons' office.

The prosecutor billed the state $10,979 in the Neely case, most of which was travel-related expenses as the trial was moved to Springfield because of pre-trial publicity.

Kravetz, A. (June 29, 2006). Bright defense cost $221,000 — But bills for the 15-month case still only half the state average. *Peoria Journal Star.* Section: City, p. 1.

Key Terms

speedy trial
plea bargain
bench trial
summary trials
jury pool
venire
voir dire
challenges for cause
peremptory challenges
nullification
real evidence
testimonial evidence
direct questioning
cross-examination
impeach
redirect examination
recross-examination
motion for a directed verdict
expert witnesses
hearsay evidence
leading questions
presentation of the defense's case
rebuttal
surrebuttal
closing argument
hung jury
mistrial
sequester
polling
truth-in-sentencing
presentence investigation

Chapter Outline

The Right to a Speedy Trial
Jury Trials: A Great American Myth
Plea Bargains
Summary and Bench Trials
The Jury Trial
Order of Trial
Sentencing
Appeals

In Chapters 7 and 8, we discussed the organization of the court systems, the roles of the various participants in those systems, and pretrial procedures. In this chapter, we describe and analyze the actual trial process by emphasizing legal requirements, some consequences of those requirements, and societal reactions to them.

The Right to a Speedy Trial

The Sixth Amendment to the U.S. Constitution guarantees defendants in federal criminal cases the right to a **speedy trial**, and the court's decision in *Klopfer v. North Carolina* (1967) extended the doctrine to the state courts. In practice, however, many criminal trials still commence months and sometimes years after the filing of formal charges or arrest.

The speedy-trial doctrine is often criticized as being vague and ambiguous, despite the fact that the Supreme Court has attempted to clarify the meaning of the doctrine through various decisions. In *Klopfer v. North Carolina* (1967), the court applied the speedy-trial doctrine to the states, recognizing it as a fundamental right of those accused of crimes. In applying this doctrine, the justices were attempting to protect the defendant from public scorn, protect the defendant's employment status, and limit the anxiety of those awaiting trial. In short, the Court clearly recognized the numerous hardships the accused might suffer if not afforded the right to a speedy trial.

In contrast, it is not uncommon for a defendant to benefit from judicial delay. The credibility and availability of witnesses diminishes with time. As a result, many defense attorneys waive their clients' rights to a speedy trial as a strategy. Can an accused use the speedy-trial doctrine as a defense if his or her attorney's actions have caused or contributed to the delay? In *Barker v. Wingo* (1972), the Court held that such cases must be decided after balancing four factors: (1) the length of the delay; (2) the reason for the delay; (3) the defendant's responsibility to assert his or her right to a speedy trial; and, (4) the prejudice resulting from the delay. Although these tests are far from objective, they do represent attempts to clarify the issue and perhaps make it more difficult for a defendant to ask for continuances or fail to object to a prosecutor's motion for continuance and still challenge the proceedings on the basis of the violation of the right to a speedy trial.

Yet another major legal issue concerning speedy trial involves the determination of when the right commences. For example, Jones burglarizes Smith's house while Smith is vacationing. Five months later, when Smith returns home, he discovers that his stereo and some money are missing. Smith reports the crime to the police, but the perpetrator is not identified. Four months later, Jones is arrested on another charge, and a subsequent search of his premises uncovers Smith's stolen property. Obviously, the time lapse between the offense and the arrest is considerable, and it may be another four or five months before the case is brought to trial. Can Jones successfully claim that his right to a speedy trial has been violated?

In *United States v. Monroe* (1971), the Court held that the time period involved does not commence until an indictment or information has been issued or the accused has been arrested for a criminal charge. Further clarification of the time period was provided by the U.S. Supreme Court in *Doggett v. United States* (1992). The Court held that a defendant who was indicted in 1980 but not arrested until 1988 had been denied his right to a speedy trial. The defendant left the country in 1980 and returned in 1982. The government thought the defendant was still absent from the country and made little effort to locate him (Reed, 2006, p. 488, 489).

Most jurisdictions employ statutes of limitations that state the maximum allowable time period between the offense and formal accusation (after which time the offender can no longer be charged with the offense). This is not to be confused with the time period for a speedy trial. Most jurisdictions also have statutes specifying the time period involved in the speedy-trial doctrine. For instance, in Illinois, a defendant held in custody must be tried within 120 days, and one out on bail has the right to have his or her case heard within 160 days (Illinois Criminal Law and Procedure, 2007, chap. 725, sec. 5/103-5). At the federal level, the Speedy Trial Act of 1974 and subsequent amendments in 1979 and 1984 state that a defendant in a federal criminal case must be brought to trial within 100 days of arrest. The 100 day federal provision involves the following limits: 30 days from arrest to initial appearance; 10 days from initial appearance to an arraignment; and 60 days from the date of an arraignment to trial (Champion, Hartley, and Rabe, 2008, pp. 357–358). Defendants can still, of course, waive their right to a speedy trial by filing motions for continuances. Only the prosecution is prohibited from prolonging the delay without good cause.

Jury Trials: A Great American Myth

One of the basic elements of the American criminal justice process is the right to a trial by jury. Like the right to a speedy trial, the right to trial by a jury of one's peers is guaranteed by the Sixth Amendment. This right was extended to defendants in state court proceedings through the Supreme Court's decision in *Duncan v. Louisiana* (1968). In a later decision, *Baldwin v. New York* (1970), the Court qualified the doctrine by holding that the right to trial by jury applies only in cases in which the defendant faces the possibility of a prison term of six months or more.

How frequently do jury trials actually occur? The vast majority of cases, about 90 percent, are actually settled by a plea of guilty that may occur at any time between the arraignment and the commencement of trial proceedings. The two major sources of guilty pleas are plea bargains and summary trials.

Plea Bargains

Although we have previously discussed plea bargaining (see Chapter 2), a closer look at the way it affects criminal trials is in order. You will recall that a **plea bargain** involves pleading guilty for some consideration. In his classic study of plea bargaining, Newman (1956) indicated that the considerations involved fall into four categories: (1) considerations concerning charge; (2) considerations concerning sentence; (3) concurrent sentences; and, (4) dropped charges. In bargaining charges, the accused agrees to plead guilty to a charge less serious than the original charge to obtain less severe punishment. In bargaining for sentence, the accused pleads guilty to the original charge with the understanding that a lenient sentence will be recommended. In bargaining for concurrent sentences, the accused pleads guilty to more than one charge in return for receiving sentences that run concurrently. For example, a defendant may be arrested for one burglary, and during a legal search of his house, the police may find evidence that he also committed five other burglaries. If burglary is punishable by 5 years of imprisonment, the burglar, if found guilty of all six burglaries, could be sentenced to 30 years in prison. In a bargain for concurrent sentences, the burglar might agree to plead guilty to all six burglaries if the prosecutor agreed to sentence him to six concurrent terms of 5 years, in which case the defendant would actually serve a maximum of 5 years. In bargaining to drop charges, the defendant may agree to plead guilty to the most serious charge if all other charges against him are dropped. For instance, Green is charged with aggravated battery, disorderly conduct, and resisting arrest. Green might plead guilty to the aggravated battery charge if the prosecutor agreed to drop the disorderly conduct and resisting arrest charges.

On several occasions, the courts have attempted to regulate plea bargaining. In *Boykin v. Alabama* (1969), the Supreme Court held that when a defendant enters a plea of guilty, it must be made in open court and the defendant must be informed of the nature of the charge, the potential sentence, and the consequences of his or her plea. The Court noted that the accused is waiving the protections of both the Fifth (against self-incrimination) and the Sixth (of trial by jury and a right to confront one's accusers) Amendments and therefore serious attempts must be made to ensure the voluntariness of the plea. As a result of the Boykin decision and a later decision in *Brady v. United States* (1970), most judges question the defendant concerning the waiver of his or her rights, inform the defendant of the possible penalties on conviction, and ask if the plea is being entered voluntarily. In *Santobello v. New York* (1971), the Court held that the prosecutor must honor promises made during negotiations or the guilty plea may be withdrawn. In a later decision, *Bordenkircher v. Hayes* (1978), the Court determined that a prosecutor's threat to seek reindictment under a habitual criminal statute, if the defendant refuses to plead guilty to a lesser charge, does not violate due process. In, *Ricketts v. Adamson* (1987), the court ruled that defendants must also live up to their terms of a plea bargain to receive leniency.

Plea bargaining is controversial for a variety of reasons. It is largely unobservable, and it eliminates citizen participation as jurors. Frequently, victims and witnesses appear at court only to find that their testimony and participation are not required because the case has been bargained. However, in many cases victims of crimes are permitted to provide input into plea bargaining at two stages of the process: when conferring with the prosecutor during plea bargaining and when addressing the court, either orally or in writing before entry of the plea (National Center for Victims of Crime, 2002). Depending upon the law in a specific State, a victim may be given the opportunity to comment on a proposed plea at either or both of these stages. Today, most states provide victims some level of prosecutorial consultation about a negotiated plea agreement. In no state is the right to confer interpreted as the right to direct the prosecution of the case or to veto decisions of the prosecutor. In at least 22 States, the victim's right to confer with the prosecutor requires a prosecutor to obtain the victim's views concerning the proposed plea (National Center for Victims of Crime, 2002). In some States, the prosecutor must inform the court of the victim's position on the plea agreement.

In some cases, plea bargaining makes a mockery of the justice network in that offenders may be convicted of charges quite different from those leading to their arrests and/or may receive punishments that are regarded as extremely lenient by victims and witnesses. Finally, some innocent parties may plead guilty to offenses they did not commit because they fear that they will be convicted on more serious charges if they maintain their innocence to the point of trial (Gorr, 2000). Although the actual incidence of such cases is probably very low, all these criticisms combined led Alaska to prohibit the practice of plea bargaining, with few if any unpleasant side effects (Rubenstein & White, 1979). Other proposals to restrict plea bargaining involve increasing court resources and requiring preplea conferences in which the judge, victim, defendant, prosecutor, police, and defense counsel all meet and discuss the issues involved in resolving the case. Palermo, White, and Wasserman (1998) concluded that in spite of its critics, and in view of the overburdened legal system, plea bargaining is here to stay. It is important to note that states that retain plea bargaining must adhere to goals related to fairness, less delay, less disparity among sentences, and sentences closer to those that would result from a trial (Reid, 2006).

Summary and Bench Trials

The Sixth Amendment and the Supreme Court's decision in *Duncan v. Louisiana* (1968) have defined the right to trial by jury in serious cases. In *Baldwin v. New York* (1970), the Court went on to define a serious case as one in which the possible penalty is more than six months of imprisonment. In *Patton v. United States* (1930), the Court ruled that a defendant can waive his or her right to trial by jury. In a later decision, *Singer v. United States* (1965), the Court upheld a federal statute requiring that the waiver of trial by jury be contingent on approval of the prosecutor. But why would a defendant waive his or her right to a jury trial? Some defendants may feel that they will receive some consideration if they save the court's time by not invoking their right to a jury trial. Others may fear a jury because they are charged with an emotion-laden crime such as child molesting. Still others may seek the perceived dispassion of a neutral judge in deciding their fate. Whatever the reason, the federal court and most state systems permit waiver of the right to trial by jury. About 40 percent of those found guilty at trial are convicted by a judge in what is commonly referred to as a **bench trial** (Cole, 1995, p. 403).

Most criminal defendants are charged with misdemeanors or petty offenses rather than felonies and are not guaranteed the right to jury trial. Justice is dispensed for these individuals at **summary trials**, which are expedient for both the court and the defendant. A large number of cases can be dealt with in a short time period during which charges are read, guilty pleas accepted, and fines levied. If we add those dealt with in summary courts to defendants who waive their right to jury trial and those pleading

A significant number of criminal cases are decided by a judge at a bench trial.
Reprinted with permission of iStockphoto.com / Jacom Stephens.

guilty for considerations, it is apparent that only a small number of criminal defendants are tried by a jury of their peers. For example, out of the 924,900 persons convicted of felonies in state courts in 2000, criminal trials accounted for only 5 percent of the convictions. The remaining 95 percent of the convictions were guilty pleas (MaGuire & Pastore, 2005).

The Jury Trial

By some estimates, jury trials have declined to less than 2 percent of all cases filed (Jones, 2004). Many attribute this decline to clogged court dockets, the costs and risks of going to trial, and to alternative forms of case resolution. The jury trial, nonetheless, remains important because it is one of the few areas in criminal justice in which members of the public are directly involved (as jurors, witnesses, and victims). Theoretically, the basic advantage of the jury trial is the assurance that the accused will be judged by a fair and impartial group. Specific procedures for selecting jurors have been developed to ensure that this occurs.

The selection of the jury involves a multistage process, the final result being a group of 12 (sometimes fewer) citizens chosen to decide the criminal case. First, a **jury pool** is randomly selected from the host community. In order for a random cross-section of the community to be maintained, a variety of lists, including tax rolls, voter registration lists, and utility lists, are used to ensure that no specific group of individuals (e.g., members of a racial or ethnic minority or gender) are systematically excluded. Recently, some jurisdictions have used licensed drivers as a source of jurors. This method is currently being used on an experimental basis in some federal courts. An individual listed in the jury pool is subject to service for a specified time period, generally three months.

Second, for each jury trial, a group of potential jurors are randomly selected, constituting the **venire**, the size of which varies according to the population of the jurisdiction. Members of the venire are legally summoned to appear in court on a specific date and will undergo yet another stage in the process to determine if they are to sit on a particular jury.

In the third and final stage of the process, both the prosecuting and the defense attorney question members of this panel in open court in the process of **voir dire** (literally, "look-speak," or to tell the truth). This process is intended to further guarantee a fair trial by allowing interested parties the opportunity to question jurors and discharge those who may be biased. For example, 30 people might be directed by the court to appear as potential jurors on a given date. In court, 12 members of this panel will be summoned to the jury box, where they must take an oath of honesty before answering questions under voir dire examination. Both attorneys will question prospective jurors concerning their knowledge about the case, their relationships with any of the participants, any opinions they may have formed about the case, and other pertinent issues. In some jurisdictions, including the federal courts, the trial judge questions the potential jurors using his or her own questions as well as those submitted by the prosecutor and the defense attorney. This method is used to promote efficiency and to avoid the attorneys' conditioning the jurors to their side of the case before the trial begins.

In determining the actual jurors, both attorneys may challenge (excuse) potential jurors by using challenges for cause and peremptory challenges. **Challenges for cause** are unlimited in number. In challenges of this type, the attorney asks the court to excuse a prospective juror because his or her responses to voir dire questions show an inability to view the case objectively. The judge makes the final decision on the basis of evidence heard during voir dire. Because challenges for cause are unlimited, most attorneys extensively question potentially hostile jurors in an attempt to prove bias and excuse such jurors.

Peremptory challenges are usually limited in number by statute. In some jurisdictions, an attorney is limited to 3 challenges, whereas in capital cases the number may range as high as 20. No reason has to be offered for a peremptory challenge, but because they are limited, most attorneys will try to save them and will challenge jurors for cause if possible. Both the state's attorney and the defense attorney have specific types of people they want to excuse, depending on the charge, and will often use peremptory challenges to exclude members of those groups. For example, in drunk driving cases prosecutors may want to exclude younger jurors because they are more likely to have recently engaged in similar behavior and will be less likely to return a conviction. In comparison, some defense attorneys will try to exclude females and deeply religious people from serving as jurors in rape cases. If the challenge for cause is not honored, the attorney may use one of his or her peremptory challenges to ensure that jurors with certain characteristics do not serve on a particular case.

Let us return to our example. Of the first 12 potential jurors, the prosecutor challenged 2 jurors, and the defense attorney challenged 3, which left 7. If both attorneys approve these 7, they will not be questioned further and will remain in the jury box until 5 more jurors have been accepted by the attorneys. Next, 5 new prospective jurors will replace those excused, and the voir dire examination will continue until 12 members have been chosen. The 12 selected will be sworn in, and the remaining members of the jury panel will be excused but are eligible to be called for future trials.

To many, the process of jury selection is one of the most important stages in the criminal process. Some attorneys attempt to stack the jury rather than to obtain a fair jury. It is common for both attorneys to employ investigators to conduct background investigations on prospective jurors so that they can conduct an extensive and complete voir dire and select a jury that is more open to their case. Additionally, in some high-profile cases, defendants will employ jury consultants. These consultants are experts who claim to be able to identify who will make the best jurors for the defendant's case.

In addition to the trial jury, many jurisdictions also select alternate jurors during voir dire. Alternate jurors remain in the courtroom and are able to replace an original juror who has to be excused during the trial. They do not participate in the deliberations unless there is a need to replace one of the 12 original jurors. This practice saves the court time and the defendant time and money because, without it, if a juror has to be excused during the trial, a mistrial would be declared and the entire process repeated.

Traditionally, juries have consisted of 12 individuals, as in our example above. The Supreme Court, however, has held that juries with 6 members do not violate constitutional guarantees (*Williams v. Florida*, 1970). The Court upheld a Florida statute permitting 6-person juries in noncapital cases. The Court contended that the 12-person jury was a historical accident and that the right to trial by jury did not specify the number of jurors. This decision does not, of course, require the use of 6-person juries, but it does permit the states to engage in the practice of using fewer than 12 jurors in noncapital cases if they so desire. Most states still employ 12-member juries, and those permitting juries of fewer than 12 often limit their use to misdemeanor cases or those in which both parties stipulate. Later, in *Ballew v. Georgia* (1978) and *Burch v. Louisiana* (1979), the Court deemed 5-member juries and nonunanimous verdicts from 6-person juries unconstitutional. The number of jurors and the issue of whether a unanimous decision is required are important; according to Dino (2000), when unanimous verdicts are required from large (12-member) juries, they seldom convict the defendant.

Another legal issue involved in jury trials centers on the composition of the jury. In *Glasser v. United States* (1942), the Court stated that a jury of one's peers means a random cross-section of the community. Thus, a white female is not entitled to be tried by a jury of all white females, but by a jury that is randomly drawn with all community members having a chance of being selected. In *Taylor v. Louisiana* (1975), the Court declared Louisiana's system of excluding females from jury service unconstitutional. Applying the Glasser ruling, we can see that this practice would not provide a cross-section of the community.

Although the Court has been explicit in demanding that jury lists not be drawn in a discriminatory manner, the use of peremptory challenges to exclude specific types of jurors remains controversial. Historically, there were no limits placed on the use of peremptory challenges, and in some instances, attorneys used peremptory challenges to fashion juries along social and racial lines. In 1986, the Supreme Court put an end to such practices in *Batson v. Kentucky*. The Court held in Batson that using peremptory challenges to eliminate jurors based on race violates the Fourteenth Amendment. Under certain circumstances, the prosecutor must now explain to the court his "race-neutral" reason for challenging a juror who is of the same race as the defendant. This procedure has received some criticism because it prolongs jury selection and interferes with the unfettered use of peremptory challenges. It has, however, become an entrenched part of the jury selection process. Recalling our discussion of voir dire, we can see why the use of peremptory challenges is limited and why attorneys consider the use of these challenges important in courtroom strategy.

Those who support the practice of trial by jury argue that juries reflect community values, reduce the potential for bias, and are politically free. Those who oppose the jury system argue, for the most part, against the way the principle is applied rather than against the principle. One of their arguments focuses on jury composition. In most jurisdictions, citizens in certain professions are systematically excluded from jury duty (e.g., doctors, lawyers, teachers, and other professionals). Other qualified jurors can ask to be excused because jury duty will cause a hardship on them or their families. Who is left to serve? Some critics claim that juries are generally composed of the elderly, the uneducated, and bored homemakers (see "In the News" 9.2).

In the News 9.2

The jury is in on feeble excuses — They don't work, though potential jurors keep trying to buck civic duty

PEORIA — After hearing the facts of the trial case, the woman took her time to carefully consider the case details, deciding whether she could be impartial and objectively judge the case as a juror.

"Yes," she meekly told Kevin Lyons — but only under one condition.

"As long as there's nothing funny," she told the Peoria County state's attorney. "Because when I laugh, I pee."

Lyons replied with a chuckle and assured her that she wouldn't have to worry about hearing anything funny — at least nothing funnier than that.

Whether true or not, some jurors will take any chance and use any excuse to get out of their civic task: jury duty.

Some jurors are chosen once in their lives, while others will serve every few years.

Jurors are chosen randomly by a computer, "so blame the computer," said Jim Ludolph, court security supervisor for the Peoria County Courthouse.

Those who opt to blow off Peoria's call can be issued summons from the sheriff and be held in contempt of court, then have to explain to the judge why they didn't serve.

The process is similar in Woodford and Tazewell counties.

"Then they serve after that," said Carol Newtson, Woodford County circuit clerk.

In Peoria County, each juror fills out a profile questionnaire, which asks things like occupation, children's names and occupations, physical impairments and if the person has any past convictions. This is a person's first chance to get out of jury duty.

The most common excuse people detail is medical reasons. A close second is a person saying they won't be paid from work when they're gone. People claim that their work simply cannot continue without them, and for some people, it's true and the excuse works.

If a person is self-employed, he or she likely will be excused. But this excuse has to be believable to actually work, instead of simply displaying a lack of creativity.

Lyons recalled a self-employed flower-shop owner who reasoned with a judge to excuse her.

About three people down the line, a man told the judge he was thinking of opening his own flower shop, so he couldn't serve, either.

Needless to say, the man's excuse didn't work.

Jurors constantly try to steal each other's excuses, said Paul Caroll, assistant court security supervisor at the Peoria County Courthouse.

"Once one gives an excuse, it's just a matter of minutes before someone else will use it," he said. "You can see the light go on."

But using work as an excuse doesn't fly with Peoria County Sheriff Mike McCoy.

"If I get hit by another truck, they'll have a new sheriff tomorrow by noon," he said, referring to a January 2006 accident in which he was struck by a pickup truck while jogging. If a person is the sole caregiver for a disabled person, he or she usually is excused, too. The judge is not sympathetic to parents who have to pick up kids from school. Citing a vacation or cruise doesn't usually work, either.

Some people are simply untruthful, Lyons said. An elderly woman was asked if any family members had been charged with an offense. After rubbing her forehead, she admitted she couldn't think of anyone.

But Lyons knew he recognized her last name. After investigating, he found that she had two children in jail: one for murder and one for attempted murder. Lyons remembered, because he represented them.

The woman's response: "Well, I didn't know you meant that kind of crime."

Of the 160 jury summons sent each week, about 115 to 125 people are available each week for the two or three weekly trials. Each trial in Peoria County gets 12 jurors and two alternates.

Carroll sees it as each person's turn to listen and make an important decision.

"It's an awesome responsibility," Carroll said. "You don't want to take that lightly."

Some people are determined not to serve because they're not interested in all the waiting at the courthouse that goes along with jury duty, claiming "their time is so valuable," Lyons said.

People tend to think of the old court system when jurors served for two weeks and would simply sit in a small room from 8 a.m. to 5 p.m. Lyons compared the experience to being a puppy in a pet store, sitting cutely, just waiting to be chosen.

Now jurors are obligated for one week and serve for two days or one trial, whichever comes first.

"It's just a non-inconvenience," he said.

By the time Peoria County jurors were reporting for duty a few weeks ago, a middle-aged man already was asleep, arms crossed, in the jury assembly room.

By a few minutes to 1 p.m., more than 30 people had filled the room. Few were smiling, and all were ready to wait for the call of a trial

After Stacy Witt, county courthouse jury commissioner, gave the rundown of what would happen throughout the day, she asked for questions.

A woman near the back quickly asked if she could be excused. Witt told her she'd have to talk to the judge.

Jurors were sworn in, then shown a video about jury duty. After the video ended, the hum of the air conditioning provided a steady soundtrack for the waiting game.

Watch TV. Read. Stare. Yawn. Sleep.

By about 2:15 p.m., Witt was back, announcing that everyone was done for the day and should report back at 9 a.m. to possibly repeat the process.

In Woodford County, people over 80 are given the option to get out, especially with a medical excuse.

Seasonal jobs also are considered, meaning teachers and students usually are called in the summer, while farmers are called in the winter.

Woodford doesn't call jurors during the popular vacation months of July and December, said Newtson, the Woodford County circuit clerk.

About 156 jurors are called each third week of the month; about 70 of those end up coming in to serve.

The extra people are called to provide schedule flexibility, Newtson said.

"I realize it's a hardship on many people, and I don't want to make it any worse," she said. Jurors serve for one week at a time, unless a trial is expected to take longer.

Between 130 and 150 people can be called each week for petit jury in Tazewell County, said Emma Zimmerman, the county's jury commissioner.

They serve one week, or whatever is required by court. If the judge says a trial will take two weeks, they're called for that two-week period.

Volunteers aren't accepted in the Tri-County Area, although some people are more than willing to perform their civic duty.

"Oh, I would love to do it every day," said Marian McCoy, the mother of Peoria County Sheriff Mike McCoy.

The appeal is simple: "It's just listening to other people's problems."

But once she's asked what her children do, she's out. She's been turned away several times, rarely getting past the question about family members involved with the police department. She has managed to serve just a few times and loved every minute of it.

"It runs in the family," she said.

While some people might never serve, no one is disqualified from getting sent a juror questionnaire, including teachers, reporters and even employees at the sheriff's office.

Even Ludolph, the court security supervisor for the Peoria County Courthouse, has served on jury duty.

"It's unusual to be picked," he said, because of his status. "But you go, you do your duty as a citizen."

Bayer, C. (August 5, 2007). **The jury is on feeble excuses — They don't work, though potential jurors keep trying to buck civic duty.** *Peoria Journal Star.* p. B1.

A further argument against juries centers on the decision-making process. Jurors receive no formal training; thus, if the charge that they are educationally unrepresentative is valid, their ability to reach a just decision is questionable. Juries have been accused of relying on characteristics of the parties involved rather than on the evidence presented to determine the outcome of cases. Also, some challenge the ability of jurors to interpret the law, arguing that since judges and attorneys who have studied and practiced for years have difficulty making legal applications it is almost impossible to expect jurors to be able to do so. Recently, there has also been much concern about the issue of jury nullification. **Nullification** occurs when jurors, who are instructed to follow the applicable law, ignore the law to reach what they perceive a correct result. There is a dispute among legal scholars as to whether jury nullification is a legitimate exercise of power by a jury. Conrad and King (2002) indicated that nullification invites jurors to devise their own defenses to a criminal charge. The Constitution does not support an enhanced law-making role for juries. Jurors have no personal constitutional right to disregard the law; otherwise they would not be required to take an oath to obey it (Conrad & King, 2002). However, according to Conrad and King (2002), legislatures and judges have rejected repeated proposals to lower barriers to jury nullification, because they understand that the costs of such changes would far outweigh the benefits.

Additional debate related to juries has developed concerning the use of cameras in the courtroom. Those in favor of cameras claim they are a tool of the media's trade like the reporters' pen and notepad (Hayslett, 2007). The cameras provide an unfiltered, unbiased method for the public to observe court proceedings and better understand

A small percentage of criminal cases are decided by juries.
Reprinted with permission of iStockphoto.com / Chris Reed.

the judicial process. Those against the use of cameras in the courtroom claim that only out-of-context sound bites are aired and that attorneys and clients play to the camera while others are distracted and intimidated (Hayslett, 2007). Camera access ranges from a presumptive right in Florida where even jurors are photographed, to a complete ban in federal courtrooms. In between these extremes are various circumstances in which courts permit and restrict the use of cameras.

Once again, we are faced with the dilemma of considering the cost of democratic involvement. Given that juries have made mistakes and have decided outcomes on the basis of nonlegal factors, is it worth the sacrifice to exclude the public from court involvement and to relinquish all power to criminal justice officials?

Order of Trial

There are well-established procedures in jury trials. As we have discussed, the voir dire examination is the first step in the process. Additional steps include opening statements, presentation of evidence, closing arguments, jury instructions, deliberation, return of the verdict, sentencing, and appeal.

Once the jury has been selected, charges will be read in open court, and the judge will ask both parties if they wish to make opening statements. Because the burden of proof rests with the state, the prosecutor makes his or her opening statement first. The defense attorney may make his or her opening remarks immediately after the prosecutor, or, in some jurisdictions, may wait until later in the proceedings. Opening statements can be waived, but this is rare in major felony trials. There are at least two good reasons for making opening remarks. First, they can provide the jury with a general overview of what the attorney intends to prove and how he or she intends to prove it. Second, the opening statement can help the attorney establish rapport with the jury if he or she maintains good eye contact, talks to the jurors in a personal manner, and explains to the jurors how important their role is in the criminal justice process. Opening statements are not to be argumentative, and lawyers are generally required to prove later, with evidence, any claims they made in opening statements.

The state has the burden of proving that a crime was committed and that the accused was the offender. The prosecutor (state's attorney or district attorney) always presents the state's case first. The prosecutor will rely on **real evidence** and testimony to present his or her case. Real evidence consists of objects that can be seen by the judge and/or jury. **Testimonial evidence** is simply evidence entered by a witness. When the prosecutor calls and questions a particular witness, he or she is engaging in **direct questioning**. The term is also applied to witnesses called and questioned by the defense attorney. Because the Sixth Amendment guarantees the accused the right to confront his or her accusers, the opposing attorney (in this case, the defense attorney) is provided an opportunity to cross-examine each witness. During **cross-examination**, attempts may be made to discredit the witness or to lessen the impact of the witness's testimony. For example, a witness testifies under direct examination that he or she saw the accused engaging in criminal activity. Under cross-examination, the defense attorney may ask questions concerning the distances involved, the witness's eyesight, or any other factor that might refute the witness's testimony. On cross-examination, the prosecutor or defense attorney in some cases will question the witness's ability to identify or recollect, or try to impeach the witness or the evidence (American Bar Association, 2007). **Impeach** means to question or reduce the credibility of the witness or the evidence that was presented in court. In order to impeach a witness it is appropriate in many states to ask the witness if they have been convicted of a felony or crime involving moral turpitude (dishonesty), since this is relevant to their credibility (American Bar Association, 2007). Cross-examination is limited in scope. The attorney administering cross-examination can ask only questions related to testimony given under direct examination; questions of untouched areas cannot be asked. Once cross-examination is completed, the party calling the witness will be provided the opportunity for redirect examination, again being limited to testimony challenged during cross-examination. **Redirect examination** is usually an attempt to clarify points challenged in cross-examination. The opposing party is also provided with a second line of questioning in **recross-examination** and is limited to evidence discussed during redirect examination. As you can see, the rules that govern testimony are specific and act as a filter in terms of the quantity of testimony covered. The prosecutor will proceed by calling all the witnesses named in disclosure and will provide the defense counsel with the opportunity to cross-examine each witness. When the prosecution has concluded calling all his or her witnesses, the state will rest its case.

Once the prosecution has rested its case, the defense attorney will usually make a **motion for a directed verdict** asking that the charges be dismissed because the state has failed to reasonably prove that the accused committed the offense. In ruling on such a motion, the trial judge is required to view the state's evidence in a light most favorable to the prosecution. Although the motion is generally denied, the judge retains the authority to halt the proceedings if he or she believes that the state has failed to prove the charges. By moving for a directed verdict at this time, the defense attorney is attempting to have the case dismissed, to lay foundation for possible postadjudicatory appeals, or both.

Before we continue with our discussion of the stages in the trial process, we need to discuss some of the rules of evidence. Evidence is a form of proof that relates to the existence or non existence of a fact. There are four traditional types of evidence: real, demonstrative, documentary and testimonial (Dicarlo, 2001). Real evidence includes such objects as weapons, fingerprints, shell casings, blood samples, and any other physical objects relevant to the proceedings. Demonstrative evidence illustrates the testimony of a witness and often involves maps, diagrams of a scene of an occurrence and animations (Dicarlo, 2001). Documentary evidence is a form of real evidence and includes public records, official documents, newspapers and certificates. The final form of evidence, testimonial evidence consists of what is stated in court by a witness deemed to be competent. Before one of the above forms of evidence can be introduced, proper foundation must be provided. For example, in a murder case, the prosecutor must establish that a homicide has occurred and the type of weapon used before the weapon can be entered into evidence. The process of laying proper foundation may be quite lengthy and involve several witnesses, including doctors, victims, witnesses, and laboratory technicians.

Closely related to the rule of laying foundation is the requirement to certify expert witnesses. **Expert witnesses** can answer hypothetical questions and render opinions, whereas lay witnesses can only testify to facts. There are two prerequisites for the admissibility of expert testimony at trial. First, the witness must be qualified by virtue of knowledge, skill, experience, training or education in the field. Second, the subject of the expert's testimony must be something outside of the knowledge and understanding of ordinary persons such as jurors, so that the testimony will help the jury to better understand the evidence and determine the facts to be decided at trial (Burnette, 2007). For example, in an arson case the questions to be qualified as an expert will involve education background, years of schooling, employment history, rank and responsibilities in an agency, number of fire scenes previously investigated, and the number of times the person has been qualified as an expert at trial. Qualifying a witness as an expert may provide greater credibility for the witness's testimony and, consequently, affect the judge's or jury's decision (Foot, Stolberg, & Shepherd, 2000). It is this concern that justifies strict control in qualifying a witness as an expert.

In television and movie trials, one often observes the attorneys objecting to the introduction of direct evidence. Normally, these issues would have been decided during pretrial suppression hearings, but the attorney may enter an objection to make that objection a part of the court record, which is generally required to preserve the issue for an appeal.

Another of the more well-known rules of evidence is the hearsay rule. Generally, **hearsay evidence** is inadmissible. A witness may testify that she saw the accused rob a liquor store but cannot testify that a third party told her that he saw the accused commit the robbery. There is a growing list of exceptions to the hearsay rule, and time and space do not permit a detailed analysis of all these exceptions. For instance, there are twenty-four exceptions to the rule against hearsay in the federal rules of evidence. Common exceptions might include excited utterances and dying declarations. Generally, the rule still applies, but we suggest that the reader consult his or her jurisdiction's criminal code to learn the exceptions.

The last rule we will cover is that of leading the witness. An attorney is prohibited from asking **leading questions**. From a practical viewpoint, this problem is rare under current practices. Most attorneys meet with their witnesses prior to the trial and coach them as to what questions will be asked and how to present their testimony. Because of the familiarity with the questions, the witness can anticipate upcoming questions and the attorney can easily avoid charges of leading the witness. Leading questions are acceptable when inquiring into background information from a witness.

Another issue that has received much discussion in recent years is whether to allow jurors to ask questions during the trial. The recent trend in some courts is to allow jurors to question witnesses on a limited basis. In fact, most states give judges the authority to allow jurors to ask questions and to set the process for such questions. The practice is prohibited in Georgia, Minnesota, Mississippi, Nebraska and Texas, according to the National Center for State Courts (Sarche, 2005). Additionally, judges have always had the authority to question witnesses.

The rules presented here represent only a portion of the many rules governing the trial and the presentation of evidence, but they are among the most frequently used.

The next stage in the proceedings is the **presentation of the defense's case**. If defense counsel did not make opening statements at the commencement of the proceedings, he or she will make them here. The defense attorney will then present his or her case in much the same manner and by the same rules of evidence as the prosecution presented its case. The defense is not required to present a case, but it normally does so to refute the state's evidence. Common strategies include offering an alibi, casting doubt on the motive, introducing contradictory testimony, or employing an affirmative defense. Once the defense has called and questioned all its witnesses, it will rest its case. At this point the prosecution or the defense can call a **rebuttal** witness to refute evidence presented by the opposing side or to attempt to reestablish the credibility of evidence that was previously challenged. After one side presents a rebuttal witness the opposing side is afforded **surrebuttal** and can call a witness to challenge the testimony of the rebuttal witness. In most cases the judge limits this part of the trial to a rebuttal and surrebuttal.

The next stage in the proceedings is the closing arguments. In some jurisdictions, the order of presentation is reversed at this stage: The defense will present closing arguments first, and the prosecution will follow. During a **closing argument**, the parties summarize their arguments and attempt to conclusively prove their version of the case. Some lawyers also employ dramatic and emotional pleas in an attempt to affect the trial's outcome. The closing arguments are the attorneys' last chance to reach the jury before deliberation, and it is often felt that the impact of closing arguments outweighs the evidence presented. There are few limitations on closing arguments, but lawyers are not allowed to do such things as make inflammatory or highly prejudicial comments or refer to a defendant's refusal to testify.

When closing arguments have concluded, the judge will charge the jury to render a true and just verdict and will provide them with legal instructions. The instructions stage requires the judge to explain the laws that apply to the case. Often juries have the option of choosing alternative forms of guilty verdicts, called lesser included offenses (Neubauer, 2005, p. 323). For example, in homicide cases the judge may have to explain differences between varying degrees of murder or between murder and manslaughter. Thus, in a murder case the jury could find the defendant guilty of 1st or 2nd degree murder, manslaughter or not guilty on all charges. In many cases the judge also instructs the jury as to what constitutes reasonable doubt. Oftentimes the parties may disagree as to the proper instructions. An instructions conference is usually held in which the lawyers submit their versions of the instructions to the judge; the judge, after listening to arguments from both parties, decides what instructions to give to the jury. Jury instructions are a common source of appeals in criminal cases. Those who argue against the jury system often contend that most jurors are incapable of understanding such instructions, which may vary in length from a few minutes to hours. In an attempt to alleviate this problem, jurors are sometimes permitted to take sets of written instructions with them into deliberations.

After they have received their instructions, the jurors retire to a private area in which they deliberate the outcome of the case. The bailiff generally serves as a link between the jury and the judge and is responsible for making sure no one attempts to communicate with the jury. A first step in most deliberations is the selection of a jury foreperson, who will preside over the deliberations and in many cases will deliver the verdict in open court. The jurors then discuss the case, examine the evidence presented, and may refer to transcripts to clear up disagreements or settle disputes. Some court rules limit or prohibit the use of transcripts in the jury room. Eventually, the jurors take a vote on the guilt or innocence of the defendant, Traditionally, votes had to be unanimous before a guilty verdict could be returned, but in *Johnson v. Louisiana* (1972) and *Apodaca v. Oregon* (1972), the Supreme Court upheld verdicts of 10 to 2 as constitutional in felony and capital cases. However, most jurisdictions still require unanimous decisions and if the first vote is not unanimous, require that the jury return to deliberation and attempt to produce a unanimous decision concerning guilt. If the jurors cannot reach such a decision, the jury is referred to as a **hung jury**, and a decision concerning retrial must be made. In most cases if the judge finds that the jury is hung, a mistrial is declared. A **mistrial** is a trial that was not completed. The trial is terminated and declared void before the jury returns a verdict (American Bar Association, 2007). A motion for a mistrial can be initiated by the prosecutor or the defense attorney. Mistrials may occur for several reasons other than the inability of a jury to agree on a verdict. These include:

1. death of a juror or attorney.
2. an impropriety in the drawing of the jury discovered during the trial.
3. a fundamental error prejudicial to the defendant that cannot be cured by appropriate instructions to the jury (highly improper remarks in an attorney's closing argument).
4. juror misconduct (e.g., having contacts with one of the parties, considering evidence not presented in the trial, conducting an independent investigation of the matter).
5. the jury's inability to reach a verdict because it is hopelessly deadlocked (hung jury). (American Bar Association, 2007)

During some trials, publicity concerning the trial becomes an issue. When publicity is extensive, the judge may feel that it is difficult to select an impartial jury and may choose to **sequester** the jurors, that is, to isolate them physically from news and other sources of information that might affect their decisions. Because sequestering is a costly operation, it is normally reserved for very highly publicized or sensitive cases. When sequestering is probable, the jury selected is at risk of including only those citizens who are willing to be separated for long periods of time from friends and relatives, and who can afford to be absent from their employment (Neubauer, 2005). Even in cases where the jury is not sequestered the judge will instruct the jurors to not read or listen to news reports concerning the case and to not discuss the case with anyone outside the jury room.

Once the jurors have reached a decision, the foreperson notifies the judge, and court is called back into session. The defendant is asked to stand, and the verdict is read aloud. The return of the verdict is a brief but important part of the trial procedure. The announcement of the verdict is usually made by the either the foreperson of the jury or the clerk of the court. Either attorney may ask that the jury be polled, although the request is usually from the losing party. The act of **polling** involves asking each juror if he or she agrees with the decision of the jury as it was announced in open court. This is to make sure that the verdict announced is the actual verdict of the jury (American Bar Association, 2007). If upon polling the jury there is not the required concurrence the judge may direct the jury to return for further deliberations, or in some cases the judge may discharge the jury. If the verdict is not guilty, charges are dismissed and the defendant is released. If the verdict is guilty, the judge usually sets a date for sentencing and then recesses. In some cases after a guilty verdict, if the defendants were released on bail, the judge will order the defendant held in custody until sentencing. If the jury returns a guilty verdict the defendant can file post-verdict motions, which are heard prior to sentencing. These motions provide the defense attorneys the option of rearguing alleged mistakes made at the trial (Neubauer, 2005). One of the most common post-verdict motions is a motion for a new trial.

Sentencing

Sentencing in most cases poses no particular problem for the judge. In cases involving plea bargaining, the judge generally accepts the recommendation of the prosecutor as to the sentence. In summary trials, penalties are often standardized by specific fines for specific offenses. In those cases resolved by criminal trial, however, sentencing is often considerably more problematic.

By and large, sentencing is the exclusive province of the judiciary. A few states provide for jury sentencing, but such sentencing is normally limited to cases involving the possibility of the death penalty. The defendant has a right to be represented by counsel at the sentencing hearing. The major complaint against current sentencing practices has to do with sentence disparities. Although some disparities are bound to occur, critics argue that sentencing disparities in many cases represent discriminatory practices, generally based on race, social class, gender, or some combination of those factors. There is little doubt that some judges do engage in discriminatory sentencing, but the judiciary is certainly not the sole body responsible for the overrepresentation of minorities and lower-social-class inmates in prison. As we have indicated before, discrimination based on these factors may occur at all levels of the criminal justice network: in reporting crimes, in making arrests, in deciding to prosecute, and so on. Differential treatment at each of these levels determines the characteristics of those individuals who proceed to the trial and sentencing stages.

Judges have considerable discretion in imposing sentences, as we have previously noted. Several factors appear to affect sentencing decisions, including the judge's view of the defendant (e.g., tough or remorseful), the ethnicity or race of the defendant (Steffensmeier & Demuth, 2000), the political ramifications of the case, the nature of the offense, the availability of prison space, and, perhaps, the gender of the judge. Songer and Crews-Meyer (2000) studied the impact of state supreme court judges' gender over a 10-year period on decisions involving obscenity and death penalty cases. They concluded that women judges tend to vote more liberally on both issues than their male counterparts and that the presence of women judges tends to increase the probability that male judges will support a more liberal position.

Although sentencing is a complex process, few law schools provide much training in sentencing, and few lawyers who become judges have much prior experience with sentencing. As a result of these shortcomings and the fact that social scientists have very little good information on the effects of various types of sentences, most judges sentence on a trial-and-error basis. There is, however, a national trend to send judges to sentencing institutes and workshops such as those provided by the National Judicial College in Reno, Nevada. Such workshops are intended to help judges better understand sentencing options and their consequences and perhaps to reduce sentencing disparities.

Another attempt to reduce the problem of disparate sentencing has been a shift from indeterminate to determinate sentencing. In indeterminate sentencing, the judge would sentence a convicted party to an indefinite period in prison (e.g., two to five years). Prison officials and parole boards actually determine the length of the sentence as a result of their involvement in granting good time and early release. In determinate sentencing, the legislature provides a range of possible sentences, and the judge must impose a specific sentence within these parameters. For example, the penalty for robbery might be 5 to 25 years, and a judge sentencing a guilty party would have to determine the specific number of years to be served (e.g., 11 years). At this point, whatever its other positive contributions, determinate sentencing does not appear to have had much impact on sentencing disparity. A number of states have implemented sentencing guidelines. These guidelines limit judicial discretion by creating sentencing grids that are based on the seriousness of the offense, the defendant's criminal history, and other relevant factors. The grids are to be strictly followed and allow little range in which to sentence each particular defendant. In another attempt to reduce sentencing disparity, some jurisdictions allow a judge to depart from the normal sentencing range, whether upward or downward, if certain exceptional circumstances exist. The sentencing guidelines approach remains controversial. Some experts believe it strips the judge of too much sentencing discretion and dehumanizes the sentencing process. Other critics charge that disparities are built into the scheme and result in inequitable impacts on certain classes of defendants. The Federal Sentencing Guidelines were established in the 1980s to ensure that the same federal crimes would receive the same punishment. However, in *U.S. v. Booker* (2005) the U.S. Supreme Court held that the mandatory nature of the Federal Sentencing Guidelines violated the Sixth Amendment because it required a judge to enhance a defendant's sentence based on facts that were neither found by a jury nor admitted by the defendant. (Bissonnette, 2006, p.1). *U.S. v. Booker* restored to judges much of the discretion that Congress took away when the mandatory sentencing guidelines were put in place (Seghetti & Smith, 2007). In essence, the Court's decision gave federal judges discretion in sentencing offenders by not requiring them to adhere to the guidelines; rather, the guidelines can now be used by judges on an advisory basis.

One of the decisions made by the judge with respect to sentencing concerns the issue of sentences for multiple offenses. The judge must decide whether such sentences will be concurrent or consecutive and in some cases whether to invoke habitual criminal statutes. Suppose, for example, that a defendant has been convicted of rape and kidnapping and is sentenced to concurrent terms of 30 years for rape and 10 years for kidnapping. The maximum time that could be served would be 30 years. If the sentences were imposed consecutively, the maximum time to be served would be 40 years. Under habitual criminal statutes, persons convicted of committing three or more felonies in a given time period may be sentenced to life imprisonment. Judges' decisions concerning whether to sentence under these statutes contribute to the controversy surrounding sentencing. (See "In the News" 9.3.)

In the News 9.3

Decatur man gets life sentence for armed robbery
47-year-old assessed under three strikes law

DECATUR — A 47-year-old Decatur man was sentenced on Wednesday to life in prison without parole for a May 2005 armed robbery.

Isaac Curry Jr. was assessed the automatic life sentence by Associate Judge Scott Diamond under Illinois' three strikes law because it was Curry's third conviction for a Class X felony. He was convicted of armed robberies in 1989 and 1995.

Last month, Curry was convicted in a May 2005 robbery of a now-closed Walgreen's store at Wood and Jasper streets. The robbery was less than three weeks after Curry had been paroled and released for his 1995 conviction.

According to police reports, Curry entered the store about 11 p.m. on May 29 and asked if the store was open so he could buy a pack of cigarettes. He then grabbed orange juice from the drink aisle and stood in a checkout line with his hands behind his back.

Once other customers left, Curry revealed he was wearing white cotton gloves and removed a large butcher knife from his clothing. He then grabbed a female employee and threatened to kill her unless another female opened the register.

After it was opened, Curry grabbed some money and fled.

Defense attorney Joseph Vigneri attempted to show another side of Curry at the sentencing hearing. Curry's sister, Linda Witherspoon, testified that her brother is a loving person.

Curry took the stand to talk about his 11 years of service in the Army and Army Reserves before he became addicted to drugs. He also testified about how he must use urostomy and colostomy bags for bodily functions because of surgeries he underwent in colon cancer treatment while in prison.

Vigneri attacked the constitutionality of the three strikes law, arguing it creates disproportionate penalties for certain crimes.

"Had he murdered somebody in cold blood, he would have received less time than what he's getting under this sentence," Vigneri argued.

But Assistant State's Attorney David Spence argued that even if no one was physically harmed in the case, society was still harmed by the robbery and Curry's past actions.

"This is an appropriate sentence," Spence said.

Tallon, M. (April 20, 2006). Decatur man gets life sentence for armed robbery: 47-year-old assessed under three strikes law. *The Herald and Review* (Decatur, IL). p. A5.

Another sentencing issue involves imposition of the death penalty. In some states with the death penalty, only one trial is held: The jury first determines innocence or guilt and, if the defendant is found guilty, then deliberates on the penalty to be imposed. In other states, a trial is first held to determine innocence or guilt and, if the defendant is found guilty, a second trial is held to determine if the death penalty or a life sentence should be imposed (Roberson, 2003, p. 442). Recent decisions by the Supreme Court appear to indicate that the death penalty may only be imposed in cases where the defendant is convicted of "first-degree-murder with aggravating circumstances" (Roberson, 2003, p. 442).

Since many sentences imposed are shortened by "good time" and by bureaucratic considerations such as overcrowding, there has been a movement to enact **truth-in-sentencing** legislation, which requires a convicted person to serve a specified portion of his or her sentence (generally 80 to 85 percent) before he or she is eligible to be released from prison. The federal government provides funds for prison construction to states that guarantee that prisoners will serve at least 85 percent of their sentence (Lippman, 2007, p. 56).

Prior to passing any sentence, the judge will normally require a **presentence investigation**. This investigation is the responsibility of the probation officer and is used to provide the judge with information on which to base a sentencing decision. The probation officer prepares a report that is made available to the judge, the prosecutor, and the defense counsel. Information contained in the report includes prior criminal record, employment, family, military history, length of residence in the community, and in some cases a recommendation from the probation officer concerning sentence. When properly conducted, the presentence investigation can be very valuable to the judge. However, two major problems characterize such investigations. First, because of heavy caseloads, some probation officers do not conduct in-depth investigations and/or fail to verify all the information contained in the report. Second, presentence reports are often highly subjective, and the biases of the probation officer simply replace those of the judge. In many cases the sentence ordered by the judge parallels the presentence report's recommendation by the probation officer If this is the case nationally, a great deal of sentencing power has been relinquished by judges.

The network approach to criminal justice makes clear the impact of the sentencing decision on various components of the network. To the extent that the judge makes an appropriate sentencing decision, the public is protected for at least some period of time from further crimes by the offender, and the police will not be involved with rearrest or the prosecutor with preparing for another trial. Further, caseloads of probation officers, prison personnel, and parole boards are largely determined by the judges' decisions at sentencing hearings. In some hearings, political ties clearly affect the judge's decision and, for that matter, may affect whether the case is heard on appeal by the higher courts. Inappropriate decisions at this stage also have obvious (and often less desirable) consequences for the various segments of the criminal justice network.

Appeals

Even after the sentence has been imposed, there is no guarantee that a criminal case is over. Convicted parties generally enjoy the right to appeal. Appellate courts review trial transcripts for legal errors, such as improper jury instructions or improperly admitted evidence, because the appellate court is limited to consideration of the trial record only. Such review does not constitute a new trial. According to Neubauer (2005) defendants win on appeal only 1 out of 8 times. The appellate court may not reverse the conviction but can order a modification of the sentence ordered by the trial judge.

Summary

1. The process of adjudication in criminal cases is complex and often controversial.

2. Most criminal cases are resolved through plea bargaining or summary trials, which involve guilty pleas.

3. In the small percentage of cases decided by a jury, both legal and nonlegal factors play a major role, as can be seen in the selection of jurors, the presentation of cases by opposing counsel, and sentencing disparities.

4. During the actual criminal trial, the order of presentation and the types of evidence admitted are governed by a set of procedural regulations.

5. The determination of sentence for those individuals found guilty is one of the most difficult duties of the judge.

6. The judge typically requires a probation officer to conduct a presentence investigation and frequently follows the recommendation of the probation officer in sentencing.

Key Terms Defined

speedy trial Trial without unreasonable delay.

plea bargain An agreement between the prosecution and defense (and sometimes the judge) concerning charges, plea, and often, sentence.

bench trial A trial in which evidence is heard and a decision rendered by a judge without a jury.

summary trials Trials in which there is no need to resolve factual issues (as when a defendant pleads guilty to a misdemeanor).

jury pool A group of citizens formed by using a number of lists in an attempt to attain a representative cross-section of potential jurors in the jurisdiction.

venire The pool of citizens from which jurors are selected for a particular trial.

voir dire Look-speak; the process of examining potential jurors to determine whether they are acceptable as actual jurors.

challenges for cause Objections to a prospective juror generally based on demonstrated (usually during voir dire) inability to view a case objectively.

peremptory challenges Objections to a prospective juror for which no cause need be stated.

nullification Occurs when jurors ignore the law to reach what they perceive a correct result.

real evidence Demonstrative evidence consisting of objects seen by the jury.

testimonial evidence Evidence given verbally by a witness.

direct questioning The initial questioning of a witness in a trial by the attorney who called the witness.

cross-examination The initial questioning of a witness called by an opposing attorney during a trial.

impeach Involves an attorney in a trial questioning or reducing the credibility of a witness or evidence.

redirect examination Additional questioning of a witness during a trial by the attorney who called the witness.

recross-examination Additional questioning of a witness during a trial by an opposing attorney.

motion for a directed verdict A motion by the defense attorney asking that the judge find that the state has failed to reasonably prove that the accused committed the offense.

expert witnesses Persons possessing special knowledge or skills who (following proper certification) are allowed to testify at a trial concerning both facts and conclusions that may be drawn from those facts.

hearsay evidence Secondhand evidence; information provided to the witness by another party that has not been substantiated by the personal observations of the witness.

leading questions Questions that lead the witness to answer in a particular way.

presentation of the defense's case The stage in a trial when defense counsel presents the case for the defendant.

rebuttal A part of the trial at the conclusion of the defendant's case in which either side is permitted to call witnesses to refute evidence presented by the opposing side.

surrebuttal The response to rebuttal by the opposing side.

closing argument A summary of the evidence presented in a trial, generally intended to indicate that the evidence presented by the attorney presenting the argument has supported his or her version of the facts in a case.

hung jury A jury that cannot reach a decision as to innocence or guilt.

mistrial A trial that was not completed.

sequester To isolate (as in isolating a jury from media presentations while the jury is deliberating a case).

polling A judge asking each juror if they agree with the verdict that was announced in open court.

truth-in-sentencing Legislation which requires a convicted person to serve a specified portion of his or her sentence (generally 80 to 85 percent) before he or she is eligible to be released from prison.

presentence investigation An investigation conducted by a probation officer to help the judge determine an appropriate sentence.

Critical Thinking Exercises

1. Several court decisions have attempted to clarify the meaning of "speedy trial." Discuss the importance of the following cases in this context: *Klopfer v. North Carolina* and *Barker v. Wingo*. Why is the concept of a speedy trial so important to defendants?

2. Plea bargaining is an important feature of the criminal justice network.

Explain the dynamics of plea bargaining, and discuss the arguments supporting and opposing plea bargaining. Do you see a future without plea bargaining?

Internet Exercises

We have discussed a number of issues and problems related to the criminal trial process in the United States. Examine some of the most current information available on the Internet for the following issues.

1. Jury nullification involves jurors, who have been instructed to follow the applicable law, ignoring the law to reach what they perceive to be the correct result. Find a web site that provides information on jury nullification. Should jurors engage in the practice of nullification? Why or why not?

2. Go to the Congressional Research Service Report to Congress (2007) concerning the Federal Sentencing Guidelines at http://www.fas.org/sgp/crs/misc/RL32766.pdf.

Should the law be amended to require federal judges to follow sentence guidelines, or should federal judges be permitted to use their discretion in sentencing?

References

American Bar Association (2007). *How courts work. Division for public education.* Available online at: http://www.abanet.org/publiced/courts/crossexam.html.

Apodaca v. Oregon, 406 U.S. 404 (1972).

Baldwin v. New York, 399 U.S. 66 (1970).

Ballew v. Georgia, 435 U.S. 223 (1978).

Barker v. Wingo, 407 U.S. 514 (1972).

Batson v. Kentucky 476 U.S. 79 (1986).

Bissonnette, G. R. (2006). "Consulting the federal sentencing guidelines after booker. *UCLA L. Rev.,53,* 1497. Available online at: http://www.uclalawreview.org/articles/archives/?view=53/6/3-1.

Bordenkircher v. Hayes, 98 S. Ct. 663 (1978).

Boykin v. Alabama, 395 U.S. 238 (1969).

Brady v. United States, 397 U.S. 742 (1970).

Burch v. Louisiana, 441 U.S. 130, 138 (1979).

Burnette, G.E. (2007). Expert testimony in an arson case. InterFire Online. Available online at: http://www.interfire.org/res_file/exptest.asp.

Carter, R. M., & Wilkins, L. T. (1967, December). Some factors in sentencing policy. *Journal of Criminal Law, Criminology, and Police Science, 58,* 503–14.

Champion, D.J., Hartley, R. D. & Rabe, G. (2008). *Criminal courts: Structure, process and issues.* Upper Saddle River, NJ: Prentice Hall.

Cole, G. F. (1995). *The American system of criminal justice.* Belmont, CA: Wadsworth.

Conrad, C.S. & King, N. (2002). Should juries nullify laws they consider unjust or excessively punitive? Palacios, W.R., Cromwell, P.F. & Dunham, R. eds. (2002). *Crime and justice in America*. Upper Saddle River, NJ: Prentice-Hall, Inc.

Dicarlo, V. (2001). Summary of rules of evidence. FindLaw. Available online at: http://library.findlaw.com/2001/Jan/1/241488.html.

Dino, G. (2000). Jury verdicts and preference diversity. *American Political Science Review, 94* (2), 395–406.

*Doggett v. United States,*550 U.S. 647 (1992).

Duncan v. Louisiana, 391 U.S. 145 (1968).

Foot, M. T., Stolberg, A. L., & Shepherd, R. (2000). Attorney and judicial perceptions of the credibility of expert witnesses in child custody cases. *Journal of Divorce and Remarriage, 33* (1/2), 31–45.

Glasser v. United States, 315 U.S. 60 (1942).

Gorr, M. (2000). The morality of plea bargaining. *Social Theory and Practice, 26* (1), 129–51.

Hayslett, J. (2007). Cameras in the courtroom: The debate continues. *Courts Today, 5* (3), 43.

Illinois Criminal Law and Procedure, (2007) Find Law, Available online at: http://www.findlaw.com/11stategov/il/laws.html.

Johnson v. Louisiana, 406 U.S. 356 (1972).

Jones, L. (2004). Fewer trials, more tribulations. *The National Law Journal.* Available online at: www.law.com/jsp/article.jsp?=1090180363092.

King, N. J. (1999). The American criminal jury. *Law and Contemporary Social Problems, 62* (2), 41–67.

Klopfer v. North Carolina, 386 U.S. 213 (1967).

Lippman, M. (2007). *Contenporary criminal law: Concepts, cases, and controversies.* Thousand Oaks, CA: Sage.

Maguire, K. & Pastore, A. (2005). *Sourcebook of criminal justice statistics 2004*. Albany, NY: The Hindelang Criminal Justice Research Center.

National Center for Victims of Crime (2002). *Victim input into plea agreements.* National Institute of Justice. Rockville, MD: U.S. Department of Justice.

Neubauer, D.W. (2005). *America's courts and the criminal justice system* (8th ed.) Belmont, CA: Thomson Wadsworth.

Newman, D. J. (1956). Pleading guilty for consideration: A study of bargain justice. *Journal of Criminal Law, Criminology, and Police Science, 46*, 780–90.

Palermo, G. B., White, M. A., & Wasserman, L. A. (1998). Plea bargaining: Injustice for all? *International Journal of Offender Therapy and Comparative Criminology*, 42 (2), 111–21.

Patton v. United States, 281 U.S. 276 (1930).

Reid, S. (2006). *Crime and criminology* (11th ed.) Boston, MA: McGraw-Hill.

Ricketts v. Adamson, 483 U.S. 1 (1987).

Roberson, C. (2003). *Criminal procedure today: Issues and cases* (2nd ed.). Upper Saddle River, NJ: Prentice Hall.

Rubinstein, M. L., & White, T. (1979). Plea bargaining: Can Alaska live without it? *Judicature, 62* (6), 266–79.

Santobello v. New York, 404 U.S. 257 (1971).

Sarche, J. (2005, May 4). Colorado Supreme Court Asked to Ban Jurors' Questioning of Witnesses. Available at: http://www.law.com/jsp/article.jsp?id=1115111117704.

Seghetti, L.M. & Smith, A. M. (2007). *Congressional research report for Congress—Federal sentencing guidelines: Background, legal analysis, and policy options.* Available online at: http://www.fas.org/sgp/crs/misc/RL32766.pdf.

Singer v. United States, 380 U.S. 24 (1965).

Songer, D. R., & Crews-Meyer, K. A. (2000). Does judge gender matter? Decision making in state supreme courts. *Social Science Quarterly, 81* (3), 750–62.

Steffensmeier, D., & Demuth, S. (2000). Ethnicity and sentencing outcomes in U. S. federal courts: Who is punished more harshly? *American Sociological Review, 65* (5), 705–29.

Tanaford, S., & Penrod, S. (1986). Jury deliberations: Discussion content and influence processes in jury decision making. *Journal of Applied Social Psychology*, 16, 322–47.

Taylor v. Louisiana, 419 U.S. 522 (1975).

United States v. Booker, 543 U.S. 220 (2005).

United States v. Monroe, 404 U.S. 307 (1971).

Williams v. Florida, 399 U.S. 78 (1970).

Suggested Readings

Brock, D. F., Sorenson, J., & Marquart, J. W. (2000). Tinkering with the machinery of death: An analysis of the impact of legislative reform on sentencing of capital murders in Texas. *Journal of Criminal Justice, 28* (5), 343–49.

Davis, A.J. (2007). *Arbitrary justice: The power of the American prosecutor.* New York, NY: Oxford Press.

Gorr, M. (2000). The morality of plea bargaining. *Social Theory and Practice*, 26 (1), 129–51.

Jonakait, R.N. (2006). *The American jury system.* New Haven, CT: Yale University Press.

Lieberman, J.D. & Sales, B.D. (2006). *Scientific jury selection.* Washington, DC: American Psychological Association.

Lippman, M. (2007). *Contemporary criminal law: Concepts, cases, and controversies.* Thousand Oaks, CA: Sage.

McConville, M. & Mirsky, C.L. (2005). *Jury trials and plea bargaining: A true history.* Houston, TX: Hart Publications.

Steffensmeier, D., & Demuth, S. (2000). Ethnicity and sentencing outcomes in U.S. federal courts: Who is punished more harshly? *American Sociological Review, 65* (5), 705–29.

Chapter Ten

Victims and Witnesses

In the News 10.1

AFRAID TO CRY OUT – LAW ENFORCEMENT RESOURCES TEND TO BE FOCUSED ON YOUNGER VICTIMS AND PERPETRATORS, EXPERTS SAY

In old age, they absorb bruises, rage — even sexual violence.

Although society has awakened to the problem of domestic violence between younger people, an entire category of victims remains, for the most part, an afterthought.

Elderly victims of violence, typically targeted by spouses and adult children, are often vulnerable and socially isolated and must rely on a safety net designed for people many years younger, the Wisconsin State Journal found in an eight-month investigation of elder abuse.

Among the newspaper's findings:

* Police, jails and courts are poorly equipped to handle elderly suspects and victims. Despite mandatory arrest rules in domestic violence cases, some police officers are reluctant to arrest elder perpetrators.

* Doctors and nurses aren't required to routinely ask elders about possible abuse, and some lack the time or training to detect problems.

* No domestic violence shelter fully meets the needs of elderly victims in Dane County and most other parts of the state, which can make them reluctant to ask for help.

The elderly are the least likely of all domestic violence victims to seek out or accept services, said Jane Raymond, who coordinates elder abuse programs for the state Department of Health and Family Services.

Like their younger counterparts, elderly victims often don't speak up because they're ashamed, they fear making an abusive relationship worse, or they believe seeking help won't change anything. But elders often face further problems — an aversion to divorce late in life, dependence on an abusive spouse or adult child and fears about what it means to send their caregiver to jail.

While elder abuse in general has been increasing in Wisconsin, reports of physical or emotional abuse have remained relatively steady over the last 10 years, numbering 575 in 2006. But at its worst, unchecked abuse usually escalates and can eventually be deadly, experts say. Last year, the state got four reports of emotional or physical abuse in cases that involved a fatality.

"At some point, the community is going to have to step up," said Shannon Barry, director of Dane County Domestic Abuse Intervention Services. "It's getting to that critical place."

Unexpected abusers

Case study

Madison Assistant Fire Chief Paul Bloom, responding to a call about an elderly man being short of breath, saw bruises as he hooked up an intravenous tube. A granddaughter ended up admitting she'd tied him to the bed "to keep him safe."

The victim never spoke up. Bloom reported the incident but believes no one sought charges.

Abusers of the elderly have many faces. They are husbands who control the money, domineer the home, isolate, mock and beat their wives or demand sex.

They're adult sons returning home after a failed marriage or job. Sometimes, a long-abused wife turns the tables if a husband becomes disabled.

Hired caregivers may be rough or demeaning with elders. Residents in long-term care homes physically attack one another. Sometimes, family members abuse elders while visiting them in a care facility.

"I see it all — dirt poor with nothing to people who have a vast amount of resources," said Jill Sweeney, an advocate for victims of domestic violence in the Dane County district attorney's office.

For years, physical and emotional abuse of seniors has been associated with the stress of caregiving, and the efforts being made to provide respite are important.

For instance, the United Way of Dane County is funding an effort to give emotional support to caregivers with a goal of reducing elder abuse 30 percent by 2012.

Training caregivers in how to deal with specialized illnesses such as Alzheimer's also could help.

But now, many experts say the desire for power and control motivates most abusers.

"The research shows it doesn't have to do with caregiver stress," Raymond said. "You're not beating your mother because you're stressed."

Reluctant reporters

Case study

An 89-year-old man who lived with his grandson and relied on his caregiving was taken to the hospital for bruising to the chest. The older man confided to a nurse that his grandson hit him, but later claimed he fell, Madison Police Detective Julie Rortvedt said. The home had multiple police calls, the grandson had a criminal record, and Rortvedt sought charges. But the district attorney's office declined for lack of evidence.

Reporting is hard for any abuse victim, but especially for frail elders, Sweeney said, because they fear even more what will happen next. A divorce may severely harm retirement savings or tap into generational anxiety about a marriage dissolving. Turning in an adult child who is your caregiver may mean you have to move into a long-term care facility.

"They want to make their marriages work," Sweeney said. "They want to stay in their home."

A long-suffering victim also may have no place to go. Elders may be reluctant to go to a traditional shelter, where they would be uncomfortable sharing space with younger women and their children or have concerns about bringing their medications or adaptive equipment, such as a walker, said Brenda Ziegler, an elder abuse investigator with Dane County.

One client struggled with physical abuse throughout her marriage, and occasionally sought refuge with a sister or adult children, but "she could never see herself in a shelter," Ziegler said.

In addition to sometimes uncooperative victims, police officers and prosecutors struggle to enforce laws involving physical abuse of the elderly because of training and other system gaps. Untrained officers may handle violence between elders differently. Jails and courts often don't meet special needs.

Under state law, police must make arrests in domestic violence cases if they believe a crime has been committed or a victim is in danger.

Earlier this year, at the first elder abuse training for Dane County sheriff's deputies, experts encouraged deputies to enforce that law.

"In some communities, it's not happening and it needs to happen," said Shelly Gillette, a domestic violence victim's advocate with the county district attorney's office. "Nobody wants to arrest grandma or grandpa. No one wants to take these people to jail. But that's when the intervention occurs."

Even if police act, prosecutors sometimes hesitate due to a reluctant witness or other reasons such as an elder victim's hardships with transportation, mental or physical problems, or the rigors of a court case.

The cases are "very difficult," Dane County Assistant District Attorney Judy Schwaemle said.

Sexual silence

Case study

A 78-year-old woman didn't resist her rapist but called 911 after the intruder left her Madison home, said Jill Poarch of Meriter Hospital's Sexual Assault Nurse Examiner Program . At the hospital, a special sexual assault nurse examiner met a female police officer who said, "I'm really sorry you were called in. I really think this woman has Alzheimer's or dreamed she was assaulted. Her story just doesn't make sense." The nurse's examination found the victim was hard of hearing and had genital and other physical traumas. A suspect was arrested and convicted of first-degree sexual assault.

Seniors who suffer sexual assault rarely report, Poarch said. In Wisconsin, there were 27 reports of sexual abuse of the elderly made to the state last year, the first time such data was kept.

Seniors are often uneasy talking about sexual issues, let alone abuse, said Lisa Rader, Dane County's elder victim advocate.

And often, seniors face more obstacles in the justice system than a younger sexual assault victim. Authorities may doubt a story because they don't believe an elderly woman would be a rape target, and many seniors recoil at the idea of opening up to police or testifying in court.

A case police detective Rortvedt described from August 2003 underscores the complications. It started when the adult children of a 75-year-old woman reported that she had been sexually assaulted by a neighbor, but the victim refused to pursue charges, Rortvedt said. Two months later, the neighbor did it again.

After the second assault, the victim cooperated with authorities. "I was resisting him, that's why I'm black and blue," she finally told officers.

Jose Gutierrez-Herrera, then 41, was charged with second- and third-degree felony sexual assault. In May, he pleaded guilty to third-degree felony sexual assault and bail jumping charges. He was sentenced to four years probation.

The second assault could have been prevented, but unless victims come forward, "we're stuck," Rortvedt said.

Intervention, "empowers (the victim)," she said. "It breaks the cycle of violence."

Key Terms

> victim compensation
> victim restitution
> victim impact statements
> victim advocacy groups
> restorative justice
> victim-offender mediation
> subpoena

Chapter Outline

> Victims in the Criminal Justice Network
> Civil Remedies
> Restitution
> Private Insurance
> State-Subsidized Compensation Programs
> A Brief Historical Overview of Victim Compensation and Restitution
> Restorative Justice Programs
> Victim-Offender Mediation
> Consequences of Dissatisfied Victims and Witnesses

Victims in the Criminal Justice Network

We have indicated repeatedly that the public plays a crucial role in the criminal justice network. There is, perhaps, no more clear-cut example of the importance of citizen participation than citizen involvement as a victim or witness. The criminal justice network is, to a great extent, dependent on crime victims and witnesses for information regarding criminal behavior. Without such information, arrests, prosecutions, and convictions are extremely difficult (Dawson & Dinovitzer, 2001). Lack of trust or confidence in the police, prosecutor, judges, and/or the procedures involved in processing defendants through the criminal justice network may lead to a decision on behalf of victims and witnesses not to cooperate with practitioners in the processing of a given case. Such lack of trust or confidence may arise from the belief that criminal law protects offenders, more than victims, from inconveniences and/or unpleasant experiences encountered in prior contacts with criminal justice practitioners, or from general confusion and misunderstanding. Cold or impersonal treatment by the police or prosecutor, delays in court proceedings, and failure of officials to notify victims concerning their rights to assistance, restitution, or compensation are among the factors commonly associated with lack of cooperation on behalf of victims and witnesses (Conway & Lohr, 1994; Sims, Yost & Abbott, 2005; Tobolowski, 1993). Other factors commonly as-

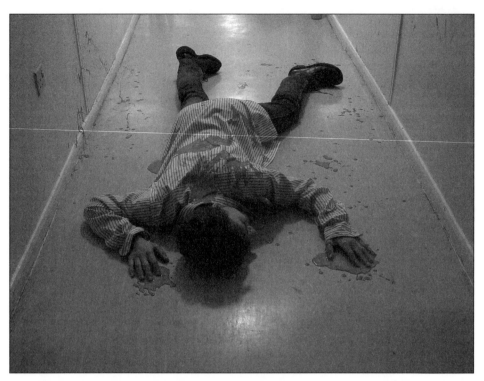

Victim and witness cooperation with practitioners in the processing of a given case
is essential to solving many cases.
Reprinted with permission of iStockphoto.com / Bart Claeys.

sociated with lack of cooperation in reporting and/or prosecuting include the belief
that the police, prosecutor, and judge will not be effective in dealing with the offender;
personal knowledge of the offender and an attendant lack of desire to see him or her
arrested and prosecuted; and fear of retribution. Whatever the cause, most prosecutors
and most police officers regard the lack of cooperation of victims and witnesses in the
prosecution of offenders as a very serious problem.

Some citizens clearly believe that the criminal justice network has an almost total
preoccupation with the rights of the criminal and largely ignores the rights of crime
victims (Jenkins, 1995; Reid, 2006, p. 424). The defendant has the right to remain silent
and to be furnished with a copy of the charges brought against him or her. On a motion by the defendant, the judge will order the prosecutor to furnish the defendant with
a list of prosecution witnesses. The defendant also has the right to a speedy trial before an impartial judge and/or jury. Society ultimately pays for the defense of the indigent defendant, as well as for the room, board, counseling, medical treatment, and
rehabilitative training or education of the defendant if he or she is incarcerated. The
law, however, does not protect the victim from being legally compelled to give testimony that may be embarrassing or self-demeaning, or that may result in considerable
pain and suffering. The rights and privileges of the victim, in short, do not appear to
be the same as those of the offender, especially from the perspective of the victim
(Brown, 1993; Kaminer, 2000).

It is, of course, quite natural for crime victims to be upset about being victimized. They have been confronted by a deliberate violation of their rights by another. To help them deal with these feelings and to improve the chances that they will assist authorities in the apprehension and prosecution of offenders, victims need to know what they can expect to receive in the way of assistance and what is expected of them should they decide to cooperate with the police and/or prosecutor. The victim is entitled to an explanation and to justice as is the person wronged (Walker, 2001, p.169–181). Each victimization tramples some fundamental personal right of the victim: the right to life, the right to personal security, the right to security of habitation and premises, or the right to retain and enjoy property.

In some ways, victims of crime in the United States constitute a minority. Crime victims are, however, unlike other minorities. They are not a cohesive group unified by religion, race, or language. Crime victims are unified only by fate. Like other minorities, however, crime victims are often misunderstood and ostracized. As is the case with other minorities, victims are often blamed for their misfortunes and accused of provoking the criminal, of not resisting strongly enough, or of resisting too strongly. Only in the last two decades have we recognized that victims do constitute a class that has rights and is entitled to have them enforced.

Within the framework of an offender-oriented criminal justice network, there is constant pressure for the police to be concerned exclusively with the offender and to view the victim only as an instrument necessary for a successful prosecution. Yet, citizens are compelled to depend on the police for protection against bodily harm and loss of property, and must rely on them to effectively ensure the safety of street and home against criminal incursion. Police protection is generally viewed as protection of the public, not of individuals with the protection of individuals typically occurring only after victimization.

The decade of the 1960s witnessed a number of U.S. Supreme Court decisions that solidified the rights of alleged offenders. Occasionally dispersed among dissenting opinions are statements noting concern about the impact the decisions might have on future crime victims. For example, in his dissenting opinion in the *Miranda v. Arizona* case in 1965 (as it applied to the ability of law enforcement officials to obtain legally admissible confessions from criminal suspects), U.S. Supreme Court Associate Justice Byron R. White predicted that "in some unknown number of cases, the Court's ruling will return a killer, a rapist, or other criminal to the streets and to the environment that produced him, to repeat his crime whenever it pleases him." Finally, White stated, with a great deal of irony, that "there is, of course, a saving factor: the next victims are uncertain, unnamed, and unrepresented in this case" (Carrington, 1975, pp. 3–4).

In an attempt to encourage victims to participate in the arrest and prosecution of offenders, a number of victim-oriented programs based on the concepts of compensation and restitution have been developed. These concepts are often used interchangeably, but, in fact, they represent two different points of view. **Victim compensation**, in the criminal-victim relationship, concerns the counterbalancing of a loss suffered by a victim as a result of criminal attack. It is basically payment for the damage or injury caused by the crime. It is an indication of the responsibility of society, and it is civil in character; thus, it represents a noncriminal goal in a criminal case. **Vic-**

tim restitution in a criminal-victim relationship involves restoring the victim to his or her position, which was damaged as a result of a criminal attack. It clearly indicates the responsibility of the offender, is penal in character, and represents a correctional goal in a criminal case. Compensation calls for action by the victim in the form of an application and payment by society; restitution calls for a decision by a criminal court and payment by the offender.

Generally, four methods of monetary recovery are available to crime victims: (1) civil remedies; (2) restitution; (3) private insurance; and, (4) state-subsidized compensation programs.

Civil Remedies

As a result of over two centuries of litigation, our criminal justice network has evolved to a stage where crime is regarded as an offense exclusively against the state. The interests of the crime victim had eroded to the point where they played little or no part in criminal procedure (though in recent years there has been progress in this area as indicated later in this chapter). Because of this, the victim was forced to seek legal remedy for his or her injury through the civil courts, where civil procedures apply. The most obvious limitation to such a system of recovery is the relatively low percentage of offenders ultimately apprehended. For the vast majority of crime victims, a tort recovery is a total impossibility. Even if the offender is apprehended, substantial obstacles to a successful civil action remain. The offender generally has few, if any, reserve funds, and most of these will be expended in the process of defense against criminal charges. If sentenced to prison, the offender has little chance to earn an income that could serve as a basis for a civil award. Finally, the civil court process itself is extremely time-consuming for the victim and may result in substantial expenditures of the victim's own funds. Only a small number of victims of crime ever collect damages from the perpetrator.

Restitution

In restitution programs, the criminal is perceived as the appropriate source of benefits for the victim of a crime. The criminal court judge has the alternative of deciding the victim's claim and incorporating a monetary settlement into the final decision. An implicit goal of restitution is to once again make the victim whole (as much as possible) by the direct action of the criminal rather than by a monetary payment by the state. It is sometimes argued that direct repayment by the criminal to the victim has the added benefit of assisting in the rehabilitation of the offender. However, as with tort recovery, restitution has proved inadequate for the majority of crime victims, mainly because the offender is either unidentified, unapprehended, or unconvicted; or without assets, employment, or skills.

An additional limitation to restitution programs is the cost involved in administering them. Some have claimed that the costs to the state of administrating a system of offender restitution to the victims of crimes would exceed the sums actually collected to reimburse the victims for their injuries and losses. The concept of offender restitution has been more popular as a theory than feasible as a practice.

Private Insurance

In the absence of a provision to the contrary, an insurance policy covering accidental injuries also covers victims of unforeseen intentional criminal attacks. However, there are a number of significant problems with respect to private insurance against crime. Many individuals cannot afford premiums to procure coverage for their basic health needs, and it is highly doubtful that they are in a position to afford the luxury of coverage against criminal attacks. Such insurance would be beyond the financial means of a substantial number of families, and making such insurance available and meaningful would require limiting the insurer's option to cancel or refuse to renew policies. Since the highest crime rates are in poverty areas, the insurance premiums would be higher for people living in these areas, even though these citizens are least likely to be able to purchase insurance. Moreover, many insurance companies refuse to issue insurance in high-crime areas. Finally, such coverage is generally inadequate to reimburse the victim for any long-term impairment; rarely is full compensation commensurate with damages attained.

State-Subsidized Compensation Programs

Because of the failure of civil suits, restitution, and private insurance as methods of assisting victims of crime, the concept of compensation by the state has gained favor. Although victim compensation also offers several drawbacks as the principal form of financial aid for victims of crime, it is felt by many to be the most equitable and consistent method of making the victim whole. Unlike civil suits and restitution schemes, compensation provides a remedy without requiring that the assailant either be apprehended and/or convicted, or financially able to repay his or her damages. All states have created victims' compensation programs to repay some of the medical costs and lost income due to victimization (Meadows, 2001, p. 201; Reid, 2006, p. 424). Although current programs vary in rationale, scope, and methods, they are sufficiently similar to warrant some general comments concerning their standards and practices. The typical crime victim compensation program serves only as a remedy of last resort to provide reimbursement of certain direct financial costs to certain victims of certain crimes. Payments are almost universally limited to unreimbursed medical expenses, loss of earnings by the victim, loss of support by the victim's dependents, and funeral and burial expenses occurring as a direct result of the criminal incident. Specifically excluded is compensation for property loss resulting from theft or vandalism; in the vast majority of states, also excluded is compensation for pain and suffering. A substantial minority of states forbid their compensation boards from making any award unless the victim would otherwise suffer financial hardship. Every jurisdiction with a compensation program has a statutory maximum award that can be made. Similarly, most states require that the victim sustain minimum out-of-pocket losses before becoming eligible for state compensation. Generally, the person must have been an innocent victim of a crime and could not have been related to or living with the offender at the time the incident occurred. After the crime takes place, the victim (or dependent) must report the crime to the police within a specified period of time (usually two to five days) and, thereafter, is obligated to cooperate fully with all law enforcement and judicial officials in the processing of the case. Additionally, the victim must file a "Notice to Apply" for compensation within a certain time interval after the occurrence of the crime (normally within one to two years). The majority of state programs are funded through general tax revenues; however, there are some states that subsidize their programs by imposing an additional fine on all convicted offenders.

Despite the political popularity of providing public assistance to innocent victims of crime, many officials have been reluctant to enact such measures because of apprehension about potential costs. Other criticisms focus on the fear that victims, knowing that they will be reimbursed for losses, may become careless; conversely, offenders, knowing that victims will be compensated, may be less hesitant about inflicting injury. Finally, there are those critics who believe that a victim compensation plan would encourage fraud. They argue that it will unavoidably result in some citizens' using the compensation plan to either report nonexistent crimes and extract "easy money" from the government, or, taking this argument to its extreme, they fear that people may deliberately injure themselves so that they might collect a check from the state.

A Brief Historical Overview of Victim Compensation and Restitution

Historical reference to victim compensation goes back at least as far as the Code of Hammurabi:

> If a man has committed robbery and is caught, that man shall be put to death. If the robber is not caught, the man who has been robbed should formally declare what he has lost and the city shall replace whatever he has lost for him. If it is the life of the owner that is lost, the city or the mayor shall pay one maneh of silver to his kinfolk. (Reiff, 1979, p.134)

Similarly, the Old Testament indicates that a criminal-victim relationship existed among the early Hebrews. If a person was injured, the perpetrator of the offense was to reimburse him for the time lost from his tasks and to be responsible for seeing to it that he had the resources to be thoroughly healed, if possible (Edelhertz & Geis, 1974, p.8).

These early systems of compensation/restitution were gradually replaced by state-run criminal prosecution that left the victim only civil remedies by which he or she might collect for injuries. One rationale for this new approach was the claim that these fines underwrote expenses incurred by the authorities in apprehending and prosecuting the offender. Schafer (1972) traces the demise of public compensation to the Middle Ages:

> It was chiefly owing to the violent greed of the feudal barons and the medieval ecclesiastical powers that the rights of the injured party were gradually infringed upon, and finally, appropriated by the authorities. These authorities exacted a double vengeance upon the offender, first by forfeiting his property to themselves instead of to his victim and then by punishing him by the dungeon, the torture, the stake, or the gibbet. But the original victim of the wrong was ignored. (p.8)

In the 1760s, Cesare Beccaria took issue with the proposition that the primary function of the criminal justice network was to serve as an aid to private action in obtaining recovery from the offender. Since the system had arisen from a social contract, it must serve the interests of society and not the individual victim. Punishment inflicted by the system should serve primarily to deter the offender from further criminal activity and to deter others from committing similar acts. Punishment was not to be imposed to redress private damages. Overall, Beccaria's principles contributed to the already declining role of victims in the criminal justice system (McDonald, 1976).

Lack of consideration for the victim on the part of the state lasted until the twentieth century. This does not mean that there were no advocates of victim rights in the meantime. Nineteenth-century writers such as Jeremy Bentham, Enrico Ferri, and Raffaele Garofalo noted the plight of victims of crime and urged the adoption of public compensation plans. However, the writings of these individuals had little effect on public policy as it applied to reforming the rights of crime victims.

Revival of active interest in compensation for crime victims in contemporary times is attributed to the work of Margaret Fry, an English magistrate and social reformer. Fry, like many others of her day, was primarily interested in restitution for victims being paid by the offender on the assumption that, "although restitution cannot undo the wrong, it will often mitigate the injury, and it has a real educative value for the offender. Repayment is the best first step toward reformation that a dishonest person can take. It is often the ideal solution" (Edelhertz & Geis, 1974, p.110). Fry felt that the "state which forbids our going armed in self-defense cannot disown all responsibility for its occasional failure to protect" (Edelhertz & Geis, 1974, p.10). State compensation, she advocated, should not interfere with the possibility of damage awards against the aggressor.

In 1959, Stephen Schafer, an American criminologist, was given a commission by the British Home Office to work on the problem of restitution/compensation. Thus, after an extended period of dormancy, the needs of crime victims once again came to the attention of governmental bodies and have received increasing attention during the past 40 years.

For example, the state of California has a Victims' Bill of Rights, that spells out entitlements for residents who suffer injury or loss as the result of a criminal act. All such victims should have the right to immediate emergency aid in the areas of medicine, law, and finances; and all victims should be protected by the police and the courts from threats or coercion on behalf of the offender or his or her supporters. Victims should be provided with timely information concerning the course of the investigation of their offense and plans for prosecution. (Governor's Office of Emergency Services, 2003) . Many other states, including Florida, New York, and Illinois have similar laws relating to victim assistance.

In 1984, Congress passed the Victims of Crime Act, establishing a fund supported by fines, half of which were to support state compensation programs and half of which were to be used for victim assistance programs (Office for Victims of Crime, 2007). In 1992, the U.S. Courts National Fine Center was computerized to help keep track of those fines.

In 1994, the Violent Crime Control Act was passed, allowing victims of federal violent and sex crimes to give **victim impact statements** (statements about how their crimes affected them) at the sentencing hearings of their offenders. A number of states also allow such statements (Meadows, 2001, p.215). In addition, in the 1990s numerous communities established **victim advocacy groups**, which provide services to the victim and/or his or her family. Such services include providing shelter and counseling, support during criminal trials, and information about compensation programs (Meadows, 2001, p.216).

The Justice for All Act of 2004 (JFAA, H.R. 5107, Public Law 108-405) was signed into law on October 30, 2004. The Act contains four major sections related to crime victims and the criminal justice process. One of these deals with victims' rights and, in 2005, the Office of the Attorney General of the United States issued a set of guidelines for victim and witness assistance based upon the JFAA (Department of Justice, 2005). These guidelines from the Crime Victim's Rights Act (part of JFAA) state that "officers and employees of the Department of Justice and other departments and agencies of the United States engaged in the detection, investigation, or prosecution of crime shall make their best efforts to see that crime victims are notified of, and accorded," their rights, which include:

1. The right to be reasonably protected from the accused.

2. The right to reasonable, accurate, and timely notice of any public court proceeding, or any parole proceeding, involving the crime or of any release or escape of the accused.

3. The right not to be excluded from any such public court proceeding, unless the court, after receiving clear and convincing evidence, determines that testimony by the victim would be materially altered if the victim heard other testimony at that proceeding.

4. The right to be reasonably heard at any public proceeding in the district court involving release, plea, [or] sentencing, or any parole proceeding.

5. The reasonable right to confer with the attorney for the Government in the case.

6. The right to full and timely restitution as provided in law.

7. The right to proceedings free from unreasonable delay.

8. The right to be treated with fairness and with respect for the victims dignity and privacy.

Further, the JFAA provides crime victims with two mechanisms for enforcing the rights enumerated above.

1. Judicial Enforcement. Crime victims, or the Government on their behalf, may move in Federal district court for an order enforcing their rights (18 U.S.C. ~ 3771(d)(3) "The district court shall take up and decide any motion asserting a victim's right forthwith. If the district court denies the relief sought, the movant may petition the court of appeals for a writ of mandamus.

2. Administrative Complaint. A crime victim may also file an administrative complaint if Department employees fail to respect the victim's rights. The Attorney General must take and "investigate complaints relating to the provision or violation of the rights of a crime victim" and provide for disciplinary sanctions for Department employees who "willfully or wantonly fail" to protect those rights (18 U.S.C. ~ 3771(f)(2)

Although these regulations apply only at the federal level, they serve as a model for action at the state level and, as we have indicated previously, all states have enacted victims' compensation legislation.

The Office of Victims of Crime (OVC, federal level) awards numerous grants to assist the states in providing victim/witness programs and services. Among these initiatives are grants for the National Program to Directly Assist Victims of Identity Theft and Financial Fraud, the Multi-Disciplinary Responses to Crime Victims with Disabilities program, and the National Training Conference on Responding to Crime Victims With Disabilities grant (OVC, 2007). There is also a National Crime Victim Bar Association which educates attorneys, victim service providers, and the general public about civil legal remedies for crime victims and refers crime victims to civil attorneys in their local area (OVC, 2007).

Restorative Justice Programs

Restorative justice advocates employ programs such as victim-offender mediation, victims' impact panels, community service, and community sentencing. The philosophy of **restorative justice** centers on the assertion that crime affects persons instead of the traditional notion that crime affects the state. In fact, restorative justice defines a "crime [as] an offense against human relationships" (The Maryland Crime Victim's Resource Center, Inc., 2006, p. 2). These programs, aimed at creating or arousing emotions within criminal offenders, are gaining momentum in the criminal justice network in the United States.

Mark Carey, director of community corrections in Dakota County, Minnesota, defines restorative justice as "a philosophical framework for responding to crime and the actions needed to mend this harm. It focuses on crime as an act against another individual or community rather than the state. It is a future-focused model that emphasizes problematic problem solving instead of 'just deserts" (Wilkinson, 1997, p.1). (See "In the News" 10.2.) In other words, restorative justice changes the focus of crime from an act against the state (which is empowered to punish wrongdoers) to a private act with the goal of preventing future crime rather than simply punishing the offenders.

In the News 10.2

Looking to break cycles of violence — Restorative justice "circles" offer means of conflict resolution

ALBANY — Xzavier Ortiz, Kiki Dancy and Missy Oliver used to be friends. They hung out with a group of friends at Albany High School.

That was before they started fighting over boys, sending nasty messages on Myspace and snapping locker room pictures of each other on their cellphones.

For the past 18 months, the girls often changed alliances and drummed up drama at the smallest offense. There was an incident in which a girl was hit in the head with a padlock inside a sock. Another girl was slashed on the face with a razor.

When John Cutro found out about the strife, he set up circles, or meetings, with the girls, their parents, teachers and anyone else who was involved in some way.

Cutro, a restorative justice expert, has tried to get the girls to stop fighting. Not be friends again. Not forgive each other.

Just stop hurting each other.

Cutro believes in restorative justice as a way to heal the community. In the past two years, he has opened more than 40 "cluster files" on groups of Albany kids who chronically fight each other.

"Each cluster can have one or two or three fights, or it can have 40 fights," Cutro said.

Many of the kids can't pinpoint why they started fighting in the first place.

"When you come from a poor community, there are a lot of things that push you downward and create anger," said Harry Corbitt, director of safe schools and violence prevention for Albany City School District. "They are angry at society, angry at culture, angry at their parents and authority. But when they let that anger out, their peers suffer."

For the police, the job is not to fix anything or to counsel, Corbitt said. "It's to respond and lodge the appropriate charges."

Restorative justice picks up where the traditional justice system leaves off, creating a venue for both the offender and the victim to learn from what happened and begin to heal.

Cutro and Dennis Mosely started their work with restorative justice in the 1990s with homeless people in Albany. At that time, for example, a man who urinated on the front door of a Lark Street business might help the business owner unload a truck or stock supplies to make up for the incident.

People who have caused harm "have to admit that they've done something wrong and then get reintegrated into the community," said Mosely, who has long been active in the social work community.

And while the goal is not to assign blame, all members of a circle must find a way to best serve their community.

"Our system is not the state versus the person," Mosely said. "We are all part of the same community. We are diverse components of the same organism."

Advocates of restorative justice see it from different perspectives. For Albany County Judge Stephen Herrick, it is a way to help a victim heal. For District Attorney David Soares, it is a way of healing the entire community and helping those who have done wrong to see how they fit in.

Soares has created a community accountability board. The board, whose volunteers include Cutro, come from various walks of life. They listen to defendants accused of a low-level, nonviolent crime and determine appropriate punishment "Offenses like disorderly conduct, noise and graffiti are not really victimless offenses at all," Soares said.

As the board resolves more cases, the district attorney's office can focus on more serious matters.

Studies have shown that those who participate in the circles are less likely to return to the same behavior.

"People are less likely to engage in criminal activity when they feel personal responsibility for what they have done," said Dennis Sullivan of Voorheesville, editor in chief of Contemporary Justice Review and co-editor with Larry Tifft of "Handbook of Restorative Justice: A Global Perspective."

Cutro is quick to point out that while restorative justice can lead to forgiveness and closure, that is not the goal of the program.

"I call forgiveness the f-word," Cutro said. "There is no such thing as closure when you've lost a loved one."

Cutro has constantly worked on a shoestring budget. Grants arrive sporadically, and Cutro often struggles to pay for circle facilitators.

"I've gotten to the point of taking out personal loans to pay for this," he said.

Herrick does not use restorative concepts as an alternative for regular penalties. It is not a get-out-of-jail-free card.

"I don't think anyone likes to think that if a person says all the right things during the process, they will be given a lighter sentence," Herrick said.

As an Albany City Court judge, Herrick often worked with Cutro, using restorative justice practices in the courtroom. Now that he is a county judge and deals with more serious cases, he doesn't have as much opportunity to use the practice, but still tries to incorporate it when he can, occasionally requiring the circles as part of a plea deal.

"It's a very workable and at times beneficial method of victims getting some benefit from the process and the perpetrator understanding what havoc they have caused," Herrick said.

For the cluster of angry girls at Albany High, there have been three circles so far. Each time, the girls have vowed to leave each other alone.

But when Ortiz, Dancy and Oliver met with a reporter recently, seething tension remained.

They didn't speak a word to each other, were reluctant to sit together and pose for a photograph. Afterward, the girls' mothers said the threats continue and they are still scared to let their children walk down the street.

"This isn't easy stuff to fix," Cutro said. "You are working against a culture of violence."

Furfaro, D. (December 26, 2006). Looking to break cycles of violence—Restorative justice "circles" offer means of conflict resolution. *The Times Union* (Albany, NY). p. B1. "Used by permission."

Restorative justice programs have been variously called community conferencing, family group conferencing, community justice, community corrections, balanced and restorative justice, and real justice, depending on the agency applying the concepts. Although community service, victims' impact panels and classes, and victims' impact statements are sometimes referred to as restorative justice programs (because they use restorative justice philosophy), there are several identifiable types of programs practiced under the restorative justice umbrella. Victim-offender mediation, sentencing or peacemaking circles, family group conferencing, and reparative probation or boards are the most popular programs using restorative justice tenets. Each of these programs views crime in the broader sense as affecting the community, the victim, and the offender rather than adhering to the traditional belief that the crime, while it clearly affects the victim, is basically an act against the state. Let's take a closer look at one of these programs.

Victim Offender Mediation

Victim-offender mediation is perhaps the most widely used restorative justice program. In 1999, there were more than 300 programs in the United States and 900 in Europe, variously called victim-offender meetings, victim-offender mediations, victim-offender reconciliation programs, and victim-offender conferences (Umbreit, 1999). According to Umbreit, (1999, p.1), "**Victim offender mediation** is a process which provides interested victims of primarily property crimes the opportunity to meet the offender, in a safe and structured setting, with the goal of holding the offender directly accountable for [his or her] behavior while providing important assistance and compensation to the victim". With the help of a mediator, the victim is allowed to tell the offender how the crime has affected his or her life and to listen to any thoughts or feelings that the offender would like to share with the victim. At the close of the mediation, it is hoped that a resolution will be obtained in which the victim receives restitution from the offender.

One of the goals of the mediation is that the victim and the offender are able to reach a mutually agreeable resolution, with little or no help from the mediator. The mediator is responsible primarily for maintaining a safe and secure atmosphere during the mediation, guiding the discussion during the mediation, and ensuring that the negotiated outcome is acceptable to both parties. A survey performed by the Center for Restorative Justice and Peacemaking of programs in 1996 and 1997 found that the most common offenses dealt with through mediation were vandalism, minor assaults, theft, and burglary. A number of the 116 programs surveyed stated that other property offenses and some violent offenses were on occasion dealt with through mediation (Umbreit, 1999).

How well does restorative justice work in practice? Walker (1998) indicates that "evaluations of experimental programs have tended to find slightly lower recidivism rates for offenders receiving restorative justice than for those given traditional sentences of prison or probation. The differences are not always consistent, however, and many questions remain regarding the implementation and outcomes of such programs" (p.224). According to Schneider (1986), between 40 and 50 percent of victims refused to participate in mediation programs. Davis, Tichane, & Grayson (1980) found no evidence that mediation reduced levels of future conflict; Roy (1993) found no differences in recidivism rates between court-based programs and victim-offender mediation programs; Niemeyer and Shicor (1996) found mixed recidivism results; and Levrant, Cullen, Fulton, and Wozniak (1999) conclude that there is little reason to hope that restorative justice programs will have a meaningful impact on recidivism. Rodriguez (2005) found that while there were some issues in the selection of offenders to participate in a restorative justice program (e.g., race/ethnicity, unemployment rate, and proportion of Spanish-speaking households in the community) offenders who took part in the restorative justice program were significantly less likely to recidivate than were offenders in a comparison group. Dzur and Wertheimer (2002), however, note that the restitution or restorative approach views crime as primarily a matter between the offender and the victim, rather than an offense against the society as a whole. In recent history, in western societies, crime has been viewed as harming society (this approach allowed us to move away from the blood feud model where individuals seek retribution to a criminal justice model). In restorative justice programs it is not clear how offenders can reconcile themselves with society or who represents society by being in a position to forgive. Dzur and Wertheimer (2002) argue that many citizens suffer from fear and are forced to engage in behaviors to avoid becoming crime victims. Thus, offenders are responsible for at least some of the costs to society in addition to the harm they impose on specific victims. To the extent that Dzur and Wertheimer (2002) are correct in their assumptions, the restorative justice model appears to stand in stark contrast to our conception of crime as a social harm which should be addressed by the society, not just by the individual victim.

Consequences of Dissatisfied Victims and Witnesses

It often occurs that the victim and witnesses in a criminal case are the only participants who have never been in a courtroom before. Frequently, being served with a **subpoena** is the victim's first indication that he or she will be required to testify, and often the victim is poorly prepared to testify because he or she has little or no knowledge of the actual courtroom environment. In many cases, once the victim leaves the courtroom, he or she has little or no further contact with the prosecutor's office. In addition, plea bargaining often allows the accused to plead guilty to some lesser offense in return for dismissal of some or all of the original charges against him or her. Although this procedure speeds up court processes and relieves the court of some scheduling burdens, it essentially neglects the interests of victims; from the point of view of the victim, it deprives him or her of the opportunity to see justice done. Because the victim is seldom apprised that a plea bargain has been arranged, it is not surprising that many victims fail to understand how offenders are found guilty of both different and lesser charges than those originally and accurately filed. Similarly, victims often fail to understand how sentences resulting from relatively serious charges can be so short or how offenders convicted of such charges can be placed on probation. As a consequence, victims may conclude that cooperation with criminal justice authorities is largely a waste of time; thus, they may fail to cooperate in future cases and/or develop a negative image of the criminal justice network. Considering the fact that in 2005, 14 percent of all U.S. households experienced one or more violent or property victimizations (Bureau of Justice Statistics, 2007), the number of citizens involved as victims is substantial and criminal justice practitioners can ill afford to alienate such large numbers of citizens. Noncooperation of victims and witnesses, when it indicates a failure of criminal justice practitioners to be responsive to the needs of citizens, then, is a serious problem.

Should the victim of a crime be allowed to intervene in criminal prosecution? Should the victim have the right to participate in hearings before the court on dismissals, guilty pleas, and sentences? The President's Task Force on Victims of Crime advocated allowing some input at the sentencing hearing for victims of violent crimes, and the federal Victims' Bill of Rights, as well as a number of states, allows crime victims (or next of kin if the victim is deceased) to attend all sentencing proceedings and to express their views concerning the crime at such hearings. Judges are to consider these views when imposing sentence.

Most victims probably do want to be kept informed with respect to the disposition of their cases even though they may not be interested in direct participation in the trial and/or sentencing process. The network perspective would lead us to anticipate a number of undesirable consequences if victims desire to be informed and heard, and are not. The criminal justice process is typically initiated by a victim reporting an offense. In many instances the process is interrupted (by plea bargaining or case dismissal) without the victim's knowledge. When this fact becomes known to the victim, he or she often feels that justice has not been done or that initiating criminal proceedings (which victims are encouraged to do by other components of the criminal justice network) is a waste of time. Should such individuals be victimized again, they might well decide not to cooperate in arresting or prosecuting the offender, which may make such arrest and prosecution less likely. Further, they might well share their experiences and views with others, who might then be less likely to cooperate with the authorities in pursuing criminal cases. At a minimum, keeping victims informed of the progress of their cases would seem a small price to pay for victim cooperation.

In January 2006, the U.S. Court of Appeals for the Ninth Circuit ruled in *Kenna* v. *United States District Court* that victims have the right to speak at sentencing hearings. The case was filed under the Crime Victims' Rights Act (CVRA), 18 U.S.C. Section 3771, and involved a father and son who pled guilty to wire fraud and money laundering. More than 60 victims submitted victim impact statements. At the father's sentencing hearing, several victims spoke about the effects of the crimes. At the son's sentencing hearing, however, the judge refused to allow victims to speak. The Court of Appeals held that the district judge should have allowed the victims to speak (*Kenna v. United States District Court*, 2006).

Summary

1. Victims and witnesses have often been overlooked by practitioners in the criminal justice network. In many cases they are not informed of important developments in their cases and they are routinely inconvenienced by delays in proceedings.

2. We can summarize current concerns for victims and witnesses in the criminal justice network by concluding that victims and witnesses should not control outcomes in lower criminal courts.

3. There is room to institute some sort of role for victims and witnesses in the decision process between the extremes of allowing them to control outcomes and the complete absence of participation that they are now afforded in most cases in most lower criminal courts. Restorative justice programs may challenge traditional conceptions of crime as a social harm in which society has a considerable stake.

Key Terms Defined

victim compensation A payment made by the state to the victim of a crime.

victim restitution A payment made by an offender to his or her victim.

victim impact statements Statements made by victims at the sentencing hearings of offenders to show how the crime committed affected their lives.

victim advocacy groups Groups that lend support to crime victims and/or their families.

restorative justice A philosophy that asserts that crime affects people rather than or in addition to the state and that those affected should be restored to wholeness through techniques such as victim confrontation.

victim-offender mediation One type of restorative justice program in which the victim and offender meet with a mediator in an attempt to resolve the victimization.

subpoena A court order that directs the recipient to appear in court.

Critical Thinking Exercises

1. How much input into the trial and sentencing of offenders should victims be allowed? What are some of the dangers in allowing too much input? Too little input?

2. Do you think the movement toward restorative justice is a step in the right direction? Do you see any dangers inherent in the process? How could the rights of restorative justice participants best be protected?

Internet Exercises

A number of websites discuss treatment of victims and witnesses by criminal justice practitioners. Many also provide instructions on where to get help, as well as on the judicial process and victim/witness advocates.

1. What type of information in this regard can you find from the website http://www.ojp.usdoj.gov/ovc/help/links.htm ?

2. Find two other websites that provide information on victims and witnesses in the criminal justice system. List the websites and provide a brief summary of their contents.

3. Is there a website that provides information on victims with disabilities? What is the website and what kinds of information does the site contain?

References

Brown, C. G. (1993). *First get mad, then get justice: The handbook for crime victims.* New York: Birch Lane Press.

Bureau of Justice Statistics (2007). National crime victimization survey. Washington, DC: U.S. Department of Justice. Available online at: http://www.ojp.usdoj.gov/bjs/pub/ascii/cnh05.txt.

Carrington, F. G. (1975). *Victims.* New Rochelle, NY: Arlington House.

Conway, M. R., & Lohr, S. L. (1994). A longitudinal analysis of factors associated with reporting violent crimes to the police. *Journal of Quantitative Criminology, 10* (1), 23–39.

Davis, R., Tichane, M. & Grayson, D. (1980). *Mediation and arbitration as alternatives to prosecution in felony cases: An evaluation of the Brooklyn Dispute Resolution Center.* New York: Vera Institute of Justice.

Dawson, M. & Dinovitzer, R. (2001). Victim cooperation and the prosecution of domestic violence in a specialized court. *Justice Quarterly: JQ, 18* (3), 593–623.

Department of Justice. (2005, May). *Guidelines for victim and witness assistance.* Available at: http://www.ojp.usdoj.gov/ovc/help/links.htm.

Dzur, A. W. & Wertheimer, A. (2002). Forgiveness and public deliberation: The practice of restorative justice. *Criminal Justice Ethics, 21* (1), 3–21.

Edelhertz, H., & Geis, G. (1974). *Public compensation to victims of crime.* New York: Praeger.

Governor's Office of Emergency Services. (2003). Available online at: http://www.oes.ca.gov/Operational/OESHome.nsf/CJPDHome?OpenForm.

Jenkins, P. (1995). Crime control and due process. In D. Close & N. Meier (Eds.). *Morality in criminal justice: An introduction to ethics,* pp.83–98. Belmont, CA: Wadsworth.

Justice for All Act. (2004). Available online at: http://www.usdoj.gov/usao/alm/Victim_Witness/justice_for_all_act.pdf.

Kaminer, W. (2000). Victims versus suspects (proposed victims' rights amendments). *American Prospect, 11* (9), 18–19.

Kenna v. United States District Court, 2006.

Levrant, S., Cullen, F. T., Fulton, B., & Wozniak, J. F. (1999). Reconsidering restorative justice: The corruption of benevolence revisited. *Crime and Delinquency, 45* (1), pp. 3–27.

Maryland Crime Victims Resource Center, Inc. (2006). *Collaborations, 13,* pp. 1–3. Available online at: http://www.mdcrimevictims.org/_pages/f_faith_based/documents/collaborative_newsletter_January_06.pdf.

McDonald, W. (1976). *Criminal justice and the victim.* Beverly Hills, CA: Sage.

Meadows, R. J. (2001). *Understanding violence and victimization* (2nd ed.). Upper Saddle River, NJ: Prentice Hall.

Miranda v. Arizona, 384 U.S. 348 (1965).

Niemeyer, M., & Shichor, D. (1996). A preliminary study of a large victim/offender reconciliation program. *Federal Probation, 60,* 30–34.

Office for Victims of Crimes. (2007). Available online at: http://www.ojp.usdoj.gov/ovc/help/links.htm.

Reid, S. T. (2006). *Crime and criminology* (11th ed.). Boston: McGraw-Hill.

Reiff, R. (1979). *The invisible victim: The criminal justice system's forgotten responsibility.* New York: Basic Books.

Rodriguez, N. (2005). Restorative justice, communities, and delinquency: Whom do we reintegrate? *Criminology & Public Policy, 4* (1), 103–131.

Roy, S. (1993). Two types of juvenile restitution programs in two midwestern counties. Federal *Probation, 57,* 48–53.

Schafer, S. (1972). *Compensation and restitution to victims of crime* (2nd ed.). Montclair, NJ: Patterson Smith.

Schneider, A. (1986). Restitution and recidivism rates of juvenile offenders: Results from four experimental studies. *Criminology, 24*, 533–52.

Sims, B. , Yost, B. , & Abbott, C. (2005). Use and nonuse of victim services programs: Implications from a statewide survey of crime victims. *Criminology and Public Policy, 4* (2), 361–384.

Tobolowski, P. M. (1993). Restitution in the federal criminal justice system. *Judicature, 77* (2), 90–95.

Umbreit, M. (1999). *Victim offender mediation and dialogue: Guidelines for victim sensitive practice.* Center for Restorative Justice and Peacemaking, School of Social Work, University of Minnesota, St. Paul. Unpublished manuscript.

Walker, S. (1998). *Sense and nonsense about crime and drugs: A policy guide* (4th ed.). Belmont, CA: West/Wadsworth.

_____(2001). Sense and nonsense about crime and drugs: A policy guide (5th ed.). Belmont, CA: West/Wadsworth.

Wilkinson, R. A. (1997). Back to basics. *Corrections Today, 59*, 6–7.

Suggested Readings

Bazemore, G. (2005). Whom and how do we reintegrate: Finding community in restorative justice. *Criminology & Public Policy, 4* (1), 131–149.

Boyes-Watson, C. (2004). The value of citizen participation in restorative/community justice: Lessons from Vermont. *Criminology & Public Policy, 3* (4), 687–692.

Meadows, R. J. (2001). *Understanding violence and victimization* (2nd ed.). Upper Saddle River, NJ: Prentice Hall.

Sarnoff, S. K. (1996). *Paying for crime: The politics and possibilites of crime victim reimbursement.* Westport, Conn.: Preager.

Stohr, M. K. (2005). Victim services programming: If it is efficacious, they will come. *Criminology & Public Policy, 4* (2), 391–398.

Strickland, R. A. (2004). *Restorative Justice.* New York: Peter Lang Publishing.

Takagi, P. & Shank, G. (2004). Critique of restorative justice. *Social Justice, 31* (3), 147–164.

Chapter Eleven

Corrections, Prisoners' Rights and Alternatives to Incarceration

In the News 11.1

AT-HOME ALCOHOL CHECKUPS VISITS ENSURE PEOPLE CONVICTED OF DUI STICK TO PROBATION TERMS

Rory Holliday passed a Breathalyzer test and got a thumbs up from four Stanislaus County probation officers who didn't find any booze in his west Modesto home Sunday afternoon.

After three convictions for driving under the influence, he has lost interest in drinking.

Holliday said he learned his lesson after the third time, when he crashed his car and spent three months in the hospital, seven months in a wheelchair and three months learning to walk again.

"I'm paying for my mistake," Holliday, 23, said as he pointed to an ankle bracelet he wears as part of a home detention monitoring system.

In the past, most people convicted of drunken driving were left alone as long as they checked in with the Probation Department once a month and attended classes as directed.

Since October, however, teams of probation officers have been making unannounced visits to offenders with felony DUI convictions.

The department is targeting people who have had four or more noninjury drunken driving convictions within 10 years or were found guilty of a drunken driving crash that caused injury or death.

A $118,766 grant from the California Office of Traffic Safety is paying for 1,995 overtime hours through June 2009. Similar programs are in 16 other counties.

The department hopes to keep 168 felony and repeat drunken drivers who were responsible for 228 drunken driving offenses sober and off the road.

"It reminds them that we're going to hold them accountable," Deputy Probation Officer Emily Boyd said.

First-time offenders who don't cause injuries typically get two days in jail, fines and must attend a class.

Those who cause injuries may spend time behind bars.

All must abstain from alcohol while on probation, which usually lasts three years. So probation officers sweep through their homes looking for booze.

Boyd and her team were welcomed at some homes, knocked on several doors and found no one at home, and learned that one of their probationers had been deported.

They poured out beer at one residence.

In west Modesto, they found Michael Day, who was sleepy and not eager for company.

Day, 26, passed a Breathalyzer, but a probation officer found a small plastic bag of marijuana in his bedroom.

That led to a string of questions but no answers. Day could face sanctions if a judge concludes he violated the terms of his probation.

"Is this your new thing?" Deputy Probation Officer Ranjit Takhar asked. "Do you know his is against the law, too? Why do you have it?"

The authorities believe repeat offenders are more likely to be involved in fatal wrecks than other motorists. But the program is seen as a deterrent to a chronic problem, not a reaction to a crime wave.

The number of people killed or injured in alcohol-related wrecks in Stanislaus County has remained relatively flat in recent years, according to the California Highway Patrol.

There were 36 deaths and 611 injuries in 2001, and 36 deaths and 541 injuries in 2005.

Natascha Roof, manager of adult probation programs, said officers are starting to know repeat offenders by sight.

Probation officers plan to tag along when law enforcement agencies set up drunken driving checkpoints on major holidays, such as Memorial Day and the Fourth of July and New Year's Eve.

They also watch to see whether offenders are driving on suspended licenses, sometimes catching them as they leave the courthouse or Probation Department.

"We now recognize them in our community, where before we would not because they were not being actively supervised," Roof said.

Nathan Wheat, 25, said he was surprised the first time probation officers came to his west Modesto house, because he had been left alone for two years after he caused a crash that injured a minister and his wife.

He was drunk that time, and that probation violation put him under house arrest for 60 days. This time, he passed a Breathalyzer and said he won't drink and drive again.

"It's not worth it," Wheat said.

Herdendeen, S. (May 21, 2007). At-home alcohol checkup visits ensure people convicted of DUI stick to probation terms. *The Modesto Bee* (CA). Local news, p. B1.

Key Terms

early release
banishment
transportation
age of enlightenment
hedonism
Walnut Street Jail
Pennsylvania prisons
Auburn prisons
retribution
specific deterrence
general deterrence
supermax security facilities
maximum security facilities
medium security facilities
minimum security facilities
recidivism rates
total institution
warehousing
civil death
hands-off doctrine
cruel and unusual punishment
good time
intermediate sanctions
boot camps
community corrections
restorative justice
drug courts
probation

intensive probation
parole

Chapter Outline

Historical Development
The Reform Movement
The Early American Experience
The Pennsylvania and Auburn Systems
Correctional Objectives
Revenge
Specific Deterrence
General Deterrence
Rehabilitation
Custody
Women in Prison
Correctional Organization
The Federal Network
State Networks
Types of Institutions
Supermax Security Facilities
Maximum Security Facilities
Medium Security Facilities
Minimum Security Facilities
Jails
History of Jails
Control and Organization
Jail Problems
Evaluating Prison Rehabilitation Programs
The Prison Society
Rehabilitation versus Custody
Education and Vocational Training in Prison
Private Prisons
Capital Punishment: Timeless Controversy, Ultimate Penalty
A Brief History of Capital Punishment
Death Penalty Arguments
Court Decisions and the Death Penalty
Civil Death and the Hands Off Doctrine
Prisoners' Rights
Freedom of Speech
Freedom of Religion
Cruel and Unusual Punishment
Due Process
Alternatives to Incarceration

Probation
Parole

At the conclusion of the trial process, a number of sentencing alternatives are available to the judge with respect to the guilty party. Among these are probation and incarceration in jail or prison. In recent years, considerable media, public, and political attention has been devoted to corrections in response to reports of overcrowding, drugs, gang violence, and riots in prisons, and in response to **early release** programs. Here, again, the fact that criminal justice is best viewed as a network is apparent. Funds used to build prisons and jails must be appropriated from the public, and prisoners who are released into society must be reintegrated if rehabilitation is one of our goals. In a nationally representative sample, Cohen, Rust, and Steen (2006) found overwhelming support for increased spending on youth prevention, drug treatment for nonviolent offenders, and police, but less support for allocating new money to building more prisons. This is of interest, first, because financial support for alternatives to incarceration comes from the public and, second, because politicians at all levels (local prosecutors to state governors to the president) have used prison construction as a political football. In Illinois, for example, communities have been involved in competition to be selected as sites for new prisons. Across the nation, lack of available space to house prisoners has led to early release for many inmates to alleviate prison and jail overcrowding. On several occasions, the media focused on stories of atrocities committed by offenders who had been released early (while conveniently overlooking the much larger number of offenders on early release who did not commit further offenses); thus, the media helped shape public opinion against such programs.

Correctional officials in the United States have been hampered by our inability to decide precisely what it is we want prisons to accomplish. We ask prison officials to focus on two, perhaps incompatible, goals—rehabilitation and custody. In the long run, however, the former depends on our willingness to accept those who have served time in prison back into society. To some extent, therefore, rehabilitation is beyond the control of prison authorities. Perhaps a look at the historical development of prisons will help us understand how some of these problems arose.

Historical Development

Forerunners of incarceration as a form of punishment were banishment and transportation. In some cases, **banishment** (exile) was reserved for the more affluent members of society who were convicted of an offense. The person being banished was pronounced civilly dead and was forced to leave the country. Return meant severe corporal punishment or death. **Transportation** emerged during the sixteenth century and was practiced until the latter part of the nineteenth century. England transported between 300 and 2,000 prisoners to America and Australia annually during this period (Hughes, 1987; Wilson, 1931). Banishment and transportation represented alternatives to corporal and capital punishment, and achieved the same result as incarceration—the isolation of offenders.

Both the English and the Dutch also developed workhouses. In England, cities or counties were required to construct bridewells to house the poor and convicts, and this practice soon spread to other parts of Europe. Conditions in these workhouses were atrocious, and no attempts were made to segregate inmates by age, gender, or type of offense. Inmates were forced to work long hours, corruption and violence were common among both guards and inmates, and disease was rampant. Nonetheless, workhouses did represent a slight shift in penal philosophy, with society assuming at least minimal responsibility for separating convicts from other citizens.

The Reform Movement

A major turning point in the history of corrections was reached in the late eighteenth and early nineteenth centuries, often referred to as the **age of enlightenment**. Efforts by Baron de Montesquieu, Francois-Marie Arouet Voltaire, Cesare Beccaria, Jeremy Bentham, and John Howard were instrumental in bringing reform to the harsh penal philosophy that had existed prior to this period. These individuals and others were concerned with human rights and limiting the coercive power of the state.

Both Montesquieu and Voltaire were concerned with the harsh punishments inflicted on French citizens. Montesquieu's treatise called for an end to such treatment, and Voltaire was actively involved in defending and appealing cases for alleged offenders. Voltaire was eventually imprisoned for his activities and then banished from France. The efforts of both Montesquieu and Voltaire had considerable impact on Beccaria, who was the person most responsible for bringing about changes in the inhumane conditions to which convicts were subjected.

Beccaria anonymously published his famous *Essays on Crimes and Punishments* in 1764, and he is remembered as the individual who directed penal philosophy away from punishment and toward corrections. Beccaria argued that humans are basically rational beings who are calculating in their behavior and controlled by the principle of **hedonism**—the desire to seek pleasurable experiences and avoid painful ones. He contended that prevention should be the goal of punishment and that the punishment should fit the crime. He abhorred torture and capital punishment, and advocated more extensive use of fines, imprisonment, and banishment. In addition, Beccaria was concerned with individual rights and with providing procedural safeguards in the trial process (Beccaria, 1953). His principles influenced many of the penologists of his time and remain an important cornerstone of corrections today.

Other contributors to the correctional reform movement include Jeremy Bentham and John Howard. Bentham, an Englishman strongly influenced by Beccaria's work, advocated a system of hedonistic calculus, which would provide graduated penalties based on the seriousness of offenses. Howard was a British sheriff in the latter part of the eighteenth century who was appalled by conditions in British jails and attempted to bring about changes in these conditions. He traveled throughout Europe to observe confinement facilities and conveyed his findings on the inhumane conditions he found everywhere. Partly because of Howard's efforts, Parliament passed the Penitentiary Act of 1779. This act provided for secure and sanitary structures and systematic inspections, among other things (Barnes & Teeters, 1959). Howard's ideas spread to continental Europe and the United States, and his legacy lives on in a contemporary reform organization bearing his name.

The Early American Experience

America's involvement with corrections stems from the early days when prisoners were transported here from England. The early settlers employed corporal punishment much like that in their home countries. One of the earliest attempts to humanize treatment of offenders resulted from the efforts of William Penn and his Quaker followers. Penn formulated the Great Law, which replaced corporal and capital punishment with imprisonment and hard labor. After Penn's death, the law was repealed and treatment of offenders once again became inhumane. However, his philosophy did not die. After the Revolution, it surfaced again to become an important part of American correctional philosophy. In fact, the reform efforts of the Quakers led the Pennsylvania legislature to declare a section of the Walnut Street Jail as a penitentiary to house convicted felons; thus the **Walnut Street Jail** became known as the first correctional institution in the United States. While housed in this institution, prisoners were permitted to work and receive wages, and were given religious instruction. Corporal punishment was prohibited, and the guards were not permitted to carry weapons. According to Menninger (1968), the Walnut Street Jail was the birthplace of the prison system. Other states adopted versions of the Walnut Street philosophy, and before long, these institutions became so overcrowded that a new system was developed.

The Pennsylvania and Auburn Systems

As a result of the overcrowding mentioned above, the Pennsylvania legislature was forced to establish new and larger institutions to house prisoners. Two new penitentiaries were established in the 1820s. The architecture of the **Pennsylvania prisons** was unique. They were designed with a central hub and numerous wings radiating from this hub. The design reflected the current attitude toward punishment, which was based on the premise that prison should be a place in which to do penance (thus, the term "penitentiary") and that the best way to achieve this end was through solitary confinement. So, each wing of the institution consisted of several cells placed back-to-back, in which inmates worked, ate, slept, and received religious instruction. It was assumed that this arrangement would give each inmate time to contemplate his crimes and repent.

At about the same time, the state of New York was also developing a prison system. The architectural design of the **Auburn prisons** differed substantially from that of the Pennsylvania prisons. The original Auburn structure was built in the shape of a U and consisted of five tiers with numerous cells on each tier. In contrast to the Pennsylvania system, prisoners in the Auburn system ate and worked with other inmates. A code of silence was enforced, and strict punishment was administered to those who violated regulations. Prisoners were placed in their own cells to sleep. Those convicted of the most serious offenses were confined to their cells, and the notion of solitary confinement as a technique for prison discipline emerged from this procedure.

A debate soon ensued over which system was better. Supporters of the Auburn system claimed their choice was more economical and that the congregation of prisoners best suited reform. Advocates of the Pennsylvania system felt their approach was more efficient and orderly. The Pennsylvania system was adopted by several European countries, whereas the Auburn system became more popular in the United States and remains the model for many of our prisons today.

In 1870, the National Prison Association (now called the American Correctional Association) met in Cincinnati to discuss prison reform. The group developed a list of 36 principles, which led to the establishment of the first reformatory in the United States, at Elmira, New York, under the direction of Z. R. Brockway. Under Brockway's leadership, educational and vocational programs were developed and instituted. Brockway also advocated individual treatment, indeterminate sentencing, and greater use of parole. Although a number of institutions adopted the name "reformatory," most did not adopt all of Brockway's principles. Nonetheless, the Elmira experiment had an impact on future correctional efforts. Brockway's attempts at reformation and rehabilitation of prisoners were forerunners of similar attempts in contemporary prisons. Numerous changes have occurred in corrections since Elmira, including the addition of professional staff members (such as behavior therapists, social workers, and psychiatrists) and greater reliance on social science research, but the emphasis on both rehabilitation and punishment remains.

Correctional Objectives

Correctional officials generally pursue two objectives: punishment and rehabilitation. The emphasis shifts from one of the objectives to the other over time with shifts in public opinion and political leadership. In general, rehabilitation received more attention than punishment in the 1960s and 1970s, but the pendulum has swung more toward punishment in recent years.

From a legal viewpoint, the court identified and discussed four objectives of punishment in the case of *Commonwealth v. Ritter* (Court of Oyer and Terminer, 1930). These objectives include revenge or retribution, specific deterrence, general deterrence, and rehabilitation or reformation. A brief look at each of these objectives is in order.

Revenge

Revenge, commonly called **retribution**, is one of the oldest known justifications for punishment. It is based on the philosophy that because the victim has suffered, so must the offender (an eye for an eye). Although it is easy to understand why revenge is a motive on the part of victims or their loved ones, how do we determine the severity of the punishment to be inflicted on the offender, and who should make that determination? Suppose Black is the victim of a hit-and-run accident. Do we adhere to a philosophy of punishment in kind? What if Black dies? Do we then execute the driver of the vehicle? What form of punishment is appropriate if Black is paralyzed? If we decide not to execute the offender, how do we determine an appropriate prison sentence? It should be apparent that making the punishment fit the crime is not always an easy task. If we add the additional factors of plea bargaining and prison overcrowding to the questions above, the issue becomes even more complex. Although revenge may be an ancient and understandable objective, in a practical sense it is difficult to achieve because punishment does not occur in a vacuum.

Specific Deterrence

Specific deterrence refers to the notion that punishment will prevent a criminal from repeating his or her crimes. You may recall from our previous discussion that Beccaria felt that punishment should be severe enough to make the potential offender refrain from engaging in crime. However, not all criminals act in a rational manner (many crimes are committed in the heat of passion, for example), and some who do apparently use a calculus different from that of most people (as may be the case when an angry husband, knowing that he will be apprehended, batters or murders his wife and her lover). In addition, severity of punishment makes a difference to potential offenders only when they believe there is a reasonable chance they will be apprehended for their crimes. According to current clearance rates for most crimes except homicide, the likelihood of detection and apprehension is not particularly great; thus, the proposed punishment, no matter how severe, is unlikely to have any great impact on the potential offender. Further, the effects of specific deterrence are very difficult to measure. Would an alternative form of punishment have increased or decreased the likelihood of an offense occurring? Research findings on the effects of punishment as a deterrent are contradictory. Chambliss (1965) argues that punishment affects some categories of shoplifters and traffic offenders, but Pittman and Gordon (1968) contend that punishment has little or no effect on drug addicts and alcoholics. The common-sense appeal of specific deterrence seems to be the basic justification for retaining it as an objective of punishment. However, a good deal of research indicates that punishment is not an effective deterrent to crime (Griffin, 2006; Nagin & Paternoster, 1991; Nagin & Pogarski, 2003). Listokin (2007), for example, notes that since criminals often fail to think about the future, the deterrence value of criminal sanctions steadily decreases as the lag between crime and punishment lengthens.

General Deterrence

The basic premise of **general deterrence** is that punishing one offender for his or her offenses will help dissuade other potential offenders from engaging in criminal conduct. Again, there is a kind of commonsense appeal to the concept, but the value of general deterrence has also been challenged. Numerous studies have been conducted in attempts to measure the deterrent effect of the death penalty as well as other forms of punishment. Most have failed to demonstrate a significant relationship between type of punishment administered and the likelihood that others will commit a similar offense (Listokin, 2007; Nagin & Paternoster, 1991; Walker, 1998; Wilson & Abrahamse, 1992). Despite this lack of scientific support for general deterrence, substantial numbers of practitioners, politicians, and citizens continue to clamor for a get-tough approach to punishment. While any given type of punishment may deter certain individuals from engaging in acts that might lead to such punishment, we currently have too little knowledge of the exact nature of this relationship to determine how best to reach those who are most likely to commit offenses.

Rehabilitation

The basic assumption underlying rehabilitation as a correctional objective is that behavior can be modified if only we know enough about the prior history of the individual involved (and about the causes of the undesirable criminal behavior). For the most part, programs aimed at rehabilitating offenders concentrate on attempting to discover the causes of the aberrant behavior to eliminate or modify the behavior through some form of therapy. Thus, a person identified as committing utilitarian burglary as a result of being a high school dropout and having no vocational skills might be placed in educational and vocational training programs that could provide skills necessary to secure and retain reasonable employment to eliminate the need to commit burglaries. Some segments of the public view rehabilitation programs as catering to criminals and as alternatives that are too lenient. Others have argued that psychological treatment programs reduce inmates to experimental animals (Lewis, 1953). Walker (1998) concludes: "In the end, the evidence on rehabilitation does not look very good. We do not seem to have devised any 'planned intervention' programs that substantially reduce recidivism rates" (p. 225). Similarly, Marlowe (2006) concludes that the effects of behavioral intervention with inmates is likely to be negligible.

Custody

Traditionally, prisons have been viewed as institutions in which prisoners are isolated or incapacitated (prevented from committing further crimes). This is the custodial as opposed to the rehabilitative function of correctional authorities, and the contradiction between these two objectives accounts for many of the problems surrounding imprisonment today. There are two major problems with the concept of incapacitation: the failure to consider crimes committed by one inmate against another, or against prison staff, as further crimes (and thousands of these are committed annually), and the fact that incapacitation is temporary, because most inmates will eventually be released whether or not they have been rehabilitated.

Women in Prison

In recent years, the number of female prison inmates has been increasing faster than the number of male inmates, though the former still constitute a small proportion of the total inmate population (Reid, 2006, p. 535). The number of women under the jurisdiction of State or Federal prison authorities increased 4.8 percent from midyear 2005, reaching 111,403 in June, 2006 (Bureau of Justice Statistics, 2007). Women made up about 23 percent of the nation's probationers (about 950,000) and 12 percent of the parolees (about 94,000) (Bureau of Justice Statistics, 2007).

Major issues for female inmates are accommodation of young children, pregnancy while incarcerated, and other health issues. In addition to the costs of creating and staffing new penal institutions for women, society often bears the added cost of rearing the minor children of female inmates, estimated at about 1.3 million in 1998 (Greenfield & Snell, 1999). Traditionally, women's prisons have lagged behind prisons for men in terms of services and programs. As a result, a number of court cases have been filed by female inmates claiming the right to equal protection (treatment). A Supreme Court decision handed down in *Craig v. Boren* (1976) has often been cited as requiring equal protection for female inmates (Cripe, 1997, p.21).

A recurring problem involving both female and male inmates is that of sexual abuse. The authority of correctional officials over their charges leaves inmates vulnerable to sexual advances and abuse. Sexual abuse of one inmate by another is common in penal institutions. Sexual favors may be granted by inmates seeking special treatment from correctional officials or from other inmates. In all of these cases, relationships are problematic for correctional officials for obvious reasons. In response to these problems, Congress passed The Prison Rape Elimination Act in 2003 which was intended to establish a zero-tolerance standard for prison rape and to "increase the accountability of prison officials who fail to detect, prevent, reduce, and punish prison rape" (Section 15602).

Correctional Organization

Although we commonly use the term "American correctional system," this is a misnomer. Correctional programs in America are actually far more fragmented than unified. There is no central authority controlling these agencies, and to some extent, they pursue different and sometimes conflicting goals.

As is the case with the courts, both the federal government and the states maintain correctional systems. Lack of centralized control is one of the major obstacles to reform, since most jurisdictions provide for autonomy of jails and prisons, which are further segmented by gender, age, and type of offense involved. Similarly, probation, parole, and diversionary programs are also largely autonomous.

The Federal Network

Congress established the Bureau of Prisons in 1930. The legislation that established the federal network resulted from serious overcrowding of existing facilities and the associated practice of leasing space from local and state facilities. Currently, the federal network is divided into six regions, with headquarters in the following cities: Dublin, California; Kansas City, Kansas; Dallas; Atlanta; Annapolis, Maryland and Philadelphia. Heads of correctional institutions and community facilities report to regional directors who are in turn responsible to the director of the Federal Bureau of Prisons. The Bureau of Prisons Central Office has nine divisions: Administration; Correctional Programs; Health Services; Human Resource Management; Industries, Education and Vocational Training; Information, Policy and Public Affairs; National Institute of Corrections; Office of General Counsel; and Program Review. Each subdivision is responsible for developing and implementing programs that are national in scope, but the daily administration of these programs is left to regional and institutional directors.

Federal institutions vary considerably in size. Those in Atlanta and Leavenworth, Kansas, are quite large, with populations of about 2,000 inmates each, and are reserved for more hardened inmates. The facility in Marion, Illinois is a medium security facility housing male inmates with an adjacent satellite prison camp that houses minimum security male offenders. The prison in Terre Haute, Indiana, was designed to house inmates thought to have considerable potential for rehabilitation. The present inmate population of federal prisons is about 199,000 (Bureau of Prisons, 2007). This includes approximately 21,000 inmates who are housed in privately-managed secure facilities. Approximately 93 percent of all inmates housed in federal facilities are male. The average federal inmate is 38 years old and approximately 54 percent of inmates are in custody for drug offenses (Bureau of Prisons, 2007). Only 3 percent of all federal inmates are in custody for homicide, aggravated assault or kidnapping offenses.

Through the National Institute of Corrections, the Federal Bureau of Prisons provides assistance to state and local networks through grants, by conducting research, by disseminating research materials, and by conducting training seminars.

State Networks

The bulk of the corrections network is located at the state level. At midyear 1999, the nation's prisons and jails incarcerated 1,860,520 persons (Beck, 2000). During the year 2005, this number surpassed 2.2 million. We are witnessing annual prison population increases of over 2 percent per year (Anonymous, 2006). As we continue to incarcerate more and more people, the costs for construction, operation, and personnel continue to escalate. State spending on corrections, which includes the costs of operating and maintaining state owned correctional facilities, was the second fastest growing component of state spending in the 1990s (Snell et. al., 2003). Rising crime rates in the 1980s and 1990s led to tougher sentencing policies and more inmates. States

There are many types of prison facilities ranging from minimum to super-max.
Reprinted with permission of iStockphoto.com / Eliza Snow.

spent more dollars to expand prisons to accommodate these policies. In the 1990s relatively new sentencing policies appeared, and included the "three strikes law" which triggered mandatory life sentences for third-time serious violent offenders and "truth in sentencing laws" which required violent offenders to serve at least 85 percent of their sentence (Snell et. al., 2003). Both sentencing concepts further impacted the prison population in states that adopted these laws. Significant increases in state spending actually leveled off and decreased slightly in some states as prison expansion projects were completed (National Conference of State Legislatures, 2003). Spending for corrections continued to grow in 2006 and is expected to grow in 2007 based on the growing number of inmates and the cost of providing inmates with adequate health care (National Conference of State Legislatures, 2007). State and federal prison populations are expected to add approximately 192,000 persons at a cost of $27.5 billion dollars between 2007 and 2011 (Public Safety Performance Project, 2007). The question we must ask ourselves is whether we can afford to pay for facilities to house and treat this increasing population. Perhaps we need to do more to prevent individuals from becoming involved in crime and to reintegrate those who have been incarcerated back in to society. A number of states that are concerned about rising prison populations are exploring or implementing programs to reduce recidivism. For example, some states are reviewing and modifying probation policies to reduce the number of violators who return to the prison system for technical violations (National Conference of State Legislatures, 2007). These issues will be discussed in greater detail later in this chapter.

Types of Institutions

A major problem with correctional facilities deals with the opportunity they provide for inmates to become more antisocial as a result of their exposure to more hardened offenders. In an attempt to deal with this problem, most jurisdictions have developed classification systems based on the amount of security required for inmates. Most commonly, prisons are divided into supermax, maximum, medium, and minimum security categories.

Supermax Security Facilities

Supermax security facilities house offenders who are extremely violent or dangerous and/or who are considered serious escape risks. They reflect the goals of revenge and incapacitation. Perimeter security typically consists of double fences and razor ribbon, electronic surveillance systems, and electric fences or walls. Movement inside these prisons is tightly controlled; inmates are placed in restraints and escorted by several staff. Contact with the outside world is restricted, the emphasis is on security and control, and treatment and rehabilitation programs are limited. Inmates may be locked down for as many as 23 hours per day.

Maximum Security Facilities

Maximum security facilities also reflect the goals of revenge and incapacitation. They are generally characterized by high concrete walls that are typically occupied by armed guards and equipped with floodlights. These institutions are generally reserved for dangerous offenders and those serving long sentences. Because of the emphasis on custody, rehabilitation programs are often present in name only in such institutions.

Medium Security Facilities

Medium security facilities have become more popular over the years in the United States. These prisons are usually smaller than maximum security prisons. Physically, they often resemble their maximum security counterparts, but they generally provide for more freedom of movement internally. These institutions house younger and less dangerous offenders and place more emphasis on rehabilitation than do maximum security facilities.

Minimum Security Facilities

Minimum security facilities house nonviolent and nontraditional offenders, for the most part. They are characterized by dormitory-style living, private rooms, and the absence of armed guards and walls. Most have been built relatively recently in comparison with maximum and medium security facilities, and they generally house fewer inmates than either of the other two types. Work and educational release are integral parts of minimum security programs, and home furlough is used frequently. These facilities, although criticized as being country clubs for white-collar and political offenders, are thought to provide better opportunities for rehabilitation than other types of prisons because they tend to maximize contact between inmates and the outside world in which they must survive after release from prison.

Jails

In terms of sheer numbers, jails are one of the most important features of the correctional network. At midyear 2006, 766,010 inmates were held in the Nation's local jails, up from 747,529 at midyear 2005. In 2006, jails reported adding 21,862 beds during the previous 12 months, bringing the total rated capacity to 810,863. From 1995 to 2005, the number of jail inmates per 100,000 U.S. residents rose from 193 to 256. From midyear 2005 to midyear 2006 the 12-month increase of 2.5 percent in the jail population was less than the average annual increase of 3.8 percent since 1995 (Bureau of Justice Statistics, 2007c).

Jails are usually the first, and sometimes the only, contact offenders have with corrections. The often deplorable conditions existing in many of these facilities have led to increased visibility in recent years. For example, Ruddell and Mays (2007) found that under-funding, overcrowding, retention and recruitment of officers and relatively high percentages of special needs inmates present significant challenges to jails with populations under 100 (numbering 1, 775). Such challenges were identified several decades ago, indicating that few structural or operational changes have been made during that period. Similarly, Tartaro and Ruddell (2006) examined the problem of suicides and attempted suicides in small jails. Their findings indicate that the prevalence of these incidents is two to five times greater than in larger jails. High rates of admissions and overcrowded facilities appeared to be related to suicide attempts.

History of Jails

Earlier, we noted that pretrial detention existed in Europe in the sixteenth century. Champion (2001 p. 82) describes these early detention facilities as providing substandard food and shelter and being plagued by malnutrition, disease, and death. These facilities were basically holding tanks rather than correctional institutions. As indicated earlier, the Walnut Street Jail was the first institution in America to be used for correctional purposes. In the seventeenth century, jails were built for the general detention of prisoners awaiting monthly court session in Jamestown, Virginia (Champion, 1998, p.306). Although Fishman documented the poor conditions existing in American jails in 1923, little public attention was devoted to them until 1970, when the first national jail census was conducted (Fishman, 1969).

In the 1980s and 1990s, many jails were cited for failure to meet jail standards relating to fire safety, health and sanitation, and various other areas. As a means to relieve overcrowding, court-ordered reductions in the number of jail inmates have become common in the past two decades.

Control and Organization

Jails have been very difficult to reform because they are normally financed and administered at the local or county level. This local autonomy has allowed jails to escape many state and federal reform movements and frequently involves jails in local politics. Traditionally, they have been low-priority items in county budgets, and they are generally under the direct supervision of the sheriff, an elected official subject to political pressures, which is important because local constituents seldom consider jails the most desirable place to expend funds (see "In the News" 11.2).

In the News 11.2

Jail space: Problems in local jails lead back to folks at Capitol

Fixing Michigan's system of correcting criminals soon will require a call to arms of the state's law-abiding citizenry. First, though, there must be a call to attention. Ingham County has one story worthy of attention; a story that touches on just part of the difficult choices taxpayers must confront.

Ingham County doesn't have enough jail space. Criminals that many citizens might want in custody are quickly cycling back to local streets.

The sheriff who runs the jail acknowledges it. The chief judge knows all about it, as does the county prosecutor.

And while these officials have ideas to reduce the problem, the apparent truth is that without fundamental changes in the Michigan Department of Corrections and the Legislature, expect to see more criminals popping out of custody.

Revolving door acknowledged

The biggest problem, says Prosecutor Stuart Dunnings III, is that after lawmakers adopted sentencing rules in 1997, people convicted of felonies such as repeat drunken drivers were directed by the guidelines into county jails, not state prisons.

Worse, says Dunnings, is that the Legislature ignored the warnings of the Sentencing Commission about demands on state prisons. The 1997 report projected a need for 65,000 prison beds in 2007, yet, Dunnings points out that the system only has a little more than 50,000.

The state Department of Corrections does lease beds from counties; 193 of the 665 beds at the Ingham County Jail are leased by the state.

The local judges, led by Chief Judge William Collette, recently appealed to the Ingham Board of Commissioners to reduce that number, so local judges could keep in custody local offenders who are now being released due to crowding.

"People in the city of Lansing deserve to be able to walk down the street or go to the store and not be assaulted by someone who will be out of jail in two hours," Collette said then.

But county officials point out that the leases earn the county about $2.5 million a year at a time when Ingham County is looking at a deficit.

Collette, Dunnings and Sheriff Gene Wriggelsworth also are proponents of building a new facility to house low-level offenders now sent to the county jail.

In separate interviews last week, both Collette and Dunnings argued that it's preferable to keep these offenders in custody than just cycle them out of the jail, even if that means more spending.

"Tax is not a four-letter word," Dunnings remarked.

Sentencing rules bite counties

Collette and Dunnings caution though that a new facility alone won't end the problems of jail crowding and of low-level offenders walking the streets.

"When I started as a circuit judge 18 years ago, the minimum sentence for a third drunken driving sentence was a year in jail. Today, the penalty for a third offense is to serve no more than 60 days. We have (sentencing) guidelines that control and dominate what we can do ... and contribute to all these early releases, too," Collette said.

Dunnings was even more pointed about sentencing rules: "The Legislature has perpetuated a sham on the state since 1997."

Gov. Jennifer Granholm has proposed a sentencing reform — a plan heavily criticized by Republican leaders in the Legislature. Dunnings, while crediting Granholm for her work, says this reform only brings the state's official position in line with the current reality of actual time served.

Legislators enact long sentences for political fanfare, says Dunnings, while the sentencing rules call for short stints.

With the state economy hurting and the state budget in deficit, huge new spending at DOC isn't an option; quite the opposite, in fact.

State leaders have to find ways to trim corrections spending and better utilize remaining dollars.

That means identifying which criminals have to stay in prison, reducing non-violent populations and pouring savings into cheaper forms of custody, rehabilitation and monitoring.

The alternative is to keep a status quo that makes life easier on state politicians and petty criminals — and much harder on everyone else.

In addition, the sheriff is both a law enforcement official and the chief correctional officer in the county, and law enforcement duties traditionally have been considered more important than jail supervision. Jail staffs frequently have little correctional training and are generally not well paid. Further, inmate-staff ratios of 40 to 1 are not uncommon in jails. It is not difficult to see why jails — with little supervision, inadequate staff, and high inmate-staff ratios — contribute little to correctional efforts.

Jail Problems

Beginning with the first jail census, investigations have consistently shown that jail populations are basically male (about 90 percent), under 35 years of age (62 percent), under- or unemployed, below the poverty level, and disproportionately from minority groups (more than 60 percent) (Bureau of Justice Statistics, 2004a). One-half of all jail inmates in 2002 were held for a violent or drug offense, nearly unchanged since 1996 (Bureau of Justice Statistics, 2004a). Jails are institutions in which inmates who cannot make bail or are not eligible for bail are housed until the time of their trial, until they have served their sentences, or until the charges against them are dropped.

In addition to their alleged criminality, many jail inmates are affected by such problems as illiteracy, substance abuse, and varying degrees of mental instability (Silverman, 2001, p. 442). Many of these problems go untreated in society and American jails become a catchall for society's problems. Thus, when nobody else can take care of the problem, the person is placed in jail (Silverman, 2001). This includes both the mentally ill for whom there are insufficient local facilities and hard-core welfare recipients who are no longer eligible for participation in the program (Parrish, 2000). A recent study of the Cook County, Illinois jail found that 6 percent of males and twelve percent of females entering the system had severe mental disorders, including schizophrenia, mania, or major depression (Daly, 2006). In addition, mentally ill inmates spend more time in jail because they tend to be homeless, have violated conditions of release and sometimes wait months for a competency evaluation (Ervin, 2006). A contributing factor to the rise in the number of inmates entering jails with mental illnesses was the nationwide deinstitutionalization of mental illness which led to the loss of 90 percent of state psychiatric beds over the last 50 years (Daly, 2006). Federal legislation and courts powered a move toward deinstitutionalization, calling on states and counties to provide resources for social services, vocational rehabilitation, and treatment services (Goin, 2007). However, the necessary community resources did not materialize anywhere near the level that was required to treat person suffering from mental illnesses. Worse, once imprisoned, people with mental illnesses are shown to have much longer incarcerations than other inmates, primarily because a prison environment and lack of treatment aggravate the very illness that has led to their objectionable or antisocial behavior (Goin, 2007).

Despite regulations, convicted offenders are frequently not segregated from pretrial detainees, and juveniles are frequently placed in cell blocks with adults. Many jails also house drunks and vagrants on a short-term basis. As a result of inadequate funding, constant turnover, and the lack of authority to require pretrial detainees (who, after all, have not been convicted of any offense) to participate, treatment programs are virtually nonexistent in most jails.

Correctional environments are increasingly becoming recognized as locations in which infectious diseases are concentrated (National Commission on Correctional Health Care, 2002). Most studies on infectious disease in correctional facilities address prisons, but infectious diseases are even more prevalent in jails (Brown, 2003). There is often a tendency to address urgent medical conditions in jails, with mental illness, drug withdrawal, and tuberculosis receiving the most attention. In many cases it is difficult to treat tuberculosis in jails due to the rapid turn over and short stays of the inmates. However, administrators are concerned about the potential spread of infectious diseases in their facilities because of the close living (and often overcrowded) conditions, the cost of medical care, and the potential spread of diseases in the communities to which inmates will return (Silverman, 2001, p. 415). Rates of HIV infection in jail detainees vary by gender and race/ethnicity but were several orders of magnitude higher for each group studied when compared to the general population (McAuley, 2004). Reasonable prevention procedures must be developed to protect staff and other inmates. The Center for Disease Control and Prevention (CDC) has issued a series of guidelines for public safety employees, including correctional officers, concerning the steps that should be initiated when working with persons who may potentially be HIV-positive or who may have other communicable diseases such as hepatitis B (Silverman, 2001). In most jails HIV-positive inmates are not separated from the general population.

Some efforts to improve jail conditions have been made. Some states have established new and stricter standards for local jails, but follow-up inspections may or may not be mandated and carried out (Mueller, 1996). A constitutionally acceptable jail environment requires adherence to standard safety codes, provides levels of supervision that adequately controls violence, and corrects situations that violate basic inmate rights (Marchese, 1990). Failure to comply with these standards often results in court imposed judgments requiring jurisdictions to budget for changes that far exceed the cost of correcting and monitoring the initial problem (Silverman, 2001).

Evaluating Prison Rehabilitation Programs

How do we determine whether or not prison rehabilitation programs are successful? Most commonly, we look at **recidivism rates**, which are based on the proportion of offenders released from prison who become involved in reported criminal behavior after their release. Many criminal justice officials believe that recidivism rates range from 50 to 75 percent, that is, that one-half to three-fourths of all offenders released from prison commit additional offenses (Silverman, 2001, p. 170; Bureau of Justice Statistics, 2002). These estimates have been challenged by some researchers. Among the first to challenge traditional conceptions of recidivism was Daniel Glaser (1964), whose research indicated that a figure of 35 percent is more reasonable. Glaser argues that recidivism rates depend on a number of factors, including the characteristics of offenders sentenced to prison, the manner in which parole is employed, and the type of institution involved. For example, in a jurisdiction that relies heavily on probation, only those offenders considered poor risks may be sentenced to prison. Similarly, if parole or early release is used extensively, some inmates may be released prematurely. Finally, when we sentence offenders to maximum instead of medium or minimum security facilities, we are making some assumptions about the likelihood of rehabilitation, and this affects recidivism rates in each of these types of institutions. Glaser makes the additional point that many ex-convicts are returned to prison not because they commit new crimes but because they commit technical violations of parole requirements, which do not necessarily indicate a return to criminal behavior.

The debate concerning recidivism rates continues, with some supporting Glaser's approach and others continuing to believe that recidivism is considerably higher than Glaser would have us believe. According to the Bureau of Justice Statistics (2002), sixty-seven percent of former inmates released from state prisons in 1994 committed at least one serious new crime within the following three years,

The problems of measuring recidivism are complex, but improved performance in the area of rehabilitation and more accurate measures of recidivism for different types of programs must be developed. What we have learned is that a number of obstacles to rehabilitation exist in the prison setting, and it is to these obstacles that we now turn our attention.

The Prison Society

The potential for successful rehabilitation in prison depends on a number of factors. Two of the most important factors are the presence of qualified staff members in sufficient numbers and creation of an atmosphere conducive to rehabilitation. Under present conditions in most prisons, neither of these conditions exists. The lack of adequately trained staff in sufficient numbers reflects the fact that prisons have not traditionally received high priority when it comes to allocation of resources. The inability of prison officials to create conditions favorable to rehabilitation results partly from inadequate staff, but equally important is the fact that most of the time spent by inmates is in the company of other inmates. Life inside prison is radically different from the prior experiences of the new inmate. In Goffman's (1961) terms, prison is a **total institution**. The inmate's identity is stripped away, and decisions that the inmate previously made concerning eating, sleeping, working, and so forth are now made by the institutional staff. Yet, when we release the offender from prison, we expect him or her to assume full responsibility for these and other decisions in the outside world. Additionally, while the inmate is in prison, he or she is subject to what may be called the inmates' code. Sykes and Messinger (1970) point out that even if the prison administration strongly supports rehabilitation, it is difficult to achieve because peer group pressure forces inmates not to support the goals of the administration (Lambropoulou, 1999). In some prisons, inmate gangs have become so powerful that they actually control the institution and the staff, making rehabilitation unlikely.

Robert Martinson (1974), after studying correctional programs, argued that very few rehabilitation programs work. Unfortunately, his remarks have been interpreted to mean that nothing can work, even though he later admitted that under certain circumstance some programs might be effective. Some have found evidence that rehabilitation can be effective under certain conditions, which, unfortunately, are seldom met (Gordon & Weldon, 2003; Visher, 2006; Walker, 1998). Others continue to support Martinson's basic premise that the effects of most rehabilitation programs are minimal (Marlowe, 2006). This debate has accompanied the accusation and perhaps rationalization that prisons have simply become warehouses where the manifest goal is the incapacitation of the convicted and the protection of the public.

In 2002, state and federal prisons in the United States were operating at between 1 and 17 percent over capacity (Harrison & Beck, 2004). The causes and ramifications of **warehousing** are severe. When warehousing occurs, the administrative agenda, the means of evaluation, and the goals are all redefined. The consequent overcrowding of the correctional system means that offenders are doubled up in cells meant for one person; packed into makeshift dormitories; and bunked in basements, corridors, converted hospital facilities, tents, trailers, warehouses, and program activity areas of the prisons (Allen & Simonsen, 2001, p. 242). Overcrowded maximum security prisons appear to be most likely to have the worst impact on prisoner health and safety (Allen & Simonsen, 2001). Prisons that have experienced violent riots are frequently overcrowded, highly authoritarian, and understaffed (Useem & Reisig, 1999).

The problem of warehousing can be explained by the network approach. First, the public and perhaps some criminal justice officials complain that too many convicted offenders are on the streets or are not receiving appropriate punishment. The legislatures respond by enacting laws requiring longer sentences and limiting other alternatives. The courts are forced to sentence more defendants to prison and for longer periods of time. Correction officials are often caught in the middle: They must accommodate the increase in prison population, but they do not receive concomitant funding to comply with prison regulations. Once the warehousing is revealed through civil suits or a riot, the public is appalled by what has happened. Although they are shocked, do they want to fund a bond issue or increase taxes to provide adequate prison care? Not likely. As illustrated, there are no easy solutions. The issue of warehousing is extremely complex, and one can see how actions and reactions in one portion of the network affect other components (Allen & Simonsen, 2001, p.242–243; Conklin, 1998; Silverman, 2001, p. 407). There are only three options for reducing prison population overcrowding: a bricks and mortar building program, prison avoidance programs (house arrest, electronic monitoring, boot camps) and back-end alternatives including early release, good-time credits, halfway houses and other alternatives (Allen & Simonsen, 2001, p. 261).

Rehabilitation versus Custody

Another obstacle to rehabilitation is the conflict that often occurs between therapeutic and correctional staff. In many institutions, the staff of one persuasion has little or no respect for those of the other, and inmates sometimes use this lack of trust and respect among staff members to their advantage. Therapeutic staff frequently regard themselves as more skilled than correctional staff and are better paid in most cases. Correctional staff often resent the fact that they take most of the risks in dealing with inmates 24 hours a day, but are not regarded as professionals and are not well paid.

Group and some individual therapy occur in most prisons; some also have social-skills training programs, and others offer family intervention and educational programs. Gordon and Weldon (2003, p. 200), for example, found that inmates who had completed vocational training had a recidivism rate of 8.75 percent, inmates who participated in both GED and vocational training reported a recidivism of 6.71 percent, and non-educational participants had a recidivism rate of 26 percent. They concluded that educational and vocational programs had a positive effect on reducing recidivism, at least in the population they studied.

Costs for these types of programs are high, and success is hampered by insufficient knowledge of the causes of crime, the fact that inmates might see a therapist/counselor less than one hour per week (the rest of the time is spent with other inmates under the supervision of correctional staff), and a lack of follow-up after the offender is released from prison. It is also somewhat ironic that we continue to provide psychological therapy to inmates when a great deal of the available evidence suggests that they are no more in need of such therapy than most of the rest of us.

Education and Vocational Training in Prison

As early as the 1830s, education was defined as one means of assisting prisoner rehabilitation, and most prisons currently offer educational programs of one type or another. Many inmates do not have high school educations, and some estimates indicate that as many as 80 percent are illiterate. Correctional populations consistently report lower levels of educational attainment compared to the general population. An estimated 40 percent of state prison inmates, 27 percent of federal inmates and 47 percent of local jail inmates had not completed high school or its equivalent compared to 18 percent of the general population who failed to attain high school graduation (Harlow, 2003). The quality of educational programs in prisons varies considerably, and some of the most outspoken critics of prison education argue that such programs are merely tools to occupy the inmates' time and that under conditions of confinement, they have little chance to succeed. An additional problem plaguing educational programs in prison is the negative experience that many inmates have had with education in the outside world. Still, it appears that some prison education programs do benefit participants by helping them deal with the stress of prison overcrowding, by helping create more positive feelings about other inmates, and by improving inmate self-esteem (Gordon & Weldon, 2003; Lawrence, 1995; Parker, 1990). Furthermore, inmates who participated in education programs while incarcerated showed lower rates of recidivism after three years (Steurer, Smith, and Tracy, 2001). They concluded that the measures of recidivism (re-arrest, re-conviction and re-incarceration) were significantly lower. This study also examined employment data and found that wages reported to the state labor departments were higher for the education participants compared to the non-participants (Steurer, et.al.,2001, p.7).

In theory, most prison work programs are designed to provide inmates with job skills that may help them secure employment on the outside. In reality, something quite different often occurs. Many of the skills prisoners are taught are obsolete by the time they are released (and some are obsolete at the time they are taught). Even when the skills they learned are current, ex-convicts often find that the stigma of having served time in prison is more important than the skills they possess. In short, no matter how skilled they are, they can't find employment because of their records.

Walker (2001) states that "no conclusive evidence indicates that locking up a lot of people actually produces the promised reduction in crime. Finally, even where some crime reduction does occur, it is not clear that it is worth the enormous dollar cost to society" (p. 144). Alternatives to the current emphasis on building new prisons must be found, and we turn attention to some of these alternatives later in this chapter.

Private Prisons

" The cost of jails and prisons is such a problem today authorities are looking for innovative ways to finance construction and maintenance of facilities as well as inmate care ... Under privatization, a profit-making company, with money from private investors, finances, builds, and owns the jail or prison or contracts to provide some service (such as food or medical care) within the institution"(Reid, 2006, p. 532). In midyear 2004, private prisons incarcerated 6.6 percent of the sentenced, adult population in the United States (Harrison & Beck, 2004). A 1999 survey of administrators who monitored private prisons in the United States (or U.S. territories) found that the private sector experienced significant problems with staff turnover, escapes, and drug use (Camp & Gaes, 2002). Others have noted quality control and cost as problems (Reid, 2006). Given the concern with public safety, these are all significant issues in privatization. At this point in time, there appears to be little convincing evidence that private prisons are superior to public prisons.

Capital Punishment:
Timeless Controversy, Ultimate Penalty

No issue in criminal justice has generated as much debate as capital punishment. Capital punishment is the ultimate sanction, the most symbolic reminder of the state's power to punish its citizens. Although the practice is perhaps as old as human life, it has been particularly controversial in the past 300 years, and the debate has been revived in the past quarter of a century as a result of several heinous and/or spectacular crimes. Some arguments are based on the morality of capital punishment, some on its deterrent effects, and some on the economic and social costs involved (Hawkins, 2006). Heinous crimes often lead to a public outcry, which usually includes a call for increased use of the death penalty. Although the details of such crimes may invoke an angry reaction in most of us, the question of whether such offenses justify the ultimate penalty is not easy to resolve.

The United States Supreme Court, in the case of *Furman v. Georgia* (1972), held that capital punishment, as it was being used, was discriminatory and, therefore, unconstitutional. The court did not rule on the issue of whether capital punishment violated the Eighth Amendment's ban on cruel and unusual punishment. The response to Furman was clear-cut. Thirty-eight states passed new legislation concerning the death penalty. Some of this legislation met with the Supreme Court's approval (*Gregg v. Georgia*, 1976), and numerous executions have occurred since. Let us briefly examine the history of capital punishment, the arguments for retaining or abolishing the death penalty, and the legal guidelines governing its use.

A Brief History of Capital Punishment

Capital punishment, an execution in the name of the state, is one of the most ancient forms of punishment. Early legal codes, such as those of Hammurabi, the Greeks, and the Romans, provided for the death penalty on conviction for a wide range of offenses (Durham, 1994; Mueller, 1955). In more recent times, the practice of banishment was sometimes equivalent to capital punishment. Convicted offenders were forced into the wilderness with very little chance of survival.

Although records are not totally reliable, it is speculated that Henry VIII had as many as 72,000 people executed during his reign. In the 1500s, the British executed convicted offenders for eight offenses: murder, robbery, rape, burglary, larceny, arson, treason, and petty treason. The popularity of the punishment peaked in the 1600s, subsided in the 1700s, and reemerged in the 1800s. Some historians estimate that the British considered as many as 200 or 300 capital offenses during this second peak. Offenses such as shoplifting, cutting down trees, and sacrilege were sometimes accorded capital status. Although the practice was not common, young children and women were occasionally executed during this period. By the 1840s, England had reduced the number of capital offenses to about 20; and in 1965, England joined many other European nations (Netherlands, 1886; Sweden, 1921; Italy, 1944; and West Germany, 1949) in abolishing the death penalty.

Early colonial codes provided for execution of those convicted of rape, man stealing, witchcraft, adultery, and other offenses, but the use of capital punishment was more restricted than in England. It appears that the framers of the Constitution accepted capital punishment as legitimate, and every state permitted the practice at the time the Constitution was ratified.

Beccaria's penal reform philosophy included a stand against the death penalty, and Americans Benjamin Rush and Edward Livingston were influenced by this abolitionist stance. Pennsylvania abolished capital punishment for all crimes except first-degree murder in 1794, and in 1834, it became the first state to ban public executions. In 1846, Michigan was the first state to abolish the death penalty, and by 1918, 11 other states had followed course. In the 1930s and 1940s, some states reinstated the death penalty. The last public execution occurred in Kentucky in 1936. The number of executions declined in the 1960s, and in 1967, a moratorium was declared on capital punishment. A decade later, Gary Gilmore was executed by a firing squad. At least 38 states (plus the federal government and U.S. Military) currently have the death penalty, and there are over 3,350 prisoners on death rows as of January 1, 2007 in the United States (Death Penalty Information Center, 2007). The slight increase in persons on death rows appears to be based on fewer executions during the last quarter of 2006. From 1976 to 2007 at total of 1095 inmates were executed in the United States (DPIC, 2007). Still, the controversy between those who wish to abolish the death penalty and those who wish to retain it rages on. This controversy has been fueled in part by the 124 exonerations or releases from death row with evidence of innocence from 1973 to 2007 (DPIC, 2007). Support for the death penalty expanded in the 1980s and 1990s, reaching a high of 80 percent in 1994 (Gallup Poll, 2007). However, since then support has declined and leveled off, and today approximately two in three Americans favor the death penalty for convicted murderers (Jones, 2007).

Death Penalty Arguments

Some of the specific issues involved in the controversy surrounding capital punishment include the following:

1. Does capital punishment violate constitutional protections against cruel and unusual punishment?
2. Is capital punishment economical?
3. What is the likelihood that an innocent person will be executed?
4. Does it meet the objectives of punishment previously stated?
5. Is it supported by the public?

The Eighth Amendment to the Constitution prohibits the use of **cruel and unusual punishment**. Is capital punishment cruel and unusual? In the Furman decision, the Court held that the death penalty was being administered in discriminatory fashion, with two of the justices (Marshall and Brennan) indicating that they believed capital punishment to be cruel and unusual. In *Gregg v. Georgia* (1976), the issue of cruel and unusual punishment was addressed directly, and the court held that the death penalty does not "invariably violate the constitution."

In discussing the relationship between the Eighth Amendment and the death penalty, we must keep in mind that cruelty and unusualness are two distinct issues. Both of these issues have been brought before the courts on numerous occasions. In *Wilkerson v. Utah* (1878), the Court held that mandatory public execution of persons who committed premeditated murder was not cruel. Later, when the electric chair was introduced, the court rejected a claim that it was unusual punishment because it had never been used before. In *Weems v. United States* (1910), the court struck down a sentence of painful labor because it was excessive (cruel). Historically, it appears, the courts have interpreted the Eighth Amendment to mean a ban on torture or other clearly inhumane treatment. At present, states with the death penalty use different methods of execution, including lethal injection, electrocution, lethal gas, hanging, and firing squads. Electrocution has recently been the subject of debate because there are reported

Does use of the electric chair constitute cruel and unusual punishment?
Reprinted with permission of iStockphoto.com / Joseph Jean Rolland Dube'.

cases of prolonged, agonizing deaths when the electric chairs fail to operate properly. Similar arguments have been raised with respect to death by lethal injection.

There are those who are claiming that capital punishment is unusual in view of the fact that there have been relatively few executions since 1967. Steiker and Steiker (2006), however, contend that despite the fact that there are few executions and a relatively small number of offenders on death row, the death penalty exerts a disproportionate influence over the rest of the US criminal justice system. According to the Bureau of Justice Statistics (2007b), in 2006, 53 persons in 14 States were executed. Texas, by a great deal, led the country with 24 executions. No other state reported more than 5 executions in 2006.

Others argue that capital punishment is administered in a cruel and unusual fashion because most of those executed are black (90 percent between the years 1930 and 1980). Bowers (1974) examined the characteristics of those executed as far back as the turn of the twentieth century and concluded that blacks have been executed for less serious crimes than whites and that many blacks were executed without appeals. According to Holcomb, Williams, and Demuth (2004, p. 877), death penalty studies continue to indicate that the race and gender of homicide victims are associated with the severity of legal responses in homicide cases even after controlling for legally relevant factors. Defendants convicted of killing white females are more likely to receive death sentences than killers of victims with other race-gender characteristics (Holcomb, Williams, and Demuth, 2004, p. 877). Of the persons executed in 2006, 32 were white,

21 were black, and all 53 inmates executed were men (Bureau of Justice Statistics, 2007b). Of persons under sentence of death in 2005, 1,805 were white, 1,372 were black, 31 were American Indian, 34 were Asian, and 12 were of unknown race (Bureau of Justice Statistics, 2007b).

Given the current average operating cost of incarceration—$22,650 per state inmate per year and $22,632 per federal inmate (Bureau of Justice Statistics, 2004b)—and the fact that a large number of offenders are sentenced to life terms, many contend that capital punishment should be employed to save money if for no other reason (Stephan, 1999). However, capital punishment does not occur immediately following sentencing. Lengthy and costly appeals are involved, and taxpayers bear the burden of these expenses, thereby reducing whatever cost benefits may be related to capital punishment. In a more general sense, during the past 20 years, the "get tough on crime" and "lock them up and throw away the key" approaches to dealing with offenders have gained momentum. We have witnessed an overhaul of sentencing procedures, which have addressed truth in sentencing (whereby an inmate is supposed to serve most of the time to which he or she is sentenced) and other issues, such as "three strikes and you're out" legislation, which requires stiff sentences for those who offend repeatedly. Mandatory sentences for those involved in drug-related offenses are another illustration of this approach. These changes have led to a need for new construction of prisons that the public continues to support through taxes. The comparison of construction costs from state to state is often difficult due to the differences in design configuration, number of stories, level of security and whether the prison is a dormitory or cell-style facility (Brown, 2005). As an example, a 500 bed maximum security institution construction costs $100,000 per bed compared with $66,000 per bed for a high security institution, and $62,500 per bed construction costs for a medium security prison (South Carolina Department of Corrections, 2007). In addition, the population of older inmates is increasing. This leads to special housing considerations, additional physical health care considerations, and additional mental health considerations brought on by the emotional stress of prison life among the aging. Largely due to increasing health care expenses, the average cost of housing an inmate over 60 years of age is $70,000 per year, or about three times the average cost for prisoners overall (Anonymous, 2005). The rapidly aging prison population in the U.S. is attributed to a number of factors: the aging of the baby boom population; tough on crime measures that impose longer sentences and mandatory terms; and an increasing number of older people being convicted of sex crimes and murder (Anonymous, 2005). It is apparent that some consideration must be given to the needs and costs involved in housing geriatric inmates, as well as to the larger issue of prison construction costs in general.

Defendants in our criminal justice network are, theoretically at least, innocent until proven guilty. It has been said that we would rather allow 100 guilty parties to go free than to convict 1 innocent person. Still, mistakes are possible, and occasionally we find that a person who has been incarcerated for a crime did not, in fact, commit the crime. As might be expected, a major argument against the death penalty is that it is irreversible. Former Governor George Ryan of Illinois announced a moratorium on the death penalty in that state. His concern was based on the fact that more death row inmates have been exonerated than executed since the death penalty was reintroduced in

1977 (Green, 2000). The American Bar Association has also proposed a moratorium on the death penalty for the same reasons (Radlet & Bedau, 1998). Not everyone agrees with the logic of this argument, however. Marquis (2005, p. 501), for example, disagrees that the death penalty is racist, that those accused of capital murder receive inadequate representation, and that many people on death row are innocent. He argues that these myths make martyrs out of murders and turn killers into victims.

Among the most heated debates concerning the death penalty are those concerning whether or not it achieves the objectives of punishment. Clearly, it precludes the possibility of rehabilitation and it deters the person executed from further crimes. It also satisfies the revenge motive. But does it deter other potential offenders? Sellin (1967), reviewing the effects of the death penalty, concluded that its abolition does not significantly jeopardize the lives of police officers, correctional personnel, or prison inmates. Bailey (1974), reviewing numerous studies of the death penalty, found no support for the deterrence hypothesis. In fact, Bailey found that in some states that had abolished the death penalty and later reinstated it, homicides actually increased in numbers. In contrast, Phillips (1981) concluded from his study of selected, highly publicized executions in London that they lowered the weekly homicide rate. However, Phillips's conclusions have been criticized because weekly homicide rates rose again two or three weeks later (Ziesel, 1982). According to Walker (1998) and others there is little hard evidence that the death penalty deters crime (Nagin and Pogarski, 2003; Griffin, 2006; and Listokin, 2007).

In spite of considerable evidence to the contrary, the American public appears to believe that executions do deter criminals. Public opinion polls have consistently shown that the public favors the death penalty. But opinion polls are just one measure of the public conscience. Some abolitionists argue that prospective jurors may attempt to avoid jury duty in capital cases. It is quite easy to support the death penalty when one is not directly involved or when one is seeking revenge. However, when one must bear the responsibility for assigning the penalty, his or her attitude may be quite different. Unnever, Cullen, and Roberts (2005) suggest that many proponents and opponents of the death penalty have weakly-held views regarding the issue and that they may change their views depending upon time and circumstances, a fact not indicated by many pollsters.

Court Decisions and the Death Penalty

As we have noted, there have been several important court cases concerning the death penalty. The effect of Furman (the United States Supreme Court decision that ruled that a degree of consistency is required in the application of the death penalty in order that the penalty not constitute cruel and unusual punishment in violation of the Eighth and Fourteenth Amendments) was to invalidate many existing death penalty statutes and to force legislators to develop more objective criteria while eliminating discrimination. The decision mandated that objective criteria and specialized procedures be incorporated into all future death penalty legislation. Of the 38 states that enacted new death penalty measures following Furman, Georgia was the first to have the new statutes tested in the courts. Favorable rulings in *Gregg v. Georgia* (1976), *Proffit v. Florida* (1976), and *Jurek v. Texas* (1976) facilitated the reinstatement of capital punishment. At the same time, however, the Supreme Court has ruled that mandatory death sentences for rape (*Coker v. Georgia*, 1972) and murder (*Woodson v. North Carolina*, 1976) constitute cruel and unusual punishment. In the 1980s, the court expedited appeal procedures by allowing death penalty appeals to take precedence on federal dockets (*Barefoot v. Estelle*, 1983), thereby eliminating the lengthy delays death row inmates have traditionally obtained by appealing their sentences to the Supreme Court. In 2002, the Supreme Court decided in *Atkins v. Virginia* that it is unconstitutional to execute mentally retarded offenders. And, in 2005, in *Roper v. Simmons,* the Supreme Court, by a five-four majority, ruled that executing a person for a crime committed before the age of 18 constitutes cruel and unusual punishment under the Eighth Amendment, resolving for the time being one of the most controversial issues in capital punishment. These decisions, taken as a group, indicate many of the controversial issues concerning the death penalty.

Civil Death and the Hands Off Doctrine

Earlier in this chapter, we noted that, historically, persons convicted of crime suffered a **civil death.** This practice was continued through the development of the penitentiary and reformatory systems and was recognized by state courts as recently as 1871 (*Ruffin v. Commonwealth,* 1871). Under the doctrine of civil death, convicted offenders were denied the right to vote, to hold public office, or to enter into contracts. Until the 1960s, the courts would not hear suits from incarcerated offenders, and inmates had no means of challenging the conditions imposed by their keepers. This refusal to hear suits from prison inmates concerning prison officials is commonly referred to as the **hands-off** doctrine. The basic assumption behind this doctrine was that corrections was not a judicial province and that convicted persons were civilly dead and had relinquished constitutional rights and privileges.

In *Cooper v. Pate* (1964), the Supreme Court ended the hands-off doctrine by ruling that inmates are protected by the Civil Rights Act, which states the following:

Every person who, under color of any statute, ordinance, regulation, custom or usage of any State or Territory subjects, or causes to be subjected, any citizen of the United States or other person within the jurisdiction thereof to the deprivation of any rights, privileges, or immunities secured by the Constitution and laws shall be liable to the party injured in an action at law, suit in equity or other proper proceeding for redress (Civil Rights Act, 42 U.S.C. 1983).

Prisoners' Rights

The result of this decision was a major change in correctional philosophy, commonly referred to as the prisoners' rights movement. The practice of allowing inmates to file actions concerning their confinement has led to numerous suits and has drastically altered some traditional correctional practices. For example, during the 1960s there were only a few hundred lawsuits filed by prisoners, but by the mid-1990s that number had swelled to nearly 40,000 cases per year. Although there was a dramatic increase in prisoner cases filed, nearly 70 percent of those cases were rejected by the courts as being frivolous. In response to this boom in prison litigation, Congress passed the Prison Litigation Reform Act (PLRA), which became effective in 1996. The purpose of the act was to limit case filings, to limit federal court jurisdiction, to order changes in prison conditions, and to return more freedom to the states to manage their prisons. While the Supreme Court attempted to curb prisoners' lawsuits, it also ruled in *Casey v. Lewis* (1996) that inmates should have access to state and federal court systems and that correctional facilities should offer them law library facilities or persons trained to help illiterate offenders prepare their legal pleadings. A study by Smith and Nelson (2002) compared survey responses of state attorneys general and federal district judges concerning the impact of the PLRA. Respondents from both groups agreed that the act had reduced prisoner lawsuits and deterred prisoners from initiating civil-rights litigation. It also limits judges' authority to order remedies in prisoners' cases.

Although very few of the suits filed produce major changes in corrections, some have had dramatic effects. Let us look at some specific changes resulting from suits in the areas of freedom of speech, freedom of religion, freedom from cruel and unusual punishment, and due process.

Freedom of Speech

Historically, prison officials have engaged in practices that denied inmates the use of mail service, censored both incoming and outgoing mail, and denied inmates access to media sources when access might have been embarrassing to such officials. Court decisions have required that such practices be altered. In *Procunier v. Martinez* (1974), the Supreme Court struck down the blanket practice of censoring all incoming and outgoing mail. The Court held that censorship could be practiced, but only if there was a substantial belief that the contents of the mail threatened security. Prior to this decision, the First Circuit Court of Appeals had outlawed a Massachusetts practice that prohibited inmates from sending letters to the news media (*Nolan v. Fitzpatrick*, 1971).

In contrast, in *Saxbe v. Washington Post* (1974), the right of an inmate to grant press interviews was denied on the grounds that it would lead to notoriety, which would undermine the attempts of authorities to provide equal treatment. In 1987, the Supreme Court ruled that inmates do not have the right to receive mail from another person and that such mail may be banned if it violates legitimate correctional interests (*Turner v. Safley*, 1987). In a related case, the Supreme Court held that prisons do not violate the First Amendment if they prohibit receipt of publications if those publications violate legitimate penalogical interests (*Thornburgh v. Abbott*, 1989).

Freedom of Religion

Historically, religion has been an important feature of prison life, yet restrictions have been placed on its exercise for economic reasons, for security reasons, and for the sake of prison officials maintaining authority. Most restrictions have been aimed at religious rituals rather than religious beliefs. Several of the suits filed were in connection with the Black Muslim religion, with the most important being *Cooper v. Pate* (1964). In this decision, the Court prohibited prison officials from completely banning religious services but did permit restricting participation for those who abuse the privilege. In *Walker v. Blackwell* (1969) and *Khan v. Carlson* (1975), federal courts upheld prison officials' refusals to provide special diets for all religious sects.

There have been contrasting decisions concerning what constitutes a religion. In *Theriault v. Carlson* (1974), the Fifth Circuit Court of Appeals ruled that the Church of the New Song and Universal Life did not constitute a religion but amounted to a mockery and a sham. However, the Eighth Circuit Court of Appeals recognized the same religion and held that its members were protected under the First Amendment (*Reemers v. Brewer*, 1974). In another case involving relgion, the Supreme Court ruled (*O'Lone v. Estate of Shabazz*, 1987) that Black Muslims' rights were not violated when work assignments made it impossible for them to attend religious services.

Cruel and Unusual Punishment

The Eighth Amendment's prohibition of cruel and unusual punishment has served as a basis for inmates' contesting the legality of prison conditions. Perhaps the most famous of these cases is *Holt v. Sarver* (1970), in which the Court ruled that conditions such as in the Cummings Prison Farm constituted cruel and unusual punishment. Later, in *Pugh v. Locke* (1976) and *Ruiz v. Estelle* (1982), courts threatened to close prison systems in Alabama and Texas, respectively, unless changes were made.

Concerning overcrowding as a form of cruel and unusual punishment, in *Bell v. Wolfish* (1979) and *Rhodes v. Chapman* (1981), the courts have upheld the practice of double bunking as long as it does not lead to filth or disease, or limit the inmate's participation in prison programs. Additional Eighth Amendment decisions have prohibited the use of corporal punishment and restricted the use of solitary confinement. For instance, in *Hudson v. McMillan* (1992), the U. S. Supreme Court ruled that inmates may file suit under the cruel and unusual clause of the 8th Amendment against prison officials who abuse them, even if the abuse does not cause significant harm. In 1993, in *Helling v. McKinney* the court held that an inmate placed in a cell with a multi-pack-a-day smoker constitutes cruel and unusual punishment (though the burden of proof remains with the plaintiff). This was followed by a decision in *Hope v. Pelzer* (2002) that chaining an inmate to a hitching post constitutes cruel and unusual punishment.

Due Process

A number of inmate suits have been concerned with the loss of privileges or good time. In *Wolff v. McDonnell* (1974), the Supreme Court held that loss of **good time** or privileges was important enough to justify some due process requirements. As a result, prison officials must now provide advance notice of charges against inmates, hold a hearing, and allow time for the inmate to call witnesses and obtain assistance in preparing a defense. In a related decision, the Court held, however, that inmates have no right to counsel in a disciplinary hearing (*Baxter v. Palmigiano*, 1976).

The requirements of due process do not apply to all prison practices. In the companion cases of *Meachurn v. Fano* (1976) and *Montaye v. Haymes* (1976), the Court upheld the practice of not providing due process in the transfer of an inmate from one institution to another. In a 1995 decision, the Supreme Court held that due process claims are limited to restraints on freedom that impose an atypical and significant hardship on an inmate in relation to the ordinary incidents of prison life (*Sandin v. Conner*, 1995). Thus, a prisoner doesn't have a due process right to prevent transfer to another facility. In turn, the prisoners' rights movement has had important implications for prison practices. Administrative practices have been altered and prison conditions improved by some of the suits filed by inmates.

Alternatives to Incarceration

In our discussion of prisons, we noted that conditions in these institutions are often less than ideal. Incarceration is also very expensive. As we mentioned earlier, conservative estimates place the annual cost of incarcerating one offender at approximately $22,600 per year (Bureau of Justice Statistics, 2004b). As an alternative to the expensive, generally ineffective, and sometimes inhumane practice of incarceration, the concepts of intermediate sanctions and community corrections have evolved.

Intermediate sanctions are those that are less severe than incarceration but more restrictive than probation (Silverman, 2001, p. 482). Such sanctions include intensive probation supervision, house arrest/home confinement, electronic monitoring, community service orders, shock incarceration/boot camp, day fines and day reporting centers. In recent years **boot camps** have received the most media attention. These camps are based on the assumption that rigorous physical training and discipline can "shock" young offenders out of criminal behavior. Sentences are typically short (less than six months), and inmates are dealt with in much the same manner as military recruits. Evaluations of the impact of boot camps have shown mixed results (Jones, 1996).

Some residential treatment centers are designed to stimulate major behavioral changes. These centers deliver highly structured treatment 24 hours a day, but generally for shorter stays of 120 days. While the major emphasis is on drug- and alcohol-related behaviors, the centers also deal with violence and anger management.

Intermediate sanctions also include probation, parole, work release centers, halfway houses, restorative justice programs, and other community-based programs. The assumption underlying **community corrections** is that rehabilitation can best be achieved if contacts are maintained between offenders and the community and family to which he or she must eventually return. Many intermediate sanction programs are administered in community settings. Although little research indicates that community corrections are more effective than prison in terms of recidivism rates, the former have the advantage of being less expensive.

Another community-based approach is the movement toward restorative justice, a program with the emphasis on restitution rather than punishment. The **restorative justice** approach attempts to resolve differences between criminals and their victims using victim-offender mediation and other techniques.

Drug courts emerged in the late 1980s as an alternative to incarceration of drug users and to address rapidly increasing court caseloads and prison overcrowding. These courts have become widespread with more than 1,500 operating in the United States (Eckley, 2006). Wolfer 's research (2006), though based on a vey small sample size, indicated that graduates of a drug court program found that the structure and random urine screens employed were beneficial to rehabilitation. Differential treatment by drug court team members and lack of respect for defendant time were deemed problematic.

Community correctional programs such as halfway houses, prerelease guidance centers, home confinement, and work release programs are designed to help reintegrate the offender into the community. According to Lurigio (2005), the community corrections population was estimated at nearly 5 million at the end of 2003 or double the number of people in jails and prisons. Those participating in community corrections programs are temporarily released to work, attend school, participate in therapy, and visit family. Although great hope has been held for such programs, their overall success rate has not been much better (in terms of recidivism) than that achieved by prisons, and, compared with probation, they are quite costly (Lurigio, 2005). In addition, it is often difficult to find neighborhoods or communities willing to support such programs because of fears that inmates will become involved in further crime and endanger area residents.

Probation

Probation is the supervised, conditional, and revocable release of an offender into the community in lieu of incarceration. It is a sanction that is served in the community instead of in prison, and if the conditions of probation are violated, the judge may modify the conditions of probation or sentence the offender to prison or jail.

Probation, as we know it, began in 1841 when a cobbler named John Augustus requested that judges let him pay fines for and supervise minor offenders. Partly because of his success, Massachusetts passed the first probation law in 1878; all states now have some form of probation.

In 2002 state courts sentenced 41 percent of convicted felons to a state prison, 28 percent to a local jail, and 31 percent to straight probation with no jail or prison time to serve (Bureau of Justice Statistics, 2004c). In 2005 approximately 4,162,500 men and women were under federal, state or local probation (Bureau of Justice Statistics, 2006).

Among the offenders on probation, 50 percent had been convicted of a felony, 40 percent of a misdemeanor, and 1 percent for other violations. Supporters believe that probation gives offenders a second chance and allows them to avoid the effects of incarceration while maintaining ties in the community to which they would eventually return if incarcerated, under the supervision of a probation officer. In addition, supporters point out that probation, even if no more effective than incarceration, costs a great deal less. Opponents claim that probation is equivalent to no punishment at all, is too widely granted, and is ineffective because most probation officers provide little or no actual supervision to probationers. In response to these charges and to the recognition that a small number of high-risk offenders commit a disproportionate amount of crime, many communities have developed the practice of **intensive probation**, which requires daily contact between probation officers and their charges. Caseloads are cut to allow probation officers to focus their efforts on a small number of offenders. Intensive probation has both positive and negative consequences. On the positive side, preliminary results show intensive supervision probation (ISP) reduces rearrest rates for probationers, reduces the costs (as compared with incarceration), and reduces the prison population. It was designed to improve the rehabilitative efforts of probation officers and to increase public protection by enhancing surveillance. At least two negative consequences have been identified. First, constant supervision of the probationer is likely to lead to discovery of more technical violations of probation. Second, reintegration into the workforce may be made more difficult by constant supervision, especially if it occurs on the work site.

Technological advances have led to the use of electronic monitoring devices for probationers. Electronic monitoring serves as a socially expedient intermediate sanction that is more punitive than traditional probation, but less harsh than incarceration (Gable & Gable, 2005). The punitive aspect of electronic monitoring is primarily a result of more rigorously enforced compliance with the conditions of community supervision (Gable & Gable, 2005, p. 1). Violations are often more easy to document with electronic monitoring than with traditional procedures. According to Nellis (2006), both the radio-frequency (RF) and the global positioning system (GPS) forms of electronic monitoring add a level of control over a probationer that typical probation supervision does not provide. The GPS form of electronic monitoring is available in two types: active, which can track an individual as much as every five minutes, or passive, which downloads offender location information once a day when the offender docks the unit at home (Rogers, 2007). While use of such devices may help prevent harm to the public, they do little to indicate respect for or trust in probationers and, thus, have no inherent rehabilitative worth (Nellis, 2006).

When a judge sentences an offender to probation, he or she specifies the maximum period of time involved, which is established by statute. Probation can be terminated early if the probationer makes satisfactory progress. The probationer is notified by the judge of the conditions of his or her probation, which are, at least in theory, tailored to the specific needs of the probationer. Common conditions of probation include the requirement to refrain from violating any criminal statute, to report or appear in person before a probation officer at certain times, to refrain from possessing a firearm, to make restitution to the injured party, to secure and retain employment, to undergo therapy, and to remain in the county or state of residence unless permitted to leave by the probation officer.

Each probationer is assigned to a probation officer, who is responsible for supervising and assisting probationers in activities such as locating employment and housing, managing finances, and dealing with other problems as they arise. Given the fact that many probation officers have caseloads of 50 to 100 probationers at any given time, the actual amount of supervision provided may be negligible, leading to some of the criticisms mentioned earlier.

Offenders who violate the conditions of their probation run the risk of having it revoked. The most common ground for revocation is the commission of another offense. The probation officer notifies the judge of the alleged violation, and a revocation hearing is held. In *Gagnon v. Scarpelli* (1973), the Supreme Court ruled that revocation hearings must be public. In an earlier decision, the Court held that an accused had the right to counsel during revocation proceedings but had avoided the issue of whether a revocation hearing was mandatory (*Mempa v. Rhay*, 1967).

Revocation hearings require that the state prove that violations of probation occurred, usually by a preponderance of evidence. Evidence is presented in open court, and the probationer has the right to be represented by counsel, to cross-examine witnesses, and to call his or her own witnesses. If the judge finds the allegations unfounded, the probationer is returned to probation under present conditions. If the allegations are substantiated, the court may modify probation conditions or send the offender to prison or jail to serve his or her original sentence.

Parole

Parole and probation are sometimes confused by the general public. Like probation, parole is supervised, revocable release; but unlike probation, it occurs after part of the original sentence has already been served in prison or jail. According to Silverman (2001), "Technically, parole is not a sentence: it is a legal status"(p. 509). If the parolee violates the conditions of his or her parole, the parolee can be returned to prison or jail to serve the remainder of the original sentence. Inmates released from prison as a result of a parole board decision dropped from 50 percent of all adults entering parole in 1995 to 31 percent in 2005 (Bureau of Justice Statistics, 2006). Determinate sentencing and mandatory release have lessened the role of the parole board in many states. By the end of 2000, 16 states had abolished their parole board authority for releasing all offenders and another four states had abolished parole board authority for releasing certain violent offenders (Bureau of Justice Statistics, 2006). Still, in those jurisdictions that retain discretionary parole boards, parole represents an important means of controlling overcrowding in prisons, which leads to frequent criticisms that release on parole depends more on the number of offenders awaiting incarceration than on the behavior of the offender released on parole. In 2005, 45 percent of parole discharges successfully completed their term of supervision, unchanged since 1995. Thirty-eight percent were returned to jail or prison and eleven percent absconded (Bureau of Justice Statistics, 2006).

The authority to grant parole is usually delegated by statute to some formal body. Most states now delegate this authority to the judge who presides over the case, but in some states a semi-autonomous parole board appointed by the governor is maintained. Qualifications for membership on parole boards vary by jurisdiction. In some areas, board members must have professional experience in corrections, law enforcement, or some other human service. In others, appointment is through patronage, and the composition of the board is highly questionable.

In those states with determinate sentencing, the duties of the parole board are minimal. Offenders serve their time minus time off for good behavior, and are released automatically. In the remaining states, the parole board has far greater latitude in deciding the release date and conditions of parole.

What factors should be considered in the parole decision? Obviously, the statutory minimum of the sentence must have been completed, but beyond this, the criteria to be employed are considerably more difficult to specify. How much weight, for example, should we give to the offender's behavior in prison, the availability of employment, family support, and support services available in the community in which the parolee will reside? Should prison overcrowding be considered in granting parole? Should the nature of the offense for which the prisoner was incarcerated be a determining factor? These and other questions make parole decisions difficult. In the final analysis, the reaction of citizens on the outside will determine the success or failure of parole, assuming that the parolee meets the conditions established to successfully complete parole. One program designed to help adult probationers and parolees reintegrate is the Opportunity to Succeed program which focuses on reducing substance abuse relapse and criminal recidivism by providing comprehensive aftercare services. The program promotes reintegration by strengthening the positive ties of participants to work, family, and community by improving coordination between parole and probation officers and other social service providers (Anonymous, 1999).

Are parolees entitled to due process? Inmates released on parole risk revocation if they are caught violating the stipulated conditions of their parole. One year prior to the Supreme Court's decision in *Gagnon v. Scarpelli* (1973), the court ruled that parolees were entitled to fundamental due process during revocation proceedings (*Morrissey v. Brewer*, 1972). The parole officer maintains discretion in determining whether or not probable cause that a violation has occurred exists. If probable cause is found, the parolee is entitled to such fundamental due process rights as notice of charges, disclosure of evidence, a hearing before a neutral and detached body, the right to appear and testify, the right to cross-examine witnesses, and written notification outlining the ruling body's decision. These rights were further extended to inmates released to relieve prison overcrowding who were not officially placed on parole (*Young v. Harper*, 1997).

The problem of prison overcrowding has placed greater demands on intermediate sanctions, probation, parole, and other forms of community corrections. Some prisons are legally forced to release inmates to avoid exceeding maximum daily population levels. The result is that some inmates may be paroled before the prison staff feel they are prepared to reenter society. This places increased pressure on the parole officer, who may already have a heavy caseload. One must question the quantity and quality of supervision the parolee receives under these conditions.

In conclusion, we would like to emphasize the importance of viewing alternatives to incarceration from the network perspective. Political decisions, public opinion, the attitudes and practices of criminal justice practitioners, and the behavior of each individual offender all play a part in determining whether alternatives to incarceration will succeed or fail and to what extent.

Summary

1. Overcrowding of prisons and jails, the high costs of incarceration, and high recidivism rates indicating the failure of correctional rehabilitation programs have all attracted the attention of the public and politicians in recent years.

2. Jail and prison populations continue to skyrocket, and rehabilitation continues to be an elusive goal.

3. Questions concerning the effectiveness of punishment as a deterrent remain basically unanswered, but the public continues to support the use of incarceration as a means of retribution or revenge.

4. Although overall conditions in jails and prisons may be better today than in the past, safety and health continue to be major issues in these institutions.

5. Inmate codes, gangs, and staff differences of opinion continue to make rehabilitation difficult, if not impossible, in most cases.

6. Educational and vocational training programs leave a good deal to be desired.

7. Capital punishment continues to be supported by the majority of the public even though a number of states have imposed, or are considering imposing, a moratorium on the death penalty, because of evidence that many of the inmates on death row may be innocent of the crimes for which they were sentenced.

8. The prisoners' rights movement and alternatives to incarceration have led to changes in our traditional conceptions of corrections.

9. A number of court decisions have improved conditions in prisons and jails, although many remain substandard.

10. In general, freedom of speech, freedom of religion, immunity from cruel and unusual punishment, and due process guarantees are the areas in which inmate suits have helped define more clearly what constitutes acceptable treatment in institutions.

11. Probation, parole, and other alternatives to incarceration have been tried in the hope that they would prove more successful than imprisonment in reintegrating offenders and in preventing recidivism. Research findings generally fail to indicate the superiority of these alternatives over incarceration, perhaps partly because alternative programs are still relatively new.

Key Terms Defined

early release The release of a prisoner before he or she has served the minimum period of time required for the offense.

banishment The process of pronouncing a person civilly dead and forcing him or her to leave the country.

transportation The practice of transporting convicts to a country other than the one in which they are citizens.

age of enlightenment The period during the late eighteenth and early nineteenth centuries when humanitarian reforms occurred with respect to the mentally ill, prisoners, juveniles, and others.

hedonism The seeking of pleasurable experiences.

Walnut Street Jail The first correctional institution in the United States.

Pennsylvania prisons Prisons designed with a central hub and numerous wings radiating from this hub, with cells in each wing placed back-to-back for the purpose of isolating prisoners from one another.

Auburn prisons U-shaped prisons with several tiers of cells; prisoners worked and ate together, and a code of silence was enforced.

retribution Exacting repayment (often with a motive of revenge); making the punishment fit the crime.

specific deterrence The notion that punishment will prevent the criminal from repeating his or her crimes.

general deterrence The notion that punishment of some will prevent others from committing crimes.

supermax security facilities Prisons housing extremely violent or dangerous offenders and/or those who are considered major escape risks.

maximum security facilities Prisons designed to isolate and maintain custody of dangerous offenders and those serving long sentences.

medium security facilities Similar to maximum security facilities, but more freedom of movement is generally allowed inmates.

minimum security facilities Prisons without walls and armed guards characteristic of medium, maximum, and supermax facilities, with emphasis on rehabilitation as opposed to custody.

recidivism rates Rates based on the proportion of offenders released from prison who become involved in reported criminal behavior after their release.

total institution An institution (such as a prison) in which all decisions concerning working, eating, sleeping, and freedom of movement are made by the staff instead of the inmates.

warehousing Placing offenders in institutions with little regard for treatment or prisoners' rights.

civil death Denial of the right to vote, the right to hold public office, and the right to enter into contracts.

hands-off doctrine Refusal of the courts to hear suits on behalf of prison inmates.

cruel and unusual punishment Punishment administered by the government that is prohibited by the Constitution.

good time Time during which an inmate abides by the rules of the institution, which is then subtracted from his or her sentence.

intermediate sanctions Sanctions less severe than incarceration but more restrictive than probation.

boot camps An intermediate sanction designed to "shock" young offenders out of criminal behavior by imposing rigorous physical activity and harsh, military-style discipline.

community corrections Correctional programs, such as probation, parole, work release, and halfway houses, in which prisoners are allowed and encouraged to maintain community and family ties.

restorative justice An intermediate sanction that attempts to resolve differences between criminals and their victims using victim-offender mediation and other techniques.

drug courts An alternative to incarceration for drug users that addresses the rapidly increasing court case loads and prison overcrowding.

probation The supervised, conditional, and revocable release of an offender into the community in lieu of incarceration.

intensive probation Probation requiring daily or very frequent face-to-face meetings between a probation officer and his or her probationers.

parole The supervised, conditional, and revocable release of an offender into the community after he or she has served part of a sentence.

Critical Thinking Exercises

1. Trace the historical development of corrections in America. What have been the most significant contributions to reform of American penal institutions?

2. American jails have been called a national scandal. Why? Suggest reforms that might improve jails. How likely are these reforms to be implemented? Why?

3. Why do rehabilitation programs prove unsuccessful with many, if not most, inmates? What changes would have to occur for such programs to be more effective?

4. Discuss the pros and cons of capital punishment. Do you support capital punishment? Why or why not?

5. What do programs such as probation, parole, and other types of community corrections attempt to accomplish? What is the rationale for such programs? What are some of the obstacles to developing successful community corrections programs? Do you believe these programs are as effective as imprisonment?

6. What kinds of changes do you think we can look forward to in the next few years in prisoners' rights and alternatives to incarceration? Will building more prisons solve the crime problem in the United States? Why or why not?

Internet Exercises

We have discussed a number of problems related to corrections in the United States. Examine some of the latest information available on the Internet on the following corrections issues:

1. Correctional education (http://www.corrections.com/).
2. HIV and AIDS in prisons (what websites did you use to obtain your nformation?).
3. Jail overcrowding (what websites did you use to obtain your information?).
4. Privatization of prisons (what websites did you use to obtain your information?).
5. Our discussion of prisoners' rights has raised a number of issues. Many of these issues are addressed by the American Civil Liberties Union (ACLU), Human Rights Watch (HRW), and other organizations.

   a. What are the latest highlights from the ACLU website (http://www.aclu.org)?

   b. What types of information are available from the HRW site (http://www.hrw.org)?

   c. What are the expressed goals of Free World Friends (http://www.free worldfriends.com) as related to prisoners?

References

Allen, H.E. & Simonsen, C.E. (2001). *Corrections in America an introduction* (9th ed.) Upper Saddle River, NJ: Prentice-Hall.

Anonymous. (1999). The impact of the opportunity to succeed program on employment success. *Alternatives to Incarceration, 5* (2), 18–21.

Anonymous. (2005). Elderly inmates swell prisons, driving up health costs. *USA Today*. Available online at: http://www.usatoday.com/news/nation/2004-02-0-28-elderly-inmates_x.htm.

Anonymous. (2006). Inmate population rises 2.6%, pushing most prisons, jails to near capacity. *Corrections Digest, 37* (20), 1–2.

Atkins v. Virginia, 536 U.S. 304 (2002).

Bailey, W. C. (1974, September). Murder and the death penalty. *Journal of Criminal Law, Criminology, and Police Science, 65,* 416–22.

Barefoot v. Estelle, 77 Led. 2d. 1090 (1983).

Barnes, H. E., & Teeters, N. K. (1959). *New horizons in criminology* (3rd ed.). Englewood Cliffs, NJ: Prentice Hall.

Baxter v. Palmigiano, 96 S. Ct. 1551 (1976).

Beccaria, C. (1953). *Essays on crimes and punishments*. Stanford, CA: Academic Reprints.

Beck, A. J. (2000, April). *Prison and jail inmates at midyear 1999*. Bureau of Justice Statistics. Washington, DC: U.S. Government Printing Office.

Bell v. Wolfish, 99 S. Ct. 1873 (1979).

Bowers, W. J. (1974). *Executions in America*. Lexington, MA: D.C. Heath.

Brown, K. (2003). Managing sexually transmitted diseases in jails. Brown medical school. Available online at: http://www.thebody.com/content/whatis/art12916.html.

Brown, M.H. (2005). Per bed prison cost. The Connecticut General Assembly, Office of legislative research. Available online at: http://www.cga.ct.gov/olr/.

Bureau of Justice Statistics. (2002). *Two-thirds of former state prisoners re-arrested for serious new crimes*. Available online at: http://www.ojp.usdoj.gov/bjs/pub/press/rpr94pr.htm.

Bureau of Justice Statistics. (2004a). *Profile of jail inmates, 2002*. Available online at: http://www.ojp.usdoj.gov/bjs/pub/press/pji02pr.htm.

Bureau of Justice Statistics. (2004b). *State prison expenditures, 2001*. Available online at: http://www.ojp.usdoj.gov/bjs/abstract/spe01.htm.

Bureau of Justice Statistics. (2004c). *Felony sentences in state courts, 2002*. Available online at: http://www.ojp.gov/bjs/pub/ascii/fssc02.txt.

Bureau of Justice Statistics. (2006). *Probation and parole statistics*. Available online at: http://www.ojp.usdoj.gov/bjs/pandp.htm.

Bureau of Justice Statistics. (2007, April). *Prison statistics*. Available online at: http://www.ojp.usdoj.gov/bjs/prisons.htm.

Bureau of Justice Statistics. (2007b, January). *Capital punishment statistics*. Available online at: http://www.ojp.usdoj.gov/bjs/cp.htm.

Bureau of Justice Statistics. (2007c). *Jail statistics*. Available online at: http://www.ojp.usdoj.gov/bjs/jails.htm.

Bureau of Prisons. (2007, August). *Weekly population report*. Available online at: http://www.bop.gov/locations/weekly_report.jsp.

Camp, G. M., & Camp, C. G. (1995). *The corrections yearbook: Adult corrections*. South Salem: NY: Criminal Justice Institute.

Camp, G. M., & Camp, C. G. (1997). *The corrections yearbook, 1997*. South Salem, NY: Criminal Justice Institute.

Camp, S. D. & Gaes, G. G. (2002). Growth and quality of U.S. private prisons: Evidence from a national survey. *Criminology & Public Policy, 1* (3), 427–450.

Casey v. Lewis, 518 U.S. 343 S. Ct. 2174 (1996).

Chambliss, W. J. (1965). *Crime and the legal process*. New York: McGraw-Hill.

Champion, D. J. (1998). *Criminal justice in the United States* (2nd ed.). Chicago: Nelson-Hall.

Champion, D. J. (2001). *Corrections in the United States: A contemporary perspective* (3rd ed.). Upper Saddle River, NJ. Prentice Hall.

Civil Rights Act, 42 U.S.C. (1983).

Cohen, M. A., Rust, R. T., & Steen, S. (2006). Prevention, crime control or cash? Public preferences towards criminal justice spending priorities. *Justice Quarterly: JQ, 23* (3), 317–334.

Coker v. Georgia, 433 U.S. 584 (1972).

Cole, G. F. (1995). *The American system of criminal justice* (7th ed.). Belmont, CA.: Wadsworth.

Conklin, J. E. (1998). *Criminology* (6th ed.). Boston: Allyn and Bacon.

_____(2006). *Criminology* (9th ed.). Boston: Allyn and Bacon.

Cooper v. Pate, 378 U.S. 546 (1964).

Court of Oyer and Terminer, Philadelphia, 13 DJC 285 (1930).

Craig v. Boren, 429 U.S. 190 (1976).

Cripe, C. A. (1997). *Legal aspects of corrections management.* Gaithersburg, MD: Aspen.

Cromwell, P. (1994, June). The greying of America's prisons. *Overcrowded Times,* 5 (3), 3.

Daly, R. (2006). Prison mental health crisis continues to grow. American Psychiatric Association. Available online at: http://pn.psychiatryonline.org/cgi/content/full/41/20/1.

Death Penalty Information Center (2007). Facts about the death penalty. Available online at: http://www.deathpenaltyinfo.org.

Durham, A. M. (1994). *Crisis and reform: Current issues in American punishment.* Boston: Little, Brown.

Eckley, T. S. (2006). Drug courts: The second decade. *Judicature, 90* (1), 43–45.

Ervin, K. (2006, November 27). Mental illness dilemma for jail. *The Seattle Times.* p.1. Available online: http://seattletimes.nwsource.com/cgibin/PrintStory.p1?document_id=2003449309&slug=h . . . .

Fishman, J. F. (1969). *Crucibles of crime: The shocking story of the American jail.* Montclair, NJ: Patterson Smith.

Four prisoners trapped in their cells are killed by smoke from fire at Missouri jail. (1991, September 15). *New York Times,* p.18.

Furman v. Georgia, 408 U.S. 238 (1972).

Gable, R.K. & Gable, R.S. (2005). Electronic monitoring: Positive intervention strategies. *Federal Probation,* 69 (1), 1–7.

Gagnon v. Scarpelli, 411 U.S. 471 (1973).

Glaser, D. (1964). *The effectiveness of a prison and parole system*. Indianapolis: Bobbs-Merrill.

Goin, M.K. (2007, July 8). The wrong place to treat mental illness. *The Washington Post*. p.B07.

Goffman, E. (1961). *Asylums*. Garden City, NY: Doubleday.

Goldfarb, R. (1975). *Jails: The ultimate ghetto*. New York: Archer Press.

Gordon, H. R. D. & Weldon, B. (2003). The impact of career and technical education programs on adult offenders: Learning behind bars. *Journal of Correctional Education, 54* (4), 200.

Green, J. (2000). Second thoughts on the death penalty: Governor of Illinois halts all executions. *American Prospect, 11* (10), 10–11.

Greenfield, L. A., & Snell, T. (1999, December). *Women offenders*. Bureau of Justice Statistics: Special Report. Washington, DC: U.S. Government Printing Office.

Gregg v. Georgia, 428 U.S. 153 (1976).

Griffin, M. L. (2006). Penal harm and unusual conditions of confinement: Inmate perceptions of 'hard time' in jail. *American Journal of Criminal Justice: AJCJ, 30* (2), 209-228.

Harlow, C.W. (2003). Education and correctional populations. Bureau of justice statistics special report. Washington, DC: U.S. Department of Justice.

Harrison, P. M. & Beck, A. J. (2004). *Private jails and prisons at midyear 2004*. Bureau of Justice Statistics. Washington, D.C.: U.S. Department of Justice.

Hawkins, B. (2006). Capital punishment and the administration of Justice: A trial prosecutor's perspective. *Judicature, 89* (5), 258–262.

Helling v. McKinney, 509 U.S. 25 (1993).

Holcomb, J. E., Williams, M. R. & Demuth, S. (2004). White female victims and death penalty disparity research. *Justice Quarterly: JQ, 21* (4), 877–903.

Holt v. Sarver, 300 F. Supp. 825 (1970).

Hope v. Pelzer, 536 U.S. 730 (2002).

Hudson v. McMillan, 503 U.S. 1 (1992).

Hughes, R. (1987). *The fatal shore*. New York: Knopf.

Irvin, K. (2006, November 27). Mental illness dilemma for jail. *The Seattle Times*, p. 1.

Jones, J.M. (2007). Support for the death penalty 30 years after the Supreme Court ruling. Princeton, NJ: The Gallup Poll. Available online at: http://www.galluppoll.com/content/?ci=23548&pg=1.

Jones, M. (1996). Do boot camp graduates make better probationers? *Journal of Crime and Justice, 19* (1), 1–14.

Jurek v. Texas, 428 U.S. 262 (1976).

Kane, S., & Dotson, C. J. (1997). HIV risk and injecting drug use: Implications for rural jails. *Crime and Delinquency, 43*, 169–85.

Khan v. Carlson, 527 F. 2d 492 (1975).

Lambropoulou, E. (1999). The sociology of prison and the self-referential approach to prison organization and to correctional reforms. *Systems Research and Behavioral Science, 16,* (3), 239–52.

Lawrence, R. A. (1995). Classrooms vs. prison cells: Funding policies for education and corrections. *Journal of Crime and Justice, 18,* 113–26.

Lewis, C. S. (1953). The humanitarian theory of punishment. *Res Judicatae 6.* In Sellars, W. & Hospers, J. (1970). *Readings in ethical theory* (2nd ed.), (pp. 646–650). NY: Appleton-Centers-Croft.

Listokin, Y. (2007). Crime and (with a lag) punishment: The implications of discounting for equitable sentencing. *The American Criminal Law Review, 44* (1), 115–141.

Lurigio, A. J. (2005). Taking stock of community corrections programs. *Criminology & Public Policy, 4* (2), 259–262.

Maguire, K., and Pastore, A. L. (1995). *Bureau of justice statistics sourcebook of criminal justice statistics:1994.* Albany, NY: Hindelang Criminal Justice Research Center.

Marchese, J.D. (1990). Emergency preparedness planning for jail officers. *Jail Operations Bulletin,* 2(9).

Marlowe, D. B. (2006). When 'what works' never did: Dodging the 'Scarlett M' in correctional rehabilitation. *Criminology & Public Policy, 5* (2), 339–347.

Marquis, J. (2005). The myth of innocence. *Journal of Criminal Law and Criminology, 95* (2), 501–522.

Martinson, R. R. (1974, Spring). What works? Questions and answers about prison reform. *The Public Interest,* 22–55.

McAuley, J. (2004). HIV/AIDS in jails and prisons. Paper presented at the 11th conference on retroviruses and opportunistic infections. San Francisco, CA.

Meacham v. Fano, 427 U.S. 215 (1976).

Mempa v. Rhay, 389 U.S. 128 (1967).

Menninger, K. (1968*). The crime of punishment.* New York: Viking Press.

Montaye v. Haymes, 427 U.S. 236 (1976).

Morrissey v. Brewer, 408 U.S. 471 (1972).

Mueller, G. O. W. (1955). Tort, crime, and the primitive law. *Journal of Criminal Law, Criminology, and Police Science, 46,* 16–19.

Mueller, J. (1996). Locking up tuberculosis. *Corrections Today, 58,* 100–101.

Nagin, D. S., & Paternoster, R. (1991). The preventive effects of perceived risk of arrest: Testing an expanded conception of deterrence. *Criminology, 29,* 561–87.

Nagin, D. S. & Pogarski, G. (2003). An experimental investigation of deterrence: Cheating, self-serving bias, and impulsivity. *Criminology, 41* (1), 167.

National Commission on Correctional Health Care (2002). The health status of soon-to-be released inmates: A report to Congress. Chicago, IL: National Commission of Correctional Health Care.

National Conference of State Legislatures (2003). State budget actions. Available online at: http://www. ncls.org/programs/fiscal/all_sba.htm.

National Conference of State Legislatures (2007). State funding for corrections in FY 2006 and FY 2007. Available online at: http://www.ncsl.org/programs/fiscal/correx07.htm.

Nellis, M. (2006). Surveillance, rehabilitation, and electronic monitoring: Getting the issues clear. *Criminology & Public Policy, 5* (1), 103–109.

Nolan v. Fitzpatrick, 451 F. 2d 545 (1971).

O'Lone v. Estate of Shabazz, 482 U.S. 342 (1987).

Parker, E. A. (1990). The social psychological impact of a college education on the prison inmate. *Journal of Correctional Education, 41,* 140–46.

Parrish, D. (2000). Colonel/Commander, Jail Division, Hillsborough Sheriffs Office. Personal communication. In Silverman, I.J. (2001). *Corrections a comprehensive view* (2nd ed.). Belmont CA: Wadsworth/Thomson Learning.

Patterson, M. J. (1983). The price of neglect is tragedy. *Corrections Magazine, 9* (1), 6–21.

Phillips, D. P. (1981). The deterrent effect of capital punishment: New evidence on an old controversy. *American Journal of Sociology, 86,* 139–48.

Pittman, D. J., & Gordon, C. W. (1968). *Revolving door.* New York: Free Press.

Procunier v. Martinez, 416 U.S. 396 (1974).

Profitt v. Florida, 428 U.S. 242 (1976).

Public Safety Performance Project (2007). Public safety, public spending: Forecasting America's prison population 2007–2011 (Washington, D.C.: Public Safety Performance Project, The Pew Charitable Trusts.

Pugh v. Locke, 406 F Supp. 318 (1976).

Radlet, M. L., & Bedau, H. A. (1998). The execution of the innocent. *Law and Contemporary Problems, 61* (4), 105–24.

Reemers v. Brewer, 494 F. 2d 1227 (1974).

Rhodes v. Chapman, 452 U.S. 337 (1981).

Rogers, D. (2007). Getting on track. *Courts Today.* 5 (3), 16.

Roper v. Simmons, 125 S. Ct. 1183 (2005).

Ruddell, R. & Mays, L. G. (2007). Rural jails: Problematic inmates, overcrowded cells, and cash-strapped counties. *Journal of Criminal Justice, 35* (3), 251.

Ruffin v. Commonwealth, 62 Va. 780 (1871).

Ruiz v. Estelle, 503 F. Supp. 1265 (1982).

Sandin v. Conner, 515 U.S. 472 (1995).

Saxbe v. Washington Post, 417 U.S. 843 (1974).

Sellin, T. (Ed). (1967). *Capital punishment*. New York: Harper and Row.

Silverman, I.J. (2001). *Corrections a comprehensive view* (2nd ed.). Belmont, CA: Wadsworth/Thomson Learning.

Smith, C. E. & Nelson, C. E. (2002). Perceptions of the consequences of the Prison Litigation Reform Act: A comparison of state attorneys general and federal district judges. *Justice System Journal, 23* (3), 295–317.

Snell, R.K., Eckl, C. & William, G. (2003). State spending in the 1990s. National conference of state legislatures, the forum of state legislatures. Available online at: http://www.ncsl.org/programs/fiscal/stspend90s.htm.

South Carolina Department of Corrections (2007). General South Carolina department of corrections operations. Available online at: www.doc.sc.gov/faqs.jsp.

Steiker, C. & Steiker, J. (2006). The effect of capital punishment on American criminal law and policy. *Judicature, 89* (5), 250–254.

Stephan, J. J. (1999, August). *State prison expenditures, 1996*. Washington, DC: Bureau of Justice Statistics.

Steurer, S.J., Smith, L. & Tracy, A. (2001). *Three state recidivism study*. Lanham, MD: Correctional Education Association.

Sykes, G., & Messinger, S. (1970). The inmate social code. In N. Johnson et al. (Eds.), *The sociology of punishment and corrections* (pp.401–408). New York: Wiley.

Tartaro, C. & Ruddell, R. (2006). Trouble in Mayberry: A national analysis of suicides and attempts in small jails. *American Journal of Criminal Justice, 31* (1), 81–104.

The Prison Rape Elimination Act of 2003 (U.S. Code, Title 42, Sections 15601 *et seq.*)

Theriault v. Carlson, 339 F. Supp. 375 (1974).

Thornburgh v. Abbott, 109 S. Ct. 1874 (1989).

Turner v. Safley, 107 S. Ct. 2254 (1987).

Unnever, J. D., Cullen, F. T., & Roberts, J. V. (2005). Not everyone strongly supports the death penalty: Assessing weakly-held attitudes about capital punishment. *American Journal of Criminal Justice, 29* (2), 187–220.

Useem, B., & Reisig, M. D. (1999). Collective action in prisons: Protests, disturbances, and riots. *Criminology, 37* (4), 735–59.

Visher, C. A. (2006). Effective reentry programs. *Criminology & Public Policy, 5* (2), 299–303.

Walker v. Blackwell, 411 F. 2d 23 (1969).

Walker, S. (1998). *Sense and nonsense about crime and drugs: A policy guide* (4th ed.). Belmont, CA: Wadsworth.

_____(2001). *Sense and nonsense about crime and drugs: A policy guide* (5th ed.). Belmont, CA: Wadsworth.

Weems v. United States, 217 U.S. 349 (1910).

Wilkerson v. Utah, 99 U.S. 130 (1878).

Wilson, J. Q., & Abrahamse, A. (1992). Does crime pay? *Justice Quarterly, 9*, 359–77.

Wilson, M. (1931). *The crime of punishment*. New York: Harcourt Brace and World.

Wolfer, L. (2006). Graduates speak: A qualitative exploration of drug court graduates' views of the strengths and weaknesses of the program. *Contemporary Drug Problems, 33* (2), 303–322.

Wolff v. McDonnell, 418 U.S. 539 (1974).

Woodson v. North Carolina, 428 U.S. 280 (1976).

Young v. Harper 520 U.S. 143 (1997).

Ziesel, H. (1982). A comment on the 'deterrent effect of capital punishment' by Phillips. *American Journal of Sociology, 88*, 167–69.

Suggested Readings

Adams, L. (2005). Death by discretion: Who decides who lives and dies in the United States of America? *American Journal of Criminal Law, 32* (3), 381–402.

Alexander, R., Jr. (1998). The impact of the Religious Freedom Restoration Act on prisons. *Journal of Criminal Justice, 26* (5), 385–98.

Anonymous. (2003). Tennessee unit for elderly hits capacity. *Corrections Digest. 34* (27), 3.

Emrey, J. A. (2007). The effects of capital punishment on the administration of justice. *Justice System Journal, 28* (1), 119–123.

Gee, J. (2006). Education in rural county jails: Need versus opportunity. *Journal of Correctional Education, 57* (4), 312–326.

Greifinger, R. B. (2006). Disabled prisoners and 'reasonable accommodation'. *Criminal Justice Ethics, 25* (1), 2–6.

Lewis, J. (2006). Correctional education: Why it is only 'promising'. *Journal of Correctional Education, 57* (4), 286–297.

Maxwell, S. R., & Gray, M. K. (2000). Deterrence: Testing the effects of perceived sanction certainty on probation violations (intensive supervision probation programs). *Sociological Inquiry, 70*, (2), 117–36.

Modley, P. (2000). NIC assists corrections with managing female offenders in the community. *Corrections Today, 62* (4), 152, 154.

Pograsky, G., Kim, K. & Paternoster, R. (2005). Perceptual change in the National Youth Survey: Lessons for deterrence theory and offender decision-making. *Justice Quarterly, 22* (1), 1–30.

Robertson, J. E. (2001). The jurisprudence of the PLRA: Inmates as 'outsiders' and the countermajoritarian difficulty. *Journal of Criminal Law & Criminology, 92* (1/2), 187–210.

St. Gerard, V. (2004). Prison boom occurred during past 20 years. *Corrections Today, 66* (4), 17.

Stolzenberg, L. & D'Alessio, S. J. (2004). Capital punishment, execution publicity and murder in Houston, Texas. *Journal of Criminal Law & Criminology, 94* (2), 351–380.

Sykes, G. M. (1958). *The society of captives: A study of a maximum security prison.* Princeton, NJ: Princeton University Press.

Visher, C. A. (2006). Effective reentry programs. *Criminology & Public Policy, 5* (2), 299–303.

Wilhelmus, D. W. (1999). Where have all the law libraries gone? Offenders' rights to access the courts in the wake of *Casey v. Lewis. Corrections Today, 61* (7), 122–24.

Chapter Twelve

Juvenile Justice

In the News 12.1

Juveniles pose special problems — Authorities face tough decisions, such as whether it's best to put out notifications.

Young Offenders.

When faced with a 15-year-old sex offender whom he believed was still dangerous, Menomonee Falls Police Chief Darick Ottow made the only decision he could, he said.

He told people about it.

"It wasn't just sexual exploration between, say, two 13-year-old boys," Ottow said about the 2005 notification involving offender Zachary Menne. "These were 8- and 9-year-old boys that he was taking advantage of. He is a sex offender."

But it wasn't an easy decision, Ottow said, to inform two schools and hundreds of Zachary's neighbors in what became the state's first community notification involving a juvenile sex offender.

"You wonder, how is the kid going to handle it once he finds out the world's found out?"

Ottow said. "If his school and his classmates find out, what are the repercussions? Is he going to be the victim of vigilantism? Are people going to seek him out for sexual favors? Is he going to run away from home or worse?"

Those are all valid concerns, said John Wabaunsee, a La Crosse public defender who has represented adult sex offenders and opposes public notification for juveniles because of the harm it could do.

"He is going to be branded," Wabaunsee said of Zachary.

Though much of the public's attention is on adult criminals, the state's registry of sex offenders also contains more than 300 juveniles convicted of serious sex crimes. Members of the public typically don't know about them, because the names of juveniles aren't included on the public Web site.

But local police agencies have access to that information, and a change in state law in 2005 allowed them to publicize it, as they have been free to do for registered adult sex offenders since 1997.

Wabaunsee said the change was a mistake because it failed to recognize that juveniles—who are less mature by definition—are not as culpable for their crimes as adult offenders.

"That is the essence of why we have a juvenile justice system," he said. "That's why we make juvenile records confidential. The people who commit these offenses when they are 15 are not the same kind of people who do it at 18 or 19."

After consulting with state officials and the parents of the known victims, Ottow said he focused less on the boy's age than on the seriousness of his crimes and his own feelings as a parent to make the decision.

"I asked myself, 'Would I want to know?' And I said, 'Yes, I would,' "Ottow said.

Like most sex offenses, Zachary's crimes were committed against victims he knew and were accomplished more with manipulation than violence.

"(Zachary) had a way of ingratiating himself with the parents of young kids,"

Ottow said. "He can carry on conversations with adults very easily. He just befriends people and they are sucked into his charm."

The incidents began when Zachary was 13 and ended with criminal charges when the boy was 15. Ottow said the boy targeted younger children from at least five families in his neighborhood—police still wonder if there were more—and persuaded them to submit to oral and anal sex in exchange for being part of his "club."

"He tried this with kids his own age and they said, 'No way,'" Ottow said. "But he could have tremendous influence over someone who was five years younger.

He functioned more like a 17-year-old than a 13- or 14-year-old."

Not everyone saw it that way, though. At a private meeting attended by about 60 people after area residents were notified by mail, a vocal minority—sitting behind the boy's parents—objected to making his case public because of his youth.

Rivedal, K. (2007, March 4). Juveniles pose special problems—Authorities face tough decisions, such as whether it's best to put out notifications. Young offenders. *Wiscon-*

sin State Journal (Madison, WI). **p. A5. "Copyright** *Wisconsin State Journal.* **Reprinted with permission."**

Key Terms

age of responsibility
mens rea
parens patriae
in loco parentis
era of socialized juvenile justice
legalists
adjudicatory hearing
dispositional hearing
delinquent acts
status offenders
petition
preliminary conference
street corner or stationhouse adjustments
detention hearing
ward of the state
social background investigation
revocation hearing
diversion programs

Chapter Outline

Juvenile Justice: A Historical Overview
Defining and Measuring Delinquency
Purpose and Scope of Juvenile Court Acts
Juvenile Justice Procedures
Current Dilemmas in Juvenile Justice

The juvenile justice network in the United States is distinct from, but not independent of, the criminal justice network. The network approach would lead us to believe that what happens to juveniles as they are processed through the juvenile justice system would have important consequences for other components of the network. If juveniles are successfully rehabilitated, they will be less likely to become problems for the police, courts, and corrections at the adult level and less likely to continue to prey on other citizens. If our efforts to assist youthful offenders fail, the consequences are equally apparent.

The juvenile justice network in the United States is almost 110 years old. Since its inception, it has been controversial with respect to objectives and procedures, because major gaps between theory and practice have emerged in the period since 1899, when the first family court was established in Cook County, Illinois. The reasons for the controversy surrounding the juvenile court and the distinction between theory and practice are apparent on review of the history of the juvenile court.

Juvenile Justice: A Historical Overview

Over 4,000 years ago, the Code of Hammurabi contained references to runaway children and youth who disowned their parents. About 2,000 years ago, Roman civil law and canon (church) law made distinctions between juveniles and adults based on the concept of **age of responsibility**. During the eleventh and twelfth centuries, distinctions were made in British common law between youth and adults. For example, children under 7 years of age were not subject to criminal sanctions because they were presumed to be incapable of forming criminal intent, or **mens rea**; children between the ages of 7 and 14 were exempt from criminal prosecution unless it could be demonstrated that they had formed criminal intent, could distinguish right from wrong, and understood the consequences of their actions (Blackstone, 1803). These issues remain important in juvenile court proceedings today. At what age is a child capable of understanding right from wrong? At what age can a child understand the consequences of his or her actions?

In the fifteenth century, chancery courts (under the direction of the king's chancellor) were created in England to grant relief and assistance to needy parties, including women and children, who were left to fend for themselves as a result of the death of a husband or father, abandonment, or divorce. The king, exercising the right of **parens patriae** (parent of the country), permitted these courts to act **in loco parentis** (in the place of parents) to provide necessary services to such women and children.

By the sixteenth century, British children could be separated from their pauper parents and apprenticed to others (Rendleman, 1974, p. 77). This practice was based on the assumption that the state has a primary interest in the welfare of children and has a right to ensure such welfare.

At about the same time, attempts were being made in England to settle, in a confidential fashion, disputes involving juveniles and to segregate youths requiring confinement from adult offenders. The former practice was to help juveniles avoid public shame and stigmatization; the latter, to avoid the harmful consequences of association with more hardened offenders. Although juveniles continued to be incarcerated in adult institutions throughout most of the 1700s, they were often segregated from adult offenders. In 1788, Robert Young established a separate institution for young offenders that was to "educate and instruct in some useful trade or occupation the children of convicts or other such infant poor as are engaged in a vagrant and criminal course of life" (Sanders, 1974, p.48).

In the United States during the 1700s, juveniles were sometimes imprisoned, but few seemed to benefit from the experience. As a result, several institutions for juveniles were established in the early and mid-1800s. These institutions were oriented toward education and treatment, and away from punishment. By the mid-1800s, these institutions were declared a great success by those who ran them (Simonsen & Gordon, 1991, p.23). Others, however, were less enthusiastic about the institutions, and in the second half of the nineteenth century, it was widely recognized that such institutions failed to reform or rehabilitate delinquents. Reform schools became the new means of dealing with delinquents, but they, too, failed to rehabilitate most delinquents.

Court decisions in the last half of the nineteenth century were in conflict over the necessity of due process for juveniles, but by the time the first family court appeared in Chicago in 1899, "the delinquent child had ceased to be a criminal and had the status of a child in need of care, protection, and discipline directed toward rehabilitation" (Cavan, 1969, p.362).

The period between 1899 and 1967 has been called the **era of socialized juvenile justice**. Emphasis on obtaining a complete picture of the delinquent to determine appropriate care, regardless of legal requirements, became paramount. Informality became the rule and was confirmed by the decision of the Supreme Court not to hear the Holmes case in 1955 on the basis that juvenile courts are not criminal courts and, therefore, the constitutional rights guaranteed to accused adults do not apply to juveniles (*In re Holmes*, 1955).

Twelve years later, however, forces opposing the extreme informality and license of the juvenile court won a major victory in the case of Gerald Gault. The problems created by extreme informality and lack of concern for constitutional guarantees became abundantly clear in the Gault case. Neither Gault nor his parents were notified properly of the charges against him, their right to counsel, their right to cross-examine witnesses, their right to remain silent, their right to a transcript of the proceedings, or their right to appeal (*In re Gault*, 1967. See appendix). The Supreme Court decision in this case left no doubt that juveniles are protected by these guarantees and brought an end to the era of socialized justice. It did not, however, end the debate between those favoring more formal juvenile court proceedings (the **legalists**) and those favoring a more informal, casework approach (the **caseworkers or therapists**). That debate rages today, with a variety of consequences for juvenile justice practitioners.

Defining and Measuring Delinquency

One of the major problems facing students of delinquency is that of arriving at a suitable definition. Without such a definition, measurement is impossible; and without accurate measurement, prevention and treatment are extremely difficult.

Two different types of definitions of delinquency have emerged over the years: legal and behavioral. Strict legal definitions hold that only those juveniles who have been officially labeled by the courts are delinquents. Such definitions are problematic because, according to self-report studies and victim survey research, the definitions do not include the vast majority of all juveniles who commit delinquent acts and, therefore, may lead us to seriously underestimate the number of delinquents. In addition, legal definitions vary from state to state and time to time. Behavioral definitions hold that juveniles who have violated or attempted to violate statutes are delinquent whether or not they are apprehended; thus, the juvenile who engages in acts of vandalism is considered delinquent even though he or she has not been officially labeled by the court. Such definitions can provide a more comprehensive picture of the extent and nature of delinquency, provided we are able to collect accurate data from unofficial as well as official sources (Cox, Allen, Hanser & Conrad, 2008).

Purpose and Scope of Juvenile Court Acts

Juvenile court acts authorize the creation of juvenile courts with the legal authority to hear certain types of cases, including delinquency, dependency, neglect or abuse, and other cases requiring authoritative intervention (a minor in need of supervision, for example). These acts establish both procedural guidelines and substantive law relative to juveniles, which are to be administered in the interests of juveniles and in the spirit of parental concern. A separate nomenclature has been developed for juvenile procedures to ensure that these goals are pursued (see Figure 12.1). An examination of the figure shows that juveniles typically have a petition filed in their interests rather than a complaint filed against them. They may be taken into custody instead of arrested, may have a preliminary conference instead of a preliminary hearing, are accused of having committed a delinquent act rather than a crime (with some exceptions), go through an **adjudicatory hearing** rather than a criminal trial, may be found delinquent rather than guilty, and participate in a **dispositional hearing** instead of a sentencing hearing.

Figure 12.1 Comparison of Juvenile Justice and Adult Criminal Justice Systems

Adult	Juvenile
Arrest	Taking into custody
Preliminary hearing	Preliminary conference/detention hearing (both optional)
Grand jury/information/indictment	Petition
Arraignment	———-
Criminal trial	Adjudicatory hearing
Sentencing hearing	Dispositional hearing
Sentence	Disposition (probation, incarceration, etc.)
Appeal	Appeal

Source: Cox, Allen, Hanser & Conrad, 2008.

In addition to establishing such guidelines and a distinct language, juvenile court acts specify the age limits within which the juvenile court has jurisdiction and the nature of the acts over which the court has authority. For example, **delinquent acts** are normally defined as acts designated criminal in terms of local, state, or federal law committed by youth under a certain age. Similarly, those considered **status offenders** are typically juveniles who commit acts that are offenses only because of their age: running away from home, being beyond the control of parents, or being incorrigible.

Juvenile Justice Procedures

Court proceedings that concern juveniles officially begin with the filing of a **petition** alleging that the juvenile is delinquent or in need of authoritative intervention of some kind (we will exclude from consideration here children who are dependent or neglected). Prior to the filing of the petition, the youth may have been taken into custody by the police and, in some states, may have been involved in a **preliminary conference** arranged by the juvenile probation officer in an attempt to settle the dispute out of court without filing a petition. Such a conference brings all parties to the dispute together (if they agree to attend), and the parties attempt to reach a settlement agreeable to all. If such a settlement cannot be reached or if the victim demands that a petition be filed, the case may be taken into juvenile court.

In any case, it is likely that delinquents who are about to have petitions filed on them will come into contact with the police. This contact may be in the form of an arrest, or may involve taking the juvenile into custody, which does not constitute an arrest (usually for the welfare of the youth involved). Typically, statutes require that the police attempt to contact the parents of any juvenile taken into custody, ensure the constitutional rights of the juvenile while he or she is in custody (including the right to counsel), and release the youth from custody as soon as possible unless they intend to detain him or her, which requires a detention hearing involving the juvenile court judge if the detention is to be for more than a few hours. It should be noted here that the majority of juvenile cases are settled either at a preliminary conference or through the use of **street corner or stationhouse adjustments** on behalf of the police. Such adjustments allow the police to process most juveniles by obtaining agreement on behalf of their parents to see that the victim is compensated in some way for any damages he or she incurred (Cox, Allen, Hanser & Conrad, 2008).

When a **detention hearing** is necessary, the state generally must prove that detention is required to protect the youth, to protect society, or to prevent flight. If the judge agrees that detention is necessary, a specified time period is involved, at the end of which the juvenile must be brought before the court or released.

If the case cannot be settled out of court, a petition is filed alleging that the youth in question is delinquent or in need of authoritative intervention. Generally speaking, any adult who has knowledge of a delinquent act or has reason to believe a delinquent act has been committed by the youth in question may file a petition. The petition gives the name and age of the juvenile, and usually the names and address(es) of the parents. It includes a statement of the facts that bring the youth under the jurisdiction of the juvenile court. The petition is then filed with the prosecutor, who decides, often in conjunction with the juvenile probation officer, whether or not to prosecute the case.

If the prosecutor decides to prosecute, proper notice must be given to the juvenile and his or her parents or guardian, as well as to all other concerned parties. The court typically issues a summons specifying the date, place, and time of the adjudicatory hearing and of the right of all parties to counsel. Notification by certified mail or publication is acceptable if the summons cannot be delivered personally.

On the date indicated on the summons, the adjudicatory hearing is held. All parties to the proceedings have the right to attend, but the public is typically excluded. Unlike adults, juveniles under the jurisdiction of the juvenile court have no right to trial by jury or to a public hearing because the courts have ruled that adjudicatory hearings are not adversary proceedings. Although this may be true in theory, it is often not true in reality, and debate continues as to the legitimacy of these restrictions. Most adjudicatory hearings are conducted by a juvenile court judge who decides matters of fact, matters of law, and proper disposition of those found delinquent. The Supreme Court has ruled that the same standard of proof employed in adult criminal trials (guilt beyond reasonable doubt) must be adhered to in delinquency proceedings (*In re Gault*, 1967; *In re Winship*, 1970).

After hearing the evidence, the juvenile court judge makes a decision as to whether the juvenile is delinquent. If the juvenile is adjudicated delinquent, he or she becomes a **ward of the state** and the court becomes the juvenile's legal guardian. At this point, the judge asks the juvenile probation officer to conduct a social background investigation, which will be used to assist in determining an appropriate disposition. The judge may also set the date for the dispositional hearing, which is typically separate from the adjudicatory hearing.

The **social background investigation** focuses on evidence, including written and oral reports, relating to the juvenile's family, environment, school history, friends, and other material that may be helpful in obtaining an accurate picture of the juvenile's circumstances. In some instances, the probation officer makes a written dispositional recommendation to the judge; in others, the probation officer simply provides the judge with his or her report without making any recommendations. In any case, the juvenile and his or her legal representative have access to the social background investigation, because there is no irrefutable presumption of accuracy attached to the investigation (*Kent v. United States*, 1966). In fact, such reports often focus on the negative aspects of the juvenile's environment and overlook positive information.

The dispositional alternatives available to the juvenile court judge are specified in each state's juvenile court act. In general, these include placement in a foster home, placement in a private or public detention facility, probation (while the child remains in his or her parent's home or while in a foster home), and commitment to a state correctional facility for juveniles. After reaching a dispositional alternative, the judge issues a dispositional order (see "In the News" 12.2).

In the News 12.2

About half of juvenile offenders ordered to stay at home.
A new family remedy:
Lower numbers (of caseloads for) probation officers plus new funding

and improved screening allow some youngsters to recover in familiar surroundings rather than in group homes.

Ruby knows the kind of troubles that can land kids in group homes.

Her mom is jailed on drug charges, and her dad's in prison. She bounced into an alternative school after ditching too many classes at her regular high school. She has a minor criminal record because police caught her tagging a wall late one night.

Then she slid into depression after her boyfriend was killed at 14 in a drive-by shooting in June 2006.

Soon after, she discovered she was pregnant with his child.

"It all got to me at one time," said the soft-spoken 15-year-old girl. "My head was twisting."

But rather than go to a group home, she began recovering with help from a team of specialists in her community. It helped her put her life back on track, providing services from counseling to bus tokens so she could get to school.

She lives with an aunt who struggles to pay the rent, but she's family. The birth of Ruby's son also gave her hope.

"She's been through a lot of devastation," her aunt said. "She's come a long way. We try to stay together so she can be OK."

Ruby is one of a growing number of youths who are reshaping their lives at home rather than in the institutions known as group homes. These facilities are supposed to meet the needs of kids with serious emotional and family problems and nowhere else to go, but critics believe they've been overused.

Now Ventura County judges are ordering about half the number of juvenile offenders to group homes than they have in the past. The number dropped from 98 in summer 2005 to 40 in spring 2007, said Mark Varela, division manager for the county Probation Agency.

Officials cite special programs that lowered caseloads for probation officers, new funding and improved screening of offenders for the shift.

"If you can keep a child in the home and provide services to the child and family, we get better results," said Donald Coleman, presiding judge of Juvenile Court.

Abused and neglected children are being sent to group homes at much lower rates as well, said Ted Myers, director of the Ventura County Human Services Agency. The monthly number stood at less than 50 this year, about half the number in the late 1990s, Myers said.

The only exception lies in the school arena. Since 2005, the number has grown from 40 to 58 for children with serious disabilities. These youngsters, many with autism or serious emotional problems, live in group homes offering special education.

"The kids being placed have pretty severe issues," said Meloney Roy, acting director of the county Behavioral Health Department. "We have much less control over the kid being placed. These are team decisions in which the parent plays a significant role."

But in the courts, judges are resisting group homes unless there is no better alternative. Among the exceptions: kids who would be returned to abusive homes, might endanger others, or would run wild because their parents cannot control them.

Kids going out of county

Critics believe no child belongs in a group home staffed by employees, rather than in a home with a family. But Myers doubts that's realistic for all.

Some troubled kids distrust adults so deeply that they feel more comfortable in an institutional setting, Myers said.

Group homes also serve kids who a foster family may be afraid to take because the child is suicidal, sets fires or could attack other children, said Jane Reimann, a Human Services Agency manager overseeing placement in group homes.

If anything, Ventura County needs more group homes, said Andrew Lang, executive director of the Guiding Our Youth homes in Simi Valley.

"There's not enough beds in Ventura County, so a lot of kids are out of county and out of state," he said.

Of the roughly 50 children now living in group homes because of abuse and neglect by their parents, half must live out of the county, some as far away as Fresno.

More spots are needed for kids ready to leave a heavily staffed, restrictive group home into a more familylike group home, Reimann said.

"It would be so much better if there were more local resources," she said.

About half of the 41 children on probation who live in group homes also must go out of the county.

Among them: pregnant girls and sex offenders.

The county has about 200 beds in group homes, but the number is misleading. Almost one-fourth are actually emergency shelter beds for kids awaiting placement in foster care. Almost 30 more spots are in a high-level treatment center outside Camarillo, leaving a little more than 100 others.

Nor do all meet the standards set by county officials who make the referrals. The Human Services Agency, for example, places kids in only about a dozen of the homes.

Tight supervision

In the coming months, state officials, advocates and others are setting out to reform group homes across California. The state needs to figure out what group homes and other congregate facilities should do for kids, said Steven Ellson, chief executive officer of Casa Pacifica, a nonprofit organization aiding troubled families in Ventura and Santa Barbara counties.

Some say in-home services coupled with tight supervision by probation officers are the answer for many children. The programs aren't necessarily cheaper than group care, which costs from $1,454 to $6,371 a month, but early results show low rates of recidivism.

One of the most well known programs is "Wraparound," a concept pioneered in Chicago 30 years ago but only recently introduced to Ventura County. The county has lagged others in California, including Los Angeles and Contra Costa.

So called because it wraps services around the family, Wraparound is assisting 50 troubled children and their families.

A team of counselors will work with the family as much as 60 hours a week. Such programs can head off placement in a group home or provide a transition once a child leaves.

"If we need to be there at 2 in the morning, we'll be there at 2 in the morning," said Stephanie Cowie, manager of the program.

Transition after therapy

Inside their tidy home in western Ventura County, a 14-year-old girl and her mom are trying to repair their stormy relationship using Wraparound. It's a transition after Alejandra finished 11 months of therapy in a high-level treatment center at Casa Pacifica.

The first month was rough, with Alejandra defying her mom's rules. But the Wraparound team helped the two build strategies to cope. One person advises Alejandra, another gives parenting tips to her mother.

Pat Stepler, a team facilitator, helps them work out differences at weekly meetings.

"We built them up," Stepler said. "We worked on strengths."

Alejandra is doing well now, overcoming years of anger over the domestic violence she witnessed. She'll be a freshman in high school in the fall and just aced her first algebra test in summer school.

Both the parents and the children have to be willing to take part, said Probation Officer Julianne Gonzalez, who also is a member of the team.

"Some parents don't want it," Gonzalez said. "It's a lot of people in your face."

But Alejandra's mom welcomed the program.

They showed her how to calm down Alejandra when she came home late and started hitting the walls in frustration.

"I felt safe and secure when they came into my home and helped me deal with my child," her mom said.

Wilson, K. (2007, July 8). About half of juvenile offenders ordered to stay at home. A new family remedy: Lower numbers of (caseloads for) probation officers plus new funding and improved screening allow some youngsters to recover in familiar surroundings rather than in group homes. *Ventura County Star* (CA). Available online at: http://www .venturacountystar.com/news/2007/jul/08/about-half-of-juvenile offenders-to-stay.

Probation is by far the most common disposition in juvenile cases, perhaps accounting for 75 to 85 percent of all such dispositions. As we have indicated previously, probation is a sentence served under specified conditions in the community, and under the supervision of the probation officer. Conditions commonly imposed on juvenile probationers require that they must attend school regularly, not leave the county or state without the approval of the probation officer, keep regular appointments with the probation officer, avoid certain places or types of places (pool halls or other game rooms, for example), find and retain part-time employment, and so on. If the conditions of probation are violated or if the youth commits another offense while on probation, then probation may be revoked. At the **revocation hearing**, the judge decides whether such violations occurred and, if they did, whether to revoke probation and send the youth to a private or public detention facility to serve the remainder of his or her time. The length of probation varies, but seldom exceeds two to three years, although in most states it may be continued until the age at which the youth is no longer under the jurisdiction of the juvenile court and sometimes longer.

Private and public detention facilities vary tremendously in terms of size, length and type of program, and cost. Some, such as boot camps, employ behavior modification or peer pressure programs; others concentrate mostly on education and vocational training; and some are basically warehouses with few, if any, rehabilitation programs. Some allow home visits and some encourage parents to visit and participate in rehabilitation efforts, while others do little along these lines. These institutions are difficult to inspect and control and some have become infamous because of the brutality and abuse that sometimes occur under these conditions.

The use of foster home placement as a disposition would appear to hold some promise for delinquents, but a variety of factors combine to limit such placement. First, many parents of teenagers are reluctant to bring a delinquent youth into their homes for fear that their children will pick up the delinquent's habits. Second, some individuals become foster parents because they mistakenly believe that they can profit financially from the experience. However, for the most part, the subsidy provided by the state or county for each youth placed in a foster home is seldom enough to totally support the youth, let alone supplement the income of the foster parents. Third, foster parents are dealing with "high risk of failure" youth when they agree to work with delinquents and not infrequently become discouraged when their efforts at rehabilitation are less successful than they intended. As a result, they may decide to withdraw from foster home programs.

The least desirable (from the point of view of most juvenile court officials) and the least frequently employed disposition is commitment to a state correctional facility for juveniles. As a rule, only those delinquents regarded as unsalvageable are so committed. Such youth include those who commit violent offenses against others, repeatedly appear in juvenile court for relatively serious offenses, and most often have failed to benefit from probation or detention of other types. Many judges believe that sending a delinquent to a state correctional facility virtually guarantees that the youth will pursue a criminal career as an adult.

Regardless of the disposition handed down by the juvenile court judge, juveniles, like adults, have the right to appeal, although in practice, appeals from juvenile courts have been rare.

Current Dilemmas in Juvenile Justice

Among the many dilemmas plaguing the juvenile court network is the perception that there has been a major increase in the past few years in violent crimes committed by juveniles though the number of violent crimes committed by juveniles dropped considerably between 1994 and 2005 (Federal Bureau of Investigation, 2006). Other factors are an increase in the visibility of street gang youth, a number of highly publicized school shootings, and fear on behalf of many adults. This environment makes reintegration of juveniles who have been found delinquent difficult at best, and has led to the passage of legislation intended to get tough with juveniles by making transfer to adult court easier and such transfer possible for younger juveniles who commit violent offenses.

There continues to be a belief that practitioners at all levels of the juvenile justice network are something less than real criminal justice officials. Police officers assigned to juvenile bureaus are often regarded as kiddie cops by other police officers, even though special dedication and expertise are required of such officers. (This perception tends to be less prevalent in areas where juvenile officers deal on a regular basis with street gang members.) Prosecutors often dislike handling juvenile cases because they are unlikely to lead to positive publicity even when an adjudication of delinquent is returned, and because preparation of such cases means time away from other cases that may be perceived as more serious or important. Defense attorneys sometimes fail to regard juvenile cases as worthy of the same preparation as adult criminal cases. Juvenile court judges are sometimes assigned this duty on a part-time basis and are sometimes unfamiliar with the requirements of the juvenile court act under which they are to operate, and many tend to overlook procedural requirements at the adjudicatory hearing on the grounds that they are interested in the total picture of the alleged delinquent. As a result, proper cross-examination of witnesses is sometimes impossible, especially if the witness happens to be an authority figure such as a teacher or a police officer, and hearsay evidence is sometimes considered. It is somewhat ironic that this should be the case when, as we have seen, it is the courts that have decided that the total picture of the delinquent may be considered only if it is obtained using the same legal procedures as are required for adults. As is the case in adult court, few judges are properly trained to decide which of the dispositional alternatives would be most beneficial to the youth in question, and so, in spite of good intentions, judges operate on a trial-and-error basis with little attempt to do follow-up research to determine the effectiveness of the dispositions they hand down (Cox, Allen, Hanser & Conrad, 2008).

Juvenile probation officers face the same dilemmas as their counterparts who work with adults. They are officers of the court and must occasionally discipline their charges, but to be effective in helping probationers, the officers must gain the probationers' confidence. As a result, the probation officer must maintain a delicate balance between the roles of counselor/friend and disciplinarian. Recognizing the difficulty of this task, many states require a college degree for juvenile probation officers, provide mandated annual training for such officers, and subsidize the officers' salaries in the hope of attracting and retaining qualified personnel. Other attempts have been and are being made to ensure better-qualified juvenile personnel. A number of states now require specialized training and specific designation for juvenile police officers. Prosecutors and juvenile court judges have their own associations, complete with national and regional meetings that address key issues confronting the juvenile justice system. In addition, specialized training programs and seminars for both judges and prosecutors are available and are frequently well attended.

Attempts to divert youth from the juvenile justice network have also been popular in recent years. **Diversion programs** are of two basic types: those that attempt to divert youth from initial involvement in delinquency and those that attempt to divert youth who have already been involved in delinquent activities from becoming further involved. Although some diversion programs claim considerable success, it is difficult to determine whether such reported success is due to selection procedures or to the programs themselves. In addition, diversion programs have been criticized for keeping youth under a microscope, that is, monitoring their behavior so closely that they become defined as delinquent for engaging in behaviors similar to those of other youth who are not defined as delinquent. It is doubtful that many of us could escape the label "delinquent" if our behaviors were closely monitored all the time. Electronic surveillance devices and intensive supervision by probation officers are two examples of such monitoring. The intent of these innovations is to reduce or maintain the cost of supervising youth in trouble while providing close supervision for those who appear to need it most.

The dilemma in juvenile corrections on whether to emphasize custody or rehabilitation is much the same as in adult corrections, and the same staff controversies exist. Further, the inmate subculture is at least as pervasive in juvenile institutions as in adult facilities, and some, if not most, juvenile correctional facilities are literally run by gangs. There is little doubt that one of the things the delinquent committed to a correctional facility learns is a wide variety of delinquent activities.

In an attempt to change the behavior of problem youth without the consequences of long-term institutionalization, boot camps, similar to those for adults, have been developed. These camps promote discipline through physical conditioning and teamwork while attempting to improve academic achievement and instill moral values. After evaluating three such programs, Bourque et al. (1996) concluded, "The evaluation team could not draw any conclusions about the programs' long-term ability to change offenders' behavior or to save money and space for the country's overburdened juvenile justice system.... Until more information is available on recidivism and the cost of alternatives to institutionalization, the impact of juvenile camps on correctional crowding and skyrocketing costs will be difficult to determine" (p.9). However, in 2006 the story of 14-year-old Martin Lee Anderson who was killed in a Panama City, FL. juvenile boot camp, where he had been sent after violating probation on charges that he

To many Americans graffiti indicates the presence of gangs.
Reprinted with permission of iStockphoto.com / Anna Bryukhanova

took his grandmother's car for a joy ride, has raised real concerns over this strategy for dealing with youth (Avila & Koch, 2007).

Although the language and structure of the juvenile justice network is intended to prevent stigmatization, in practice, it occurs routinely. While the public is excluded from juvenile court proceedings, the press may attend, and the identities of delinquents may be disclosed through this medium either directly or indirectly. Further, in the case of youth adjudicated delinquent, school officials and other public agency officials are routinely informed of this decision. In many cases, youth involved publicize their adjudication as a symbol of their toughness. Even in the case of youth who avoid such publicity, weekly visits to or from the probation officer make it difficult to conceal the label.

The public has become increasingly concerned about violent offenses committed by juveniles. We have become, to some extent, afraid of our own children. As a result, the public has called for more severe penalties for youth involved in violent offenses. It is increasingly easy to automatically transfer youth who commit such offenses to adult court, thereby negating the philosophy of treat, educate, and rehabilitate instead of punish. As indicated above, there is precious little evidence to prove that such transfers or increasingly severe punishment have any major impact on juvenile offenders, but as the network approach would indicate, when there is a perceived threat, any or all components of the network may react. In this case, public fear has resulted in pressure on legislators to pass laws mandating severe punishment for violent youth. To the extent that judges impose more severe sentences on youth or waive them to adult courts, which may lead to incarceration, correctional officials have larger numbers of inmates to deal with. Already overcrowded facilities, combined with federal and state standards for jails and prisons, may lead to cursory attempts at rehabilitation or outright early release of some offenders (Cox, Allen, Hanser & Conrad, 2008). When such offenders recidivate, the press focuses attention on them, public concern is once again aroused, and the cycle begins again. (See "In the News" 12.3.)

In the News 12.3

Houston is first Utah juvenile facing life without parole; some wonder if sentence is fair to teen convicts

CLEARFIELD — Robert Cameron Houston, who was 17 when he committed aggravated murder, earned an infamous spot in Utah history last week.

According to the Department of Corrections, he is the first juvenile offender to enter the Utah State Prison with no hope of dying anywhere but in prison.

Houston was sentenced by a jury to life in prison without parole after pleading guilty in March to the aggravated murder of Raechale Elton on Feb. 15, 2006. She was a counselor in a youth home where Houston lived.

Since 2005, when capital punishment of juvenile offenders was declared cruel and unusual and therefore unconstitutional, human rights groups in the U.S. have turned their efforts to fighting life without parole sentences levied against juveniles.

More than 2,200 individuals in the U.S. are serving life without parole sentences for crimes they committed as juveniles, according to a report by Human Rights Watch and Amnesty International. The report states that such sentences for juveniles are nearly non-existent anywhere else in the world.

There are signs of changing attitudes, however. In the U.S., eight states and the District of Columbia forbid life without parole penalties for juveniles.

California's legislature is considering a bill that would make it the ninth state to ban the sentence.

Supporters of the harsh sentence say Houston's crime is arguably the most vile crime ever committed by a juvenile in Utah, so his sentence is appropriate.

One Episcopalian priest, who lobbied the California legislature last week, said the possibility of parole is about more than human rights: It affects souls of America's children.

James Tramel was imprisoned in California for the violent stabbing death of a homeless man in 1983 when he was 17. He was convicted of second-degree murder, but in 1983, neither California nor many other states allowed life without parole sentences for juvenile offenders.

He was sentenced to 15 years to life in prison, a so-called indeterminate sentence that allows parole hearings and a possibility of release. He was released last year.

Tramel, who was ordained in prison and is now the rector of a San Francisco church, said children need a sense that society believes they can be reformed in order to seek redemption in the eyes of the law and God.

"If someone is confined to no hope of parole from prison ... he's going to forever be in a place that is violent. In that environment, people die a moral death and act out of the most basic survival instincts, which always comes out as aggressive animal behavior," Tramel said in a telephone interview with the Standard-Examiner.

"In the case of a juvenile ... it is my feeling that it is morally wrong for us as a society to sentence them to life without the possibility of parole. We lose nothing by offering them the hope, however slim, of redemption and reconciliation....

For juveniles, a life without the possibility of parole is really a sentence of death without execution."

Tramel agrees that juveniles who commit heinous crimes most often should not be released.

However, he said, all of them, regardless of their crime, ought to be considered for release after years of incarceration.

Houston's mother, Carol Houston, agrees. She said Cameron, as she calls him, is confused and "feels like everyone hates him." Barely able to utter the words, she said the sentence her son received is just as cruel as executing him would be.

"If he's just going be stuck there without parole and not eligible for any rehabilitation programs whatsoever.... I can't see the difference. He's just going to waste away," she said. "My family has still not stopped crying."

Tramel said his possibility of parole enabled him to enter programs that eventually led to his ordination as a priest.

'Mercy of the system'

State Sen. Greg Bell, R-Fruit Heights, who chairs the Utah Senate Judiciary, Law Enforcement and Criminal Justice Committee, said he feels life without parole sentences are merciful. Speaking to Houston's case, he said the young man is lucky he did not face capital punishment.

"He's very fortunate, I think, that he wasn't a few months older and subject to capital punishment," Bell said. "Therein is the mercy of the system."

Houston's mother disagrees. A prison official who testified at her son's trial said prisoners who have option of parole are not eligible for rehabilitation programs, education programs and the like.

"That's not mercy," Carol Houston said. "There is no mercy in making a juvenile spend the rest of his life behind bars with no rehabilitation and no help, no nothing. Because he got the life without parole, not eligible for anything the Utah State Prison has to offer."

Davis County prosecutor Ryan Perkins said life without parole sentences offer mercy to someone than the offender: the victim's family.

"The victim's family no longer has to participate in a process. It provides closure for the community and for the family," said Perkins, a prosecutor at Houston's sentencing hearing.

Adult crime

According to the 2005 Human Rights Watch and Amnesty International report, the idea of trying juveniles in adult courts is a new one. The idea caught on during a spike in juvenile crime in the 1980s and 1990s, the report states. In 1986, 965 gun-related homicides were committed by juveniles. By 1994, that number had jumped to 3,337.

By 1997, the report states, all but three states had changed laws to push more juveniles into adult court.

However, the laws changed just as the crime wave declined. By 1997, youth gun-related homicides had dropped below 1970 levels.

Utah's "direct file" system was enacted during this era. The juvenile Court Act of 1996 laid out 10 crimes for which juveniles would automatically be tried as adults.

The debate

Bell said he believes kids who commit adult crimes should be punished like adults. He said public safety, deterrence and punishment justify the harsh penalty.

Weber State University professor and child psychologist Dr. Jim Bird has done evaluations of juvenile offenders for 25 years. He and others like him are brought in when there is a question of whether the youth should be tried as an adult.

Utah pushes too many juveniles into adult court, he said.

"Sometimes I feel that the system is very, very wrong in trying to adjudicate somebody as an adult when they have no business doing so," Bird said.

"Sometimes it seems they (politicians and prosecutors) are doing that to look good in the public eye, to say, 'We're tough on crime.' "

Bird said Houston's case was appropriate to try in adult court, but he still has reservations about the sentence.

Politics best explain the existence of life without parole sentences for juveniles, he said, since what is known about children's brains does not. Stiffer penalties do not deter juveniles from committing crimes because they have poor impulse control and insight into their lives, he said.

"As our current system is, it is extremely expensive and does not serve anything besides revenge," Bird said. "It's not going to prevent people or youths from doing the crime.... When people start saying 'never-ever-ever should this person see the light of day,' that's getting a little severe. You can't predict the future."

Mental disorders

Mental disorders are more complicated to see and understand than, say, a brain tumor, Bird said, but their biological natures are the same. Both can cause individuals to commit crimes they would not otherwise commit. He said new research will turn up new causes for mental illness and new treatments or cures.

Houston has been diagnosed with depression throughout his life and obsessive-compulsive disorder during his trial.

Bird said he's not suggesting that psychology can cure Houston and therefore he should be released. But, he said, psychology can treat Houston, and for that reason, his release should at least be considered as the decades pass.

Perkins disagrees and said it's the privilege of the jury to predict if an individual could ever be reformed, and it ought to stay that way.

Predicting?

Predicting is something Carol Houston said no one can do.

"I don't think anybody can say where Cameron will be in 10 or 20 years down the road," she said. "It changes his whole life, being in prison."

In 2005, matters of child psychology, culpability and predicting the future of juvenile offenders prompted the Supreme Court to ban the possibility of executing them.

Hundreds of youth offenders, many who were by then adults still awaiting execution, were removed from death row as a result.

Houston's defense attorney, Rich Gallegos, said much of the rationale the court used to find executions of youth to be "cruel and unusual" also apply to life without parole.

"The troubling thing was, yeah, they didn't give them the death penalty, but they changed their sentences to life in prison without parole," he said. "That's troubling. I don't think we've gone far enough as far as juveniles are concerned."

Would it ever happen? Could the U.S. Supreme Court declare life without parole sentences for juvenile offenders unconstitutional?

Gallegos is doubtful, but hopeful. In determining whether executing juvenile offenders was "unusual," Gallegos said, the Supreme Court determined that more than half the states had already outlawed the practice.

Those states that hadn't, the court said, rarely used it anyway.

As it stands now, only eight states, maybe soon nine, outlaw life without parole for juveniles. That's not likely to change quickly, Perkins said.

"When you put a fine point on it, the people — any person — would be more comfortable making decisions about life without parole rather than taking a person's life," he said.

Nonetheless, Perkins and Gallegos agree the Supreme Court could someday nullify the more than 2,200 life without parole sentences held by juvenile offenders.

If that happens, Gallegos said, Houston's sentence likely would revert to 20 years to life in prison, the only other sentencing option jurors had to consider in his case.

Fruhwirth, J. (2007, May 5). Houston is first Utah juvenile facing life without parole; some wonder if sentence is fair to teen convicts, *Standard-Examiner* (Ogden, UT). Available online at: http://www.standard.net/live/textarticle

One of the continuing dilemmas in juvenile justice involves the use of capital punishment. In March 2005, in the case of *Roper v. Simmons*, the U.S. Supreme Court reversed a 1989 precedent and struck down the death penalty for crimes committed by people under the age of 18 years. On being taken into custody, Christopher Simmons confessed to the murder of Shirley Crook and the guilt phase of the trial in Missouri state court was uncontested (Bradley, 2006). The U.S. Supreme Court held that "evolving standards of decency" govern the prohibition of cruel and unusual punishment and found that "capital punishment must be limited to those offenders who commit a narrow category of the most serious crimes and whose extreme culpability makes them the most deserving of execution" (Death Penalty Information Center, n.d.). The Court further found that there is a scientific consensus that teenagers have "an underdeveloped sense of responsibility" and that it is unreasonable to classify them among the most culpable offenders: "From a moral standpoint, it would be misguided to equate the failings of a minor with those of an adult, for a greater possibility exists that a minor's character deficiencies will be reformed" (Death Penalty Information Center, n.d.). In addition, the Court concluded that it would be extremely difficult for jurors to distinguish between juveniles whose crimes reflect immaturity and those whose crimes reflect "irreparable corruption." (Bradley, 2006). Finally, the Court pointed out that only seven countries in the world have executed juveniles since 1990, and even those countries now disallow the juvenile death penalty. Thus, the United States was the only country to still permit it. The pros and cons of this decision are still being debated but suffice it to say now that the decision in this case furthered the considerable controversy that has characterized the juvenile justice network since its inception (Cox, Allen, Hanser, & Conrad, 2008). Following the Supreme Court decision, Simmons was sentenced to life in prison without the possibility of parole.

In some jurisdictions, the decision to transfer youth to adult court rests with the prosecutor rather than the judge. While this action may help streamline the transfer process, once such a transfer occurs, the protections offered in juvenile court cease to exist. The juvenile's trial is public, as are records related to the case. Long-term incarceration and loss of civil rights are possibilities, and individualized treatment and rehabilitation become less likely. Opportunities to associate with, and learn from, hardened criminals increase. As a result of such risks, a full hearing before a judge who makes the final waiver decision is probably in the best interests of juveniles. Nonetheless, community pressure supporting the current concept of transfer is considerable because many observers believe that juvenile offenders are coddled by the juvenile justice network, even when they commit serious violations.

A number of remedies have been put forth for the problems confronting the juvenile justice network. Many of these remedies are based on overreaction to the inaccurate perception that there has been a recent increase in violent juvenile crime. "Get-tough" policies have been adopted in a number of states as a result of the mistaken belief that the more severe the punishment, the less likely the offender is to commit an offense. As noted above, there is little evidence to indicate that this return to the classical approach (based on assumptions of free will, the rationality of human beings, and a relationship between severity of punishment and likelihood of crime) will produce the desired results. In the meantime, the goals of the juvenile justice network may be set aside or overlooked.

At the beginning of the twenty-first century, those interested in the juvenile court can be divided into two basic groups: those who believe the juvenile court should be abolished and those who believe it should be reformed. Some of those in the former group believe that the juvenile court has never fulfilled the promise of the original juvenile court to protect and rehabilitate youth. Others believe the court has failed to guarantee the constitutional rights of juveniles. Still others believe the court is incapable of dealing with contemporary youth, who differ in many ways from the clients envisioned by the original framers of the juvenile court. Hatchett (1998), for example, concludes that, "There is little argument that the current juvenile justice system is indeed in turmoil and lacks the foresight and preventive measures required for lasting reform.... The challenge before us is to move from the rhetoric to the reality of what we are going to do to save their [juveniles'] lives and our collective futures" (Hatchett, 1998, pp. 83–84; see also Feld, 2003).

Bilchik (1998) concluded that "A revitalized juvenile justice system needs to be put into place and brought to a scale that will ensure immediate and appropriate sanctions, provide effective treatment, reverse trends in juvenile violence, and rebuild public confidence in and support for the juvenile justice system" (p.89). Such a system would include swift intervention with early offenders, an individualized comprehensive needs assessment, transfer of serious or chronic offenders, and intensive aftercare. This system would require the coordinated efforts of law enforcement, treatment, correctional, judicial, and social service personnel. This approach to delinquency control represents a form of community programming that might help reintegrate troubled youth into mainstream society rather than further isolate and alienate them (Bazemore & Washington, 1995; Farrington, 2005; Zaslaw & Balance, 1996). Accomplishing this goal will require the best efforts of the various components of the adult and juvenile justice networks as well as the support of the public.

Summary

1. The juvenile justice network in the United States is a separate network just over 100 years old.

2. The underlying philosophy of the juvenile justice network is based on principles developed in England and transported to this country.

3. These principles include parens patriae, in loco parentis, chancery/equity or protection, treatment, and rehabilitation of women and children.

4. The first family court in the United States was established in 1899 in Cook County, Illinois.

5. Since the inception of the juvenile justice network, there has been debate about how official or informal the proceedings should be, and the courts have taken first one position and then the other.

6. At present, the legalists appear to have the advantage because the courts now require a considerable degree of formality in delinquency proceedings.

7. Protection of juveniles from stigmatization; recruitment, training, and retention of qualified personnel; and a current wave of public fear of violent youth are problems confronting the juvenile justice network as we enter the twenty-first century.

Key Terms Defined

age of responsibility The age at which children are assumed to be responsible (in a legal sense) for their actions.

mens rea A criminal or guilty state of mind.

parens patriae The right of the government to take care of those who cannot legally care for themselves.

in loco parentis In the place of parents.

era of socialized juvenile justice The period between 1899 and 1967, during which juvenile courts emphasized getting the total picture of the juvenile as opposed to adhering only to legal requirements.

legalists Those favoring a formal approach to juvenile justice.

adjudicatory hearing A hearing in juvenile cases at which the judge determines whether the youth in question is delinquent, dependent, abused, or otherwise in need of intervention.

dispositional hearing A hearing in juvenile cases at which the judge decides on appropriate placement for the juvenile in question.

delinquent acts Acts committed by youth under a specified age that violate a federal, state, or municipal law.

status offenders Those who commit acts that constitute an offense only because of the age of the offender.

petition A written request for action directed to the juvenile court.

preliminary conference A conference of interested parties at which a juvenile probation officer attempts to adjust juvenile cases without taking official action.

street corner or stationhouse adjustments Adjustments in juvenile cases made by a police officer and other interested parties in lieu of taking further official action.

detention hearing A hearing at which the state generally must prove that detention is required to protect the youth, to protect society, or to prevent flight.

ward of the state A juvenile whose guardian is the court.

social background investigation An investigation which focuses on evidence, including written and oral reports, relating to the juvenile's family, environment, school history, friends, and other material that may be helpful in obtaining an accurate picture of the juvenile's circumstances.

revocation hearing A hearing at which the judge decides whether probation violations occurred and, if they did, whether to revoke probation and send the youth to a private or public detention facility to serve the remainder of his or her time.

diversion programs Programs intended to divert (redirect) youth from the official juvenile justice network.

Critical Thinking Exercises

1. Do you think the juvenile justice system is capable of handling the kinds of cases presented before it today? Is juvenile court the appropriate place for youth who commit violent offenses in which people lose their lives? If not, at what age do you think youth should be transferred to adult court and for what kinds of offenses?

2. How important are the concepts of rehabilitation, treatment, and education as applied to juveniles today? Can get-tough policies and harsh punishment accomplish the goals of the juvenile court? Present both sides of the argument regarding these types of policies. Which arguments do you find most persuasive?

Internet Exercises

Juveniles are often treated differently from adults in the justice network because they have unique problems and unique status.

1. Can you find a website that provides information for troubled teens and/or their parents? Please provide the website and a brief summary of the information contained at the site.

2. What types of recent information concerning delinquents are available from http://www.crime-times.org?

3. If you wanted to know more about the processing of juveniles in the federal system, could you find that information from http://www.ojd.usdoj.gov? What other information concerning juveniles is available from this source?

References

Avila, J. & Koch, S. (2007, February 7). Boot camp death—caught on tape. *ABC News.* Available online at: http://www.abcnews.go.com/2020/story?id=2751785&page=1.

Bazemore, G., & Washington, C. (1995, Spring). Charting the future of the juvenile justice system: Reinventing mission and management. *Spectrum, 68,* 51–66.

Bilchik, S. (1998). A juvenile justice system for the 21st century. *Crime and Delinquency, 44,* (1), 89–101.

Blackstone, W. (1803). *Commentaries on the laws of England* (12th ed.). London: Strahan.

Bourque, B. B., Cronin, R.C., Felker, D. B., Han, M. & Hill, S.M. (1996). Boot camps for juvenile offenders: An implementation evaluation of three demonstration programs. *Research in Brief.* Washington, DC: National Institute of Justice.

Bradley, C. M. (2006, March/April). The right decision on the juvenile death penalty. *Judicature, 89,* 302–305.

Cavan, R. S. (1969). *Juvenile delinquency: Development, treatment, control* (2nd ed.). Philadelphia: Lippincott.

Cox, S.M., Allen, J.M., Hanser, R. D., & Conrad, J.J. (2008). *Juvenile justice: A guide to theory, policy, and practice.* (6th ed.). Thousand Oaks, CA: Sage Publications Inc.

Death Penalty Information Center. (n.d.) U.S. Supreme Court: *Roper v. Simmons.* Available online at http://www.deathpenaltyinfo.org/article.php?scid=388cdid=885.

Farrington, D. P. (2005). Early identification and preventive intervention: How effective is this strategy? *Criminology & Public Policy, 4* (2), 237–249.

Federal Bureau of Investigation. (2006). *Crime in the United States, 2005.* Available on line at: http://www.fbi.gov/ucr/ucr.htm#cius.

Feld, B. C. (2003). The politics of race and juvenile justice: The "due process revolution" and the conservative reaction. *Justice Quarterly: JQ, 20* (4), 765.

Hatchett, G. (1998). Why we can't wait: The juvenile court in the new millenium. *Crime and Delinquency, 44,* (1), 83–88.

In re Gault, 387 U.S. 1, 49–50; 87 S. Ct. 1428, 1455 (1967).

In re Holmes, 379 Pa. 599, 109 A. 2d. 523 (1954); cert denied, 348 U.S. 973, 75 S. Ct. 535 (1955).

In re Winship, 397 U.S. 358, 90 S. Ct. 1068 (1970).

Kent v. United States, 383 U.S. 541, 86 S. Ct. 1045, 16 L. Ed. 2d. 84 (1966).

Moon, M. M., Sundt, J. L., Cullen, F. T., & Wright, J. P. (2000). Is child saving dead? Public support for juvenile rehabilitation. *Crime and Delinquency, 46,* (1), 38–60.

Rendleman, D. R. (1974). Parens patriae: From chancery to the juvenile court. In F. L. Faust & P. J. Brantingham (Eds.), *Juvenile justice philosophy* (pp. 72–117). St. Paul, MN: West.

Sanders, W. B. (1974). Some early beginnings of the children's court movement in England. In F. L. Faust & P. J. Brantingham (Eds.), *Juvenile justice philosophy* (pp.46–47). St. Paul, MN: West.

Simonsen, C. E., & Gordon, M. S. (1991). *Juvenile justice in America* (2nd ed.). New York: Macmillan.

Zaslaw, J. G., & Balance, G. S. (1996, February). The socio-legal reponse: A new approach to juvenile justice in the '90s. *Corrections Today, 58*, 72.

Suggested Readings

Cox, S. M., Allen, J.M., Hanser, R.D., & Conrad, J.J. (2008). *Juvenile justice: A guide to theory, policy, and practice* (6th ed.). Thousand Oaks, CA: Sage.

Feld, B. C. (2003). The politics of race and juvenile justice: The "due process revolution" and the conservative reaction. *Justice Quarterly: JQ, 20* (4), 765.

Mays, G. L., & Winfree, L. T., Jr. (2000). *Juvenile justice*. Boston: McGraw-Hill.

Wooden, W. S., & Blazak, R. (2001). *Renegade kids, suburban outlaws*. Belmont, CA: Wadsworth.

Appendix

The U.S. Constitution and Selected Landmark Decisions

Constitution of the United States of America: Preamble

We, the People of the United States, in Order to form a more perfect Union, establish justice, insure domestic tranquility, provide for the common defence, promote the general welfare, and secure the blessings of liberty to ourselves and our posterity, do ordain and establish this Constitution for the United States of America.

Article I

Section 1

All legislative Powers herein granted shall be vested in a Congress of the United States, which shall consist of a Senate and House of Representatives.

Section 2

The House of Representatives shall be composed of Members chosen every second Year by the People of the several States, and the Electors in each State shall have the Qualifications requisite for Electors of the most numerous Branch of the State Legislature.

No Person shall be a Representative who shall not have attained to the Age of twenty-five Years, and been seven Years a Citizen of the United States, and who shall not, when elected, be an Inhabitant of that State in which he shall be chosen.

Representatives and direct Taxes shall be apportioned among the several States which may be included within this Union, according to their respective Numbers, which shall be determined by adding to the whole Number of free Persons, including those bound to Service for a Term of Years, and excluding Indians not taxed, three-fifths of all other Persons. The actual Enumeration shall be made within three Years after the first Meeting of the Congress of the United States, and within every subsequent Term of ten Years, in such Manner as they shall by Law direct. The Number of Representatives shall not exceed one for every thirty Thousand, but each State shall have at Least one Representative; and until such enumeration shall be made, the State of New Hampshire shall be entitled to choose three, Massachusetts eight, Rhode-Island and Providence Plantations one, Connecticut five, New-York six, New Jersey four, Pennsylvania eight, Delaware one, Maryland six, Virginia ten, North Carolina five, South Carolina five, and Georgia three.

When vacancies happen in the Representation from any State, the Executive Authority thereof shall issue Writs of Election to fill such Vacancies.

The House of Representatives shall choose their Speaker and other Officers; and shall have the sole Power of Impeachment.

Section 3

The Senate of the United States shall be composed of two Senators from each State, chosen by the Legislature thereof, for six Years; and each Senator shall have one Vote.

Immediately after they shall be assembled in Consequence of the first Election, they shall be divided as equally as may be into three Classes. The Seats of the Senators of the first Class shall be vacated at the Expiration of the second Year, of the second Class at the Expiration of the fourth Year, and of the third Class at the Expiration of the sixth Year, so that one-third may be chosen every second Year; and if Vacancies happen by Resignation, or otherwise, during the Recess of the Legislature of any State, the Executive thereof may make temporary Appointment until the next Meeting of the Legislature, which shall then fill such Vacancies.

No Person shall be a Senator who shall not have attained to the Age of thirty Years, and been nine Years a Citizen of the United States, and who shall not, when elected, be an Inhabitant of that State for which he shall be chosen.

The Vice-President of the United States shall be President of the Senate, but shall have no Vote, unless they be equally divided.

The Senate shall choose their other Officers, and also a President pro tempore, in the Absence of the Vice-President, or when he shall exercise the Office of President of the United States.

The Senate shall have the sole Power to try all Impeachments. When sitting for that Purpose, they shall be on Oath or Affirmation. When the President of the United States is tried, the Chief Justice shall preside: And no Person shall be convicted without the Concurrence of two-thirds of the Members present.

Judgment in Cases of Impeachment shall not extend further than to removal from Office, and disqualification to hold and enjoy any Office of honor, Trust or Profit under the United States: but the Party convicted shall nevertheless be liable and subject to Indictment, Trial, Judgment and Punishment, according to Law.

Section 4

The Times, Place and Manner of holding Elections for Senators and Representatives, shall be prescribed in each State by the Legislature thereof; but the Congress may at any time by Law make or alter such Regulations, except as to the Places of choosing Senators.

The Congress shall assemble at least once in every Year, and such Meeting shall be on the first Monday of December, unless they shall by Law appoint a different day.

Section 5

Each House shall be the Judge of the Elections, Returns and Qualifications of its own Members, and a Majority of each shall constitute a Quorum to do Business; but a smaller Number may adjourn from day to day, and may be authorized to compel the Attendance of absent Members, in such Manner, and under such Penalties as each House may provide.

Each House may determine the Rules of its Proceedings, punish its Members for disorderly Behaviour, and, with the Concurrence of two-thirds, expel a Member.

Each House shall keep a Journal of its Proceedings, and from time to time publish the same, excepting such Parts as may in their Judgment require Secrecy; and the Yeas and Nays of the Members of either House on any question shall, at the Desire of one-fifth of those Present, be entered on the Journal.

Neither House, during the Session of Congress, shall, without the Consent of the other, adjourn for more than three days, nor to any other Place than that in which the two Houses shall be sitting.

Section 6

The Senators and Representatives shall receive a Compensation for their Services, to be ascertained by Law, and paid out of the Treasury of the United States. They shall in all Cases, except Treason, Felony and Breach of the Peace, be privileged from Arrest during their Attendance at the Session of their respective Houses, and in going to and returning from the same; and for any Speech or Debate in either House, they shall not be questioned in any other Place.

No Senator or Representative shall, during the Time for which he was elected, be appointed to any civil Office under the Authority of the United States, which shall have been created, or the Emoluments whereof shall have been increased during such time; and no Person holding any Office under the United States, shall be a Member of either House during his Continuance in Office.

Section 7

All Bills for raising Revenue shall originate in the House of Representatives; but the Senate may propose or concur with Amendments as on other Bills.

Every Bill which shall have passed the House of Representatives and the Senate shall, before it becomes a Law, be presented to the President of the United States; if he approve, he shall sign it, but if not, he shall return it, with his Objections, to that House in which it shall have originated, who shall enter the Objections at large on their Journal, and proceed to reconsider it. If after such Reconsideration two-thirds of the House shall agree to pass the Bill, it shall be sent, together with the Objections, to the other House, by which it shall likewise be reconsidered, and if approved by two-thirds of that House, it shall become a Law. But in all such Cases the Votes of both Houses shall be determined by Yeas and Nays and the Names of the Persons voting for and against the Bill shall be entered on the Journal of each House respectively. If any Bill shall not be returned by the President within ten Days (Sundays excepted) after it shall have been presented to him, the Same shall be a Law, in like Manner as if he had signed it, unless the Congress by their Adjournment prevent its Return, in which Case it shall not be a law.

Every Order, Resolution, or Vote to which the Concurrence of the Senate and House of Representatives may be necessary (except on a question of Adjournment) shall be presented to the President of the United States; and before the Same shall take Effect, shall be approved by him, or being disapproved by him, shall be repassed by two-thirds of the Senate and House of Representatives, according to the Rules and Limitations prescribed in the Case of a Bill.

Section 8

The Congress shall have Power: To lay and collect Taxes, Duties, Imposts and Excises, to pay the Debts and provide for the common Defence and general Welfare of the United States; but all Duties, Imposts and Excises shall be uniform throughout the United States.

- To borrow Money on the credit of the United States;
- To regulate Commerce with foreign Nations, and among the several States, and with the Indian Tribes;
- To establish a uniform Rule of Naturalization, and uniform Laws on the subject of Bankruptcies throughout the United States;
- To coin Money, regulate the Value thereof, and of foreign Coin, and fix the Standard of Weights and Measures;
- To provide for the Punishment of counterfeiting the Securities and current Coin of the United States;
- To establish Post Offices and post Roads;
- To promote the Progress of Science and useful Arts, by securing for limited Times to Authors and Inventors the exclusive Right to their respective Writings and Discoveries;
- To constitute Tribunals inferior to the Supreme Court;
- To define and punish Piracies and Felonies committed on the high Seas, and Offences against the Law of Nations;
- To declare War, grant Letters of Marque and Reprisal, and make Rules concerning Captures on Land and Water;
- To raise and support Armies, but no Appropriation of Money to the Use shall be for a longer Term than two Years;
- To provide and maintain a Navy;
- To make Rules for the Government and Regulation of the land and naval Forces;
- To provide for calling forth the Militia to execute the Laws of the Union, suppress Insurrections and repel Invasions;

- To provide for organizing, arming, and disciplining the Militia, and for governing such Part of them as may be employed in the Service of the United States, reserving to the States respectively, the Appointment of the Officers, and the Authority of training the Militia according to the Discipline prescribed by Congress;
- To exercise exclusive Legislation in all Cases whatsoever, over such District (not exceeding ten Miles square) as may, by Cession of particular States, and the Acceptance of Congress, become the Seat of Government of the United States, and to exercise like Authority over all Places purchased by the Consent of the Legislature of the State in which the Same shall be, for the Erection of Forts, Magazines, Arsenals, dock-Yards, and other needful Buildings;—And

- To make all Laws which shall be necessary and proper for carrying into Execution the foregoing Powers, and all other Powers vested by this Constitution in the Government of the United States, or in any Department or Officer thereof.

Section 9

The Migration or Importation of such Persons as any of the States now existing shall think proper to admit, shall not be prohibited by the Congress prior to the Year one thousand eight hundred and eight, but a Tax or duty may be imposed on such Importation, not exceeding ten dollars for each Person.

The Privilege of the Writ of Habeas Corpus shall not be suspended, unless when in Cases of Rebellion or Invasion the public Safety may require it.

No Bill of Attainder or ex post facto Law shall be passed.

No Capitation, or other direct, Tax shall be laid, unless in Proportion to the Census or Enumeration herein before directed to be taken.

No Tax on Duty shall be laid on Articles exported from any State.

No Preference shall be given by any Regulation of Commerce or Revenue to the Ports of one State over those of another; nor shall Vessels bound to, or from, one State, be obliged to enter, clear, or pay Duties in another.

No Money shall be drawn from the Treasury, but in Consequence of Appropriations made by Law; and a regular Statement and Account of the Receipts and Expenditures of all public Money shall be published from time to time.

No Title of Nobility shall be granted by the United States; And no Person holding any Office of Profit or Trust under them, shall, without the Consent of the Congress, accept of any present, Emolument, Office, or Title, of any kind whatever, from any King, Prince, or foreign State.

Section 10

No State shall enter into any Treaty, Alliance, or Confederation; grant Letters of Marque and Reprisal; coin Money; emit Bills of Credit; make any Thing but gold and silver Coin a Tender in Payment of Debts; pass any Bill of Attainder, ex post facto Law, or Law impairing the Obligation of Contracts, or grant any Title of Nobility.

No State shall, within the Consent of the Congress, lay any Imposts or Duties on Imports or Exports, except what may be absolutely necessary for executing its inspection Laws; and the net Produce of all Duties and Imposts, laid by any State on Imports or Exports, shall be for the Use of the Treasury of the United States; and all such Laws shall be subject to the Revision and Control of the Congress.

No State shall, without the Consent of Congress, lay any Duty of Tonnage, keep Troops, or Ships of War in Time of Peace, enter into any Agreement or Compact with another State, or with a foreign Power, or engage in War, unless actually invaded, or in such imminent Danger as will not admit of Delay.

Article II

Section 1

The executive Power shall be vested in a President of the United States of America. He shall hold his Office during the Term of four Years, and, together with the Vice-President, chosen for the same Term, be elected, as follows:

Each State shall appoint, in such Manner as the Legislature thereof may direct, a Number of Electors, equal to the whole Number of Senators and Representatives to which the State may be entitled in the Congress: but no Senator or Representative, or Person holding an Office of Trust or Profit under the United States, shall be appointed an Elector.

The Electors shall meet in their respective States, and vote by Ballot for two Persons, of whom one at least shall be an Inhabitant of the same State with themselves. And they shall make a List of all the Persons voted for, and of the Number of Votes for each; which List they shall sign and certify, and transmit sealed to the Seat of the Government of the United States, directed to the President of the Senate. The President of the Senate shall, in the Presence of the Senate and House of Representatives, open all the Certificates, and the Votes shall then be counted. The Person having the greatest Number of Votes shall be the President, if such Number be a Majority of the whole Number of Electors appointed; and if there be more than one who have such Majority, and have an equal Number of Votes, then the House of Representatives shall immediately choose by Ballot one of them for President; and if no Person have a Majority, then from the five highest on the List the said House shall in like Manner choose the President. But in choosing the President, the Votes shall be taken by States, the Representation from each State having one Vote. A Quorum for this Purpose shall consist of a Member or Members from two-thirds of the States, and a Majority of all the States shall be necessary to a Choice. In every Case, after the Choice of the President, the Person having the greatest Number of Votes of the Electors shall be the Vice-President. But if there should remain two or more who have equal Votes, the Senate shall choose from them by Ballot the Vice-President.

The Congress may determine the Time of choosing the Electors, and the Day on which they shall give their Votes; which Day shall be the same throughout the United States.

No Person except a natural born Citizen, or a Citizen of the United States, at the time of the Adoption of this Constitution, shall be eligible to the Office of President;

neither shall any Person be eligible to that Office who shall not have attained to the Age of thirty-five Years, and been fourteen Years a Resident within the United States.

In Case of the Removal of the President from Office, or of his Death, Resignation, or Inability to discharge the Powers and Duties of the said Office, the Same shall devolve on the Vice-President, and the Congress may by Law provide for the Case of Removal, Death, Resignation or Inability, both of the President and Vice-President, declaring what Officer shall then act as President, and such Officer shall act accordingly, until the Disability be removed, or a President shall be elected.

The President shall, at stated Times, receive for his Services, a Compensation which shall neither be increased nor diminished during the Period for which he shall have been elected, and he shall not receive within that Period any other Emolument from the United States, or any of them.

Before he enter on the Execution of his Office, he shall take the following Oath or Affirmation—"I do solemnly swear (or affirm) that I will faithfully execute the office of the President of the United States, and will, to the best of my Ability, preserve, protect and defend the Constitution of the United States."

Section 2

The President shall be Commander in Chief of the Army and Navy of the United States, and of the Militia of the several States, when called into actual Service of the United States; he may require the Opinion, in writing, of the principal Office in each of the executive Departments, upon any Subject relating to the Duties of their respective Offices, and he shall have Power to grant Reprieves and Pardons for Offences against the United States, except in Cases of Impeachment.

He shall have Power, by and with the Advice and Consent of the Senate, to make Treaties, provided two-thirds of the Senators present concur; and he shall nominate, and by and with the Advice and Consent of the Senate, shall appoint Ambassadors, other public Ministers and Consuls, Judges of the Supreme Court, and all other Officers of the United States, whose Appointments are not herein otherwise provided for, and which shall be established by Law: but the Congress may by Law vest the Appointment of such inferior Officers, as they think proper, in the President alone, in the Courts of Law, or in the Heads of Departments.

The President shall have Power to fill up all Vacancies that may happen during the Recess of the Senate, by granting Commissions which shall expire at the End of their next Session.

Section 3

He shall from time to time give to the Congress Information of the State of the Union, and recommend to their Consideration such Measures as he shall judge necessary and expedient; he may, on extraordinary Occasions, convene both Houses, or either of them, and in Case of Disagreement between them, with Respect to the Time of Adjournment, he may adjourn them to such Time as he shall think proper; he shall receive Ambassadors and other public Ministers; he shall take Care that the Laws be faithfully executed, and shall Commission all the Officers of the United States.

Section 4

The President, Vice-President and all civil Officers of the United States, shall be removed from Office on Impeachment for, and Conviction of, Treason, Bribery, or other high Crimes and Misdemeanors.

Article III

Section 1

The judicial Power of the United States shall be vested in one Supreme Court, and in such inferior Courts as the Congress may from time to time ordain and establish. The Judges, both of the Supreme and inferior Courts, shall hold their Offices during good Behavior, and shall, at stated Times, receive for their Services, a Compensation, which shall not be diminished during their Continuance in Office.

Section 2

The judicial Power shall extend to all Cases, in Law and Equity, arising under this Constitution, the Laws of the United States, and Treaties made, or which shall be made, under their Authority;—to all Cases affecting Ambassadors, other public Ministers and Consuls;—to all Cases of admiralty and maritime Jurisdiction;—to Controversies to which the United States shall be a Party;—to Controversies between two or more States;—between a State and Citizens of another State;—between Citizens of different States;—between Citizens of the same State claiming Lands under Grants of different States, and between a State, or the Citizens thereof, and foreign States, Citizens or Subjects.

In all Cases affecting Ambassadors, other public Ministers and Consuls, and those in which a State shall be Party, the Supreme Court shall have original Jurisdiction. In all the other Cases before mentioned, the Supreme Court shall have appellate Jurisdiction, both as to Law and Fact, with such Exceptions, and under such Regulations as the Congress shall make.

The Trial of all Crimes, except in Cases of Impeachment, shall be by Jury; and such Trial shall be held in the State where the said Crimes shall have been committed; but where not committed within any State, the Trial shall be at such Place or Places as the Congress may by Law have directed.

Section 3

Treason against the United States, shall consist only in levying War against them, or in adhering to their Enemies, giving them Aid and Comfort. No Person shall be convicted of Treason unless on the Testimony of two Witnesses to the same overt Act, or of Confession in open Court.

The Congress shall have Power to declare the Punishment of Treason, but no Attainder of Treason shall work Corruption of Blood, or Forfeiture except during the Life of the Person attained.

Article IV

Section 1

Full Faith and Credit shall be given in each State to the public Acts, Records and judicial Proceedings of every other State. And the Congress may by general Laws prescribe the Manner in which such Acts, Records and Proceedings shall be proved, and the Effect thereof.

Section 2

The Citizens of each State shall be entitled to all Privileges and Immunities of Citizens in the several States.

A Person charged in any State with Treason, Felony, or other Crime, who shall flee from Justice, and be found in another State, shall on Demand of the executive Authority of the State from which he fled, be delivered up, to be removed to the State having Jurisdiction of the Crime.

No Person held to Service or Labour in one State, under the Laws thereof, escaping into another, shall, in Consequence of any Law or Regulation therein, be discharged from such Service or Labour, but shall be delivered up on Claim of the Party to whom such Service of Labour may be due.

Section 3

New States may be admitted by the Congress into this Union; but no new States shall be formed or erected within the Jurisdiction of any other State; nor any State be formed by the Junction of two or more States, or Parts of States, without the Consent of the Legislatures of the States concerned as well as of the Congress.

The Congress shall have Power to dispose of and make all needful Rules and Regulations respecting the Territory or other Property belonging to the United States; and nothing in this Constitution shall be so construed as to prejudice any Claims of the United States, of any particular State.

Section 4

The United States shall guarantee to every State in this Union a Republican Form of Government, and shall protect each of them against Invasion; and on Application of the Legislature, or of the Executive (when the Legislature cannot be convened) against domestic Violence.

Article V

The Congress, whenever two-thirds of both Houses shall deem it necessary, shall propose Amendments to this Constitution, or, on the Application of the Legislatures of two-thirds of the several States, shall call a Convention for proposing Amendments, which, in either Case, shall be valid to all Intents and Purposes, as Part of this Constitution, when ratified by the Legislatures of three-fourths of the several States, or by Conventions in three-fourths thereof, as the one or the other Mode of Ratification may be proposed by the Congress; Provided *that no Amendment which may be made prior to the Year One thousand eight hundred and eight* shall in any Manner affect the first and fourth Clauses in the Ninth Section of the first Article; and that no State, without its Consent, shall be deprived of its equal Suffrage in the Senate.

Article VI

All Debts contracted and Engagements entered into, before the Adoption of this Constitution, shall be as valid against the United States under this Constitution, as under the Confederation.

This Constitution, and the Laws of the United States which shall be made in Pursuance thereof and all Treaties made, or which shall be made, under the Authority of the United States, shall be the supreme Law of the Land; and the Judges in every State shall be bound thereby, any Thing in the Constitution or Laws of any State to the Contrary notwithstanding.

The Senators and Representatives before mentioned, and the Members of the several State Legislatures, and all executive and judicial Officers, both of the United States and of the several States, shall be bound by Oath or Affirmation, to support this Constitution; but no religious Test shall ever be required as a Qualification to any Office or public Trust under the United States.

Article VII

The Ratification of the Conventions of nine States, shall be sufficient for the Establishment of this Constitution between the States so ratifying the Same.

DONE in Convention by the Unanimous Consent of the States present the Seventeenth Day of September in the Year of our Lord one thousand seven hundred and Eighty-seven and of the Independence of the United States of America the Twelfth. In witness whereof We have hereunto subscribed our Names,

Attest William Jackson Secretary

G° Washington —

Presidt. and deputy

from Virginia

New Hampshire

John Langdon

Nicholas Gilman

Massachusetts

Nathaniel Gorham

Rufus King

Connecticut

Wm. Saml. Johnson

Roger Sherman

New York

Alexander Hamilton

New Jersey

Wil: Livingston

David Brearley.

Wm. Paterson.

Jona: Dayton

Pennsylvania

B. Franklin

Thomas Mifflin

Robt. Morris

Geo. Clymer

Thos. FitzSimons

Jared Ingersoll

James Wilson

Gouv Morris

Delaware

Geo: Read

Gunning Bedford Jun

John Dickinson

Richard Bassett

Jaco: Broom

Maryland

James McHenry

Dan of St. Thos Jenifer

Danl. Carroll

Virginia

John Blair —

James Madison Jr.

North Carolina

Wm. Blount

Richd. Dobbs Spaight.

Hu Williamson

South Carolina

J. Rutledge

Charles Cotesworth Pinckney

Charles Pinckney

Pierce Butler

Georgia

William Few

Abr Baldwin

Amendments to the Constitution of the United States of America

Amendment I

Congress shall make no law respecting an establishment of religion, or prohibiting the free exercise thereof; abridging the freedom of speech, or of the press; or of the right of the people peaceably to assemble and to petition the Government for a redress of grievances.

Amendment II

A well regulated Militia, being necessary to the security of a free State, the right of the people to keep and bear Arms, shall not be infringed.

Amendment III

No Soldier shall, in time of peace be quartered in any house, without the consent of the Owner, nor in time of war, but in a manner to be prescribed by law.

Amendment IV

The right of the people to be secure in their persons, houses, papers, and effects, against unreasonable searches and seizures, shall not be violated, and no Warrants shall issue, but upon probable cause, supported by Oath or affirmation and particularly describing the place to be searched, and the persons or things to be seized.

Amendment V

No person shall be held to answer for a capital, or otherwise infamous crime, unless on a presentment or indictment of a Grand Jury, except in cases arising in the land or naval forces, or in the Militia, when in actual service in time of War or public danger; nor shall any person be subject for the same offence to be twice put in jeopardy of life or limb; nor shall be compelled in any criminal case to be a witness against himself, nor be deprived of life, liberty, or property, without due process of law; nor shall private property be taken for public use, without just compensation.

Amendment VI

In all criminal prosecutions, the accused shall enjoy the right to a speedy and public trial, by an impartial jury of the State and district wherein the crime shall have been committed, which district shall have been previously ascertained by law, and to be informed of the nature and cause of the accusation: to be confronted with the witnesses against him; to have compulsory process for obtaining witnesses in his favor, and to have the Assistance of Counsel for his defence.

Amendment VII

In suits at common law, where the value in controversy shall exceed twenty dollars, the right of trial by jury shall be preserved, and no fact tried by jury, shall be otherwise reexamined in any Court of the United States, than according to the rules of the common law.

Amendment VIII

Excessive bail shall not be required, nor excessive fines imposed, nor cruel and unusual punishments inflicted.

Amendment IX

The enumeration in the Constitution, of certain rights, shall not be construed to deny or disparage others retained by the people.

Amendment X

The powers not delegated to the United States by the Constitution, nor prohibited by it to the States, are reserved to the States respectively, or to the people.

(Ratification of first ten amendments completed December 15, 1791.)

Amendment XI

The Judicial power of the United States shall not be construed to extend to any suit in law or equity, commenced or prosecuted against one of the United States by Citizens of another State, or by Citizens or Subjects of any Foreign State.

(Declared ratified January 8, 1798.)

Amendment XII

The electors shall meet in their respective states and vote by ballot for President and Vice-President, one of whom, at least, shall not be an inhabitant of the same state with themselves; they shall name in their ballots the person voted for as President, and in distinct ballots the person voted for as Vice-President, and they shall make distinct lists of all persons voted for as President, and of all persons voted for as Vice-President, and of the number of votes for each, which lists they shall sign and certify, and transmit sealed to the seat of the government of the United States, directed to the President of the Senate;—The President of the Senate shall, in presence of the Senate and House of Representatives, open all the certificates and the votes shall then be counted;—The person having the greatest number of votes for President, shall be the President, if such number be a majority of the whole number of Electors appointed; and if no person have such majority, then from the persons having the highest numbers not exceeding three on the list of those voted for as President, the House of Representatives shall choose immediately, by ballot, the President. But in choosing the President, the votes shall be taken by states, the representation from each state having one vote; a quorum for this purpose shall consist of a member or members from two-thirds of the states, and a majority of all the states shall be necessary to a choice. *[and if the House of Representatives shall not choose a President whenever the right of choice shall devolve upon them, before the fourth day of March next following, then the Vice-President shall act as President, as in the case of the death or other constitutional disability of the President.] — The person having the greatest number of votes as Vice-President, shall be the Vice-President, if such number be a majority of the whole number of Electors appointed, and if no person have a majority, then from the two highest numbers on the list, the Senate shall choose the Vice-President; a quorum for the purpose shall consist of two-thirds of the whole number of Senators, and a majority of the whole number shall be necessary to a choice. But no person constitutionally ineligible to the office of President shall be eligible to that of Vice-President of the United States.

(Declared ratified September 25, 1804.)

Amendment XIII

Section 1

Neither slavery nor involuntary servitude, except as a punishment for crime whereof the party shall have been duly convicted, shall exist within the United States, or any place subject to their jurisdiction.

Section 2

Congress shall have power to enforce this article by appropriate legislation.

(Declared ratified December 18, 1865.)

Amendment XIV

Section 1

All persons born or naturalized in the United States, and subject to the jurisdiction thereof, are citizens of the United States and of the State wherein they reside. No State shall make or enforce any law which shall abridge the privileges or immunities of citizens of the United States; nor shall any State deprive any person of life, liberty, or property, without due process of law; nor deny to any person within its jurisdiction the equal protection of the laws.

Section 2

Representatives shall be apportioned among the several States according to their respective numbers, counting the whole number of persons in each State, excluding Indians not taxed. But when the right to vote at any election for the choice of electors for President and Vice-President of the United States, Representatives in Congress, the Executive and Judicial officers of a State, or the members of the Legislature thereof, is denied to any of the male inhabitants of such State, being twenty-one years of age, and citizens of the United States, or in any way abridged, except for participation in rebellion, or other crime, the basis of representation therein shall be reduced in the proportion which the number of such male citizens shall bear to the whole number of male citizens twenty-one years of age in such State.

Section 3

No person shall be a Senator or Representative in Congress, or elector of President and Vice-President, or hold any office, civil or military, under the United States, or under any State, who, having previously taken an oath, as a member of Congress, or as an officer of the United States, or as a member of any State legislature, or as an executive or judicial officer of any State, to support the Constitution of the United States, shall have engaged in insurrection or rebellion against the same, or given aid or comfort to the enemies thereof. But Congress may by a vote of two-thirds of each House, remove such disability.

Section 4

The validity of the public debt of the United States, authorized by law, including debts incurred for payment of pensions and bounties for services in suppressing insurrection or rebellion, shall not be questioned. But neither the United States nor any State shall assume or pay any debt or obligation incurred in aid of insurrection or rebellion against the United States, or any claim for the loss or emancipation of any slave; but all such debts, obligations and claims shall be held illegal and void.

Section 5

The Congress shall have power to enforce, by appropriate legislation, the provisions of this article.

(Declared ratified July 28, 1868.)

Amendment XV

Section 1

The right of citizens of the United States to vote shall not be denied or abridged by the United States or by any State on account of race, color, or previous condition of servitude—

Section 2

The Congress shall have power to enforce this article by appropriate legislation.

(Declared ratified March 30, 1870.)

Amendment XVI

The Congress shall have power to lay and collect taxes on incomes, from whatever source derived, without apportionment among the several States, and without regard to any census or enumeration.

(Declared ratified February 25, 1913.)

Amendment XVII

The Senate of the United States shall be composed of two Senators from each State, elected by the people thereof, for six years; and each Senator shall have one vote. The electors in each State shall have the qualifications requisite for electors of the most numerous branch of the State legislatures.

When vacancies happen in the representation of any State in the Senate, the executive authority of such State shall issue writs of election to fill such vacancies: Provided, That the legislature of any State may empower the executive thereof to make temporary appointments until the people fill the vacancies by election as the legislature may direct.

This amendment shall not be so construed as to affect the election or term of any Senator chosen before it becomes valid as part of the Constitution.

(Declared ratified May 31, 1913.)

Amendment XVIII

Section 1

After one year from the ratification of this article the manufacture, sale, or transportation of intoxicating liquors within, the importation thereof into, or the exportation thereof from the United States and all territory subject to the jurisdiction thereof for beverage purposes is hereby prohibited.

Section 2

The Congress and the several States shall have concurrent power to enforce this article by appropriate legislation.

Section 3

This article shall be inoperative unless it shall have been ratified as an amendment to the Constitution by the legislatures of the several States, as provided in the Constitution, within seven years from the date of submission hereof to the States by the Congress]*

(Declared ratified January 29, 1919.)

Amendment XIX

The right of citizens of the United States to vote shall not be denied or abridged by the United States or by any State on account of sex.

Congress shall have power to enforce this article by appropriate legislation.

(Declared ratified August 26, 1920.)

Amendment XX

Section 1

The terms of the President and Vice-President shall end at noon on the 20th day of January, and the terms of Senators and Representatives at noon on the 3d day of January, of the years in which such terms would have ended if this article had not been ratified; and the terms of their successors shall then begin.

Section 2

The Congress shall assemble at least once in every year, and such meeting shall begin at noon on the 3d day of January, unless they shall by law appoint a different day.

Section 3

If, at the time for the beginning of the term of the President, the President elect shall have died, the Vice-President elect shall become President. If a President shall not have been chosen before the time fixed for the beginning of his term, or if the President elect shall have failed to qualify, then the Vice-President elect shall act as President until a President shall have qualified; and the Congress may by law provide for the case wherein neither a President elect nor a Vice-President elect shall have qualified, declaring who shall then act as President, or the manner in which one who is to act shall be selected, and such person shall act accordingly until a President or Vice-President shall have qualified.

Section 4

The Congress may by law provide for the case of the death of any of the persons from whom the House of Representatives may choose a President whenever the right of choice shall have devolved upon them and for the case of the death of any of the persons from whom the Senate may choose a Vice-President whenever the right of choice shall have devolved upon them.

Section 5

Sections 1 and 2 shall take effect on the 15th day of October following the ratification of this article.

Section 6

This article shall be inoperative unless it shall have been ratified as an amendment to the Constitution by the legislatures of three-fourths of the several States within seven years from the date of its submission.

(Declared ratified February 6, 1933.)

Amendment XXI

Section 1

The eighteenth article of amendment to the Constitution of the United States is hereby repealed.

Section 2

The transportation or importation into any State, Territory, or possession of the United States for delivery or use therein of intoxicating liquors, in violation of the laws thereof, is hereby prohibited.

Section 3

This article shall be inoperative unless it shall have been ratified as an amendment to the Constitution by conventions in the several States, as provided in the Constitution, within seven years from the date of the submission hereof to the States by the Congress.

(Declared ratified December 5, 1933.)

Amendment XXII

Section 1

No person shall be elected to the office of the President more than twice, and no person who has held the office of President, or acted as President, for more than two years of a term to which some other person was elected President shall be elected to the office of the President more than once. But this article shall not apply to any person holding the office of President when this Article was proposed by the Congress, and shall not prevent any person who may be holding the office of President, or acting as President, during the term within which this Article becomes operative from holding the office of President or acting as President during the remainder of such term.

Section 2

This article shall be inoperative unless it shall have been ratified as an amendment to the Constitution by the legislatures of three-fourths of the several States within seven years from the date of its submission to the States by the Congress.

(Declared ratified March 1, 1951.)

Amendment XXIII

Section 1

The District constituting the seat of Government of the United States shall appoint in such manner as the Congress may direct:

A number of electors of President and Vice President equal to the whole number of Senators and Representatives in Congress to which the District would be entitled if it were a State, but in no event more than the least populous State; they shall be in addition to those appointed by the States, but they shall be considered, for the purposes of the election of President and Vice President, to be electors appointed by a State; and they shall meet in the District and perform such duties as provided by the twelfth article of amendment.

Section 2

The Congress shall have power to enforce this article by appropriate legislation.

(Declared ratified April 3, 1961.)

Amendment XXIV

Section 1

The right of citizens of the United States to vote in any primary or other election for President or Vice President, for electors for President or Vice President, or for Senator or Representative in Congress, shall not be denied or abridged by the United States or any State by reason of failure to pay any poll tax or other tax.

Section 2

The Congress shall have power to enforce this article by appropriate legislation.

(Declared ratified February 4, 1962.)

Amendment XXV

Section 1

In case of the removal of the President from office or of his death or resignation, the Vice President shall become President.

Section 2

Whenever there is a vacancy in the office of the Vice President, the President shall nominate a Vice President who shall take office upon confirmation by a majority vote of both Houses of Congress.

Section 3

Whenever the President transmits to the President pro tempore of the Senate and the Speaker of the House of Representatives his written declaration that he is unable to discharge the powers and duties of his office, and until he transmits to them a written declaration to the contrary, such powers and duties shall be discharged by the Vice President as Acting President.

Section 4

Whenever the Vice President and a majority of either the principal officers of the executive departments or of such other body as Congress may by law provide, transmit to the President pro tempore of the Senate and the Speaker of the House of Representatives their written declaration that the President is unable to discharge the powers and duties of his office, the Vice President shall immediately assume the powers and the duties of the office as Acting President.

Thereafter, when the President transmits to the President pro tempore of the Senate and the Speaker of the House of Representatives his written declaration that no inability exists, he shall resume the power and duties of his office unless the Vice President and a majority of either the principal officers of the executive department or of such other body as Congress may by law provide, transmit within four days to the President pro tempore of the Senate and the Speaker of the House of Representatives their written declaration that the President is unable to discharge the powers and duties of his office. Thereupon Congress shall decide the issue, assembling within forty-eight hours for that purpose if not in session. If the Congress, within twenty-one days after receipt of the latter written declaration, or, if Congress is not in session, within twenty-one days after Congress is required to assemble, determines by two-thirds vote of both Houses that the President is unable to discharge the powers and duties of his office, the Vice President shall continue to discharge the same as Acting President; otherwise, the President shall resume the powers and duties of his office.

(Declared ratified February 10, 1967.)

Amendment XXVI

Section 1

The right of citizens of the United States, who are eighteen years of age or older, to vote shall not be denied or abridged by the United States or by any state on account of age.

Section 2

The Congress shall have the power to enforce this article by appropriate legislation. (Declared Ratified, 1971.)

Amendment XXVII

No law, varying the compensation for the services of the Senators and Representatives, shall take effect, until an election of Representatives shall have intervened.

Mapp v. Ohio

Supreme Court of the United States.
367 U.S. 643, 81 S.Ct. 1684, 6 L.Ed.2d 1081 (1961).

Mr. Justice CLARK delivered the opinion of the Court....

On May 23, 1957, three Cleveland police officers arrived at appellant's residence in that city pursuant to information that "a person [was] hiding out in the home, who was wanted for questioning in connection with a recent bombing, and that there was a large amount of police paraphernalia being hidden in the home." ... Upon their arrival at that house, the officers knocked on the door and demanded entrance but appellant, after telephoning her attorney, refused to admit them without a search warrant. They advised their headquarters of the situation and undertook a surveillance of the house.

The officers again sought entrance three hours later when four or more additional officers arrived on the scene. When Miss Mapp did not come to the door immediately, at least one of the several doors to the house was forcibly opened and the policemen gained admittance. Meanwhile Miss Mapp's attorney arrived, but the officers, having secured their own entry, and continuing in their defiance of the law, would permit him neither to see Miss Mapp nor to enter the house. It appears that Miss Mapp was halfway down the stairs from the upper floor to the front door when the officers, in this high-handed manner, broke into the hall. She demanded to see the search warrant. A paper, claimed to be a warrant, was held up by one of the officers. She grabbed the "warrant" and placed it in her bosom. A struggle ensued in which the officers recovered the piece of paper and as a result of which they handcuffed appellant because she had been "belligerent" in resisting their official rescue of the "warrant" from her person. Running roughshod over appellant, a policeman "grabbed" her, "twisted [her] hand," and she "yelled [and] pleaded with him" because "it was hurting." Appellant, in handcuffs, was then forcibly taken upstairs to her bedroom where the officers searched a dresser, a chest of drawers, a closet and some suitcases. They also looked into a photo album and through personal papers belonging to the appellant. The search spread to the rest of the second floor including the child's bedroom, the living room, the kitchen and a dinette. The basement of the building and a trunk found therein were also searched. The obscene materials for possession of which she was ultimately convicted were discovered in the course of that widespread search.

At the trial no search warrant was produced by the prosecution, nor was the failure to produce one explained or accounted for. At best, "There is, in the record, considerable doubt as to whether there ever was any warrant for the search of defendant's home." ...

... [T]his Court in *Weeks v. United States*, 232 U.S. 383, 34 S.Ct. 341, 58 L.Ed. 652 (1914), stated that "the Fourth Amendment ... put the courts of the United States and Federal officials, in the exercise of their power and authority, under limitations and restraints [and] ... forever secure[d] the people, their persons, houses, papers and effects against all unreasonable searches and seizures under the guise of law ... and the duty of giving to it force and effect is obligatory upon all entrusted under our Federal system with the enforcement of the laws." At pp. 391-392.

Specifically dealing with the use of the evidence unconstitutionally seized, the Court concluded:

> "If letters and private documents can thus be seized and held and used in evidence against a citizen accused of an offense, the protection of the Fourth Amendment declaring his right to be secure against such searches and seizures is of no value, and, so far as those thus placed are concerned, might as well be stricken from the Constitution. The efforts of the courts and their officials to bring the guilty to punishment, praiseworthy as they are, are not to be aided by the sacrifice of those great principles established by years of endeavor and suffering which have resulted in their embodiment in the fundamental law of the land." At p.393.

"The striking outcome of the *Weeks* case and those which followed it was the sweeping declaration that the Fourth Amendment, although not referring to or limiting the use of evidence in courts, really forbade its introduction if obtained by government officers through a violation of the Amendment." ...

In 1949, 35 years after *Weeks* was announced, this Court, in

...

Wolf v. Colorado,..., again for the first time, discussed the effect of the Fourth Amendment upon the States through the operation of the Due Process Clause of the Fourteenth Amendment. It said:

> "[W]e have no hesitation in saying that were a State affirmatively to sanction such police incursion into privacy it would run counter to the guaranty of the Fourteenth Amendment." ...

Nevertheless, ... the Court decided that the Weeks exclusionary rule would not then be imposed upon the States as "an essential ingredient of the right." ... While in 1949, prior to the Wolf case, almost two-thirds of the States were opposed to the use of the exclusionary rule, now, despite the Wolf case, more than half of those since passing upon it, by their own legislative or judicial decision, have wholly or partly adopted or adhered to the Weeks rule.... Significantly, among those now following the rule is California, which, according to its highest court, was "compelled to reach that conclusion because other remedies have completely failed to secure compliance with the constitutional provisions...."

...

Today we once again examine *Wolfs* constitutional documentation of the right to privacy free from unreasonable state intrusion, and, after its dozen years on our books, are led by it to close the only courtroom door remaining open to evidence secured by official lawlessness in flagrant abuse of that basic right, reserved to all persons as a specific guarantee against that very same unlawful conduct. We hold that all evidence obtained by searches and seizures in violation of the Constitution is, by that same authority, inadmissible in a state court.

Since the Fourth Amendment's right of privacy has been declared enforceable against the States through the Due Process Clause of the Fourteenth, it is enforceable against them by the same sanction of exclusion as is used against the Federal Government. Were it otherwise, then just as without the Weeks rule the assurance against unreasonable federal searches and seizures would be "a form of words," valueless and undeserving of mention in a perpetual charter of inestimable human liberties, so too, without that rule the freedom from state invasions of privacy would be so ephemeral and so neatly severed from its conceptual nexus with the freedom from all brutish means of coercing evidence as not to mend this Court's high regard as a freedom "implicit in the concept of ordered liberty." ... In short, the admission of the new constitutional right by *Wolf* could not consistently tolerate denial of its most important constitutional privilege, namely, the exclusion of the evidence which an accused had been forced to give by reason of the unlawful seizure. To hold otherwise is to grant the right but in reality to withhold its privilege and enjoyment. Only last year the Court itself recognized that the purpose of the exclusionary rule "is to deter—to compel respect for the constitutional guaranty in the only effectively available way—by removing the incentive to disregard it."

  ...

There are those who say, as did Justice (then Judge) Cardozo, that under our constitutional exclusionary doctrine "[t]he criminal is to go free because the constable has blundered." *People v. Defore*, 242 N.Y., at 21, 150 N.E., at 587. In some cases this will undoubtedly be the result. But, as was said in Elkins, "there is another consideration—the imperative of judicial integrity." 364 U.S., at 222. The criminal goes free, if he must, but it is the law that sets him free. Nothing can destroy a government more quickly than its failure to observe its own laws, or worse, its disregard of the charter of its own existence. As

Mr. Justice Brandeis, dissenting, said in *Olmstead v. United States*, 277 U.S. 438, 485, 48 S.Ct. 564, 72 L.Ed. 944 (1928): "Our Government is the potent, the omnipresent teacher. For good or for ill, it teaches the whole people by its example.... If the Government becomes a lawbreaker, it breeds contempt for law; it invites every man to become a law unto himself; it invites anarchy." Nor can it lightly be assumed that, as a practical matter, adoption of the exclusionary rule fetters law enforcement....

The ignoble shortcut to conviction left open to the State tends to destroy the entire system of constitutional restraints on which the liberties of the people rest. Having once recognized that the right to privacy embodied in the Fourth Amendment is enforceable against the States, and that the right to be secure against rude invasions of privacy by state officers, is, therefore, constitutional in origin, we can no longer permit that right to remain an empty promise. Because it is enforceable in the same manner and to like effect as other basic rights secured by the Due Process Clause, we can no longer permit it to be revocable at the whim of any police officer who, in the name of law enforcement itself, chooses to suspend its enjoyment. Our decision, founded on reason and truth, gives to the individual no more than that which the Constitution guarantees him, to the police officer no less than that to which honest law enforcement is entitled, and, to the courts, that judicial integrity so necessary in the true administration of justice.

The judgement of the Supreme Court of Ohio is reversed and the cause remanded for further proceedings not inconsistent with this opinion.

Reversed and remanded.

Miranda v. Arizona

Supreme Court of the United States, 1966.
384 U.S. 436, 86 S.Ct. 1602, 16 L.Ed.2d 694.

Mr. CHIEF JUSTICE WARREN delivered the opinion of the Court.

The cases before us raise questions which go to the roots of our concepts of American criminal jurisprudence: the restraints society must observe consistent with the Federal Constitution in prosecuting individuals for crime. More specifically, we deal with the admissibility of statements obtained from an individual who is subjected to custodial police interrogation and the necessity for procedures which assure that the individual is accorded his privilege under the Fifth Amendment to the Constitution not to be compelled to incriminate himself.

We dealt with certain phases of this problem recently in *Escobedo v. State of Illinois*, 378 U.S. 478, 84 S.Ct. 1758, 12 L.Ed.2d 977 (1964). There, as in the four cases before us, law enforcement officials took the defendant into custody and interrogated him in a police station for the purpose of obtaining a confession. The police did not effectively advise him of his right to remain silent or of his right to consult with his attorney. Rather, they confronted him with an alleged accomplice who accused him of having perpetrated a murder. When the defendant denied the accusation and said "I didn't shoot Manuel, you did it," they handcuffed him and took him to an interrogation room. There, while handcuffed and standing, he was questioned for four hours until he confessed. During this interrogation, the police denied his request to speak to his attorney, and they prevented his retained attorney, who had come to the police station, from consulting with him. At his trial, the State, over his objection, introduced the confession against him. We held that the statements thus made were constitutionally inadmissible.

This case has been the subject of judicial interpretation and spirited legal debate since it was decided two years ago. Both state and federal courts, in assessing its implications, have arrived at varying conclusions. A wealth of scholarly material has been written tracing its ramifications and underpinnings. Police and prosecutor have speculated on its range and desirability. We granted certiorari in these cases, 382 U.S. 924, 925, 937, 86 S.Ct. 318, 320, 395, 15 L.Ed.2d 338, 339, 348, in order further to explore some facets of the problems, thus exposed, of applying the privilege against self-incrimination to in-custody interrogation, and to give concrete constitutional guidelines for law enforcement agencies and courts to follow.

. . .

Our holding will be spelled out with some specificity in the pages which follow but briefly stated it is this: the prosecution may not use statements, whether exculpatory or inculpatory, stemming from custodial interrogation of the defendant unless it demonstrates the use of procedural safeguards effective to secure the privilege against self-incrimination. By custodial interrogation, we mean questioning initiated by law enforcement officers after a person has been taken into custody or otherwise deprived of his freedom of action in any significant way. As for the procedural safeguards to be employed, unless other fully effective means are devised to inform accused persons of their right of silence and to assure a continuous opportunity to exercise it, the following measures are required. Prior to any questioning, the person must be warned that he has a right to remain silent, that any statement he does make may be used as evidence against him, and that he has a right to the presence of an attorney, either retained or appointed. The defendant may waive effectuation of these rights, provided the waiver is made voluntarily, knowingly and intelligently. If, however, he indicates in any manner and at any stage of the process that he wishes to consult with an attorney before speaking there can be no questioning. Likewise, if the individual is alone and indicates in any manner that he does not wish to be interrogated, the police may not question him. The mere fact that he may have answered some questions or volunteered some statements on his own does not deprive him of the right to refrain from answering any further inquiries until he has consulted with an attorney and thereafter consents to be questioned.

I

The constitutional issue we decide in each of these cases is the admissibility of statements obtained from a defendant questioned while in custody or otherwise deprived of his freedom of action in any significant way. In each, the defendant was questioned by police officers, detectives, or a prosecuting attorney in a room in which he was cut off from the outside world. In none of these cases was the defendant given a full and effective warning of his rights at the outset of the interrogation process. In all the cases, the questioning elicited oral admissions, and in three of them, signed statements as well which were admitted at their trials. They all thus share salient features—incommunicado interrogation of individuals in a police-dominated atmosphere, resulting in self-incriminating statements without full warnings of constitutional rights.

An understanding of the nature and setting of this in-custody interrogation is essential to our decisions today. The difficulty in depicting what transpires at such interrogations stems from the fact that in this country they have largely taken place incommunicado. From extensive factual studies undertaken in the early 1930's, including the famous Wickersham Report to Congress by a Presidential Commission, it is clear that police violence and the "third degree" flourished at that time. In a series of cases decided by this Court long after these studies, the police resorted to physical brutality—beatings, hanging, whipping—and to sustained and protracted questioning incommunicado in order to extort confessions. The Commission on Civil Rights in 1961 found much evidence to indicate that "some policemen still resort to physical force to obtain confessions," 1961 Comm'n on Civil Rights Rep., Justice, pt. 5, 17. The use of physical brutality and violence is not, unfortunately, relegated to the past or to any part of the country. Only recently in Kings County, New York, the police brutally beat, kicked and placed lighted cigarette butts on the back of a potential witness under interrogation for the purpose of securing a statement incriminating a third party. *People v. Portelli*, 15 N.Y.2d 235, 257 N.Y.S.2d 931, 205 N.E.2d 857 (1965).

The examples given above are undoubtedly the exception now, but they are sufficiently widespread to be the object of concern. Unless a proper limitation upon custodial interrogation is achieved—such as these decisions will advance—there can be no assurance that practices of this nature will be eradicated in the foreseeable future.

...

Again we stress that the modern practice of in-custody interrogation is psychologically rather than physically oriented. As we have stated before, "*Since Chambers v. State of Florida,* 309 U.S. 227, 60 S.Ct. 472, 84 L.Ed. 716, this Court has recognized that coercion can be mental as well as physical, and that the blood of the accused is not the only hallmark of an unconstitutional inquisition." *Blackburn v. State of Alabama,* 361 U.S. 199, 206, 80 S.Ct. 274, 279, 4 L.Ed.2d 242 (1960). Interrogation still takes place in privacy. Privacy results in secrecy and this in turn results in a gap in our knowledge as to what in fact goes on in the interrogation rooms. A valuable source of information about present police practices, however, may be found in various police manuals and texts which document procedures employed with success in the past, and which recommend various other effective tactics. These texts are used by law enforcement agencies themselves as guides. It should be noted that these texts professedly present the most enlightened and effective means presently used to obtain statements through custodial interrogation. By considering these texts and other data, it is possible to describe procedures observed and noted around the country.

The officers are told by the manuals that the "principal psychological factor contributing to a successful interrogation is privacy—being alone with the person under interrogation." The efficacy of this tactic has been explained as follows:

> "If at all practicable, the interrogation should take place in the investigator's office or at least in a room of his own choice. The subject should be deprived of every psychological advantage. In his own home he may be confident, indignant, or recalcitrant. He is more keenly aware of his rights and more reluctant to tell of his indiscretions or criminal behavior within the walls of his home. Moreover his family and other friends are nearby, their presence lending moral support. In his office, the investigator possesses all the advantages. The atmosphere suggests the invincibility of the forces of the law."

To highlight the isolation and unfamiliar surroundings, the manuals instruct the police to display an air of confidence in the suspect's guilt and from outward appearance to maintain only an interest in confirming certain details. The guilt of the subject is to be posited as a fact. The interrogator should direct his comments toward the reasons why the subject committed the act, rather than court failure by asking the subject whether he did it. Like other men, perhaps the subject has had a bad family life, had an unhappy childhood, had too much to drink, had an unrequited desire for women. The officers are instructed to minimize the moral seriousness of the offense, to cast blame on the victim or on society. These tactics are designed to put the subject in a psychological state where his story is but an elaboration of what the police purport to know already—that he is guilty. Explanations to the contrary are dismissed and discouraged.

The texts thus stress that the major qualities an interrogator should possess are patience and perseverance. One writer describes the efficacy of these characteristics in this manner:

> "In the preceding paragraphs emphasis has been placed on kindness and stratagems. The investigator will, however, encounter many situations where the sheer weight of his personality will be the deciding factor. Where emotional appeals and tricks are employed to no avail, he must rely on an oppressive atmosphere of dogged persistence. He must interrogate steadily and without relent, leaving the subject no prospect of surcease. He must dominate his subject and overwhelm him with his inexorable will to obtain the truth. He should interrogate for a spell of several hours pausing only for the subject's necessities in acknowledgement of the need to avoid a charge of duress that can be technically substantiated. In a serious case, the interrogation may continue for days, with the required intervals for food and sleep, but with no respite from the atmosphere of domination. It is possible in this way to induce the subject to talk without resorting to duress or coercion. The method should be used only when the guilt of the subject appears highly probable."

The manuals suggest that the suspect be offered legal excuses for his actions in order to obtain an initial admission of guilt. Where there is a suspected

revenge-killing, for example, the interrogator may say:

"Joe, you probably didn't go out looking for this fellow with the purpose of shooting him. My guess is, however, that you expected something from him and that's why you carried a gun — for your own protection. You knew him for what he was, no good. Then when you met him he probably started using foul, abusive language and he gave some indication that he was about to pull a gun on you, and that's when you had to act to save your own life. That's about it, isn't it, Joe?"

Having then obtained the admission of shooting, the interrogator is advised to refer to circumstantial evidence which negates the self-defense explanation. This should enable him to secure the entire story. One text notes that "Even if he fails to do so, the inconsistency between the subject's original denial of the shooting and his present admission of at least doing the shooting will serve to deprive him of a self-defense 'out' at the time of trial."

When the techniques described above prove unavailing, the texts recommend they be alternated with a show of some hostility. One ploy often used has been termed the "friendly-unfriendly" or the "Mutt and Jeff" act:

"In this technique, two agents are employed. Mutt, the relentless investigator, who knows the subject is guilty and is not going to waste any time. He's sent a dozen men away for this crime and he's going to send the subject away for the full term. Jeff, on the other hand, is obviously a kindhearted man. He has a family himself. He has a brother who was involved in a little scrape like this. He disapproves of Mutt and his tactics and will arrange to get him off the case if the subject will cooperate. He can't hold Mutt off for very long. The subject would be wise to make a quick decision. The technique is applied by having both investigators present while Mutt acts out his role.

Jeff may stand by quietly and demur at some of Mutt's tactics. When Jeff makes his plea for cooperation, Mutt is not present in the room."

The interrogators sometimes are instructed to induce a confession out of trickery. The technique here is quite effective in crimes which require identification or which run in series. In the identification situation, the interrogator may take a break in his questioning to place the subject among a group of men in a line-up. "The witness or complainant (previously coached, if necessary) studies the line-up and confidently points out the subject as the guilty party." Then the questioning resumes "as though there were now no doubt about the guilt of the subject." A variation on this technique is called the "reverse line-up":

"The accused is placed in a line-up, but this time he is identified by several fictitious witnesses or victims who associated him with different offenses. It is expected that the subject will become desperate and confess to the offense under investigation in order to escape from the false accusations."

The manuals also contain instructions for police on how to handle the individual who refuses to discuss the matter entirely or who asks for an attorney or relatives. The examiner is to concede him the right to remain silent. "This usually has a very undermining effect. First of all, he is disappointed in his expectation of an unfavorable reaction in the part of the interrogator. Secondly, a concession of this right to remain silent impresses the subject with the apparent fairness of his interrogator." After this psychological conditioning, however, the officer is told to point out the incriminating significance of the suspect's refusal to talk:

"Joe, you have the right to remain silent. That's your privilege and I'm the last person in the world who'll try to take it away from you. If that's the way you want to leave this, O.K. But let me ask you this. Suppose you were in my shoes and I were in yours and you called me in to ask me about this and I told you,

'I don't want to answer any of your questions.' You'd think I had something to hide, and you'd probably be right in thinking that. That's exactly what I'll have to think about you, and so will everybody else. So let's sit here and talk this whole thing over."

Few will persist in their initial refusal to talk, it is said, if this monologue is employed correctly.

In the event that the subject wishes to speak to a relative or an attorney, the following advice is tendered:

"[T]he interrogator should respond by suggesting that the subject first tell the truth to the interrogator himself rather than get anyone else involved in the matter. If the request is for an attorney, the interrogator may suggest that the subject save himself or his family the expense of any such professional service, particularly if he is innocent of the offense under investigation. The interrogator may also add, 'Joe, I'm only looking for the truth, and if you're telling the truth, that's it. You can handle this by yourself.'"

From these representative samples of interrogation techniques, the setting prescribed by the manuals and observed in practice becomes clear. In essence, it is this: To be alone with the subject is essential to prevent distraction and to deprive him of any outside support. The aura of confidence in his guilt undermines his will to resist. He merely confirms the preconceived story the police seek to have him describe. Patience and persistence, at times relentless questioning, are employed. To obtain a confession, the interrogator must "patiently maneuver himself or his quarry into a position from which the desired objective may be attained." When normal procedures fail to produce the needed result, the police may resort to deceptive stratagems such as giving false legal advice. It is important to keep the subject off balance, for example, by trading on his insecurity about himself or his surroundings. The police then persuade, trick, or cajole him out of exercising his constitutional rights.

Even without employing brutality, the "third degree" or the specific stratagems described above, the very fact of custodial interrogation exacts a heavy toll on individual liberty and trades on the weakness of individuals. This fact may be illustrated simply by referring to three confession cases decided by this Court in the Term immediately preceding our *Escobedo* decision. In *Townsend v. Sain*, 372 U.S. 293, 83 S.Ct. 745, 9 L.Ed.2d 770 (1963), the defendant was a 19-year-old heroin addict, described as a "near mental defective," id., at 307-310, 83 S.Ct. at 754-755. The defendant in *Lynumn v. State of Illinois*, 372 U.S. 528, 83 S.Ct. 917, 9 L.Ed.2d 922 (1963), was a woman who confessed to the arresting officer after being importuned to "cooperate" in order to prevent her children from being taken by relief authorities. This Court as in those cases reversed the conviction of a defendant in *Haynes v. State of Washington*, 373 U.S. 503, 83 S.Ct. 1336, 10 L.Ed.2d 513 (1963), whose persistent request during his interrogation was to phone his wife or attorney. In other settings, these individuals might have exercised their constitutional rights. In the incommunicado police-dominated atmosphere, they succumbed.

In the cases before us today, given this background, we concern ourselves primarily with this interrogation atmosphere and the evils it can bring. In No. 759, *Miranda v. Arizona*, the police arrested the defendant and took him to a special interrogation room where they secured a confession. In No. 760, *Vignera v. New York*, the defendant made oral admissions to the police after interrogation in the afternoon, and then signed an inculpatory statement upon being questioned by an assistant district attorney later the same evening. In No. 761, *Westover v. United States*, the defendant was handed over to the Federal Bureau of Investigation by local authorities after they had detained and interrogated him for a lengthy period, both at night and the following morning. After some two hours of questioning, the federal officers had obtained signed statements from the defendant. Lastly, in No. 584, *California v. Stewart*, the local police held the defendant five days in the station and interrogated him on nine separate occasions before they secured his inculpatory statement.

In these cases, we might find the defendants' statements to have been involuntary in traditional terms. Our concern for adequate safeguards to protect precious Fifth Amendment rights is, of course, not lessened in the slightest. In each of the cases, the defendant was thrust into an unfamiliar atmosphere and run through menacing police interrogation procedures. The potentiality for compulsion is forcefully apparent, for example, in *Miranda*, where the indigent Mexican defendant was a seriously disturbed individual with pronounced sexual fantasies, and in Stewart, in which the defendant was an indigent Los Angeles Negro who had dropped out of school in the sixth grade. To be sure, the records do not evince overt physical coercion or patent psychological ploys. The fact remains that in none of these cases did the officers undertake to afford appropriate safeguards at the outset of the interrogation to insure that the statements were truly the product of free choice.

It is obvious that such an interrogation environment is created for no purpose other than to subjugate the individual to the will of his examiner. This atmosphere carries its own badge of intimidation. To be sure, this is not physical intimidation, but it is equally destructive of human dignity. The current practice of incommunicado interrogation is at odds with one of our Nation's most cherished principles — that the individual may not be compelled to incriminate himself. Unless adequate protective devices are employed to dispel the compulsion inherent in custodial surroundings, no statement obtained from the defendant can truly be the product of his free choice.

...

III

Today, then, there can be no doubt that the Fifth Amendment privilege is available outside of criminal court proceedings and serves to protect persons in all settings in which their freedom of action is curtailed in any significant way from being compelled to incriminate themselves. We have concluded that without proper safeguards the process of in-custody interrogation of persons suspected or accused of crime contains inherently compelling pressures which work to undermine the individual's will to resist and to compel him to speak where he would not otherwise do so freely. In order to combat these pressures and to permit a full opportunity to exercise the privilege against self-incrimination, the accused must be adequately and effectively apprised of his rights and the exercise of those rights must be fully honored.

It is impossible for us to foresee the potential alternatives for protecting the privilege which might be devised by Congress or the States in the exercise of their creative rule-making capacities. Therefore we cannot say that the Constitution necessarily requires adherence to any particular solution for the inherent compulsions of the interrogation process as it is presently conducted. Our decision in no way creates a constitutional strait-jacket which will handicap sound efforts at reform, nor is it intended to have this effect. We encourage Congress and the States to continue their laudable search for increasingly effective ways of protecting the rights of the individual while promoting efficient enforcement of our criminal laws. However, unless we are shown other procedures which are at least as effective in apprising accused persons of their right of silence and in assuring a continuous opportunity to exercise it, the following safeguards must be observed.

At the outset, if a person in custody is to be subjected to interrogation, he must first be informed in clear and unequivocal terms that he has the right to remain silent. For those unaware of the privilege, the warning is needed simply to make them aware of it — the threshold requirement for an intelligent decision as to its exercise. More important, such a warning is an absolute prerequisite in overcoming the inherent pressures of the interrogation atmosphere. It is not just the subnormal or woefully ignorant who succumb to an interrogator's imprecations, whether implied or expressly stated, that the interrogation will continue until a confession is obtained or that silence in the face of accusation is itself damning and will bode ill when presented to a jury. Further, the warning will show the individual that his interrogators are prepared to recognize his privilege should he choose to exercise it.

The Fifth Amendment privilege is so fundamental to our system of constitutional rule and the expedient of giving an adequate warning as to the availability of the privilege so simple, we will not pause to inquire in individual cases whether the defendant was aware of his rights without a warning being given. Assessments of the knowledge the defendant possessed, based on information as to his age, education, intelligence, or prior contact with authorities, can never be more than speculation; a warning is a clearcut fact. More important, whatever the background of the person interrogated, a warning at the time of the interrogation is indispensable to overcome its pressures and to insure that the individual knows he is free to exercise the privilege at that point in time.

The warning of the right to remain silent must be accompanied by the explanation that anything said can and will be used against the individual in court. This warning is needed in order to make him aware not only of the privilege, but also of the consequences of forgoing it. It is only through an awareness of these consequences that there can be any assurance of real understanding and intelligent exercise of the privilege. Moreover, this warning may serve to make the individual more acutely aware that he is faced with a phase of the adversary system—that he is not in the presence of persons acting solely in his interest.

The circumstances surrounding in-custody interrogation can operate very quickly to overbear the will of one merely made aware of his privilege by his interrogators. Therefore, the right to have counsel present at the interrogation is indispensable to the protection of the Fifth Amendment privilege under the system we delineate today. Our aim is to assure that the individual's right to choose between silence and speech remains unfettered throughout the interrogation process. A once-stated warning, delivered by those who will conduct the interrogation, cannot itself suffice to that end among those who most require knowledge of their rights. A mere warning given by the interrogators is not alone sufficient to accomplish that end. Prosecutors themselves claim that the admonishment of the right to remain silent without more "will benefit only the recidivist and the professional." Brief for the National District Attorneys Association as amicus curiae, p.14. Even preliminary advice given to the accused by his own attorney can be swiftly overcome by the secret interrogation process. Cf. *Escobedo v. State of Illinois*, 378 U.S. 478, 485, n. 5, 84 S.Ct. 1758, 1762. Thus, the need for counsel to protect the Fifth Amendment privilege comprehends not merely a right to consult with counsel prior to questioning, but also to have counsel present during any questioning if the defendant so desires.

The presence of counsel at the interrogation may serve several significant subsidiary functions as well. If the accused decides to talk to his interrogators, the assistance of counsel can mitigate the dangers of untrustworthiness. With a lawyer present the likelihood that the police will practice coercion is reduced, and if coercion is nevertheless exercised the lawyer can testify to it in court. The presence of a lawyer can also help to guarantee that the accused gives a fully accurate statement to the police and that the statement is rightly reported by the prosecution at trial. See *Crooker v. State of California*, 357 U.S. 433, 443-448, 78 S.Ct. 1287, 1293-1296, 2 L.Ed.2d 1448 (1958) (Douglas, J., dissenting).

An individual need not make a pre-interrogation request for a lawyer. While such request affirmatively secures his right to have one, his failure to ask for a lawyer does not constitute a waiver. No effective waiver of the right to counsel during interrogation can be recognized unless specifically made after the warnings we here delineate have been given. The accused who does not know his rights and therefore does not make a request may be the person who most needs counsel. As the California Supreme Court has aptly put it:

"Finally, we must recognize that the imposition of the requirement for the request would discriminate against the defendant who does not know his rights. The defendant who does not ask for counsel is the very defendant who most needs counsel. We cannot penalize a defendant who, not understanding his constitutional rights, does not make the formal request and by such failure demonstrates his helplessness. To require the request would be to favor the defendant whose sophistication or status had fortuitously prompted him to make it." *People v. Dorado*, 62 Cal.2d 338, 351, 42 Cal.Rptr. 169, 177-178, 398 P.2d 361, 369-370, (1965) (Tobriner, J.).

In *Carnley v. Cochran*, 369 U.S. 506, 513, 82 S.Ct. 884, 889, 8 L.Ed.2d 70 (1962), we stated: "[I]t is settled that where the assistance of counsel is a constitutional requisite, the right to be furnished counsel does not depend on a request." This proposition applies with equal force in the context of providing counsel to protect an accused's Fifth Amendment privilege in the face of interrogation. Although the role of counsel at trial differs from the role during interrogation, the differences are not relevant to the question whether a request is a prerequisite.

Accordingly we hold that an individual held for interrogation must be clearly informed that he has the right to consult with a lawyer and to have the lawyer with him during interrogation under the system for protecting the privilege we delineate today. As with the warnings of the right to remain silent and that anything stated can be used in evidence against him, this warning is an absolute prerequisite to interrogation. No amount of circumstantial evidence that the person may have been aware of this right will suffice to stand in its stead. Only through such a warning is there ascertainable assurance that the accused was aware of this right.

If an individual indicates that he wishes the assistance of counsel before any interrogation occurs, the authorities cannot rationally ignore or deny his request on the basis that the individual does not have or cannot afford a retained attorney. The financial ability of the individual has no relationship to the scope of the rights involved here. The privilege against self-incrimination secured by the Constitution applies to all individuals. The need for counsel in order to protect the privilege exists for the indigent as well as the affluent. In fact, were we to limit these constitutional rights to those who can retain an attorney, our decisions today would be of little significance. The cases before us as well as the vast majority of confession cases with which we have dealt in the past involve those unable to retain counsel. While authorities are not required to relieve the accused of his poverty, they have the obligation not to take advantage of indigence in the administration of justice. Denial of counsel to the indigent at the time of interrogation while allowing an attorney to those who can afford one would be no more supportable by reason or logic than the similar situation at trial and on appeal struck down in *Gideon v. Wainwright*, 372 U.S. 335, 83 S.Ct. 792, 9 L.Ed.2d 799 (1963), and *Douglas v. People of State of California*, 372 U.S. 353, 83 S.Ct. 814, 9 L.Ed.2d 811 (1963).

In order fully to apprise a person interrogated of the extent of his rights under this system then, it is necessary to warn him not only that he has the right to consult with an attorney, but also that if he is indigent a lawyer will be appointed to represent him. Without this additional warning, the admonition of the right to consult with counsel would often be understood as meaning only that he can consult with a lawyer if he has one or has the funds to obtain one. The warning of a right to counsel would be hollow if not couched in terms that would convey to the indigent—the person most often subjected to interrogation—the knowledge that he too has a right to have counsel present. As with the warnings of the right to remain silent and of the general right to counsel, only by effective and express explanation to the indigent of this right can there be assurance that he was truly in a position to exercise it.5

Once warnings have been given, the subsequent procedure is clear. If the individual indicates in any manner, at any time prior to or during questioning, that he wishes to remain silent, the interrogation must cease.6 At this point he has shown that he intends to exercise his Fifth Amendment privilege; any statement taken after the person invokes his privilege cannot be other than the product of compulsion, subtle or otherwise. Without the right to cut off questioning, the setting of in-custody interrogation operates on the individual to overcome free choice in producing a statement after the privilege has been once invoked. If the individual states that he wants an attorney, the interrogation must cease until an attorney is present. At that time, the individual must have an opportunity to confer with the attorney and to have him present during any subsequent questioning. If the individual cannot obtain an attorney and he indicates that he wants one before speaking to police, they must respect his decision to remain silent.

This does not mean, as some have suggested, that each police station must have a "station house lawyer" present at all times to advise prisoners. It does mean, however, that if police propose to interrogate a person they must make known to him that he is entitled to a lawyer and that if he cannot afford one, a lawyer will be provided for him prior to any interrogation. If authorities conclude that they will not provide counsel during a reasonable period of time in which investigation in the field is carried out, they may refrain from doing so without violating the person's Fifth Amendment privilege so long as they do not question him during that time.

If the interrogation continues without the presence of an attorney and a statement is taken, a heavy burden rests on the government to demonstrate that the defendant knowingly and intelligently waived his privilege against self-incrimination and his right to retained or appointed counsel. *Escobedo v. State of Illinois*, 378 U.S. 478, 490, n. 14, 84 S.Ct. 1758, 1764, 12 L.Ed.2d 977. This Court has always set high standards of proof for the waiver of constitutional rights, *Johnson v. Zerbst*, 304 U.S. 458, 58 S.Ct. 1019, 82 L.Ed. 1461 (1938), and we reassert these standards as applied to in-custody interrogation. Since the State is responsible for establishing the isolated circumstances under which the interrogation takes place and has the only means of making available corroborated evidence of warnings given during incommunicado interrogation, the burden is rightly on its shoulders.

An express statement that the individual is willing to make a statement and does not want an attorney followed closely by a statement could constitute a waiver. But a valid waiver will not be presumed simply from the silence of the accused after warnings are given or simply from the fact that a confession was in fact eventually obtained. A statement we made in *Carnley v. Cochran*, 369 U.S. 506, 516, 82 S.Ct. 884, 890, 8 L.Ed.2d 70 (1962), is applicable here:

"Presuming waiver from a silent record is impermissible. The record must show, or there must be an allegation and evidence which show, that an accused was offered counsel but intelligently and understandingly rejected the offer. Anything less is not waiver."

See also *Glasser v. United States*, 315 U.S. 60, 62 S.Ct. 457, 86 L.Ed. 680 (1942). Moreover, where in-custody interrogation is involved, there is no room for the contention that the privilege is waived if the individual answers some questions or gives some information on his own prior to invoking his right to remain silent when interrogated.

Whatever the testimony of the authorities as to waiver of rights by an accused, the fact of lengthy interrogation or incommunicado incarceration before a statement is made is strong evidence that the accused did not validly waive his rights. In these circumstances the fact that the individual eventually made a statement is consistent with the conclusion that the compelling influence of the interrogation finally forced him to do so. It is inconsistent with any notion of a voluntary relinquishment of the privilege. Moreover, any evidence that the accused was threatened, tricked, or cajoled into a waiver will, of course, show that the defendant did not voluntarily waive his privilege. The requirement of warnings and waiver of rights is a fundamental with respect to the Fifth Amendment privilege and not simply a preliminary ritual to existing methods of interrogation.

The warnings required and the waiver necessary in accordance with our opinion today are, in the absence of a fully effective equivalent, prerequisites to the admissibility of any statement made by a defendant. No distinction can be drawn between statements which are direct confessions and statements which amount to "admissions" of part or all of an offense. The privilege against self-incrimination protects the individual from being compelled to incriminate himself in any manner; it does not distinguish degrees of incrimination. Similarly, for precisely the same reason, no distinction may be drawn between inculpatory statements and statements alleged to be merely "exculpatory." If a statement made were in fact truly exculpatory it would, of course, never be used by the prosecution. In fact, statements merely intended to be exculpatory by the defendant are often used to impeach his testimony at trial or to demonstrate untruths in the statement given under interrogation and thus to prove guilt by implication. These statements are incriminating in any meaningful sense of the word and may not be used without the full warnings and effective waiver required for any other statement. In *Escobedo* itself, the defendant fully intended his accusation of another as the slayer to be exculpatory as to himself.

The principles announced today deal with the protection which must be given to the privilege against self-incrimination when the individual is first subjected to police interrogation while in custody at the station or otherwise deprived of his freedom of action in any significant way. It is at this point that our adversary system of criminal proceedings commences, distinguishing itself at the outset from the inquisitorial system recognized in some countries. Under the system of warnings we delineate today or under any other system which may be devised and found effective, the safeguards to be erected about the privilege must come into play at this point.

Our decision is not intended to hamper the traditional function of police officers in investigating crime. See *Escobedo v. State of Illinois*, 378 U.S. 478, 492, 84 S.Ct. 1758, 1765. When an individual is in custody on probable cause, the police may, of course, seek out evidence in the field to be used at trial against him. Such investigation may include inquiry of persons not under restraint. General on-the-scene questioning as to facts surrounding a crime or other general questioning of citizens in the fact-finding process is not affected by our holding. It is an act of responsible citizenship for individuals to give whatever information they may have to aid in law enforcement. In such situations the compelling atmosphere inherent in the process of in-custody interrogation is not necessarily present.

In dealing with statements obtained through interrogation, we do not purport to find all confessions inadmissible. Confessions remain a proper element in law enforcement. Any statement given freely and voluntarily without any compelling influences is, of course, admissible in evidence. The fundamental import of the privilege while an individual is in custody is not whether he is allowed to talk to the police without the benefit of warnings and counsel, but whether he can be interrogated. There is no requirement that police stop a person who enters a police station and states that he wishes to confess to a crime, or a person who calls the police to offer a confession or any other statement he desires to make. Volunteered statements of any kind are not barred by the Fifth Amendment and their admissibility is not affected by our holding today.

To summarize, we hold that when an individual is taken into custody or otherwise deprived of his freedom by the authorities in any significant way and is subjected to questioning, the privilege against self-incrimination is jeopardized. Procedural safeguards must be employed to protect the privilege and unless other fully effective means are adopted to notify the person of his right of silence and to assure that the exercise of the right will be scrupulously honored, the following measures are required. He must be warned prior to any questioning that he has the right to remain silent, that anything he says can be used against him in a court of law, that he has the right to the presence of an attorney, and that if he cannot afford an attorney one will be appointed for him prior to any questioning if he so desires. Opportunity to exercise these rights must be afforded to him throughout the interrogation. After such warnings have been given, and such opportunity afforded him, the individual may knowingly and intelligently waive these rights and agree to answer questions or make a statement. But unless and until such warnings and waiver are demonstrated by the prosecution at trial, no evidence obtained as a result of interrogation can be used against him.

IV

A recurrent argument made in these cases is that society's need for interrogation outweighs the privilege. This argument is not unfamiliar to this Court. See, e.g., *Chambers v. State of Florida*, 309 U.S. 227, 240-241, 60 S.Ct. 472, 478-479, 84 L.Ed. 716 (1940). The whole thrust of our foregoing discussion demonstrates that the Constitution has prescribed the rights of the individual when confronted with the power of government when it provided in the Fifth Amendment that an individual cannot be compelled to be a witness against himself. That right cannot be abridged. As Mr. Justice Brandeis once observed:

"Decency, security, and liberty alike demand that government officials shall be subjected to the same rules of conduct that are commands to the citizen. In a government of laws, existence of the government will be imperilled if it fails to observe the law scrupulously. Our government is the potent, the omnipresent teacher. For good or for ill, it teaches the whole people by its example. Crime is contagious. If the government becomes a lawbreaker, it breeds contempt for law; it invites every man to become a law unto himself; it invites anarchy. To declare that in the administration of the criminal law the end justifies the means ... would bring terrible retribution. Against that pernicious doctrine this court should resolutely set its face." *Olmstead v. United States*, 277 U.S. 438, 485, 48 S.Ct. 564, 575, 72 L.Ed. 944 (1928) (dissenting opinion).[7] In this connection, one of our country's distinguished jurists has pointed out: "The quality of a nation's civilization can be largely measured by the methods it uses in the enforcement of its criminal law."

If the individual desires to exercise his privilege, he has the right to do so. This is not for the authorities to decide. An attorney may advise his client not to talk to police until he has had an opportunity to investigate the case, or he may wish to be present with his client during any police questioning. In doing so an attorney is merely exercising the good professional judgment he has been taught. This is not cause for considering the attorney a menace to law enforcement. He is merely carrying out what he is sworn to do under his oath—to protect to the extent of his ability the rights of his client. In fulfilling this responsibility the attorney plays a vital role in the administration of criminal justice under our Constitution.

In announcing these principles, we are not unmindful of the burdens which law enforcement officials must bear, often under trying circumstances. We also fully recognize the obligation of all citizens to aid in enforcing the criminal laws. This Court, while protecting individual rights, has always given ample latitude to law enforcement agencies in the legitimate exercise of their duties. The limits we have placed on the interrogation process should not constitute an undue interference with a proper system of law enforcement. As we have noted, our decision does not in any way preclude police from carrying out their traditional investigatory functions. Although confessions may play an important role in some convictions, the cases before us present graphic examples of the overstatement of the "need" for confessions. In each case authorities conducted interrogations ranging up to five days in duration despite the presence, through standard investigating practices, of considerable evidence against each defendant.

...

It is also urged that an unfettered right to detention for interrogation should be allowed because it will often redound to the benefit of the person questioned. When police inquiry determines that there is no reason to believe that the person has committed any crime, it is said, he will be released without need for further formal procedures. The person who has committed no offense, however, will be better able to clear himself after warnings with counsel present than without. It can be assumed that in such circumstances a lawyer would advise his client to talk freely to police in order to clear himself.

Custodial interrogation, by contrast, does not necessarily afford the innocent an opportunity to clear themselves. A serious consequence of the present practice of the interrogation alleged to be beneficial for the innocent is that many arrests "for investigation" subject large numbers of innocent persons to detention and interrogation. In one of the cases before us, No. 584, *California v. Stewart*, police held four persons, who were in the defendant's house at the time of the arrest, in jail for five days until defendant confessed. At that time they were finally released. Police stated that there was "no evidence to connect them with any crime." Available statistics on the extent of this practice where it is condoned indicate that these four are far from alone in being subjected to arrest, prolonged detention, and interrogation without the requisite probable cause.

Over the years the Federal Bureau of Investigation has compiled an exemplary record of effective law enforcement while advising any suspect or arrested person, at the outset of an interview, that he is not required to make a statement, that any statement may be used against him in court, that the individual may obtain the services of an attorney of his own choice and, more recently, that he has a right to free counsel if he is unable to pay. A letter received from the Solicitor General in response to a question from the Bench makes it clear that the present pattern of warnings and respect for the rights of the individual followed as a practice by the FBI is consistent with the procedure which we delineate today. It states:

"At the oral argument of the above cause, Mr. Justice Fortas asked whether I could provide certain information as to the practices followed by the Federal Bureau of Investigation. I have directed these questions to the attention of the Director of the Federal Bureau of Investigation and am submitting herewith a statement of the questions and of the answers which we have received.

"'(1) When an individual is interviewed by agents of the Bureau, what warning is given to him?

"'The standard warning long given by Special Agents of the FBI to both suspects and persons under arrest is that the person has a right to say nothing and a right to counsel, and that any statement he does make may be used against him in court. Examples of this warning are to be found in the *Westover* case at 342 F.2d 684 (1965), and *Jackson v. United States*, [119 U.S.App.D.C. 100] 337 F.2d 136 (1964), cert. den. 380 U.S.935, 85 S.Ct. 1353.

"'After passage of the Criminal Justice Act of 1964, which provides free counsel for Federal defendants unable to pay, we added to our instructions to Special Agents the requirement that any person who is under arrest for an offense under FBI jurisdiction, or whose arrest is contemplated following the interview, must also be advised of his right to free counsel if he is unable to pay, and the fact that such counsel will be assigned by the Judge. At the same time, we broadened the right to counsel warning to read counsel of his own choice, or anyone else with whom he might wish to speak.

"'(2) When is the warning given?

"'The FBI warning is given to a suspect at the very outset of the interview, as shown in the Westover case, cited above. The warning may be given to a person arrested as soon as practicable after the arrest, as shown in the Jackson case, also cited above, and in United *States v. Konigsberg*, 336 F.2d 844 (1964), cert. den. [*Celso v. United States*] 379 U.S. 933 [85 S.Ct. 327, 13 L.Ed.2d 342] but in any event it must precede the interview with the person for a confession or admission of his own guilt.

"'(3) What is the Bureau's practice in the event that (a) the individual requests counsel and (b) counsel appears?

"'When the person who has been warned of his right to counsel decides that he wishes to consult with counsel before making a statement, the interview is terminated at that point, *Schultz v. United States*, 351 F.2d 287 ([10 Cir.] 1965). It may be continued, however, as to all matters other than the person's own guilt or innocence. If he is indecisive in his request for counsel, there may be some question on whether he did or did not waive counsel. Situations of this kind must necessarily be left to the judgment of the interviewing Agent. For example, in *Hiram v. United States*, 354 F.2d 4 ([9 Cir.] 1965), the Agent's conclusion that the person arrested had waived his right to counsel was upheld by the courts.

"'A person being interviewed and desiring to consult counsel by telephone must be permitted to do so, as shown in *Caldwell v. United States*, 351 F.2d 459

([1 Cir.] 1965). When counsel appears in person, he is permitted to confer with his client in private.

"'(4) What is the Bureau's practice if the individual requests counsel, but cannot afford to retain an attorney?

"'If any person being interviewed after warning of counsel decides that he wishes to consult with counsel before proceeding further the interview is terminated, as shown above. FBI Agents do not pass judgment on the ability of the person to pay for counsel. They do, however, advise those who have been arrested for an offense under FBI jurisdiction, or whose arrest is contemplated following the interview, of a right to free counsel if they are unable to pay, and the availability of such counsel from the Judge.'"8

The practice of the FBI can readily be emulated by state and local enforcement agencies. The argument that the FBI deals with different crimes than are dealt with by state authorities does not mitigate the significance of the FBI experience.

The experience in some other countries also suggests that the danger to law enforcement in curbs on interrogation is overplayed. The English procedure since 1912 under the Judges' Rules is significant. As recently strengthened, the Rules require that a cautionary warning be given an accused by a police officer as soon as he has evidence that affords reasonable grounds for suspicion; they also require that any statement made be given by the accused without questioning by police. The right of the individual to consult with an attorney during this period is expressly recognized.

The safeguards present under Scottish law may be even greater than in England. Scottish judicial decisions bar use in evidence of most confessions obtained through police interrogation. In India, confessions made to police not in the presence of a magistrate have been excluded by rule of evidence since 1872, at a time when it operated under British law. Identical provisions appear in the Evidence Ordinance of Ceylon, enacted in 1895. Similarly, in our country the Uniform Code of Military Justice has long provided that no suspect may be interrogated without first being warned of his right not to make a statement and that any statement he makes may be used against him. Denial of the right to consult counsel during interrogation has also been proscribed by military tribunals. There appears to have been no marked detrimental effect on criminal law enforcement in these jurisdictions as a result of these rules. Conditions of law enforcement in our country are sufficiently similar to permit reference to this experience as assurance that lawlessness will not result from warning an individual of his rights or allowing him to exercise them. Moreover, it is consistent with our legal system that we give at least as much protection to these rights as is given in the jurisdictions described. We deal in our country with rights grounded in a specific requirement of the Fifth Amendment of the Constitution, whereas other jurisdictions arrived at their conclusions on the basis of principles of justice not so specifically defined.

It is also urged upon us that we withhold decision on this issue until state legislative bodies and advisory groups have had an opportunity to deal with these problems by rule making. We have already pointed out that the Constitution does not require any specific code of procedures for protecting the privilege against self-incrimination during custodial interrogation. Congress and the States are free to develop their own safeguards for the privilege, so long as they are fully as effective as those described above in informing accused persons of their right of silence and in affording a continuous opportunity to exercise it. In any event, however, the issues presented are of constitutional dimensions and must be determined by the courts. The admissibility of a statement in the face of a claim that it was obtained in violation of the defendant's constitutional rights is an issue the resolution of which has long since been undertaken by this Court. See *Hopt v. People of Territory of Utah*, 110 U.S. 574, 4 S.Ct. 202, 28 L.Ed. 262 (1884). Judicial solutions to problems of constitutional dimension have evolved decade by decade. As courts have been presented with the need to enforce constitutional rights, they have found means of doing so. That was our responsibility when Escobedo was before us and it is our responsibility today. Where rights secured by the Constitution are involved, there can be no rule making or legislation which would abrogate them.

V

Because of the nature of the problem and because of its recurrent significance in numerous cases, we have to this point discussed the relationship of the Fifth Amendment privilege to police interrogation without specific concentration on the facts of the cases before us. We turn now to these facts to consider the application to these cases of the constitutional principles discussed above. In each instance, we have concluded that statements were obtained from the defendant under circumstances that did not meet constitutional standards for protection of the privilege.

No. 759. *Miranda v. Arizona.*

On March 13, 1963, petitioner, Ernesto Miranda, was arrested at his home and taken into custody to a Phoenix police station. He was there identified by the complaining witness. The police then took him to "Interrogation Room

No. 2" of the detective bureau. There he was questioned by two police officers. The officers admitted at trial that Miranda was not advised that he had a right to have an attorney present.9 Two hours later, the officers emerged from the interrogation room with a written confession signed by Miranda. At the top of the statement was a typed paragraph stating that the confession was made voluntarily, without threats or promises of immunity and "with full knowledge of my legal rights, understanding any statement I make may be used against me."10

At his trial before a jury, the written confession was admitted into evidence over the objection of defense counsel, and the officers testified to the prior oral confession made by Miranda during the interrogation. Miranda was found guilty of kidnapping and rape. He was sentenced to 20 to 30 years' imprisonment on each count, the sentences to run concurrently. On appeal, the Supreme Court of Arizona held that Miranda's constitutional rights were not violated in obtaining the confession and affirmed the conviction. 98 Ariz. 18, 401 P.2d 721. In reaching its decision, the court emphasized heavily the fact that Miranda did not specifically request counsel.

We reverse. From the testimony of the officers and by the admission of respondent, it is clear that Miranda was not in any way apprised of his right to consult with an attorney and to have one present during the interrogation, nor was his right not to be compelled to incriminate himself effectively protected in any other manner. Without these warnings the statements were inadmissible. The mere fact that he signed a statement which contained a typed-in clause stating that he had "full knowledge" of his "legal rights" does not approach the knowing and intelligent waiver required to relinquish constitutional rights.

. . .

No. 760. *Vignera v. New York*

Petitioner, Michael Vignera, was picked up by New York police on October 14, 1960, in connection with the robbery three days earlier of a Brooklyn dress shop. They took him to the 17th Detective Squad headquarters in Manhattan. Sometime thereafter he was taken to the 66th Detective Squad. There a detective questioned Vignera with respect to the robbery. Vignera orally admitted the robbery to the detective. The detective was asked on cross-examination at trial by defense counsel whether Vignera was warned of his right to counsel before being interrogated. The prosecution objected to the question and the trial judge sustained the objection. Thus, the defense was precluded from making any showing that warnings had not been given. While at the 66th Detective Squad, Vignera was identified by the store owner and a saleslady as the man who robbed the dress shop. At about 3 p.m. he was formally arrested. The police then transported him to still another station, the 70th Precinct in Brooklyn, "for detention." At 11 p.m. Vignera was questioned by an assistant district attorney in the presence of a hearing reporter who transcribed the questions and Vignera's answers. This verbatim account of these proceedings contains no statement of any warnings given by the assistant district attorney. At Vignera's trial on a charge of first degree robbery, the detective testified as to the oral confession. The transcription of the statement taken was also introduced in evidence. At the conclusion of the testimony, the trial judge charged the jury in part as follows:

> "The law doesn't say that the confession is void or invalidated because the police officer didn't advise the defendant as to his rights. Did you hear what I said? I am telling you what the law of the State of New York is."

> Vignera was found guilty of first degree robbery. He was subsequently adjudged a third-felony offender and sentenced to 30 to 60 years' imprisonment. The conviction was affirmed without opinion by the Appellate Division, Second Department, 21 A.D.2d 752, 252 N.Y. S.2d 19, and by the Court of Appeals, also without opinion, 15 N.Y.2d 970, 259 N.Y.S.2d 857, 207 N.E.2d 527, remittitur amended, 16 N.Y. 2d 614, 261 N.Y.S.2d 65, 209 N.E.2d 110. In argument to the Court of Appeals, the State contended that Vignera had no constitutional right to be advised of his right to counsel or his privilege against self-incrimination.

We reverse. The foregoing indicates that Vignera was not warned of any of his rights before the questioning by the detective and by the assistant district attorney. No other steps were taken to protect these rights. Thus he was not effectively apprised of his Fifth Amendment privilege or of his right to have counsel present and his statements are inadmissible.

No. 761. *Westover v. United States.*

At approximately 9:45 p.m. on March 20, 1963, petitioner, Carl Calvin Westover, was arrested by local police in Kansas City as a suspect in two Kansas City robberies. A report was also received from the FBI that he was wanted on a felony charge in California. The local authorities took him to a police station and placed him in a line-up on the local charges, and at about 11:45 p.m. he was booked. Kansas City police interrogated Westover on the night of his arrest. He denied any knowledge of criminal activities. The next day local officers interrogated him again throughout the morning. Shortly before noon they informed the FBI that they were through interrogating Westover and that the FBI could proceed to interrogate him. There is nothing in the record to indicate that Westover was ever given any warning as to his rights by local police. At noon, three special agents of the FBI continued the interrogation in a private interview room of the Kansas City Police Department, this time with respect to the robbery of a savings and loan association and a bank in Sacramento California. After two or two and one-half hours, Westover signed separate confessions to each of these two robberies which had been prepared by one of the agents during the interrogation. At trial one of the agents testified, and a paragraph on each of the statements state that the agents advised Westover that he did not have to make a statement, that any statement he made could be used against him, and that he had the right to see an attorney.

Westover was tried by a jury in federal court and convicted of the California robberies. His statements were introduced at trial. He was sentenced to 15 years' imprisonment on each count, the sentences to run consecutively. On appeal, the conviction was affirmed by the Court of Appeals for the Ninth Circuit. 342 F.2d 684.

We reverse. On the facts of this case we cannot find that Westover knowingly and intelligently waived his rights to remain silent and his right to consult with counsel prior to the time he made the statement. At the time the FBI agents began questioning Westover, he had been in custody for over 14 hours and had been interrogated at length during that period. The FBI interrogation began immediately upon the conclusion of the interrogation by Kansas City police and was conducted in local police headquarters. Although the two law enforcement authorities are legally distinct and the crimes for which they interrogated Westover were different, the impact on him was that of a continuous period of questioning. There is no evidence of any warning given prior to the FBI interrogation nor is there any evidence of an articulated waiver of rights after the FBI commenced its interrogation. The record simply shows that the defendant did in fact confess a short time after being turned over to the FBI following interrogation by local police. Despite the fact that the FBI agents gave warnings at the outset of their interview, from Westover's point of view the warnings came at the end of the interrogation process. In these circumstances an intelligent waiver of constitutional rights cannot be assumed.

We do not suggest that law enforcement authorities are precluded from questioning any individual who has been held for a period of time by other authorities and interrogated by them without appropriate warnings. A different case would be presented if an accused were taken into custody by the second authority removed both in time and place from his original surroundings, and then adequately advised of his rights and given an opportunity to exercise them. But here the FBI interrogation was conducted immediately following the state interrogation in the same police station—in the same compelling surroundings. Thus, in obtaining a confession from Westover the federal authorities were the beneficiaries of the pressure applied by the local in-custody interrogation. In these circumstances the giving of warnings alone was not sufficient to protect the privilege.

No. 584. *California v. Stewart.*

In the course of investigating a series of purse-snatch robberies in which one of the victims had died of injuries inflicted by her assailant, respondent, Roy Allen Stewart, was pointed out to Los Angeles police as the endorser of dividend checks taken in one of the robberies. At about 7:15 p.m., January 31, 1963, police officers went to Stewart's house and arrested him. One of the officers asked Stewart if they could search the house, to which he replied, "Go ahead." The search turned up various items taken from the five robbery victims. At the time of Stewart's arrest, police also arrested Stewart's wife and three other persons who were visiting him. These four were jailed along with Stewart and were interrogated. Stewart was taken to the University Station of the Los Angeles Police Department where he was placed in a cell. During the next five days, police interrogated Stewart on nine different occasions. Except during the first interrogation session, when he was confronted with an accusing witness, Stewart was isolated with his interrogators.

During the ninth interrogation session, Stewart admitted that he had robbed the deceased and stated that he had not meant to hurt her. Police then brought Stewart before a magistrate for the first time. Since there was no evidence to connect them with any crime, the police then released the other four persons arrested with him.

Nothing in the record specifically indicates whether Stewart was or was not advised of his right to remain silent or his right to counsel. In a number of instances, however, the interrogating officers were asked to recount everything that was said during the interrogations. None indicated that Stewart was ever advised of his rights.

Stewart was charged with kidnapping to commit robbery, rape, and murder. At his trial, transcripts of the first interrogation and the confession at the last interrogation were introduced in evidence. The jury found Stewart guilty of robbery and first degree murder and fixed the penalty as death. On appeal, the Supreme Court of California reversed. 62 Cal.2d 571, 43 Cal.Rptr. 201, 400 P.2d 97. It held that under this Court's decision in *Escobedo*, Stewart should have been advised of his right to remain silent and of his right to counsel and that it would not presume in the face of a silent record that the police advised Stewart of his rights.

We affirm. In dealing with custodial interrogation, we will not presume that a defendant has been effectively apprised of his rights and that his privilege against self-incrimination has been adequately safeguarded on a record that does not show that any warnings have been given or that any effective alternative has been employed. Nor can a knowing and intelligent waiver of these rights be assumed on a silent record. Furthermore, Stewart's steadfast denial of the alleged offenses through eight of the nine interrogations over a period of five days is subject to no other construction than that he was compelled by persistent interrogation to forego his Fifth Amendment privilege.

Therefore, in accordance with the foregoing, the judgments of the Supreme Court of Arizona in No. 759, of the New York Court of Appeals in No. 760, and of the Court of Appeals for the Ninth Circuit in No. 761 are reversed. The judgment of the Supreme Court of California in No. 584 is affirmed. It is so ordered.

Judgments of Supreme Court of Arizona in No. 759, of New York Court of Appeals in No. 760, and of the Court of Appeals for the Ninth Circuit in No. 761 reversed.

Judgment of Supreme Court of California in No. 584 affirmed.

Miranda notes:

5. While a warning that the indigent may have counsel appointed need not be given to the person who is known to have an attorney or is known to have ample funds to secure one, the expedient of giving a warning is too simple and the rights involved too important to engage in ex post facto inquiries into financial ability when there is any doubt at all on that score.

6. If an individual indicates his desire to remain silent, but has an attorney present, there may be some circumstances in which further questioning would be permissible. In the absence of evidence of overbearing, statements then made in the presence of counsel might be free of the compelling influence of the interrogation process and might fairly be construed as a waiver of the privilege for purposes of these statements.

7. In quoting the above from the dissenting opinion of Mr. Justice Brandeis we, of course, do not intend to pass the constitutional questions involved in the *Olmstead* case.

8. We agree that the interviewing agent must exercise his judgment in determining whether the individual waives his right to counsel. Because of the constitutional basis of the right, however, the standard for waiver is necessarily high. And, of course, the ultimate responsibility for resolving this constitutional question lies with the courts.

9. Miranda was also convicted in a separate trial on an unrelated robbery charge not presented here for review. A statement introduced at that trial was obtained from Miranda during the same interrogation which resulted in the confession involved here. At the robbery trial, one officer testified that during the interrogation he did not tell Miranda that anything he said would be held against him or that he could consult with an attorney. The other officer stated that they had both told Miranda that anything he said would be used against him and that he was not required by law to tell them anything.

10. One of the officers testified that he read this paragraph to Miranda. Apparently, however, he did not do so until after Miranda had confessed orally.

Chimel v. California

Supreme Court of the United States, 1969.
395 U.S. 752, 89 S. Ct. 2034, 23 L. Ed. 2d 685.

Mr. Justice STEWART delivered the opinion of the Court.

. . .

Approval of a warrantless search incident to a lawful arrest seems first to have been articulated by the Court in 1914 as dictum in *Weeks v. United States* . . . in which the Court stated:

"What then is the present case? Before answering that inquiry specifically it may be well by a process of exclusion to state what it is not. It is not an assertion of the right on the part of the Government, always recognized under English and American law, to search the person of the accused when legally arrested to discover and seize the fruits of evidences of crime." . . .

That statement made no reference to any right to search the place where an arrest occurs, but was limited to a right to search the "person." Eleven years later the case of *Carroll v. United States*, 267 U.S. 132 (1925), brought the following embellishment of the Weeks statement:

"When a man is legally arrested for an offense, whatever is found upon his person or in his control which it is unlawful for him to have and which may be used to prove the offense may be seized and held as evidence in the prosecution." (Emphasis added.) . . .

Still, that assertion too was far from a claim that the "place" where one is arrested may be searched so long as the arrest is valid. Without explanation, however, the principle emerged in expanded form a few months later in *Agnello v. United States*, 269 U.S. 20 (1925)-although still by way of dictum:

"The right without a search warrant contemporaneously to search persons lawfully arrested while committing crime and to search the place where the arrest is made in order to find and seize things connected with the crime as its fruits or as the means by which it was committed, as well as weapons and other things to effect an escape from custody, is not to be doubted." And in Marron v. United States two years later, the dictum of Agnello appeared to be the foundation of the Court's decision. In that case federal agents had secured a search warrant authorizing the seizure of liquor and certain articles used in its manufacture. When they arrived at the premises to be searched, they say "that the place was used for retailing and drinking intoxicating liquors." They proceeded to arrest the person in charge and to execute the warrant. In searching a closet for the items listed in the warrant they came across an incriminating ledger, concededly not covered by the warrant, which they also seized. The Court upheld the seizure of the ledger by holding that since the agents had made a lawful arrest, "[t]hey had a right without a warrant contemporaneously to search the place in order to find and seize the things used to carry on the criminal enterprise." . . .

That the Marron opinion did not mean all that it seemed to say became evident, however, a few years later in *Go-Bart Importing Company v. United States*, 282 U.S. 344 (1931), and *United States v. Lefkowitz*, 285 U.S. 452 (1932). . . . In *Go-Bart*, agents had searched the office of persons whom they had lawfully arrested and had taken several papers from a desk, a safe, and other parts of the office. The Court noted that no crime had been committed in the agents' presence, and that although the agent in charge "had an abundance of information and time to swear out a valid [search] warrant, he failed to do so." . . . In holding the search and seizure unlawful, the Court stated:

"Plainly the case before us is essentially different from *Marron v. United States*. . . . There, officers executing a valid search warrant for intoxicating liquors found and arrested one Birdsall who in pursuance of a conspiracy was actually engaged in running a saloon. As an incident to the arrest they seized a ledger in a closet where the liquor or some of it was kept and some bills beside the cash register. These things were visible and accessible and in the offender's immediate custody. There was no threat of force or general search or rummaging of the place." . . .

This limited characterization of Marron was reiterated in Lefkowitz, a case in which the Court held unlawful a search of desk drawers and cabinet despite the fact that the search had accompanied a lawful arrest. . . .

The limiting views expressed in *Go-Bart* and *Lefkowitz* were thrown to the winds, however, in *Harris v. United States*, 331 U.S. 145, decided in 1947. In that case, officers had obtained a warrant for Harris' arrest on the basis of his alleged involvement with the cashing and interstate transportation of a forged check. He was arrested in the living room of his four-room apartment, and in an attempt to recover two canceled checks thought to have been used in effecting the forgery, the officers undertook a thorough search of the entire apartment. Inside a desk drawer they found a sealed envelope marked "George Harris, personal papers." The envelope, which was then torn open, was found to contain altered Selective Service documents, and those documents were used to secure Harris' conviction for violating the Selective Training and Service Act of 1940. The Court rejected Harris' Fourth Amendment claim, sustaining the search as "incident to arrest." . . .

Only a year after Harris, however, the pendulum swung again. In *Trupiano v. United States*, 334 U.S. 699 (1948), agents raided the site of an illicit distillery, saw one of several conspirators operating the still, and arrested him, contemporaneously "seiz[ing] the illicit distillery." . . . The Court held that the arrest and others made subsequently had been valid, but that the unexplained failure of the agents to procure a search warrant-in spite of the fact that they had had more than enough time before the raid to do so-rendered the search unlawful. The opinion stated:

"It is a cardinal rule that, in seizing goods and articles, law enforcement agents must secure and use search warrants wherever reasonably practicable. . . . This rule rests upon the desirability of having magistrates rather than police officers determine when searches and seizures are permissible and what limitations should be placed upon such activities. . . ." To provide the necessary security against unreasonable intrusions upon the private lives of individuals, the framers of the Fourth Amendment required adherence to judicial processes wherever possible. And subsequent history has confirmed the wisdom of that requirement.

. . .

"A search or seizure without a warrant as an incident to a lawful arrest had always been considered to be a strictly limited right. It grows out of the inherent necessities of the situation at the time of the arrest. But there must be something more in the way of necessity than merely a lawful arrest.". . .

In 1950, two years after *Trupiano*, came *United States v. Rabinowitz*, 339 U.S. 56, the decision upon which California primarily relies in the case now before us. In *Rabinowitz*, federal authorities had been informed that the defendant was dealing in stamps bearing forged overprints. On the basis of that information they secured a warrant for his arrest, which they executed at his one-room business office. At the time of the arrest, the officers "searched the desk, safe, and file cabinets in the office for about an hour and a half" . . . and seized 573 stamps with forged overprints. The stamps were admitted into evidence at the defendant's trial, and this Court affirmed his conviction, rejecting the contention that the warrantless search had been unlawful. The Court held that the search in its entirety fell within the principle giving law enforcement authorities "[t]he right 'to search the place where the arrest is made in order to find and seize things connected with the crime. . . .'" . . . Harris was regarded as "ample authority" for that conclusion. . . . The opinion rejected the rule of Trupiano that "in seizing goods and articles, law enforcement agents must secure and use search warrants wherever reasonably practicable." The test, said the Court, "is not whether it is reasonable to procure a search warrant, but whether the search was reasonable." . . .

Rabinowitz has come to stand for the proposition, inter alia, that a warrantless search "incident to a lawful arrest" may generally extend to the area that is considered to be in the "possession" or under the "control" of the person arrested. And it was on the basis of that proposition that the California courts upheld the search of the petitioner's entire house in this case. That doctrine, however, at least in the broad sense in which it was applied by the California courts in this case, can withstand neither historical nor rational analysis.

Even limited to its own facts, the Rabinowitz decision was, as we have seen, hardly founded on an unimpeachable line of authority. As Mr. Justice Frankfurter commented in dissent in that case, the "hint" contained in Weeks was, without persuasive justification, "loosely turned into dictum and finally elevated to a decision." . . . And the approach taken in cases such as Go-Bart, Lefkowitz, and Trupiano was essentially disregarded by the Rabinowitz Court.

Nor is the rationale by which the State seeks here to sustain the search of the petitioner's house supported by a reasoned view of the background and purpose of the Fourth Amendment. Mr. Justice Frankfurter wisely pointed out in his Rabinowitz dissent that the Amendment's proscription of "unreasonable searches and seizures" must be read in light of "the history that gave rise to the words"-history of "abuses so deeply felt by the Colonies as to be one of the potent causes of the Revolution. . . ." The Amendment was in large part a reaction to the general warrants and warrantless searches that had so alienated the colonists and had helped speed the movement for independence. In the scheme of the Amendment, therefore, the requirement that "no Warrants shall issue, but upon probable cause," plays a crucial part. As the Court put it in *McDonald v. United States*, 335 U.S. 451 (1948):

"We are not dealing with formalities. The presence of a search warrant serves a high function. Absent some grave emergency, the Fourth Amendment has interposed a magistrate between the citizen and the police. This was done not to shield criminals nor to make the home a safe haven for illegal activities. It was done so that an objective mind might weigh the need to invade that privacy in order to enforce the law. The right of privacy was deemed too precious to entrust to the discretion of those whose job is the detection of crime and the arrest of criminals. . . . And so the Constitution requires a magistrate to pass on the desires of the police before they violate the privacy of the home. We cannot be true to that constitutional requirement and excuse the absence of a search warrant without a showing by those who seek exemption from the constitutional mandate that the exigencies of the situation made that course imperative." . . . Even in the Agnello case the Court relied upon the rule that "[b]elief, however well founded, that an article sought is concealed in a dwelling house, furnishes no justification for a search of that place without a warrant. And such searches are held unlawful notwithstanding facts unquestionably showing probable cause." . . . Clearly, the general requirement that a search warrant be obtained is not lightly to be dispensed with, and "the burden is on those seeking [an] exemption [from the requirement] to show the need for it. . . ."

. . .

. . . When an arrest is made, it is reasonable for the arresting officer to search the person arrested in order to remove any weapons that the latter might seek to use in order to resist arrest or effect his escape. Otherwise, the officer's safety might well be endangered, and the arrest itself frustrated. In addition, it is entirely reasonable for the arresting officer to search for and seize any evidence on the arrestee's person in order to prevent its concealment or destruction. And the area into which an arrestee might reach in order to grab a weapon or evidentiary items must, of course, be governed by a like rule. A gun on a table or in a drawer in front of one who is arrested can be as dangerous to the arresting officer as one concealed in the clothing of the person arrested. There is ample justification, therefore, for a search of the arrestee's person and the area "within his immediate control"-construing that phrase to mean the area from within which he might gain possession of a weapon or destructible evidence.

There is no comparable justification, however, for routinely searching any room other than that in which an arrest occurs-or, for that matter, for searching through all the desk drawers or other closed or concealed areas in that room itself. Such searches, in the absence of well-recognized exceptions, may be made only under the authority of a search warrant. The "adherence to judicial processes" mandated by the Fourth Amendment requires no less.

. . .

It is argued in the present case that it is "reasonable" to search a man's house when he is arrested in it. But that argument is founded on little more than a subjective view regarding the acceptability of certain sorts of police conduct, and not on considerations relevant to Fourth Amendment interests. Under such an unconfined analysis, Fourth Amendment protection in this area would approach the evaporation point. It is not easy to explain why, for instance, it is less subjectively "reasonable" to search a man's house when he is arrested on his front lawn-or just down the street-than it is when he happens to be in the house at the time of arrest.

. . .

It would be possible, of course, to draw a line between Rabinowitz and Harris on the one hand, and this case on the other. For Rabinowitz involved a single room, and Harris a four-room apartment, while in the case before us an entire house was searched. But such a distinction would be highly artificial. The rationale that allowed the searches and seizures in Rabinowitz and Harris would allow the searches and seizures in this case. No consideration relevant to the Fourth Amendment suggests any point of rational limitation, once the search is allowed to go beyond the area from which the person arrested might obtain weapons or evidentiary items. The only reasoned distinction is one between a search of the person arrested and the area within his reach on the one hand, and more extensive searches on the other.

The petitioner correctly points out that one result of decisions such as Rabinowitz and Harris is to give law enforcement officials the opportunity to engage in searches not justified by probable cause, by the simple expedient of arranging to arrest suspects at home rather than elsewhere. We do not suggest that the petitioner is necessarily correct in his assertion that such a strategy was utilized here, but the fact remains that had he been arrested earlier in the day, at his place of employment rather than at home, no search of his house could have been made without a search warrant. In any event, even apart from the possibility of such police tactics, the general point so forcefully made by Judge Learned Hand in *United States v. Kirschenblatt* remains:

"After arresting a man in his house, to rummage at will among his papers in search of whatever will convict him, appears to us to be indistinguishable from what might be done under a general warrant; indeed, the warrant would give more protection, for presumably it must be issued by a magistrate. True, by hypothesis the power would not exist, if the supposed offender were not found on the premises; but it is small consolation to know that one's papers are safe only so long as one is not at home." . . .

Rabinowitz and Harris have been the subject of critical commentary for many years, and have been relied upon less and less in our own decisions. It is time, for the reasons we have stated, to hold that on their own facts, and insofar as the principles they stand for are inconsistent with those that we have endorsed today, they are no longer to be followed.

Application of sound Fourth Amendment principles to the facts of this case produces a clear result. The search here went far beyond the petitioner's person and the area from within which he might have obtained either a weapon or something that could have been used as evidence against him. There was no constitutional justification, in the absence of a search warrant, for extending the search beyond that area. The scope of the search was, therefore, "unreasonable" under the Fourth and Fourteenth Amendments and the petitioner's conviction cannot stand.

Reversed.

[Mr. Justice Harlan wrote a concurring opinion.]

[Mr. Justice White, with whom Mr. Justice Black joined, dissented.]

In Re Gault

Supreme Court of the United States, 1967.

387 U.S. 1, 87 S.Ct. 1428, 18 L.Ed.2d 527.

Mr. Justice Fortas delivered the opinion of the Court.

This is an appeal under 28 U.S.C. § 1257(2) from a judgment of the Supreme Court of Arizona affirming the dismissal of a petition for a writ of habeas corpus. 99 Ariz. 181, 407 P.2d 760 (1965). The petition sought the release of Gerald Francis Gault, appellants' 15-year-old son, who had been committed as a juvenile delinquent to the State Industrial School by the Juvenile Court of Gila County, Arizona. The Supreme Court of Arizona affirmed dismissal of the writ against various arguments which included an attack upon the constitutionality of the Arizona Juvenile Code because of its alleged denial of procedural due process rights to juveniles charged with being "delinquents." The Court agreed that the constitutional guarantee of due process of law is applicable in such proceedings. It held that Arizona's Juvenile Code is to be read as "impliedly" implementing the "due process concept." It then proceeded to identify and describe "the particular elements which constitute due process in a juvenile hearing." It concluded that the proceedings ending in commitment of Gerald Gault did not offend those requirements. We do not agree, and we reverse. We begin with a statement of the facts.

I

On Monday, June 8, 1964, at about 10 a.m., Gerald Francis Gault and a friend, Ronald Lewis, were taken into custody by the Sheriff of Gila County. Gerald was then still subject to a six months' probation order which had been entered on February 25, 1964, as a result of his having been in the company of another boy who had stolen a wallet from a lady's purse. The police action on June 8 was taken as the result of a verbal complaint by a neighbor of the boys, Mrs. Cook, about a telephone call made to her in which the caller or callers made lewd or indecent remarks. It will suffice for purposes of this opinion to say that the remarks or questions put to her were of the irritatingly offensive, adolescent, sex variety.

At the time Gerald was picked up, his mother and father were both at work. No notice that Gerald was being taken into custody was left at the home. No other steps were taken to advise them that their son had, in effect, been arrested. Gerald was taken to the Children's Detention Home. When his mother arrived home at about 6 o'clock, Gerald was not there. Gerald's older brother was sent to look for him at the trailer home of the Lewis family. He apparently learned then that Gerald was in custody. He so informed his mother. The two of them went to the Detention Home. The deputy probation officer, Flagg, who was also superintendent of the Detention Home, told Mrs. Gault "why Jerry was there" and said that a hearing would be held in Juvenile Court at 3 o'clock the following day, June 9.

Officer Flagg filed a petition with the court on the hearing day, June 9, 1964. It was not served on the Gaults. Indeed, none of them saw this petition until the habeas corpus hearing on August 17, 1964. The petition was entirely formal. It made no reference to any factual basis for the judicial action which it initiated. It recited only that "said minor is under the age of eighteen years, and is in need of the protection of this Honorable Court; [and that] said minor is a delinquent minor." It prayed for a hearing and an order regarding "the care and custody of said minor." Officer Flagg executed a formal affidavit in support of the petition.

On June 9, Gerald, his mother, his older brother, and Probation Officers Flagg and Henderson appeared before the Juvenile Judge in chambers. Gerald's father was not there. He was at work out of the city. Mrs. Cook, the complainant, was not there. No one was sworn at this hearing. No transcript or recording was made. No memorandum or record of the substance of the proceedings was prepared. Our information about the proceedings and the subsequent hearing on June 15, derives entirely from the testimony of the Juvenile Court Judge, Mr. and Mrs. Gault and Officer Flagg at the habeas corpus proceeding conducted two months later. From this, it appears that at the June 9 hearing Gerald was questioned by the judge about the telephone call. There was conflict as to what he said. His mother recalled that Gerald said he only dialed Mrs. Cook's number and handed the telephone to his friend, Ronald. Officer Flagg recalled that Gerald had admitted making the lewd remarks. Judge McGhee testified that Gerald "admitted making one of these [lewd] statements." At the conclusion of the hearing, the judge said he would "think about it." Gerald was taken back to the Detention Home. He was not sent to his own home with his parents. On June 11 or 12, after having been detained since June 8, Gerald was released and driven home. There is no explanation in the record as to why he was kept in the Detention Home or why he was released. At 5 p.m. on the day of Gerald's release, Mrs. Gault received a note signed by Officer Flagg. It was on plain paper, not letterhead. Its entire text was as follows:

"Mrs. Gault:

"Judge McGHEE has set Monday June 15, 1964 at 11:00 a.m. as the date and time for further Hearings on Gerald's delinquency"

"/s/Flagg"

At the appointed time on Monday, June 15, Gerald, his father and mother, Ronald Lewis and his father, and Officers Flagg and Henderson were present before Judge McGhee. Witnesses at the habeas corpus proceeding differed

in their recollections of Gerald's testimony at the June 15 hearing. Mr. and Mrs. Gault recalled that Gerald again testified that he had only dialed the number and that the other boy had made the remarks. Officer Flagg agreed that at this hearing Gerald did not admit making the lewd remarks. But Judge McGhee recalled that "there was some admission again of some of the lewd statements. He — he didn't admit any of the more serious lewd statements." Again, the complainant, Mrs. Cook, was not present. Mrs. Gault asked that Mrs. Cook be present "so she could see which boy that done the talking, the dirty talking over the phone." The Juvenile Judge said "she didn't have to be present at that hearing." The judge did not speak to Mrs. Cook or communicate with her at any time. Probation Officer Flagg had talked to her once — over the telephone on June 9.

At this June 15 hearing a "referral report" made by the probation officers was filed with the court, although not disclosed to Gerald or his parents. This listed the charge as "Lewd Phone Calls." At the conclusion of the hearing, the judge committed Gerald as a juvenile delinquent to the State Industrial School "for the period of his minority [that is, until 21], unless sooner discharged by due process of law." An order to that effect was entered. It recites that "after a full hearing and due deliberation the Court finds that said minor is a delinquent child, and that said minor is of the age of 15 years."

No appeal is permitted by Arizona law in juvenile cases. On August 3, 1964, a petition for a writ of habeas corpus was filed with the Supreme Court of Arizona and referred by it to the Superior Court for hearing.

At the habeas corpus hearing on August 17, Judge McGhee was vigorously cross-examined as to the basis for his actions. He testified that he had taken into account the fact that Gerald was on probation. He was asked "under what section of ... the code you found the boy delinquent?"

His answer is set forth in the margin.1 In substance, he concluded that Gerald came within ARS § 8—201, subsec. 6(a), which specifies that a "delinquent child" includes one "who has violated a law of the state or an ordinance or regulation of a political subdivision thereof." The law which Gerald was found to have violated is ARS § 13—377. This section of the Arizona Criminal Code provides that a person who "in the presence or hearing of any woman or child ... uses vulgar, abusive or obscene language, is guilty of a misdemeanor...." The penalty specified in the Criminal Code, which would apply to an adult, is $5 to $50, or imprisonment for not more than two months. The judge also testified that he acted under ARS § 8—201, subsec. 6(d) which includes in the definition of a "delinquent child" one who, as the judge phrased it, is "habitually involved in immoral matters."2

Asked about the basis for his conclusion that Gerald was "habitually involved in immoral matters," the judge testified, somewhat vaguely, that two years earlier, on June 2, 1962, a "referral" was made concerning Gerald, "where the boy had stolen a baseball glove from another boy and lied to the Police Department about it." The judge said there was "no hearing," and "no accusation" relating to this incident, "because of lack of material foundation." But it seems to have remained in his mind as a relevant factor. The judge also testified that Gerald had admitted making other nuisance phone calls in the past which, as the judge recalled the boy's testimony, were "silly calls, or funny calls, or something like that."

The Superior Court dismissed the writ, and appellants sought review in the Arizona Supreme Court. That court stated that it considered appellants' assignments of error as urging (1) that the Juvenile Code, ARS § 8—201 to

§ 8—239, is unconstitutional because it does not require that parents and children be apprised of the specific charges, does not require proper notice of a hearing, and does not provide for an appeal; and (2) that the proceedings and order relating to Gerald constituted a denial of due process of law because of the absence of adequate notice of the charge and the hearing; failure to notify appellants of certain constitutional rights including the rights to counsel and to confrontation, and the privilege against self-incrimination; the use of unsworn hearsay testimony; and the failure to make a record of the proceedings. Appellants further asserted that it was [an] error for the Juvenile Court to remove Gerald from the custody of his parents without a showing and finding of their unsuitability, and alleged a miscellany of other errors under state law.

The Supreme Court handed down an elaborate and wide-ranging opinion affirming dismissal of the writ and stating the court's conclusions as to the issues raised by appellants and other aspects of the juvenile process. In their jurisdictional statement and brief in this Court, appellants do not urge upon us all of the points passed upon by the Supreme Court of Arizona. They urge that we hold the Juvenile Code of Arizona invalid on its face or as applied in this case because, contrary to the Due Process Clause of the Fourteenth Amendment, the juvenile is taken from the custody of his parents and committed to a state institution pursuant to proceedings in which the Juvenile Court has virtually unlimited discretion, and in which the following basic rights are denied:

1. Notice of the charges;
2. Right to counsel;
3. Right to confrontation and cross-examination;
4. Privilege against self-incrimination;
5. Right to a transcript of the proceedings; and
6. Right to appellate review.

We shall not consider other issues which were passed upon by the Supreme Court of Arizona. We emphasize that we indicate no opinion as to whether the decision of that court with respect to such other issues does or does not conflict with requirements of the Federal Constitution.

II

The Supreme Court of Arizona held that due process of law is requisite to the constitutional validity of proceedings in which a court reaches the conclusion that a juvenile has been at fault, has engaged in conduct prohibited by law, or has otherwise misbehaved with the consequence that he is committed to an institution in which his freedom is curtailed. This conclusion is in accord with the decisions of a number of courts under both federal and state constitutions.

This Court has not heretofore decided the precise question. In *Kent v. United States*, 383 U.S. 541, 86 S.Ct. 1045, 16 L.Ed.2d 84 (1966), we considered the requirements for a valid waiver of the "exclusive" jurisdiction of the Juvenile Court of the District of Columbia so that a juvenile could be tried in the adult criminal court of the District. Although our decision turned upon the language of the statute, we emphasized the necessity that "the basic requirements of due process and fairness" be satisfied in such proceedings. *Haley v. State of Ohio*, 332 U.S. 596, 68 S.Ct. 302, 92 L.Ed. 224 (1948), involved the admissibility, in a state criminal court of general jurisdiction, of a confession by a 15-year-old boy. The Court held that the Fourteenth Amendment applied to prohibit the use of the coerced confession. Mr. Justice Douglas said, "Neither man nor child can be allowed to stand condemned by methods which flout constitutional requirements of due process of law." To the same effect is *Gallegos v. State of Colorado*,

370 U.S. 49, 82 S.Ct. 1209, 8 L.Ed.2d 325 (1962). Accordingly, while these cases relate only to restricted aspects of the subject, they unmistakably indicate that, whatever may be their precise impact, neither the Fourteenth Amendment nor the Bill of Rights is for adults alone.

We do not in this opinion consider the impact of these constitutional provisions upon the totality of the relationship of the juvenile and the state. We do not even consider the entire process relating to juvenile "delinquents." For example, we are not here concerned with the procedures or constitutional rights applicable to the prejudicial stages of the juvenile process, nor do we direct our attention to the post-adjudicative or dispositional process. We consider only the problems presented to us by this case. These relate to the proceedings by which a determination is made as to whether a juvenile is a "delinquent" as a result of alleged misconduct on his part, with the consequence that he may be committed to a state institution. As to these proceedings, there appears to be little current dissent from the proposition that the Due Process Clause has a role to play. The problem is to ascertain the precise impact of the due process requirement upon such proceedings.

In view of this, it would be extraordinary if our Constitution did not require the procedural regularity and the exercise of care implied in the phrase "due process." Under our Constitution, the condition of being a boy does not justify a kangaroo court. The traditional ideas of Juvenile Court procedure, indeed, contemplated that time would be available and care would be used to establish precisely what the juvenile did and why he did it—was it a prank

of adolescence or a brutal act threatening serious consequences to himself or society unless corrected? Under traditional notions, one would assume that in a case like that of Gerald Gault, where the juvenile appears to have a home, a working mother and father, and an older brother, the Juvenile Judge would have made a careful inquiry and judgment as to the possibility that the boy could be disciplined and dealt with at home, despite his previous transgressions.3 Indeed, so far as appears in the record before us, except for some conversation with Gerald about his school work and his "wanting to go to ... Grand Canyon with his father," the points to which the judge directed his attention were little different from those that would be involved in determining any charge of violation of a penal statute. The essential difference between Gerald's case and a normal criminal case is that safeguards available to adults were discarded in Gerald's case. The summary procedure as well as the long commitment was possible because Gerald was 15 years of age instead of over 18.

If Gerald had been over 18, he would not have been subject to Juvenile Court proceedings. For the particular offense immediately involved, the maximum punishment would have been a fine of $5 to $50, or imprisonment in jail for not more than two months. Instead, he was committed to custody for a maximum of six years. If he had been over 18 and had committed an offense to which such a sentence might apply, he would have been entitled to substantial rights under the Constitution of the United States as well as under Arizona's laws and constitution. The United States Constitution would guarantee him rights and protections with respect to arrest, search, and seizure, and pretrial interrogation. It would assure him of specific notice of the charges and adequate time to decide his course of action and to prepare his defense. He would be entitled to clear advice that he could be represented by counsel, and, at least if a felony were involved, the State would be required to provide counsel if his parents were unable to afford it. If the court acted on the basis of his confession, careful procedures would be required to assure its voluntariness. If the case went to trial, confrontation and opportunity for cross-examination would be guaranteed. So wide a gulf between the State's treatment of the adult and of the child requires a bridge sturdier than mere verbiage, and reasons more persuasive than cliche can provide. As Wheeler and Cottrell have put it, "The rhetoric of the juvenile court movement has developed without any necessarily close correspondence to the realities of court and institutional routines."

In *Kent v. United States*, supra, we stated that the Juvenile Court Judge's exercise of the power of the state as *parens patriae* was not unlimited. We said that "the admonition to function in a 'parental' relationship is not an invitation to procedural arbitrariness." With respect to the waiver by the Juvenile Court to the adult court of jurisdiction over an offense committed by a youth, we said that "there is no place in our system of law for reaching a result of such tremendous consequences without ceremony—without hearing, without effective assistance of counsel, without a statement of reasons." We announced with respect to such waiver proceedings that while "We do not mean ... to indicate that the hearing to be held must conform with all of the requirements of a criminal trial or even of the usual administrative hearing; but we do hold that the hearing must measure up to the essentials of due process and fair treatment." We reiterate this view, here in connection with a juvenile court adjudication of "delinquency," as a requirement which is part of the Due Process Clause of the Fourteenth Amendment of our Constitution.4

We now turn to the specific issues which are presented to us in the pres-ent case.

III. Notice of Charges

Appellants allege that the Arizona Juvenile Code is unconstitutional or alternatively that the proceedings before the Juvenile Court were constitutionally defective because of failure to provide adequate notice of the hearings. No notice was given to Gerald's parents when he was taken into custody on Monday, June 8. On that night, when Mrs. Gault went to the Detention Home, she was orally informed that there would be a hearing the next afternoon and was told the reason why Gerald was in custody. The only written notice Gerald's parents received at any time was a note on plain paper from Officer Flagg delivered on Thursday or Friday, June 11 or 12, to the effect that the judge had set Monday, June 15, "for further Hearings on Gerald's delinquency."

A "petition" was filed with the court on June 9 by Officer Flagg, reciting only that he was informed and believed that "said minor is a delinquent minor and that it is necessary that some order be made by the Honorable Court for said minor's welfare." The applicable Arizona statute provides for a petition to be filed in Juvenile Court, alleging in general terms that the child is "neglected, dependent or delinquent." The statute explicitly states that such a general allegation is sufficient, "without alleging the facts." There is no requirement that the petition be served and it was not served upon, given to, or shown to Gerald or his parents.

The Supreme Court of Arizona rejected appellants' claim that due process was denied because of inadequate notice. It stated that "Mrs. Gault knew the exact nature of the charge against Gerald from the day he was taken to the detention home." The court also pointed out that the Gaults appeared at the two hearings "without objection." The court held that because "the policy of the juvenile law is to hide youthful errors from the full gaze of the public and bury them in the graveyard of the forgotten past," advance notice of the specific charges or basis for taking the juvenile into custody and for the hearing is not necessary. It held that the appropriate rule is that "the infant and his parents or guardian will receive a petition only reciting a conclusion of delinquency. But no later than the initial hearing by the judge, they must be advised of the facts involved in the case. If the charges are denied, they must be given a reasonable period of time to prepare."

We cannot agree with the court's conclusion that adequate notice was given in this case. Notice, to comply with due process requirements, must be given sufficiently in advance of scheduled court proceedings so that reasonable opportunity to prepare will be afforded, and it must "set forth the alleged misconduct with particularity." It is obvious, as we have discussed above, that no purpose of shielding the child from the public stigma of knowledge of his having been taken into custody and scheduled for hearing is served by the procedure approved by the court below. The "initial hearing" in the present case was a hearing on the merits. Notice at that time is not timely; and even if there were a conceivable purpose served by the deferral proposed by the court below, it would have to yield to the requirements that the child and his parents or guardian be notified, in writing, of the specific charge or factual allegations to be considered at the hearing, and that such written notice be given at the earliest practicable time, and in any event sufficiently in advance of the hearing to permit preparation. Due process of law requires notice of the sort we have described — that is, notice which would be deemed constitutionally adequate in a civil or criminal proceeding. It does not allow a hearing to be held in which a youth's freedom and his parents' right to his custody are at stake without giving them timely notice, in advance of the hearing, of the specific issues that they must meet. Nor, in the circumstances of this case, can it reasonably be said that the requirement of notice was waived.

IV. Right to Counsel

Appellants charge that the Juvenile Court proceedings were fatally defective because the court did not advise Gerald or his parents of their right to counsel, and proceeded with the hearing, the adjudication of delinquency and the order of commitment in the absence of counsel for the child and his parents or an express waiver of the right thereto. The Supreme Court of Arizona pointed out that "[t]here is disagreement [among the various jurisdictions] as to whether the court must advise the infant that he has a right to counsel." It noted its own decision in *Arizona State Dept. of Public Welfare v. Barlow*, 80 Ariz. 249, 296 P.2d 298 (1956), to the effect "that the parents of an infant in a juvenile proceeding cannot be denied representation by counsel of their choosing." (Emphasis added.) It referred to a provision of the Juvenile Code which it characterized as requiring "that the probation officer shall look after the interests of neglected, delinquent and dependent children," including representing their interests in court. The court argued that "The parent and the probation officer may be relied upon to protect the infant's interests." Accordingly it rejected the proposition that "due process requires that an infant have a right to counsel." It said that juvenile courts have the discretion, but not the duty, to allow such representation; it referred specifically to the situation in which the Juvenile Court discerns conflict between the child and his parents as an instance in which this discretion might be exercised. We do not agree. Probation officers, in the Arizona scheme, are also arresting officers. They initiate proceedings and file petitions which they verify, as here, alleging the delinquency of the child; and they testify, as here, against the child. And here the probation officer was also superintendent of the Detention Home. The probation officer cannot act as counsel for the child. His role in the adjudicatory hearing, by statute and in fact, is as arresting officer and witness against the child. Nor can the judge represent the child. There is no material difference in this respect between adult and juvenile proceedings of the sort here involved. In adult proceedings, this contention has been foreclosed by decisions of this Court. A proceeding where the issue is whether the child will be found to be "delinquent" and subjected to the loss of his liberty for years is comparable in seriousness to a felony prosecution. The juvenile needs the assistance of counsel to cope with problems of law, to make skilled inquiry into the facts, to insist upon regularity of the proceedings, and to ascertain whether he has a defense and to prepare and submit it. The child "requires the guiding hand of counsel at every step in the proceedings against him." Just as in *Kent v. United States*, supra, 383 U.S., at 561-562, 86 S.Ct., at 1057-1058, we indicated our agreement with the United States Court of Appeals for the District of Columbia Circuit that the assistance of counsel is essential for purposes of waiver proceedings, so we hold now that it is equally essential for the determination of delinquency, carrying with it the awesome prospect of incarceration in a state institution until the juvenile reaches the age of 21.5

During the last decade, court decisions, experts, and legislatures have demonstrated increasing recognition of this view. In at least one-third of the States, statutes now provide for the right of representation by retained counsel in juvenile delinquency proceedings, notice of the right, or assignment of counsel, or a combination of these. In other States, court rules have similar provisions.

The President's Crime Commission has recently recommended that in order to assure "procedural justice for the child," it is necessary that "Counsel ... be appointed as a matter of course wherever coercive action is a possibility, without requiring any affirmative choice by child or parent."6 As stated by the authoritative "Standards for Juvenile and Family Courts," published by the Children's Bureau of the United States Department of Health, Education, and Welfare:

"As a component part of a fair hearing required by due process guaranteed under the 14th amendment, notice of the right to counsel should be required at all hearings and counsel provided upon request when the family is financially unable to employ counsel." Standards, p.57.

This statement was "reviewed" by the National Council of Juvenile Court Judges at its 1965 Convention and they "found no fault" with it. The New York Family Court Act contains the following statement:

"This act declares that minors have a right to the assistance of counsel of their own choosing or of law guardians in neglect proceedings under article three and in proceedings to determine juvenile delinquency and whether a person is in need of supervision under article seven. This declaration is based on a finding that counsel is often indispensable to a practical realization of due process of law and may be helpful in making reasoned determinations of fact and proper orders of disposition."

The Act provides that "At the commencement of any hearing" under the delinquency article of the statute, the juvenile and his parent shall be advised of the juvenile's "right to be represented by counsel chosen by him or his parent ... or by a law guardian assigned by the court...." The California Act (1961) also requires appointment of counsel.

We conclude that the Due Process Clause of the Fourteenth Amendment requires that in respect of proceedings to determine delinquency which may result in commitment to an institution in which the juvenile's freedom is curtailed, the child and his parents must be notified of the child's right to be represented by counsel retained by them, or if they are unable to afford counsel, that counsel will be appointed to represent the child.

At the habeas corpus proceeding, Mrs. Gault testified that she knew that she could have appeared with counsel at the juvenile hearing. This knowledge is not a waiver of the right to counsel which she and her juvenile son had, as we have defined it. They had a right expressly to be advised that they might retain counsel and to be confronted with the need for specific consideration of whether they did or did not choose to waive the right. If they were unable to afford to employ counsel, they were entitled in view of the seriousness of the charge and the potential commitment, to appointed counsel, unless they chose waiver. Mrs. Gault's knowledge that she could employ counsel was not an "intentional relinquishment or abandonment" of a fully known right.7

V. Confrontation, Self-Incrimination, Cross-Examination

Appellants urge that the writ of habeas corpus should have been granted because of the denial of the rights of confrontation and cross- examination in the Juvenile Court hearings, and because the privilege against self-incrimination was not observed. The Juvenile Court Judge testified at the habeas corpus hearing that he had proceeded on the basis of Gerald's admission at the two hearings. Appellants attack this on the ground that the admissions were obtained in disregard of the privilege against self-incrimination. If the confession is disregarded, appellants argue that the delinquency conclusion, since it was fundamentally based on a finding that Gerald had made lewd remarks during the phone call to Mrs. Cook, is fatally defective for failure to accord the rights of confrontation and cross-examination which the Due Process Clause of the Fourteenth Amendment of the Federal Constitution guarantees in state proceedings generally.

Our first question, then, is whether Gerald's admission was improperly obtained and relied on as the basis of decision, in conflict with the Federal Constitution. For this purpose, it is necessary briefly to recall the relevant facts.

Mrs. Cook, the complainant, and the recipient of the alleged telephone call, was not called as a witness. Gerald's mother asked the Juvenile Court Judge why Mrs. Cook was not present and the judge replied that "she didn't have to be present." So far as appears, Mrs. Cook was spoken to only once, by Officer Flagg, and this was by telephone. The judge did not speak with her on any occasion. Gerald had been questioned by the probation officer after having been taken into custody. The exact circumstances of this questioning do not appear but any admissions Gerald may have made at this time do not appear in the record. Gerald was also questioned by the Juvenile Court Judge at each of the two hearings. The judge testified in the habeas corpus proceeding that Gerald admitted making "some of the lewd statements ... [but not] any of the more serious lewd statements." There was conflict and uncertainty among the witnesses at the habeas corpus proceeding—the Juvenile Court Judge, Mr. and Mrs. Gault, and the probation officer—as to what Gerald did or did not admit.

We shall assume that Gerald made admissions of the sort described by the Juvenile Court Judge, as quoted above. Neither Gerald nor his parents were advised that he did not have to testify or make a statement, or that an incriminating statement might result in his commitment as a "delinquent."

The Arizona Supreme Court rejected appellants' contention that Gerald had a right to be advised that he need not incriminate himself. It said: "We think the necessary flexibility for individualized treatment will be enhanced by a rule which does not require the judge to advise the infant of a privilege against self-incrimination."

In reviewing this conclusion of Arizona's Supreme Court, we emphasize again that we are here concerned only with a proceeding to determine whether a minor is a "delinquent" and which may result in commitment to a state institution. Specifically, the question is whether, in such a proceeding, an admission by the juvenile may be used against him in the absence of clear and unequivocal evidence that the admission was made with knowledge that he was not obliged to speak and would not be penalized for remaining silent. In light of *Miranda v. State of Arizona*, 384 U.S. 436, 86 S.Ct. 1602, 16 L.Ed.2d 694 (1966), we must also consider whether, if the privilege against self-incrimination is available, it can effectively be waived unless counsel is present or the right to counsel has been waived.

It has long been recognized that the eliciting and use of confessions or admissions require careful scrutiny. Dean Wigmore states:

"The ground of distrust of confessions made in certain situations is, in a rough and indefinite way, judicial experience. There has been no careful collection of statistics of untrue confessions, nor has any great number of instances been even loosely reported ... but enough have been verified to fortify the conclusion, based on ordinary observation of human conduct, that under certain stresses a person, especially one of defective mentality or peculiar temperament, may falsely acknowledge guilt. This possibility arises wherever the innocent person is placed in such a situation that the untrue acknowledgment of guilt is at the time the more promising of two alternatives between which he [is] obliged to choose; that is, he chooses any risk that may be in falsely acknowledging guilt, in preference to some worse alternative associated with silence.

"The principle, then, upon which a confession may be excluded is that it is, under certain conditions, testimonially untrustworthy.... [T]he essential feature is that the principle of exclusion is a testimonial one, analogous to the other principles which exclude narrations as untrustworthy...."

This Court has emphasized that admissions and confessions of juveniles require special caution. In *Haley v. State of Ohio*, 332 U.S. 596, 68 S.Ct. 302, 92 L.Ed. 224, where this Court reversed the conviction of a 15-year-old boy for murder, Mr. Justice Douglas said:

"What transpired would make us pause for careful inquiry if a mature man were involved. And when, as here, a mere child — an easy victim of the law — is before us, special care in scrutinizing the record must be used. Age 15 is a tender and difficult age for a boy of any race. He cannot be judged by the more exacting standards of maturity. That which would leave a man cold and unimpressed can overawe and overwhelm a lad in his early teens. This is the period of great instability which the crisis of adolescence produces. A 15-year-old lad, questioned through the dead of night by relays of police, is a ready victim of the inquisition. Mature men possibly might stand the ordeal from midnight to 5 a.m. But we cannot believe that a lad of tender years is a match for the police in such a contest. He needs counsel and support if he is not to become the victim first of fear, then of panic. He needs someone on whom to lean lest the overpowering presence of the law, as he knows it, crush him. No friend stood at the side of this 15-year-old boy as the police, working in relays, questioned him hour after hour, from midnight until dawn. No lawyer stood guard to make sure that the police went so far and no farther, to see to it that they stopped short of the point where he became the victim of coercion. No counsel or friend was called during the critical hours of questioning."

In *Haley*, as we have discussed, the boy was convicted in an adult court, and not a juvenile court. In notable decisions, the New York Court of Appeals and the Supreme Court of New Jersey have recently considered decisions of Juvenile Courts in which boys have been adjudged "delinquent" on the basis of confessions obtained in circumstances comparable to those in Haley. In both instances, the State contended before its highest tribunal that constitutional requirements governing inculpatory statements applicable in adult courts do not apply to juvenile proceedings. In each case, the State's contention was rejected, and the juvenile court's determination of delinquency was set aside on the grounds of inadmissibility of the confession. *In Matters of W. and S.*, 19 N.Y.2d 55, 277 N.Y.S.2d 675, 224 N.E.2d 102 (1966) (opinion by Keating, J.), and *In Interests of Carlo and Stasilowicz*, 48 N.J. 224, 225 A.2d 110 (1966) (opinion by Proctor, J.).

The privilege against self-incrimination is, of course, related to the question of the safeguards necessary to assure that admissions or confessions are reasonably trustworthy, that they are not the mere fruits of fear or coercion, but are reliable expressions of the truth. The roots of the privilege are, however, far deeper. They tap the basic stream of religious and political principle because the privilege reflects the limits of the individual's attornment to the state and — in a philosophical sense — insists upon the equality of the individual and the state. In other words, the privilege has a broader and deeper thrust than the rule which prevents the use of confessions which are the product of coercion because coercion is thought to carry with it the danger of unreliability. One of its purposes is to prevent the state, whether by force or by psychological domination, from overcoming the mind and will of the person under investigation and depriving him of the freedom to decide whether to assist the state in securing his conviction.

It would indeed be surprising if the privilege against self-incrimination were available to hardened criminals but not to children. The language of the Fifth Amendment, applicable to the States by operation of the Fourteenth Amendment, is unequivocal and without exception. And the scope of the privilege is comprehensive. As Mr. Justice White, concurring, stated in *Murphy v. Waterfront Commission*, 378 U.S. 52, 94, 84 S.Ct. 1594, 1611, 12 L.Ed.2d 678 (1964):

"The privilege can be claimed in any proceeding, be it criminal or civil, administrative or judicial, investigatory or adjudicatory ... it protects any *disclosures* which the witness may reasonably apprehend could be used in a criminal prosecution or which *could lead to other evidence that might be so used*." (Emphasis added.)

With respect to juveniles, both common observation and expert opinion emphasize that the "distrust of confessions made in certain situations" to which Dean Wigmore referred in the passage quoted supra, at 1453, is imperative in the case of children from an early age through adolescence. In New York, for example, the recently enacted Family Court Act provides that the juvenile and his parents must be advised at the start of the hearing of his right to remain silent. The New York statute also provides that the police must attempt to communicate with the juvenile's parents before questioning him, and that absent "special circumstances" a confession may not be obtained from the child prior to notifying his parents or relatives and releasing the child either to them or to the Family Court. In *In Matters of W. and S.*, referred to above, the New York Court of Appeals held that the privilege against self-incrimination applies in juvenile delinquency cases and requires the exclusion of involuntary confessions, and that *People v. Lewis*, 260 N.Y. 171, 183 N.E. 353, 86 A.L.R. 1001 (1932), holding the contrary, had been specifically overruled by statute.

The authoritative "Standards for Juvenile and Family Courts" concludes that, "Whether or not transfer to the criminal court is a possibility, certain procedures should always be followed. Before being interviewed [by the police], the child and his parents should be informed of his right to have legal counsel present and to refuse to answer questions or be fingerprinted if he should so decide."

Against the application to juveniles of the right to silence, it is argued that juvenile proceedings are "civil" and not "criminal," and therefore the privilege should not apply. It is true that the statement of the privilege in the Fifth Amendment, which is applicable to the States by reason of the Fourteenth Amendment, is that no person "shall be compelled in any *criminal case* to be a witness against himself." However, it is also clear that the availability of the privilege does not turn upon the type of proceeding in which its protection is invoked, but upon the nature of the statement or admission and the exposure which it invites. The privilege may, for example, be claimed in a civil or administrative proceeding, if the statement is or may be inculpatory.

It would be entirely unrealistic to carve out of the Fifth Amendment all statements by juveniles on the ground that these cannot lead to "criminal" involvement. In the first place, juvenile proceedings to determine "delinquency," which may lead to commitment to a state institution, must be regarded as "criminal" for purposes of the privilege against self-incrimination. To hold otherwise would be to disregard substance because of the feeble enticement of the "civil" label-of-convenience which has been attached to juvenile proceedings. Indeed, in over half of the States, there is not even assurance that the juvenile will be kept in separate institutions, apart from adult "criminals." In those States juveniles may be placed in or transferred to adult penal institutions after having been found "delinquent" by a juvenile court. For this purpose, at least, commitment is a deprivation of liberty. It is incarceration against one's will, whether it is called "criminal" or "civil." And our Constitution guarantees that no person shall be "compelled" to be a witness against himself when he is threatened with deprivation of his liberty—a command which this Court has broadly applied and generously implemented in accordance with the teaching of the history of the privilege and its great office in mankind's battle for freedom.

In addition, apart from the equivalence for this purpose of exposure to commitment as a juvenile delinquent and exposure to imprisonment as an adult offender, the fact of the matter is that there is little or no assurance in Arizona, as in most if not all of the States, that a juvenile apprehended and interrogated by the police or even by the Juvenile Court itself will remain outside of the reach of adult courts as a consequence of the offense for which he has been taken into custody. In Arizona, as in other States, provision is made for Juvenile Courts to relinquish or waive jurisdiction to the ordinary criminal courts. In the present case, when Gerald Gault was interrogated concerning violation of a section of the Arizona Criminal Code, it could not be certain that the Juvenile Court Judge would decide to "suspend" criminal prosecution in court for adults by proceeding to an adjudication in Juvenile Court.

It is also urged, as the Supreme Court of Arizona here asserted, that the juvenile and presumably his parents should not be advised of the juvenile's right to silence because confession is good for the child as the commencement of the assumed therapy of the juvenile court process, and he should be encouraged to assume an attitude of trust and confidence toward the officials of the juvenile process. This proposition has been subjected to widespread challenge on the basis of current reappraisals of the rhetoric and realities of the handling of juvenile offenders.

In fact, evidence is accumulating that confessions by juveniles do not aid in "individualized treatment," as the court below put it, and that compelling the child to answer questions, without warning or advice as to his right to remain silent, does not serve this or any other good purpose. In light of the observations of Wheeler and Cottrell, and others, it seems probable that where children are induced to confess by "paternal" urgings on the part of officials and the confession is then followed by disciplinary action, the child's reaction is likely to be hostile and adverse—the child may well feel that he has been led or tricked into confession and that despite his confession, he is being punished.

Further, authoritative opinion has cast formidable doubt upon the reliability and trustworthiness of "confessions" by children. This Court's observations in *Haley v. State of Ohio* are set forth above. The recent decision of the New York Court of Appeals referred to above, *In Matters of W. and S.* deals with a dramatic and, it is to be hoped, extreme example. Two 12-year-old Negro boys were taken into custody for the brutal assault and rape of two aged domestics, one of whom died as the result of the attack. One of the boys was schizophrenic and had been locked in the security ward of a mental institution at the time of the attacks. By a process that may best be described as bizarre, his confession was obtained by the police. A psychiatrist testified that the boy would admit "whatever he thought was expected so that he could get out of the immediate situation." The other 12-year-old also "confessed." Both confessions were in specific detail, albeit they contained various inconsistencies. The Court of Appeals, in an opinion by Keating, J., concluded that the confessions were products of the will of the police instead of the boys. The confessions were therefore held involuntary and the order of the Appellate Division affirming the order of the Family Court adjudging the defendants to be juvenile delinquents was reversed.

A similar and equally instructive case has recently been decided by the Supreme Court of New Jersey. *In Interests of Carlo and Stasilowicz*, supra. The body of a 10-year-old girl was found. She had been strangled. Neighborhood boys who knew the girl were questioned. The two appellants, aged 13 and 15, confessed to the police, with vivid detail and some inconsistencies. At the Juvenile Court hearing, both denied any complicity in the killing. They testified that their confessions were the product of fear and fatigue due to extensive police grilling. The Juvenile Court Judge found that the confessions were voluntary and admissible. On appeal, in an extensive opinion by Proctor, J., the Supreme Court of New Jersey reversed. It rejected the State's argument that the constitutional safeguard of voluntariness governing the use of confessions does not apply in proceedings before the Juvenile Court. It pointed out that under New Jersey court rules, juveniles under the age of 16 accused of committing a homicide are tried in a proceeding which "has all of the appurtenances of a criminal trial," including participation by the county prosecutor, and requirements that the juvenile be provided with counsel, that a stenographic record be made, etc. It also pointed out that under New Jersey law, the confinement of the boys after reaching age 21 could be extended until they had served the maximum sentence which could have been imposed on an adult for such a homicide, here found to be second-degree murder carrying up to 30 years' imprisonment. The court concluded that the confessions were involuntary, stressing that the boys, contrary to statute, were placed in the police station and there interrogated; that the parents of both boys were not allowed to see them while they were being interrogated; that inconsistencies appeared among the various statements of the boys and with the objective evidence of the crime; and that there were protracted periods of questioning. The court noted the State's contention that both boys were advised of their constitutional rights before they made their statements, but it held that this should not be given "significant weight in our determination of voluntariness." Accordingly, the judgment of the Juvenile Court was reversed.

In a recent case before the Juvenile Court of the District of Columbia, Judge Ketcham rejected the proffer of evidence as to oral statements made at police headquarters by four juveniles who had been taken into custody for alleged involvement in an assault and attempted robbery. *In the Matter of Four Youths*, Nos. 28—776—J, 28—778—J, 28—783—J, 28—859—J. Juvenile Court of the District of Columbia, April 7, 1961. The court explicitly stated that it did not rest its decision on a showing that the statements were involuntary, but because they were untrustworthy. Judge Ketcham said:

"Simply stated, the Court's decision in this case rests upon the considered opinion—after nearly four busy years on the Juvenile Court bench during which the testimony of thousands of such juveniles has been heard—that the statements of adolescents under 18 years of age who are arrested and charged with violations of law are frequently untrustworthy and often distort the truth."

We conclude that the constitutional privilege against self-incrimination is applicable in the case of juveniles as it is with respect to adults. We appreciate that special problems may arise with respect to waiver of the privilege by or on behalf of children, and that there may well be some differences in technique—but not in principle—depending upon the age of the child and the presence and competence of parents. The participation of counsel will, of course, assist the police, juvenile courts and appellate tribunals in administering the privilege. If counsel was not present for some permissible reason when an admission was obtained, the greatest care must be taken to assure that the admission was voluntary, in the sense not only that it was not coerced or suggested, but also that it was not the product of ignorance of rights or of adolescent fantasy, fright or despair.

The "confession" of Gerald Gault was first obtained by Officer Flagg, out of the presence of Gerald's parents, without counsel and without advising him of his right to silence, as far as appears. The judgment of the Juvenile Court was stated by the judge to be based on Gerald's admissions in court. Neither "admission" was reduced to writing, and, to say the least, the process by which the "admissions," were obtained and received must be characterized as lacking the certainty and order which are required of proceedings of such formidable consequences. Apart from the "admission," there was nothing upon which a judgment or finding might be based. There was no sworn testimony. Mrs. Cook, the complainant, was not present. The Arizona Supreme Court held that "sworn testimony must be required of all witnesses including police officers, probation officers and others who are part of or officially related to the juvenile court structure." We hold that this is not enough. No reason is suggested or appears for a different rule in respect of sworn testimony in juvenile courts than in adult tribunals. Absent a valid confession adequate to support the determination of the Juvenile Court, confrontation and sworn testimony by witnesses available for cross-examination were essential for a finding of "delinquency" and an order committing Gerald to a state institution for a maximum of six years.

The recommendations in the Children's Bureau's "Standards for Juvenile and Family Courts" are in general accord with our conclusions. They state that testimony should be under oath and that only competent, material and relevant evidence under rules applicable to civil cases should be admitted in evidence. The New York Family Court Act contains a similar provision.

As we said in *Kent v. United States*, 383 U.S. 541, 554, 86 S.Ct. 1045, 1053, 16 L.Ed.2d 84 (1966), with respect to waiver proceedings, "there is no place in our system of law for reaching a result of such tremendous consequences without ceremony...." We now hold that, absent a valid confession, a determination of delinquency and an order of commitment to a state institution cannot be sustained in the absence of sworn testimony subjected to the opportunity for cross-examination in accordance with our law and constitutional requirements.

VI. Appellate Review and Transcript of Proceedings

Appellants urge that the Arizona statute is unconstitutional under the Due Process Clause because, as construed by its Supreme Court, "there is no right of appeal from a juvenile court order...." The court held that there is no right to a transcript because there is no right to appeal and because the proceedings are confidential and any record must be destroyed after a prescribed period of time. Whether a transcript or other recording is made, it held, is a matter for the discretion of the juvenile court.

This Court has not held that a State is required by the Federal Constitution "to provide appellate courts or a right to appellate review at all." In view of the fact that we must reverse the Supreme Court of Arizona's affirmance of the dismissal of the writ of habeas corpus for other reasons, we need not rule on this question in the present case or upon the failure to provide a transcript or recording of the hearings — or, indeed, the failure of the Juvenile Judge to state the grounds for his conclusion. Cf. *Kent v. United States*, supra, 383 U.S., at 561, 86 S.Ct., at 1057, where we said, in the context of a decision of the juvenile court waiving jurisdiction to the adult court, which by local law, was permissible: " ... it is incumbent upon the Juvenile Court to accompany its waiver order with a statement of the reasons or considerations therefor." As the present case illustrates, the consequences of failure to provide an appeal, to record the proceedings, or to make findings or state the grounds for the juvenile court's conclusion may be to throw a burden upon the machinery for habeas corpus, to saddle the reviewing process with the burden of attempting to reconstruct a record, and to impose upon the Juvenile Judge the unseemly duty of testifying under cross-examination as to the events that transpired in the hearings before him.

For the reasons stated, the judgment of the Supreme Court of Arizona is reversed and the cause remanded for further proceedings not inconsistent with this opinion. It is so ordered.

Judgment reversed and cause remanded with directions.

Gault Notes:

1. "Q. All right. Now, Judge, would you tell me under what section of the law or tell me under what section of—of the code you found the boy delinquent?

"A. Well, there is a—I think it amounts to disturbing the peace. I can't give you the section, but I can tell you the law, that when one person uses lewd language in the presence of another person, that it can amount to—and I consider that when a person makes it over the phone, that it is considered in the presence. I might be wrong, that is one section. The other section upon which I consider the boy delinquent is Section 8—201, Subsection (d), habitually involved in immoral matters."

. ARS § 8—201. subsec. 6, the section of the Arizona Juvenile Code which defines a delinquent child, reads: "'Delinquent child' includes:

"(a) A child who has violated a law of the state or an ordinance or regulation of a political subdivision thereof.

"(b) A child who, by reason of being incorrigible, wayward or habitually disobedient, is uncontrolled by his parent, guardian or custodian.

"(c) A child who is habitually truant from school or home.

"(d) A child who habitually so deports himself as to injure or endanger the morals or health of himself or others."

3. The Juvenile Judge's testimony at the habeas corpus proceeding is devoid of any meaningful discussion of this. He appears to have centered his attention upon whether Gerald made the phone call and used lewd words. He was impressed by the fact that Gerald was on six months' probation because he was with another boy who allegedly stole a purse—a different sort of offense, sharing the feature that Gerald was "along." And he even referred to a report which he said was not investigated because "there was no accusation" "because of lack of material foundation." With respect to the possible duty of a trial court to explore alternatives to involuntary commitment in a civil proceeding, cf. *Luke v. Cameron*, 124 U.S. App.D.C. 264, 364 F.2d 657 (1966), which arose under statutes relating to treatment of the mentally ill.

4. The Nat'l Crime Comm'n Report recommends that "Juvenile courts should make fullest feasible use of preliminary conferences to dispose of cases short of adjudication." Id., at 84. See also D.C. Crime Comm'n Report, pp.662-665. Since this "consent decree" procedure would involve neither adjudication of delinquency nor institutionalization, nothing we say in this opinion should be construed as expressing any views with respect to such procedure. The problems of preadjudication treatment of juveniles, and of post-adjudication disposition, are unique to the juvenile process; hence what we hold in this opinion with regard to the procedural requirements at the adjudicatory stage has no necessary applicability to other steps of the juvenile process.

5. This means that the commitment, in virtually all cases, is for a minimum of three years since jurisdiction of juvenile courts is usually limited to age 18 and under.

6. Nat'l Crime Comm'n Report, pp.86-87. The Commission's statement of its position is very forceful:

"The Commission believes that no single action holds more potential for achieving procedural justice for the child in the juvenile court than provision of counsel. The presence of an independent legal representative of the child, or of his parent, is the keystone of the whole structure of guarantees that a minimum system of procedural justice requires. The rights to confront one's accusers, to cross-examine witnesses, to present evidence and testimony of one's own, to be unaffected by prejudicial and unreliable evidence, to participate meaningfully in the dispositional decision, to take an appeal have substantial meaning for the overwhelming majority of persons brought before the juvenile court only it they are provided with competent lawyers who can invoke those rights effectively. The most informal and well-intentioned of judicial proceedings are technical; few adults without legal training can influence or even understand them; certainly children cannot. Papers are drawn and charges expressed in legal language. Events follow one another in a manner that appears arbitrary and confusing to the uninitiated. Decisions, unexplained, appear too official to challenge. But with lawyers come records of proceedings; records make possible appeals which, even if they do not occur, impart by their possibility a healthy atmosphere of accountability.

"Fears have been expressed that lawyers would make juvenile court proceedings adversary. No doubt this is partly true, but it is partly desirable. Informality is often abused. The juvenile courts deal with cases in which facts are disputed and in which, therefore, rules of evidence, confrontation of witnesses, and other adversary procedures are called for. They deal with many cases involving conduct that can lead to incarceration or close supervision for long periods, and therefore juveniles often need the same safeguards that are granted to adults. And in all cases children need advocates to speak for them and guard their interest, particularly when disposition decisions are made. It is the disposition stage at which the opportunity arises to offer individualized treatment plans and in which the danger inheres that the court's coercive power will be applied without adequate knowledge of the circumstances. "Fears also have been expressed that the formality lawyers would bring into juvenile court would defeat the therapeutic aims of the court. But informality has no necessary connection with therapy; it is a device that has been used to approach therapy, and it is not the only possible device. It is quite possible that in many instances lawyers, for all their commitment to formality, could do more to further therapy for their clients than can the small, overworked social staffs of the courts.

. . .

"The Commission believes it is essential that counsel be appointed by the juvenile court for those who are unable to provide their own. Experience under the prevailing systems in which children are free to seek counsel of their choice reveals how empty of meaning the right is for those typically the subjects of juvenile court proceedings. Moreover, providing counsel only when the child is sophisticated enough to be aware of his need and to ask for one or when he fails to waive his announced right [is] not enough, as experience in numerous jurisdictions reveal.

"The Commission recommends:

"COUNSEL SHOULD BE APPOINTED AS A MATTER OF COURSE WHEREVER COERCIVE ACTION IS A POSSIBILITY, WITHOUT REQUIRING ANY AFFIRMATIVE CHOICE BY CHILD OR PARENT."

7. *Johnson v. Zerbst*, 304 U.S. 458, 464, 58 S.Ct. 1019, 1023, 82 L.Ed. 1461 (1938); *Carnley v. Cochran*, 369 U.S. 506, 82 S.Ct. 884, 8 L.Ed.2d 70 (1962); *United States ex rel. Brown v. Fay*, 242 F.Supp. 273 (D.C.S.D.N.Y. 1965.

Name and Case Index

Subject Index